Prose by Victorian Women

GARLAND REFERENCE LIBRARY OF THE HUMANITIES
VOLUME 1893

PROSE BY VICTORIAN WOMEN
AN ANTHOLOGY

EDITED BY
ANDREA BROOMFIELD AND SALLY MITCHELL

GARLAND PUBLISHING, INC.
NEW YORK AND LONDON
1996

Library of Congress Cataloging-in-Publication Data
Prose by Victorian women : an anthology / edited by Andrea Broomfield
    and Sally Mitchell.
            p.   cm. — (Garland reference library of the humanities ; vol.
    1893)
        ISBN 0-8153-1970-3 (hardcover)—
        ISBN 0-8153-1967-3 (paperback)
        1. English prose literature—Women authors.   2. English prose lit-
    erature—19th century.   I. Broomfield, Andrea.   II. Mitchell, Sally,
    1937–   .   III. Series.
    PR1286.W6P76   1996
    828'.8080809287—dc20   95-24400
                                                                          CIP

Cover illustration: A lady reading. Reprinted by permission of Tate Gallery,
London/Art Resource, NY.

Printed on acid-free, 250-year-life paper
Manufactured in the United States of America

Contents

Foreword

Although the editions and texts that can be used to teach Victorian fiction and Victorian poetry have changed dramatically over the past two or three decades, anthologies of Victorian prose still offer only a small and traditional list of "men of letters." How would our conception of nineteenth-century British intellectual life change if the women who also took part in public discussions of philosophy, religion, aesthetics, literature, and social questions were brought into the classroom? With that question in mind, *Prose by Victorian Women: An Anthology* had its origin in two graduate seminars conducted by Sally Mitchell at Temple University in 1989 and 1991. Students were given lists of Victorian women writers and made responsible for generating bibliographies, tracking down essays in primary sources, proposing and defending selections to include, agreeing on editorial guidelines, and writing the biographical introductions and headnotes. Some seminar students did what might be called negative research—they spent a semester working diligently on authors who were ultimately not included. To an extent, space governed the selection. In addition, however, the "negative research" had its own value: it demonstrated that for most topics of interest to Victorians a multitude of voices contested to be heard.

A few Victorian essayists not covered in the seminars have been added to the anthology, thus drawing in the work of additional scholars. Some seminar participants have moved on to permanent jobs or graduate programs elsewhere. The name of the person responsible for an individual essayist appears at the end of each biographical introduction. All of the seminar members, however, made authentic and valuable contributions to the process of creating *Prose by Victorian Women: An Anthology*. They are: Mare Fallon Adams, Craig Bennett, Andrea Broomfield, John Dern, Kathleen Dillon,Walter Hajduk, John Hallock,

Noreen Groover Lape, Lauren McKinney, Richard Moses, Herbert Northcote, Bettina Pedersen, Christine Palumbo, Esther Schwartz-McKenzie, Sylvia Skaggs, Carolyn Sundstrom, Mary Timmins, Alison Valtin, Katharine Walke Gillespie, and Laurie Zierer.

Sally Mitchell would like to thank the two graduate chairs of Temple's English department who cheerfully agreed to her teaching a course for which she was unable to provide a reading list, Daniel O'Hara and Susan Wells. In addition, a Faculty Summer Research Grant helped her to do editing, checking, verification, and some negative research of her own in the British Library.

Andrea Broomfield would like to extend her thanks to Eastern New Mexico University for supplying her with a research assistant, Amy Scrivner, who diligently typed out and helped proof many of the essays from the original periodicals. She would also like to thank Margaret Willen for her assistance with numerous French translations, and Shoshana Milgram Knapp and Solveig Robinson for their extensive and detailed footnotes. Thanks also goes to Charles Broomfield for providing some of the equipment necessary to make this project go more smoothly, and to Vincent Miller for his endless patience with helping to type, proofread, and produce the final draft of this manuscript.

Introduction

Prose by Victorian Women: An Anthology is more than a collection of women's writing on a variety of topics; its very existence attests to scholars' increased willingness to challenge the rigidity of the Victorian "separate spheres" paradigm. By having available for the first time an anthology of women's critical and theoretical writing on aesthetics, race, criminal justice, women's issues, animal rights, trade unions, nationalism, religion, travel, education, and government, we can encourage readers to examine the assumption that Victorian middle- and upper-middle-class women, ensconced in domesticity, were not familiar enough with "worldly" events to write serious nonfiction. Rather (the assumption goes), women authors saw the novel as an optimum genre for depicting the joys and dilemmas of the parlor and nursery, while their talented husbands, brothers, and fathers, moving through the throngs of humanity, were best equipped to write essays about social and political questions.

Certainly Victorian women wrote hundreds of novels. Gaye Tuchman and Nina Fortin note that until the 1870s, women serialized almost six times as many of them in *Macmillan's Magazine* as did men. Only in the 1880s, when the novel was increasingly viewed as "serious" art, did *Macmillan's* publish more novels by men than by women.[1] Throughout most of the nineteenth century, Tuchman and Fortin maintain, nonfiction remained "the preserve of serious male authors." However, increasing research in Victorian periodicals is beginning to demonstrate otherwise. In spite of the difficulty women endured while breaking into the nonfiction marketplace, several succeeded by first gaining authority in careers outside their homes and then by publishing articles which drew on their special knowledge. Professional women, like many educated men, earned money and influence through active participation in what is known as the "higher journalism." By writing lengthy essays for prominent periodicals, they engaged their colleagues and readers in a variety of topical debates.

Dozens of women essayists whose work was known by nineteenth-century contemporaries have slipped into invisibility in the twentieth century, for a variety of reasons. The most significant may be the institutionalization of Victorian literary studies in the United States. Courses in Victorian prose were offered as early as the 1930s, especially after the publication of C.F. Harrold's and W.D. Templeman's *English Prose of the Victorian Period* (1938). However, widespread interest in Victorian prose was a later development, incited partly by significant studies of what is known as Victorian "prophetic" or "sage" prose. John Holloway's *The Victorian Sage: Studies in Argument* (1953), in particular, offered an insightful analysis of nonfiction by Thomas Carlyle, Matthew Arnold, and John Henry Newman.[2] Holloway also offered a defense for reading these authors' works as literature, rather than as history, criticism, theology, or philosophy—categories used by Victorians themselves when discussing nonfiction. Except on rare occasions, twentieth-century students were exposed to nonfiction written by an elite group of gentlemen who associated with other like-minded gentlemen.

Women essayists also disappeared from twentieth-century scholarship because of the increasing inaccessibility of Victorian periodicals, the repository of nonfiction prose produced by hundreds of "noncanonical" writers (both women and men). As more periodicals were transferred to microfilm, fewer students and teachers were inclined to conduct the tedious research needed to rediscover lost, seemingly unimportant essays. Furthermore, most articles written in the early and middle nineteenth century were anonymous; the difficulty of attribution inhibited scholarship on all but that small group of regularly anthologized Victorian male prophets.

What has undoubtedly triggered an overdue study of women essayists—aside from the impact of feminist literary criticism in general—was the completion of Walter Houghton's massive *Wellesley Index to Victorian Periodicals* (5 vols., 1966–90), which has accomplished that seemingly impossible task of attributing thousands of unsigned periodical essays to their authors. Although it is clear that women's essays were not printed nearly so frequently as men's in this select group of intellectual and well-known periodicals covered by the *Wellesley Index*, several women's names do appear frequently throughout the volumes. Dozens, if not hundreds, of other women essayists remain to be found in the plethora of specialized, popular, sectarian, and other periodicals which are as yet unindexed.

The information about authorship in the *Wellesley Index*, however, has made possible recent studies such as Thaïs Morgan's collection *Victorian Sages and Cultural Discourse: Renegotiating Gender and Power* (1990). Morgan's collection, which includes essays on women's prose, as well as essays which dissect the supposedly "masculine" nature of this genre, has helped establish a theoretical framework for reading women's nonfiction as more than historical documentation of issues and attitudes.

Yet the effectiveness of such recent theoretical scholarship and the ease of bringing it into the classroom have been hindered by the unwillingness of publishers to reprint Victorian women's nonfiction. Theory, after all, can have little impact unless supported by primary texts. Without available editions of women's nonfiction, it is not only more convenient to continue teaching the handful of anthologized male Victorian prophets, but it is also convenient to perpetuate the myth that Victorian women did not excel at serious prose but were best equipped (given their domestic isolation) to write novels. Publishers have recently begun to make some progress. There are, for example, some volumes of travel writing by Isabella Bird Bishop and Mary Kingsley and critical editions of nonfiction prose by George Eliot and Florence Nightingale, as well as a few other reprinted selections, although largely available in expensive library editions.

Prose by Victorian Women: An Anthology, is intended primarily for classroom use, to introduce readers to the variety and scope of women's nonfiction and to the work of some of Victorian Britain's most influential activists and thinkers. Several of the writers included here, such as Frances Power Cobbe, Eliza Lynn Linton, and Harriet Martineau, were editors or staff reporters for newspapers and periodicals, and thus developed a loyal following. Others, including Clementina Black and Edith Simcox (both intimately involved with trade union organizing), were prominent activists. George Eliot, invariably studied as a novelist rather than an essayist, wrote important studies of such issues as nationalism and discrimination against English Jews. Helen Taylor, Mona Caird, and Sarah Grand were committed women's rights activists whose essays on the woman question provoked controversy and compelled readers to reconsider the laws and customs which curtailed women's lives. Mary Mitford, Elizabeth Eastlake, Anne Thackeray Ritchie, Margaret Oliphant, and Vernon Lee gained influence by defining and critiquing various literary and aesthetic trends. Isabella Bird Bishop provided invaluable records of journeys—often unaccompanied—through remote parts of Japan, Hawaii, Korea, and other countries. Alice Bodington, along with several other late Victorians, wrote about Great Britain's imperialist mission; in doing so, she popularized theories about race and eugenics that remain as controversial and conflicted today as they were when she wrote them. Most of these women were involved in several other activities as well: Simcox was a regular book reviewer for the *Academy*; Lynn Linton was arguably the most influential Victorian critic of women's rights; Eliot and Oliphant were prolific novelists; Eastlake, Lee, Cobbe, and Martineau were respected travel writers. Thus, this anthology is designed to give readers a sense of both the variety of women's public lives and the diversity of their prose styles.

As is the case with all such collections, we have had to struggle with the limits of space. Readers may rightly wonder why certain writers have been left out in favor of others. A number of influential women's names are indeed missing, most often because their volume-length works did not lend themselves well to excerpting. Notable excluded authors include Florence Nightingale, Mary Kingsley, Anna Jameson, Mary Somerville, Josephine Butler, Annie Besant, and Emily Davies. We make no claims to create another restrictive canon of prose, but have instead attempted to provide access to varied essays by accomplished writers in hopes that students and scholars will look more carefully at nonfiction prose by many women—those included in this edition and those who are not.

This anthology can be used either as a companion to other collections of Victorian prose or on its own in courses which focus on women's writing. Thus, chapters from Isabella Bird Bishop's *Tracks in Japan* can be read in conjunction with chapters from Martineau's *Society in America*, as well as in conjunction with selections from Charles Darwin's writings on South America. Likewise, Elizabeth Eastlake's extensive critique of Ruskin's *Modern Painters* can be read in conjunction with Vernon Lee's essays on aesthetics, as well as with Ruskin's *Modern Painters* itself. Most of the selections are unabridged essays reprinted from the periodicals in which they first appeared. The remainder are complete chapters taken from the authors' books (and are so designated). Our decision to keep each essay or chapter complete rather than print short extracts (which would have allowed us to include many more authors and topics) will allow readers to study technique and style as well as content.

Finally, we have made no editorial modernizations. Essays have been reprinted here exactly as they first appeared, thus letting readers study the writing in a form as near to the original as possible. Authors' idiosyncratic spelling variations or the misspelling of proper nouns are followed by a "sic." Only the most obvious typographical errors have been corrected. Furthermore, each author's selections are preceded by an introduction and headnotes designed to acquaint readers with the author's background and the historical context of her writing. With such information, as well as with added bibliographic sources, we hope that readers of this anthology will gain a more complicated and rich understanding of the viewpoints and theories espoused by British intellectuals in the Victorian period.

Andrea L. Broomfield,
Eastern New Mexico University

Notes

1.   Tuchman, Gaye with Nina E. Fortin. *Edging Women Out: Victorian Novelists, Publishers, and Social Change.* (Yale UP, 1989), pp. 146-47.

2.   Holloway does examine George Eliot's fiction, but he neglects any extended discussion of women's nonfiction.

I. Mary Russell Mitford

(1787–1855)

Mary Russell Mitford is best known for the informal essays, or sketches, she wrote describing the local characters and environs of her village, Three Mile Cross. Compiled into a series of volumes entitled *Our Village: Sketches of Rural Life, Character, and Scenery*, these essays had a wide and admiring contemporary readership, and later writers and critics credited Mitford with inventing a new literary genre: the geographically descriptive essay. Her "sketches" are valuable for both content and technique. The bulk of her freshest work was written between 1819 and 1830, before the railroads and the First Reform Bill; for this reason, later Victorians saw Mitford's writing as offering one of the last views of pre-industrial England.

She was born in Alresford, Hampshire to Mary Russell Mitford, heiress of a moderate fortune, and George Mitford, a non-practicing physician with a propensity for gambling. Mary was their only child and was considered something of a prodigy; she could read before age three. When she was ten, her parents sent her to Mrs. St. Quintin's school in London, where Caroline Lamb and Laetitia Landon (L.E.L.) were also educated. After four years at Mrs. St. Quintin's, Mitford continued her education on her own. The record of the circulating library in Reading, where the family lived at the time, indicates that Mitford checked out fifty-five books in one month.

Mitford started publishing her poetry in 1810, when her small volume, *Poems*, appeared. Shortly before 1820, she also began writing plays, keeping a detailed journal, and submitting essays to periodicals. By this time, Mitford's father had gambled away or spent all of the £20,000 in Irish lottery money that Mitford had won at age ten; thus, her interests were of necessity turning towards a writing career.

Economic straits also forced the Mitfords to move to a simple cottage in Three Mile Cross, the location that proved so rich a source of material for *Our Village*. Mitford continued to write sketches until near the end of her life; she also corresponded prolifically with other literary figures, including John Ruskin and Elizabeth Barrett Browning.

Although Mitford's father was a vociferous Whig, she herself never sided overtly with any political party, and indeed she ridicules one-sided politicians in the *Our Village* sketch, "The Election." Nevertheless, she developed an undidactic but strong affinity toward the laboring classes; she commented once that Balzac's settings were too frequently the boudoir and opera, and that he had no love for the people. This affinity showed itself through a sensitive if perhaps too rosy interpretation of the lives of country laborers, instead of through activism or politically specific tracts. At the same time, Mitford eschewed sentimentality and sometimes mimicked pastoral ideas of "the country" in her writing.

Compared with later Victorian thinkers, Mitford does not on the surface appear intellectual, simply because she rarely discusses ideas in the abstract. She focused her thoughts on the specifics of her local world, allowing her wide literary background to subtly deepen that view. Although Mitford wrote some poetry in the 1810s and some tragedies in the 1820s, her most innovative work is the descriptive sketch, as found in the *Our Village* compilations, which were published in five volumes as they were written: in 1824, 1826, 1828, 1830, and 1832. Many of the sketches were initially published in *Lady's Magazine*. Later sketches followed the same vein but are generally considered stilted: *Belford Regis* in 1834 and *Country Stories* in 1837. The uniqueness of Mitford's *Our Village* sketches lies in their spontaneity (written "on the spot and at the moment," as she writes in the preface to the first volume), and in an extraordinary detail that by no means diminishes the fresh, unlabored style. Thus, Mitford paints a thorough and multidimensional verbal picture of her locale.

Although Mitford's goal was to exclude what she called sentimentality and pathos, it is not always clear whether she achieved it. H.F. Chorley, a close friend of Mitford's, admitted that she "enamels too brightly." By all accounts, though, her work was received well by contemporary casual readers; the circulation of *Lady's Magazine* increased from 250 to 2,000 upon publication of her essays. By midcentury, Mitford had also come to the attention of critics. Elizabeth

Barrett Browning called Mitford a "sort of prose Crabbe in the sun." Tennyson was so enchanted by her sketch "Dora Creswell," that he adapted it for his poem "Dora." Many less well-known writers in midcentury claimed their indebtedness to her prose style, including S.C. Hall, who wrote popular sketches on Ireland, and Susannah Moody, who recorded the trials of frontier life in Canada.

Mitford's *Our Village* deserves attention for several reasons: its innovative style, its popularity among Mitford's contemporaries, the critical consideration it received, and its direct influence on other writers. Mitford's domestic subject matter and her informal, rambling style have probably prevented her work from being considered "serious." It is clear, however, that the sketches resonated deeply with later Victorians due to the wholeness and clarity of her interpretations of village life. Although everyday life was not a proper subject for adherents to Ruskin's aesthetics, even Ruskin himself praised Mitford for "finding history enough in the life of the butcher's boy, and romance enough in the story of the miller's daughter." In other words, what later Victorians nostalgically perceived as the innocence of lost village life was preserved for them in Mitford's prose.

Mitford's letters, edited by L'Estrange in 1870 under the title *The Life of Mary Russell Mitford, Told in Her Letters*, are useful for understanding the social and literary circles in which she moved. Her *Recollections of a Literary Life* (1852) is more an entertaining narrative of the people Mitford knew than it is a literary autobiography. The only biography of Mitford, written by Vera Watson and published in 1949, is most valuable for the interweaving of passages of Mitford's letters, entries in her unpublished diary (housed in the Reading Public Library), and the usual chronological information. Although Watson has cleared up some factual ambiguities, her biography is not a critical study of Mitford's texts. W.J. Keith devotes a chapter to Mitford in *The Rural Tradition: A Study of the Non-Fiction Prose Writers of the English Countryside* (1974). Shelagh Hunter, in *Victorian Idyllic Fiction: Pastoral Strategies* (1984), sees Mitford as a fiction writer, and she discusses Mitford's point of view in *Our Village*. The most recent work on Mitford is P.D. Edwards' *Idyllic Realism from Mary Russell Mitford to Hardy* (1988)—a discussion which draws connections between passages in her sketches and particulars of British social history.

Lauren D. McKinney,
Eastern Mennonite University

---

1. Our Village

Introduction

"Our Village" is one of Mary Mitford's earliest sketches, published initially in the first volume of *Our Village* (1824), and reprinted here from *The Works of Mary Mitford* (Philadelphia, 1841).[1] In her leisurely style, Mitford introduces the village that is the subject of her subsequent essays in the series. Mitford uses the opening paragraph to outline her own aesthetics of narrative. As with Jane Austen, she contends that a confined locale is the most pleasing setting to read and write about because of the thoroughness and familiarity that enrich and propel both activities. In this piece—the most panoramic of the *Our Village* essays—the organizing structure is a literal walk through the town, with the narrator assuming that the reader is her willing companion on the journey. Commenting on such varying topics as the neighbors' personalities and idiosyncrasies, the brilliance of the local flowers, the effects of the evening sun, and her own role in selecting the stories, "Our Village" serves not only as an introduction to the milieu, but also as a sampler of the viewpoints Mitford adopts in the essays to follow.

Our Village

Of all situations for a constant residence, that which appears to me most delightful is a little village far in the country; a small neighbourhood, not of fine mansions finely peopled, but of cottages and cottage-like houses, "messuages or tenements," as a friend of mine calls such ignoble and nondescript dwellings, with inhabitants whose faces are as familiar to us as the flowers in our garden; a little world of our own, close-packed and insulated like ants in an ant-hill, or bees in a hive, or sheep in a fold, or nuns in a convent, or sailors in a ship; where we know every one, are known to every one, interested in every one, and authorized to hope that every one feels an interest in us. How pleasant it is to slide into these true-hearted feelings from the kindly and unconscious influence of habit, and to learn to know and to love the people about us, with all their peculiarities, just as we learn to know and to love the nooks and turns of the shady lanes and sunny commons that we pass every day. Even in books I like a confined locality, and so do the critics when they talk of the unities. Nothing is so tiresome as to be whirled half over Europe at the chariot wheels of a hero, to go to sleep at Vienna, and awaken at Madrid; it produces a real fatigue, a weariness of spirit. On the other hand, nothing is so delightful as to sit down in a country village in one of Miss Austen's delicious novels, quite sure before we leave it to become intimate with every spot and every person it contains; or to ramble with Mr. White[2] over his own parish of Selborne, and form a friendship with the fields and coppices, as well as with the birds, mice, and squirrels, who inhabit them; or to sail with Robinson Crusoe to his island, and live there with him and his goats and his man Friday;—how much we dread any new comers, any fresh importation of savage or sailor! we never sympathise for a moment in our hero's want of company, and are quite grieved when he gets away;—or to be shipwrecked with Ferdinand on that other lovelier island—the island of Prospero, and Miranda, and Caliban, and Ariel, and nobody else, none of Dryden's exotic inventions;—that is best of all. And a small neighbourhood is as good in sober waking reality as in poetry or prose; a village neighbourhood, such as this Berkshire Hamlet in which I write, a long, straggling winding street at the bottom of a fine eminence, with a road through it, always abounding in carts, horsemen, and carriages, and lately enlivened by a stage-coach from

B___ to S___, which passed through about ten days ago, and will I suppose return some time or other. There are coaches of all varieties now-a-days; perhaps this may be intended for a monthly diligence, or a fortnight fly. Will you walk with me through our village, courteous reader? The journey is not long. We will begin at the lower end, and proceed up the hill.

The tidy, square, red cottage on the right hand, with the long well-stocked garden by the side of the road, belongs to a retired publican from a neighbouring town; a substantial person with a comely wife; one who piques himself on independence and idleness, talks politics, reads newspapers, hates the minister, and cries out for reform. He introduced into our peaceable vicinage the rebellious innovations of an illumination on the queen's acquittal. Remonstrance and persuasion were in vain; he talked of liberty and broken windows—so we all lighted up. Oh! how he shone that night with candles and laurel, and white bows, and gold paper, and a transparency (originally designed for a pocket handkerchief) with a flaming portrait of her Majesty, hatted and feathered, in red ochre. He had no rival in the village, that we all acknowledged; the very bonfire was less splendid; the little boys reserved their best crackers to be expended in his honour, and he gave them full sixpence more than any one else. He would like an illumination once a month; for it must not be concealed that, in spite of gardening, of newspaper reading, of jaunting about in his little cart, and frequenting both church and meeting, our worthy neighbour begins to feel the weariness of idleness. He hangs over his gate, and tries to entice passengers to stop and chat; he volunteers little jobs all round, smokes cherry-trees to cure the blight, and traces and blows up all the wasp-nests in the parish. I have seen a great many wasps in our garden to-day, and shall enchant him with the intelligence. He even assists his wife in her sweepings and dustings. Poor man! he is a very respectable person, and would be a very happy one, if he would add a little employment to his dignity. It would be the salt of life to him.

Next to his house, though parted from it by another long garden with a yew arbour at the end, is the pretty dwelling of the shoemaker, a pale, sickly-looking, black-haired man, the very model of sober industry. There he sits in his little shop from early morning till late at night. An earthquake would hardly stir him: the illumination did not. He stuck immoveably to his last, from the first lighting up, through the long blaze and the slow decay, till his large solitary candle was the only light in the place. One cannot conceive any thing more perfect than the contempt which the man of transparencies and the man of shoes must have felt for each other on that evening. There was at least as much vanity in the sturdy industry as in the strenuous idleness, for our shoemaker is a man of substance; he employs three journeymen, two lame, and one a dwarf, so that his shop looks like an hospital; he has purchased the lease of his commodious dwelling, some even say that he has bought it out and out; and he has only one pretty daughter, a light, delicate, fair-haired girl of fourteen, the champion, protectress, and playfellow of every brat under three years old, whom she jumps, dances, dandles, and feeds all day long. A very attractive person is that child-loving girl. I have never seen any one in her station who possessed so thoroughly that undefinable charm, the lady-look. See her on a Sunday in her simplicity and her white frock, and she might pass for an earl's daughter. She likes flowers too, and has a profusion of white stocks under her window, as pure and delicate as herself.

The first house on the opposite side of the way is the blacksmith's; a gloomy dwelling, where the sun never seems to shine; dark and smoky within and without, like a forge. The blacksmith is a high officer in our little state, nothing less than a constable: but, alas! alas! when tumults arise, and the constable is called for, he will commonly be found in the thickest of the fray. Lucky would it be for his wife and her eight children if there were no public-house in the land: an inveterate inclination to enter those bewitching doors is Mr. Constable's only fault.

Next to this official dwelling is a spruce brick tenement, red, high, and narrow, boasting, one above another, three sash windows, the only sash windows in the village, with a clematis on one side and a rose on the other, tall and narrow like itself. That slender mansion has a fine genteel look. The little parlour seems made for Hogarth's old maid and her stunted footboy; for tea and card-parties,—it would just hold one table: for the rustle of faded silks, and the splendour of old China; for the delight of four by honours, and a little snug quiet scandal between the deals; for affected gentility and real starvation. This should have been its destiny; but fate has been unpropitious: it belongs to a plump, merry, bustling dame, with four fat, rosy, noisy children, the very essence of vulgarity and plenty.

Then comes the village shop, like other village shops, multifarious as a bazaar; a repository for bread, shoes, tea, cheese, tape, ribands, and bacon; for every thing, in short, except the one particular thing which you happen to want at the moment, and will be sure not to find. The people are civil and thriving, and frugal withal; they have let the upper part of their house to two young women (one of them is a pretty blue-eyed girl) who teach little children their A B C, and make caps and gowns for their mammas,—parcel schoolmistress, parcel mantuamaker.[3] I believe they find adorning the body a more profitable vocation than adorning the mind.

Divided from the shop by a narrow yard, and opposite the shoemaker's, is a habitation, of whose inmates I shall say nothing. A cottage—no—a miniature house, with many additions, little odds and ends of places, pantries, and what not; all angles, and of a charming in-and-outness; a little bricked court before one half, and a little flower-yard before the other; the walls old and weatherstained, covered with hollyhocks, roses, honey-suckles, and a great apricot tree; the casements full of geraniums; (ah, there is our superb white cat peeping out from amongst them!) the closets (our landlord has the assurance to call them rooms) full of contrivances and corner-cupboards; and the little garden behind full of common flowers, tulips, pinks, larkspurs, pionies, stocks, and carnations, with an arbour of privet, not unlike a sentry-box, where one lives in a delicious green light, and looks out on the gayest of all gay flower-beds. That house was built on purpose to show in what an exceedingly small compass comfort may be packed. Well, I will loiter there no longer.

The next tenement is a place of importance, the Rose inn; a white-washed building, retired from the road behind its fine swinging sign, with a little bow-window room coming out on one side, and forming, with our stable on the other, a sort of open square, which is the constant resort of carts, wagons, and return chaises. There are two carts there now, and mine host is serving them with beer in his eternal red waistcoat. He is a thriving man, and a portly, as his waistcoat attests, which has been twice let out within this twelvemonth. Our landlord has a stirring wife, a hopeful son, and a daughter, the belle of the village; not so pretty as the fair nymph of the shoe-shop, and far less elegant, but ten times as fine; all curl-papers in the morning, like a porcupine, all curls in the afternoon, like a poodle, with more flounces than curl-papers, and more lovers than curls. Miss Phoebe is fitter for town than country; and, to do her justice, she has a consciousness of that fitness, and turns her steps town-ward as often as she can. She is gone to B___ to-day with her last and principal lover, a recruiting serjeant—a man as tall as Serjeant Kite, and as impudent. Some day or other he will carry off Miss Phoebe.

In a line with the bow-window room is a low garden wall, belonging to a house under repair:—the white house opposite the collarmaker's shop, with four lime trees before it, and a wagon-load of bricks at the door.—That house is the plaything of a wealthy, well-meaning, whimsical person, who lives about a mile off. He has a passion for brick and mortar, and, being too wise to meddle with his own residence, diverts himself with altering and re-altering, improving and re-improving, doing and undoing here. It is a perfect Penelope's web. Carpenters and bricklayers have been at work for these eighteen months, and yet I sometimes stand and wonder whether any thing has really been done. One exploit in last June was, however, by no means equivocal. Our good neighbour fancied that the limes shaded the rooms, and made them dark, (there was not a creature in the house but the workmen,) so he had all the leaves stripped from every tree. There they stood, poor miserable skeletons, as bare as Christmas under the glowing midsummer sun. Nature revenged herself in her own sweet and gracious manner; fresh leaves sprang out, and at early Christmas the foliage was as brilliant as when the outrage was committed.

Next door lives a carpenter, "famed ten miles round, and worthy all his fame,"—few cabinet-makers surpass him, with his excellent wife, and their little daughter Lizzy, the plaything and queen of the village, a child three years old according to the register, but six in size and strength and intellect, in power and in self-will. She manages every body in the place, her schoolmistress included; turns the wheeler's children out of their own little cart, and makes them draw her; seduces cakes and lollypops from the very shop-windows; makes the lazy carry her, the silent talk to her, the grave romp with her; does any thing she pleases; is absolutely irresistible. Her chief attraction lies in her exceeding power of loving, and her firm reliance on the love and indulgence of others. How impossible it would be to disappoint the dear little girl when she runs to meet you, slides her pretty hand into yours, looks up gladly in your face, and says, "Come!" You must go: you cannot help it. Another part of her charm is her singular beauty. Together with a good deal of the character of Napoleon, she has something of his square, sturdy, upright form, with the finest limbs in the world, a complexion purely English, a round laughing face, sunburnt and rosy, large merry blue eyes, curling brown hair, and a wonderful play of countenance. She has the imperial attitudes too, and loves to stand with her hands behind her, or folded over her bosom; and sometimes, when she has a little touch of shyness, she clasps them together on the top of her head, pressing down her shining curls, and looking so exquisitely pretty! Yes, Lizzy is queen of the village! She has but one rival in her dominions, a certain white grey-hound called May-flower, much her friend, who resembles her in beauty and strength, in playfulness, and almost in sagacity, and reigns over the animal world as she over the human. They are both coming with me, Lizzy and Lizzy's "pretty May." We are now at the end of the street; a cross lane, a rope-walk, shaded with limes and oaks, and a cool clear pond overhung with elms, lead us to the bottom of the hill. There is still one house round the corner, ending in a picturesque wheeler's shop. The dwelling-house is more ambitious. Look at the fine flowered window-blinds, the green door with the brass knocker, and the somewhat prim but very civil person, who is sending off a labouring man with sirs and curtsies enough for a prince of the blood. Those are the curate's lodgings—apartments, his landlady would call them: he lives with his own family four miles off, but once or twice a week he comes to his neat little parlour to write sermons, to marry, or to bury, as the case may require. Never were better or kinder people than his host and hostess; and there is a reflection of clerical importance about them, since their connection with the church, which is quite edifying—a decorum, a gravity, a solemn politeness. Oh, to see the worthy wheeler carry the gown after his lodger on a Sunday, nicely pinned up in his wife's best handkerchief!—or to hear him rebuke a squalling child or a squabbling woman! The curate is nothing to him. He is fit to be perpetual churchwarden.

We must now cross the lane into the shady rope-walk. That pretty white cottage opposite, which stands straggling at the end of the village, in a garden full of flowers, belongs to our mason, the shortest of men, and his handsome, tall wife: he, a dwarf, with the voice of a giant; one starts when he begins to talk as if he were shouting through a speaking-trumpet; she, the sister, daughter, and granddaughter, of a long line of gardeners, and no contemptible one herself. It is very magnanimous in me not to hate her; for she beats me in my own way, in chrysanthemums, and dahlias, and the like gauds. Her plants are sure to live; mine have a sad trick of dying, perhaps because I love them, "not wisely, but too well," and kill them with over-kindness. Half-way up the hill is another detached cottage, the residence of an officer and his beautiful family. That eldest boy, who is hanging over the gate, and looking with such intense childish admiration at my Lizzy, might be a model for a Cupid.

How pleasantly the road winds up the hill, with its broad green borders and hedge-rows so thickly timbered! How finely the evening sun falls on that sandy excavated bank, and touches the farm-house on the top of the eminence! and how clearly defined and relieved is the figure of the man who is just coming down! It is poor John Evans, the gardener—an excellent gardener till about ten years ago, when he lost his wife, and became insane. He was sent to St. Luke's, and dismissed as cured; but his power was gone and his strength; he could no longer manage a garden, nor submit to the restraints, nor encounter the fatigue of regular employment; so he retreated to the work-house, the pensioner and factotum of the village, amongst whom he divides his services. His mind often wanders, intent on some fantastic and impracticable plan, and lost to present objects; but he is perfectly harmless, and full of a child-like simplicity, a smiling contentedness, a most touching gratitude. Every one is kind to John Evans, for there is that about him which must be loved; and his unprotectedness, his utter defencelessness, have an irresistible claim on every better feeling. I know nobody who inspires so deep and tender a pity; he improves all around him. He is useful, too, to the extent of his little power; will do any thing, but loves gardening best, and still piques himself on his old arts of pruning fruit-trees, and raising cucumbers. He is the happiest of men just now, for he has the management of a melon bed—a melon bed!—fie! What a grand pompous name was that for three melon plants under a handlight! John Evans is sure that they will succeed. We shall see: as the chancellor said, "I doubt."

We are on the very brow of the eminence close to the Hill-house and its beautiful garden. On the outer edge of the paling, hanging over the bank that skirts the road, is an old thorn—such a thorn! The long sprays covered with snowy blossoms, so graceful, so elegant, so lightsome, and yet so rich! There only wants a pool under the thorn to give a still lovelier reflection, quivering and trembling, like a tuft of feathers, whiter and greener than the life, and more prettily mixed with the bright blue sky. There should indeed be a pool; but on the dark grass-plat, under the high bank, which is crowned by that magnificent plume, there is something that does almost as well,—Lizzy and May-flower in the midst of a game at romps, "making a sun-shine in the shady place;" Lizzy rolling, laughing, clapping her hands, and glowing like a rose; May-flower playing about her like summer lightning, dazzling the eyes with her sudden turns, her leaps, her bounds, her attacks and her escapes. She darts round the lovely little girl, with the same momentary touch that the swallow skims over the water, and has exactly the same power of flight, the same matchless ease and strength and grace. What a pretty picture they would make; what a pretty foreground they do make to the real landscape! The road winding down the hill with a slight bend, like that in the High-street at Oxford; a wagon slowly ascending, and a horseman passing it at a full trot—(ah! Lizzy, May-flower will certainly desert you to have a gambol with that blood-horse!)—half-way down, just at the turn, the red cottage of the lieutenant, covered with vines, the very image of comfort and content; farther down, on the opposite side, the small white dwelling of the little mason; then the limes and the rope-walk; then the village street, peeping through the trees, whose clustering tops hide all but the chimneys, and various roofs of the houses, and here and there some angle of a wall: farther on, the elegant town of B___ , with its fine old church towers and spires; the whole view shut in by a range of chalky hills; and over every part of the picture, trees so profusely scattered, that it appears like a woodland scene, with glades and villages intermixed. The trees are of all kinds and all hues, chiefly the finely shaped elm, of so deep and bright a green, the tips of whose high outer branches droop down with such a crisp and garland-like richness, and the oak, whose stately form is just now so splendidly adorned by the sunny colouring of the young leaves. Turning again up the hill, we find ourselves on that peculiar charm of English scenery, a green common, divided by the road; the right side fringed by hedge-rows and trees, with cottages and farm-houses irregularly placed, and terminated by a double avenue of noble oaks: the left, prettier still, dappled by bright pools of water, and islands of cottages and cottage-gardens, and sinking gradually down to corn-fields and meadows, and an old farm-house, with pointed roofs and clustered chimneys, looking out from its blooming orchard, and backed by woody hills. The common is itself the prettiest part of the prospect; half covered with low furze, whose golden blossoms reflect so intensely the last beams of the setting sun, and alive with cows and sheep, and two sets of cricketers: one of young men, surrounded with spectators, some standing, some sitting, some stretched on the grass, all taking a delightful interest in the game; the other, a merry group of little boys, at an humble distance, for whom even cricket is scarcely lively enough, shouting, leaping, and enjoying themselves to their hearts' content. But cricketers and country boys are too important persons in our village to be talked of merely as figures in the landscape. they deserve an individual introduction—an essay to themselves—and they shall have it. no fear of forgetting the good-humoured faces that meet us in our walks every day.

Notes

1.   Subsequent Mitford selections in this anthology are also reprinted from *The Works of Mary Mitford.* (Philadelphia, 1841).

2.   White's Natural History and Antiquities of Selborne; one of the most fascinating books ever written. I wonder that no naturalist has adopted the same plan. [Mitford's note]

3.   One who makes mantuas—a loose-fitting gown open in the front to reveal the underskirt of a woman's dress.

---

2. Rosedale

Introduction

First published in *New Monthly Magazine* in December, 1824, under the title "Rosedale and Its Tenants," Mary Mitford's "Rosedale" was then reprinted in the fourth volume of *Our Village* (1830). This sketch serves as an example of Mitford's running commentary on manners, which is interwoven with her accounts of local scenery. Not pretending to be as spontaneously written as her other sketches in *Our Village*, "Rosedale" is rather a deliberately drawn portrait of what Mitford sees as social and aesthetic folly: namely, Rosedale occupants' pretentious mimicking of classical styles and sentimental pastoralism, which clash comically with the exigencies of living in the country. Mitford's good-natured critique of citified people's ways of constructing the country came from a sensibility that had been informed by a familiarity with literature; for example, her likening Laura to an "opera shepherdess without a crook" and the description of her dress as "Arcadian" reflect an irreverent familiarity with the pastoral tradition, and a quick eye for its imitation. Mitford's love of simplicity is a "late Romantic" sensibility; her taste is not one that could have tolerated the mid-Victorians' love of the Albert Memorial.

Rosedale

I don't know how it happened when we were house-hunting the other day, that nobody ever thought of Rosedale. I should have objected to it, both as out of distance—it's a good six miles off; and as being utterly unrecommendable by one rational person to another. Rosedale! the very name smacks of the Minerva Press,[1] and gives token of the nonsense and trumpery thereunto belonging. Rosedale Cottage! the man who, under that portentous title takes that house, cannot complain of lack of warning.

Nevertheless is Rosedale one of the prettiest cottages that ever sprung into existence in brick or on paper. All strangers go to see it, and few "cots of spruce gentility" are so well worth seeing. Fancy a low irregular white rough-cast building thatched with reeds, covered with roses, clematis, and passion-flowers, standing on a knoll of fine turf, amidst flower-beds and shrubberies and magnificent elms, backed by an abrupt hill, and looking over lawny fields to a green common, which is intersected by a gay high road, dabbled with ponds of water, and terminated by a pretty village edging off into rich woodlands: imagine this picture of a place tricked out with ornaments of all sorts, conservatories, roseries, rustic seats, American borders, Gothic dairies, Spanish hermitages, and flowers stuck as close as pins in a pincushion, with every thing, in short, that might best become the walls of an exhibition room, or the back scene of a play: conceive the interior adorned in a style of elegance still more fanciful, and it will hardly appear surprising that this "unique bijou," as the advertisement calls it, should seldom want a tenant. The rapid succession of these occupiers is the more extraordinary matter. Every body is willing to come to Rosedale, but nobody stays.

For this, however, it is not difficult to assign very sufficient cause. In the first place, the house has the original sin of most ornamented cottages, that of being built on the foundation of a real labourer's dwelling; by which notable piece of economy the owner saved some thirty pounds, at the expense of making half his rooms mere nut-shells, and the house incurably damp,—to say nothing of the inconvenience of the many apartments which were erected as afterthoughts, the addenda of the work, and are only to be come at by outside passages and French window-doors. Secondly, that necessary part of a two-story mansion, the staircase, was utterly forgotten by architect, proprietor, and builder, and never missed by any person, till the ladder being one day taken away at the dinner hour, an Irish labourer, accidentally left behind, was discovered by the workmen on their return, perched like a bird on the top of the roof, he having taken the method of going up the chimney as the quickest way of getting down. This adventure occasioned a call for the staircase, which was at length inserted by the by, and is as much like a step-ladder in a dark corner as any thing well can be.[2] Thirdly, and lastly, this beautiful abode is in every way most thoroughly inconvenient and uncomfortable. In the winter one might find as much protection in the hollow of a tree—cold, gusty, sleety, wet; snow threatening from above like an avalanche; water gushing up from below like a fountain; a house of card-paper would be the solider refuge, a gipsy's tent by far the more snug. In summer it is proportionably close and hot, giving little shade and no shelter; and all the year round it is overdone with frippery and finery, a toy-shop in action, a Brobdignagian baby-house.

Every room is in masquerade: the saloon Chinese, full of jars and mandarins and pagodas; the library Egyptian, all covered with hieroglyphics, and swarming with furniture crocodiles and sphynxes. Only think of a crocodile couch, and a sphynx sofa! They sleep in Turkish tents, and dine in a Gothic chapel.[3] Now English ladies and gentlemen in their every-day apparel look exceedingly out of place amongst such mummery. The costume wont [sic] do. It is not in keeping. Besides, the properties themselves are apt to get shifted from one scene to another, and all manner of anomalies are the consequence. The mitred chairs and screens of the chapel, for instance, so very upright, and tall, and carved, and priestly, were mixed up oddly enough with the squat Chinese bonzes; whilst by some strange transposition a pair of nodding mandarins figured amongst the Egyptian monsters, and by the aid of their supernatural ugliness really looked human.

Then the room taken up by the various knicknackery, the unnamed and unnameable generation of gew-gaws! It always seemed to me to require more house-maids than the house would hold. And the same with the garden. You are so begirt with garlands and festoons, flowers above and flowers below, that you walk about under a perpetual sense of trespass, of taking care, of doing mischief, now bobbing against a sweet-briar, in which rencontre you have the worst; now flapped in the face by a woodbine to the discomfiture of both parties, now revenging these vegetable wrongs by tripping up an unfortunate balsam; bonnets, coatskirts and flounces in equal peril! The very gardeners step gingerly, and tuck their aprons tightly round them before they venture into that fair demesne of theirs, which is, so to say, over-peopled. In short, Rosedale is a place to look at, rather than live in; a fact which will be received without dispute by some score of tenants, by the proprietor of the county newspaper who keeps the advertisement of this matchless villa constantly set, to his no small emolument, and by the neighbourhood at large, to whom the succession of new faces, new liveries, and new equipages driving about our rustic lanes, and sometimes occupying a very tasty pew in the parish church, has long supplied a source of conversation as unfailing and as various as the weather.

The first person who ascertained, by painful experience, that Rosedale was uninhabitable, was the proprietor, a simple young man from the next town, who unluckily took it into his head that he had a taste for architecture and landscape gardening, and so forth; and falling into the hands of a London upholsterer and a country nurseryman, produced the effort of genius that I have endeavoured to describe. At the end of a month he found that nobody could live there; and with the advice of the nurseryman and the upholsterer began to talk of re-building and new-modelling; nay, he actually went so far as to send for the brick-layer; but fortunately for our man of taste he had a wife of more sense than himself, who seized the moment of disappointment to disgust him with improvements and improvers, in which feat she was greatly aided by the bills of his late associates; put a stop at once to his projects and his complaints: removed with all speed to their old residence, an ugly, roomy, comfortable red brick house in the market-place at B___; drew up a flaming advertisement, and turned the grumbling occupant into a thriving landlord. Lucky for him was the day in which William Walker, Esquire, married Miss Bridget Tomkins, second daughter of Mr. Samuel Tomkins, attorney at law! And lucky for Mr. Samuel Tomkins was the hour in which he acquired a son-in-law more profitable in the article of leases than the two lords to whom he acted as steward both put together!

First on the list of tenants was a bride and bridegroom come to spend the early months of their nuptial life in this sweet retirement. They arrived towards the end of August with a great retinue of servants, horses, dogs, and carriages, well bedecked with bridal favours. The very pointers had white ribbons round their necks, so splendid was their rejoicing, and had each, as we were credibly informed, eaten a huge slice of wedding-cake when the happy couple returned from church. The bride, whom every body except myself called plain, and whom I thought pretty, had been a great heiress, and had married for love the day she came of age. She was slight of form and pale of complexion, with a profusion of brown hair, mild hazel eyes, a sweet smile, a soft voice, and an air of modesty that clung about her like a veil. I never saw a more loveable creature. He was dark and tall and stout and bold, with an assured yet gentlemanly air, a loud voice, a confident manner, and a real passion for shooting. They stayed just a fortnight, during which time he contrived to get warned off half the manors in the neighbourhood, and cut down the finest elm in the lawn one wet morning to open a view of the high road. I hope the marriage has turned out a happy one, for she was a sweet gentle creature. I used to see her leaning over the gate watching his return from shooting with such a fond patience! And her hound to meet him when he did appear! And the pretty coaxing playfulness with which she patted and chided her rivals the dogs! Oh I hope she is happy! but I fear, I fear.

Next succeeded a couple from India, before whom floated reports golden and gorgeous as the clouds at sunset. Inexhaustible riches; profuse expenditure; tremendous ostentation; unheard-of luxury; ortolans; beccaficos; French-beans at Christmas; green-peas at Easter; strawberries always; a chariot and six; twelve black footmen; and parrots and monkeys beyond all count. These were amongst the most moderate of the rumours that preceded them; and every idle person in the country was preparing to be a hanger-on; and every shop-keeper in B. on the watch for a customer; when up drove a quiet-looking old gentleman in a pony-chaise, with a quiet-looking old lady at his side, and took possession, their retinue following in a hack post-chaise. Whether the habits of this Eastern Crœsus corresponded with his modest debût, or his magnificent reputation, we had not time to discover, although from certain indications, I conceive that much might be said on both sides. They arrived in the middle of a fine October, while the China roses covered the walls, and the China-asters, and dahlias, and fuchsias, and geraniums in full blow, gave a summer brilliancy to the lawn; but scarcely had a pair of superb Common-prayer-books, bound in velvet, and a bible with gold clasps entered in possession of the pew at church, before "there came a frost, a nipping frost," which turned the China-asters, and the China-roses brown, and the dahlias and geraniums black, and the nabob and the nabobess blue. They disappeared the next day, and have never been seen or heard of since.

Then arrived a fox-hunting Baronet, with a splendid stud and a splendid fortune. A young man, a single man, a handsome man! Every speculating mamma in the country fixed her eyes on Sir Robert for a son-in-law; papas were sent to call; brothers were enjoined to go out hunting, and get acquainted; nay, even certain of the young ladies themselves (I grieve to say it!) showed symptoms of condescension which might almost have made their grandmothers start from their graves. But what could they do? How could they help it, poor pretty things? The Baronet, with the instinct of a determined bachelor, avoided a young lady as a sparrow does a hawk, and discovering this shyness, they followed their instinct as the hawk would do in a similar case, and pursued the coy bird. It was what sportsmen call a fine open season, which being translated, means every variety of wintry weather except frost—dirty, foggy, sleety, wet; so such of our belles as looked well on horse-back, took the opportunity to ride, to cover and see the hounds throw off; and such as shone more as pedestrians would take an early walk, exquisitely dressed, for their health's sake, towards the general rendezvous. Still Sir Robert was immovable. He made no morning calls, accepted no invitations, spoke to no mortal till he had ascertained that there was neither sister, daughter, aunt, nor cousin in the case. He kept from every petticoat as if it contained the contagion of the plague, shunned ball-rooms and drawing-rooms, as if they were pest-houses, and finally, had the comfort of leaving Rosedale without having even bowed to a female during his stay. The final cause of his departure has been differently reported; some hold that he was frightened away by Miss Amelia Singleton, who had nearly caused him to commit involuntary homicide, (is that the word for killing a woman?) by crossing and recrossing before his hunter in Sallow-field-lane, thereby putting him in danger of a coroner's inquest; whilst others assert that his landlord, Mr. Walker, happening to call one day, found his tenant in dirty boots on the sphynx sofa, and a Newfoundland dog, dripping with mud, on the crocodile couch, and gave him notice to quit on the spot. For my part I regard this legend as altogether apocryphal, invented to save the credit of the house by assuming that one of its many inhabitants was turned out, contrary to his own wish. My faith goes entirely with the Miss Amelia version of the history; the more so, as that gentle damsel was so inconsolable as to marry a former beau, a small Squire of the neighbourhood, rather weather-beaten, and not quite so young as he had been, within a month after she had the ill luck not to be run over by Sir Robert.

However that may have been, "thence ensued a vacancy" in Rosedale, which was supplied the same week by a musical family, a travelling band, drums, trumpets, harps, pianos, violins, violincellos, trombones, and German flutes—noise personified! an incarnation of din! The family consisted of three young ladies who practised regularly six hours a day; a governess who played on some instruments or other from morning till night; one fluting brother; one fiddling ditto; a violin-celloing music-master; and a singing papa. The only quiet person among them, the "one poor half-penny-worth of bread to this monstrous quantity of sack," was the unfortunate mamma, sole listener, as it seemed, of her innumerous choir. Oh, how we pitied her! She was a sweet placid-looking woman, and younger in appearance than either of her daughters, with a fair open forehead, full dark eyes, lips that seemed waiting to smile, a deep yet cool colour, and a heavenly composure of countenance, resembling in features, expression, and complexion, the small Madonnas of Raphael. We never ceased to wonder at her happy serenity until we found out that the good lady was deaf, a discovery which somewhat diminished the ardour of our admiration. How this enviable calamity befell her, I did not hear,—but of course that din! The very jars and mandarins cracked under the incessant vibration; I only wonder that the poor house did not break the drum of its ears; did not burst from its own report, and explode like an overloaded gun. One could not see that unlucky habitation half a mile off, without such a feeling of noise as comes over one in looking at Hogarth's enraged musician.[4] To pass it was really dangerous. One stage-coach was overturned, and two post-chaises ran away in consequence of their uproarious doings; and a sturdy old-fashioned country gentleman, who rode a particularly anti-musical, startlish, blood-horse, began to talk of indicting Rosedale as a nuisance, when just at the critical moment, its tenants had the good fortune to discover, that although the hermitage with its vaulted roof made a capital concert-room, yet that there was not space enough within doors for their several practisings, that the apartments were too small, and the partitions too thin, so that concord was turned into discord, and harmonies went crossing each other all over the house—Mozart jostled by Rossini, and Handel put down by Weber. And away they went also.

Our next neighbours were two ladies, not sisters, except as one of them said in soul; kindred spirits determined to retire from the world, and emulate in this sweet retreat the immortal friendship of the ladies of Llangollen.[5] The names of our pair of friends were Jackson and Jennings, Miss Laura Jackson (I wonder whether Laura really was her name! She signed herself so in prose and in verse, and would certainly for more reasons than one have disliked an appeal to the Register! besides, she ought to know; so Laura it shall be!) Miss Laura Jackson and Miss Barbara Jennings, commonly called Bab. Both were of that unfortunate class of young ladies, whom the malicious world is apt to call old maids; both rich, both independent, and both in the fullest sense of the word cockneys. Laura was tall and lean, and scraggy and yellow, dressing in an Arcadian sort of way, pretty much like an opera shepherdess without a crook, singing pastoral songs prodigiously out of tune, and talking in a deep voice, with much emphasis and astounding fluency all sorts of sentimentalities all the day long. Miss Barbara on the other hand was short and plump and round-faced and ruddy, inclining to vulgarity as Laura to affectation, with a great love of dancing, a pleasant chuckling laugh, and a most agreeable habit of assentation. Altogether Bab was a likeable person in spite of some nonsense, which is more than could honestly be said for her companion.

Juxtaposition laid the corner-stone of this immortal friendship, which had already lasted four months and a half, and cemented by resemblance of situation, and dissimilarity of character, really bade fair to continue some months longer. Both had been heartily weary of their previous situations: Laura keeping house for a brother in Aldersgate-street, where as she said she was overwhelmed by odious vulgar business; Barbara living with an aunt on Fish-street Hill, where she was tired to death of having nothing to do. Both had a passion for the country. Laura, who, except one jaunt to Margate, had never been out of the sound of Bow-bell, that she might ruralize after the fashion of the poets, sit under trees and gather roses all day long; Bab, who in spite of yearly trips to Paris and Brussels and Amsterdam and Brighton, had hardly seen a green field except through a coach-window, was on her side possessed with a mania for notability and management; *she yearned to keep cows*, fatten pigs, breed poultry, grow cabbages, make hay, brew and bake, and wash and churn. Visions of killing her own mutton flitted over her delighted fancy; and when one evening at a ball in the Borough her favorite partner had deserted her to dance with her niece, and Miss Laura, who had been reading Miss Seward's letters, proposed to her to retire from the world and its vanities in imitation of the illustrious recluses of Llangollen, Miss Barbara, caught above all things with the prospect of making her own butter every morning for breakfast,[6] acceded to the proposal most joyfully.

The vow of friendship was taken, and nothing remained but to look out for a house. Barbara wanted a farm, Laura a cottage; Barbara talked of cows and clover, Laura of nightingales and violets; Barbara sighed for Yorkshire pastures, Laura for Welsh mountains; and the scheme seemed likely to go off for want of an habitation, when Rosedale in all the glory of advertisement shone on Miss Laura in the Morning Post, and was immediately engaged by the delighted friends on a lease of seven, fourteen, or one-and-twenty years.

It was a raw blowy March evening, when the fair partners arrived at the cottage. Miss Laura made a speech in her usual style on taking possession, an invocation to friendship and rural nature, and a deprecation of cities, society and men; at the conclusion of which Miss Barbara underwent an embrassade;[7] and having sufficiently admired the wonders within they sallied forth with a candle and lanthorn to view their ruralities without. Miss Laura was better satisfied with this ramble than her companion. She found at least trees and primroses, whilst the country felicities of ducks and chickens were entirely wanting. Bab, however, reconciled the matter by supposing they were gone to roost, and a little worn out by the journey wisely followed their example.

The next day saw Miss Laura obliged to infringe her own most sacred and inviolable rule, and admit a man—the apothecary—into this maiden abode. She had sate under a tree the night before listening not to, but for a nightingale, and was laid up by a most unpastoral fit of the rheumatism. Barbara in the meanwhile was examining her territory by day-light, and discovering fresh cause of vexation at every step. Here she was in the country, in a cottage "compromising," as the advertisement set forth, "all manner of convenience and accommodation," without grass or corn, or cow or sheep, or pig or chicken, or turkey or goose;—no laundry, no brew-house, no pig-stye [sic], no poultry-yard! not a cabbage in the garden! not a useful thing about the house! Imagine her consternation!

But Barbara was a person of activity and resource. She sallied out forthwith to the neighbouring village, bought utensils and livestock; turned the coach-house into a cow-stall; projected a pig-sty in the rosery; installed her ducks and geese in the orangery; introduced the novelty of real milk-pans, churns and butter-prints amongst the old china, Dutch-tiles and stained glass of that make-believe toy the Gothic dairy; placed her brewing vessels in 'the housekeeper's room,' which to accord with the genius of the place had been fitted up to represent a robber's cave; deposited her washing-tubs in the butler's pantry, which with a similar regard to congruity had been decorated with spars and shells like Nereid's grotto;[8] and finally, in spite of all warning and remonstrance, drove her sheep into the shrubbery, and tethered her cows upon the lawn.

This last stroke was too much for the gardener's patience. He betook himself in all haste to B. to apprise Mr. Walker; and Mr. Walker armed with Mr. Samuel Tompkins and a copy of the lease made his appearance with breathless speed at Rosedale. Barbara, in spite of her usual placidity, made good battle on this occasion. She cried and scolded and reasoned and implored; it was as much as Mr. Walker, and Mr. Samuel Tomkins [sic], aided by their mute witness the lease, and that very clamorous auxiliary the gardener, could do to out-talk her. At last, however, they were victorious. Poor Miss Bab's livestock were forced to make a rapid retreat, and she would probably have marched off at the same time, had not an incident occurred which brought her visions of rural felicity much nearer to reality than could have been anticipated by the liveliest imagination.

The farmer's wife of whom she had made her purchases, and to whom she unwillingly addressed herself to resume them, seeing to use her own words, "how much Madam seemed to take on at parting with the poor dumb things," kindly offered to accommodate them as boarders at a moderate stipend, volunteering also lessons in the chicken-rearing and pig-feeding department, of which the lady did to be sure stand rather in need.

Of course Barbara closed with this proposal at a word. She never was so happy in her life; her cows, pigs, and poultry, en pension, close by, where she might see them every hour if she liked, and she herself with both hands full, learning at the farm, and ordering at the cottage, and displaying all that can be imagined of ignorance and good-humour at both.

Her mistakes were innumerable. Once for instance, she carried away by main force from a turkey, whose nest she had the ill-luck to discover, thirteen eggs, just ready to hatch, and after a severe combat with the furious and injured hen, brought them home to Rosedale as fresh-laid—under a notion rather new in natural history, that turkeys lay all their eggs in one day. Another time she discovered a hoard of choice double-dahlia roots in a tool-house belonging to her old enemy the gardener, and delivered them to the cook for Jerusalem artichokes, who dressed them as such accordingly. No end to Barbara's blunders! but her good-humour, her cheerfulness, her liberality, and the happy frankness with which she laughed at her own mistakes, carried her triumphantly through. Every body liked her, especially a smug little curate who lodged at the very farm-house where her pigs and cattle were boarded, and said twenty times a day that Miss Barbara Jennings was the pleasantest woman in England. Barbara was never so happy in her life.

Miss Laura, on her part, continued rheumatic and poorly, and kept closely to her bedchamber, the Turkish tent, with no other consolations than novels from the next town and the daily visits of the apothecary. She was shocked at Miss Barbara's intimacy with the farm people, and took every opportunity of telling her so. Barbara, never very fond of her fair companion's harangues, and not the more reconciled to them from their being directed against her own particular favourites, ran away as often as she could. So that the two friends had nearly arrived at the point of not speaking, when they met one afternoon by mutual appointment in the Chinese saloon. Miss Barbara blushed and looked silly, and seemed trying to say something which she could not bring out. Miss Laura tried to blush rather unsuccessfully. She however could talk at all times, her powers of speech were never known to fail; and at the end of an oration in which she proved, as was pretty evident, that they had been mistaken in supposing the company of each all-sufficient to the other as well as in their plan of seclusion from the world, she invited Miss Barbara, after another vain attempt at a blush, to pay the last honours to their friendship by attending her to the hymeneal altar, whither she had promised to accompany Mr. Opodeldoc on the morning after the next.

"I can't," replied Miss Barbara.

"And why not?" resumed Miss Laura. "Surely Mr. Opodel——"

"Now, don't be angry!" interrupted our friend Bab. "I can't be your bridemaid the day after to-morrow, because I am going to be married to-morrow myself."

And so they left Rosedale, and I shall leave them.

Notes

1.   Minerva Press and Minerva Library, started by William Lane in 1770, produced inexpensive, light romances, written chiefly by women for other women. See Adburgham's *Women in Print* for a detailed account of Lane and his publications.

2.   This instance of forgetfulness is not unexampled. A similar accident is said to have happened to Madame d'Arblay in the erection of a cottage built from the profits of her admirable Camilla. [Mitford's note]

3.   Some of the pleasantest days of my life have been spent in a house so furnished. But then it was of fitting dimensions, and the delightful persons to whom it belonged had a house in London, and a mansion in the country, and used their fancy villa much as one would use a marquee or a pleasure-boat, for gay parties in fine weather. Rosedale, unlucky place, was built to be lived in. [Mitford's note]

4.   William Hogarth (1697–1764), an English artist who satirized 18th-century life with comic zeal.

5.   I need not, I trust, disclaim any intention of casting the lightest shade of ridicule on the remarkable instance of female friendship to which I have alluded in the text. An union enduring as that has done, from youth to age, adorned by rank, talent, and beauty, cemented by cheerfulness and good-humour, and consecrated by benevolence and virtue, can fear no one's censure, and soars far beyond my feeble praise. Such a friendship is the very poetry of life. But the heartless imitation, the absurd parody of the noble and elevating romance, is surely fair game, the more so, as it tends like all parodies to bring the original into undeserved disrepute. [Mitford's note]

6.   Vide Anna Seward's Correspondence. [Mitford's note]

7.   A French word, meaning embrace, hug; kissing, or a kiss.

8.   Sea nymphs, the daughters of Nereus and Doris. According to Bulfinch, they played, danced, and were wooed by the Tritons.

3. Walks in the Country: The Wood

Introduction

Published in the second volume of *Our Village* (1826), Mary Mitford's "The Wood" is one of her few sketches that represent nature as threatened; in this case, the ancient oaks that shelter the wood sorrel are destroyed by the woodman's axe. The narrator and her fellow traveller stumble across the scene in the course of their wanderings; they both feel awed by the power of the saw over the majestic trees. The essay places this destruction in a disturbing context which wrenches the reader and the country travelers from the pleasant sights they have just seen in the wood. Nature is personified as an entity angry over its own demise at the hands of the axe. This poignant, sobering scene of the trees' destruction is amplified when we realize that at the time the sketch was written, rural England was on the brink of great and sudden changes, such as the introduction of farm machines that sparked riots by displaced farm laborers in the 1830s, the advent of the railways in the 1840s, and the increasing migration of the population to the cities.

Walks in the Country: The Wood

April 20th.—Spring is actually come now, with the fulness and almost the suddenness of a northern summer. To-day is completely April;—clouds and sunshine, wind and showers; blossoms on the trees, grass in the fields, swallows by the ponds, snakes in the hedge-rows, nightingales in the thickets, and cuckoos every where. My young friend Ellen G. is going with me this evening to gather wood sorrel. She never saw that most elegant plant, and is so delicate an artist that the introduction will be a mutual benefit; Ellen will gain a subject worthy of her pencil, and the pretty weed will live;—no small favour to a flower, almost as transitory as the gum cistus; duration is the only charm which it wants, and that Ellen will give it. The weather is, to be sure, a little threatening, but we are not people to mind the weather when we have an object in view; we shall certainly go in quest of the wood-sorrel, and will take May, provided we can escape May's follower; for, since the adventure of the lamb, Saladin has had an affair with a gander, furious in defence of his goslings, in which recontre the gander came off conqueror; and as geese abound in the wood to which we are going (called by the country people the Pinge,) and the victory may not always incline to the right side, I should be very sorry to lead the Soldan to fight his battles over again. We will take nobody but May.[1]

So saying, we proceeded on our way through winding lanes, between hedge-rows tenderly green, till we reached the hatch-gate, with the white cottage beside it embosomed in fruit-trees, which forms the entrance to the Pinge, and in a moment the whole scene was before our eyes.

"Is not this beautiful, Ellen?" The answer could hardly be other than a glowing rapid "Yes!"—A wood is generally a pretty place; but this wood—Imagine a smaller forest, full of glades and sheep-walks, surrounded by irregular cottages with their blooming orchards, a clear stream winding about the brakes, and a road intersecting it, and giving life and light to the picture; and you will have a faint idea of the Pinge. Every step was opening a new point of view, a fresh combination of glade and path and thicket. The accessories too were changing every moment. Ducks, geese, pigs, and children, giving way, as we advanced into the wood, to sheep and forest ponies; and they again disappearing as we became more entangled in its mazes, till we heard nothing but the song of the nightingale, and saw only the silent flowers.

What a piece of fairy land! The tall elms overhead just bursting into tender vivid leaf, with here and there a hoary oak or a silver-barked beech, every twig swelling with the brown buds, and yet not quite stripped of the tawny foliage of Autumn; tall hollies and hawthorn beneath, with their crisp brilliant leaves mixed with the white blossoms of the sloe, and woven together with garlands of woodbines and wild briars;—what a fairy land!

Primroses, cowslips, pansies, and the regular open-eyed white blossom of the wood anemone (or to use the more elegant Hampshire name, the windflower) were set under our feet as thick as daisies in a meadow; but the pretty weed we came to seek was coyer; and Ellen began to fear that we had mistaken the place or the season.—At last she had herself the pleasure of finding it under a brake of holly—"Oh look! look! I am sure that this is the wood-sorrel! Look at the pendent white flower, shaped like a snow-drop and veined with purple streaks, and the beautiful trefoil leaves folded like a heart,—some, the young ones, so vividly yet tenderly green that the foliage of the elm and the hawthorn would show dully at their side,—others of a deeper tint, and lined, as it were, with a rich and changeful purple!—Don't you see them?" pursued my dear young friend, who is a delightful piece of life and sunshine, and was half inclined to scold me for the calmness with which, amused by her enthusiasm, I stood listening to her ardent exclamations—"Don't you see them? Oh how beautiful! and in what quantity! what profusion! See how the dark shade of the holly sets off the light and delicate colouring of the flower!—And see that other bed of them springing from the rich moss in the roots of that old beech tree! Pray let us gather some. Here are baskets." So quickly and carefully we began gathering, leaves, blossoms, roots and all, for the plant is so fragile that it will not brook separation!—quickly and carefully we gathered, encountering divers petty misfortunes in spite of all our care, now caught by the veil in a holly bush, now hitching our shawls in a bramble, still gathering on, in spite of scratched fingers, till we had nearly filled our baskets and began to talk of our departure:—

"But where is May? May! May! No going home without her. May! Here she comes galloping, the beauty!"—(Ellen is almost as fond of May as I am.)—"What has she got in her mouth? that rough, round, brown substance which she touches so tenderly? What can it be? A bird's nest? Naughty May!"

"No! as I live, a hedgehog! Look, Ellen, how it has coiled itself into a thorny ball! Off with it May! Don't bring it to me!"—And May, somewhat reluctant to part with her prickly prize, however troublesome of carriage, whose change of shape seemed to me to have puzzled her sagacity more than any event I ever witnessed, for in general she has perfectly the air of understanding all that is going forward—May at last dropt the hedgehog; continuing however to pat it with her delicate cat-like paw, cautiously and daintily applied, and caught back suddenly and rapidly after every touch, as if her poor captive had been a red-hot coal. Finding that these pats entirely failed in solving the riddle, (for the hedgehog shammed dead, like the lamb the other day, and appeared entirely motionless), she gave him so spirited a nudge with her pretty black nose, that she not only turned him over, but sent him rolling some little way along the turfy path,—an operation which that sagacious quadruped endured with the most perfect passiveness, the most admirable non-resistance. No wonder that May's discernment was at fault: I myself, if I had not been aware of the trick, should have said that the ugly rough thing which she was trundling along, like a bowl or a cricket-ball, was an inanimate substance, something devoid of sensation and of will. At last my poor pet thoroughly perplexed and tired out, fairly relinquished the contest, and came slowly away, turning back once or twice to look at the object of her curiosity, as if half inclined to return and try the event of another shove. The sudden flight of a wood-pigeon effectually diverted her attention; and Ellen amused herself by fancying how the hedgehog was scuttling away, till our notice was also attracted by a very different object.

We had nearly threaded the wood, and were approaching an open grove of magnificent oaks on the other side, when sounds other than of nightingales burst on our ear, the deep and frequent strokes of the woodman's axe, and emerging from the Pinge we discover the havoc which that axe had committed. About twenty of the finest trees lay stretched on the velvet turf. There they lay in every shape and form of devastation: some, bare trunks stripped ready for the timber carriage, with the bark built up in long piles at the side; some with the spoilers busy about them, stripping, hacking, hewing; others with their noble branches, their brown and fragrant shoots all fresh as if they were alive—majestic corses, the slain of to-day! The grove was like a field of battle. The young lads who were stripping the bark, the very children who were picking up the chips, seemed awed and silent, as if conscious that death was around them. The nightingales sang faintly and interruptedly—a few low frightened notes like a requiem.

Ah! here we are at the very scene of murder, the very tree that they are felling; they have just hewn round the trunk with those slaughtering axes, and are about to saw it asunder. After all it is a fine and thrilling operation, as the work of death usually is. Into how grand an attitude was that young man thrown as he gave the final stroke round the root; and how wonderful is the effect of that supple and apparently powerless saw, bending like a riband, and yet overmastering that giant of the woods, conquering and overthrowing that thing of life! Now it has passed half through the trunk, and the woodman has begun to calculate which way the tree will fall; he drives a wedge to direct its course;—now a few more movements of the noiseless saw; and then a larger wedge. See how the branches tremble! Hark how the trunk begins to crack? Another stroke of the huge hammer on the wedge, and the tree quivers, as with a mortal agony, shakes, reels, and falls. How slow and solemn and awful it is! How like to death, to human death in its grandest form! Cæsar in the Capitol, Seneca in the bath, could not fall more sublimely than that oak.

Even the heavens seem to sympathise with the devastation. The clouds have gathered into one thick low canopy, dark and vapoury as the smoke which overhangs London; the setting sun just gleaming underneath with a dim and bloody glare, and the crimson rays spreading upwards with a lurid and portentous grandeur, a subdued and dusky glow, like the light reflected on the sky from some vast conflagration. The deep flush fades away, and the rain begins to descend; and we hurry homeward rapidly yet sadly, forgetful alike of the flowers, the hedgehog, and the wetting, thinking and talking only of the fallen tree.

Notes

1. May is the greyhound who appeared in "Our Village." Saladin and Brindle are two other greyhounds who like to walk with Mary. The greyhounds often get into trouble chasing lambs into ditches.

II. Harriet Martineau
(1802–1876)

When writing her own obituary for the *Daily News*, Harriet Martineau categorized herself as a popularizer of other people's ideas. She concluded that her "original power was nothing more than was due to earnestness and intellectual clearness within a certain range. . . . In short, she could popularise, while she could neither discover or invent" (June 29, 1876). Martineau did indeed gain a reputation as a popularizer of others' ideas; however, she was also an intellectual in her own right. Over the course of her lifetime she espoused theories on a vast array of subjects, including theology, political economy, the woman question, abolition of slavery, household management, and invalidism. No matter what her topic, Martineau worked to advance the cause of rationality, often employing positivism and utilitarianism to help explain human behavior. Although considered by her contemporaries to be a social reformer, Martineau did not believe political legislation could lead to change; she argued instead that if people were educated to think rationally, without emotion or convention interfering with their logic, reform would follow naturally. Ultimately, Martineau's arguments for public education, laissez-faire economics, and female equality directly influenced discussion and reform in her time, thus making her one of Victorian Britain's most influential women of letters.

Harriet Martineau was born on June 12, 1802, in Norwich, to Thomas and Elizabeth Rankin Martineau. She was the sixth of eight children. A sickly child, susceptible to periods of depression and loneliness, she sought the comforts of religion as well as the companionship of her younger brother, James, to help counteract her melancholia. Martineau initially was educated at home under the tutelage of her older siblings. She learned French, Latin, writing, and arithmetic before being sent at age eleven to a Unitarian school conducted by Isaac Perry. When the school closed two years later, she resumed studying at home with professional tutors. Throughout her adolescence, Martineau maximized her opportunity to obtain an education superior to that given to most nineteenth-century middle-class girls.

In spite of her enthusiasm for education and reading, Martineau's depression worsened when she realized that she was losing her hearing. By age sixteen, she was almost deaf. In an attempt to help their daughter improve her health, the Martineaus sent her to live with an aunt in Bristol. While there, Martineau became a protégé of the Unitarian minister Lant Carpenter, who exposed her to the writings of Locke, Hartley, and Priestley. During her time in Bristol, Martineau began coming to terms with her deafness, and at the same time devoted herself to studying utilitarian and necessarian philosophies.

Martineau started writing when she returned home from Bristol in 1818. At the urging of James, she drafted essays and tales, working late at night after she had completed her obligatory household chores. Her first published essays, "Female Writers on Practical Divinity" (1822) and "On Female Education" (1823), appeared in the dissident *Monthly Repository*. After her father's death in 1826 and the virtual failure of his manufacturing business, Martineau had good reason to consider writing as a career. Due in part to the favorable response that her tales *The Turn-Out* and *The Rioters* (1827) generated among a working-class audience, Martineau began creating a series of fictionalized tales, each illustrating a specific lesson in political economy. It was the 1832 publication of *Life in the Wilds*, the first of the twenty-five volume *Illustrations of Political Economy* (1832–34), which made Martineau phenomenally popular. In spite of the tales' didactic, overly simplistic approach to economic principles espoused by Malthus, Smith, and Ricardo, Martineau became recognized as a leading proponent of the utilitarian principle, "the greatest happiness of the greatest number."

As with many authors in Victorian Britain, Martineau was able to support herself by writing. The population's increasing literacy created a demand for books and periodicals, and because Martineau could popularize ideas that were formerly the province of an educated upper class, her writing was in high demand. Martineau often directed her attention to the lower and middle classes, documenting their lives, means of survival, family and social interactions, occupations, struggles, and accomplishments. *Illustrations of Political Economy* was Martineau's most popular attempt at working-class fiction, and it anticipated the works of Elizabeth Gaskell and Charles Dickens. Furthermore, Martineau's histories, especially *The History of England during the Thirty Years' Peace, 1816–1846* (1849–50), are among the first to record the social and economic aspects of English society, rather than just the political, military, or intellectual history of a people. From 1822 up to 1864, Martineau published articles in a variety of periodicals, including the *Edinburgh Review*, *Household Words*, *Monthly Repository*, *Once A Week*, *People's Journal*, the *Westminster Review*, and *Zoist: A Journal of Cerebral Psychology and Mesmerism*.

The diversity, popularity, and influence of Martineau's work made her a major literary figure in Victorian Britain. Certainly the study of that age would be incomplete without considering her, both as a writer and as a social reformer. Her writing contributed to the emergence of the middle and working classes as legitimate literary subjects, and thus, is important to our study of both the British novel and intellectual prose. Furthermore, her *Society in America* (1837) serves as one of the most important sociological documents of nineteenth-century American culture and history. Although sorely neglected today, it equalled Alexis de Tocqueville's *Democracy in America* (1835;1840) in popularity and influence.

Scholarship on Martineau is extensive. However, the most revealing study remains Martineau's own *Autobiography* (1877). *Harriet Martineau's Letters to Fanny Wedgwood*, edited by Elisabeth Sanders Arbuckle (1983), is equally informative. Many of Martineau's contemporaries also wrote about her life and work. John Stuart Mill's "Miss Martineau's Summary of Political Economy" (*Monthly Repository*, 1834) offers valuable criticism of Martineau's economic theory, while Florence Fenwick Miller's *Harriet Martineau* (1884) serves as an extensive account of Martineau's social activism. More recent studies include two significant intellectual biographies: Robert K. Webb's *Harriet Martineau: A Radical Victorian* (1960), and Valerie Kossew Pichanick's *Harriet Martineau: The Woman and Her Work, 1802–76* (1980). Deirdre David's *Intellectual Women and Victorian Patriarchy: Harriet Martineau, Elizabeth Barrett Browning, and George Eliot* (1987) considers Martineau's concessions, as well as her resistance, to Victorian patriarchal constructs. Valerie Sanders's *Reason Over Passion: Harriet Martineau and the Victorian Novel* (1986) examines Martineau's fiction and argues her importance as an innovative novelist.

Herbert Northcote,
Temple University

4. Prison Discipline

Introduction

Harriet Martineau's "Prison Discipline" first appeared in the *Monthly Repository* in 1832, and is reprinted here from her *Miscellanies* (2 vols., Boston, 1836). "Prison Discipline" is in part Martineau's review of *The Eighth Report of the Committee of the Society for the Improvement of Prison Discipline* (1832), and *Punishment of Death: A Series of Short Articles, &ct.* (1832); however, as was the case with many Victorian-era reviews, "Prison Discipline" is also an essay in its own right. Martineau examines how the British education system actually helps to produce criminals, and how the prison system promotes, instead of inhibits, crime. As with many of her contemporaries, Martineau was keenly aware that seemingly disparate entities, in this case class, education, and criminal behavior, were actually interconnected. "Prison Discipline" was a timely discussion that offered readers insight into why prisons were in dire need of reform, as well as why persons turned to crime in the first place.

Prison Discipline[1]

While, as a nation, we are setting to work in earnest to prepare for ourselves institutions which will, in all probability, lessen the amount of crime within our borders, the greater number of us are little aware how barbarous are those of our regulations which relate to the custody and punishment of criminals. Our ignorance is not the less because we venerate the names of Howard and Romilly. If this had been enough, their philanthropic successors would not now have had to deplore that the work begun by them has made little progress, in comparison with the time which has elapsed since they set it on foot; and that our treatment of the sinning part of our population is as largely compounded of folly and cruelty, as if our Christianity were no more than a name, and our civilization a false and conceited assumption. As a nation, we have not even arrived at the principle of punishment; we are blind to its objects, and therefore erring in the use of its means. The lowest classes among us look upon punishment as sheer cruelty, inflicted by those who have power, for some unknown purpose of gratification or advantage. Those a little above them regard punishment as vengeance; others, as something connected with crime by an unknown moral necessity; others, more enlightened, see in it a benevolent purpose of preventing more evil by the infliction of less. Few, very few, question whether any right exists to inflict punishment at all, except in as far as punishment is involved in the regulations by which the orderly part of society is secured from aggression. Of all these, the lower classes know most of the facts of the treatment of our criminals; and all that they know is so corroborative of their notions of punishment being either gratuitous cruelty or vengeance, that we must not expect them to improve their conceptions till we have amended our management. In order to bring about this amendment, the comparatively enlightened classes must be more fully informed than they are of the actual state of our criminal policy; and such of them as are practised in tracing institutions to their principles must be loudly called upon to apply their philosophy where it has never yet been applied by more than a few individuals, who, groaning in spirit, have taken upon themselves as much as individuals might bear of the responsibilities of a nation. It is not enough to carry on Howard's department of the work, or even to perpetuate the labors of Romilly;

for, like all other moral labors, this grows upon the hands. It is not enough (though, alas! it is still much wanted) to go into our prisons, and see that the inmates have air, and light, and food, and water. It is not enough, though it is much, to see that they are not confined month after month, year after year, before there is so much as an attempt to prove a charge against them. It is not enough, though it is much, to strive to free our penal code from the barbarities and absurdities of former ages. Further than this, it ought to be, it must be, ascertained what constitutes crime in the present age; how society may be best guarded from its aggressions; and whether that kind of punishment which consists in the arbitrary infliction of suffering serves the purpose of security, or any other purpose; and whether, therefore, such infliction is authorized.

It is clearly the duty of a government to protect its subjects from the aggressions of crime; and, in consequence, to seclude, or otherwise render powerless, its criminal members. This appears to us to be the limit of its authority, in the first instance. This should be the object, not only in the process of arrest and custody previous to trial, but after conviction. We cannot discern whence is given the power to inflict arbitrary suffering in the case of guilt, more than in any other case. A just direction of natural consequences answers all the good purposes ever contemplated in the institution of arbitrary punishments, and refers the responsibility whither it ought to rest,—on that Providence which has ordained misery to be the natural consequence of guilt. A man breaks into his neighbour's dwelling to steal his goods: we punish him with death. This certainly secures society from his future trespasses; but it does much more,—much more, that we can perceive no warrant for our doing. It destroys a life which we recognise no commission to take; and which, for aught we know, might be made useful to the community and happy to the individual: it perplexes the notions of moral cause and effect, right and wrong, duty and Providence, in the minds of multitudes; and excites tumults of angry passions: thus demoralizing instead of warning, and tending to the propagation instead of the repression of evil. How different are the effects of punishment by natural consequence!

The man has done his neighbour wrong, and must therefore be secluded, that he may not again do an injury. This is the reason of his imprisonment, which is longer or shorter, in proportion to the apparent probabilities of his repeating the offence,—that is, to the aggravation of the circumstances and to the offender's known character. In prison, he must not be a burden to the community, and must work, not only for his bread, but for the expenses which he has caused to be incurred in secluding him. This is the reason of his being condemned to hard labor. If, in his seclusion, he attempts further injury to those yet within his reach, a closer confinement is ordered for the same purpose as the first. Hence solitary confinement, and, if ever necessary, fetters. The other regulations of his prison arise, some out of the position in which the culprit has placed himself, and not out of the will of his judges and jailers; and others out of their responsibility for his benefit, that he shall re-enter the world no worse, as far as in them lies, than when he quitted it. Hence arise the circumstances of his abode, his employments, his recreations,—in short, the routine of his prison-life. Is not this what is wanted for the security of society? Is not this still punishment,—most irksome punishment to the offender, while it allows him to feel himself, not the victim of tyranny, but the ward of justice? Is not this the discipline to satisfy instead of revolting the injured, to obviate the oppressions of the agents of the law, to educate the moral sense of the community, while it answers all the proposed objects of an arbitrary penal system? Is it not easy to be understood in its purpose and in its workings?—far more easy than the inexplicable and empirical method,—if method it may be called,—according to which justice is at present administered?

That human governments will in time bring their penal rule into an analogy with the divine, we cannot doubt. The divine government ordained arbitrary punishments in the infancy of the peculiar people, and afterwards withdrew its ordinances, when they became capable of recognising and anticipating natural consequences; and thus ought it to be with human governments. In barbarous ages and countries, crimes are little less arbitrary than punishments; as in Russia, not very long ago, the wearing of shoe-strings was punishable with imprisonment, and in India the killing of a cow, with death. In proportion as States approximate to a right application of the eternal principles of morals, should their penal government approximate to the divine rule of natural consequence; for which precisely the same reasons exist as that a parent should lay aside the rod and the holiday-treat when his child grows up into the youth.

It is a difficult task to arrange the penal government of a nation like ours in its present state, combining as it does the wisdom of manhood and the lowest ignorance and folly of infancy,—much of the refinement of advanced civilization, and some of the brutalization of a savage state. It is difficult to provide punishments which it does not shock the consciences and sensibilities of the injured to inflict, and which may at the same time be prospectively dreadful to the aggressor. This difficulty, great at the best, we aggravate to the utmost,—first, by not procuring the universal education of the people, and next, by making the worst of such regulations as we have; administering our punishments capriciously, and enhancing their mischiefs by bad modes of infliction. Two great works, then, have to be achieved, in preparation for the enlightened penal system of which our philosophers and philanthropists descry a glimpse in a coming age:—the nation must be educated into a state of moral discernment: and, while this is doing, our present penal institutions must be purified from the executive abuses which render them ten times more cruel and pernicious than the most barbarous of their originators intended, or than there is any occasion for them to be made.

We quote some remarks from the Report before us, on the first of the two objects we have specified:—

The distressed condition of juvenile offenders on their discharge from prison has continued to occupy the attention of the Committee, and they have afforded such relief to these necessitous objects as the very limited state of the funds would allow. The prevalence of crime among the youth of the lower orders is well known to be alarmingly great. On the causes which contribute to this evil, the Committee have fully enlarged in their former Reports. Whatever operates to the production of indigence among the adult poor, has, of course, a most unfavorable effect on the moral condition of their families; and the juvenile depravity, which now unhappily prevails, derives its origin and strength from circumstances too deeply rooted in the present state of society to be materially diminished by any plans, however wise, for the mere punishment of the offender. The diffusion of education is, in every point of view, the most efficacious remedy for the prevention of crime. By education is meant, not merely instruction in the elementary arts of reading and writing, but a course of moral training which shall impart religious impressions, control the passions, and amend the heart. In their previous Reports, the Committee have enlarged on the benefits which the establishment of Infant Schools is calculated to impart to the most indigent classes, and especially in those crowded parts of the metropolis where a single room often contains several families. Beset on every side by the most profligate associations, breathing a moral atmosphere the most corrupt, no benefits can be conceived more precious than those which are presented by these Institutions; and it is therefore to be regretted that, notwithstanding their obvious importance, they should not have become universally established. In regard to the education of the poor generally, it must be acknowledged that the experience of the last thirty years has proved the inefficiency of the exertions made for this purpose, as well by public associations as by private individuals. In the metropolis and populous towns throughout the kingdom, the want of education is severely felt, while in the agricultural districts a large proportion of the working classes are in a state of profound ignorance and great moral debasement. But a slight consideration of the subject will show that the moral and religious education of the people is an object too vast in its importance to the well-being of the State, to be left to the voluntary exertions of benevolent individuals and charitable associations. An Education Act, framed on broad and liberal principles, and securing the concurrence of all sects and parties, would be one of the greatest blessings which the legislature could confer; and it is earnestly hoped that the period has at length arrived when a national measure of this high character will provide for every child throughout the kingdom an education comprising the elements of useful knowledge, and based on the solid foundation of Christian principles.—pp. 85–87.

Our business, then, is to favor infant and other schools to the utmost, and to go on thanking government for the Irish School Bill, and reminding it that we want more, till general education becomes the law of our English land. Then there will be, among an incalculable number of other advantages, a wide opening for an improvement in our penal government.

The second great object, that of rendering our penal institutions no worse than they need be, is that which the Prison Discipline Society[2] espouses.

None of the objects, with a view to which imprisonment should be conducted, can possibly be answered by the methods which prevailed before the Society began its exertions, and which have not yet given place sufficiently to the better system of discipline which they have partially introduced, and are striving to make general. Those objects are,

1st. The security of the community.

2d. The reformation of the offender.

3d.—(a subordinate, though still important object)—That the resources of the community should not be uselessly consumed by its criminals.

The security of a community is little promoted by a system which lodges a man in prison a debtor, and brings him out a ruffian; which imprisons him erring, and discharges him depraved; or turns a merely suspected man into a guilty one. Of the 120,000 prisoners yearly contained within the jails of the United Kingdom, a very large number must have gone in, in a moral condition less threatening to society than that of many whom they were about to join. Thousands of them were only debtors, thousands were young, many guilty of a first offence only, many innocent. For the short protection afforded to society by the temporary confinement of these 120,000, how dearly must it pay on their return to it! Some of its foes are removed by the gallows, others are sent abroad to spread the contagion of their vices elsewhere; but in compensation of this riddance, the debtors come out ready to steal as well as defraud; the young educated to crime; the once over-tempted now hardened; the innocent corrupted. Thus is moral evil propagated by the very mode adopted to confine it, and society injured by the means ordained for its protection. The remedy must be found in classification, in restriction of intercourse, in keeping our prisons as clear as possible of offenders whose misdeeds are not of so bad a character as to render their seclusion necessary to the peace of the community, and in shortening, as much as possible, the period of imprisonment previous to trial.

"In respect to classification," observes the Report, "the prison-act directs that in every county jail or house of correction, the prisoners shall be divided into ten classes; and where these prisons are united together, twelve classes are required:" it is further enacted that "such further means of classification shall be adopted as the justices shall deem conducive to good order and discipline." "It appears, however, from the jail returns, that upwards of forty prisons have not even the lowest scale of classification required by law; and that there are only twenty-two united county prisons in which the *minimum* is exceeded. Wherever the numbers are large, a further division of classes in respect to age, character, and degrees of crime, is indispensable, in order to promote individual reformation, and prevent the mischievous effects of contamination."—p. 23. There is much to be done then in rectifying the execution of the law while waiting for the amendment of the penal code.

The difficulties in the way of classification are much increased by the crowded state of too many of our jails,—an evil not wholly arising from the increase of crime, but from an increased disposition in the magistracy to avoid the responsibility of bailing offenders who are brought before them; so that stealers of hedge-stakes and boys guilty of street-rows are shut up in a school of corruption for weeks, instead of awaiting, under better influences, the punishment of their offences. It should be remembered that every committal to jail is a misfortune to the community as well as to the culprit, and therefore a deed not to be needlessly done. "There cannot be a question," says the Report, "that the number of untried prisoners—the most unmanageable class—might, by the general acceptance of bail, be reduced to one-half, or even a third, with no injury to the community, with great benefit to the individual, and with material advantage to the discipline of prisons. The large proportion which the number of persons discharged by grand juries, and of those acquitted, bears to the whole number committed, affords strong presumptive evidence of the unsoundness of the present system." And this, though much greater license of bailing is allowed by law than formerly.

An analogous evil is the infrequency of jail-deliveries. Something has of late been done, and more is, we trust, in the way to be done towards rectifying the inequality of the law under which a prisoner belonging to a certain county may be kept in prison a year before trial, while the perpetrator of a similar offence in London is tried in six weeks; but, in the meanwhile, incalculable injury has been and continues to be done to the safety of society by the congregation of numbers, of whom such as are not guilty are exasperated, and therefore prepared for guilt, and all of whom are suffering gross injustice. Magna Charta was framed with a view to other results than this: it provided that justice should not be *delayed*, any more than denied or sold.

It is evident that these grievances, which affect the security of society, have an immediate bearing on the moral state of the offender. As long as they exist, the reformation of the criminal cannot be looked for. It is plain that, previous to trial, before he is subjected to any other infliction than the loss of liberty, every precaution should be taken to avoid his sustaining any kind of injury. He should have means to pursue his own employments; instruction should be within his reach;

and he should have liberty to decline society which he dislikes. None of these dues are afforded in any fair proportion to the untried inmates of our jails. After sentence, the infliction (as long as the right of infliction is recognised and acted upon) should be arranged with a view to a higher object still,—that the criminal should leave the prison a better man than he entered it. That this object may be, and therefore ought universally to be, attained under the present law, is proved by the degree of success of which the Penitentiary at Millbank has been productive, though more animating examples are before us in other directions. That which, through lapse of time, may be best depended on, is at Auburn, in the state of New York, a brief summary of the plans and results of which is found at page 7 of this Report, conveying as much valuable fact as the more copious details which may be met with elsewhere:—

At sunrise, the convicts proceed in regular order to the several workshops, where they remain under vigilant superintendence until the hour of breakfast, when they repair to the common hall. When at their meals, the prisoners are seated at table in single rows, with their backs towards the centre, so that there can be no interchange of signs. From one end of the work-rooms to the other, upwards of five hundred convicts may be seen without a single individual being observed to turn his head towards a visitor. Not a whisper is heard throughout the apartments. At the close of day, labor is suspended, and the prisoners return in military order to their solitary cells: there they have the opportunity of reading Scriptures, and of reflecting in silence on their past lives. The chaplain occasionally visits the cells, instructing the ignorant, and administering the reproofs and consolations of religion. The influence of these visits is described to be most beneficial; and the effect of the entire discipline is decidedly successful in the prevention of crime, both by the dread which imprisonment inspires, as well as by the reformation of the offender. Inquiries have been instituted relative to the conduct of prisoners released from the Auburn Penitentiary— the prison at which this system has been longest observed—and of two hundred and six discharged, who have been watched over for the space of three years, one hundred and forty-six have been reclaimed, and maintained reputable characters in society.

A large proportion;—to which should be added all who, instead of being corrupted on the reëntrance of these offenders into the world, are warned by their past and encouraged by their present example.

It would seem to be the very least that the authorities of a civilized country could do, to provide against the further corruption of the criminals who are made such, in a large degree, by the vices of that country's institutions; yet, among us, not only have the authorities failed to discharge this essential part of their duty, but they have hindered or omitted to support the exertions of benevolent societies and individuals. The jails in Scotland remain unimproved, and most of the prisons attached to corporate jurisdictions are in a state so disgraceful as necessarily to corrupt all committed to them. In some of these there is no employment, no inspection, no separation of the men from the women, of murderers from truant boys, or even of the sick from the healthy. In some, the jailer does not reside. In others, irons are illegally used because the walls are tumbling down. It is a very old analogy between the disease of the body and the spirit; but it is one so complete and well-grounded, that it will bear a perpetual application. What should we think of the justice and humanity of first throwing a man into the very centre of a plague contagion; then, as soon as sick, removing him into an hospital with the ostensible purpose of relieving society and curing himself; then, instead of putting him into a clean separate bed, and applying proper means for his recovery, shutting him up with patients worse than himself, in heat and dirt, untended and uncared for; and, finally, turning him out into the world again, when the disease had reached its height, to spread it wherever he goes? Yet this is precisely our management of those afflicted with that kind of malady which is to the patient as much the result of natural causes as physical disease, while it is at the same time productive of worse evils, and more certainly curable. The root of this grievance lies deep,—even in the mistaken notions generally prevailing of the origin and nature of virtue and vice; but thousands who cannot reach or discern the principle of the mischief can help to ameliorate the practice. Without arguing how the criminal became a criminal, they may perceive and apply the means of curing him of his criminality: thus fulfilling the second great object which imprisonment should be made to effect.

If our nation were in the most prosperous state conceivable, it would still be an injustice to charge it with the gratuitous maintenance of even the few offenders who would then be found in its prisons; but, in the condition of difficulty and want in which our population finds itself at present, the support of 120,000 prisoners per annum is a burden which ought to be declared intolerable. If it be considered that advantages of every kind attend the enforcement of productive labor in prisons, while evils of all sorts arise in its absence, it becomes difficult to conceive how so many have been permitted to spend their months and years of captivity in idleness,—why the sentence of hard labor has been so largely evaded,—and how it is that the necessary working apparatus has not been made a part of the furniture of every prison. The objection that the labor of prisons, like work-house labor, deranges, in a certain degree, the operation of demand and supply, and thereby injures the innocent laborer and capitalist, is of small weight in comparison with that of maintaining prisoners in idleness: moreover, it would become of less weight perpetually, were prison labor properly regulated and enforced, since the number of prisoners would decrease. Let us once, like the Auburn authorities, send out 146 reformed out of 206 committed, and the productions of our offenders' industry would shortly occupy a very small space in the market. There would result, from such an arrangement, a sensible relief to the community,—already sufficiently injured by the acts of the offender,—and a new efficiency in our penal institutions, to the great benefit both of the criminal and of society at large.

The one great thing to be borne in mind throughout the contemplation of the subject before us,—throughout the doings of the daily life of the benevolent,—is that the amelioration or renovation of our penal system lies, in some measure, between the hands of every man. Let the government be aroused to the utmost vigilance and activity,—let the Prison Discipline Society continue its virtuous labors,—let individuals visit the prisoner, and towns and cities unite to keep their magistracies up to their duty; much yet remains to be done by those who may, for reasons or excuses of their own, abstain from joining in any of these efforts to accomplish a great good. As much may be done indirectly as directly for an object which may be reached by so many ramifications as this. Injudicious charity, overgrown luxury, waste, aristocratic idleness, all cause poverty somewhere; and poverty causes crime. Commercial restrictions, unequal taxation, profuse government expenditure, all cause poverty somewhere; and poverty causes crime. Cruel, inconsistent, perplexed laws, imperfect representation, aristocratic privilege, all cause oppression; and oppression is not only crime in the tyrant, but causes crime in the oppressed. Temporal hardship perpetuates ignorance; and ignorance causes crime. Thus it appears that every one who moves in society with more or less of influence, does something for or against the improvement in principle and practice of our penal system. Every one does something towards sending some other one to prison or helping him out,—and towards determining his condition when there. Every one is, consciously or unconsciously, enlisted with the Prison Discipline Society or against it. The alms-giver, the land-proprietor, the merchant, the manufacturer, the elector, the head of a family, school committees, charitable, literary, commercial associations of every kind, are all concerned in aiding or injuring the interest of that most pitiable, the criminal, class of society; and it is for these to look to it that they act not only with a benevolent intention, but with a wise benevolence. Whoever gives to street beggars helps to fill our prisons, and therefore to corrupt their inmates. Whoever votes for the continuance of the Corn Laws,[3] or the East India Charter, helps to fill our prisons, though he may be a member of the Society for the Suppression of Vice. On the other hand, every man, woman, or child, who helps to uphold schools, to ascertain the true nature and workings of our institutions and customs, who encourages industry, discountenances waste, and assists intercourse between different classes of the community, does much, very much for which the advocates of the prisoner will be grateful. They, however, are the best benefactors, who unite direct with indirect efforts: who petition and petition till they obtain a partial abolition of the punishment of death; who, animated instead of satisfied by this success, go on till they shall have obtained its total abolition, and an equalization of the penal system altogether; who, meanwhile, visit the prisons, and advocate the rights of their inmates in and out of doors: who do what in them lies to lighten the temporal burdens of the poorer classes, and above all, give them moral light, and strength to discern and pursue their best interests. Many of the best men in France are using their new liberties with a view to these objects. Germany has set about the same work with the wisdom, and is pursuing it with the vigor and perseverance, which might be expected from the usual character of her enterprises. America is still so far before all other co[u]ntries in this branch of her legislation as well as her executive, that we must long consider it a sufficient praise to be seen to follow in her steps. She is not unwilling, we believe, to have her penal system made the test of her political state. Great Britain must make haste to get rid of the shame which would arise from having a similar test applied in her case. Since we cannot allow it to be a fair one, let us frankly admit our penal system to be an anomaly; and by a diligent and perpetual renovation, bring it at length into an accordance with the best of our social institutions.

Notes

1. The Eighth Report of the Committee of the Society for the Improvement of Prison Discipline. 1832.
Punishment of Death. A Series of short Articles, &c. 1832. [Martineau's note]
2. One of the hundreds of reform or social societies which worked on prison reform.
3. The Corn Laws regulated the importation of all cereal grains into Britain. Enacted to protect British agriculture, they were suspended during the Napoleonic Wars, and again in 1846 during the Irish famine. They were permanently abolished in 1849.

5. Letter to the Deaf

Introduction

Harriet Martineau's "Letter to the Deaf" first appeared in *Tait's Edinburgh Magazine* in April, 1834, and is reprinted here from that periodical. The essay, published several times in the nineteenth century, was used extensively by charitable and cooperative organizations to address the concerns of deaf readers. Although she chose to publish this work in a mainstream periodical, Martineau states that she, as a deaf person, is specifically addressing a deaf audience. As in her autobiographical writings, Martineau eloquently relates her feelings and experiences, thus enabling her to reach the reader on an emotional, as well as on an intellectual, level.

Letter to the Deaf

My Dear Companions,

The deafness under which I have now for some years past suffered, has become, from being an almost intolerable grievance, so much less of one to myself and my friends, than such a deprivation usually is, that I have often of late longed to communicate with my fellow-sufferers, in the hope of benefiting, by my experience, some to whom the discipline is newer than to myself.

I have for some time done what I could in private conversation; but it never occurred to me to print what I had to say, till it was lately not only suggested to me, but urged upon me as a duty. I adopt this method as the only means of reaching you all; and I am writing with the freedom which I should use in a private letter to each of you. It does not matter what may be thought of anything I now say, or of my saying it in this manner, by those who do not belong to our fraternity. I write merely for those who are deeply concerned in the subject of my letter. The time may come when I shall tell the public some of our secrets, for other purposes than those which are now before me. At present I address only you; and as there is no need for us to tell our secrets to one another, there may be little here to interest any but ourselves. I am afraid I have nothing to offer to those of you who have been deaf from early childhood. Your case is very different from mine, as I have reason to know through my intimacy with a friend who became deaf at five years old. Before I was so myself, I had so prodigious a respect for this lady, (which she well deserves,) that if she could have heard the lightest whisper in which a timid girl ever spoke, I should not have dared to address her. Circumstances directed her attention towards me, and she began a correspondence, by letter, which flattered me, and gave me courage to converse with her when we met, and our acquaintance grew into an intimacy which enabled me at last to take a very bold step;—to send her a sonnet, in allusion to our common infirmity; my deafness being then new, and the uppermost thing in my mind day and night. I was surprised and mortified at her not seeming to enter into what I had no doubt in the world must touch her very nearly; but I soon understood the reason. When we came to compare our experiences, we were amused to find how differently we felt, and had always felt, about our privation. Neither of us, I believe, much envies the other, though neither of us pretends to strike the balance of evil. She had suffered the most privations, and I the most pain.

Nothing can be more different than the two cases necessarily are. Nine-tenths of my miseries arose from false shame; and, instead of that false shame, the early deaf entertain themselves with a sort of pride of singularity, and usually contrive to make their account of this, as of other infirmities, by obtaining privileges and indulgences, for which they care much more than for advantages which they have never known and cannot appreciate. My friend and I have principles, major and minor, on which our methods of managing our infirmity are founded; but some of the minor principles, and all the methods, are as different as might be expected from the diversity of the experience which has given rise to them. Nothing can be better for her than her own management, and, of course, I think the same of my own for myself, or I should change it. Before I dismiss this lady, I must mention that I am acquainted with several deaf ladies; so that no one but herself and our two families can know whom I have been referring to.

I am afraid some of you may be rather surprised at the mention of plans, and methods, and management,—for, alas! we are but too apt to shrink from regularly taking in hand our own case. We are left to our own weakness in this respect. We can have but little help,—and we usually have none, but much hinderance. I do not mean by this, to find any fault with our neighbours. I have met with too much sympathy, (as far as sympathy is possible,) with too much care, and generosity, and tenderness, to have the least inclination to complain of any body connected with me. I only mean that this very tenderness is hurtful to us in as far as it encourages us to evade our enemy, instead of grappling with it; to forget our infirmity, from hour to hour, if we can, and to get over the present occasion somehow, without thinking of the next. This would be considered a strange way of meeting any other kind of evil; and its consequences in our case are most deplorable. If we see that the partially deaf are often unscrupulous about truth, inquisitive, irritable, or morose, suspicious, low-spirited, or ill-mannered, it is owning to this. It is impossible for *us* to deny that if principles are ever needed, if methods are ever of use as supports and guides, it must be in a case where each of us must stand alone in the midst of temptations and irritations which beset us every hour, and against which no defence of habit has been set up, and no bond of companionship can strengthen us. What these temptations and irritations are, we all know:—the almost impossibility of not seeming to hear when we do not,—the persuasion that people are taking advantage of us in what they say,—that they are discussing us, or laughing at us,—that they do not care for us as long as they are merry,—that the friend who takes the pains to talk to us might make us less conspicuous if he would,—the vehement desire that we might be let alone, and the sense of neglect if too long let alone; all these, absurd and wicked fancies as they are seen to be when fairly set down, have beset us all in our time; have they not? For my own part, though I am never troubled with them now, I have so vivid a remembrance of them all, that I believe a thousand years would not weaken the impression. Surely that degree of suffering which lashes us into a temporary misanthropy when our neighbours are happiest, which makes us fly to our chambers, and lock ourselves in, to hide the burning tears which spring at the mirth of those we love best, which seduces us into falsehood or thanklessness to God and man, is enough to justify and require the most careful fixing of principles, and framing of methods. We might as well let our hearts and minds—our happiness—take their chance without discipline in this.

The first thing to be done is to fix upon our principle. This is easy enough. To give the least possible pain to others is the right principle: how to apply it requires more consideration. Let me just observe, that we are more inexcusable in forsaking our principle here than in any other case, and than the generality of people are in the generality of cases. Principles are usually forsaken from being forgotten,—from the occasion for them not being perceived. We have no such excuse while beginning to act upon our principle. We cannot forget,—we cannot fail to perceive the occasion, for five minutes together, that we spend in society. By the time that we become sufficiently at ease to be careless, habit may, if we choose, have grown up to support our principle, and we may be safe.

Our principle requires that we should boldly review our case, and calmly determine for ourselves what we will give up, and what struggle to retain. It is a miserable thing to get on without a plan from day to day, nervously watching whether our infirmity lessens or increases, or choosing to take for granted that we shall be rid of it; or hopelessly and indolently giving up every thing but a few selfish gratifications, or weakly refusing to resign what we can no longer enjoy. We must ascertain the probability for the future, if we can find physicians humane enough to tell us the truth: and where it cannot be ascertained, we must not delay making provision for the present. The greatest difficulty here arises from the mistaken kindness of friends. The physician had rather not say, as mine said to me, "I consider yours a bad case." The parent entreats to be questioned about any thing that passes; brothers and sisters wish that music should be kept up; and, what is remarkable, every body has a vast deal of advice to give, if the subject be fairly mentioned; though every body helps, by false tenderness, to make the subject too sacred an one to be touched upon. We sufferers are the persons to put an end to all this delusion and mismanagement. Advice must go for nothing with us in a case where nobody is qualified to advise. We must cross-question our physician, and hold him to it till he has told us all. We must destroy the sacredness of the subject, by speaking of it ourselves; not perpetually and sentimentally, but, when occasion arises, boldly, cheerfully, and as a plain matter of fact. When every body about us gets to treat it as a matter of fact, our daily difficulties are almost gone; and when we have to do with strangers, the simple, cheerful declaration, "I am very deaf," removes almost all trouble. Whether there was ever as much reluctance to acknowledge defective sight as there now is defective hearing,—whether the mention of spectacles was ever as hateful as that of a trumpet is now, I do not know; but I was full as much grieved as amused lately at what was said to me in a shop where I went to try a new kind of trumpet: "I assure you, Ma'am," said the shopkeeper, "I dread to see a deaf person come into my shop. They all expect me to find them some little thing that they may put into their ears, that will make them hear every thing, without any body finding out what is the matter with them."

Well, what must be given up, and what may be struggled for?

The first thing which we are disposed to give up is the very last which we ought to relinquish—society. How many good reasons we are apt to see,—are we not?—why we should not dine out; why it is absurd to go into an evening party; why we ought to be allowed to remain quiet up stairs when visitors are below! This will not do. Social communication must be kept up through all its pains, for the sake of our friends as well as for our own. It can never be for the interest of our friends that we should grow selfish, or absorbed in what does not concern our day and generation, or nervous, dependant, and helpless in common affairs. The less able we become to pick up tidings of man and circumstance, the more diligently we must go in search of the information. The more our sympathies are in danger of contraction, the more must we put ourselves in the way of being interested by what is happening all about us. Society is the very last thing to be given up; but it must be sought, (and I say it with deep sympathy for those of you to whom the effort is new,) under a bondage of self-denial, which annihilates for a time almost all the pleasures. Whatever may be our fate,—whether we may be set down at the end of a half circle, where nobody comes to address us, or whether we may be placed beside a lady who cannot speak above her breath, or a gentleman who shouts till every body turns to see what is the matter; whether one well meaning friend says across the room, in our behalf, "do tell that joke over again to _____," and all look to see how we laugh when they have done; or another kind person says, "how I wish you could hear that song,"—or "that harp in the next room," or "those sweet nightingales," if we happen to be out of doors,—whether any or all these doings and sayings befal [sic] us, we must bravely go on taking our place in society.

Taking our place, I say. What is our place? It is difficult to decide. Certainly, not that of chief talker any more than that of chief listener. We must make up our minds for a time to hold the place that we may chance to be put into,—to depend on the tact and kindness of those near us. This is not very pleasant; but if we cannot submit to it for a while, we cannot boast much of our humility, nor of our patience. We must submit to be usually insignificant, and sometimes ridiculous. Do not be dismayed, dear companions. This necessity will not last long, and it is well worth while undergoing it. Those who have strength of mind to seek society under this humiliation, and to keep their tempers through it, cannot long remain insignificant there. They must rise to their proper place, if they do but abstain from pressing beyond it. It is astonishing how everything brightens sooner or later. The nightingales and the harp will be still out of the question, but they will be given up almost without pain, because it is a settled matter to every body present that they *are* out of the question. Friends will have discovered that jokes are not the things to be repeated; and that which is repeated will be taken as coming in due course, and will at length consist of all that has been really worth hearing of what has been said. Other people may laugh without occasioning a nervous distortion in your countenance; and it is quite certain that if your temper have stood your trial, you will never pass an evening without meeting with some attention which will touch, some frank kindness which will elevate your feelings, and send you home wiser and happier than you came forth.

This can only be, however, if you have stood your trial well, if you bring an open temper and an open countenance. It is a matter of wonder that we are addressed so much as we are; and if, in addition to the difficulty of making us hear, we offer the disagreeableness of (not a constrained, that will be pitied, but) a frowning countenance, we may betake ourselves to the books of prints on the table, but may as well give up all hope of conversation. As a general rule, nothing can be worse than for people to think at all about their countenances; but in our case it is worth while, for a time, and to a certain extent. I was kindly told, a few years ago, that many people wished to converse with me, but that I looked as if I had rather not be spoken to. Well I might; for I then discovered that in trying to check one bad habit, I had fallen into another. I had a trick of sighing, to cover which I used to twist my fingers out of joint, (and so do you, I dare say,) and the pain of this process very naturally made me frown. My friend's hint put me on my guard. Instead of twisting my fingers, I recalled my vow of patience, and this made me smile; and the world has been a different place to me since. Some such little rule as turning every sigh into a smile will help you over a multitude of difficulties, and save you, at length, the trouble of thinking about either smiling or sighing.

It has always been my rule *never* to ask what is going forward; and the consequence has well compensated all I had to go through from the reproaches of kind friends, who were very anxious that I should trouble them in that way. Our principle plainly forbids the practice; and nothing can therefore justify it. There is at first no temptation, for we had then rather miss the sayings of the wise men of Greece, than obtain them by such means; but the practice once begun, there is no telling where it will stop. Have we not seen—it sickens me to think of it—restless, inquisitive, deaf people, who will have every insignificant thing repeated to them, to their own incessant disappointment, and the suffering of every body about them, whom they make, by their appeals, almost as ridiculous as themselves. I never could tolerate the idea of any approach to the condition of one of these. I felt, besides, that it was impossible for me to judge of what might fairly be asked for, and what had better be let pass. I therefore obstinately adhered to my rule; and I believe that no one whom I have met in any society, (and I have seen a great deal,) has been enabled to carry away more that is valuable, or to enjoy it more thoroughly than myself. I was sure that I might trust to the kindness of my neighbours, if I was but careful not to vex and weary it; and my confidence has been fully justified. The duty extends to not looking as if you wanted to be amused. Your friends can have little satisfaction in your presence, if they believe that when you are not conversing you are no longer amused. "I wonder every day," said a young friend to me, when I was staying in a large well-filled country house, "what you do with yourself during our long dinners, when we none of us talk with you, because we have talked so much more comfortably on the lawn all the morning. I cannot think how you help going to sleep." "I watch how you help the soup," was my inconsiderate reply—I was not aware how inconsiderate, till I saw how she blushed every day after on taking up the ladle. I mentioned the soup only as a specimen of my occupations during dinner. There were also the sunset lights and shadows on the lawn to be watched, and the never ceasing play of human countenances,—our grand resource when we have once gained ease enough to enjoy them at leisure. There were graceful and light-headed girls, and there was an originality of action in the whole family which amused me from morning till night. The very apparatus of the table, and the various dexterities of the servants, are matters worth observing when we have nothing else to do. I never yet found a dinner too long, whether or not my next neighbour might be disposed in a tête-a-tête—never, I mean, since the time when every social occupation was to me full of weariness and constraint.

Another rule which I should recommend is always to wait to be addressed, except in our own houses, where the exception must be made with our guests. Some, I know, adopt a contrary rule, for this reason, that if we ask a question to which we can anticipate the answer, the awkwardness of a failure at the outset is prevented. But my own feeling is against obliging any one to undertake the trouble of conversing with us. It is perfectly easy to show, at the moment of being addressed, that we are socially disposed, and grateful for being made companions; and I, at least, feel the pleasure to be greater for its having been offered me.

I think it best for us to give up also all undertakings and occupations in which we cannot mark and check our own failures;— teaching any thing which requires ear, preaching, and lecturing, and music. I gave up music, in opposition to much entreaty, some reproach, and strong secret inclination; because I knew that my friends would rather put up with a wrong bass in my playing, and false time in my singing, than deprive me of a resource. Our principle clearly forbids this kind of indulgence; therefore, however confident we may be of our musical ear, let us be quite sure that we shall never again be judges of our own music, or our own oratory, and avoid all wish of making others suffer needlessly by our privations. Listen to no persuasions, dear companions, if you are convinced that what I have said is right. No one *can* judge for you. Be thankful for the kind intentions of your friends; but propose to enjoy their private eloquence instead of offering you own in public; and please yourselves with their music, as long as you can, without attempting to rival it. These are matters in which we have a right to be obstinate, if we are sure of the principle we go upon; for we are certainly much better able to judge what will be for the happiness of our friends, in their common circumstances, than they can be of ours, in our uncommon ones.

How much less pain there is in calmly estimating the enjoyments from which we must separate ourselves, of bravely saying, for once and for ever, "Let them go," than in feeling them waste and dwindle, till their very shadows escape from our grasp! With the best management, there is quite enough, for some of us, of this wasting and dwindling, when we find, at the close of each season, that we are finally parting with something, and at the beginning of each that we have lost something since the last. We miss first the song of the skylark, and then the distant nightingale, and then one bird after another, till the loud thrush itself seems to have vanished; and we go in the way of every twittering under the eaves, because we know that that will soon be silenced too. But I need not enlarge upon this to you. I only mean to point out the prudence of lessening this kind of pain to the utmost, by making a considerable effort at first; and the most calculating prudence becomes a virtue, when it is certain that as much must at best be gone through as will afflict our friends, and may possibly overpower ourselves, our temper and deportment, if not our principles and our affections. I do not know how sufficiently to enforce these sacrifices being made with frankness and simplicity; and nothing so much needs enforcing. If our friends were but aware how cruel an injury is the false delicacy which is so common, they would not encourage our false shame as they do. If they have known anything of the bondage of ordinary false shame, they may imagine something of our suffering in circumstances of irremediable singularity. Instead of putting the singularity out of sight, they should lead us to acknowledge it in words, prepare for it in habits, and act upon it in social intercourse. If they will not assist us here, we must do it for ourselves. Our principle, again, requires this. Thus only can we save others from being uneasy in our presence, and sad when they think of us. That we can thus alone make ourselves sought and beloved is an inferior consideration, though an important one to us, to whom warmth and kindliness are as peculiarly animating as sunshine to the caged bird. This frankness, simplicity, and cheerfulness, can only grow out of a perfect acquiescence in our circumstances. Submission is not enough. Pride fails at the most critical moment. Nothing short of acquiescence will preserve the united consistency and cheerfulness of our acknowledgment of infirmity. Submission will bemoan it while making it. Pride will put on indifference while making it. But hearty acquiescence cannot fail to bring forth cheerfulness. The thrill of delight which arises during the ready agreement to profit by pain—(emphatically the joy with which no stranger intermeddleth)—must subside like all other emotions; but it does not depart without leaving the spirit lightened and cheered; and every visitation leaves it in a more genial state than the last.

And now, what may we struggle for? I dare say the words of the moralist lie as deep down in your hearts as in my own: "We must not repine, but we may lawfully struggle!" I go further, and say that we are bound to struggle. Our principle requires it. We must struggle for whatever may be had, without encroaching on the comfort of others. With this limitation, we must hear all we can, for as long as we can. Yet how few of us will use the helps we might have! How seldom is a deaf person to be seen with a trumpet! I should have been diverted, if I had not been too much vexed, at the variety of excuses that I have heard on this head since I have been much in society. The trumpet makes the sound disagreeable; or is of no use; or is not wanted in a noise, because we hear better in a noise; nor in quiet, because we hear very fairly in quiet; or we think our friends do not like it; or we ourselves do not care for it, if it does not enable us to hear general conversation; or—a hundred other reasons just as good. Now, dear friends, believe me these are but excuses. I have tried them all in turn, and I know them to be so. The sound soon becomes anything but disagreeable; and the relief to the nerves, arising from the use of such a help, is indescribable. None but the totally deaf can fail to find some kind of trumpet that will be of use of them, if they choose to look for it properly, and give it a fair trial. That it is not wanted in a noise is usually true; but we are seldom in a noise; and quiet is our greatest enemy, (next to darkness, when the play of the countenance is lost to us.) To reject a tête-à-tête in comfort because the same means will not afford us the pleasure of general conversation, is not very wise. Is it? As for the fancy, that our friends do not like it, it is a mistake, and a serious mistake. I can speak confidently of this. By means of galvanism,[1] (which I do not, from my own experience, recommend,) I once nearly recovered my hearing for a few weeks. It was well worth while being in a sort of nervous fever during those weeks, and more deaf than ever afterwards, for the enlightenment which I gained during the interval on various subjects, of which the one that concerns us now, is,—the toil that our friends undergo on our account. This is the last topic on which I should speak to you, but for the prevalent unwillingness in our fraternity to use such helps as much as their own nerves. Of course, my friends could not suddenly accommodate their speech to my improved hearing; and I was absolutely shocked when I found what efforts they had been making for my sake. I vowed that I would never again bestow an unkind thought on their natural mistakes, or be restive under their inapplicable instructions; and, as for carrying a trumpet, I like it no better than my brethren till then; but now, if it would in any degree ease my friends that I should wear a fool's cap and bells, I would do it. Any of you who may have had this kind of experience, are, I should think, using trumpets. I entreat those of you who have not been so made aware of your state, to take my word for what you are obliging your friends to undergo. You know that we can be no judges of the degree of effort necessary to make us hear. We might as well try to echo the skylark. I speak plainly, it may seem harshly; but I am sure you would thank me ere long if I could persuade you to encounter this one struggle to make the most of your remnant of one of God's prime blessings.

Another struggle must be to seize or make opportunities for preserving or rectifying our associations, as far as they are connected with the sense which is imperfect. Hunger and thirst after all sounds that you can obtain, without trouble to others, and without disturbing your own temper; and do it the more strenuously and cheerfully, the more reason you have to apprehend the increase of your infirmity. The natural desire to obtain as much pleasure as we can, while we can, would prompt us to this; but my appetite was much sharpened during the interval I spoke of; as yours would be, if you had such an interval. I was dismayed to find, not only what absurd notions I had formed on some small points, but how materially some very important processes of association had been modified by the failure of the sense of hearing. In consequence of the return and increase of the infirmity, I have now no distinct notion of what these intellectual faults are: but the certainty then impressed that they exist, has taught me more than one lesson. I carry about with me the consciousness of an intellectual perversion which I can never remedy in this world, and of which neither I nor any one else can ascertain the extent, nor even the nature. This does not afflict me, because it would be as unreasonable to wish it otherwise, as to pray for wings which should carry us up to the milky-way; but it has stimulated me to devise every possible means of checking and delaying the perversion. We ought all to do so; losing no opportunity of associating sounds with other objects of sense, and of catching every breath of sound that passes us. We should note street cries; we should entice children to talk to us; we should linger in the neighbourhood of barrel organs, and go out of our way to walk by a dashing stream. We cannot tell how much wisdom we may at last find ourselves to have gained, by running out among the trees, when the quick coming and going of the sunshine tells us that the winds are abroad. Some day will show us from how much folly the chirp of an infant's voice may have saved us. I go so far as to recommend, certainly not any place of worship for purposes of experiment, but the theatre and the House of Commons; even when "the sough[2] of words without the sense" is all that can be had. The human voice is music, and carries sense, even then; and every tone is worth treasuring, when tones are likely to become scarce, or to cease. You will understand that it is only to those who can rule their own spirits that I recommend such an exercise as this last. If you cannot bear to enjoy less than the people about you, and in a different manner; or if you neglect what you came for, in mourning what you have lost, you are better at home. Nothing is worth the sacrifice of your repose of mind.

What else may we struggle for? For far more in the way of knowledge than I can now even intimate. I am not going to make out, as some would have me, that we lose nothing after all; that what we lose in one way we gain in another, and so on; pursuing a line of argument equally insulting to our own understandings, and to the wisdom and benignity of Him who framed that curious instrument, the ear, and strung the chords of its nerves, and keeps up the perpetual harmonies of the atmosphere for its gratification. The ear was not made that men should be happier without it. To attempt to persuade *you* so, would above all be folly. But, in some sense, there is a compensation to us, if we choose to accept it; and it is to improve this to the utmost that I would urge you and stimulate myself. We *have* some accomplishments which we may gratefully acknowledge, while the means by which we gain them must prevent our being proud of them. We are good physiognomists—good perceivers in every way, and have (if we are not idle) rather the advantage over others in the power of abstract reasoning. This union of two kinds of power, which in common cases are often cultivated at the expense of each other, puts a considerable amount of accurate knowledge within easier reach of us than of most other people. We must never forget what a vast quantity we must forego, but neither must we lose sight of whatever is peculiarly within our power. We have more time, too, than anybody else: more than the laziest lordling, who does nothing but let his ears be filled with nonsense from morning till night. The very busiest of our fraternity has, I should think, time every day for as much thought as is good for him, between the hours of rising and of rest.

These advantages make it incumbent upon us to struggle for such compensation as is placed before us. We must set ourselves to gather knowledge from whatever we see and touch, and to digest it into wisdom during the extra time which is our privilege. What the sage goes out into the field at eventide to seek, we can have at table, or in the thronged streets at noonday,—opportunity for meditation, one of the chief means of wisdom. If to us the objects of sight are more vivid in their beauty, and more distinct in their suggestions than to others,—if to us there is granted more leisure, and stronger inducement to study the movements of the mind within, from us may be expected a degree of certain kinds of attainment, in which it is as much of a sin as a misfortune for us to be deficient.

Finally, we, like all who are placed in uncommon circumstances, are so situated that our mental and moral constitution can scarcely fail of being either very weak or very strong. If we are dull and slow of observation, and indolent in thought, there is little chance of our being much wiser than infants; whereas, if we are acute and quick of observation, (and for us there is no medium,) and disposed for thought, nothing is likely to prevent our going on to be wiser continually. In like manner, there is an awful alternative as to our morals. If we cannot stand our trial, we must become selfish in principle, sour in temper, and disagreeable in manners. If we are strong enough for our discipline, we cannot fail to come out of it with principles strengthened, affections expanded, temper under control, and manners graced by the permanent cheerfulness of a settled mind and a heart at ease. If you can make this last your lot, you have little more to fear. If you have brought vigour out of this conflict, you are not likely to be unnerved. If, in your enforced solitude, you have cultivated instead of losing your sympathies, you can scarcely afterwards grow selfish. If, as your enjoyments were failing you, you have improved your serenity, your cheerfulness will probably be beyond the reach of circumstances. The principal check which must be put upon these happy anticipations, is the fear that while the privations cannot be lessened, the pain of it may disappear too soon and too entirely. I now suffer little of no pain from my privation, (except at moments when comparisons are forced upon me before I am ready for them;) and I cannot help dreading a self-deception, to avoid which I would gladly endure over again all I have suffered. I had infinitely rather hear the perpetual sense of privation than become unaware of any thing that is true,—of my intellectual deficiencies, of my disqualifications for society, of my errors in matters of fact, and of the burdens which I necessarily impose on those who surround me. My dependence for being reminded of these things is,—not on those who incur trouble and sacrifice for my sake, but on the few occasional mortifications which I still meet with, and which are always welcomed for the sake of their office. We can never get beyond the necessity of keeping in full view the worst and the best that can be made of our lot. The worst is, either to sink under the trial, or to be made callous by it. The best is, to be as wise as is possible under a great disability, and as happy as is possible under great privation. Believe me, with deep respect,

> Your affectionate sister,
> Harriet Martineau.
> March 16, 1834.

Notes

1.   An application of electricity; usually the application of electric stimulation to the nerves.

2. The OED defines "sough" as "a rushing or murmuring sound, as of wind, water, or the like . . ."

6. Society in America
Section VI: Citizenship of People of Colour
Section VII: Political Non-Existence of Women

Introduction

The following sections are reprinted from Volume 1 of Harriet Martineau's *Society in America* (2nd ed., New York, 1837). Martineau embarked on a two-year trip to the United States in 1834, where she travelled throughout the nation, recording her observations of American life. As with Alexis de Tocqueville in *Democracy in America*, Martineau attempted to comment objectively on American society and government. As she notes in the lengthy introduction to this work, she wished "to compare the existing state of society in America with the principles on which it is professedly founded; thus testing Institutions, Morals, and Manners by an indisputable, instead of an arbitrary standard, and securing to myself the same point of view with my readers of both nations." Martineau was understandably disillusioned by much of what she observed, precisely because of discrepancies between American principle and practice. "Citizenship of People of Colour" is especially significant, because in examining the treatment of free New England blacks, Martineau disabuses her readers of the myth that northern whites were more principled than southern slave owners. In the next section, "Political Non-Existence of Women," Martineau observes that American women's lack of rights is a stark example of how American democratic ideology falls far short of American democratic practice.

Society in America
Section VI: Citizenship of People of Colour

Before I entered New England, while I was ascending the Mississippi, I was told by a Boston gentleman that the people of colour in the New England States were perfectly well-treated; that the children were educated in schools provided for them; and that their fathers freely exercised the franchise. This gentleman certainly believed he was telling me the truth. That he, a busy citizen of Boston, should know no better, is now as striking an exemplification of the state of the case to me as a correct representation of the facts would have been. There are two causes for his mistake. He was not aware that the schools for the coloured children in New England are, unless they escape by their insignificance, shut up, or pulled down, or the school-house wheeled away upon rollers over the frontier of a pious State, which will not endure that its coloured citizens should be educated. He was not aware of a gentleman of colour, and his family, being locked out of their own hired pew in a church, because their white brethren will not worship by their side. But I will not proceed with an enumeration of injuries, too familiar to Americans to excite any feeling but that of weariness; and too disgusting to all others to be endured. The other cause of this gentleman's mistake was, that he did not, from long custom, feel some things to be injuries, which he would call anything but good treatment, if he had to bear them himself. Would he think it good treatment to be forbidden to eat with fellow-citizens; to be assigned to a particular gallery in his church; to be excluded from college, from municipal office, from professions, from scientific and literary associations? If he felt himself excluded from every department of society, but its humiliations and its drudgery, would he declare himself to be "perfectly well-treated in Boston?" Not a word more of statement is needed.

A Connecticut judge lately declared on the bench that he believed people of colour were not considered citizens in the laws. He was proved to be wrong. He was actually ignorant of the wording of the acts by which people of colour are termed citizens. Of course, no judge could have forgotten this who had seen them treated as citizens: nor could one of the most eminent statesmen and lawyers in the country have told me that it is still a doubt, in the minds of some high authorities, whether people of colour are citizens. He is as mistaken as the judge. There has been no such doubt since the Connecticut judge was corrected and enlightened. The error of the statesman arose from the same cause; he had never seen the coloured people treated as citizens. "In fact," said he, "these people hold an anomalous situation. They are protected as citizens when the public service requires their security; but not otherwise treated as such." Any comment would weaken this intrepid statement.

The common argument, about the inferiority of the coloured race, bears no relation whatever to this question. They are citizens. They stand, as such, in the law, and in the acknowledgment of every one who knows the law. They are citizens, yet their houses and schools are pulled down, and they can obtain no remedy at law. They are thrust out of offices, and excluded from the most honourable employments, and stripped of all the best benefits of society by fellow-citizens who, once a year, solemnly lay their hands on their hearts, and declare that all men are born free and equal, and that rulers derive their just powers from the consent of the governed.

This system of injury is not wearing out. Lafayette, on his last visit to the United States, expressed his astonishment at the increase of the prejudice against colour. He remembered, he said, how the black soldiers used to mess with the whites in the revolutionary war. The leaders of that war are gone where principles are all,—where prejudices are nothing. If their ghosts could arise, in majestic array, before the American nation, on their great anniversary, and hold up before them the mirror of their constitution, in the light of its first principles, where would the people hide themselves from the blasting radiance? They would call upon their holy soil to swallow them up, as unworthy to tread upon it. But not all. It should ever be remembered that America is the country of the best friends the coloured race has ever had. The more truth there is in the assertions of the oppressors of the blacks, the more heroism there is in their friends. The greater the excuse for the pharisees of the community, the more divine is the equity of the redeemers of the coloured race. If it be granted that the coloured race are naturally inferior, naturally depraved, disgusting, cursed,—it must be granted that it is a heavenly charity which descends among them to give such solace as it can to their incomprehensible existence. As long as the excuses of the one party go to enhance the merit of the other, the society is not to be despaired of, even with this poisonous anomaly at its heart.

Happily, however, the coloured race is not cursed by God, as it is by some factions of his children. The less clear-sighted of them are pardonable for so believing. Circumstances, for which no living man is answerable, have generated an erroneous conviction in the feeble mind of man, which sees not beyond the actual and immediate. No remedy could ever have been applied, unless stronger minds than ordinary had been brought into the case. But it so happens, wherever there is an anomaly, giant minds rise up to overthrow it: minds gigantic, not in understanding, but in faith. Wherever they arise, they are the salt of their earth, and its corruption is retrieved. So it is now in America. While the mass of common men and women are despising, and disliking, and fearing, and keeping down the coloured race, blinking the fact that they are citizens, the few of Nature's aristocracy are putting forth a strong hand to lift up this degraded race out of oppression, and their country from the reproach of it. If they were but one or two, trembling and toiling in solitary energy, the world afar would be confident of their success. But they number hundreds and thousands; and if ever they feel a passing doubt of their progress, it is only because they are pressed upon by the meaner multitude. Over the sea, no one doubts of their victory. It is as certain as that the risen sun will reach the meridian. Already are there overflowing colleges, where no distinction of colour is allowed;—overflowing, *because* no distinction of colour is allowed. Already have people of colour crossed the thresholds of many whites, as guests, not as drudges or beggars. Already are they admitted to worship, and to exercise charity, among the whites.

The world has heard and seen enough of the reproach incurred by America, on account of her coloured population. It is now time to look for the fairer side. The crescent streak is brightening towards the full, to wane no more. Already is the world beyond the sea beginning to think of America, less as the country of the double-faced pretender to the name of Liberty, than as the home of the single-hearted, clear-eyed Presence which, under the name of Abolitionism, is majestically passing through the land which is soon to be her throne.

Society in America
Section VII: Political Non-Existence of Women

One of the fundamental principles announced in the Declaration of Independence is, that governments derive their just powers from the consent of the governed. How can the political condition of women be reconciled with this?

Governments in the United States have power to tax women who hold property; to divorce them from their husbands; to fine, imprison, and execute them for certain offences. Whence do these governments derive their powers? They are not "just," as they are not derived from the consent of the women thus governed.

Governments in the United States have power to enslave certain women; and also to punish other women for inhuman treatment of such slaves. Neither of these powers are "just;" not being derived from the consent of the governed.

Governments decree to women in some States half their husbands' property; in others one-third. In some, a woman, on her marriage, is made to yield all her property to her husband; in others, to retain a portion, or the whole, in her own hands. Whence do governments derive the unjust power of thus disposing of property without the consent of the governed?

The democratic principle condemns all this as wrong; and requires the equal political representation of all rational beings. Children, idiots, and criminals, during the season of sequestration, are the only fair exceptions.

The case is so plain that I might close it here; but it is interesting to inquire how so obvious a decision has been so evaded as to leave to women no political rights whatever. The question has been asked, from time to time, in more countries than one, how obedience to the laws can be required of women, when no woman has, either actually or virtually, given any assent to any law. No plausible answer has, as far as I can discover, been offered; for the good reason, that no plausible answer can be devised. The most principled democratic writers on government have on this subject sunk into fallacies, as disgraceful as any advocate of despotism has adduced. In fact, they have thus sunk from being, for the moment, advocates of despotism. Jefferson in America, and James Mill at home, subside, for the occasion, to the level of the author of the Emperor of Russia's Catechism for the young Poles.

Jefferson says,[1] "Were our State a pure democracy, in which all the inhabitants should meet together to transact all their business, there would yet be excluded from their deliberations,

"1. Infants, until arrived at years of discretion;

"2. Women, who, to prevent depravation of morals, and ambiguity of issue, could not mix promiscuously in the public meetings of men;

"3. Slaves, from whom the unfortunate state of things with us takes away the rights of will and of property."

If the slave disqualification, here assigned, were shifted up under the head of Women, their case would be nearer the truth than as it now stands. Woman's lack of will and of property, is more like the true cause of her exclusion from the representation, than that which is actually set down against her. As if there could be no means of conducting public affairs but by promiscuous meetings! As if there would be more danger in promiscuous meetings for political business than in such meetings for worship, for oratory, for music, for dramatic entertainments,—for any of the thousand transactions of civilized life! The plea is not worth another word.

Mill says, with regard to representation, in his Essay on Government, "One thing is pretty clear; that all those individuals, whose interests are involved in those of other individuals, may be struck off without inconvenience. . . . In this light, women may be regarded, the interest of almost all of whom is involved, either in that of their fathers or in that of their husbands."

The true democratic principle is, that no person's interests can be, or can be ascertained to be, identical with those of any other person. This allows the exclusion of none but incapables.

The word "almost," in Mr. Mill's second sentence, rescues women from the exclusion he proposes. As long as there are women who have neither husbands nor fathers, his proposition remains an absurdity.

The interests of women who have fathers and husbands can never be identical with theirs, while there is a necessity for laws to protect women against their husbands and fathers. This statement is not worth another word.

Some who desire that there should be an equality of property between men and women, oppose representation, on the ground that political duties would be incompatible with the other duties which women have to discharge. The reply to this is, that women are the best judges here. God has given time and power for the discharge of all duties; and, if he had not, it would be for women to decide which they would take, and which they would leave. But their guardians follow the ancient fashion of deciding what is best for their wards. The Emperor of Russia discovers when a coat of arms and title do not agree with a subject prince. The King of France early perceives that the air of Paris does not agree with a free-thinking foreigner. The English Tories feel the hardship that it would be to impose the franchise on every artizan, busy as he is in getting his bread. The Georgian planter perceives the hardship that freedom would be to his slaves. And the best friends of half the human race peremptorily decide for them as to their rights, their duties, their feeling, their powers. In all these cases, the persons thus cared for feel that the abstract decision rests with themselves; that, though they may be compelled to submit, they need not acquiesce.

It is pleaded that half of the human race does acquiesce in the decision of the other half, as to their rights and duties. And some instances, not only of submission, but of acquiescence, there are. Forty years ago, the women of New Jersey went to the poll, and voted, at state elections. The general term, "inhabitants," stood unqualified;—as it will again, when the true democratic principle comes to be fully understood. A motion was made to correct the inadvertence; and it was done, as a matter of course; without any appeal, as far as I could learn, from the persons about to be injured. Such acquiescence proves nothing but the degradation of the injured party. It inspires the same emotions of pity as the supplication of the freed slave who kneels to his master to restore him to slavery, that he may have his animal wants supplied, without being troubled with human rights and duties. Acquiescence like this is an argument which cuts the wrong way for those who use it.

But this acquiescence is only partial; and, to give any semblance of strength to the plea, the acquiescence must be complete. I, for one, do not acquiesce. I declare that whatever obedience I yield to the laws of the society in which I live is a matter between, not the community and myself, but my judgment and my will. Any punishment inflicted on me for the breach of the laws, I should regard as so much gratuitous injury; for to those laws I have never, actually or virtually, assented. I know that there are women in England who agree with me in this—I know that there are women in America who agree with me in this. The plea of acquiescence is invalidated by us.

It is pleaded that, by enjoying the protection of some laws, women give their assent to all. This needs but a brief answer. Any protection thus conferred is, under woman's circumstances, a boon bestowed at the pleasure of those in whose power she is. A boon of any sort is no compensation for the privation of something else; nor can the enjoyment of it bind to the performance of anything to which it bears no relation. Because I, by favour, may procure the imprisonment of the thief who robs my house, am I, unrepresented, therefore bound not to smuggle French ribbons? The obligation not to smuggle has a widely different derivation.

I cannot enter upon the commonest order of pleas of all;—those which relate to the virtual influence of woman; her swaying the judgment and will of man through the heart; and so forth. One might as well try to dissect the morning mist. I knew a gentleman in America who told me how much rather he had be a woman than the man he is;—a professional man, a father, a citizen. He would give up all this for a woman's influence. I thought he was mated too soon. He should have married a lady, also of my acquaintance, who would not at all object to being a slave, if ever the blacks should have the upper hand; "it is so right that the one race should be subservient to the other!" Or rather,—I thought it a pity that the one could not be a woman, and the other a slave; so that an injured individual of each class might be exalted into their places, to fulfil and enjoy the duties and privileges which they despise, and, in despising, disgrace.

The truth is, that while there is much said about "the sphere of woman," two widely different notions are entertained of what is meant by the phrase. The narrow, and, to the ruling party, the more convenient notion is that sphere appointed by men, and bounded by their ideas of propriety;—a notion from which any and every woman may fairly dissent. The broad and true conception is of the sphere appointed by God, and bounded by the powers which he has bestowed. This commands the assent of man and woman; and only the question of powers remains to be proved.

That woman has power to represent her own interests, no one can deny till she has been tried. The modes need not be discussed here: they must vary with circumstances. The fearful and absurd images which are perpetually called up to perplex the question,—images of women on wool-sacks in England, and under canopies in America, have nothing to do with the matter. The principle being once established, the methods will follow, easily, naturally, and under a remarkable transmutation of the ludicrous into the sublime. The kings of Europe would have laughed mightily, two centuries ago, at the idea of a commoner, without robes, crown, or sceptre, stepping into the throne of a strong nation. Yet who dared to laugh when Washington's super-royal voice greeted the New World from the presidential chair, and the old world stood still to catch the echo?

The principle of the equal rights of both halves of the human race is all we have to do with here. It is the true democratic principle which can never be seriously controverted, and only for a short time evaded. Governments can derive their just powers only from the consent of the governed.

Notes

1.   Correspondence vol. iv. p. 295. [Martineau's note]

III. Lady Elizabeth Eastlake
(1809–1893)

Elizabeth Rigby Eastlake was a central figure in the Victorian art scene. As a practitioner of *Kunstgeschichte*, or art history, she translated the works of German art scholars Johann David Passavant and Gustav Friedrich Waagan into English. She also wrote articles on the utilitarian versus the aesthetic functions of art, the influence of new waves in German painting upon British artists, and the assimilation of photography into artistic practice. Eastlake, along with her husband, painter and scholar Charles Eastlake, sat at the hub of the "Eastlake Circle" comprised of J. M.W. Turner, John Ruskin, Harriet Martineau, Anna Jameson, William Makepeace Thackeray, Thomas Carlyle, Thomas Babington Macaulay, Robert Browning, and countless others.

Elizabeth Rigby was born in Norwich on November 17, 1809, to Anne Palgrave Rigby and Edward Rigby, a prominent obstetrician. Dr. Rigby died when Eastlake was eleven, and from that point she and her seven surviving siblings were raised solely by their mother. The Rigby children were encouraged to fraternize with the many intellectual and professional visitors who frequented the family's residence, and the children's formal education was itself quite rigorous. They were tutored by masters in French, Italian, mathematics, and geography. It is believed, however, that Eastlake was too young to have benefitted much from such instruction; at one point she characterized her own education as very deficient. After Dr. Rigby's death, the family retired to Framingham, and Mrs. Rigby allowed her children to pursue their own education, with the help of a French governess. Although interested in languages and literature, Eastlake's first passion was art. She began drawing at age eight and by time of her death had produced over two thousand works.

At age eighteen, Eastlake contracted typhoid fever; her mother and a sister accompanied her to Heidelberg, Germany, for a convalescence. They remained in Germany for two and one-half years, and while there, Eastlake learned German. Shortly after her returning home she put her new language to use by translating Passavant's *Kunstreise durch England und Belgien* (1832). In 1835, Eastlake again visited Germany, and while there she wrote a condemnatory article on Goethe, published in the *Foreign Quarterly Review* in 1836. This article is representative of the critical study she began making of German thought and culture.

Always eager to travel, Eastlake next embarked on a trip to Russia in 1838 to visit one of her sisters. She stayed in Reval (Tallinn, Estonia) in the Baltic provinces, and also visited Petersburg where she met the Czar. From Russia, Eastlake wrote long letters to her mother, which were published by John Murray in 1841 under the title *A Residence on the Shores of the Baltic; Described in a Series of Letters*. These Baltic letters, which provided a vivid picture of Russian customs and manners, were a great success in Britain. They reached a second edition in only a few months and are considered the true starting point of Eastlake's literary career. Murray sent the manuscript to J.G. Lockhart at the *Quarterly Review*, who wrote back: "I have no doubt she is the cleverest female writer now in England, the most original in thought and expression too. . . ." Lockhart's enthusiasm marked the beginning of Eastlake's long affiliation with the *Quarterly Review* as its sole female contributor; she ultimately published over thirty-four articles in this prestigious periodical.

While on a visit to London in 1846, Elizabeth met Sir Charles Eastlake, a well-known painter and art academician. The two were married in 1849 and went on to become one of Britain's most illustrious couples. Through Sir Charles's legendary directorship of the fledgling National Gallery from 1854 until his death, Elizabeth Eastlake was able to help develop that institution into a world-famous collection of art; during her husband's presidency of the Royal Academy, Eastlake consolidated the role of hostess into one which allowed her to exercise her criticism on art. She also acted as a facilitator between artists and collectors, and between collectors and the Crown.

Due to her talent as both artist and writer, Eastlake influenced Victorian opinion on the subject of aesthetics. Her early *Quarterly Review* article "Modern German Painting" (1846) was commissioned by Lockhart because he considered Eastlake to be the writer most in touch with contemporary art currents. Her negative opinion of the famous Düsseldorf show of the new German "Nazarenes" not only set up a much-needed critical polemic to counter John Ruskin's opinions about the social function of art, but it also attacked art which she described as "laborious idleness"—a criticism which later influenced the Pre-Raphaelites in their own rebellion against the English painting tradition. Eastlake's quarrel with Ruskin's aesthetic theory culminated in her review of his *Modern Painters*, which she published in the *Quarterly Review* in 1856. As a whole, Eastlake's art criticism speaks of a sensibility that was both in tune with contemporary issues and in anticipation of future currents. Her application of Waagan and Passavant's *kunstgeschichte* resulted in a series of revisionary, iconoclastic critiques of Leonardo da Vinci, Michelangelo, Albrecht Dürer, Titian, and Raphael. Furthermore, Eastlake's writings are first-rate examples of modern art criticism—a discipline that was then being codified and used to build national treasures, preserve classical works and identify the important contemporary artists. Testament to Eastlake's authority in the Victorian art world lies in the fact that she was asked to complete Anna Jameson's ambitious work on Christian art, *The History of Our Lord* (1864), after Jameson's death in 1860. Eastlake referred to this project as her *magnum opus*, and indeed, it remains a fixture in the field of art criticism.

Eastlake's writing was not confined to the subject of art. Her understanding of the interrelatedness of culture, national character, history and the individual lent itself well to characterizing foreign societies. Her reflections on German, Italian, and Russian culture resulted in several essays, including "Germany, Present and Past," (*Edinburgh Review*, 1880), "Venice: Her Institutions and Private Life" (*Quarterly Review*, 1889), and "Russia: Its People and Government" (*Quarterly Review*, 1891). While analyzing German culture, Eastlake identified such national characteristics as militarism and an anti-modernism which she rightly viewed as ominous. In addition, Eastlake established her reputation as an influential literary critic when the *Quarterly Review* published her attack on Charlotte Brontë's *Jane Eyre* in December, 1848.

Eastlake's exclusion from the Victorian prose canon stems from the old belief that her views were the product of her husband's mind and not her own. Unfortunately, Eastlake helped propagate this theory by writing in the brief preface to her *Five Great Painters* (1883) that she "founds her claim to the indulgence of the reader on no study or thought of her own, but solely on the advantages enjoyed by her for long years at the side of the late Sir Charles L. Eastlake." With the exception of her vociferous critics, however, Eastlake's reading audience as well as her editors and publishers did indeed champion her originality and individuality. In fact, some present-day art historians believe that Eastlake's influence on her *husband's* career was profound. In any event, she demands more attention for the roles she played in Victorian thought and society, both as a pioneer art critic and as a stylist of important magnitude.

One of the first to recognize Eastlake and her works as deserving a permanent place in literary history was her nephew Charles Eastlake Smith. His introduction and textual comments on her *Journals and Correspondence* (1895) provide an excellent source of information on Eastlake's life and work. John Steegman's classic *Victorian Taste: A Study of the Arts and Architecture from 1830 to 1870* (1970) offers further information on Eastlake's contribution to the aesthetic debates of her day. Also of note is David Robertson's detailed study, *Sir Charles Eastlake and the Victorian Art World* (1978). Like Steegman, Robertson relies heavily on Elizabeth Eastlake's journals for his insight into the mid-nineteenth-century art scene. He recognizes Eastlake's value as a writer and devotes considerable discussion to her work. For more extensive biography, consult "The Memoir of Sir Charles Eastlake," written by Eastlake herself and included in Sir Charles's *Contributions to the Literature of Fine Arts* (1870). Lady Eastlake actually found the Queen reading this Memoir one afternoon in 1870 when she visited her at Westminster.

Katharine Walke Gillespie,
State University of New York
at Buffalo

7. Modern Painters

Introduction

Elizabeth Eastlake's review of John Ruskin's *Modern Painters* appeared anonymously in the March, 1856, *Quarterly Review* and is reprinted here from that periodical. As Eastlake points out in *Journals and Correspondence*, her critical aim was "to show and to refute [Ruskin's] elementary errors regarding the principles and purposes of Art." In her review, she criticizes Ruskin for his "erroneous statement" that "'painting, or art generally, with all its technicalities, difficulties, and particular ends, is nothing but a noble and expressive language, invaluable as the vehicle of thought, but by itself nothing.'" She goes on to condemn his "wrong reasoning in the comparison of two unanalogous things, viz. the language of the painter and that of the poet." Eastlake's rebuttal of Ruskin's critical premises rests with her belief that "the language of painting is comparatively of no value as the vehicle of thought, which is a faculty conveyed much better by its own proper medium—the written forms of speech." In her defense of the aesthetic object as meaningful in and of itself, Eastlake may be viewed as working in a line of descent which originated with Immanuel Kant and culminated in the Art-for-Art's-Sake Movement. Like Kant before her and Oscar Wilde after, Eastlake sought to define a realm of human experience to and for which only art could speak, whereas Ruskin believed that art should serve and reflect Christian morality and social utility.

Modern Painters

There are many reasons for the popularity of Mr. Ruskin's works. In the first place he is a thinker—a character sufficiently rare to obtain—we do not say to deserve, for that depends on the issue—that class of thoughtful readers of whom a writer may be justly proud. In the next place he is a very positive and confident thinker—also a comparatively rare phenomenon—and any positive man or opinion commands, at least for a time, a certain amount of followers, for people naturally trust those who trust themselves. And further, he is a positive and confident thinker on a subject which is now engaging the attention of a large class of the educated English public. But in proportion to the increasing love for art is the consciousness of ignorance about it, and in proportion to the consciousness of ignorance is the prevalence of self-distrust; and here we arrive at a more interesting, because a more earnest section of readers, including especially the young and uncritical, who gratefully follow the guidance of any one who suggests thought and lays down principle on a subject on which many can feel, but few have the power or opportunity to reason. But while the arts enjoy the advantage of being at this time a reality of the most earnest and almost sacred kind to many, they suffer, as must always be the case, the disadvantage of being a fashion of the most empty and pedantic sort to many more. Here the reasons are at once apparent which furnish Mr. Ruskin with another class of readers more numerous than any we have mentioned; for fashion cannot think, and must talk, and is therefore the eager adherent of those who save the brains and supply the tongue on the favourite topic of the day. And, lastly, while art is now temporarily in fashion, it must be borne in mind that strange and new doctrines on any subject in the world are always the fashion, and this accounts at once for the most prolific source of Mr. Ruskin's popularity, and discloses a class of readers larger than all the foregoing put together.

There are also many reasons why Mr. Ruskin has not been more generally or broadly answered—we will not say more effectually, for that he has been on particular points in several of the monthly and weekly journals. The pure and enthralling power exercised by art over the imagination and the emotions is supposed, and not always erroneously, to be purchased somewhat at the expense of the prosier faculties of the mind. The lover of art, like all true lovers, is, on that point at least, a shy and sensitive being. He can confess his passion, but little more. Nor is art a worship in which there is any duty to give a reason for the faith that is in us. Taste is rightly defined by Hazlitt as "a sensibility to the excellences of art;" and our sensibilities to anything, from the relish for poetry to that for an orange, are facts in ourselves, the grounds of which we are not required to define. Why we believe in any given thing we bound to know, but why we feel involves no such responsibility. A man may therefore say of art, as, in the song, the *innamorato* of his mistress, "I love you, because I love you," and yet not be thought deficient either in enthusiasm or in understanding, but rather the reverse. Artists themselves are seldom able to define in words the principles which their works triumphantly exemplify. And thus it is that the lovers and followers too of art present the anomaly of being at once the most devoted of adherents, and yet often the least able or inclined to fight for the cause. It is certain also that discussion and criticism, unless of a most enlightened, and therefore most rare, description, is more depressing than stimulating to the producers of art, while to encourage litigation and debate among the classes who are constituted its judges is to encourage that which most unfits them for the privilege. Freedom of opinion, like true freedom in anything, can do art no harm,—though, from the fact that the greatest period of art was that of the greatest religious and political thraldom, it is evident that freedom is a condition on which it is in no way dependent,—while all that licence which abuses the name of liberty is incalculably pernicious to it. This is one of the profounder reasons why, in the economy of European civilization, art, as a means of public education, was sent before letters, and this is why now, and at all times, its best friends will abstain from that war of words which is foreign to its nature, adverse to its promotion, and incompatible with the temper necessary for its enjoyment.

These are the reasons that may be said to apply to the subject of art in general: as to those which especially withold many an answer to Mr. Ruskin, they lie chiefly in the imagination of the persons who are otherwise admirably qualified to controvert him. As a thinker, mechanically considered, of the most able and elaborate class, Mr. Ruskin is supposed to require much of that same faculty to refute him; while, as a controversialist, of the rudest manners, many an antagonist is deterred by the supposition that something of the Ruskin is needed, at all events in process, to catch a Ruskin. It would, however, be as useless to meet this writer with the same properties of thought, as undesirable to use the mere style of argument which he wields, and a victory so achieved would be but an additional subject of regret. Mr. Ruskin reminds us of the tale of the Emperor's clothes in the "Fairy Legends" of Andersen. Like the cunning weavers, he persuades his readers that it is the test of their religion and morality to see as he sees, and the delusion is kept up till some one not more clever, but more simple, ventures to speak the plain truth. The real way, therefore, to face Mr. Ruskin, is not with those weapons he has selected from the mental armoury, but with those he has left, and thus accoutred the humblest adversary has nothing to fear. And this requires us to be the more plainspoken in the consideration of his writings, for downright and unvarnished truth is doubly necessary in the conflict with sophistry and irony, and doubly justified towards one who by his treatment of others has in reality forfeited all title to courtesy.

We must commence with a short but necessary analysis of the author himself, before proceeding to his works. Mr. Ruskin's own mind, judging from his writings, is an extreme exemplification of that which is pronounced—we do not stop to consider whether rightly or wrongly—the defect of the present age, and to which the absence of all *greatness* in the various departments of life is now-a-days imputed. The period is declared to be one rather of brilliant intellectual talents than of great moral qualities—those qualities which, though they cut no figure in debate, and make no show in print, yet lead a man to prefer duty to fame, and truth to everything. Now, Mr. Ruskin's intellectual powers are of the most brilliant description; but there is, we deliberately aver, not one single great moral quality in their application: on the contrary, he appears so far more destitute than others, like himself, more intellectually than morally gifted men, of these higher aims, as not even to recognise the necessity for feigning them. Where the truth of a conclusion is no object in the process of reasoning, there no restraint exists on that activity of the thinking faculty, which can never lead to better things than itself without a higher principle to enlighten it. Nay, there is something at once sad and consoling in the fact that the intellect cannot even ripen itself. Mr. Ruskin's writings have all the qualities of premature old age—its coldness, callousness, and contraction. There is no development apparent in all he has written. Even in his first volume, the most able, and therefore the most favourable to himself, his overbearing spirit has nothing of the self-excusing insolence of youth. In his crotchety contradictions and peevish paradoxes there is nothing of the perverse, but often charming, conflict between the arrogance and the timidity of a juvenile reasoner—between the high spirit and tender mouth of the young courser in the race of thought. His contradictions and false conclusions are from the beginning those of a cold and hardened habit, in which no enthusiasm involuntarily leads astray, and no generosity instinctively leads aright. His revilings of all that is most sacred in the past, and his insults to all who are most sensitive in the present, bear the stamp of proceeding rather from an unfeeling heart than a hasty judgment; while such, necessarily, have been the vitiating effects on himself of the unrestrained indulgence of these habits, that his latter works, as we shall have occasion to prove, show him to have arrived at a blind rhodomontade of reasoning and a reckless virulence of language almost unparalleled in the annals of literature.

It will, however, sufficiently answer all our purposes of justice, and better those of equity, to form our estimate of Mr. Ruskin's title to be considered an authority on the matters he treats, chiefly from his first volume. From this we abundantly gather those qualities by which we may define him as a writer, viz. active thought, brilliant style, wrong reasoning, false statement, and unmannerly language.

After this definition, it will not surprise the reader to find us start with the declaration that Mr. Ruskin's principles, as applied to art, are unsound from the outset; and that, the foundation having a radical defect, it follows that the structure he has raised upon it, however showy, is untenable. Throughout, therefore, as a consequence of this false beginning, we observe a prevailing unfitness between the means of investigation he uses and the object for which he uses them. His tests may be ingeniously compounded, and have all the qualities of care and thought, but it stands to reason that a test is not a test unless applied to the right substance. Now, art is a thing which, as we have said already, appeals more to the heart, the seat of emotion, than to the head, the seat of thought, and is, therefore, more dreamt and raved about than reasoned about. Still it contains principles and admits of tests which, though utterly superfluous for the guidance of the artist—for he is not an artist at all with whom these principles and tests are not more or less intuitive—yet are interesting to an educated public, and necessary as a refutation of such teaching as Mr. Ruskin's. We need hardly state that we have no romantic project of doing battle to all the fallacies Mr. Ruskin has penned. Life is short, and if art be long it is in its practice, not in its theory: all that we have time or occasion to deal with are the errors of his fundamental principles; knowing that, if these main fortresses of his modes of thinking can be demolished, there will be little to fear from all that labyrinth of specious argument which depends upon them. Further, it is only with the errors of his fundamental principles, as applied to *Painting*, that we propose to deal at all; his Architecture and other subjects would require a separate campaign.

In the first chapter after his Introduction, Vol. i., page 7, the first fundamental false principle will be found, viz.—

that painting, or art generally, with all its technicalities, difficulties, and particular ends, is nothing but a noble and expressive language, invaluable as the vehicle of thought, but by itself nothing. He who has learned what is commonly considered the whole art of painting—that is, the art of representing any natural object faithfully—has as yet only learned the language in which his thoughts are to be expressed. He has done just as much towards being that which we ought to respect as a great painter, as a man who has learned to express himself grammatically and melodiously has towards being a great poet.

Here we have an erroneous statement, namely, that "the language of painting is invaluable as the vehicle of thought, but by itself nothing;" and wrong reasoning in the comparison of two unanalogous things, viz. the language of the painter and that of the poet. We begin with the first.

The only way to arrive at the true end for which an art is valuable at all is by determining those qualities which no other art but itself can express, and which are therefore to be considered as *proper* to it. Now thought, having a language proper to itself, cannot possibly be defined as the great specific excellence or purpose of the art of painting. On the contrary, the slightest reflection will show that thought when expressed by painting is, by the inherent conditions of the art of painting itself, restricted in range, depth, and originality,—those very qualities which are the great essentials of thought itself. No picture, whether good or bad, that does seek to embody depth and range of thought, even in the very limited degree possible, can be deciphered without borrowing another language, in addition to its own, in the shape of a glossary; while, so far from original thought being even a recommendation, the whole history of art shows that it is the *familiar* thought which is sure to be the most attractive. The best pictures the world ever saw or perhaps will see, repeat, as in the innumerable Madonnas and Holy Families, the same thought over and over again; while with the Greeks, not only the same thought, but the same motive or particular mode of expressing the thought, was handed down from one generation to another. Indeed, were we required to answer Mr. Ruskin's proposition as positively and broadly as he has made it, we should be far nearer the truth by denying it altogether, and declaring that the language of painting is comparatively of no value as the vehicle of thought, which is a faculty conveyed much better by its own proper medium—the written forms of speech; but that the language of painting being capable of utterance where every other art is silent is in itself *everything*.

That there is, however, a certain measure of thought compatible with, and separate from the language of, painting, we shall be the last to deny. But here we are stopped by the vagueness of the term itself; for though Mr. Ruskin urges, further on, that "it must be the part of a judicious critic carefully to distinguish what is language and what is thought, and to rank and praise pictures chiefly for the latter" (vol. i, p. 10); yet such is the confusion and contradiction prominent in his own thoughts and language that it becomes no easy task to ascertain what he really means by "thought," "ideas," "subject of intellect," &c., as applied to painting. All we can do, therefore, is to try his meaning by certain pictorial attributes connected with the domain of thought, but distinct from the language of painting itself: thus, for instance, by the word commonly acknowledged to convey the topic a painter has chosen—viz., the *subject* of his picture—and under this head to show how very little thought even in this sense is either admissible or endurable by defining how very much is neither the one nor the other.

For this purpose we have only to glance at the different fields of thought—moral, speculative, theoretic, poetic, epigrammatic—those which must occupy the thinking faculty. Assuming, therefore, that it is not necessary that the thought which the painter's language is to express be original (which no little diminishes its value as a vehicle), we perceive at once that such men as Aristotle, Bacon, Paley, and Pope—each the representative of certain fields of thought—offer as thinkers no subject to which the painter's powers of expression can be applied. Here, therefore, we should rather say that the department of thought proper—thought "by itself"—far from being indebted to the language of painting for an "invaluable vehicle," is not so much as able to make any use of it at all, and would not suffer one iota in its means of conveyance to the human understanding were painting even blotted from the creation.

But lest it should be supposed that there is something too untangible and diffuse in this class of general thought to come within that grasp of positive representation which constitutes a subject for a picture, let us next look at that most essential and compact form in which thought can be condensed—that which is defined as "the thought of one and the wisdom of many," as often taking the form of an image as of a moral reflection—and we find the Proverb equally untransmittable by the painter's vehicle. Teniers,[1] for one, committed the mistake of trying to depict the proverb, if not as the entire subject of his picture—a landscape—yet as the principal subject of his foreground; and with all his skill in adorning the commonest, the vulgarest, and the most unthoughtful circumstances of life, he failed the moment he attempted the region of thought itself, the picture remaining a record of his folly.[2]

We come now to the very frontiers of what we may term the picturesque in thought—that class of mental conceptions which are always poetical, and sometimes representable. But even they do not stand the test of investigation. For the Allegory is a form of subject from which, when seen on canvas, the eye turns coldly or impatiently away, and which requires the utmost strength of art itself to carry what is essentially so unfit to be conveyed. This is why it will never be found successful, except with glorious colourists and splendid draughtsmen—in short, with such men as Titian and Rubens, who occupy us so completely with the attractions proper to the art, as to render us indifferent to the unattractiveness consequent on the thought.

And next we turn to the very garden of poetic thought and imagination—that beautiful land where, by means of scenes described and images raised, the painter's and the poet's materials are in some measure identical, and the confines of vocal and visible language partially united. But indeed they meet here on such amicable terms as to be equally lenders and borrowers in turn. To say, therefore, that that portion of poetry where natural scenes and objects are attempted to be painted in words is the thought proper for the painter's language to convey, would be a very false and absurd illustration of Mr. Ruskin's definition, for it must be remembered that the materials of poetry are here borrowed from the picture—real or imaginary—and that in reversing the process the painter's language only resumes what belongs not to thought, but to itself.

Still, as we need not inform the reader, there are, in all lofty and imaginative poetry, ideas and images which the painter delights to interpret into his own tongue, and does so with the utmost success, provided always he have the taste and instinct to select such subjects as are adapted to his vocabulary, and especially to steer clear of those in which the poet has invested, not the least, but the most thought. For the truer the artist the more intuitively he knows that he must be chary in the use of this element, and that, wherever a poet's thought is complete and thoroughly worked out in itself, the language of painting becomes not an invaluable vehicle, but a superfluous load. And especially as regards a poetical image—that form of thought in which the highest poet will ever most excel, and the best poetry be found most replete—here especially the painter will deliberate. For though the tangible forms under which the poet has imaged the abstract thought seem all ready fitted to his hand, yet the subject he may attempt to form from them will be found after all but the illustration of an illustration, and, in that intermediate step, utterly removed from the parent thought which ought to give the meaning to the whole. We may instance this by referring the reader to the new edition of Moore's Irish Melodies, the title-page of which contains an illustration by Mulready of the lines—

> A type that blends
> Three godlike friends,
> Wit, valour, love, for ever.[3]

As a work of art, the drawing is so perfect, and the execution so refined, that one cares not what the motive which has set such a pleasure-giving hand to work; but as the illustration of an illustration, and that one complete in itself, the painter's language, being superfluous, becomes necessarily unintelligible. Had the type been resolved back into its archetype—the shamrock—the painter, however little he would have had to do, would have been intelligible. As it is, however, in the literal representation of a perfect poetical image, the "type that blends three godlike friends" is quite as like three figures engaged in the performance of a very common feat in the saltant art, as the abstract ideas of wit, valour, and love; and thus, while the painter has been evidently puzzled how to convey the thought at all, the mere transfer to his vehicle has utterly put it out of joint. A very little reflection upon favourite thoughts and images in poetry will convince the reader how little, therefore, at best, even this popular source of pictorial inspiration can safely supply, and account for many a mistake in the painter's selection, for which his language—far from being nothing by itself— can alone indemnify us.

And this brings us to a natural law inherent in the science of art, and upon which hangs all the philosophy of true selection and composition of subject. For a work of art can but hold a certain amount of interest, beyond which the mind of the spectator, its real correlative, though strained to comprehend, cannot be forced to enjoy—a measure undefinable and incalculable in itself but perfectly understood by the painter and the spectator, and which, more than anything else, establishes the right sympathy between them. This being accepted as a *law*, we suspect that wherever an art admits of marriage with another art, or another faculty, the union can only be effected by dividing the field between them; in other words, that the more of art the less of superadded thought will a picture be found capable of containing, and *vice versâ*. It is so, if we consider, with music. The composer of a song expressly selects words so far devoid of any depth or completeness of thought as to give the music scope for itself. We cannot imagine a musical composition to be too full of the beauties proper to music itself; but, having these in the fullest measure—being like a symphony by Beethoven or Mozart, *all music*—words, or the thoughts expressed by words, are superfluous. Nor can we imagine a picture too replete with the qualities proper to painting—form, colour, light and shade, and expression; but having these in the utmost perfection, thought itself becomes a *hors d'œuvre*, to use a gastronomic term, for which there is no appetite left. Look at the picture which combines all these qualities more fully than any other we know, the Sistine Madonna, and the subject itself, as referable to thought, will be found to be of very minor importance. The Madonna and Child are looking abstractedly out of the picture; a glory of angels is behind; a papal saint is pointing, it may be to the spectator, on the one side, a female saint is looking down on the other, and two little angels are gazing up from below—thoughts, considered as a subject, of the commonest order, especially in the age of

Raphael, and which in a bad picture we should not look at twice. Nay, so strong were the old masters in the instinctive principles of art, that they never hesitated even to do violence to thought, and to conceive a subject which, viewed in that light, is utterly unjustifiable and absurd. The scene of the Sistine Madonna, for instance, is in heaven, or, at all events, in the sky: the figures rest on clouds, and a fathomless vista of the heavenly host is behind them. So far our imaginations can consent to the thought, and so far any one to whom we may describe it can follow; but when we add that between the Madonna and the heavenly host there is on each side a green stuff curtain looped up to invisible rods, and that the little angels below—the most spiritually abstracted winged children that art has ever produced—lean on a common wooden shelf in the foreground, we at once perceive the incongruity, and are forced to admit, by demonstration if not by feeling, that the painter's language, when perfect in itself, is not only exonerated from the conveyance of anything consistent in the shape of thought, but may even indulge in solecisms by way of subject utterly at variance with all those rules of probability, if not possibility, which are the first conditions of the thinking faculty.[4]

Frequently also the compatibility between the language of the painter and the thought conveyed by the subject is effected by the spectator not perceiving, or, if passively perceiving, not attending to the thought at all. This is the case in Titian's exquisite picture of the Three Ages in Lord Ellesmere's Gallery, where the thought is all very well as an excuse for painting a youth and a maiden in front, and lovely naked children in the middle distance, in the sweetest tones nature could teach or art portray, while an old man and a skull, being both unattractive objects, are rightly put into airy background. But the thought which forms the subject is no part of the pleasure or merit. Had the arrangement been accidental, or the three groups the idealised portraits of three generations of one family, we should enjoy the picture quite as intensely, for there is as much in the painter's language alone as the mind can enjoy at once.[5]

Enough, it appears to us, has been said to show that it is not the *subject* of a picture to which Mr. Ruskin alludes by the term "thought," and in comparison with which the language is "nothing by itself;" for this slight investigation proves that the subjects of the finest pictures existing embody the simplest, the least original, or even the least consistent thoughts, and that it is, on the contrary, the language itself, which, far from being an inferior attribute, can alone exalt the commonest, or recommend the most mistaken subject a painter may choose.

But before proceeding to try another pictorial definition of thought, we must examine Mr. Ruskin's notion of this said language of the painter a little closer. We therefore take the reader back to the concluding paragraph of that same quotation to the illogical nature of which we have already referred, and where he repudiates all benefit of that vagueness under which he might otherwise have found shelter.

He who has learned what is commonly considered as the whole art of painting—that is, the art of representing any natural object faithfully—has as yet only learned the language by which his thoughts are to be expressed. He has done just as much towards being what we ought to respect as a great painter, as a man who has learned to express himself grammatically and melodiously has towards being a great poet.

Whether "what is commonly considered the whole art of painting" be intended for a sneer at those time-honoured works and opinions which Mr. Ruskin delights to assault, we must leave undecided, the difficulty of knowing when he is in jest or earnest being one of the minor objections to his style of writing: nor does it matter— the reasoning of this sentence is, under any view, false from beginning to end. In what, we would ask, does the force of an illustration consist, but in the analogy upon the point at issue of the two things compared? Here all analogy fails. Are we obliged to remind Mr. Ruskin of the essential difference between the language of the painter and that of the poet? *Words*, or the language of the great writer called a poet, are mere arbitrary signs and ciphers differing in different countries—having no meaning good or evil of their own, until invested with one or the other by the thought they are summoned to express[6]—while *things*, or the language of the great imitator called a painter, being the very copy and mirror of Nature herself, are vocal with the eloquence of her voice, and rich with the varied treasures of her meaning—needing no further process by which to reach our understandings—immediate interpreters of that inexhaustible creation beyond which the wildest flights of the painter cannot soar, and without which his simplest inventions cannot be expressed—which, though they have neither speech nor language in the common sense of the terms, yet send forth a sound, and that a joyous one, throughout all lands. Therefore he who has learned what is commonly considered the whole art of painting—that is, the art of representing any natural object faithfully—that is, the art of representing form, colour, light and shadow and expression, for these are the great and sole constituents of *every* natural object—*is* a great painter already, for Raphael himself could learn no more.

To attempt therefore to separate the whole art, or the language—for with Mr. Ruskin, as with ourselves, they are synonymous—from the thought of the painter, seems to us the emptiest mistake into which the teacher or even learner of art could possibly fall. Art is not a trade which is taught in two distinct stages. A man does not first learn to paint, and then to think, as a tailor's apprentice learns first to stitch a garment, and then to shape it. If his language and his thought do not grow hand in hand in equal strength, he will never be a painter at all. If even there be any precedence in the matter, it is far more frequently the thought that gets before the utterance, letting "I *cannot* wait upon I would." And this is also in some measure a hopeless condition; for in truth the painter's language Mr. Ruskin despises is not so much to be considered as "invaluable" for his thoughts, as *indispensable* for them. For as the language of music involves the idea conveyed by it, and the loftier the composer's sound the loftier his meaning; so the language of the painter, wielding as it does the qualities of colour, form, light and shade, and expression, *includes* the idea that these qualities express; for there is not one of these four chief pictorial elements which does not teem with thought, meaning, feeling, emotion—all that it is possible for the language of painting to contain, and impossible to detach from itself;—so that it is false to say that thought can be all, and language nothing, since the painter who speaks the finest language must in that utter the finest ideas, and what Nature has joined together let no sophistry sunder!

What, we would ask, distinguishes the ideas of a great painter from those of his feebler follower? those of Raphael from those of his scholars? those of Leonardo da Vinci from those of Luini? or those of Rembrandt from those of his imitator Eckhout?[7] What, when the subjects are identical and endeavoured to be expressed by the same qualities in art, brings the grace of the one down to the mere gracefulness of the other, changes the grandeur of the one into the sweetness of the other, or transforms the mysterious chiaroscuro of the one into the nothing-suggesting shadow of the other? What but the difference in their language? What indeed makes the distinction between the original and the copy, so that the idea you delight in in the first, you find all enfeebled or utterly gone in the last—but the difference in the language?

Nevertheless, though it is our entire conviction that any attempt to distinguish the painter's language from his thoughts would, even in the hands of a judicious critic, be an unprofitable proceeding, and is, in Mr. Ruskin's, a mischievous one—we will try him by another test, and assume that *expression*, in the highest physiognomical and intellectual sense of the word,—that which we consider as the highest element of the painter's language,—is in reality separate from and superior to it. But here we are at once met by a passage which leads us to suspect that this test will prove no more successful than the last. For, speaking of "painting or literature"—a false parallel in itself—he says, not only that "the highest thoughts are those which are least dependent on language," but that "the dignity of any composition and praise to which it is entitled are in exact proportion to its independency of (a painter's or poet's) language or expression." This sounds very much as if that state of inarticulation which a sheet of white paper best typifies were the state most to be coveted in art or literature. It is, however, possible that Mr. Ruskin does not here mean that same element of expression to which we refer; though what he does mean it would puzzle us to define. To test the word at all we must test it in its most indubitable and elevated sense—that expression, namely, which is found in the highest painter's highest productions, and on the elevation, purity, or sweetness of which all the world of taste, past and present, is so agreed, that juvenile enthusiasts might be well excused for a few romantic speculations as to its being the work of some agency independent of the painter's art. But here there is no further doubt at all; for, far from having hit upon the author's real meaning by that element of expression best illustrated by Raphael—for instance in the Madonna della Seggiola—that picture, and other works, as we shall hereafter show more fully, are especially the objects of Mr. Ruskin's most scornful contempt. So that it is evident that, instead of acknowledging our concession of expression from the domain of art to that of thought, it would rather be resented as a concession which he altogether rejects.

A further test will make this doubly sure; for, of all the elements of the painter's language, expression must be allowed to be that in which the *idea* conveyed to the spectator is most intimately involved; since it is chiefly by the expression of the faces that the leading intention of the subject can be told. Far, however, from apprehending the real value or condition of the idea a great painter, by means of expression, can convey, Mr. Ruskin not only despises the purest ideas that expression has ever conveyed, but proceeds, a few pages further on, to insist on the *number* of the ideas or thoughts in the same picture as a proof of its merit. "The picture which has the nobler and more numerous ideas, however awkwardly expressed, is a greater and better picture than that which has the less noble and the less numerous ideas, however beautifully expressed." (vol. i, p. 10.) Now, however round this passage may read, and moral it may sound, it is but the more ingeniously erroneous both in statement and conclusion. We deny altogether the compatibility of "the nobler and more numerous ideas" in one picture. The higher we go in art, the more assuredly do we find that the nobler the idea—whether of devotion, as in the masters before Raphael, of supernatural grandeur, as in the Sistine Madonna, of beauty, or grace, or sweetness, as in other pictures by this most complete of masters—the more single and alone it stands. It is in truth this unity and prevalence of one idea that gives the old masters such a hold upon the mind. One idea at a time was all they in their wisdom, practical and theoretical, sought to embody. We look on the Sistine Madonna again as the triumphant exemplification of this. In the all-engrossing aim at the expression of supernatural grandeur, Raphael has even foregone the temptation, if such occurred to him, of introducing any of those sweet incidents of nature in the representation of which he was equally unrivalled. The Mother and the Child have forgotten their human relation in the Divinity that transfigures them. This is why the picture stands still higher as a work of art than the Madonna della Seggiola, where the exquisitely natural action of the Child's feet, and its hands buried in the mother's bosom, by so much lessen, because they by so much sweeten, the idea of supernatural grandeur.

And if this was the case with Raphael, it is still more characteristic of Michael Angelo, who, scorning all minor things, throws the whole weight of his gigantic power into the shaping and strengthening of one idea. Hence that very autocratic grandeur peculiar to him, and hence too that baldness of all accessory incident, or dramatic variety equally observable in his works.

But here we come upon another glimpse of Mr. Ruskin's meaning. For though the actions or incidents of nature we have just alluded to in the Madonna della Seggiola are too commonly observable in any young infant to be dignified in the painter's adoption of them by the term "thought," and though Mr. Ruskin's ostentatious contempt for the whole Dutch school further proves that the mere common and homely incidents of life are the last things he would think of so dignifying; yet there is no doubt that there are incidents—what we should rather call "allusion," or "double-meaning"—which are the result of thought, and are also separate from the painter's language. For this we refer to Mr. Ruskin's description of a picture by Sir Edwin Landseer, where he starts with that fallacious identification of poetry and painting which has been raised and refuted—and, being wrong, oftener raised than refuted—over and over again before Mr. Ruskin's time:—

> Take, for instance, one of the most perfect poems or pictures (I use the words as synonymous) which modern times has seen—"The Old Shepherd's Chief Mourner."—Here the exquisite execution of the glossy and crisp hair of the dog, the bright, sharp touching of the green bough beside it, the clear painting of the wood of the coffin and of the folds of the blanket, are language—language clear and expressive in the highest degree. But the close pressure of the dog's breast against the wood, the convulsive clinging of the paw which has dragged the blanket off the tressel, the total powerlessness of the head laid close and motionless upon its folds, the fixed and tearful fall of the eye in its utter hopelessness, the rigidity of repose that marks that there has been no motion or change in the trance of agony since the last blow was struck on the coffin-lid, the quietness and gloom of the chamber, the spectacles marking the place where the Bible was last closed, indicating how lonely had been the life, how unwatched the departure of him who is now laid solitary in his sleep,—these are all thoughts by which the picture is separated at once from hundreds of equal merit as far as mere painting goes, by which it ranks as a work of high art, and stamps the author, not as the neat imitator of the texture of a skin or the fold of a drapery, but as the man of mind.[8]

We are tempted to claim the quietness and gloom of the chamber and whole expression of the dog as beautiful thoughts inherent in such a painter's language. Also to ask Mr. Ruskin what idea he really attaches to expression when he declares the painting of the dog's hair, of the wood of the coffin, and of the folds of the blanket to be "language—language clear and expressive in the highest degree;" for what, after all, does such painting express, but hair, wood, and wool? But we leave this to speak for itself, and rather draw the reader's attention to the fact that, in the vividness with which Mr. Ruskin's own language has brought such few incidents as this picture contains, distinct from the painter's language, before our eyes, lies the proof that Sir Edwin's language would have been ill employed if alone on that which there are better and shorter means of rendering. And it is precisely here that we have the whole key at last to Mr. Ruskin's meaning of the word "thought" as separable from the art of painting. For it is not the incident that Raphael or the Dutch masters introduce—given in its refinement by the one, in its vulgarity by the other, and in its simplicity by both—it is not even the touching allusion which Raphael introduced in the folded hands of the sleeping saint in his Deliverance of St. Peter, or the erudite allusion in the actions of Plato and Aristotle in his School of Athens, and of which he forbore all use in the Disputà and the Parnassus—it is not even such incidents or allusions which a painter may discreetly use for the enrichment of a picture to which Mr. Ruskin does honour; but it is the incident that will bear description, expatiation, and speculation—the incident that will furnish a text for those arbitrary interpretations and egotistical rhapsodies so foreign to the real simplicity of art, which fill Mr. Ruskin's books—the incident for which there is least space in the highest productions, simply because it does represent that thought which is independent of the painter's language, and of which, therefore, the greater the number in one picture the more the author's purpose and praise is secured.

There is but one form in which the old masters, who were compelled occasionally to address themselves to superstition at the expense of true taste, made the mistake of attempting to combine a number of thoughts, incidents, allusions—call them what we may—in one picture. This was the case in their representations of the Last Judgment, such as that by Fra Angelico in Lord Ward's gallery, where the side of the Condemned far outweighs in number of thoughts, and those not his own, that of the Blessed, and we need not say at what expense of nobility and every other desirable attribute of art.[9] Indeed, the more the subject is considered, the more we are persuaded it will appear that numerous thoughts in one picture are only to be found in the *lower* walks of art, and that the further we descend the scale the greater the quantity of that element, in Mr. Ruskin's sense. Our Hogarth[10] may be cited as a unique example of the successful application of painting to quantity of subject and number of allusions, and those of a high moral order. Nor are we in the least disposed to agree with the German lecturer who said of him that he "badly painted capital satires;" but, on the contrary, are astonished at the beauties of the painter that have been overlooked in the fame of the moralist. At the same time it must be admitted that Hogarth stands at best but at the head—however far in advance of—that class of art in which multiplicity of thought, or what we may define as *illustration*, is the painter's principal object. Nor is there any halting in the downward course, or avoiding of that extreme but actual result to which this principle tends; for if number of thoughts be admitted as the one great merit in a work of art (and number and nobility we perceive cannot go together), there is no denying that the caricature, with its point, allusion, wit, meaning, and double meaning in every line, is, by Mr. Ruskin's reasoning, proved to be as much the highest in the scale of excellence as Michael Angelo is the lowest.

But now we are reminded of another principle which Mr. Ruskin ignores altogether, and to which any painter who may be misled to follow out his doctrines must inevitably do violence. For if the real test of *style*, according to the philosophical meaning of the word, be defined as that form of art which suggests no want, as for instance, the Sistine Madonna, it may be equally defined as that form of art which suggests no superfluity. Thus we return to the fundamental law of the incapacity of the mind to enjoy more than a certain amount of interest at once, and, as a necessary consequence, to the fundamental necessity of diminishing one source of interest in proportion as another is added; and applying this to the present question, we arrive irresistibly at the conclusion that, where numerous thoughts are presented to the spectator at all in one picture, the *painter's* language, far from being invaluable, is partially superfluous. The thoughts or incidents of Hogarth are almost, if not quite as intelligible to us in the form of an engraving, while for more elaborate themes and still more numerous allusions the slightest light and shade, or the mere outline, as in Cruikshank or Retsch, is all-sufficient.[11] And here at all events the author ratifies the conclusion of his views at which we have arrived, by the following rather paradoxical passage:—"Speaking with strict propriety, therefore, we should call a man a greater painter only as he excelled in precision and force in the language of lines." (vol. i. p. 8.)

We trust we have demonstrated that, as, where the thought or idea is highest and singlest, the painter's language is not "invaluable" but indispensable, so where the thoughts are lower because more numerous, and therefore capable of expression by a simpler form of art, the painter's language is in great measure superfluous.

But to turn now from those reasons for the exclusion, or very limited admission of thoughts in a painting, which are inherent in the art of painting, to such as may be said to be rather facts of experience. Is that to be considered the highest attribute and purpose of a picture which has the greatest number of ignorant and vulgar admirers? Yet, as regards the subject, the story, the thought in a picture, such does experience prove to be the case. Not only do we observe this in the crowds that gather round that stronghold of Mr. Ruskin's principle—viz., the greater the number of thoughts, however awkwardly expressed, the greater the merit—the caricature-shop, but every exhibition shows that the story is all the uneducated care for. Follow a *laquais de place* [12] marshalling a party through a foreign gallery, and his whole jargon is of what is represented. It is dull work for him and his listeners when he has only to tell that that is St. Peter, that St. Lawrence, and that figure behind St. Roch; but the party brightens up if he can explain that the figure of St. Clara is a portrait of the painter's wife, and is quite happy when there is some such knotty allegory to untie as that in the Garofalo in our National Gallery, where St. Augustine is endeavouring to comprehend the mystery of the Trinity, and a child showing him that it would be just as easy to empty the ocean with a spoon. Nay, even the most trivial story, not in the picture but about it, is eagerly listened to, and the anecdote that such a prince offered to cover the canvas with napoleons, remembered with far more interest than the picture itself. Not that there is anything blameable or surprising in this. A painter's aim is not, like a cook's, obvious to the commonest understanding. We may like a dish to have a pleasant appearance, but everybody knows that is not its real purpose. As soon, however, might we judge of a dish by our eyes and not by our palates as exclusively exalt the thought of a picture and cry down its language. Were the subject, or the rendering of the subject, the highest merit in a work of art, connoisseurship would be attained without much study, and far fewer mistakes made in the formation of collections. Far, however, from this being the case, it was the saying of the most cultivated and felicitous private collector that England has yet known—the late Samuel Rogers—that if a picture bore an eloquent description he did not want to see it. Though, therefore, it would be great folly, as well as ignorance, to be indifferent to the thought or allusion of a great painter—for any fact, characteristic, or even tradition about a fine picture is interesting, however collaterally so—yet it is far greater folly and ignorance to pronounce the one to be all and the other nothing; and on this road no one will ever rise above the herd in the understanding or enjoyment of art.

We are not, however, intending either to excuse or to insult Mr. Ruskin by comparing him with this common herd whom he misleads. In the error that has led him to lay down the principles we have endeavoured to confute, he is rather to be regarded as the type of a class of minds, frequent now and common always—men who, leading lives in the study of some particular pursuit or hobby, are ignorant of the legitimate sources of interest in a picture, and seek only for those which we may define by the vague and often-used term of "the pleasures of association." But it is the pleasures in which art differs from other forms of human intelligence, and not those in which she accidentally agrees with them, that we must seek; therefore not for thought, nor erudition, nor history, nor antiquarian lore, nor anything which, though a picture may contain, it is altogether independent of. These, it is true, have their interest and value as connecting a work of art with the scholarship, the superstition, or the fashion of its time, but are so far from constituting any essential part of its merits, that not one of these concomitants, however ingenious and abundant, could render a picture endurable if it happened to be vile as a work of art. But though Mr. Ruskin may be classed with these minds in the false conclusions they form, he has no right to the real excuses they may plead. They are occupied with other pursuits distinct from the world of art: he professes to live only in it, and (how generously!) only for it. They err from ignorance, and are, generally speaking, ready to acknowledge it,—he from a quality which is apt to prove a barrier even to that lowest stage of wisdom.

We have dwelt thus at length on this first chapter for obvious reason that here lies that organic defect which renders the whole body of Mr. Ruskin's criticism morbid and diseased. He who pronounces the painter's thought to be everything, and his language nothing, must of course next attempt to force upon art a moral and not a pictorial responsibility. We are at once stopped by this in the preface to the second edition, which is strictly consequent on this first chapter. Having assumed that the state of religion was better in Italy during the immobility of Byzantine art than in the time of Michael Angelo and

Benvenuto Cellini—a question the historian may answer—he thus proceeds:—[13]

It appears to me that a rude symbol is oftener more efficient than a refined one in touching the heart, and that, as pictures rise in rank as works of art, they are regarded with less devotion and more curiosity.

But, however this may be, and whatever influence we may be disposed to admit in the great works of sacred art, no doubt can, I think, be reasonably entertained as to the utter inutility of all that has been hitherto accomplished by the painters of landscape. No moral end has been answered, no permanent good effected, by any of their works. They may have amused the intellect, or exercised the ingenuity, but they never have spoken to the heart. Landscape art has never taught us one deep or holy lesson; it has not recorded that which is fleeting, nor penetrated that which was hidden, nor interpreted that which was obscure; it has never made us feel the wonder, nor the power, nor the glory of the universe; it has not prompted to devotion, nor touched with awe; its power to move and exalt the heart has been fatally abused, and perished in the abusing. That which ought to have been a witness to the omnipotence of God has become an exhibition of the dexterity of man, and that which should have lifted our thoughts to the throne of the Deity has encumbered them with the inventions of his creatures.

If we stand for a little time before any of the more celebrated works of landscape, listening to the comments of the passers by, we shall hear numberless expressions relating to the skill of the artist, but very few relating to the perfection of nature. Hundreds will be voluble in admiration, for one who will be silent in delight; multitudes will laud the composition, and depart with the praise of Claude on their lips—not one will feel as if it were *no* composition, and depart with the praise of God in his heart.[14]

These are the signs of a debased, mistaken, and false school of painting. The skill of the artist, and the perfection of his art, are never proved until both are forgotten. The artist has done nothing till he has concealed himself—the art is imperfect which is visible—the feelings are but feebly touched, if they permit us to reason on the methods of their excitement. In the reading of a great poem, in the hearing of a noble oration, it is the subject of the writer and not his skill—his passion, not his power— on which our minds are fixed. We see as he sees, but we see not him. We become part of him, feel with him, judge, behold with him; but we think *of* him as little as of ourselves. Do we think of Aeschylus while we wait on the silence of Cassandra, or of Shakespeare while we listen to the wailing of Lear? Not so. The power of the masters is shown by their self-annihilation. It is commensurate with the degree in which they themselves appear not in their work. The harp of the minstrel is untruly touched, if his own glory is all that it records. Every great writer may be at once known by his guiding the mind far from himself, to the beauty which is not of his creation, and the knowledge which is past his finding out.

And must it ever be otherwise with painting? for otherwise it has ever been. Her subjects have been regarded as mere themes on which the artist's power is to be displayed; and that power, be it of imitation, composition, idealization, or of whatever other kind, is the chief object of the spectator's observation. It is man and his fancies, man and his trickeries, man and his inventions—poor, paltry, weak, self-sighted man— which the connoisseur for ever seeks and worships. Among potsherds and dunghills, among drunken boors and withered beldames, through every scene of debauchery and degradation, we follow the erring artist, not to receive one wholesome lesson, not to be touched with pity, nor moved with indignation, but to watch the dexterity of the pencil, and gloat over the glittering of the hue.

I speak not only of the works of the Flemish school—I wage no war with their admirers; they may be left in peace to count the spiculæ of haystacks and the hairs of donkeys: it is also of works of real mind that I speak—works in which there are evidences of genius and workings of power—works which have been held up as containing all the beautiful that art can reach or man conceive. And I assert with sorrow that all hitherto done in landscape, by those commonly conceived its masters, has never prompted one holy thought in the minds of nations. It has begun and ended in exhibiting the dexterities of individuals, and conventionalities of system. Filling the world with the honour of Claude and Salvator, it has never once tended to the honour of God.

Were Mr. Ruskin amenable to those rules of consistency which with other writers forbid the penning of many a magnificent paragraph, we should have been spared this rhapsody of plausible sophistry and careful alliteration. He would have halted, as we do, at his first sentence, and, admitting that "as pictures rise in rank as works of art they are regarded with less devotion and more curiosity," he would either have shrunk from an argument which involves the necessity of keeping art undeveloped and barbarous, as the Greek Church to this day does; or, knowing that it is only in the development of any art that we can perceive its real aim, he would have looked a little closer at that "curiosity," or, in other words, at that other source of interest, separate from religion, which, by his own admission, increases in strength in proportion as pictures increase in merit.

But this is begging the whole question; for to have interposed such considerations between Mr. Ruskin and his arguments would have been to interdict them altogether. We take them, therefore, as they are, and boldly meet the accusation of the religious and moral shortcomings of landscape art, or any art, by the utter denial and denunciation not of those shortcomings, which we gladly confess, but of those doctrines which so mischievously misrepresent the real mission of art. Whether sacred or historical, landscape or domestic, art was *not* given to man either to teach him religion or morality; and wherever he is found professing to learn one or the other from her something worse than that spiritual indifference which Mr. Ruskin laments—namely, false and morbid fervours—and something worse than that human interest he despises—namely, cold and selfish abstractions—will be found. As the minister of those ineffable pleasures which stand in sweet reconciliation midway between the senses and the soul; as the stirrer of those humanising emotions which harmonise equally with man's highest spiritual aspirations and his commonest daily impressions—which have none of the dangers of selfish sensibility or the penalties of false excitement;—as all this, and infinitely more, art is indeed to be looked upon as a gift of inappreciable price to a race who need those pure pleasures which recall their forfeited innocence, quite as much as those moral lessons which point to its loss; but beyond this she happily gives and teaches nothing. For if outward Nature herself, with all her blessed influences, never really, except in an infidel novel, taught a man to fear God, love his neighbour, and correct himself; if from the beginning of the world men never really listened to the voice of the creation as the means of moral and religious teaching—for if they had, St. Paul would not have been sent to the Gentiles—neither will they to the best painter's best echo of it. "For art is the shadow of His wisdom, and but copieth His resources." He, therefore, who would wrest art from her real field and purposes—he who with brilliantly-strung words and active sophistry of thought would misrepresent the real scheme of Providence, *putting one thing for another*, would, if we can imagine followers numerous enough to constitute him a leader, bring about just that false state of society and just that idolatry of shadows for which he now professes to pity us. For he who advocates false motives, and assigns false sources for the teaching of religion and morality, does in fact weaken and obscure, though he may not openly deny, the faith in those only motives and sources which have been revealed to us.

What too, we have a right to ask, have been the results of all the supposed religious and moral teaching of art upon the writer himself?

Let the nature of the creed be tested by its influence on the believer. Independent of all the attacks upon painters, living or dead, which we shall presently investigate, and which may be considered the substance of his works, the mere incidental and accessory portions teem with a malice, bitterness, and uncharitableness, which is as uncalled for as it is unjustifiable. Mr. Ruskin may talk of love for trees, stones, and clouds, and profess an impious horror for those who do not represent them according to his ideas of truth, but where, throughout his writings, do we find one spark of that love for *man, woman,* or *child* which is foremost among all the precepts and the fruits of religion and morality? How comes it that the man who lives under the influence of him whom he pronounces "the greatest landscape-painter the world has yet seen;" and further, as he owns, "more among mountains than among men," and therefore under nature's immediate teaching—how comes he to have formed such low and contemptuous notions of his fellow-creatures as appear directly and indirectly in every chapter he has written? Considering the little company he professes to keep, how comes it to be only of that kind as to wring from him the declaration that "There never yet was a generation of men (savage or civilized), who, taken as a body, so woefully fulfilled the words, 'having no hope and living without God in the world,' as the present civilized European race;" that "a Red Indian or Otaheitan savage has more sense of a Divine existence round him, or government over him, than the plurality of refined Londoners and Parisians?" (vol. iii. p. 258.)

Again, that "I truly believe that there never yet was idolatry of stock or stone so utterly unholy as this our idolatry of shadows;" nor can he think that "of those who burnt incense under oaks, and poplars, and elms, it could in any wise be more justly or sternly declared, "The wind hath bound them up in her wings, and they shall be ashamed because of their sacrifices." (iii. 72.)

How does it happen that this man never descends from his mountains—"the pure and holy hills" as he calls them—without stumbling on that particular kind "of young lady who, rising in the middle of the day, jaded by her last night's ball, and utterly incapable of any wholesome religious exercise, can still gaze into the dark eyes of the Madonna di S. Sisto, or dream over the whiteness of a crucifix, and who returns to the course of her daily life in the full persuasion that her morning's feverishness has atoned for her evening's folly?" (iii. 57.) Or upon that type of "the fashionable lady who will write five or six pages in her diary respecting the effect of such and such an ideal upon her mind?" Or on that of "the shallow fine lady or fine gentleman to whom the beauty of the Apollo Belvedere or the Venus de Medicis is perfectly palpable" (which we doubt), though they would have perceived none in the face of an old weather-beaten St. Peter, or "Grandmother Lois" (iii. 69)? Or, worse still, upon that rather exceptional example of "the modern English lady, who, if she does *not* beat her servant or her rival about the ears, it is oftener because she is too weak or too proud than because she is of purer mind than Homer's Juno? She will not strike them, but she will overwork the one and slander the other without pity." (iii. 179.)

Are these the "holy thoughts" which a right feeling for art is to prompt? Is this the language of a man whose heart and mind have been refined even by the commonest and most legitimate influences of art? If so the world must be weaker and wickeder even than Mr. Ruskin believes it, not to feel it a matter of duty as well as self-interest to repudiate doctrines which bear such unpalatable fruits in the person of their especial apostle!

Mr. Ruskin professes to have written his first two volumes for the express purpose of defending Turner, which, considering that this great painter received while living the unfeigned and unstinted admiration of every British artist worthy the name, and a larger share of that of the cultivated public than usually falls to the lot of artistic genius—considering, too, that this was an admiration so far from barren that he lived to afford to be fastidious as to the individuals from whom he would accept commissions, and died possessed of a larger fortune than any English painter has ever accumulated—appears somewhat unnecessary. Nevertheless, had Mr. Ruskin performed this self-imposed task honestly and sincerely, the world would have been indebted to him for a work of much beauty and interest, and Turner grateful even for services not needed. As it is, however, Mr. Ruskin has taught us that there is an admiration and love more worthy both of Turner's works and Turner's memory, and that is one which resents the use of his name as the pretext for the most unmannerly vituperation of all those great painters who occupy that genealogical tree of art on which Turner's shield now hangs proudly aloft. No enthusiasm for Turner can ever justify, because none can ever really cause, the offensive sentiments levelled at such men as Claude, Poussin, Canaletto, Wilson, Cuyp, Hobbema, and Ruysdael, or the ill-disguised contempt of higher names still.[15] If to honour Turner it be necessary to assert of Claude that his pictures are "the evidence of classic poison upon a weak mind" (i. 123); that he has "the industry and intelligence of a Sèvres china painter;" that a background city by him is strikingly like that which Mr. Ruskin has the faint recollection of having delineated in the first page of a spelling-book when he was four years of age! (i. 191)—of Poussin, that "distances like his are mere meaningless tricks of clever execution, which, when once discovered, the artist may repeat over and over again with mechanical contentment and perfect satisfaction to himself and his superficial admirers, with no more awakening of feeling or exertion of intellect than any tradesman has in multiplying some ornamental pattern of furniture" (i. 194);—of the glorious Dutch oak-painter, that "one dusty roll of Turner's brush is more truly expressive of the infinity of foliage than the niggling of Hobbema could have rendered his canvas if he had worked on till doomsday" (i. 199);—of our own Wilson, that "his pictures are diluted adaptations from Poussin and Claude, without the dignity of the one or the elegance of the other" (i. 91)—for he will praise those he elsewhere most abuses, if it be at the expense of another, and then withdraw this very praise again, as in this instance, by calling Claude's "a foolish grace," and Poussin's "a dull dignity" (iii. 332);—if it were necessary to speak of Rubens with an insulting apology for "his unfortunate want of seriousness and incapability of true passion" (i. 162);—of the great Italian masters, not excepting Titian and Paul Veronese,[16] with a lament too absurd to be otherwise than ludicrous for "their blunt and feelingless eyes and untaught imaginations" (i. 210);—of all the French, Dutch, and Flemish landscape-painters in a lump, with a declaration that "they passed their lives in jugglery;" that "the deception of the senses was the first and great end of all their art;" that "they had neither love of nature nor feeling of her beauty;["] that "they looked at her coldest and most commonplace effects because they were easiest to imitate, and for her most vulgar forms because they were most easily to be recognised by the untaught eyes of those whom they alone could hope to please;" that "they did it, like the Pharisee of old, to be seen of men, and they had their reward" (i. 74); and, finally, as the climax of indecent contempt, that "I conceive that the best patronage that any modern monarch could bestow on the arts would be to collect the whole body of them into a grand gallery and burn it to the ground" (i. 90);—if, we again say, it was necessary for the exaltation of Turner, thus ignorantly, flippantly, and malignantly (and to a far greater extent than any quotations can show) to vilify those without whom Turner would never have been Turner,—then better were it that the great painter's name, and even his glorious works too, had been buried in oblivion, than raised up to notice in such odious association. It is no slight proof of the previous appreciation of Turner's merits, that even Mr. Ruskin's defence of them has not been able to lower them in public estimation. By the same rule also, indignant as we may be that any one should be found in our times impious enough to blacken these great benefactors—for, with the debt of gratitude which all sound lovers of art must acknowledge, we can only so designate such an act—yet there is no fear that Mr. Ruskin can really bay one of these luminaries one hair's breadth out of his sphere, or that the adherents he can agitate for Turner will be any loss to Claude, Poussin, Wilson, and Hobbema.

Let, however, Mr. Ruskin's style of criticism be laid to its own account—the nature of his own mind. Art may be his excuse, but the man who scatters about "firebrands and arrows" will never want an excuse, and will plead earnestness, quite as much as sport. Let us rather pursue the reasoning of him who has pronounced the painter's language to be of no value by itself. Holding this doctrine, it is evident that, however he may affect to despise, he is in reality incapacitated from the enjoyment of a school in which the language of painting is so entirely all in all, that you must love it for that, or cannot love it at all. It is but too easy for ignorance or pedantry to sneer at the men who painted "stagnant ditches, pollard willows, and stupid boors;" but it would have been far wiser to have acknowledged that benevolence which has sent a handmaiden amongst us who is dependent neither on the aristocracy of Nature nor of mind, who can dwell in the lowliest scenes, and thrive on the homeliest fare, and hold her Court with as much state, splendour, and refinement too, as regards some of her attributes, in the commonest kitchen, in the prosiest court-yard, beside a spinning-wheel or cradle, along a flat meadow all striped with bleaching linen, in short, wherever man with his pleasures, occupations, and affections is to be found, as among saints and madonnas, mountains and thunderstorms. We have no wish to gloss over Ostade's and Teniers' drinking boors, or to be less honest than those great painters themselves, who, as their lot was cast in the fens of Holland, painted Dutchmen, drunk or sober, just as they found them, not thinking themselves in their simplicity called upon to invent fictitious proprieties, or their art defiled by speaking the truth.[17]

But it is not to "beldames and boors" that he confines his virtuous indignation; he must forsooth abuse Claude for letting porters be found carrying so very improper a burden as "iron-bound boxes" along so very improbable a locality as a common landing-pier; and further, "can scarce but be angered" when Claude bids him stand on this same "paltry, chipped, and chiselled quay, with porters and wheelbarrows running against him, to watch a weak, rippling, bound, and barriered water, that has not strength enough in one of its waves to upset the flower-pots on the wall, or even to fling one jet of spray over the confining stone."—vol. i. p. 76.

It is unfortunate for Mr. Ruskin, not for Turner, who can well afford to be unfortunate for once, that the great painter's best work, in his own estimation, hangs by his own wish precisely next [to] one of these "weak, rippling, bound, and barriered" seas of Claude. We might compare the skies of each to Claude's great advantage, but that Mr. Ruskin admits, as we do, that this sulphury mass is not a fair specimen of Turner. We do compare the buildings—Claude's, the lustrous walls on which a succession of Italian suns and moons have lingered, and linger still—Turner's mere tenements of clay which neither sun illumines nor shadows enliven. But more than all the comparison is forced upon us when we look at that exquisite sea—weak, or rather calm with excess of strength—clear, cool, and above all dark with excess of purity—true in its roll of varied monotony as none but Claude ever did or can paint the sea—whose murmur, however placid, is but the lull of its awful roar, and whose ripples, however gentle, are but the repose of its dreadful strength, and then turn to that sluggish pool in Turner's Carthage, with no movement, yet with no reflections, and ripples thick with crusted edges, and glaring with prismatic light, the apparent refuse of some neighbouring factory, which our great painter has placed beside it.

And here let the reader judge whether the incident which occurs in the foreground of this very pool, namely, children swimming some toy-boats, as an allusion to the future greatness of Carthage, be really and alone sufficient to give Turner "an intellectual superiority above Claude, which no powers of the draughtsman or the artist (supposing that such existed in his antagonist (!)) could ever wrest from him" (vol. i. p. 29). Or whether this toy-boat incident, with all its ingenuity, be not to common sense and justice incalculably outweighed by that grand *idea* of the stupendous element itself which Claude impresses upon the mind by the mere unassisted characters of his glorious language.

But let us now consider more especially that particular excellence in Turner, by virtue of which, according to Mr. Ruskin, he stands alone as the painter of landscape. There is no fear of our handling Turner too freely, for his greatness, as we have said before, can afford all truth to be spoken of him. We have always looked upon Turner, even before Mr. Ruskin was born, as one of the greatest landscape-painters in the world, and great especially in that particular aspect of Nature which had not been before expressed. The early Italian and Flemish masters had given

> The spacious firmament on high,
> And all the blue ethereal sky,

as none, we fear, will ever give it again. The Venetians had arrested many a gorgeous effect—cool with light and radiant with heat; Claude had set the very sun in the heavens; Cuyp had depicted the rarified pulsation of still-noon heat, and the solemn all-massing vapour of a golden afternoon; Berghem had piled up those stately masses which the winds drive together, and then leave for hours undisturbed; Poussin had gathered the thunder-charged clouds, showing deep within the lurid chamber whence the bolt is ready to fall; Rubens had spanned the rainbow; Wilson had painted daylight in every gradation, from the rising of the sun to the setting of the same; Ruysdael had given the sky which heightens the idea of solitude; Van de Welde and Backhuysen, that which we most remark at sea—each had their favourite phase best in keeping with their favourite object; while to Turner was reserved not only the desire of expressing every phase (excepting always the unfathomable vault of the early masters), and of rendering every form of cloud that floats under heaven, but also of arresting those evanescent and fantastic forms of vapour and mist which never had been aimed at before.

For doing that entirely, which none had done but partially, and for perpetuating those wonderful effects which none had arrested at all, Turner does indeed stand alone. But as this is the secret of his perfection, so it is the secret of his imperfection too. Turner dwelt so much aloft; his eye was so saturated with light, air, and vapour; so practised in the imitation of delicacy, evanescence, and unsubstantiality, that it descended to earth incapacitated for recognising the common conditions of our common mother. Every object he saw, as he himself has told us, was outlined to his vision in prismatic colour. What wonder, therefore, that his earth, however replete with all that botanical and geological truth which Mr. Ruskin so much overrates, should be wanting in that first truth of all proper to it, viz., substantiality. What wonder then that, however exquisitely he traces the bramble and veins the rocks, the scene below is often but the secondary accompaniment to the still more elaborately worked out scene above. Not that Turner did this by deliberate choice; on the contrary, he could not have done otherwise; he had chosen one world for his brush to delight in, and he knew that no picture could contain two. To have made out the substance of this Terra firma with the same solidity, precision, care, and detail according to its nature, as he did that of clouds according to theirs; to have rendered earth earth, as he rendered sky sky, would have been to paint what no eye, and, least of all his, could have endured.

In this he fell under that same inherent law we have adverted to before as regulating the proportions of art and thought; for where there is the preponderance even of one part of the painter's speech, there must be the deficiency of another. It is true that this double detail of earth and sky, this delicacy of the feathered cloud above your head, which he so marvellously possessed, and this solidity of the clod at your foot, which he so generally evaded, are thought to be compatible in Nature. But this is owing not to any capacity in her for reconciling things irreconcilable in a picture, but simply to the spectator's own freedom of eye. We are very Arguses when we contemplate this fair world itself: the power of shifting our vision gives us a hundred eyes, and a hundred pictures in which only one principal thing is seen at a time, in less than as many seconds. It is true that a picture *can* represent with equal prominence all that Nature presents, and *can* therefore give you with equal detail earth and sky, and all that therein is; but then, instead of being true to Nature, the picture becomes in so far false that it forces upon you that which in Nature you have the power to escape from. But here Art comes to the rescue; for, as a completely finished picture *must* contain more than in Nature you would care to look at in one moment, she also provides the power of concealing what she cannot leave out. This is the secret of all the half-finished pictures or drawings by the amateur; he shows his feeling by stopping when he has advanced far enough for his pleasure—but his ignorance in not knowing how to deal with all beyond that; while those who, like the professional artist, have to fight the battle in earnest, count it one of their greatest victories to have acquired, by slight treatment, skilful chiaroscuro, or any other means, the power of getting rid of the troublesome surplus. It would be an interesting inquiry to ascertain how far two such opposite means as Rembrandt's shadow and Turner's light both conduced to the same end of concealment or subordination to a principal object. At all events, we may unhesitatingly declare that the unsubstantiality of Turner's earth— the ethereal vision it presents as compared with what it really is— however exquisite, is an imperfection consequent on the perfection of his skies; and that therefore, though he differed from all other painters in the particular choice of his principal object, he only followed in all their steps in making that principal object—no matter what—the most true, and therefore the most prominent thing in his picture. To arraign, therefore, the old landscape painters, and the old painters in general—for no name is sacred to Mr. Ruskin—for not elaborately depicting the details of the sky as Turner did—for not introducing "the region of the Cirrus," 1stly, with "Symmetry;" 2ndly, with "Sharpness of edge;" 3rdly, with "Multitude;" 4thly, with "Variety;" and that with the most studied inequality, with "the most delicate symmetry," and "with the most elaborate contrast," till it becomes, as he admits, "a picture in itself" (vol. i. p. 226)—is to arraign them for principles in which, far from differing, they agree with him, and principles which, however he may have practised, they had established.

In all the eloquence, therefore, with which Mr. Ruskin has treated the subject of clouds—a chapter generally quoted as his best— there is the unpleasant association that his end is to mislead; and that, like an able counsel, he increases in parade of zeal, roundabout ingenuity of invective, and simulated indignation, in proportion as he knows his case to be unsound. Accordingly, after all this weary length of words—this wonder, "how little people in general know about the sky"—this lament over "the feebly-developed intelligence and ill-regulated observation," as well as over "the blank and feelingless eyes," and untaught imaginations of the great old masters—this playful irony, that the massive clouds of the old master, not excepting Titian and Paul Veronese, "may be broad, may be grand, may be beautiful, artistical, and in every way desirable—I don't say it is not, I merely say it is a concentration of every kind of falsehood" (vol. i. p. 230)—these doubts, whether they had any other motive for not anticipating Turner in his skies "beyond the extreme facility with which acres of canvas might be covered without any troublesome exertion of thought;" this ostentatious word-painting—a far easier art than is generally supposed—of some of Turner's splendid sky-effects; this needless inquiry, in the tone of triumphant condemnation, as to whether Claude has the same; these witticisms upon "half-crowns," "ropes," "cauliflowers," and "turnips;" these lamentations over "abuses of nature and abortions of art;" these epithets of "childish," "abominable," "painful," "degrading," "criminal," and "lying"—to all this tirade, as far as regards the not having studied the sky in the same sense as Turner, there is the very short and simple answer, that the comparison is unfair from beginning to end; that the old masters had different objects; and that while they often neglected that which Turner accomplished, they accomplished what he as often neglected. Theirs is the earth which the husbandman tills and the miner bores—Turner's, a radiant sphere where no such operations are possible or needed; their skies are the beautiful, the appropriate, or, in some of the earlier masters, only the negative accessories to the picture— Turner's often, by the very rule of Ruskin, the picture itself. Nay, even where his skies cannot be called the chief object—having scarcely any objects in them, but only serene gradation of colour, with perhaps a few brilliant wind-swept forms overhead—yet, from the habit of the painter's eye, the earth is equally unsubstantial; and, though exquisitely graduated in scale from distance to foreground, yet false in the position of the scale itself.

As regards the merits of their skies, it would be useless insisting on the fact, that, as far as they go, they are every whit as true and as beautiful as Turner's. As Mr. Ruskin says of colour, "one man may see yellow where another sees blue, and yet neither can be said to see falsely, because the colour is not in the thing, but in the thing and them together;" so as respects the forms, colours, and substances of clouds—proverbially rather mutable bodies—Mr. Ruskin may see half-crowns and ropes where another sees what is appropriate for the scene and the hour; for the secret of recognising what is true lies not in the thing, but in the thing and the spectator together. While also his loss is so much our gain, we shall be the last to combat his opinions. We know that he prefers rough seas to smooth, "and can scarce but be angered" at the painter who has given us the mere heave of its placid slumber: in another part of his works, present or future, we may find that he prefers smooth seas to rough, for no better reason than to deride their portrayer. In either case he has a right to his opinion, and a right

also to change his opinion. There is no law to prohibit bad taste or
absurd inconsistency, and it is against the needless offensiveness with
which he expresses those tastes and inconsistencies, and not against
themselves, that we protest. When, therefore, he takes us to the
National Gallery, and bids us see childishness in one great painter,
imbecility in another, and bold broad falsehood in a third, and the fruit
of our examination is to raise all three higher than ever in our
admiration and gratitude, we have nothing to say, but to thank God who
has made us like other men—publicans included—rather than like Mr.
Ruskin. But when—as an example of their skies being "systematically
wrong"—he points to Poussin's grand picture of the Sacrifice of Isaac,
and vents a page of contempt upon it, all based upon the assertion that
the time in the picture is "high-noon, as is shown by the shadows of
the figures,"—we convict him of building erroneous theories upon a
perversion of facts. We, therefore, assert that the whole basis of his
abuse of this picture falls to the ground, for that the time is *not* high-
noon. Noon shadows are under the feet; these of Abraham and Isaac are
as long as themselves, being moreover shortened by the fact of their
ascending a hill. There are also shadows from tall trees on the left
slanting across the whole foreground; the time may be, therefore,
considered either late afternoon or early morning—the latter, considering
the journey before them, most probable; these two periods of the day
being in Italy so alike, that the keeping and lighting of the picture may
represent either; and as Mr. Ruskin's word and our own here
diametrically differ, the shadows themselves—the earliest clocks known
to man, and still the source and proof of all accuracy in time—
fortunately become the real witnesses. To them, therefore, we refer the
reader; and while examining them, we should not be surprised if he
came to the conclusion that instead of their being an example of
Poussin's want of veracity as a painter, they serve rather as an example
of Mr. Ruskin's want of the most ordinary care or candour as an
observer.

   Altogether the vicinity of the National Gallery is inconvenient to
the stability of this writer's facts. When he tells the reader that he "may
search through the foregrounds of Claude, from one end of Europe to
another, and not find the shadow of one leaf cast upon another," (vol. i.
p. 176) the magnitude of the task disposes him rather to take Mr.
Ruskin's word for the fact, than to undertake the labour of testing it.
But no such labour is wanted. The answer is neither at Rome or Naples,

nor even at Dresden or Berlin, but in the National Gallery here in London, where, in the picture of David at the cave of Adullam, the reader will find, directly in the foreground, a tall large-leaved foxglove-like plant, with certain dark appearances thrown by one leaf upon another, as like shadows as anything Turner or the photograph ever rendered.

But though a man may be "systematically wrong" in his facts, it does not follow that he must be so in his opinions. "A little peculiarity of taste," according to Mr. Ruskin's admirers, must be allowed for, as more or less with all original thinkers. Very well: let Mr. Ruskin have all the benefit of peculiarity in this respect; let us see whether we have not to allow for a little peculiarity of Vision also. At page 52 of the chapter on "Truth not easily discerned"—a heading singularly suitable, and *à propos* of a lament which curiously illustrates our own feelings regarding his treatment of the Poussin picture above, that a man of "deadened moral sensation" may "even coin causes to account for impressions which have no existence at all"—we find this:—

How many people are misled, by what has been said or sung, of the serenity of Italian skies, to suppose that they must be more *blue* than the skies of the North, and think they see them so. Whereas, the sky of Italy is far more dull and grey in colour than the skies of the North, and is distinguished only by its intense repose of light. And this is confirmed by Benvenuto Cellini, who, I remember, on his first entering France is especially struck with the clearness of the sky, as contrasted with the *mist* of Italy.

Here we have, without question, a slight peculiarity of vision, and one for which no Italian traveller we ever met with will be disposed to make allowance. Mr. Ruskin's reference to Benvenuto Cellini also, in whose journal truth may be considered as "not easily discerned," is unfortunate; especially as the allusion to the clearness of the French sky, as contrasted with the *mist* of Italy, is in reference to an apparition of the Virgin which was granted to the Münchhausen sculptor, and a consequent halo round his own head which accompanied him wherever he went, and was apparent "to every kind of person to whom I chose to show it—*quali sono stati pochissimi*" ! ! That such a phænomenon as a brightness round the head has been remarked we are not going to dispute. Goethe alludes to it as seen by persons crossing dewy meadows at sunrise, and, in suggesting the laws of refraction for its solution, shows not the clearness, but the vapoury and misty condition of the atmosphere that gives rise to it. The definition also of "intense repose of light" is not entirely compatible with the conditions of a daylight sky in any part of the world. Repose of light, like the *nuits blanches* [18] of northern summers, is that abeyance of the luminary which may be considered, at all events, as an approach to darkness; the more "intense" the one, therefore, the more "intense" the other. Add to this the fact of the dullness and greyness Mr. Ruskin insists upon, and instead of a bright Italian day, which is the time that this deep blue appears to the common misled eye, we have something far more like a cloudy English night. However, mist or no mist, dull grey or deep blue, intense repose of light or intense brightness of light—which is right and which is wrong is not the point; all we contend for is, that where the vision of one man differs from the vision of the multitude, and those of the most educated classes of society, it comes under the denomination of peculiarity of vision. But after reading what Mr. Ruskin says of the grey and dull skies and the repose of light which he sees in Italy, and bearing in mind his regret that people should be so misled, what are we to think of the following marvellous passage, which we find at page 84, concerning a picture by Giovanni Bellini? "It is," Mr. Ruskin says, "remarkable for the *absolute truth of the sky*, whose *blue*, clear as crystal, and, though *deep* in tone, *bright* as the open air, is graduated to the horizon," &c. This passage occurs very properly under the heading of "General Application of the foregoing Principles."

We turn now to another accusation against the old masters, touching their supposed non-observance of the laws of nature, which argues equal want of knowledge or fairness on the part of the accuser, and which it is important to clear up. Under the head of "Truth of Chiaroscuro," Mr. Ruskin prefers an indictment against "the ancients" for having "set at defiance" the great fact of the existence of shadows. We are told that if we look at an object in full sunshine, and therefore with deep shadows upon it, and then retire backward from it, the forms of its shadows will remain quite distinct to the eye long after those of its real substance have ceased to be so:—

Now this may serve to show you the immense prominence and importance of shadows where there is anything like bright light. They are, in fact, commonly far more conspicuous than the thing which casts them; for being as large as the casting object, and altogether made up of a blackness deeper than the darkest part of the casting object (while that object is also broken up with positive and reflected lights), their large, broad, unbroken spaces tell strongly upon the eye, especially as all form is rendered partially, often totally, invisible within them, and as they are suddenly terminated by the strongest lines which Nature can show. For no outline of objects whatsoever is so sharp as the edge of a close shadow.— vol. i. p. 172.

If there had been any candour in the writer we should again not have been favoured with arguments which he raises only to refute. Let us examine his words as to "the immense prominence and importance of shadows where there is anything like bright light," that "they are in fact commonly far more conspicuous than the thing that casts them;" that they are "as large as the casting object, and altogether made up of a blackness deeper than the darkest part of the casting object;" that "all form is rendered partially, often totally, invisible within them" and finally that "they are suddenly terminated by the sharpest lines that nature can show." One would think Mr. Ruskin were pleasantly testing the reader's apprehension of a joke. The accusations against these delinquents is the best defence they can set up. In Benedict fashion, the old masters may ask "for which of these bad parts" are they to be enamoured of shadows? Because they chose certain exquisite appearances in Nature to produce a desired effect, are they to be rated for avoiding another appearance which would have ruined the effect altogether? Yet such, in point of fact, was the deliberate plan on which they acted; and no reasons they themselves could have urged for the incompatibility of strong-cast shadows with their other and higher views could have been stronger than those Mr. Ruskin has urged for them. With his arguments at hand we need hardly refer the reader to Leonardo da Vinci on the same subject, who agrees marvellously with Mr. Ruskin as to the nature of shadows, and only differs from him by drawing a diametrically opposite conclusion as to their fitness for a picture. But whichever of the two— Ruskin or Leonardo—be right, the first thing a modern critic is bound to do in attempting to reason, far more to animadvert, upon any fact, whether of commission or omission in the great schools of the past, is to ascertain which object they had especially in view; otherwise, as in this instance, he may commit the blunder of exposing that as a grand fault which, in reality, it was their highest pride to have attained.

We will take the Venetians as an example. Light was regarded by them simply as the means for showing form and colour, and not as an object in itself. To have aimed at direct sunlight, and its consequence, intense and defined cast-shadows, would have been to sacrifice that which exactly constitutes the beauty of their school. For what form of distinct outline could have been preserved under the condition of shadows "far more conspicuous than the thing that cast them?" and what local colour could have been retained if subjected to "a blackness deeper than the blackest part of the casting object?" But while these masters knew better than to renounce the greater beauty for the less, they accomplished the compromise at no expense of truth. They knew that form and colour were best discerned in their integrity at that hour when both bright light and deep shadow cease; when the low or hidden sun diffuses a shadow-extinguishing glow upon every object; and they lived, moreover, in that land where the habits of the people happen to bring them forth at an hour when the heat of the day is over, and its greatest beauty begins. Instead, therefore, of not having the perception of the truth of shadows, as Mr. Ruskin affects to believe, they knew that it was at best but a very inferior truth, and had rather the perception to avoid it. Take any Venetian picture as an illustration—that gem of a Palma Vecchio, in Lord Ellesmere's gallery; or his Three Ages, by Titian, already mentioned; or the "Noli me tangere," bequeathed by Mr. Rogers to the National Gallery—imagine the faces orange on one side with sun, and blue or black on the other with shadow.[19] Imagine strong black masses cast by one figure upon the other, the landscape dotted with intensely dark patches, with "outlines stronger than anything else which Nature ever shows;" and instead of all the noble distinctness and refined breadth which are the fundamental beauties of these pictures we have the gross Michael Angelo Caravaggio at once. See too the time of day, the sun setting or hidden behind tranquil masses of evening cloud, and only its glow on the figures and on the "deepening landscape" behind. For *shade*, it must be remembered, these great masters painted better than any—witness that "Venetian Shade," which Agostino Carracci's sonnet has rendered proverbial. It was the *shadow*, in Mr. Ruskin's sense—the *tenebre*, which Leonardo da Vinci carefully distinguishes from the *ombre*—which they especially shunned when under those very conditions for which Mr. Ruskin would have them introduced. But there are proofs enough in many a background that the Italian masters could paint sunshine and shadow if they pleased. In Mr. Rogers's "Noli me tangere," both are introduced where they could not possibly disturb the principal subject, viz., in the buildings in the middle distance.

If the practice of the avoidance of deep shadows began earlier than Leonardo da Vinci, it may be traced down to those landscape-painters who, like Claude and Poussin, looked to Italy as the fountain of true art, and, we may venture to say, will never cease while painters continue to labour under the same desirable delusion. It is true this excellence could not continue unbroken in descent; when perfectly worked out it yielded, as much by the law of change as of progress, to others. Among the Italian painters, Correggio may be cited as the great innovator in this respect.[20] He it was who first stepped out of the beaten track, and made, if not the largest amount of shadow, yet that entire gradation of the whole scale of shadow, or, as we feel it in his works, of lesser light, his chief aim. Doubtless this was the inborn tendency of the man; though looking at his works with that wish to account for certain characteristics so natural to the mind, it may be said that he adopted his glorious system of chiaroscuro as a substitute for those previously cultivated beauties he could not attain; and that feeling his incapacity for that elevation of form which light had merely been the means for distinctly showing, he forsook the end for the means, and made that—namely, light—his great excellence, which, like love, covers a multitude of sins.

Let us therefore reject the puerile cavilling against men for not doing before what is done now, as the absurd hope of their doing now what has been done before. The futile reproach and the visionary expectation are both equally opposed to the true history and philosophy of the human mind. Even had the great Italian masters been as far below all who have come since as they are above them, it would be sufficient for candour and common sense that they had worked out the object they had in view, and that the object most consistent with the habits of the society and the climate of the country to which they belonged.

Thus far the name of Turner has most unjustly been made to serve as a shield for those sallies of invective in which Mr. Ruskin most delights. Now, in his third volume—though so early as the second page to the preface to it he deliberately prefers charges concerning Turner's "critics" which he, not only better than most people, knows to be unfounded, but for the honour of the great painter had much better have let alone[21]—now, in the third volume, this shield must be laid aside. It might be thought that the power of presumption, as regards the attacks upon hard-earned and proudly-established reputations could no further go; but Mr. Ruskin is like the fisherman's wife—having proceeded step by step in profane aspiration from one great luminary to another, he now discharges his arrow at the greatest of all; and the reader is startled by the announcement, that Raphael himself is the greatest criminal in the world of art.

But there is nothing really surprising in this. On the contrary, if Mr. Ruskin's proselytes be consistent they are bound to admit that such a climax is not only probable but inevitable. Let any one pervert the principles and deny the purposes of any art or system, and they not only may but must condemn everything in this world, from a school of art to the scheme of Providence. It is, therefore, only the natural consequence of Mr. Ruskin's assertion that art is intended as a means of moral religious teaching, that when it becomes most admirable in itself it should present the most reprehensible aspect in his eyes. We are accordingly favoured with elaborate commendations of the edifying powers and conscientious purposes of the painter, at a time—that of the illuminating of manuscripts—when all the answer we need give is that art was *not* art; and taking us through a strictly-graduated path of improving means on the one hand, and degenerating ends on the other, he finally overwhelms us with the indignant denunciations of that awful period, when, having reached the guilty summit of perfection, Art altogether ceased to do what from the beginning it had never been intended to do.

The progress as to cause and effect is curious. The earliest cause the author instances was the miniature painter, or illuminator, who, "having learned the rudiments of his art without pain, and employed them without pride"—having, in other words, learned to represent figures utterly unlike figures, standing or lying, as no one could stand or lie, breathing an air consisting of a stiff-panelled pattern, enclosed in a kind of architectural bower infested with dragons and nondescripts, and all upheld in the bowels of an illegible P—having learned this "without pain, and practised it without pride, his spirit was left free to express, as far as it was capable of them, the reaches of higher thought." The effect being, that the spectator gazed upon his work "without having his faith in the actual and unrepresented scene obscured for a moment"—a result in which we thoroughly concur. "But as soon as art obtained the power of realisation, it attained that of *assertion* (!). As fast as the painter advanced in skill he gained also in credibility," "and representation, which had been innocent in discrepancy, became guilty in consistency." Taking, therefore, base advantage of this state of things, the imagination, which Mr. Ruskin informs us "is chiefly warped and dishonoured by being allowed to create false images," actually indulged in something so foreign to its nature, and seduced such painters as Francia and Perugino "to devote all their skill to the delineation of an impossible scene"—representing the Virgin as "a beautiful and queenly lady, her dress embroidered with gold, and with a crown of jewels upon her hair, kneeling on a floor of inlaid and precious marbles before a crowned child" (vol. iii. p. 49).[22] These being the deplorable circumstances, it followed that "the continual presentment to the mind of such beautiful and fully-realised imagery more and more chilled its power of apprehending the real truth"—. . . . "that all true grounds of faith were gradually undermined, and the beholder was either enticed into mere luxury of fanciful enjoyment, believing nothing, or left in his confusion of mind, the prey of vain tales and traditions," till "with no sense of the real cause of his error, he bowed himself, in prayer or adoration, to the lovely lady on her golden throne, when he would never have dreamed of doing so to the Jewish girl in her outcast poverty, or, in her simple household, to the carpenter's wife" (vol. iii. p. 50).

But though "a shadow of increasing darkness fell upon the human mind as art proceeded to still more perfect realisation," yet these painters, erring as they might be, were not yet utterly depraved; "for they only darkened faith, but never hardened *feeling*." This was reserved for that stage of wickedness "when the greater his powers became, the more the mind of the painter was absorbed in their attainment, and complacent in their display"—when "accurate shade, and subtle colour, and perfect anatomy, and complicated perspective, having become necessary to the work, the artist's whole energy was employed in learning the laws of them, and his whole pleasure in exhibiting them"—when "his life was devoted, not to the objects of art, but to the cunning of it"—and when "without perception on the part of any one of the abyss to which all were hastening, a fatal change of aim took place throughout the whole world of art. In early times *art was employed for the display of religious facts*— now *religious facts were employed for the display of art*" (the horror-expressing italics are the author's)—"the transition, though imperceptible, was consummate; it involved the entire destiny of painting. It was passing from the paths of life to the paths of death" (vol. iii. p. 51); and this transition was the advent of Raphael! Hear Mr. Ruskin on this topic:—

And this change was all the more fatal, because at first veiled by an appearance of greater dignity and sincerity than were possessed by the older art. One of the earliest results of the new knowledge was the putting away the greater part of the *unlikelihoods* and fineries of the ancient pictures, and an apparently closer following of nature and probability. All the phantasy which I have just been blaming as disturbant of the simplicity of faith, was first subdued, then despised, and cast aside. The appearances of nature were more closely followed in everything; and the crowned Queen-Virgin of Perugino sank into a simple Italian mother in Raphael's Madonna of the Chair.

Was not this, then, a healthy change? No. It *would* have been healthy if it had been effected with a pure motive, and the new truths would have been precious if they had been sought for truth's sake. But they were not sought for truth's sake, but for pride's; and truth which is sought for display may be just as harmful as truth which is spoken in malice. The glittering childishness of the old art was rejected, not because it was false, but because it was easy; and still more, because the painter had no longer any religious passion to express. He could think of the Madonna now very calmly, with no desire to pour out the treasures of earth at her feet, or crown her brows with the golden shafts of heaven. He could think of her as an available subject for the display of transparent shadows, skilfull tints, and scientific foreshortenings—as a fair woman, forming, if well painted, a pleasant piece of furniture for the corner of a boudoir, and best imagined by combination of the beauties of the prettiest contadinas. He could think of her, in her last maternal agony, with academical discrimination; sketch in first her skeleton, invest her, in serene science, with the muscles of misery and the fibres of sorrow; then cast the grace of antique drapery over the nakedness of her desolation, and fulful, with studious lustre of tears and delicately-painted pallor, the perfect type of the "Mater Dolorosa."

It was thus that Raphael thought of the Madonna.

Now observe, when the subject was thus scientifically completed, it became necessary, as we have just said, to the full display of all the power of the artist, that it should in many respects be more faithfully imagined than it had been hitherto. "Keeping," "expression," "historical unity," and such other requirements, were enforced on the painter, in the same tone, and with the same purpose, as the purity of his oil, and the accuracy of his perspective. He was told that the figure of Christ should be "dignified," those of the Apostles "expressive," that of the Virgin "modest," and those of children "innocent." All this was perfectly true; and, in obedience to such directions, the painter proceeded to manufacture certain arrangements of apostolic sublimity, virginal mildness, and infantine innocence, which, being free from the quaint imperfection and contradictiveness of the early art, were looked upon by the European public as true things, and trustworthy representations of the events of religious history.—vol. iii. p. 53.

Here the patience of the reader must fail, even if ours did not. To such language and sentiments as these we have nothing to say; for though every line be as opposed to sense, and piety, as it is to his own maxims of education in art, when laid down for the abuse of the old landscape-painters, or for the praise of that modern school which has the misfortune to excite his approbation; yet, taken altogether, they reach that sum of the *profane* on which argument is wasted. Let us leave, therefore, that sweet, pure, Italian mother to defend him who, to the everlasting gratitude and wonder of all true believers in art, placed her in that well-known chair; let us leave that piteous Mater Dolorosa to excuse the humble and reverential care with which Raphael approached the subject of her sufferings. Let us leave all that true "apostolic dignity," "virginal mildness, and infantine innocence," to fight their best painter's battle to sound hearts if not to cultivated tastes. The only cause for regret, however great the cause for condemnation, is, that, as the old saying has it, "dirty water cannot run without leaving a stain." We do not allude to those examples among the young whom we know by experience to have derived the greatest hindrance in their artistic education from the poison of Mr. Ruskin's works, leading them to perverse and sophistical dreams, instead of earnest action, and instilling no principle but that of contempt for all established authority. We are rather thinking of others who, with the greatest abhorrence of such sentiments and language, will yet not be able, when they next stand before a Raphael, entirely to divest themselves of the recollection of them, feeling as some have done, who, by inadvertence or accident, have read a page of some noted infidel work, that, however they may abhor the ribaldry of sacred things, the mere knowledge of it is polluting.

But though we leave Mr. Ruskin in his glory, as the scoffer of Raphael's highest productions, and the condemner of his worthiest and most profitable title to a student's imitation, yet we must inflict upon the reader a continuation of the same theme, though on a different chord, were it only to endeavour to refute some of those empty assertions, without which Mr. Ruskin would be at a loss to carry on that system of contradiction to all received opinion, which is the only consistent thing in his writings.

Now, neither they (the cartoons of Raphael) nor any other work of the period were representations either of historical or of possible fact. They were, in the strictest sense of the word, "compositions"—cold arrangements of propriety and agreeableness, according to academical formulas, the painter never in any case making the slightest effort *to conceive the thing as it really must have happened* (the italics are ours), but only to gather together graceful lines and beautiful faces, in such compliance with commonplace ideas of the subject as might obtain for the whole an "epic unity," or some such other form of scholastic perfectness.

Mr. Ruskin here instances the subject of Christ's showing himself to the disciples at the Lake of Galilee, and continues:—

They had gone back to their daily work, thinking still their business lay netwards—unmeshed from the literal rope and drag. "Simon Peter saith unto them, 'I go a fishing.'" They say unto him "We also go with thee." True words enough, and having far echo beyond the Galilean hills. That night they caught nothing; but when the morning came, in the clear light of it, behold, a figure stood on the shore. They were not thinking of anything but their fruitless hauls. They had no guess who it was. It asked them simply if they had caught anything? They said no. And it tells them to cast yet again. And John shades his eyes from the morning sun with his hand, to look who it is; and though the glinting of the sea, too, dazzles him, he makes out who it is at last; and poor Simon, not to be outrun this time, tightens his fisher's coat about him, and dashes in, over his nets. One would have liked to see him swim those hundred yards, and stagger to the beach.

Well the others get to the beach too, in time, in such slow way as men in general do yet in this world, to its true shore, much impeded by that wonderful "dragging the net with fishes;" but they get there—seven of them in all—first, the Denier, and then the slowest believer, and then the quickest believer, and then the two throne-seekers, and two more, we know not who.

They sit down on the shore face to face with Him, and eat their broiled fish as He bids. And then, to Peter, all dripping still, shivering, and amazed, staring at Christ in the sun, on the other side of the coal fire, thinking a little, perhaps, of what happened by another coal fire, when it was colder, and having had no word once changed with Him by his master since that look of His—to him, so amazed, comes the question, "Simon, lovest thou me?" Try to feel that a little, and think of it till it is true to you; and then take up that infinite monstrosity and hypocrisy, Raphael's cartoon of the charge to Peter. Note, first, the bold fallacy—the putting *all* the Apostles there—a mere lie to serve the Papal heresy of the Petric supremacy, but putting them all in the background while Peter receives the charge, and making them all witnesses to it. Note the handsomely-curled hair and neatly-tied sandals of the men who had been out all night in the sea-mists and on the slimy decks. Note their convenient dresses for going a-fishing, with trains that lie a yard along the ground, and goodly fringes, all made to match—an apostolic fishing costume. Note how, Peter especially (whose chief glory was in his wet coat *girt* about him, and naked limbs), is enveloped in folds and fringes, so as to kneel and hold his keys with grace. No fire of coals at all, nor lonely mountain shore, but a pleasant Italian landscape, full of villas and churches, and a flock of sheep to be pointed at; and the whole group of Apostles, not round Christ, as they would have been naturally, but straggling away in a line, that they may all be shown.—vol. iii. p. 55.

Now, we pass over the circumstance that the representation of sacred subjects was not considered by the old masters so much historical as poetical in nature, and so far removed from "possible fact," that the scene was as often laid in heaven as in earth, or, as in the Sistine Madonna, in both at once. Our attention is chiefly drawn to the author's ignorance of the real limits as well as purposes of a work of art by the fact of his expatiating, by way of reproof to Raphael, upon the materials for half a dozen pictures instead of one. Whether these materials be good or bad for pictorial purposes is another question, which, however, as in the matter of shadows, Mr. Ruskin has sufficiently answered himself. For let us try, indeed, to fancy but one of the moments he has described, that of St. Peter, all dripping, shivering, and amazed, with slip-shod sandals and slimy garments, and hair all draggled to the life over his eyes, and a correct coal-fire burning at his side, and setting aside Raphael's moral and religious objections as a man to such a conception of the sacred person of any Apostle, far more of that of the great head of the Roman Church, we perfectly realise all his objections as a painter. In Raphael's time, at least, such a principle of composition would have been condemned as much by the laws of art as of religion, and so we suspect it will ever be (and, as usual, Mr. Ruskin condemns his own creed by the example he gives,[23]) as long as right art and right feeling go together. What kind of criticism, too, is this, which charges that as a crime to Raphael, namely, his belief "in the Papal heresy of the Petric supremacy," which was, and is, and ever will be, the chief corner-stone of a Roman Catholic's faith. As for the great painter's reason for departing from that historical probability of representation in his Charge to Peter, which he observed in his St. Paul preaching at Athens, the Death of Ananias and Sapphira, and others, we may be sure that it was nothing less than that strongest reason of all in a painter's creed, and that which governed Poussin in his representation of the same subject, namely, its unfitness for pictorial purposes. And here we utterly deny that a painter is bound to try and "conceive the thing as it really must have happened," unless this suits his pictorial purposes better than any other way. If Poetry, as regards history or anything that comes under the denomination of fact, be entitled to her poetic licenses, Painting, incomparably more circumscribed in limits as she is, is tenfold entitled to her pictorial licenses. Two modes of representation are, therefore, always open to a painter—one the real, or the thing as it *might* have happened, the other the symbolical. Who does not see, therefore, that Raphael has here purposely adopted the symbolical, and that all that Mr. Ruskin is pleased to designate as "infinite monstrosity and hypocrisy," and "mere lie," is no untruer in that sense than the actual sheep behind the figures, or the actual keys in the hand of St. Peter. In short, here, as everywhere throughout Mr. Ruskin's writings, we are stopped by the false tests and false conclusions consequent on false premises. Impute to Art responsibilities that do not belong to her, whether of teaching religion, morality, or even history, and, of course, it is easy to convict her of not acting up to them.

Yet even in this case Mr. Ruskin is caught in his own arguments; for grant that Francia and Bellini partially, and Raphael wholly, misled the spectator, as for instance, concerning the real history and circumstances of the Madonna's life and condition. Grant that the spectator really "bowed in prayer and adoration to the lovely lady on the golden throne," whom Francia had invested with all the adornments so foreign to her actual condition; or to "the simple Italian mother in the chair," on whom Raphael had bestowed "transparent shadows, skilful tints, scientific foreshortenings," "keeping," "expression," and every other true excellence in the painter's language; still we deny that the same man would not have done the same "to the Jewish girl in her poverty, or, in her simple household, to the carpenter's wife." Let us, for one moment, investigate this in a philosophical point of view.

The imagination is a faculty which is powerful to deceive, and by the exercise of which every one at all possessed of it deceives himself. If exercised upon matters of fact—history—pounds, shillings and pence, &c.—where the judgment is required, it deceives us to our harm; if upon the world of fancy—in poetry or painting—where the emotions are concerned, to our pleasure. Thus it would be just as absurd to look for matter-of-fact truth in a poem or picture, or to mistake such delightful deceits as they convey for matter-of-fact truths, as it would be to credit verbatim a lover's description of his mistress. Not that the lover or the imagination can really present "false images" in the mendacious sense Mr. Ruskin means; the lover does not depict his mistress with black eyes instead of blue, nor the imagination the Madonna as merry and masculine instead of dignified and feminine. The vocation of each is not to alter in kind, but in degree; not to change the reality, but to heighten the ideality, rendering the blue eye bluer still, or the dignified and feminine character more dignified and feminine still. In this exaggeration lies what is called the deluding power of the imaginative faculty, and this deluding power is what makes it so much in request. Hero worship, saint worship, man or woman worship, all alike call upon the imagination to deck up their idols for them, simply because they know that there are no suits of clothing so bright as those she can supply. Therefore, whether in thinking of their object, describing it, or depicting it, love, faith, and admiration never do strip it to its real conditions, because it is not their nature so to do; while indifference and satiety, being influenced by just the contrary feeling, not only strip it at once but rob it beside. But in all this, if the love, the faith, or admiration be well founded—and when applied to sacred or divine persons, we know it must be so—it is the greatest possible mistake to say that any harm can ensue. The imagination after all only heightens the ideal, *because* the real is not there, and it is only in the character of a proxy that it is cherished at all. It is, therefore, utterly fallacious to assert with Mr. Ruskin that he who had bowed himself in prayer or adoration to the representation of the Madonna, when clothed in the best suits that the fondness of imagination or the skill of art could supply, "would never dream of doing the same to the Jewish girl in her outcast poverty, or in her simple household to the carpenter's wife." Of course this argument in one respect applies only to the Roman Catholic, with whom prayer or adoration are supposed duties. But whether Catholic or Protestant—whether viewing the Madonna falsely with faith as a mediator, or simply with reverence as the most blessed among women—let any reader ask himself if his faith or his reverence had been kindled by the painter's imagination in the one case, whether it would not far *more* kindle at the reality in the other. For then the fact that it was *herself* in her ineffable truth before him—no matter what the poverty, the household, or dress—would be stronger, millions of times, than all the strength of the imagination; and what she might have lost in the blind but loving deckings of faith, would be utterly extinguished and swallowed up in the overwhelming brightness of sight.

It is, indeed, in proportion to the adoration with which he would worship or pay homage to the Divine or sacred persons, could they be suddenly present, that a painter or poet will invest them with the most radiant gifts of his imagination while absent; while the Ruskin disciple, whose heart could or would not rise above the cold and rational conception "of the thing as it really must have happened,"—who, remembering that St. Paul's presence, in his own words, was "mean," could depict him so; and that St. Peter was a mere dirty fisherman, who had been out all night, could bring him before us, as Mr. Ruskin recommends, all "slimy," "dripping and shivering,"—he, who knowing the Virgin to have been but a poor Jewish maiden, could represent her under the usual menial conditions of poverty—such a man or painter would as certainly, could his life be turned eighteen centuries back and he transformed into an Israelite of that time, be found among those who said, in their reason and unbelief, "Is not this the carpenter's son?"

And, if there were no other arguments against this doctrine of literal representation and "positive fact," that language of the painter which Mr. Ruskin has condemned as "nothing by itself" here rises up as an invincible impediment. The ideas of a painter and his language being *inseparable*, at all events in aim, he can never at once depict what is mean, dirty, and squalid, and yet suggest that grandeur, power, sweetness, or grace which, as connected with the persons of Holy Writ, is infinitely more important for us to dwell upon than all the trivial facts that hung, like the dust upon their shoes, to the circumstances of their human condition.

The old masters are not without examples of the carrying out of this false principle, though not to that depth of abjectness which Mr. Ruskin advocates. Lord Ward's gallery at once furnishes one in a picture by Teniers, Christ mocked by the Soldiers. The painter here represents the Saviour as an ordinary and homely, but still a meek and suffering person, seated in a room with dirty floor and walls, and surrounded with those coarse figures and physiognomies, who, in his other pictures, stand with their backs to great fires, or sit with card, bottle, and pipe around a table. But that the scene is a Dutch guard-house, and the

figures Dutch boors, does not matter; for with all his condemnation of
painters who do not represent subjects as they really must have
happened, he elsewhere says, "in earnest seriousness, that if a painter
cannot make a Madonna out of a British girl of the 19th century (or a
Jewish soldier out of a Dutch boor of the 17th century), he cannot paint
one at all" (vol. i. p. 122). At all events, considered merely as dirty
floors and walls, and as rude and unsymmetrical figures, it is not only
possible but probable that such are far nearer the truth of "the common
hall" into which the Saviour was taken, and the brutal soldiery by
whom he was mocked, than the marble floors and pillars and
classically-formed athletes of the Italian painters. Nevertheless we turn
disgusted from the representation, and are quite sure that all with sound
mental organizations will do the same, simply because not being the
real scene, there is nothing to satisfy our imagination in the substitute
the picture supplies.

The mistake on Teniers' part lies here. When a painter proposes
to himself a subject, he considers it partly in its fitness to pictorial
purposes and partly in its fitness to the language in which he most
delights. Now there is a fitness between Raphael's purity of expression
and grace of form, and his highly spiritual Holy Family subjects; there
is a fitness between Titian's transparent flesh tones and refined breadth
of colour, and his lovely Madonna and Infant subjects; there is a fitness
between Paul Veronese's gorgeousness of garment and dignity of
bearing, and his pompous historical subjects; and there is a fitness
between Teniers' love of broad common character and broken
picturesqueness of colour, and his carousing boor and old iron and
earthenware subjects. But, by the same rule, there is no fitness between
this language, in which he especially delighted and excelled, and the
sacred subject he has attempted at Lord Ward's; and next to choosing a
subject unfit for painting at all, a painter can commit no greater
mistake than that of choosing one for which he has not the suitable
powers of expression.

Having thus endeavoured to show how impossible morally, and
how intolerable practically, it would be for any true painter to strip a
scene, especially if sacred, to the bare bones of "positive fact," we must
add how doubly absurd it is to accuse such men of seeking their own
praise, instead of that of God, by the delighted exercise of that power of
pictorial utterance, which, whether of form, colour, chiaroscuro, or
expression, is alike to them the gift of God. On the contrary, it may be

taken as a necessary consequence, that where a painter's language has really given no delight to himself, it will as surely give no delight to the spectator. And here we may refer to that mis-called pre-Raphaelite school, we have hitherto forborne to criticise—their merits being, in our judgment, great, and their faults sufficiently censured by Mr. Ruskin's praise—for the principal cause of the unfavourable impression they generally leave, is the circumstance that the language they speak appears to have given no pleasure to themselves, but rather a pain and weariness, producing the irresistible feeling in the spectator that the art is held down rather to the grindstone of unloving slavery, than borne up on the wings of willing power.

It becomes time for us to quit this subject, but before doing so we have a few words to say on a pamphlet by Mr. Ruskin upon the pictures in the last summer's exhibition of the Royal Academy. Here Mr. Ruskin displays in great force his worst qualities, without gilding them with that ingenuity of thought or brilliancy of style which are elsewhere so conspicuous. We have not the slightest intention of defending the merits of those living painters he has there assailed. They can only feel it a compliment to be held worthy to stand in those condemned ranks which are headed by Raphael. He is welcome, therefore, as before, to opinions by which he alone is the loser; he is welcome to arraign Creswick for imperfections which he justifies (vol. i. p. 186) in Turner; he is welcome to asperse Faed's Mitherless Bairn as "throughout the most common-place Wilkieism—white spots everywhere," which was a necessary prelude to the sententious "*I* expected better things from this painter;"[24] he is welcome to all such sentiments, in which he only differs from the educated public for difference sake; but as before, in the case of Poussin, he is not welcome to assert what is not true, and to condemn a great painter upon a false assumption. We pass over, therefore, all his opinions as to the expression and drawing of Mr. Herbert's Lear and Cordelia,[25] shallow and unmannerly as they are, and solicit the reader's particular attention to the following passage:—

It is a thing not a little to be pondered upon, that the men who attempt these highest things are always those who cannot do the least things well. Around the brow of this firwood figure there is a coronet, and in the coronet five jewels; I thought that, according to Royal Academy principles in a "High Art" picture, this Rundell and Bridge portion of it should have been a little less conspicuous. However, as we find these unideal emeralds and rubies thus condescendingly touched, let us see *how* they are touched. Each stone has a white spot, or high light upon it. Now that flash is always the reflection of the highest light to which the jewel is turned, and here in the tent it must be an opening on the left-hand side. Now, as the jewels are set round the brow, each in a different position, each would reflect this tent-door from a different spot on its surface. This change in the position of the reflection would be one of the principal means by which nature would indicate the curve of the coronet. Now, look at the painting— every gem has actually the high light in the same spot on the left-hand side all round the brow!

The dimness of pictorial capacity indicated by such a blunder as this, is very marvellous; for a painter of the slightest power, even though he had not drawn the gems from nature, would infallibly have varied the flash for his own pleasure and in an instinctive fulfillment of the eternal law of change.—p. 19.

Now if the reader will follow us a little carefully we shall have no difficulty in showing him, what one look at the picture itself would show in a moment, *viz.*, that Mr. Herbert had precisely those grounds which Mr. Ruskin represents him as ignorant of, for *not* varying the place of that flash of light even "for his own pleasure." A coronet is a circular thing, which of course when seen upon a head level with the spectator's eye, presents to his view only half its circle at once, the centre of which half-circle is nearest the eye, and the sides receding. In this view five points of the coronet are seen, each point tipped with a jewel. The jewel on the centre point presents its front face to you, the jewel on each point right and left of the centre presents its opposite three-quarter face, and the jewels on the two outermost points of the half-circle (thus making five jewels) present their opposite profiles. What is the consequence? The light which comes in from an aperture on the left, strikes, as Mr. Ruskin says, "upon the same spot on the left-hand side all round the brow;" but in his haste to deride he forgets to add, yet upon a different part of each jewel! For that same spot upon the *apparent* left-hand side of each jewel falls *in reality* upon the centre of the profile jewel nearest the light—rather to the left of the centre of the next three-quarter jewel—midway between the centre and edge of the centre jewel, still nearer the edge of the next three-quarter jewel, and completely on the edge of the profile jewel furthest from the light. Thus while the light has necessarily stood still, it is the jewels which have turned, and while the light has apparently struck on the same left-hand edge of each jewel, it has in reality been reflected from a different spot on the surface of all five. To deride a painter, therefore, for "not varying the flash for his own pleasure," under these circumstances, is simply to deride him for not making the light enter at five different parts of the tent instead of one, and such a derision is the best compliment that can be paid to one who is not only great in the great things of art but right in the least things also.

Nothing can be more degradingly low, both as regards art and manners, than the whole tone of this pamphlet, calculated only to mislead those who are as conceited as they are ignorant, which unfortunately includes a large number. Even granting that Herbert had erred in the highlight of a jewel, or Maclise (for with equal injustice Mr. Ruskin accuses the one of the breach of that principle of perspective the observance of which he abuses in the other), in the drawing of a border pattern, even granting this, what does it prove?[26] A picture is not a culprit to be cross-examined and detected by a trap here and a slip there. Mr. Ruskin's ideas of truth and falsehood as applied to art (all traceable to his false start as to the nature and purposes of art) are utterly futile and nonsensical. Falsehood only becomes such when there is the power in the deceiver to pervert the truth, or in the deceived to believe the lie. Now a man may paint grass red, but in the first place he could not conceal that he had not made it green—in the next place nobody would believe it to be green—and finally and chiefly he would be no painter to do such a thing at all. Of such blunders as a real painter, from oversight or inadvertence, may make, a picture may be full and yet not be a whit the worse for it, or from everything of the kind it may be scrupulously free and yet be an untrue and wretched daub. Raphael's frescoes in the Vatican would furnish a rich harvest of little inaccuracies to such wretched spies and informers, while no painter was more fallible in such matters than Turner, who once even painted the sun on the north side.

It is not therefore the man who makes a blunder *in* a picture, but he who makes a false statement *about* a picture, who is the real offender. The one commits a mechanical fault which does not even harm himself, far less his neighbour—the other, as far as in him lies, inflicts a wanton and undeserved injury. Mr. Ruskin, however, might have spared himself the boast, that when once he had marked an artist's reputation for his prey it was of no use trying to save it.[27] Setting aside the malice which is so obviously the leading principle in this pamphlet, the mere fact that he was driven to such paltry modes of criticism, is the highest encomium that living artists could receive. As Hazlitt has wisely said, "To take a pride and pleasure in nothing but defects (and those, perhaps, of the most paltry, obvious, and mechanical kind)—in the disappointment and tarnishing of our faith in excellence— in proofs of weakness, not of power—is not a sign of uncommon refinement but of unaccountable perversion of taste."

One great proof, were there no other, of the falseness of Mr. Ruskin's reasoning, is its quantity. Only on the wrong road could so much have been said at all. As we observed before, if art be long, it is in practice not in theory. Separate what is really to be thought and said about art from false assumption, futile speculation, contradictory argument, crotchety views, and romantic rubbish, and ninety-nine hundredths of what Mr. Ruskin writes, and one-half of what most write, will fall to the ground. But, it may be asked, are not the precepts of common sense applicable to art as well as to everything else? To this we readily agree; but the truth is, that all the common sense as to diligence, sincerity of purpose, recognition of their own powers, and observation of nature, which is so much obscured under Mr. Ruskin's jargon of "love," "wisdom," "fear and gladness," "firm words, true message, unstinted fulness and unfailing faith," have been said to and by painters over and over again, and, if not realized, at all events steadily aimed at by all deserving the name.

As regards quantity, however, it is easy to foresee that Mr. Ruskin will always have the advantage. Nature has given him the mechanism of thinking in a most peculiar degree. The exercise of this faculty, which is always more or less an exertion and strain to other minds, is none to his; and no wonder, for sophistry travels on roads where, however much dust, there are neither stones nor tolls. Though, therefore, the broad false principles he has laid down may be easily refuted, yet it may be doubted whether any mind will have the patience to follow all the windings of one who thinks equally without consistency and without weariness. A man may attack from bars, oak doors, or stone walls, and hope with energy and perseverance to break his way through, but to follow a thin thread, which leads him through winding and slippery paths, and is always snapping at an honest touch, requires a strength of nerve and tenacity of purpose which Mr. Ruskin's writings will hardly inspire or their refutation reward.

Not that we are in the least inclined to magnify the importance of unsound ideas and absurd conclusions upon the subject of art. Art, not being a direct moral agent at all, can only do real harm in proportion as it can do real good—its debasement can only be the index of a frivolous or ignorant state of society—never in any way its cause. As regards Mr. Ruskin in particular, he will mislead no mind and injure no career which would not have been misled or injured equally without him. For those who have no eyes, it matters little how entirely the pseudo moral at the end of his chapter is purchased by the flimsy fallacy at the beginning, while those who possess these organs to any purpose will soon forget both the one and the other. It would have been well, therefore, for Mr. Ruskin had he erred in nothing but what may thus be harmlessly swallowed or easily rejected; but it is the terrible penalty of the propagators of slander that their evil deeds should remain—for no evil, as no good, can fall into our moral world without fruits of which none can compute the length or the strength; in either case, in proportion to the good or evil, is the return or the recoil upon the author, and upon Mr. Ruskin the recoil has begun already.

Notes

1.   David Teniers, "the Younger," (1610–90). A painter of the peasant genre who was directly influenced by Adriaen Brouwer.

2.   A picture at Belvoir Castle. [Eastlake's note]

3.   Thomas Moore. *Irish Melodies* (1866).

4.   We have mentioned the Sistine Madonna as an example which none (except Mr. Ruskin) can question, but the larger Francia, in our National Gallery will prove the same, or the great St. Justina, by Pordenone, in the Vienna Gallery, or the picture called Palma Veechio's Three Daughters in the Dresden Gallery, or half the Titian Holy Families one best remembers, or most of that class of composition called a *Santa Conversazione* by any master—all with subjects too utterly simple to be considered the offspring or representation of thought, and, if with any incident at all, of the most trivial or incongruous nature. [Eastlake's note]

5.   We had abstained from reading Mr. Leslie's admirable "Handbook for young Painters" until after the completion of this article. We now rejoice to find our meaning thus further illustrated by the following passage:—"In the 'Cephalus and Aurora' of Nicolo Poussin, in our National Gallery, the substitution of Apollo for the rising sun, as he has managed it, is in the highest degree poetic. But the thought alone is a mere imitation of the poet's, which might have occurred to the most prosaic mind. It is

entirely, therefore, to the technical treatment—to the colour and to the manner in which the forms of the chariot and horses of the god melt into the shapes of clouds—in fact, to the chiaroscuro—that the incident as connected with the picture owes its poetry." Mr. Leslie adds one more to the number of accomplished men, who, like Sir Joshua Reynolds, write as admirably as they paint. Though the title of his "Handbook" might lead to the inference that it was only adapted for artists, it will be read with delight and instruction by every person who has any enjoyment in pictures. [Eastlake's note]

6.   As this article is going through the press, we find that in this passage we have almost verbatim expressed the sentiments of Mr. Leslie, p. 173. The coincidence being entirely accidental, we do not attempt to alter the phraseology, but are proud to be found agreeing, in form as well as in substance, with such an authority. [Eastlake's note]

7.   Bernardino Luini (1475–1531/2). A minor painter who was a contemporary of Leonardo da Vinci. Gerbrand van den Eeckhout, or Eckhout (1621–74), was Rembrandt's pupil. [cited by Frank Young]

8.   This excerpt appears in Ruskin's *Modern Painters*. Volume I, Chapter ii: "Definition of Greatness in Art."

9.   Fra Giovanni da Fiesole, also known as Fra Angelico (1387?-1455). A Dominican Friar noted for his *Madonna* (1433) and his frescoes.

10.   William Hogarth (1697–1794). An English artist who satirized all social classes.

11.   George Cruikshank (1792–1878). A British caricaturist best known for his illustrations of Charles Dickens's works. Retsch, or Retzsch, most likely refers to Friedrich Moritz August Retzsch (1779–1857), a Dresden artist who illustrated editions of the works of Shakespeare, Gessner, Fouque, and Goethe. [cited by Frank Young]

12.   Lackey in residence.

13.   Benvenuto Cellini (1500–71). Florentine sculptor and goldsmith who is considered by many art historians to be a more exquisite craftsman than artist.

14.   Claude Gellée, called Claude Lorrain (1600–82), was considered a French painter, although he spent his entire working career in Italy. He is known for his landscape paintings, in particular, *Seaport Scene* (1639).

15.   Ruskin discusses all of these painters in *Modern Painters*. Vol. I. Nicholas Poussin (1594–1665) revolted against the extreme Baroque style of painting. Giovanni Antonio Canal, called Canaletto (1697–1768) was an Italian landscape painter. Richard Wilson (1713–82) was a British landscape painter. Aelbert Cuyp (1620–91), Meindert Hobbema (1638–1709), and Salomon van Ruysdael (1600–70) were all Dutch landscape painters.

16.   Peter Paul Rubens, German-Flemish painter (1577–1640), who made Flanders a main center of art in the 17th century. Paul, or Paolo

Veronese (1528–88), along with Titian and Tintoretto, form the famous triad of Venetian Cinquecento painters.

17. Could refer to either Isaac (1621–49) or Adriaen Ostade (1610–85). Both were Dutch painters who specialized in the peasant genre.

18. Literally, "white nights."

19. Jacopo (or Giacomo) Negreti, known as Palma Vecchio (1480?-1523), was most likely a pupil of Giovanni Bellini. Many of Palma's paintings were finished by other artists.

20. Antonio Allegri, called Correggio (1489/94–1534), had a major influence on North Italian artists of his and later generations.

21. As one of the executors appointed in Turner's will, Mr. Ruskin can plead no ignorance as to the fact that the "length of funeral disposed throug[h] Ludgate," which he stigmatises as the act of Turner's critics (Preface to vol. iii. p. 2), was only the carrying out of the testator's own express and to be regretted commands. Mr. Ruskin employed a legal gentleman to examine the will; the consequence being that he threw up that trust which the friend for whom he affects such zeal had bequeathed to him, and moreover, as we are assured, endeavoured to have the expenses of his lawyer's investigation defrayed from Turner's estate. [Eastlake's note]

22. Francesco Francia (1450?-1517) was an Italian painter of the Ferraresa tradition, as well as a goldsmith. Pietro Vannucci, called Il Perugino (1445/50–1523), was invited to paint several frescoes for the Sistine Chapel in Rome in 1480.

23. Hunt's picture, *The Light of the World.* [Eastlake's note]

24. John Faed (1820–1902) was a Scottish painter best known for his works depicting Scottish history, poetry, and romance.

25. John Rogers Herbert (1810–90) was an English painter who received a commission to paint the frescoes in the new Houses of Parliament. Among the most notable is *King Lear.*

26. Daniel Maclise (1811–70). A Scottish-Irish painter primarily remembered for his portraits.

27. In the second edition of "*Notes on some of the principal Pictures exhibited in the rooms of the Royal Academy,*" occurs this passage:— "Hereafter it will be known, that when I have thought fit to attack a picture, the worst policy that the friends of the artist can adopt is to *defend* it." [Eastlake's note]

8. Photography

Introduction

Elizabeth Eastlake's "Photography," published in the April, 1857, *Quarterly Review,* and reprinted here from that periodical, shows an early usage of such now-standard photographic terms as "negative," "positive," and "develop." However, a more notable feature of "On Photography" is its style. Eastlake combines the scientific terms of the medium's technological development with a colorful elucidation of its effects in such a way that reflects the quasi-scientific/quasi-artistic nature she discovered in photography itself. Although Eastlake failed to predict the exact historical course of development that photography would take, she did succeed in imagining the poetic potential of a medium which pairs the individual eye with the natural force of sunlight.

Interestingly enough, Eastlake was as much an early subject for photography as photography was for her. She wrote in a letter that a Talbotype of her done by D.O. Hill and Robert Adamson, entitled "Elizabeth Rigby" (1844–45), was the first specimen of the photographic art that the Prince Consort saw. Furthermore, one of the most arresting images of the handsome, six-foot-tall Eastlake exists in a photograph of her with her mother, taken by D.O. Hill in 1844.

Photography

It is now more than fifteen years ago that specimens of a new and mysterious art were first exhibited to our wondering gaze. They consisted of a few heads of elderly gentlemen executed in a bistre-like colour upon paper. The heads were not above an inch long, they were little more than patches of broad light and shade, they showed no attempt to idealise or soften the harshnesses and accidents of a rather rugged style of physiognomy—on the contrary, the eyes were decidedly contracted, the mouths expanded, and the lines and wrinkles intensified. Nevertheless we examined them with the keenest admiration, and felt that the spirit of Rembrandt had revived. Before that time little was the existence of a power, availing itself of the eye of the sun both to discern and to execute, suspected by the world—still less that it had long lain the unclaimed and unnamed legacy of our own Sir Humphry Davy.[1] Since than photography has become a household word and a household want; is used alike by art and science, by love, business, and justice; is found in the most sumptuous saloon, and in the dingiest attic—in the solitude of the Highland cottage, and in the glare of the London gin-palace—in the pocket of the detective, in the cell of the convict, in the folio of the painter and architect, among the papers and patterns of the millowner and manufacturer, and on the cold brave breast on the battle-field.

The annals of photography, as gathered from the London Directory, though so recent, are curious. As early as 1842 one individual, of the name of Beard, assumed the calling of a daguerreotype artist. In 1843 he set up establishments in four different quarters of London, reaching even to Wharf Road, City Road, and thus alone supplied the metropolis until 1847. In 1848 Claudet and a few more appear on the scene, but, owing to then existing impediments, their numbers even in 1852 did not amount to more than seven. In 1855 the expiration of the patent and the influence of the Photographic Society swelled them to sixty-six—in 1857 photographers have a heading to themselves and stand at 147.

These are the higher representatives of the art. But who can number the legion of petty dabblers, who display their trays of specimens along every great thoroughfare in London, executing for our lowest servants, for one shilling, that which no money could have commanded for the Rothschild bride of twenty years ago? Not that photographers flock especially to the metropolis; they are wanted everywhere and found everywhere. The large provincial cities abound with the sun's votaries, the smallest town is not without them; and if there be a village so poor and remote as not to maintain a regular establishment, a visit from a photographic travelling van gives it the advantages which the rest of the world are enjoying. Thus, where not half a generation ago the existence of such a vocation was not dreamt of, tens of thousands (especially if we reckon the purveyors of photographic materials) are now following a new business, practising a new pleasure, speaking a new language, and bound together by a new sympathy.

For it is one of the pleasant characteristics of this pursuit that it unites men of the most diverse lives, habits, and stations, so that whoever enters its ranks finds himself in a kind of republic, where it needs apparently but to be a photographer to be a brother. The world was believed to have grown sober and matter-of-fact, but the light of photography has revealed an unsuspected source of enthusiasm. An instinct of our nature, scarcely so worthily employed before, seems to have been kindled, which finds something of the gambler's excitement in the frequent disappointments and possible prizes of the photographer's luck. When before did any motive short of the stimulus of chance or the greed of gain unite in one uncertain and laborious quest the nobleman, the tradesman, the prince of blood royal, the innkeeper, the artist, the manservant, the general officer, the private soldier, the hard-worked member of every learned profession, the gentleman of leisure, the Cambridge wrangler, the man who bears some of the weightiest responsibilities of this country on his shoulder, and, though last, not least, the fair woman whom nothing but her own choice obliges to be more than the fine lady? The records of the Photographic Society, established in 1853, are curiously illustrative of these incongruities. Its first chairman, in order to give the newly instituted body the support and recognition which art was supposed to owe it, was chosen expressly from the realms of art. Sir Charles Eastlake therefore occupied the chair for two years; at the end of which the society selected a successor quite as interested and efficient from a sphere of life only so far connected with art or science as being their very antipodes, namely, Sir Frederick Pollock, the Chief Baron of England. The next chairman may be a General fresh from the happy land where they photograph the year round; the fourth, for aught that can be urged to the contrary, the Archbishop of Canterbury. A clergyman of the Established Church has already been the editor to the journal of the society. The very talk of these photographic members is unlike that of any other men, either of business or pleasure. Their style is made up of the driest facts, the longest words, and the most high-flown rhapsodies. Slight improvements in processes, and slight varieties in conclusions, are discussed as if they involved the welfare of mankind. They seek each other's sympathy, and they resent each other's interference, with an ardour of expression at variance with all the sobrieties of business, and the habits of reserve; and old-fashioned English *mauvaise honte*[2] is extinguished in the excitement, not so much of a new occupation as of a new state. In one respect, however, we can hardly accuse them of the language of exaggeration. The photographic body can no longer be considered only a society, it is becoming "one of the institutions of the country." Branches from the parent tree are flourishing all over the United Kingdom. Liverpool assists Norwich, Norwich congratulates Dublin, Dublin fraternises with the Birmingham and Midland Institute, London sympathises with each, and all are looking with impatience to Manchester. Each of these societies elect their officers, open their exhibitions, and display the same encouraging medley of followers. The necessity too for regular instruction in the art is being extensively recognised. The Council of King's College have instituted a lectureship of photography. Photographic establishments are attached to the Royal Arsenal at Woolwich; a photographic class is opened for the officers of the Royal Artillery and Engineers; lectures are given at the Royal Institution, and popular discourses at Mechanics' Institutes. Meanwhile British India has kept pace with the mother country. The Photographic Society at Bombay is only second in period of formation to that of London. Calcutta, Madras, Bengal, and minor places all correspond by means of societies. The Elphinstone Institution has opened a class for instruction. Nor is the feeling of fellowship confined to our own race. The photographic and the political alliance with France and this country was concluded at about the same period, and we can wish nothing more than that they may be maintained with equal cordiality. The Duke de Luynes, a French nobleman of high scientific repute, has placed the sum of 10,000 francs at the disposal of the Paris Photographic Society, to be divided into two prizes for objects connected with the advance of the art,—the prizes open to the whole world. The best landscape photographs at the *Exposition des Beaux Arts* were English, the best architectural specimens in the London Exhibitions are French. The Exhibition at Brussels last October was more cosmopolitan than Belgian. The Emperors of Russia and Austria, adopting the old way for paying new debts, are bestowing snuff-boxes on photographic merit. These are but a few of the proofs that could be brought forward of the wide dissemination of the new agent, and of the various modes of its reception, concluding with a juxtaposition of facts which almost ludicrously recall paragraphs from the last speech from the throne; for while our Queen has sent out a complete photographic apparatus for the use of the King of Siam, the King of Naples alone, of the whole civilised world, has forbidden the practice of the works of light in his dominions!

Our chief object at present is to investigate the connexion of photography with art—to decide how far the sun may be considered an artist, and to what branch of imitation his powers are best adapted. But we must first give a brief history of those discoveries which have led to the present efficiency of the solar pencil. It appears that the three leading nations—the French, the English, and the Germans—all share in the merit of having first suggested, then applied, and finally developed the existence of the photographic element. It may not be superfluous to all our readers to state that the whole art in all its varieties rests upon the fact of the blackening effects of light upon certain substances, and chiefly upon silver, on which it acts with a decomposing power. The silver being dissolved in a strong acid, surfaces steeped in the solution became encrusted with minute particles of the metal, which in this state darkened with increased rapidity. These facts were first ascertained and recorded, as regards chloride of silver, or silver combined with chlorine, in 1777, by Scheele, a native of Pomerania, and in 1801, in connexion with nitrate of silver, by Ritter of Jena. Here therefore were the raw materials for the unknown art; the next step was to employ them. And now we are at once met by that illustrious name to which we have alluded. Sir Humphry Davy was the first to make the practical application of these materials, and to foresee their uses. In conjunction with Mr. Thomas Wedgwood, only less eminent than his brother Josiah, Sir Humphry succeeded, by means of a camera abscura, in obtaining images upon paper, or white leather prepared with nitrate of silver—of which proceeding he has left the most interesting record in the Journal of the Royal Society for June,

1802.[3] Their aim, as the title shows, was not ambitious; but the importance lay in the first stain designedly traced upon the prepared substance, not in the thing it portrayed. In one sense, however, it was very aspiring, if colour as well as form were sought to be transferred, as would appear from the attempt to copy coloured glass; otherwise it is difficult to account for their selecting this particular material.

Besides showing the possibility of imprinting the forms of objects thus reflected in the camera, the paper in question proceeds to describe the process since known as "Photographic Drawing," by which leaves, or lace, or the wings of insects, or any flat and semi-transparent substances, laid upon prepared paper, and exposed to the direct action of the sun, will leave the perfect tracery of their forms. But having thus conjured up the etherial spirit of photography, they failed in all attempts to retain it in their keeping. The charm once set agoing refused to stop—the slightest exposure to light, even for the necessary purposes of inspection, continued the action, and the image was lost to view in the darkening of the whole paper. In short, they wanted the next secret, that of rendering permanent, or, in photographic language, of *fixing* the image. Here, therefore, the experiment was left to be taken up by others, though not without a memento of the prophetic light cast on the mind's eye of the great elucidator; for Sir Humphry observes, "Nothing but a method of preventing the unshaded parts of the delineation from being coloured by the exposure to the day is wanted to render this process as useful as it is elegant."

Meanwhile, in 1803, some remarkable experiments were made by Dr. Wollaston, proving the action of light upon a resinous substance known in commerce as "gum guaiacum;" and in due time another workman entered the field who availed himself of this class of materials. The name of Joseph Nicéphore de Niepce is little known to the world as one of the founders of the now popular art, his contributions being exactly of that laborious and rudimental nature which later inventions serve to conceal.[4] He was a French gentleman of private fortune, who lived at Châlons-sur-Saone, and pursued chemistry for his pleasure. Except also in the sense of time, he cannot be called a successor to Davy and Wedgwood; for it is probable that the path they had traced was unknown to him. Like them, however, he made use of the camera to cast his images; but the substance on which he received them was a polished plate of pewter, coated with a thin bituminous surface. His process is now rather one of the curiosities of photographic history; but, such as it was, it gained the one important step of rendering his creations permanent. The labours of the sun in his hands remained spell-bound, and remain so still. He began his researches in 1814, and was ten years before he attained this end. To M. Niepce also belongs the credit of having at once educed the high philosophic principle, since then universally adopted in photographic practice, which put faith before sight—the conviction of what must be before the appearance of what is. His pictures, on issuing from the camera, were invisible to the eye, and only disengaged by the application of a solvent which removed those shaded parts unhardened by the action of the light. Nor do they present the usual reversal of the position of light and shade, know in photographic language as a *negative* appearance; but whether taken from nature or from an engraving, are identical in effect, or what is called *positives*. But though, considering all these advantages, the art of Heliography, as it was called by its author, was at that early period as great a wonder as any that have followed it, yet it was deficient in those qualities which recommend a discovery to an impatient world. The process was difficult, capricious, and tedious. It does not appear that M. Niepce ever obtained an image from nature in less than between seven to twelve hours, so that the change in lights and shadows necessarily rendered it imperfect; and in a specimen we have seen, the sun is shining on opposite walls. Deterred probably by this difficulty from any aspirations after natural scenes, M. Niepce devoted his discovery chiefly to the copying of engravings. To this he sought to give a practical use by converting his plate, by means of the application of an acid, into a surface capable of being printed by the ordinary methods. Here again he was successful, as specimens of printed impressions still show, though under circumstances too uncertain and laborious to encourage their adoption. Thus the comparative obscurity in which his merits have remained is not difficult to comprehend; for while he conquered many of the greater difficulties of the art, he left too many lesser ones for the world to follow in his steps. To these reasons may be partially attributed the little sensation which the efforts of this truly modest and ingenious gentleman created in this country, which he visited in 1827, for the purpose, he states, of exhibiting his results to the Royal Society, and of rendering homage of his discovery to his Britannic Majesty. A short memorial, drawn up by himself, was therefore forwarded, with specimens, to the hands of George IV.; but a rule on the part of the Royal Society to give no attention to a discovery which involves a secret proved a barrier to the introduction of M. Niepce's results to that body. Dr. Wollaston was the only person of scientific eminence to whom they appear to have been exhibited; and, considering their intrinsic interest, as well as the fact of his being in some sort their progenitor, it is difficult to account for the little attention he appears to have paid them. M. Niepce therefore returned to his own country, profoundly convinced of the English inaptitude for photographic knowledge.

In the mean time the indiscretion of an optician revealed to the philosopher of Châlons the fact that M. Daguerre, a dioramic artist by profession, was pursuing researches analogous to his own in Paris.[5] This led to an acquaintance between the two, and finally to a legal partnership in the present pains and possible profits of the new art. M. Niepce died in 1833 without, it seems, contributing any further improvement to the now common stock; and M. Daguerre, continuing his labours, introduced certain alterations which finally led to a complete change in the process. Suffice it to say that, discarding the use of the bituminous varnish, and substituting a highly polished tablet of silver, he now first availed himself of that great agent in photographic science, the action of iodine, by means of which the sensitiveness of his plate was so increased as to render the production of the image an affair of fewer minutes than it had previously been of hours. At the same time the picture, still invisible, was brought to light by the application of the fumes of mercury, after which a strong solution of common salt removed those portions of the surface which would otherwise have continued to darken, and thus rendered the impression permanent.

Here, therefore, was a representation obtained in a few minutes by a definite and certain process, which was exquisitely minute and clear in detail, capable of copying nature in all her stationary forms, and also true to the natural conditions of light and shade. For the fumes of mercury formed minute molecules of a white colour upon those parts of the iodised tablet darkened by the light, thus producing the lights to which the silver ground supplied the shades.

In 1839 the results of M. Daguerre's years of labour, called after himself the Daguerreotype, came forth fully furnished for use; and in the June of that year gave rise to a remarkable scene in the French Chambers. The question before the deputies was this: MM. Daguerre and Niepce jun. (for the partnership gave all the advantages of M.

Daguerre's discovery to the son of his late colleague) were possessed of a secret of the utmost utility, interest, and novelty to the civilised world—a secret for which immense sacrifices of time, labour, and money had been made, but which, if restricted by patent for their protection, would be comparatively lost to society. A commission had therefore been appointed by the French Government to inquire into its merits, and the secret itself intrusted to M. Arago, who succeeded at once in executing a beautiful specimen of the art.[6] Thus practically convinced, he addressed the Chamber in a speech which is a masterpiece of scientific summary and philosophic conclusion. He pointed out the immense advantages which might have been derived, "for example, during the expedition to Egypt, by a means of reproduction so exact and so rapid." He observed that "to copy the millions and millions of hieroglyphics which entirely cover the great monuments at Thebes, Memphis, and Carnac, &c., would require scores of years and legions of artists; whereas with the daguerreotype a single man would suffice to bring this vast labour to a happy conclusion." He quoted the celebrated painter De la Roche in testimony of "the advantage to art by designs perfect as possible, and yet broad and energetic—where a finish of inconceivable minuteness in no respect disturbs the repose of the masses, nor impairs in any manner the general effect." The scene was French in the highest sense—at once scientific, patriotic, and withal dramatic,—France herself treating for the creations of genius on the one hand, and on the other dispensing them, "a gift to the whole world." It was repeated in the Chamber of Peers, who, in addition to the other arguments addressed to them by M. Gay-Lussac, were reminded, with a true French touch, that "even a field of battle in all its phases may be thus delineated with a precision unattainable by any other means!" The result was that a pension of 10,000 francs was awarded for the discovery—6000 to M. Daguerre, 4000 to M. Niepce. The seals which retained the secret were broken, and the daguerreotype became the property of the world.

We unwillingly recall a fact which rather mars the moral beauty of this interesting proceeding, viz., that by some chicanery a patent for the daguerreotype was actually taken out in England, which for a time rendered this the only country which did not profit by the liberality of the French Government. The early history of photography is not so generous in character as that of its maturity.

It may be added that all that has been since done for the daguerreotype are improvements in the same direction. It has that mark of a great invention—not to require or admit of any essential deviation from its process. Those who have contributed to perfect it are also of the same race as the inventor. The names of M. Fizeau and M. Claudet are associated with its present state.[7] The first, by using a solution of chloride of gold, has preserved the daguerreotype from abrasion, and given it a higher tone and finish; while M. Claudet, who has variously contributed to the advance of the art, by the application of chloride of bromine with iodine, has accelerated a hundred-fold the action of the plate; at the same time, by a prolongation of a part of the process, he has, without the aid of mercury, at once converted the image into a positive, the silver ground now giving the lights instead, as before, of the shades of the picture.

We may now turn to England, and to those discoveries which, though less brilliant in immediate result, yet may be said to have led to those practical uses which now characterise the new agent. The undivided honour of having first successfully worked out the secret of photography in England belongs to Mr. Fox Talbot.[8] He also is a private gentleman, living in the country, and pursuing chemical researches for his own pleasure. In his case it may be strictly said that he took up the ground to which Davy and Wedgwood had made their way. Paper was the medium he adhered to from the beginning, and on which he finally gained the victory. We have no account of the repeated essays and disappointments by which this gentleman advanced step by step to the end in view. All we know is that the French success on metal and the English success on paper were, strange to say, perfectly coincident in date. Daguerre's discovery was made know in Paris in January, 1839; and in the same month Mr. Fox Talbot sent a paper to the Royal Society, giving an account of a method by which he obtained pictures on paper, rendered them unalterable by light, and by a second and simple process, which admitted of repetition to any extent, restored the lights and shadows to their right conditions.

This announcement fell, like the pictures of light themselves, upon ground highly excited in every way to receive and carry it forward. It was immediately taken up by Sir John Herschel, who commenced a series of experiments of the utmost practical importance to photography and science in general, one of the first results of which was the discovery of the hyposulphate of soda as the best agent for dissolving the superfluous salts, or, in other words, of fixing the picture. This was one of those steps which has met with general adoption. Another immediate impulse was given by a lecture read at the London Institution in April, 1839, and communicated by the Rev. J. B. Reade, recommending the use of gallic acid in addition to iodide or chloride of silver as a means of greatly increasing the sensitiveness of the preparation. Again, Mr. Robert Hunt, since known as the author of the work that heads this article, published at the British Association at Plymouth, in 1841, another sensitive process, in which the ferrocyanate of potash was employed; and in 1844 the important use of the protosulphate of iron in bringing out, or, as it is termed, *developing* the latent picture.[9] Other fellow-labourers might be mentioned, too, all zealous to offer some suggestion of practical use to the new-born art. Meanwhile Mr. Fox Talbot, continuing to improve on his original discovery, thought fit in 1842 to make it the subject for a patent, under the name of the calotype process. In this he is accused of having incorporated the improvements of others as well as his own, a question on which we have nothing to say, except that at this stage of the invention the tracks of the numerous exploring parties run too close to each other to be clearly identified. As to the propriety of the patent itself, no one can doubt Mr. Fox Talbot's right to avail himself of it, though the results show that the policy may be questioned. For this gentleman reaped a most inadequate return, and the development of the art was materially retarded. In the execution of a process so delicate and at best so capricious as that of photography, the experience of number, such as only free-trade can secure, is required to define the more or less practical methods. Mr. F. Talbot's directions, though sufficient for his own pre-instructed hand, were too vague for the tyro; and an enlistment into the ranks of the "Pilgrims of the Sun" seldom led to any result but that of disappointment. Thus, with impediments of this serious nature, photography made but slow way in England; and the first knowledge to many even of her existence came back to us from across the Border. It was in Edinburgh where the first earnest, professional practice of the art began, and the calotypes of Messrs. Hill and Adamson remain to this day the most picturesque specimens of the new discovery.[10]

It was at this crisis that a paper published in the "Philosophical Transactions" of May, 1844, by Mr. George Cundell, gave in great measure the fresh stimulus that was needed. The world was full of the praise of the daguerreotype, but Mr. Cundell stood forth as the advocate of the calotype or paper process, pointed out its greater simplicity and inexpensiveness of apparatus, its infinite superiority in the power of multiplying its productions, and then proceeded to give those careful directions for the practice, which, though containing no absolutely new element, yet suggested many a minute correction where every minutia is important. With the increasing band of experimentalists who arose— for all photographers are such—now ensued the demand for some material on which to receive their pictures less expensive than the silver plate, and less capricious than paper. However convenient as a medium, this latter, from the miscellaneous nature of its antecedents, was the prolific parent of disappointment. Numerous expedients were resorted to to render it more available,—it was rubbed, polished, and waxed, but, nevertheless, blotches and discolorations would perpetually appear, and that at the very moment of success, which sorely tried the photographic heart. The Journal of the Society sends up at this time one vast cry of distress on this subject, one member calling unto another for help against the common enemy. Under these circumstances many a longing eye was fixed upon glass as a substitute; and numerous experiments, among which those by Sir John Herschel were the earliest and most successful, were tried to render this material available. But glass itself was found to be an intractable material; it has no powers of absorption, and scarcely any affinities. The one thing evidently needed was to attach some transparent neutral coating of extreme tenuity to its surface, and in due time the name of Niepce again appears supplying the intermediate step between failure and success. M. Niepce de St. Victor, nephew to the inventor of heliography, is known as the author of the albumen process, which transparent and adhesive substance being applied to glass, and excited with the same chemical agents as in the calotype process, is found to produce pictures of great beauty and finish. But, ingenious as is the process, and often as it is still used, it fails of that unsurpassable fitness which alone commands universal adoption. The amalgamation of the substances is tedious and complicated, and the action of the light much slower. The albumen process was a great step, and moreover a step in the right direction; for it pointed onward to that discovery which has reduced the difficulties of the art to the lowest sum, and raised its powers, in one respect at all events, to the highest possibility, viz. to the use of collodion. The Daguerre to this Niepce was a countryman of our own—Mr. Scott Archer—who is entitled to fame not only for this marvellous improvement, but for the generosity with which he threw it open to the public. The character of the agent, too, adds interest to the invention. The birth and parentage of collodion are both among the recent wonders of the age. Gun-cotton—partly a French, partly a German discovery—is but a child in the annals of chemical science; and collodion, which is a solution of this compound in ether and alcohol, is its offspring.[11] Its first great use was, as is well known, in the service of surgery; its second in that of photography. Not only did the adoption of this vehicle at once realise the desires of the most ardent photographer—not only, thus applied, did it provide a film of perfect transparency, tenuity, and intense adhesiveness—not only was it found easy of manipulation, portable and preservable—but it supplied that element of rapidity which more than anything else has given the miraculous character to the art. Under the magician who first attempted to enlist the powers of light in his service, the sun seems at best to have been but a sluggard; under the sorcery of Niepce he became a drudge in a twelve-hours' factory. On the prepared plate of Daguerre and on the sensitive paper of Fox Talbot the great luminary concentrates his gaze for a few earnest minutes; with the albumen-sheathed glass he takes his time more leisurely still; but at the delicate film of collodion—which hangs before him finer than any fairy's robe, and potent only with invisible spells—he literally does no more than wink his eye, tracing in that moment, with a detail and precision beyond all human power, the glory of the heavens, the wonders of the deep, the fall, not of the avalanche, but of the apple, the most fleeting smile of the babe, and the most vehement action of the man.

Further than this the powers of photography can never go; they are already more nimble than we need. Light is made to portray with a celerity only second to that with which it travels; it has been difficult to contrive the machinery of the camera to keep pace with it, and collodion has to be weakened in order to clog its wheels.

While these practical results occupied the world, more fundamental researches had been carried on. By the indefatigable exertions of Sir John Herschel and Mr. Hunt the whole scale of mineral and other simple substances were tested in conjunction with tried and untried chemical processes, showing how largely nature abounds with materials for photographic action. Preparations of gold, platinum, mercury, iron, copper, tin, nickel, manganese, lead, potash, &c., were found more or less sensitive, and capable of producing pictures of beauty and distinctive character. The juices of beautiful flowers were also put into requisition, and paper prepared with the colours of the Corchorus japonica, the common ten-weeks' stock, the marigold, the wallflower, the poppy, the rose, the Senecio splendens, &c., has been made to receive delicate though in most cases fugitive images. By these experiments, though tending little to purposes of utility, the wide relations and sympathies of the new art have been in some measure ascertained, and its dignity in the harmonious scale of natural phenomena proportionably raised.

When once the availability of one great primitive agent is thoroughly worked out, it is easy to foresee how extensively it will assist in unravelling other secrets in natural science. The simple principle of the stereoscope, for instance, might have been discovered a century ago, for the reasoning which led to it was independent of all the properties of light, but it could never have been illustrated, far less multiplied as it now is, without photography.[12] A few diagrams, of sufficient identity and difference to prove the truth of the principle, might have been constructed by hand for the gratification of a few sages, but no artist, it is to be hoped, could have been found possessing the requisite ability and stupidity to execute the two portraits, or two groups, or two interiors, or two landscapes, identical in every minutia of the most elaborate detail, and yet differing in point of view by the inch between the two human eyes, by which the principle is brought to the level of any capacity. Here, therefore, the accuracy and the insensibility of a machine could alone avail; and if in the order of things the cheap popular toy which the stereoscope now represents was necessary for the use of man, the photograph was first necessary for the service of the stereoscope.

And while photography is thus found ready to give its aid to other agencies, other agencies are in turn ready to co-operate with that. The invention now becoming familiar to the public by the name of photo-galvanic engraving is a most interesting instance of this reciprocity of action. That which was the chief aim of Niepce in the humblest dawn of the art, viz. to transform the photographic plate into a surface capable of being printed, which had been *bonâ fide* realised by Mr. Fox Talbot, M. Niepce de St. Victor, and others, but by methods too complicated for practical use, is now by the co-operation of electricity with photography done with the simplicity and perfection which fulfil all conditions. This invention is the work of M. Pretsch of Vienna, and deserves a few explanatory words.[13] It differs from all other attempts for the same purpose in not operating upon the photographic tablet itself, and by discarding the usual means of varnishes and bitings in. The process is simply this. A glass tablet is coated with gelatine diluted till it forms a jelly, and containing bichromate of potash, nitrate of silver and iodide of potassium. Upon this when dry is placed, face downwards, a paper positive, through which the light, being allowed to fall, leaves upon the gelatine a representation of the print. It is then soaked in water, and while the parts acted upon by the light are comparatively unaffected by the fluid, the remainder of the jelly swells, and rising above the general surface gives a picture in relief, resembling an ordinary engraving upon wood. Of this intaglio a cast is now taken in gutta-percha, to which the electro process in copper being applied, a plate or matrix is produced bearing on it an exact repetition of the original positive picture.[14] All that now remains to be done is to repeat the electro process, and the result is a copper plate, in the necessary relievo, of which, as the company who have undertaken to utilise the invention triumphantly set forth, nature furnishes the materials, and science the artist, the inferior workman being only needed to roll it through the press.

And here, for the present, terminate the more important steps of photographic development, each in its turn a wonder, and each in its turn obtained and supported by wonders only a little older than itself. It was not until 1811 that the chemical substance called iodine, on which the foundations of all popular photography rest, was discovered at all; bromine, the only other substance equally sensitive, not till 1826. The invention of the electro process was about simultaneous with that of photography itself. Gutta-percha only just preceded the substance of which collodion is made; the ether and chloroform, which are used in some methods, that of collodion. We say nothing of the optical improvements purposely contrived or adapted for the service of the photograph—the achromatic lenses, which correct the discrepancy between the visual and chemical foci; the double lenses, which increase the force of the action; the binocular lenses, which do the work of the stereoscope; nor of the innumerable other mechanical aids which have sprung up for its use; all things, great and small, working together to produce what seemed at first as delightful, but as fabulous, as Aladdin's ring, which is now as little suggestive of surprise as our daily bread. It is difficult now to believe that the foundations of all this were laid within the memory of a middle-aged gentleman, by a few lonely philosophers, incognizant of each other, each following a glimmer of light through years of toil, and looking upward to that Land of Promise to which beaten tracks and legible handposts now conduct an army of devotees. Nevertheless, there is no royal road thrown open yet. Photography is, after all, too profoundly interwoven with the deep things of Nature to be entirely unlocked by any given method. Every individual who launches his happiness on this stream finds currents and rocks not laid down in the chart. Every sanguine little couple who set up a glass-house at the commencement of summer, call their friends about them, and toil alternately in broiling light and stifling gloom, have said before long, in their heart, "Photography, thy name is disappointment!" But the photographic back is fitted to the burden. Although all things may be accused in turn—their chemicals, their friends, and even Nature herself—yet with the next fine day there they are at work again, successively in hope, excitement, and despair, for, as Schiller says,—

> Etwas furchten [sic], und hoffen, und sorgen
> Muss der Mensch für den kommenden Morgen.[15]

At present no observation or experience has sufficed to determine the state of atmosphere in which the photographic spirits are most propitious; no rule or order seems to guide their proceedings. You go out on a beautifully clear day, not a breath stirring, chemicals in order, and lights and shadows in perfection; but something in the air is absent, or present, or indolent, or restless, and you return in the evening only to develop a set of blanks. The next day is cloudy and breezy, your chemicals are neglected, yourself disheartened, hope is gone, and with it the needful care; but here again something in the air is favourable, and in the silence and darkness of your chamber pictures are summoned from the vasty deep which at once obliterate all thought of failure. Happy the photographer who knows what is his enemy, or what is his friend; but in either case it is too often "something," he can't tell what; and all the certainty that the best of experience attains is, that you are dealing with one of those subtle agencies which, though Ariel-like it will serve you bravely, will never be taught implicitly to obey.

As respects the time of the day, however, one law seems to be thoroughly established. It has been observed by Daguerre and subsequent photographers that the sun is far more active, in a photographic sense, for the two hours before, than for the two hours after it has passed the meridian. As a general rule, too, however numerous the exceptions, the cloudy day is better than the sunny one. Contrary, indeed, to all preconceived ideas, experience proves that the brighter the sky that shines above the camera the more tardy the action within it. Italy and Malta do their work slower than Paris. Under the brilliant light of a Mexican sun, half an hour is required to produce effects which in England would occupy but a minute. In the burning atmosphere of India, though photographical the year round, the process is comparatively slow and difficult to manage; while in the clear, beautiful, and, moreover, cool light of the higher Alps of Europe, it has been proved that the production of a picture requires many more minutes, even with the most sensitive preparations, than in the murky atmosphere of London. Upon the whole, the temperate skies of this country may be pronounced most favourable to photographic action, a fact for which the prevailing characteristic of our climate may partially account, humidity being an indispensable condition for the working state both of paper and chemicals.

But these are at most but superficial influences—deeper causes than any relative dryness or damp are concerned in these phenomena. The investigation of the solar attributes, by the aid of photographic machinery, for which we are chiefly indebted to the researches of Mr. Hunt and M. Claudet, are, scientifically speaking, the most interesting results of the discovery. By these means it is proved that besides the functions of light and heat the solar ray has a third, and what may be called photographic function, the cause of all the disturbances, decompositions, and chemical changes which affect vegetable, animal, and organic life. It had long been known that this power, whatever it may be termed—energia—actinism—resided more strongly, or was perhaps less obstructed, in some of the coloured rays of the spectrum than in others—that solutions of silver and other sensitive surfaces were sooner darkened in the violet and the blue than in the yellow and red portions of the prismatic spectrum. Mr. Hunt's experiments further prove that mere light, or the luminous ray, is little needed where the photographic or "chemical ray" is active, and that sensitive paper placed beneath the comparative darkness of a glass containing a dense purple fluid, or under that deep blue glass commonly used as a finger-glass, is photographically affected almost as soon as if not shaded from the light at all. Whereas, if the same experiment be tried under a yellow glass or fluid, the sensitive paper, though robbed neither of light nor heat, will remain a considerable time without undergoing any change.[16]

We refer our readers to this work for results of the utmost interest—our only purpose is to point out that the defects or irregularities of photography are as inherent in the laws of Nature as its existence—being coincident with the first created of all things. The prepared paper or plate which we put into the camera may be compared to a chaos, without form and void, on which the merest glance of the sun's rays calls up image after image till the fair creation stands revealed: yet not revealed in the order in which it met the solar eye, for while some colours have hastened to greet his coming, others have been found slumbering at their posts, and have been left with darkness in their lamps. So impatient have been the blues and violets to perform their task upon the recipient plate, that the very substance of the colour has been lost and dissolved in the solar presence; while so laggard have been the reds and yellows and all tints partaking of them, that they have hardly kindled into activity before the light has been withdrawn. Thus it is that the relation of one colour to another is found changed and often reversed, the deepest blue being altered from a dark mass into a light one, and the most golden-yellow from a light body into a dark.

It is obvious, therefore, that however successful photography may be in the closest imitation of light and shadow, it fails, and must fail, in the rendering of true chiaroscuro, or the true imitation of light and dark. And even if the world we inhabit, instead of being spread out with every variety of the palette, were constituted but of two colours— black and white and all their intermediate grades—if every figure were seen in monochrome like those that visited the perturbed vision of the Berlin Nicolai—photography could still not copy them correctly. Nature, we must remember, is not made up only of actual lights and shadows; besides these more elementary masses, she possesses innumerable reflected lights and half-tones, which play around every object, rounding the hardest edges, and illuminating the blackest breadths, and making that sunshine in a shady place, which it is the delight of the practised painter to render. But of all these photography gives comparatively no account. The beau ideal of a Turner and the delight of a Rubens are caviar to her. Her strong shadows swallow up all timid lights within them, as her blazing lights obliterate all intrusive half-tones across them; and thus strong contrasts are produced, which, so far from being true to Nature, it seems one of Nature's most beautiful provisions to prevent.

Nor is this disturbance in the due degree of chiaroscuro attributable only to the different affinities for light residing in different colours, or to the absence of true gradation in light and shade. The quality and texture of a surface has much to do with it. Things that are very smooth, such as glass and polished steel, or certain complexions and parts of the human face, or highly-glazed satin-ribbon—or smooth leaves, or brass-buttons—everything on which the light *shines*, as well as everything that is perfectly white, will photograph much faster than other objects, and thus disarrange the order of relation. Where light meets light the same instantaneous command seems to go forth as that by which it was at first created, so that, by the time the rest of the picture has fallen into position, what are called the high lights have so rioted in action as to be found far too prominent both in size and intensity.

And this brings us to the artistic part of our subject, and to those questions which sometimes puzzle the spectator, as to how far photography is really a picturesque agent, what are the causes of its successes and its failures, and what in the sense of art are its successes and failures? And these questions may be fairly asked now when the scientific processes on which the practice depends are brought to such perfection that, short of the coveted attainment of colour, no great improvement can be further expected. If we look round a photographic exhibition we are met by results which are indeed honourable to the perseverance, knowledge, and in some cases to the taste of man. The small, broadly-treated, Rembrandt-like studies representing the sturdy physiognomies of Free Church Ministers and their adherents, which first cast the glamour of photography upon us, are replaced by portraits of the most elaborate detail, and of every size not excepting that of life itself. The little bit of landscape effect, all blurred and uncertain in forms, and those lost in a confused and discoloured ground, which was nothing and might be anything, is superseded by large pictures with minute foregrounds, regular planes of distance, and perfectly clear skies. The small attempts at architecture have swelled into monumental representations of a magnitude, truth, and beauty which no art can surpass—animals, flowers, pictures, engravings, all come within the grasp of the photographer; and last, and finest, and most interesting of all, the sky with its shifting clouds, and the sea with its heaving waves, are overtaken in their course by a power more rapid than themselves.

But while ingenuity and industry—the efforts of hundreds working as one—have thus enlarged the scope of the new agent, and rendered it available for the most active, as well as for the merest still life, has it gained in an artistic sense in like proportion? Our answer is not in the affirmative, nor is it possible that it should be so. Far from holding up the mirror to nature, which is an assertion usually as triumphant as it is erroneous, it holds up that which, however beautiful, ingenious, and valuable in powers of reflection, is yet subject to certain distortions and deficiencies for which there is no remedy. The science therefore which has developed the resources of photography, has but more glaringly betrayed its defects. For the more perfect you render an imperfect machine the more must its imperfections come to light: it is superfluous therefore to ask whether Art has been benefited, where Nature, its only source and model, has been but more accurately falsified. If the photograph in its early and imperfect scientific state was more consonant to our feelings for art, it is because, as far as it went, it was more true to our experience of Nature. Mere broad light and shade, with the correctness of general forms and absence of all convention, which are the beautiful conditions of photography, will, when nothing further is attempted, give artistic pleasure of a very high kind; it is only when greater precision and detail are superadded that the eye misses the further truths which should accompany the further finish.

For these reasons it is almost needless to say that we sympathise cordially with Sir William Newton, who at one time created no little scandal in the Photographic Society by propounding the heresy that pictures taken slightly out of focus, that is, with slightly uncertain and undefined forms, "though less *chemically*, would be found more *artistically* beautiful." Much as photography is supposed to inspire its votaries with æsthetic instincts, this excellent artist could hardly have chosen an audience less fitted to endure such a proposition. As soon could an accountant admit the morality of a false balance, or a seampstress the neatness of a puckered seam, as your merely scientific photographer be made to comprehend the possible beauty of "a slight *burr*." His mind proud science never taught to doubt the closest connexion between cause and effect, and the suggestion that the worse photography could be the better art was not only strange to him, but discordant. It was hard too to disturb his faith in his newly acquired powers. Holding, as he believed, the keys of imitation in his camera, he had tasted for once something of the intoxicating dreams of the artist; gloating over the pictures as they developed beneath his gaze, he had said in his heart "anch' io son pittore." Indeed there is no lack of evidence in the Photographic Journal of his believing that art had hitherto been but a blundering groper after that truth which the cleanest and precisest photography in his hands was now destined to reveal. Sir William Newton, therefore, was fain to allay the storm by qualifying his meaning to the level of photographic toleration, knowing that, of all the delusions which possess the human breast, few are so intractable as those about art.

But let us examine a little more closely those advances which photography owes to science—we mean in an artistic sense. We turn to the portraits, our *premiers amours*, now taken under every appliance of facility both for sitter and operator. Far greater detail and precision accordingly appear. Every button is seen—piles of stratified flounces in most accurate drawing are there,—what was at first only suggestion is now all careful making out,—but the likeness to Rembrandt and Reynolds is gone! There is no mystery in this. The first principle in art is that the most important part of a picture should be best done. Here, on the contrary, while the dress has been rendered worthy of a fashion-book, the face has remained, if not so unfinished as before, yet more unfinished in proportion to the rest. Without referring to M. Claudet's well-known experiment of a falsely coloured female face, it may be averred that, of all the surfaces a few inches square the sun looks upon, none offers more difficulty, artistically speaking, to the photographer, than a smooth, blooming, clean washed, and carefully combed human head. The high lights which gleam on this delicate epidermis so spread and magnify themselves, that all sharpness and nicety of modelling is obliterated—the fineness of skin peculiar to the under lip reflects so much light, that in spite of its deep colour it presents a light projection, instead of a dark one—the spectrum or intense point of light on the eye is magnified to a thing like a cataract. If the cheek be very brilliant in colour, it is as often as not represented by a dark stain. If the eye be blue, it turns out as colourless as water; if the hair be golden or red, it looks as if it had been dyed, if very glossy it is cut up into lines of light as big as ropes. This is what a fair young young girl has to expect from the tender mercies of photography—the male and the older head, having less to lose, has less to fear. Strong light and shade will portray character, though they mar beauty. Rougher skin, less glossy hair, Crimean moustaches and beard overshadowing the white under lip, and deeper lines, are all so much in favour of a picturesque result. Great grandeur of feature too, or beauty of *pose* and sentiment, will tell as elevated elements of the picturesque in spite of photographic mismanagement. Here and there also a head of fierce and violent contrasts, though taken perhaps from the meekest of mortals, will remind us of the Neapolitan or Spanish school, but, generally speaking, the inspection of a set of faces, subject to the usual conditions of humanity and the camera, leaves us with the impression that a photographic portrait, however valuable to relative or friend, has ceased to remind us of a work of art at all.

And, if further proof were wanted of the artistic inaptitude of this agent for the delineation of the human countenance, we should find it in those magnified portraits which ambitious operators occasionally exhibit to our ungrateful gaze. Rightly considered, a human head, the size of life, of average intelligence, and in perfect drawing, may be expected, however roughly finished, to recall an old Florentine fresco of four centuries ago. But, "ex nihilo, nihil fit:"[17] the best magnifying lenses can in this case only impoverish in proportion as they enlarge, till the flat and empty Magog which is born of this process is an insult, even in remotest comparison with the pencil of a Masaccio.

The falling off of artistic effect is even more strikingly seen if we consider the department of landscape. Here the success with which all accidental blurs and blotches have been overcome, and the sharp perfection of the object which stands out against the irreproachably speckless sky, is exactly as detrimental to art as it is complimentary to science. The first impression suggested by these buildings of rich tone and elaborate detail, upon a glaring white background without the slightest form or tint, is that of a Chinese landscape upon looking-glass. We shall be asked why the beautiful skies we see in the marine pieces cannot be also represented with landscapes; but here the conditions of photography again interpose. The impatience of light to meet light is, as we have stated, so great, that the moment required to trace the forms of the sky (it can never be traced in its cloudless gradation of tint) is too short for the landscape, and the moment more required for the landscape too long for the sky. If the sky be given, therefore, the landscape remains black and underdone; if the landscape be rendered, the impatient action of the light has burnt out all cloud-form in one blaze of white. But it is different with the sea, which, from the liquid nature of its surface, receives so much light as to admit of simultaneous representation with the sky above it. Thus the marine painter has both hemispheres at his command, but the landscape votary but one; and it is but natural that he should prefer Rydal Mount and Tintern Abbey to all the baseless fabric of tower and hill which the firmament occasionally spreads forth. But the old moral holds true even here. Having renounced heaven, earth makes him, of course, only an inadequate compensation. The colour green, both in grass and foliage, is now his great difficulty. The finest lawn turns out but a gloomy funeral-pall in his hands; his trees, if done with the slower paper process, are black, and from the movement, uncertain webs against the white sky,—if by collodion, they look as if worked in dark cambric, or stippled with innumerable black and white specks; in either case missing all the breadth and gradations of nature. For it must be remembered that every leaf reflects a light on its smooth edge or surface, which, with the tendency of all light to over-action, is seen of a size and prominence disproportioned to things around it; so that what with the dark spot produced by the green colour, and the white spot produced by the high light, all intermediate grades and shades are lost. This is especially the case with hollies, laurels, ivy, and other smooth-leaved evergreens, which form so conspicuous a feature in English landscape gardening—also with foreground weeds and herbage, which, under these conditions, instead of presenting a sunny effect, look rather as if strewn with shining bits of tin, or studded with patches of snow.

For these reasons, if there be a tree distinguished above the rest of the forest for the harshness and blueness of its foliage, we may expect to find it suffer less, or not at all, under this process. Accordingly, the characteristic exception will be found in the Scotch fir, which, however dark and sombre in mass, is rendered by the photograph with a delicacy of tone and gradation very grateful to the eye. With this exception it is seldom that we find any studies of trees, in the present improved state of photography, which inspire us with the sense of pictorial truth. Now and then a bank of tangled brushwood, with a deep, dark pool beneath, but with no distance and no sky, and therefore no condition of relation, will challenge admiration. Winter landscapes also are beautiful, and the leafless Burnham beeches a real boon to the artist; but otherwise such materials as Hobbema, Ruysdael, and Cuyp converted into pictures unsurpassable in picturesque effect are presented in vain to the improved science of the photographic artist.[18] What strikes us most frequently is the general *emptiness* of the scene he gives. A house stands there, sharp and defined like a card-box, with black blots of trees on each side, all rooted in a substance far more like burnt stubble than juicy, delicate grass. Through this winds a white spectral path, while staring palings or linen hung out to dry (oh! how unlike the luminous spots on Ruysdael's bleaching-grounds!), like bits of the white sky dropped upon the earth, make up the poverty and patchiness of the scene. We are aware that there are many partial exceptions to this; indeed, we hardly ever saw a photograph in which there was not something or other of the most exquisite kind. But this brings us no nearer the standard we are seeking. Art cares not for the right finish unless it be in the right place. Her great aim is to produce a whole: the more photography advances in the execution of parts, the less does it give the idea of completeness.

There is nothing gained either by the selection of more ambitious scenery. The photograph seems embarrassed with the treatment of several gradations of distance. The finish of background and middle distance seems not to be commensurate with that of the foreground; the details of the simplest light and shadow are absent; all is misty and bare, and distant hills look like flat, grey moors washed in with one gloomy tint. This emptiness is connected with the rapidity of collodion, the action of which upon distance and middle ground does not keep pace with the hurry of the foreground. So much for the ambition of taking a picture. On the other hand, we have been struck with mere studies of Alpine masses done with the paper process, which allows the photograph to take its time, and where, from the absence of all foreground or intermediate objects, the camera has been able to concentrate its efforts upon one thing only—the result being records of simple truth and precision which must be invaluable to the landscape-painter.

There is no doubt that the forte of the camera lies in the imitation of one surface only, and that of a rough and broken kind. Minute light and shade, cognisant to the eye, but unattainable by hand, is its greatest and easiest triumph—the mere texture of stone, whether rough in the quarry or hewn on the wall, its especial delight. Thus a face of rugged rock, and the front of a carved and fretted building, are alike treated with a perfection which no human skill can approach; and if asked to say what photography has hitherto best succeeded in rendering, we should point to everything near and rough—from the texture of the sea-worn shell, of the rusted armour, and the fustian jacket, to those glorious architectural pictures of French, English, and Italian subjects, which, whether in quality, tone, detail, or drawing, leave nothing to be desired.

Here, therefore, the debt to Science for additional clearness, precision, and size may be gratefully acknowledged. What photography can do, is now, with her help, better done than before; what she can but partially achieve is best not brought too elaborately to light. Thus the whole question of success and failure resolves itself into an investigation of the capacities of the machine, and well may we be satisfied with the rich gifts it bestows, without straining it into a competition with art. For everything for which Art, so-called, has hitherto been the means but not the end, photography is the allotted agent—for all that requires mere manual correctness, and mere manual slavery, without any employment of the artistic feeling, she is the proper and therefore the perfect medium. She is made for the present age, in which the desire for art resides in a small minority, but the craving, or rather necessity, for cheap, prompt, and correct facts in the public at large. Photography is the purveyor of such knowledge to the world. She is the sworn witness of everything presented to her view. What are her unerring records in the service of mechanics, engineering, geology, and natural history, but facts of the most sterling and stubborn kind? What are her studies of the various stages of insanity—pictures of life unsurpassable in pathetic truth—but facts as well as lessons of the deepest physiological interest? What are her representations of the bed of the ocean, and the surface of the moon—of the launch of the Marlborough, and of the contents of the Great Exhibition—of Charles Kean's now destroyed scenery of the "Winter's Tale," and of Prince Albert's now slaughtered prize ox—but facts which are neither the province of art nor of description, but of that new form of communication between man and man—neither letter, message, nor picture—which now happily fills up the space between them? What indeed are nine-tenths of those facial maps called photographic portraits, but accurate landmarks and measurements for loving eyes and memories to deck with beauty and animate with expression, in perfect certainty, that the ground-plan is founded upon fact?

In this sense no photographic picture that ever was taken, in heaven, or earth, or in the waters underneath the earth, of any thing, or scene, however defective when measured by an artistic scale, is destitute of a special, and what we may call an historic interest. Every form which is traced by light is the impress of one moment, or one hour, or one age in the great passage of time. Though the faces of our children may not be modelled and rounded with that truth and beauty which art attains, yet minor things—the very shoes of the one, the inseparable toy of the other—are given with a strength of identity which art does not even seek. Though the view of a city be deficient in those niceties of reflected lights and harmonious gradations which belong to the facts of which Art takes account, yet the facts of the age and of the hour are there, for we count the lines in that keen perspective of telegraphic wire, and read the characters on that playbill or manifesto, destined to be torn down on the morrow.

Here, therefore, the much-lauded and much-abused agent called Photography takes her legitimate stand. Her business is to give evidence of facts, as minutely and as impartially as, to our shame, only an unreasoning machine can give. In this vocation we can as little overwork her as we can tamper with her. The millions and millions of hieroglyphics mentioned by M. Arago may be multiplied by millions and millions more,—she will render all as easily and as accurately as one. When people, therefore, talk of photography as being intended to supersede art, they utter what, if true, is not so in the sense they mean. Photography *is* intended to supersede much that art has hitherto done, but only that which it was both a misappropriation and deterioration of Art to do. The field of delineation, having two distinct spheres, requires two distinct labourers; but though hitherto the freewoman has done the work of the bondwoman, there is no fear that the position should be in future reversed. Correctness of drawing, truth of detail, and absence of convention, the best artistic characteristics of photography, are qualities of no common kind, but the student who issues from the academy with these in his grasp stands, nevertheless, but on the threshold of art. The power of selection and rejection, the living application of that language which lies dead in his paint-box, the marriage of his own mind with the object before him, and the offspring, half stamped with his own features, half with those of Nature, which is born of the union— whatever appertains to the free-will of the intelligent being, as opposed to the obedience of the machine,—this, and much more than this, constitutes that mystery called Art, in the elucidation of which photography can give valuable help, simply by showing what it is not.

There is, in truth, nothing in that power of literal, unreasoning imitation, which she claims as her own, in which, rightly viewed, she does not relieve the artist of a burden rather than supplant him in an office. We do not even except her most pictorial feats—those splendid architectural representations—from this rule. Exquisite as they are, and fitted to teach the young, and assist the experienced in art, yet the hand of the artist is but ignobly employed in closely imitating the texture of stone, or in servilely following the intricacies of the zigzag ornament. And it is not only in what she can do to relieve the sphere of art, but in what she can sweep away from it altogether, that we have reason to congratulate ourselves. Henceforth it may be hoped that we shall hear nothing further of that miserable contradiction in terms "bad art"—and see nothing more of that still more miserable mistake in life "a bad artist." Photography at once does away with anomalies with which the good sense of society has always been more or less at variance. As what she does best is beneath the doing of a real artist at all, so even in what she does worst she is a better machine than the man who is nothing but a machine.

Let us, therefore, dismiss all mistaken ideas about the harm which photography does to art. As in all great and sudden improvements in the material comforts and pleasures of the public, numbers, it is true, have found their occupation gone, simply because it is done cheaper and better in another way. But such improvements always give more than they take. Where ten self-styled artists eked out a precarious living by painting inferior miniatures, ten times that number now earn their bread by supplying photographic portraits. Nor is even such manual skill as they possessed thrown out of the market. There is no photographic establishment of any note that does not employ artists at high salaries—we understand not less than 1£ a day—in touching, and colouring, and finishing from nature those portraits for which the camera may be said to have laid the foundation. And it must be remembered that those who complain of the encroachments of photography in this department could not even supply the demand. Portraits, as is evident to any thinking mind, and as photography now proves, belong to that class of facts wanted by numbers who know and care nothing about their value as works of art. For this want, art, even of the most abject kind, was, whether as regards correctness, promptitude, or price, utterly inadequate. These ends are not only now attained, but, even in an artistic sense, attained far better than before.

The coloured portraits to which we have alluded are a most satisfactory coalition between the artist and the machine. Many an inferior miniature-painter who understood the mixing and applying of pleasing tints was wholly unskilled in the true drawing of the human head. With this deficiency supplied, their present productions, therefore, are far superior to anything they accomplished, single-handed, before. Photographs taken on ivory, or on substances invented in imitation of ivory, and coloured by hand from nature, such as are seen at the rooms of Messrs. Dickinson, Claudet, Mayall, Kilburn, &c., are all that can be needed to satisfy the mere portrait want, and in some instances may be called artistic productions of no common kind besides. If, as we understand, the higher professors of miniature-painting—and the art never attained greater excellence in England than now—have found their studios less thronged of late, we believe that the desertion can be but temporary. At all events, those who in future desire their exquisite productions will be more worthy of them. The broader the ground which the machine may occupy, the higher will that of the intelligent agent be found to stand. If, therefore, the time should ever come when art is sought, as it ought to be, mainly for its own sake, our artists and our patrons will be of a far more elevated order than now: and if anything can bring about so desirable a climax, it will be the introduction of Photography.

Notes

1.   Humphry Davy (1778–1829) was a renowned English chemist who served as President of the Royal Society of London.
2.   French for self-consciousness or bashfulness.
3.   An account of a method of copying paintings upon glass and of making *profiles* by the agency of light upon nitrate of silver, with observations by Humphry Davy. [Eastlake's note]
4.   Joseph Nicéphore Niepce (1765–1833) invented photography in the camera and heliogravure. He used a camera with lens as early as 1816.
5.   Louis Daguerre (1789–1851).
6.   Francois Arago (1786–1853) was a pioneer French photographer.

7. Hippolyte Louis Fizeau (1819–96) was by profession a French physicist. Antoine Francois Jean Claudet (1797–1867) was a French daguerreotypist and early professional photographer.

8. William Henry Fox Talbot (1800–77) published *The Pencil of Nature* (1844)—the first book published for profit to include photographs.

9. Sir John Herschel (1792–1867) was a British astronomer and pioneer photographic chemist. He coined the word "photography" in 1839. Joseph Bancroft Reade (1801–70) was a British astronomer, microscopist, and pioneer photographer. Robert Hunt (1807–87) wrote some of the earliest and best known studies on photography. He was a founder of the British Royal Photographic Society.

10. David Octavius Hill (1802–70), a Scottish painter, and Robert Adamson (1820–48), became photographers and produced portraits and genre scenes. They helped ensure that photography become an accepted art form.

11. Collodion is a highly flammable syrupy solution used to make photographic plates. As Eastlake notes, Gun-cotton, or nitrocellulose, is used in the manufacture of collodion.

12. A stereoscope contains two eyepieces used to impart a three-dimensional effect to two photographs of the same scene from slightly different angles.

13. Paul Pretsch (1808–73) was an Austrian printer, photographer and photomechanical inventor.

14. Guttapercha is a substance used as an electrical insulator.

15. A literal translation of Friedrich Schiller's poem reads: "A person needs to have some fear, hope, and concern for the coming day."

16. We may add, though foreign to our subject, that the same experiment applied by Mr. Hunt to plants has been attended with analogous results. Bulbs of tulips and ranunculuses have germinated beneath yellow and red glasses, but the plant has been weakly and has perished without forming buds. Under a green glass (blue being a component part of the colour) the plants have been less feeble, and have advanced as far as flower-buds; while beneath the blue medium perfectly healthy plants have grown up, developing their buds, and flowering in perfection. [Eastlake's note]

17. Latin for "Nothing comes from nothing."

18. Meindert Hobbema (1638–1709), Salomon van Ruysdael (1600–70), and Aelbert Cuyp (1620–91) were Dutch landscape painters.

IV. George Eliot
(Marian Evans)
(1819–1880)

Marian Evans—who as "George Eliot" wrote fiction that distinguished her as a leading novelist of the age and a founder of what F.R. Leavis called "The Great Tradition"—began and ended her writing career with politically and philosophically significant works of nonfiction prose. Although her achievement in fiction has eclipsed her translations of Strauss and Feuerbach, her contributions to periodicals, and her final book, *Impressions of Theophrastus Such*, Eliot's nonfiction prose reveals intellectual ambition and integrity, passionate and painstaking scholarship, and intense engagement in contemporary issues that she believed to be of timeless value. In book reviews that compose a large portion of her writing, Eliot renders justice to the immediate text and places it in a fuller context, much as her character Lydgate aspired "to do good small work for Middlemarch, and great work for the World" (*Middlemarch*, Ch. 14). The result is a body of work that not only explicates and supports her novels, but that can be read independently as the record of a formidable mid-Victorian mind, weighing, sifting, and judging the work of other minds.

Born in the parish of Calton, Warwickshire, on November 22, 1819, and raised in neighboring Nuneaton, Marian Evans was the fifth and last daughter of Charles Evans, a self-educated estate agent, and Christiana Pearson, his second wife. Marian underwent more than ten years of formal education in a succession of boarding schools, in addition to a strenuous program of self-education through reading. In Coventry in her twenties, she developed close, fruitful friendships with Charles Bray (author of *The Philosophy of Necessity*, 1841), his wife Caroline Hennell Bray, and her brother Charles Hennell (author of *An*

Inquiry into the Origins of Christianity, 1838). Marian Evans's religious views shifted from an acceptance of her family's conventional Anglicanism to a zealous, Puritanically severe form of Evangelicalism, and then to a resolute, outspoken rejection of mysticism, eternal damnation, Biblical literalism, religious ritual, and dogma. Ultimately, she became an adherent to the moral ideas and actions she associated with Christianity. Her behavior in her religious crisis was paradigmatic: in January, 1842, she refused to accompany her father to church, proclaiming herself unable to profess a lie and willing to suffer any consequences, including expulsion from their home; several months later, upon seeing his distress and regretting what she later called the "narrowness of . . . intellectual superiority" that had impelled her to hurt him, she agreed to go to church, but insisted that she would continue to hold her free-thinking opinions. In her later conduct, as well as in her writing, she repeated the same rule: although principle would appear to dictate a given course of action, an abstraction could be properly outweighed, temporarily and in particular circumstances, by personal and social history.

Through the invitation of her Coventry friends, Eliot was invited to translate *Das Leben Jesu* (1846), a 1,550–page treatise by David Friedrich Strauss. Eliot ultimately embraced an interpretation of the Bible as literature (to be cherished as a cultural myth, created not by an individual mind but by some sort of collective consciousness) rather than history (to be adopted, in violation of our understanding of causality, as literally true).

After her father's death in 1849, Eliot spent a winter in Geneva and then settled in London, where she served for two years as secret editor of and frequent contributor to John Chapman's *Westminster Review*. In the early 1850s, she met such figures as Harriet Martineau, William Hale White, Eliza Lynn (later Linton), Bessie Rayner Parkes, and Barbara Leigh Smith (later Bodichon)—an advocate for women's education and suffrage who became her intimate friend and her closest personal link to the women's suffrage movement. Herbert Spencer, then subeditor of the *Economist* and later the author of the multivolume *System of Synthetic Philosophy* (1862–93), also became Eliot's friend and life-long intellectual colleague whose writings on politics, ethics, psychology, and education alternately evoked her agreement and inspired her opposition.

In 1852, Eliot became close to Spencer's friend George Henry Lewes, a journalist, historian, philosopher, biographer, and pioneer psychologist. In 1854, as their relationship deepened, Eliot read his work and shared with him her own, including her translation of Ludwig Feuerbach's *Das Wesen des Christenthums*, which was published in 1854 by Chapman as *The Essence of Christianity*, by Marian Evans— the only time her name was to appear on one of her books. Her decision later in 1854 to share her life with Lewes (who, already married, was unable to obtain a divorce because he had condoned his wife's adultery) brought her into contact with thinkers and artists on the Continent, but removed her for many years from the social circles in which she had flourished as writer and editor; her uncomfortable social status contributed to her wish to write anonymously or pseudonymously.

After completing a translation of Spinoza's 1677 treatise *Ethica* (which remained unpublished during her lifetime) and contributing additional reviews and articles to the *Westminster Review*, she wrote "The Sad Fortunes of Amos Barton" in 1856 and began, as "George Eliot," a new career in fiction, continuing in 1857 with the publication of "Mr. Gilfil's Love Story" and "Janet's Repentance" (the second and third tales which make up *Scenes of Clerical Life*). Even during her years as a novelist, which culminated in 1876 with the publication of *Daniel Deronda*, "George Eliot" returned on regular occasion to her first career of nonfiction prose.

As a reviewer and essayist, Eliot wrote for the *Coventry Herald and Observer*, produced at least seventeen individual or omnibus reviews for the *Westminster Review* (1851–52, 1855–57), at least thirty-three brief reviews for the *Leader* (1851, 1854–56), two pieces on Weimar culture for *Fraser's Magazine* (1855), four reviews for the *Saturday Review* (1856), four essays for the *Pall Mall Gazette* (1865), two reviews for the *Fortnightly Review* (1865), and "Address to Working Men, by Felix Holt" for *Blackwood's* (1868). Only the late works bear the name "George Eliot," and the rest were published anonymously. (The numbers here are a lower limit, based on conservative attribution; the actual numbers may be somewhat higher.) *Impressions of Theophrastus Such* (1879)—a plotless collection of eighteen thematically related sketches on such topics as literary controversy, plagiarism, moral judgement, and psychological volatility—is written in male persona. This last book recalls Eliot's earliest writings for the *Coventry Herald*, which published her essays as "Poetry and Prose from the Notebook of an Eccentric."

Eliot's periodical contributions are remarkable for the breadth of her reach and for the consistency of her viewpoint. The longest pieces, all written for the *Westminster Review*, deal with a variety of topics, including Victor Cousin's biography of Madame de Sablé, as well as her review of six 1856 novels that she saw as representative of unfortunate trends ("Silly Novels by Lady Novelists," 1856). In brief notices of novels, poetry, and nonfiction, and in longer essays on a similar range of topics, Eliot measures the quality of a work's content by the standard of truthfulness, and the power of a work's presentation by the standard of sympathy.

For Eliot, truthfulness in history entails accuracy of detail and emphasis, while truthfulness in politics and philosophy demands a comprehensive field of inquiry and scrupulous balance in the weighing of information. In judging the truthfulness of a novel or painting, Eliot praises in her reviews a naturalistic aesthetic: shaping one's characters and narrative to fit the limits of the actual.

The criterion of sympathy, as Eliot uses it to evaluate the works she reviews, requires the writer to address primarily the universal features of human experience and to show how social relationships outweigh individual considerations, purposes, or achievements. In political and social history, the historian must stress universal laws and trends, eschew partisan pleading, and minimize disconnected melodrama. The roots of an individual, of a family, or of a nation are compelling; one pays a price for uprooting oneself. In literature, to be sympathetic is to construct fictions in which individuals are socially identified, engaged, and enmeshed—with the ability, perhaps, to adjust the tension of their social bonds or to choose among their myriad obligations, but not to uphold their own concerns as paramount and fundamental.

The largest published selection of Eliot's nonfiction prose, most of which addresses the above philosophies, is *Essays of George Eliot*, edited by Thomas Pinney (1963), which includes a list of her periodical contributions. *George Eliot: A Writer's Notebook 1854–1879 and Uncollected Writings*, edited by Joseph Wiesenfarth (1981), includes additional articles. Two recent collections—*George Eliot: Selected Essays, Poems and Other Writings*, edited by A.S. Byatt and Nicholas Warren (1990), and *George Eliot: Selected Critical Writings*, edited by Rosemary Ashton (1992)—contain representative selections and intelligent notes. *Impressions of Theophrastus Such*, edited by Nancy Henry, has been published by the University of Iowa Press (1995).

Of course, the critical writings on George Eliot are numerous, as well as daunting in content and scope. However, the best source of information regarding the events of Eliot's life and writing history remains Gordon S. Haight's biography (1968), in conjunction with his nine-volume edition of her letters (1954–78). For discussions of Eliot's reviews, consult William Myers's "George Eliot's Essays and Reviews 1849–57," in *Prose Studies 1800–1900*, I (1978): 5–20; G. Robert Strange's "The Voices of the Essayist," in *Nineteenth-Century Fiction*, 35 (1980): 312–30; and Susan Rowland Tush's *George Eliot and the Conventions of Popular Fiction: A Serious Literary Response to the "Silly Novels by Lady Novelists"* (1993). James D. Rust's Ph.D. dissertation (Yale, 1945), "George Eliot's Periodical Contributions," surveys the range of Eliot's work, but includes within the total count and analysis twenty-nine pieces that may not in fact be hers.

Shoshana Milgram Knapp,
Virginia Polytechnic Institute
and State University

9. Natural History of German Life: Riehl

Introduction

George Eliot's "Natural History of German Life: Riehl" went through several editions in the nineteenth century. It first appeared in the *Westminster Review* in July, 1856, was reprinted in *The Essays of 'George Eliot', Complete*, edited by Nathan Sheppard (1883), and then appeared in an edition selected and revised by George Eliot, *Essays and Leaves from a Notebook* (1884). The text here is taken from a 1907–08 edition published in Boston and reprinted in 1970 by AMS Press.

In her enthusiastic review of new editions of Wilhelm Heinrich von Riehl's *Die Bürgerliche Gesellschaft* (1851) and *Land und Leute* (1853), Eliot praises Riehl (1823–97) for performing, on behalf of the German people, the task she recommends to "some future or actual student of our own people": an accurate description of the physical, social, and moral development of the peasants. Riehl lays claim to a truth analogous to scientific truth, and, through the presentation of a "true conception of the popular character," can "guide our sympathies rightly" and "check our theories, and direct us in their application." By promoting a natural history of society, Eliot, in the spirit of Auguste Comte's positivism and Johann Gottfried von Herder's cultural evolution, is placing social analysis in the context of the geological studies of Charles Lyell, the *Origin of Species* of Charles Darwin, and R.W. Mackay's *The Progress of Intellect*. In endorsing Riehl's analysis of the German peasant's "natural" conservatism, Eliot presents gradualist reform as not only judicious and prudent, but based on an understanding of evolution at work in history.

Natural History of German Life: Riehl

It is an interesting branch of psychological observation to note
the images that are habitually associated with abstract or collective
terms—what may be called the picture-writing of the mind, which it
carries on concurrently with the more subtle symbolism of language.
Perhaps the fixity or variety of these associated images would furnish a
tolerably fair test of the amount of concrete knowledge and experience
which a given word represents, in the minds of two persons who use it
with equal familiarity. The word *railways*, for example, will probably
call up, in the mind of a man who is not highly locomotive, the image
either of a "Bradshaw,"[1] or of the station with which he is most
familiar, or of an indefinite length of tram-road; he will alternate
between these three images, which represent his stock of concrete
acquaintance with railways. But suppose a man to have had successively
the experience of a "navvy," an engineer, a traveller, a railway director
and shareholder, and a landed proprietor in treaty with a railway
company and it is probable that the range of images which would by
turns present themselves to his mind at the mention of the *word*
"railways" would include all the essential facts in the existence and
relations of the *thing*. Now it is possible for the first-mentioned
personage to entertain very expanded views as to the multiplication of
railways in the abstract, and their ultimate function in civilization. He
may talk of a vast network of railways stretching over the globe, of
future "lines" in Madagascar, and elegant refreshment-rooms in the
Sandwich Islands, with none the less glibness because his distinct
conceptions on the subject do not extend beyond his one station and his
indefinite length of tram-road. But it is evident that if we want a railway
to be made, or its affairs to be managed, this man of wide views and
narrow observation will not serve our purpose.

Probably, if we could ascertain the images called up by the terms
"the people," "the masses," "the proletariat," "the peasantry," by many
who theorize on those bodies with eloquence, or who legislate for them
without eloquence, we should find that they indicate almost as small an
amount of concrete knowledge—that they are as far from completely
representing the complex facts summed up in the collective term, as the
railway images of our non-locomotive gentleman. How little the real
characteristics of the working classes are known to those who are

outside them, how little their natural history has been studied, is sufficiently disclosed by Art, as well as by our political and social theories. Where, in our picture exhibitions, shall we find a group of true peasantry? What English artist even attempts to rival in truthfulness such studies of popular life as the pictures of Teniers or the ragged boys of Murillo?[2] Even one of the greatest painters of the pre-eminently realistic school, while, in his picture of "The Hireling Shepherd,"[3] he gave us a landscape of marvellous truthfulness, placed a pair of peasants in the foreground who were not much more real than the idyllic swains and damsels of our chimney ornaments. Only a total absence of acquaintance and sympathy with our peasantry could give a moment's popularity to such a picture as "Cross Purposes," where we have a peasant girl who looks as if she knew L.E.L.'s[4] poems by heart, and English rustics, whose costume seems to indicate that they are meant for ploughmen, with exotic features that remind us of a handsome *primo tenore*.[5] Rather than such Cockney sentimentality as this, as an education for the taste and sympathies, we prefer the most crapulous group of boors that Teniers ever painted. But even those among our painters who aim at giving the rustic type of features, who are far above the effeminate feebleness of the "Keepsake" style, treat their subjects under the influence of tradition and prepossessions rather than of direct observation.[6] The notion that peasants are joyous, that the typical moment to represent a man in a smock-frock is when he is cracking a joke and showing a row of sound teeth, that cottage matrons are usually buxom, and village children necessarily rosy and merry, are prejudices difficult to dislodge from the artistic mind, which looks for its subjects into literature instead of life. The painter is still under the influence of idyllic literature, which has always expressed the imagination of the cultivated and town-bred, rather than the truth of rustic life. Idyllic ploughmen are jocund when they drive their team afield; idyllic shepherds make bashful love under hawthorn-bushes; idyllic villagers dance in the chequered shade and refresh themselves, not immoderately, with spicy nut-brown ale. But no one who has seen much of actual ploughmen thinks them jocund; no one who is well acquainted with the English peasantry can pronounce them merry. The slow gaze, in which no sense of beauty beams, no humour twinkles,— the slow utterance, and the heavy slouching walk, remind one rather of that melancholy animal the camel than of the sturdy countryman, with striped stockings, red waistcoat, and hat aside, who represents the traditional English peasant. Observe a company of haymakers. When you see them at a distance, tossing up the forkfuls of hay in the golden light, while the waggon creeps slowly with its increasing burthen over the meadow, and the bright green space which tells of work done gets larger and larger, you pronounce the scene "smiling," and you think these companions in labour must be as bright and cheerful as the picture to which they give animation. Approach nearer, and you will certainly find that haymaking-time is a time for joking, especially if there are women among the labourers; but the coarse laugh that bursts out every now and then, and expresses the triumphant taunt, is as far as possible from your conception of idyllic merriment. That delicious effervescence of the mind which we call fun has no equivalent for the northern peasant, except tipsy revelry; the only realm of fancy and imagination for the English clown exists at the bottom of the third quart-pot.

The conventional countryman of the stage, who picks up pocket-books and never looks into them, and who is too simple even to know that honesty has its opposite, represents the still lingering mistake that an unintelligible dialect is a guarantee for ingenuousness, and that slouching shoulders indicate an upright disposition. It is quite true that a thresher is likely to be innocent of any adroit arithmetical cheating, but he is not the less likely to carry home his master's corn in his shoes and pocket;[7] a reaper is not given to writing begging-letters, but he is quite capable of cajoling the dairymaid into filling his small-beer bottle with ale. The selfish instincts are not subdued by the sight of buttercups, nor is integrity in the least established by that classic rural occupation, sheep-washing. To make men moral, something more is requisite than to turn them out to grass.

Opera peasants, whose unreality excites Mr. Ruskin's indignation, are surely too frank an idealization to be misleading;[8] and since popular chorus is one of the most effective elements of the opera, we can hardly object to lyric rustics in elegant laced bodices and picturesque motley, unless we are prepared to advocate a chorus of colliers in their pit costume, or a ballet of charwomen and stocking-weavers. But our social novels profess to represent the people as they are, and the unreality of their representations is a grave evil. The greatest benefit we owe to the artist, whether painter, poet, or novelist, is the extension of our sympathies. Appeals founded on generalizations and statistics require a sympathy ready-made, a moral sentiment already in activity; but a picture of human life, such as a great artist can give, surprises even the trivial and the selfish into that attention to what is apart from themselves, which may be called the raw material of moral sentiment. When Scott takes us into Luckie Mucklebackit's cottage, or tells the story of "The Two Drovers,"—when Wordsworth sings to us the reverie of "Poor Susan,"—when Kingsley shows us Alton Locke gazing yearningly over the gate which leads from the highway into the first wood he ever saw,—when Hornung paints a group of chimney-sweepers,—more is done towards linking the higher classes with the lower, towards obliterating the vulgarity of exclusiveness, than by hundreds of sermons and philosophical dissertations.[9] Art is the nearest thing to life; it is a mode of amplifying experience and extending our contact with our fellow men beyond the bounds of our personal lot. All the more sacred is the task of the artist when he undertakes to paint the life of the People. Falsification here is far more pernicious than in the more artificial aspects of life. It is not so very serious that we should have false ideas about evanescent fashions—about the manners and conversation of beaux and duchesses; but it *is* serious that our sympathy with the perennial joys and struggles, the toil, the tragedy, and the humour, in the life of our more heavily laden fellow men, should be perverted, and turned towards a false object instead of the true one.

This perversion is not the less fatal because the misrepresentation which gives rise to it has what the artist considers a moral end. The thing for mankind to know is not what are the motives and influences which the moralist thinks *ought* to act on the labourer or the artisan, but what are the motives and influences which *do* act on him. We want to be taught to feel, not for the heroic artisan or the sentimental peasant, but for the peasant in all his coarse apathy, and the artisan in all his suspicious selfishness.

We have one great novelist who is gifted with the utmost power of rendering the external traits of our town population; and if he could give us their psychological character—their conceptions of life, and their emotions—with the same truth as their idiom and manners, his books would be the greatest contribution Art has ever made to the awakening of social sympathies. But while he can copy Mrs. Plornish's[10] colloquial style with the delicate accuracy of a sun-picture, while there is the same startling inspiration in his description of the gestures and phrases of "Boots,"[11] as in the speeches of Shakespeare's mobs or numskulls, he scarcely ever passes from the humorous and external to the emotional and tragic, without becoming as transcendent in his unreality as he was a moment before in his artistic truthfulness. But for the precious salt of his humour, which compels him to reproduce external traits that serve, in some degree, as a corrective to his frequently false psychology, his preternaturally virtuous poor children and artisans, his melodramatic boatmen and courtesans, would be as noxious as Eugène Sue's idealized proletaires in encouraging the miserable fallacy that high morality and refined sentiment can grow out of harsh social relations, ignorance, and want;[12] or that the working classes are in a condition to enter at once into a millennial state of *altruism*, wherein every one is caring for every one else, and no one for himself.[13]

If we need a true conception of the popular character to guide our sympathies rightly, we need it equally to check our theories, and direct us in their application. The tendency created by the splendid conquests of modern generalization, to believe that all social questions are merged in economical science, and that the relations of men to their neighbours may be settled by algebraic equations,[14]—the dream that the uncultured classes are prepared for a condition which appeals principally to their moral sensibilities,—the aristocratic dilettanteism[15] which attempts to restore the "good old times" by a sort of idyllic masquerading, and to grow feudal fidelity and veneration as we grow prize turnips, by an artificial system of culture,—none of these diverging mistakes can coexist with a real knowledge of the People, with a thorough study of their habits, their ideas, their motives. The landholder, the clergyman, the mill-owner, the mining-agent, have each an opportunity for making precious observations on different sections of the working classes; but unfortunately their experience is too often not registered at all, or its results are too scattered to be available as a source of information and stimulus to the public mind generally. If any man of sufficient moral and intellectual breadth, whose observations would not be vitiated by a foregone conclusion, or by a professional point of view, would devote himself to studying the natural history of our social classes, especially of the small shopkeepers, artisans, and peasantry,—the degree in which they are influenced by local conditions, their maxims and habits, the points of view from which they regard their religious teachers, and the degree in which they are influenced by religious doctrines, the interaction of the various classes on each other, and what are the tendencies in their position towards disintegration or towards development,—and if, after all this study, he would give us the result of his observations in a book well nourished with specific facts, his work would be a valuable aid to the social and political reformer.

What we are desiring for ourselves has been in some degree done for the Germans by Riehl, the author of the very remarkable books the titles of which are placed at the bottom of this page;[16] and we wish to make these books known to our readers, not only for the sake of the interesting matter they contain and the important reflections they suggest, but also as a model for some future or actual student of our own people. By way of introducing Riehl to those who are unacquainted with his writings, we will give a rapid sketch from his picture of the German peasantry, and perhaps this indication of the mode in which he treats a particular branch of his subject may prepare them to follow us with more interest when we enter on the general purpose and contents of his works.

In England, at present, when we speak of the peasantry, we mean scarcely more than the class of farm-servants and farm-labourers; and it is only in the most primitive districts—as in Wales, for example—that farmers are included under the term. In order to appreciate what Riehl says of the German peasantry, we must remember what the tenant-farmers and small proprietors were in England half a century ago, when the master helped to milk his own cows, and the daughters got up at one o'clock in the morning to brew,—when the family dined in the kitchen with the servants, and sat with them round the kitchen fire in the evening. In those days the quarried parlour was innocent of a carpet, and its only specimens of art were a framed sampler and the best tea-board; the daughters even of substantial farmers had often no greater accomplishment in writing and spelling than they could procure at a dame-school; and, instead of carrying on sentimental correspondence, they were spinning their future table-linen, and looking after every saving in butter and eggs that might enable them to add to the little stock of plate and china which they were laying in against their marriage. In our own day, setting aside the superior order of farmers, whose style of living and mental culture are often equal to that of the professional class in provincial towns, we can hardly enter the least imposing farmhouse without finding a bad piano in the "drawing-room," and some old annuals, disposed with a symmetrical imitation of negligence, on the table; though the daughters may still drop their *h*'s, their vowels are studiously narrow; and it is only in very primitive regions that they will consent to sit in a covered vehicle without springs, which was once thought an advance in luxury on the pillion.

The condition of the tenant-farmers and small proprietors in Germany is, we imagine, about on a par, not, certainly, in material prosperity, but in mental culture and habits, with that of the English farmers who were beginning to be thought old-fashioned nearly fifty years ago; and if we add to these the farm-servants and labourers, we shall have a class approximating in its characteristics to the *Bauernthum*, or peasantry, described by Riehl.

In Germany, perhaps more than in any other country, it is among the peasantry that we must look for the historical type of the national physique. In the towns this type has become so modified to express the personality of the individual that even "family likeness" is often but faintly marked. But the peasants may still be distinguished into groups by their physical peculiarities. In one part of the country we find a longer-legged, in another a broader-shouldered race, which has inherited these peculiarities for centuries. For example, in certain districts of Hesse are seen long faces, with high foreheads, long straight noses, and small eyes with arched eyebrows and large eyelids. On comparing these physiognomies with the sculptures in the church of Saint Elizabeth, at Marburg, executed in the thirteenth century, it will be found that the same old Hessian type of face has subsisted unchanged, with this distinction only, that the sculptures represent princes and nobles, whose features then bore the stamp of their race, while that stamp is now to be found only among the peasants. A painter who wants to draw mediæval characters with historic truth must seek his models among the peasantry. This explains why the old German painters gave the heads of their subjects a greater uniformity of type than the painters of our day: the race had not attained to a high degree of individualization in features and expression. It indicates, too, that the cultured man acts more as an individual; the peasant, more as one of a group. Hans drives the plough, lives, and thinks just as Kunz does; and it is this fact, that many thousands of men are as like each other in thoughts and habits as so many sheep or oysters, which constitutes the weight of the peasantry in the social and political scale.

In the cultivated world each individual has his style of speaking and writing. But among the peasantry it is the race, the district, the province, that has its style—namely, its dialect, its phraseology, its proverbs, and its songs, which belong alike to the entire body of the people. This provincial style of the peasant is again like his physique, a remnant of history to which he clings with the utmost tenacity. In certain parts of Hungary there are still descendants of German colonists of the twelfth and thirteenth centuries, who go about the country as reapers, retaining their old Saxon songs and manners, while the more cultivated German emigrants in a very short time forget their own language, and speak Hungarian. Another remarkable case of the same kind is that of the Wends, a Sclavonic race settled in Lusatia, whose numbers amount to 200,000, living either scattered among the German population or in separate parishes. They have their own schools and churches, and are taught in the Sclavonic tongue. The Catholics among them are rigid adherents of the Pope; the Protestants not less rigid adherents of Luther, or *Doctor* Luther, as they are particular in calling him—a custom which, a hundred years ago, was universal in Protestant Germany. The Wend clings tenaciously to the usages of his Church, and perhaps this may contribute not a little to the purity in which he maintains the specific characteristics of his race. German education, German law and government, service in the standing army, and many other agencies, are in antagonism to his national exclusiveness; but the *wives* and *mothers* here, as elsewhere, are a conservative influence, and the habits temporarily laid aside in the outer world are recovered by the fireside. The Wends form several stout regiments in the Saxon army; they are sought far and wide, as diligent and honest servants; and many a weakly Dresden or Leipzig child becomes thriving under the care of a Wendish nurse. In their villages they have the air and habits of genuine, sturdy peasants, and all their customs indicate that they have been, from the first, an agricultural people. For example, they have traditional modes of treating their domestic animals. Each cow has its own name, generally chosen carefully, so as to express the special qualities of the animal; and all important family events are narrated to the *bees*—a custom which is found also in Westphalia. Whether by the help of the bees or not, the Wend farming is especially prosperous; and when a poor Bohemian peasant has a son born to him, he binds him to the end of a long pole and turns his face towards Lusatia, that he may be as lucky as the Wends who live there.

The peculiarity of the peasant's language consists chiefly in his retention of historical peculiarities, which gradually disappear under the friction of cultivated circles. He prefers any proper name that may be given to a day in the calendar, rather than the abstract date, by which he very rarely reckons. In the baptismal names of his children he is guided by the old custom of the country, not at all by whim and fancy. Many old baptismal names, formerly common in Germany, would have become extinct but for their preservation among the peasantry, especially in North Germany; and so firmly have they adhered to local tradition in this matter that it would be possible to give a sort of topographical statistics of proper names, and distinguish a district by its rustic names as we do by its Flora and Fauna. The continuous inheritance of certain favourite proper names in a family, in some districts forces the peasant to adopt the princely custom of attaching a numeral to the name, and saying, when three generations are living at once, Hans I, II, and III; or, in the more antique fashion, Hans the elder, the middle, and the younger. In some of our English counties there is a similar adherence to a narrow range of proper names; and as a mode of distinguishing collateral branches in the same family, you will hear of Jonathan's Bess, Thomas's Bess, and Samuel's Bess—the three Bessies being cousins.[17]

The peasant's adherence to the traditional has much greater inconvenience than that entailed by a paucity of proper names. In the Black Forest and in Hüttenberg you will see him in the dog-days wearing a thick fur cap, because it is an historical fur cap—a cap worn by his grandfather. In the Wetterau, that peasant-girl is considered the handsomest who wears the most petticoats. To go to field-labour in seven petticoats can be anything but convenient or agreeable, but it is the traditionally correct thing; and a German peasant-girl would think herself as unfavourably conspicuous in an untraditional costume as an English servant-girl would now think herself in a "linsey-woolsey" apron or a thick muslin cap. In many districts no medical advice would induce the rustic to renounce the tight leather belt with which he injures his digestive functions; you could more easily persuade him to smile on a new communal system than on the unhistorical invention of braces. In the eighteenth century, in spite of the philanthropic preachers of potatoes, the peasant for years threw his potatoes to the pigs and the dogs, before he could be persuaded to put them on his own table. However, the unwillingness of the peasant to adopt innovations has a not unreasonable foundation in the fact that for him experiments are practical, not theoretical, and must be made with expense of money instead of brains—a fact that is not, perhaps, sufficiently taken into account by agricultural theorists who complain of the farmer's obstinacy. The peasant has the smallest possible faith in theoretic knowledge; he thinks it rather dangerous than otherwise, as is well indicated by a Lower Rhenish proverb: "One is never too old to learn, said an old woman; so she learned to be a witch."

Between many villages an historical feud—once perhaps the occasion of much bloodshed—is still kept up under the milder form of an occasional round of cudgelling, and the launching of traditional nicknames. An historical feud of this kind still exists, for example, among many villages on the Rhine and more inland places in the neighbourhood. *Rheinschnacke* (of which the equivalent is perhaps "water-snake") is the standing term of ignomiy for the inhabitant of the Rhine village, who repays it in kind by the epithet "karst" (mattock) or "kukuk" (cuckoo), according as the object of his hereditary hatred belongs to the field or the forest. If any Romeo among the "mattocks" were to marry a Juliet among the "water-snakes," there would be no lack of Tybalts and Mercutios to carry the conflict from words to blows, though neither side knows a reason for the enmity.

A droll instance of peasant conservatism is told of a village on the Taunus, whose inhabitants from time immemorial had been famous for impromptu cudgelling. For this historical offence the magistrates of the district had always inflicted the equally historical punishment of shutting-up the most incorrigible offenders, not in prison, but in their own pig-sty. In recent times, however, the Government, wishing to correct the rudeness of these peasants, appointed an "enlightened" man as magistrate, who at once abolished the original penalty above-mentioned. But this relaxation of punishment was so far from being welcome to the villagers that they presented a petition praying that a more energetic man might be given them as a magistrate, who would have the courage to punish according to law and justice, "as had been beforetime." And the magistrate who abolished incarceration in the pig-sty could never obtain the respect of the neighbourhood. This happened no longer ago than the beginning of the present century.

But it must not be supposed that the historical piety of the German peasant extends to anything not immediately connected with himself. He has the warmest piety towards the old tumble-down house which his grandfather built, and which nothing will induce him to improve; but towards the venerable ruins of the old castle that overlooks his village he has no piety at all, and carries off its stones to make a fence for his garden, or tears down the Gothic carving of the old monastic church, which is "nothing to him," to mark off a footpath through his field. It is the same with historical traditions. The peasant has them fresh in his memory, so far as they relate to himself. In districts where the peasantry are unadulterated, you discern the remnants of the feudal relations in innumerable customs and phrases, but you will ask in vain for historical traditions concerning the Empire, or even concerning the particular princely house to which the peasant is subject. He can tell you what "half-people and whole people" mean; in Hesse you will still hear of "four horses making a whole peasant," or of "four-day and three-day peasants"; but you will ask in vain about Charlemagne and Frederic Barbarossa.

Riehl well observes that the feudal system, which made the peasant the bondman of his lord, was an immense benefit in a country the greater part of which had still to be colonized,—rescued the peasant from vagabondage, and laid the foundation of persistency and endurance in future generations. If a free German peasantry belongs only to modern times, it is to his ancestor who was a serf, and even, in the earliest times a slave, that the peasant owes the foundation of his independence,—namely, his capability of a settled existence,—nay, his unreasoning persistency, which has its important function in the development of the race.

Perhaps the very worst result of that unreasoning persistency is the peasant's inveterate habit of litigation. Every one remembers the immortal description of Dandie Dinmont's importunate application to Lawyer Pleydell to manage his "bit lawsuit," till at length Pleydell consents to help him ruin himself, on the ground that Dandie may fall into worse hands.[18] It seems, this is a scene which has many parallels in Germany. The farmer's lawsuit is his point of honour; and he will carry it through, though he knows from the very first day that he shall get nothing by it. The litigious peasant piques himself, like Mr. Saddletree, on his knowledge of the law, and this vanity is the chief impulse to many a lawsuit.[19] To the mind of the peasant, law presents itself as the "custom of the country," and it is his pride to be versed in all customs. *Custom with him holds the place of sentiment, of theory, and, in many cases, of affection.* Riehl justly urges the importance of simplifying law proceedings, so as to cut off this vanity at its source, and also of encouraging, by every possible means, the practice of arbitration.

The peasant never begins his lawsuit in summer, for the same reason that he does not make love and marry in summer,—because he has no time for that sort of thing. Anything is easier to him than to move out of his habitual course, and he is attached even to his privations. Some years ago, a peasant youth, out of the poorest and remotest region of the Westerwald, was enlisted as a recruit, at Weilburg in Nassau. The lad having never in his life slept in a bed, when he had to get into one for the first time began to cry like a child; and he deserted twice because he could not reconcile himself to sleeping in a bed, and to the "fine" life of the barracks: he was homesick at the thought of his accustomed poverty and his thatched hut. A strong contrast this with the feeling of the poor in towns, who would be far enough from deserting because their condition was too much improved! The genuine peasant is never ashamed of his rank and calling; he is rather inclined to look down on every one who does not wear a smock-frock, and thinks a man who has the manners of the gentry is likely to be rather windy and unsubstantial. In some places, even in French districts, this feeling is strongly symbolized by the practice of the peasantry, on certain festival days, to dress the images of the saints in peasants' clothing. History tells us of all kinds of peasant insurrections, the object of which was to obtain relief for the peasants from some of their many oppressions; but of an effort on their part to step out of their hereditary rank and calling, to become gentry, to leave the plough and carry on the easier business of capitalists or Government functionaries, there is no example.

The German novelists who undertake to give pictures of peasant life fall into the same mistake as our English novelists; they transfer their own feelings to ploughmen and woodcutters, and give them both joys and sorrows of which they know nothing. The peasant never questions the obligation of family ties,—he questions *no custom;*—but tender affection, as it exists amongst the refined part of mankind, is almost as foreign to him as white hands and filbert-shaped nails. That the aged father who has given up his property to his children on condition of their maintaining him for the remainder of his life is very far from meeting with delicate attentions is indicated by the proverb current among the peasantry—"Don't take your clothes off before you go to bed."[20] Among rustic moral tales and parables, not one is more universal than the story of the ungrateful children who made their grey-headed father, dependent on them for a maintenance, eat at a wooden trough because he shook the food out of his trembling hands. Then these same ungrateful children observed one day that their own little boy was making a tiny wooden trough; and when they asked him what it was for, he answered—that his father and mother might eat out of it, when he was a man and had to keep them.

Marriage is a very prudential affair, especially among the peasants who have the largest share of property. Politic marriages are as common among them as among princes; and when a peasant-heiress in Westphalia marries, her husband adopts her name, and places his own after it with the prefix *geboren* (*né*). The girls marry young, and the rapidity with which they get old and ugly is one among the many proofs that the early years of marriage are fuller of hardships than of conjugal tenderness. "When our writers of village stories," says Riehl, "transferred their own emotional life to the peasant, they obliterated what is precisely his most predominant characteristic—namely, that with him general custom holds the place of individual feeling."

We pay for greater emotional susceptibility too often by nervous diseases of which the peasant knows nothing. To him headache is the least of physical evils, because he thinks head-work the easiest and least indispensable of all labour. Happily, many of the younger sons in peasant families, by going to seek their living in the towns, carry their hardy nervous system to amalgamate with the overwrought nerves of our town population, and refresh them with a little rude vigour. And a return to the habits of peasant life is the best remedy for many moral as well as physical diseases induced by perverted civilization. Riehl points to colonization as presenting the true field for this regenerative process. On the other side of the ocean a man will have the courage to begin life again as a peasant, while at home, perhaps, opportunity as well as courage will fail him. Apropos of this subject of emigration, he remarks the striking fact that the native shrewdness and mother-wit of the German peasant seem to forsake him entirely when he has to apply them under new circumstances, and on relations foreign to his experience. Hence it is that the German peasant who emigrates, so constantly falls a victim to unprincipled adventurers in the preliminaries to emigration; but if once he gets his foot on the American soil, he exhibits all the first-rate qualities of an agricultural colonist; and among all German emigrants, the peasant class are the most successful.

But many disintegrating forces have been at work on the peasant character, and degeneration is unhappily going on at a greater pace than development. In the wine districts especially, the inability of the small proprietors to bear up under the vicissitudes of the market, or to ensure a high quality of wine by running the risks of a late vintage, and the competition of beer and cider with the inferior wines, have tended to produce that uncertainty of gain which, with the peasant, is the inevitable cause of demoralization. The small peasant proprietors are not a new class in Germany, but many of the evils of their position are new. They are more dependent on ready money than formerly: thus, where a peasant used to get his wood for building and firing from the common forest, he has now to pay for it with hard cash; he used to thatch his own house, with the help perhaps of a neighbour, but now he pays a man to do it for him; he used to pay taxes in kind, he now pays them in money. The chances of the market have to be discounted, and the peasant falls into the hands of money-lenders. Here is one of the cases in which social policy clashes with a purely economical policy.

Political vicissitudes have added their influence to that of economical changes in disturbing that dim instinct, that reverence for traditional custom, which is the peasant's principle of action. He is in the midst of novelties for which he knows no reason—changes in political geography, changes of the Government to which he owes fealty, changes in bureaucratic management and police regulations. He finds himself in a new element before an apparatus for breathing in it is developed in him. His only knowledge of modern history is in some of its results—for instance, that he has to pay heavier taxes from year to year. His chief idea of a government is of a power that raises his taxes, opposes his harmless customs, and torments him with new formalities. The source of all this is the false system of "enlightening" the peasant which has been adopted by the bureaucratic governments. A system which disregards the traditions and hereditary attachments of the peasant, and appeals only to a logical understanding which is not yet developed in him, is simply disintegrating and ruinous to the peasant character. The interference with the communal regulations has been of this fatal character. Instead of endeavouring to promote to the utmost the healthy life of the commune, as an organism the conditions of which are bound up with the historical characteristics of the peasant, the bureaucratic plan of government is bent on improvement by its patent machinery of state-appointed functionaries, and off-hand regulations in accordance with modern enlightenment. The spirit of communal exclusiveness— the resistance to the indiscriminate establishment of strangers—is an intense traditional feeling in the peasant. "This gallows is for us and our children" is the typical motto of this spirit. But such exclusiveness is highly irrational and repugnant to modern liberalism; therefore a bureaucratic government at once opposes it, and encourages to the utmost the introduction of new inhabitants in the provincial communes. Instead of allowing the peasants to manage their own affairs, and, if they happen to believe that five and four make eleven, to unlearn the prejudice by their own experience in calculation, so that they may gradually understand processes, and not merely see results, bureaucracy comes with its "Ready Reckoner"[21] and works all the peasant's sums for him—the surest way of maintaining him in his stupidity, however it may shake his prejudice.

Another questionable plan for elevating the peasant is the supposed elevation of the clerical character, by preventing the clergyman from cultivating more than a trifling part of the land attached to his benefice,—that he may be as much as possible of a scientific theologian, and as little as possible of a peasant. In this, Riehl observes, lies one great source of weakness to the Protestant Church as compared with the Catholic, which finds the great majority of its priests among the lower orders; and we have had the opportunity of making an analogous comparison in England, where many of us can remember country districts in which the great mass of the people were Christianized by illiterate Methodist and Independent ministers; while the influence of the parish clergyman among the poor did not extend much beyond a few old women in scarlet cloaks, and a few exceptional church-going labourers.

Bearing in mind the general characteristics of the German peasant, it is easy to understand his relation to the revolutionary ideas and revolutionary movements of modern times. The peasant in Germany, as elsewhere, is a born grumbler. He has always plenty of grievances in his pocket, but he does not generalize those grievances; he does not complain of "government" or "society," probably because he has good reason to complain of the burgomaster. When a few sparks from the first French Revolution fell among the German peasantry, and in certain villages of Saxony the country people assembled together to write down their demands, there was no glimpse in their petition of the "universal rights of man," but simply of their own particular affairs as Saxon peasants. Again, after the July Revolution of 1830, there were many insignificant peasant insurrections; but the object of almost all was the removal of local grievances. Toll-houses were pulled down; stamped paper was destroyed; in some places there was a persecution of wild boars, in others of that plentiful tame animal, the German *Rath*, or councillor who is never called into council. But in 1848 it seemed as if the movements of the peasants had taken a new character; in the small western states of Germany it seemed as if the whole class of peasantry was in insurrection. But, in fact, the peasant did not know the meaning of the part he was playing. He had heard that everything was being set right in the towns, and that wonderful things were happening there, so he tied up his bundle and set off. Without any distinct object or resolution, the country people presented themselves on the scene of commotion, and were warmly received by the party leaders. But, seen from the windows of ducal palaces and ministerial hotels, these swarms of peasants had quite another aspect, and it was imagined that they had a common plan of co-operation. This, however, the peasants had never had. Systematic co-operation implies general conceptions, and a provisional subordination of egoism, to which even the artisans of towns have rarely shown themselves equal, and which are as foreign to the mind of the peasant as logarithms or the doctrine of chemical proportions. And the revolutionary fervour of the peasant was soon cooled. The old mistrust of the towns was reawakened on the spot. The Tyrolese peasants saw no great good in the freedom of the press and the constitution, because these changes "seemed to please the gentry so much." Peasants who had given their voices stormily for a German parliament asked afterwards, with a doubtful look, whether it were to consist of infantry or cavalry. When royal domains were declared the property of the State, the peasants in some small principalities rejoiced over this, because they interpreted it to mean that every one would have his share in them, after the manner of the old common and forest rights.

The very practical views of the peasants, with regard to the demands of the people, were in amusing contrast with the abstract theorizing of the educated townsmen. The peasant continually withheld all State payments until he saw how matters would turn out, and was disposed to reckon up the solid benefit, in the form of land or money, that might come to him from the changes obtained. While the townsman was heating his brains about representation on the broadest basis, the peasant asked if the relation between tenant and landlord would continue as before, and whether the removal of the "feudal obligations" meant that the farmer should become owner of the land?

It is in the same naïve way that Communism is interpreted by the German peasantry. The wide spread among them of communistic doctrines, the eagerness with which they listened to a plan for the partition of property, seemed to countenance the notion that it was a delusion to suppose the peasant would be secured from this intoxication by his love of secure possession and peaceful earnings. But, in fact, the peasant contemplated "partition" by the light of an historical reminiscence rather than of novel theory. The golden age, in the imagination of the peasant, was the time when every member of the commune had a right to as much wood from the forest as would enable him to sell some, after using what he wanted in firing,—in which the communal possessions were so profitable that, instead of his having to pay rates at the end of the year, each member of the commune was [sic] something in pocket. Hence the peasants in general understood by "partition" that the State lands, especially the forests, would be divided among the communes, and that, by some political legerdemain or other, everybody would have free firewood, free grazing for his cattle, and, over and above that, a piece of gold without working for it. That he should give up a single clod of his own to further the general "partition" had never entered the mind of the peasant communist; and the perception that this was an essential preliminary to "partition" was often a sufficient cure for his Communism.

In villages lying in the neighborhood of large towns, however, where the circumstances of the peasantry are very different, quite another interpretation of Communism is prevalent. Here the peasant is generally sunk to the position of the proletaire, living from hand to mouth; he has nothing to lose, but everything to gain by "partition." The coarse nature of the peasant has here been corrupted into bestiality by the disturbance of his instincts, while he is as yet incapable of principles; and in this type of the degenerate peasant is seen the worst example of ignorance intoxicated by theory.

A significant hint as to the interpretation the peasants put on revolutionary theories may be drawn from the way they employed the few weeks in which their movements were unchecked. They felled the forest trees and shot the game; they withheld taxes; they shook off the imaginary or real burdens imposed on them by their mediatized princes, by presenting their "demands" in a very rough way before the ducal or princely "Schloss"; they set their faces against the bureaucratic management of the communes, deposed the Government functionaries who had been placed over them as burgomasters and magistrates, and abolished the whole bureaucratic system of procedure, simply by taking no notice of its regulations, and recurring to some tradition—some old order or disorder of things. In all this it is clear that they were animated not in the least by the spirit of modern revolution, but by a purely narrow and personal impulse towards reaction.

The idea of constitutional government lies quite beyond the range of the German peasant's conceptions. His only notion of representation is that of a representation of ranks—of classes; his only notion of a deputy is of one who takes care, not of the national welfare, but of the interests in his own order. Herein lay the great mistake of the democratic party, in common with the bureaucratic Governments, that they entirely omitted the peculiar character of the peasant from their political calculations. They talked of the "people," and forgot that the peasants were included in the term. Only a baseless misconception of the peasant's character could induce the supposition that he would feel the slightest enthusiasm about the principles involved in the reconstitution of the Empire, or even about that reconstitution itself. He has no zeal for a written law, as such, but only so far as it takes the form of a living law—a tradition. It was the external authority which the revolutionary party had won in Baden that attracted the peasants into a participation in the struggle.

Such, Riehl tells us, are the general characteristics of the German peasantry—characteristics which subsist amidst a wide variety of circumstances. In Mecklenburg, Pomerania, and Brandenburg, the peasant lives on extensive estates; in Westphalia he lives in large isolated homesteads; in the Westerwald and in Sauerland, in little groups of villages and hamlets; on the Rhine, land is for the most part parcelled out among small proprietors, who live together in large villages. Then, of course, the diversified physical geography of Germany gives rise to equally diversified methods of land-culture; and out of these various circumstances grow numerous specific differences in manner and character. But the generic character of the German peasant is everywhere the same: in the clean mountain-hamlet and in the dirty fishing-village on the coast; in the plains of North Germany and in the backwoods of America. "Everywhere he has the same historical character—everywhere custom is his supreme law. Where religion and patriotism are still a naïve instinct—are still a sacred *custom*—there begins the class of the German Peasantry."

*   *   *

Our readers will perhaps already have gathered from the foregoing portrait of the German peasant that Riehl is not a man who looks at objects through the spectacles either of the doctrinaire or the dreamer; and they will be ready to believe what he tells us in his Preface— namely, that years ago he began his wanderings over the hills and plains of Germany for the sake of obtaining, in immediate intercourse with the people, that completion of his historical, political, and economical studies which he was unable to find in books. He began his investigations with no party prepossessions, and his present views were evolved entirely from his own gradually amassed observations. He was, first of all, a pedestrian, and only in the second place a political author. The views at which he has arrived by this inductive process, he sums up in the term—*social-political-conservatism*; but his conservatism is, we conceive, of a thoroughly philosophical kind. He sees in European society *incarnate history*, and any attempt to disengage it from its historical elements must, he believes, be simply destructive of social vitality.[22] What has grown up historically can only die out historically, by the gradual operation of necessary laws. The external conditions which society has inherited from the past are but the manifestation of inherited internal conditions in the human beings who compose it; the internal conditions and the external are related to each other as the organism and its medium, and development can take place only by the gradual consentaneous development of both. Take the familiar example of attempts to abolish titles, which have been about as effective as the process of cutting off poppyheads in a corn-field. *"Jedem Menschen,"* says Riehl, *"ist sein Zopf angeboren, warum soll denn der sociale Sprachgebrauch nicht auch seinen Zopf haben?"*— which we may render—"As long as snobbism runs in the blood, why should it not run in our speech?" As a necessary preliminary to a purely rational society, you must obtain purely rational men, free from the sweet and bitter prejudices of hereditary affection and antipathy; which is as easy as to get running streams without springs, or the leafy shade of the forest without the secular growth of trunk and branch.

The historical conditions of society may be compared with those of language. It must be admitted that the language of cultivated nations is in anything but a rational state; the great sections of the civilized world are only approximatively intelligible to each other, and even that, only at the cost of long study; one word stands for many things, and many words for one thing; the subtle shades of meaning, and still subtler echoes of association, make language an instrument which scarcely anything short of genius can wield with definiteness and certainty. Suppose, then, that the effort which has been again and again made to construct a universal language on a rational basis has at length succeeded, and that you have a language which has no uncertainty, no whims of idiom, no cumbrous forms, no fitful shimmer of many-hued significance, no hoary archaisms "familiar with forgotten years"[23]—a patent deodorized and non-resonant language, which effects the purpose of communication as perfectly and rapidly as algebraic signs. Your language may be a perfect medium of expression to science, but will never express *life*, which is a great deal more than science. With the anomalies and inconveniences of historical language, you will have parted with its music and its passion, with its vital qualities as an expression of individual character, with its subtle capabilities of wit, with everything that gives it power over the imagination; and the next step in simplification will be the invention of a talking watch, which will achieve the utmost facility and dispatch in the communication of ideas by a graduated adjustment of ticks, to be represented in writing by a corresponding arrangement of dots. A melancholy "language of the future"! The sensory and motor nerves that run in the same sheath are scarcely bound together by a more necessary and delicate union than that which binds men's affections, imagination, wit, and humour, with the subtle ramifications of historical language. Language must be left to grow in precision, completeness, and unity, as minds grow in clearness, comprehensiveness, and sympathy. And there is an analogous relation between the moral tendencies of men and the social conditions they have inherited. The nature of European men has its roots intertwined with the past, and can only be developed by allowing those roots to remain undisturbed while the process of development is going on, until that perfect ripeness of the seed which carries with it a life independent of the root.[24] This vital connection with the past is much more vividly felt on the Continent than in England, where we have to recall it by an effort of memory and reflection; for though our English life is in its core intensely traditional, Protestantism and commerce have modernized the face of the land and the aspects of society in a far greater degree than in any Continental country: "Abroad," says Ruskin, "a building of the eighth or tenth century stands ruinous in the open street; the children play around it, the peasants heap their corn in it, the buildings of yesterday nestle about it, and fit their new stones in its rents, and tremble in sympathy as it trembles. No one wonders at it, or thinks of it as separate, and of another time; we feel the ancient world to be a real thing, and one with the new; antiquity is no dream; it is rather the children playing about the old stones that are the dream. But all is continuous, and the words, 'from generation to generation,' understandable here."[25] This conception of European society, as incarnate history, is the fundamental idea of Riehl's books.

After the notable failure of revolutionary attempts conducted from the point of view of abstract democratic and socialistic theories, after the practical demonstration of the evils resulting from a bureaucratic system which governs by an undiscriminating, dead mechanism, Riehl wishes to urge on the consideration of his countrymen a social policy founded on the special study of the people as they are—on the natural history of the various social ranks. He thinks it wise to pause a little from theorizing, and see what is the material actually present for theory to work upon. It is the glory of the Socialists—in contrast with the democratic doctrinaires who have been too much occupied with the general idea of "the people" to inquire particularly into the actual life of the people—that they have thrown themselves with enthusiastic zeal into the study at least of one social group—namely, the factory operatives; and here lies the secret of their partial success. But, unfortunately, they have made this special study of a single fragment of society the basis of a theory which quietly substitutes for the small group of Parisian proletaires or English factory-workers, the society of all Europe—nay, of the whole world. And in this way they have lost the best fruit of their investigations. For, says Riehl, the more deeply we penetrate into the knowledge of society in its details, the more thoroughly we shall be convinced that *a universal social policy has no validity except on paper*, and can never be carried into successful practice. The conditions of German society are altogether different from those of French, of English, or of Italian society; and to apply the same social theory to these nations indiscriminately is about as wise a procedure as Triptolemus Yellowley's application of the agricultural directions in Virgil's "Georgics" to his farm in the Shetland Isles.[26]

It is the clear and strong light in which Riehl places this important position that in our opinion constitutes the suggestive value of his books for foreign as well as German readers. It has not been sufficiently insisted on that in the various branches of Social Science there is an advance from the general to the special, from the simple to the complex, analogous with that which is found in the series of the sciences, from Mathematics to Biology.[27] To the laws of quantity comprised in Mathematics and Physics are superadded, in Chemistry, laws of quality; to these again are added, in Biology, laws of life; and lastly, the conditions of life in general branch out into its special conditions, or Natural History, on the one hand, and into its abnormal conditions, or Pathology, on the other. And in this series or ramification of the sciences, the more general science will not suffice to solve the problems of the more special. Chemistry embraces phenomena which are not explicable by Physics; Biology embraces phenomena which are not explicable by Chemistry; and no biological generalization will enable us to predict the infinite specialities produced by the complexity of vital conditions. So Social Science, while it has departments which in their fundamental generality correspond to mathematics and physics—namely, those grand and simple generalizations which trace out the inevitable march of the human race as a whole, and, as a ramification of these, the laws of economical science—has also, in the departments of government and jurisprudence, which embrace the conditions of social life in all their complexity, what may be called its Biology, carrying us on to innumerable special phenomena which outlie the sphere of science, and belong to Natural History. And just as the most thorough acquaintance with physics, or chemistry, or general physiology will not enable you at once to establish the balance of life in your private vivarium, so that your particular society of zoöphytes, molluscs, and echinoderms may feel themselves, as the Germans say, at ease in their skin; so the most complete equipment of theory will not enable a statesman or a political and social reformer to adjust his measures wisely, in the absence of a special acquaintance with the section of society for which he legislates, with the peculiar characteristics of the nation, the province, the class whose well-being he has to consult. In other words, a wise social policy must be based not simply on abstract social science, but on the Natural History of social bodies.

Riehl's books are not dedicated merely to the argumentative maintenance of this or of any other position; they are intended chiefly as a contribution to that knowledge of the German people on the importance of which he insists. He is less occupied with urging his own conclusions than with impressing on his readers the facts which have led him to those conclusions. In the volume entitled "Land und Leute," which, though published last, is properly an introduction to the volume entitled "Die Bürgerliche Gesellschaft," he considers the German people in their physical-geographical relations; he compares the natural divisions of the race, as determined by land and climate, and social traditions, with the artificial divisions which are based on diplomacy; and he traces the genesis and influences of what we may call the ecclesiastical geography of Germany—its partition between Catholicism and Protestantism. He shows that the ordinary antithesis of North and South Germany represents no real ethnographical distinction, and that the natural divisions of Germany, founded on its physical geography, are threefold—namely, the low plains, the middle mountain region, and the high mountain region, or Lower, Middle, and Upper Germany; and on this primary natural division all the other broad ethnographical distinctions of Germany will be found to rest. The plains of North or Lower Germany include all the seaboard the nation possesses; and this, together with the fact that they are traversed to the depth of six hundred miles by navigable rivers, makes them the natural seat of a trading race. Quite different is the geographical character of Middle Germany. While the northern plains are marked off into great divisions, by such rivers as the Lower Rhine, the Weser, and the Oder, running almost in parallel lines, this central region is cut up like a mosaic by the capricious lines of valleys and rivers. Here is the region in which you find those famous roofs from which the rain-water runs towards two different seas, and the mountain-tops from which you may look into eight or ten German States. The abundance of water-power and the presence of extensive coal-mines allow of a very diversified industrial development in Middle Germany. In Upper Germany, or the high mountain region, we find the same symmetry in the lines of the rivers as in the north; almost all the great Alpine streams flow parallel with the Danube. But the majority of these rivers are neither navigable nor available for industrial objects, and instead of serving for communication, they shut off one great tract from another. The slow development, the simple peasant-life of many districts, is here determined by the mountain and the river. In the southeast, however, industrial activity spreads through Bohemia towards Austria, and forms a sort of balance to the industrial districts of the Lower Rhine. Of course, the boundaries of these three regions cannot be very strictly defined; but an approximation to the limits of Middle Germany may be obtained by regarding it as a triangle, of which one angle lies in Silesia, another in Aix-la-Chapelle, and a third at Lake Constance.

This triple division corresponds with the broad distinctions of climate. In the northern plains the atmosphere is damp and heavy; in the southern mountain region it is dry and rare, and there are abrupt changes of temperature, sharp contrasts between the seasons, and devastating storms; but in both these zones men are hardened by conflict with the roughnesses of the climate. In Middle Germany, on the contrary, there is little of this struggle; the seasons are more equable, and the mild, soft air of the valleys tends to make the inhabitants luxurious and sensitive to hardships. It is only in exceptional mountain districts that one is here reminded of the rough, bracing air on the heights of Southern Germany. It is a curious fact that, as the air becomes gradually lighter and rarer from the North German coast towards Upper Germany, the average of suicides regularly decreases. Mecklenburg has the highest number, then Prussia, while the fewest suicides occur in Bavaria and Austria.

Both the northern and southern regions have still a large extent of waste lands, downs, morasses, and heaths; and to these are added, in the south, abundance of snow-fields and naked rock; while in Middle Germany culture has almost overspread the face of the land, and there are no large tracts of waste. There is the same proportion in the distribution of forests. Again, in the north we see a monotonous continuity of wheat-fields, potato-grounds, meadow-lands, and vast heaths; and there is the same uniformity of culture over large surfaces in the southern table-lands and the Alpine pastures. In Middle Germany, on the contrary, there is a perpetual variety of crops within a short space; the diversity of land surface, and the corresponding variety in the species of plants, are an invitation to the splitting up of estates, and this again encourages to the utmost the motley character of the cultivation.

According to this threefold division, it appears that there are certain features common to North and South Germany in which they differ from Central Germany, and the nature of this difference Riehl indicates by distinguishing the former as *Centralized Land* and the latter as *Individualized Land*—a distinction which is well symbolized by the fact that North and South Germany possess the great lines of railway which are the medium for the traffic of the world, while Middle Germany is far richer in lines for local communication, and possesses the greatest length of railway within the smallest space. Disregarding superficialities, the East Frieslanders, the Schleswig-Holsteiners, the Mecklenburgers, and the Pomeranians are much more nearly allied to the old Bavarians, the Tyrolese, and the Styrians, than any of these are allied to the Saxons, the Thuringians, or the Rhinelanders. Both in North and South Germany original races are still found in large masses, and popular dialects are spoken; you still find there thoroughly peasant districts, thorough villages, and also, at great intervals, thorough cities; you still find there a sense of rank. In Middle Germany, on the contrary, the original races are fused together or sprinkled hither and thither; the peculiarities of the popular dialects are worn down or confused; there is no very strict line of demarcation between the country and the town population, hundreds of small towns and large villages being hardly distinguishable in their characteristics; and the sense of rank, as part of the organic structure of society, is almost extinguished. Again, both in the north and south there is still a strong ecclesiastical spirit in the people, and the Pomeranian sees Antichrist in the Pope as clearly as the Tyrolese sees him in Doctor Luther; while in Middle Germany the confessions are mingled—they exist peaceably side by side in very narrow space, and tolerance or indifference has spread itself widely even in the popular mind. And the analogy, or rather the causal relation, between the physical geography of the three regions and the development of the population goes still further:—

"For," observes Riehl, "the striking connection which has been pointed out between the local geological formations in Germany and the revolutionary disposition of the people, has more than a metaphorical significance. Where the primeval physical revolutions of the globe have been the wildest in their effects, and the most multiform strata have been tossed together or thrown one upon the other, it is a very intelligible consequence that on a land surface thus broken up, the population should sooner develop itself into small communities, and that the more intense life generated in these smaller communities should become the most favourable nidus for the reception of modern culture, and with this a susceptibility for its revolutionary ideas; while a people settled in a region where its groups are spread over a large space will persist much more obstinately in the retention of its original character. The people of Middle Germany have none of that exclusive one-sidedness which determines the peculiar genius of great national groups, just as this one-sidedness or uniformity is wanting to the geological and geographical character of their land."

This ethnographical outline Riehl fills up with special and typical descriptions, and then makes it the starting-point for a criticism of the actual political condition of Germany. The volume is full of vivid pictures, as well as penetrating glances into the maladies and tendencies of modern society. It would be fascinating as literature, if it were not important for its facts and philosophy. But we can only commend it to our readers, and pass on to the volume entitled "Die Bürgerliche Gesellschaft," from which we have drawn our sketch of the German peasantry. Here Riehl gives us a series of studies in that natural history of the people, which he regards as the proper basis of social policy. He holds that, in European society, there are *three natural ranks or estates:* the hereditary landed aristocracy, the citizens or commercial class, and the peasantry or agricultural class. By *natural ranks* he means ranks which have their roots deep in the historical structure of society, and are still, in the present, showing vitality above ground; he means those great social groups which are not only distinguished externally by their vocation, but essentially by their mental character, their habits, their mode of life,—by the principle they represent in the historical development of society. In his conception of the "Fourth Estate" he differs from the usual interpretation, according to which it is simply equivalent to the proletariat, or those who are dependent on daily wages, whose only capital is their skill or bodily strength—factory operatives, artisans, agricultural labourers, to whom might be added, especially in Germany, the day-labourers with the quill, the literary proletariat. This, Riehl observes, is a valid basis of economical classification, but not of social classification. In his view, the Fourth Estate is a stratum produced by the perpetual abrasion of the other great social groups; it is the sign and result of the decomposition which is commencing in the organic constitution of society. Its elements are derived alike from the aristocracy, the bourgeoisie, and the peasantry. It assembles under its banner the deserters of historical society, and forms them into a terrible army, which is only just awaking to the consciousness of its corporate power. The tendency of this Fourth Estate, by the very process of its formation, is to do away with the distinctive historical character of the other estates, and to resolve their peculiar rank and vocation into a uniform social relation founded on an abstract conception of society. According to Riehl's classification, the day-labourers, whom the political economist designates as the Fourth Estate, belong partly to the peasantry or agricultural class, and partly to the citizens or commercial class.

Riehl considers, in the first place, the peasantry and aristocracy as the "Forces of social persistence," and, in the second, the bourgeoisie and the "fourth estate" as the "Forces of social movement."

The aristocracy, he observes, is the only one among these four groups which is denied by others besides Socialists to have any natural basis as a separate rank. It is admitted that there was once an aristocracy which had an intrinsic ground of existence; but now, it is alleged, this is an historical fossil, an antiquarian relic, venerable because grey with age. In what, it is asked, can consist the peculiar vocation of the aristocracy, since it has no longer the monopoly of the land, of the higher military functions, and of Government offices, and since the service of the Court has no longer any political importance? To this Riehl replies that in great revolutionary crises, the "men of progress" have more than once "abolished" the aristocracy. But remarkably enough, the aristocracy has always reappeared. This measure of abolition showed that the nobility were no longer regarded as a real class, for to abolish a real class would be an absurdity. It is quite possible to contemplate a voluntary breaking-up of the peasant or citizen class in the socialistic sense, but no man in his senses would think of straightway "abolishing" citizens and peasants. The aristocracy, then, was regarded as a sort of cancer, or excrescence of society. Nevertheless, not only has it been found impossible to annihilate an hereditary nobility by decree; but also, the aristocracy of the eighteenth century outlived even the self-destructive acts of its own perversity. A life which was entirely without object, entirely destitute of functions, would not, says Riehl, be so persistent. He has an acute criticism of those who conduct a polemic against the idea of an hereditary aristocracy while they are proposing an "aristocracy of talent," which after all is based on the principle of inheritance. The Socialists are, therefore, only consistent in declaring against an aristocracy of talent. "But when they have turned the world into a great Foundling Hospital, they will still be unable to eradicate the 'privileges of birth.'" We must not follow him in his criticism, however; nor can we afford to do more than mention hastily his interesting sketch of the mediæval aristocracy, and his admonition to the German aristocracy of the present day, that the vitality of their class is not to be sustained by romantic attempts to revive mediæval forms and sentiments, but only by the exercise of functions as real and salutary for actual society as those of the mediæval aristocracy were for the feudal age. "In modern society the divisions of rank indicate *division of labour*, according to that distribution of functions in the social organism which the historical constitution of society has determined. In this way the principle of differentiation and the principle of unity are identical."

The elaborate study of the German bourgeoisie which forms the next division of the volume must be passed over; but we may pause a moment to note Riehl's definition of the social *Philister* (Philistine), an epithet for which we have no equivalent—not at all, however, for want of the object it represents.[28] Most people who read a little German know that the epithet *Philister* originated in the *Burschen-Leben*, or student-life of Germany and that the antithesis of *Bursch* and *Philister* was equivalent to the antithesis of "gown" and "town"; but since the word has passed into ordinary language, it has assumed several shades of significance which have not yet been merged in a single absolute meaning; and one of the questions which an English visitor in Germany will probably take an opportunity of asking is, "What is the strict meaning of the word *Philister?*" Riehl's answer is that the *Philister* is one who is indifferent to all social interests, all public life, as distinguished from selfish and private interests; he has no sympathy with political and social events except as they affect his own comfort and prosperity, as they offer him material for amusement or opportunity for gratifying his vanity. He has no social or political creed, but is always of the opinion which is most convenient for the moment. He is always in the majority, and is the main element of unreason and stupidity in the judgement of a "discerning public." It seems presumptuous in us to dispute Riehl's interpretation of a German word, but we must think that, in literature, the epithet *Philister* has usually a wider meaning than this—includes his definition and something more. We imagine the *Philister* is the personification of the spirit which judges everything from a lower point of view than the subject demands—which judges the affairs of the parish from the egotistic or purely personal point of view—which judges the affairs of the nation from the parochial point of view, and does not hesitate to measure the merits of the universe from the human point of view. At least, this must surely be the spirit to which Goethe alludes in a passage cited by Riehl himself, where he says that the Germans need not be ashamed of erecting a monument to him as well as to Blücher; for if Blücher had freed them from the French, he (Goethe) had freed them from the nets of the *Philister:* —

> "Ihr mögt mir immer ungescheut
> Gleich Blüchern Denkmal setzen!
> Von Franzosen hat er euch befreit,
> Ich von Philister-netzen."[29]

Goethe could hardly claim to be the apostle of public spirit; but he is eminently the man who helps us to rise to a lofty point of observation, so that we may see things in their relative proportions.

The most interesting chapters in the description of the "Fourth Estate," which concludes the volume, are those on the "Aristocratic Proletariat" and the "Intellectual Proletariat." The Fourth Estate in Germany, says Riehl, has its centre of gravity not, as in England and France, in the day-labourers and factory operatives, and still less in the degenerate peasantry. In Germany, the *educated* proletariat is the leaven that sets the mass in fermentation; the dangerous classes there go about, not in blouses, but in frock-coats; they begin with the impoverished prince and end in the hungriest *littérateur*. The custom that all the sons of a nobleman shall inherit their father's title necessarily goes on multiplying that class of aristocrats who are not only without function but without adequate provision, and who shrink from entering the ranks of the citizens by adopting some honest calling. The younger son of a prince, says Riehl, is usually obliged to remain without any vocation; and however zealously he may study music, painting, literature, or science, he can never be a regular musician, painter, or man of science; his pursuit will be called a "passion," not a "calling," and to the end of his days he remains a dilettante. "But the ardent pursuit of a fixed practical calling can alone satisfy the active man." Direct legislation cannot remedy this evil. The inheritance of titles by younger sons is the universal custom, and custom is stronger than law. But if all Government preference for the "aristocratic proletariat" were withdrawn, the sensible men among them would prefer emigration, or the pursuit of some profession, to the hungry distinction of a title without rents.

The intellectual proletaires Riehl calls the "church militant" of the Fourth Estate in Germany. In no other country are they so numerous; in no other country is the trade in material and industrial capital so far exceeded by the wholesale and retail trade, the traffic and the usury, in the intellectual capital of the nation. *Germany yields more intellectual produce than it can use and pay for.*

"This overproduction, which is not transient but permanent, nay, is constantly on the increase, evidences a diseased state of the national industry, a perverted application of industrial powers, and is a far more pungent satire on the national condition than all the poverty of operatives and peasants. . . . Other nations need not envy us the preponderance of the intellectual proletariat over the proletaires of manual labour. For man more easily becomes diseased from over-study than from the labour of the hands; and it is precisely in the intellectual proletariat that there are the most dangerous seeds of disease. This is the group in which the opposition between earnings and wants, between the ideal social position and the real, is the most hopelessly irreconcileable."

We must unwillingly leave our readers to make acquaintance for themselves with the graphic details with which Riehl follows up this general statement; but before quitting these admirable volumes, let us say, lest our inevitable omissions should have left room for a different conclusion, that Riehl's conservatism is not in the least tinged with the partisanship of a class, with a poetic fanaticism for the past, or with the prejudice of a mind incapable of discerning the grander evolution of things to which all social forms are but temporarily subservient. It is the conservatism of a clear-eyed, practical, but withal large-minded man—a little caustic, perhaps, now and then in his epigrams on democratic doctrinaires who have their nostrum for all political and social diseases, and on communistic theories which he regards as "the despair of the individual in his own manhood, reduced to a system," but nevertheless able and willing to do justice to the elements of fact and reason in every shade of opinion and every form of effort. He is as far as possible from the folly of supposing that the sun will go backward on the dial, because we put the hands of our clock backward; he only contends against the opposite folly of decreeing that it shall be midday, while in fact the sun is only just touching the mountain-tops, and all along the valley men are stumbling in the twilight.

Notes

1. A monthly railway guide issued by George Bradshaw.
2. David Teniers the Younger (1610–90). Flemish painter of scenes of peasant life. Bartolomé Estéban Murillo (1617–82). Spanish painter of religious scenes.
3. Painting exhibited in 1852 by William Holman Hunt (1827–1910), a Pre-Raphaelite painter whose style of symbolism matched Ruskin's aesthetic views.
4. Letitia Elizabeth Landon (1802–38). Sentimental poet admired by Rosamond in *Middlemarch* (Ch. 27), to the amusement of the more sophisticated Lydgate.
5. Principal tenor singer (by analogy with prima donna).
6. "Keepsake" style: the insipid prettiness of the verse, prose, and illustrations. of literary annuals popular in the early nineteenth century.
7. In *Adam Bede* (Ch. 53), Ben Tholoway is "detected more than once in carrying away his master's corn in his pockets."
8. Mr. Ruskin's indignation: See *Modern Painters* (1856), Vol. IV, Part V, Ch. 19, Section 6.
9. Scott: The Mucklebackit family's cottage appears in Ch. 31 of *The Antiquary* (1816). "The Two Drovers" is part of the First Series of *Chronicles of the Canongate* (1826). "Poor Susan": Wordsworth's "The Reverie of Poor Susan" (1797, revised 1800). Alton Locke: Charles Kingsley's *Alton Locke, Tailor and Poet* (1850), Ch. 11. Locke refuses to give the "picturesque" portrait required by the "rules of modern art." Chimney-sweepers: "The Little Chimney-Sweep" by Joseph Hornung (1792–1870), Swiss painter.
10. A character in Dickens's *Little Dorrit* (published in parts from December 1855–July 1857).
11. Name for hotel servant in charge of cleaning shoes and boots. Probably Cobbs, of the story "The Boots," which Dickens contributed to the extra Christmas number of *Household Words* entitled "The Holly-Tree Inn" (1855).
12. Eugène Sue (1804–57) wrote melodramatic romances of underground Parisian life, notably *Les Mystères de Paris* (1842–43),which influenced Victor Hugo's *Les Misérables*.
13. *altruism*: neologism devised by Auguste Comte to denote exclusive regard for others (as opposed to self) as a principle of action, and first used in English in Lewes's book *Comte's Philosophy of the Sciences* (1853).
14. Allusion to Jeremy Bentham's "felicific calculus," a utilitarian belief George Eliot mocks as an "inherent imbecility of feeling" ("Janet's Repentance," Ch. 22).
15. Allusion to the "Young England" movement inaugurated by Benjamin Disraeli's *Coningsby* (1844).

16. *Die Bürgerliche Gesellschaft.* Von W.H. Riehl. Dritte Auflage, 1855.
Land und Leute. Von W. H. Riehl. Dritte Auflage, 1856. [Eliot's note]

17. The three Bessies being cousins: as with Chad's Bess and Timothy's Bess in *Adam Bede*.

18. Dandie Dinmont is a character in Scott's *Guy Mannering, or the Astrologer* (1815), Ch. 38.

19. Bartoline Saddletree is a character in Scott's *The Heart of Midlothian* (1818).

20. This proverb is common among the English farmers also. [Eliot's note]

21. A collection of arithmetic tables showing the result of common business and household calculations.

22. Throughout this article, in our statement of Riehl's opinions, we must be understood not as quoting Riehl, but as interpreting and illustrating him. [Eliot's note]

23. A line from William Wordsworth's *The Excursion* (1814), I, 276.

24. In this paragraph and the preceding one, Eliot summarizes Riehl's view of history as an organic development in which everything—notably society and language—can be seen to follow natural laws of growth.

25. John Ruskin. *Modern Painters*, IV (1856), Part V, Ch. 1, Section 5.

26. Triptolemus Yellowley's application: Walter Scott's *The Pirate* (1822), Ch. 4.

27. Comte develops this positivist model of the sciences in *Cours de philosophie positive* (1830–42).

28. *Philister*: Eliot's extension of Riehl's term (which he interprets as political apathy) to mean "the personification of the spirit which judges everything from a lower point of view than the subject demands" anticipates Matthew Arnold's use of the term "Philistinism" in his essay "Heinrich Heine" (1863).

29. Pinney notes that this passage is slightly misquoted from Number 112 of Goethe's *Sprüche* (*Hamburger Ausgabe*, I, 322). Ashton says the date is approximately 1832. Byatt translates the passage as follows: "You may, without shame, still put up a monument to me, / Similar to Blucher's! / He freed you from the French, / I from the nets of the Philistines."

10. The Modern Hep! Hep! Hep![1]

Introduction

First published in 1879 by Blackwood, *Impressions of Theophrastus Such* has been republished in editions of George Eliot's works. The text here is taken from an 1889 edition, *Romola and Theophrastus Such*, published in Chicago by Belford, Clarke & Co. A scholarly edition, edited by Nancy Henry, has now been published by the University of Iowa Press (1995).

In the final essay of this final book, Eliot condemns negative stereotypes regarding Jews and also considers the general issue of history and national identity. In acknowledging the fears of many British citizens that Jews have conquered in both commerce and politics, Eliot maintains that the proposed "cure" of restricting immigration for Jews and other foreigners may be worse than what she admits to be a disease—the "threatened danger" or "affliction" of foreign contamination of the language and political and social life. In support of her analysis, Eliot invokes contemporary historians who emphasize ancestry, and, by implication, she also invokes the eighteenth-century German historian Johann Gottfried von Herder, as well as Samuel Taylor Coleridge and John Stuart Mill. She also, without naming them, contradicts David Friedrich Strauss (whose *Das Leben Jesu* she had translated, and who published articles blaming Jewish victims for inciting persecution through their financial chicanery), and Wilhelm von Riehl (whose books on German social history she had reviewed enthusiastically while omitting any reference to his attacks on the German Jews as "the Cossacks of modern civilization").

Impressions of Theophrastus Such appears to have been in part a response to the fashion of the character book; in 1870, R.C. Jebb had published a revised translation, with notes, entitled *The Characters of Theophrastus*. "The Modern Hep! Hep! Hep!" shares with earlier pieces such common themes as the relation between the individual and the group, the presence of the past in the present, and the tolerance of diversity.

The Modern Hep! Hep! Hep!

To discern likeness amidst diversity, it is well known, does not require so fine a mental edge as the discerning of diversity amidst general sameness. The primary rough classification depends on the prominent resemblances of things: the progress is toward finer and finer discrimination according to minute differences.

Yet even at this stage of European culture one's attention is continually drawn to the prevalence of that grosser mental sloth which makes people dull to the most ordinary prompting of comparison—the bringing things together because of their likeness. The same motives, the same ideas, the same practices, are alternately admired and abhorred, lauded and denounced, according to their association with superficial differences, historical or actually social: even learned writers treating of great subjects often show an attitude of mind not greatly superior in its logic to that of the frivolous fine lady who is indignant at the frivolity of her maid.

To take only the subject of the Jews: it would be difficult to find a form of bad reasoning about them which has not been heard in conversation or been admitted to the dignity of print; but the neglect of resemblances is a common property of dullness which unites all the various points of view—the prejudiced, the puerile, the spiteful, and the abysmally ignorant.

That the preservation of national memories is an element and a means of national greatness, that their revival is a sign of reviving nationality, that every heroic defender, every patriotic restorer, has been inspired by such memories and has made them his watchword, that even such a corporate existence as that of a Roman legion or an English regiment has been made valorous by memorial standards,—these are the glorious commonplaces of historic teaching at our public schools and universities, being happily ingrained in Greek and Latin classics. They have also been impressed on the world by conspicuous modern instances. That there is a free modern Greece is due—through all infiltration of other than Greek blood—to the presence of ancient Greece in the consciousness of European men; and every speaker would feel his point safe if he were to praise Byron's devotion to a cause made glorious by ideal identification with the past;[2] hardly so, if he were to insist that the Greeks were not to be helped further because their history shows that they were anciently unsurpassed in treachery and lying, and that many modern Greeks are highly disreputable characters, while others are disposed to grasp too large a share of our commerce. The same with Italy: the pathos of his country's lot pierced the youthful soul of Mazzini, because, like Dante's, his blood was fraught with the kinship of Italian greatness, his imagination filled with a majestic past that wrought itself into a majestic future.[3] Half a century ago, what was Italy? An idling-place of dilettanteism or of itinerant motiveless wealth, a territory parceled out for papal sustenance, dynastic convenience, and the profit of an alien government. What were the Italians? No people, no voice in European counsels, no massive power in European affairs: a race thought of in English and French society as chiefly adapted to the operatic stage, or to serve as models for painters; disposed to smile gratefully at the reception of halfpence; and by the more historical remembered to be rather polite than truthful, in all probability a combination of Machiavelli, Rubini, and Masaniello.[4] Thanks chiefly to the divine gift of a memory which inspires the moments with a past, a present, and a future, and gives the sense of corporate existence that raises man above the otherwise more respectable and innocent brute, all that, or most of it, is changed.

Again, one of our living historians[5] finds just sympathy in his vigorous insistence on our true ancestry, on our being the strongly marked heritors in language and genius of those old English seamen who, beholding a rich country with a most convenient seaboard, came doubtless with a sense of divine warrant, and settled themselves on this or the other side of fertilizing streams, gradually conquering more and more of the pleasant land from the natives who knew nothing of Odin, and finally making unusually clean work in ridding themselves of those prior occupants. "Let us," he virtually says, "let us know who were our forefathers, who it was that won the soil for us, and brought the good seed of those institutions through which we should not arrogantly but gratefully feel ourselves distinguished among the nations as possessors of long-inherited freedom; let us not keep up an ignorant kind of naming which disguises our true affinities of blood and language, but let us see thoroughly what sort of notions and traditions our forefathers had, and what sort of song inspired them. Let the poetic fragments which breathe forth their fierce bravery in battle and their trust in fierce gods who helped them, be treasured with affectionate reverence. These seafaring, invading, self-asserting men were the English of old time, and were our fathers who did rough work by which we are profiting. They had virtues which incorporated themselves in wholesome usages to which we trace our own political blessings. Let us know and acknowledge our common relationship to them, and be thankful that over and above the affections and duties which spring from our manhood, we have the closer and more constantly guiding duties which belong to us as Englishmen."

To this view of our nationality most persons who have feeling and understanding enough to be conscious of the connection between the patriotic affection and every other affection which lifts us above emigrating rats and free-loving baboons, will be disposed to say Amen. True, we are not indebted to those ancestors for our religion: we are rather proud of having got that illumination from elsewhere. The men who planted our nation were not Christians, though they began their work centuries after Christ; and they had a decided objection to Christianity when it was first proposed to them: they were not monotheists, and their religion was the reverse of spiritual. But since we have been fortunate enough to keep the island-home they won for us, and have been on the whole a prosperous people, rather continuing the plan of invading and spoiling other lands than being forced to beg for shelter in them, nobody has reproached us because our fathers thirteen hundred years ago worshipped Odin, massacred Britons, and were with difficulty persuaded to accept Christianity, knowing nothing of Hebrew history and the reasons why Christ should be received as the Savior of mankind. The Red Indians, not liking us when we settled among them, might have been willing to fling such facts in our faces, but they were too ignorant, and besides, their opinions did not signify, because we were able, if we liked, to exterminate them. The Hindoos also have doubtless had their rancors against us and still entertain enough ill-will to make unfavorable remarks on our character, especially as to our historic rapacity and arrogant notions of our own superiority; they perhaps do not admire the usual English profile, and they are not converted to our way of feeding; but though we are a small number of an alien race profiting by the territory and produce of these prejudiced people, they are unable to turn us out; at least, when they tried we showed them their mistake. We do not call ourselves a dispersed and punished people; we are a colonizing people, and it is we who have punished others.

Still the historian guides us rightly in urging us to dwell on the virtues of our ancestors with emulation, and to cherish our sense of common descent as a bond of obligation. The eminence, the nobleness of a people, depends on its capability of being stirred by memories, and of striving for what we call spiritual ends—ends which consist not in immediate material possession, but in the satisfaction of a great feeling that animates the collective body as with one soul. A people having the seed of worthiness in it must feel an answering thrill when it is adjured by the deaths of its heroes who died to preserve it national existence; when it is reminded of its small beginnings and gradual growth through past labors and struggles, such as are still demanded of it in order that the freedom and well-being thus inherited may be transmitted unimpaired to children and children's children; when an appeal against the permission of injustice is made to great precedents in its history and to the better genius breathing in its institutions. It is this living force of sentiment in common which makes a national consciousness. Nations so moved will resist conquest with the very breasts of their women, will pay their millions and their blood to abolish slavery, will share privation in famine and all calamity, will produce poets to sing "some great story of a man," and thinkers whose theories will bear the test of action. An individual man, to be harmoniously great, must belong to a nation of this order, if not in actual existence yet existing in the past, in memory, as a departed, invisible, beloved ideal, once a reality, and perhaps to be restored. A common humanity is not yet enough to feed the rich blood of various activity which makes a complete man. The time is not come for cosmopolitanism to be highly virtuous, any more than for communism to suffice for social energy. I am not bound to feel for a Chinaman as I feel for my fellow-countryman: I am bound not to demoralize him with opium, not to compel him to my will by destroying or plundering the fruits of his labor on the alleged ground that he is not cosmopolitan enough, and not to insult him for his want of my tailoring and religion when he appears as a peaceable visitor on the London pavement. It is admirable in a Briton with a good purpose to learn Chinese, but it would not be a proof of fine intellect in him to taste Chinese poetry in the original more than he tastes the poetry of his own tongue. Affection, intelligence, duty, radiate from a center, and nature has decided that for us English folk that center can be neither China nor Peru.[6] Most of us feel this unreflectingly; for the affectation of undervaluing everything native, and being too fine for one's own country, belongs only to a few minds of no dangerous leverage. What is wanting is, that we should recognize a corresponding attachment to nationality as legitimate in every other people, and understand that its absence is a privation of the greatest good.

For, to repeat, not only the nobleness of a nation depends on the presence of this national consciousness, but also the nobleness of each individual citizen. Our dignity and rectitude are proportioned to our sense of relationship with something great, admirable, pregnant with high possibilities, worthy of sacrifice, a continual inspiration to self-repression and discipline by the presentation of aims larger and more attractive to our generous part than the securing of personal ease or prosperity. And a people possessing this good should surely feel not only a ready sympathy with the effort of those who, having lost the good, strive to regain it, but a profound pity for any degradation resulting from its loss; nay, something more than pity when happier nationalities have made victims of the unfortunate whose memories nevertheless are the very fountain to which the persecutors trace their most vaunted blessings.

These notions are familiar: few will deny them in the abstract, and many are found loudly asserting them in relation to this or the other particular case. But here as elsewhere, in the ardent application of ideas, there is a notable lack of simple comparison or sensibility to resemblance. The European world has long been used to consider the Jews as altogether exceptional, and it has followed naturally enough that they have been excepted from the rules of justice and mercy, which are based on human likeness. But to consider a people whose ideas have determined the religion of half the world, and that the more cultivated half, and who made the most eminent struggle against the power of Rome, as a purely exceptional race, is a demoralizing offense against rational knowledge, a stultifying inconsistency in historical interpretation. Every nation of forcible character—*i.e.,* of strongly marked characteristics, is so far exceptional. The distinctive note of each bird-species is in this sense exceptional, but the necessary ground of such distinction is a deeper likeness. The superlative peculiarity in the Jews admitted, our affinity with them is only the more apparent when the elements of their peculiarity are discerned.

From whatever point of view the writings of the Old Testament may be regarded, the picture they present of a national development is of high interest and speciality, nor can their historic momentousness be much affected by any varieties of theory as to the relation they bear to the New Testament or to the rise and constitution of Christianity. Whether we accept the canonical Hebrew books as a revelation or simply as part of an ancient literature,[7] makes no difference to the fact that we find there the strongly characterized portraiture of a people educated from an earlier or later period to a sense of separateness unique in its intensity, a people taught by many concurrent influences to identify faithfulness to its national traditions with the highest social and religious blessings. Our too scanty sources of Jewish history, from the return under Ezra to the beginning of the desperate resistance against Rome, show us the heroic and triumphant struggle of the Maccabees, which rescued the religion and independence of the nation from the corrupting sway of the Syrian Greeks, adding to the glorious sum of its memorials, and stimulating continuous efforts of a more peaceful sort to maintain and develop that national life which the heroes had fought and died for, by internal measures of legal administration and public teaching.[8] Thenceforth the virtuous elements of the Jewish life were engaged, as they had been with varying aspects during the long and changeful prophetic period and the restoration under Ezra, on the side of preserving the specific national character against a demoralizing fusion with that of foreigners whose religion and ritual were idolatrous and often obscene. There was always a Foreign party reviling the National party as narrow, and sometimes manifesting their own breadth in extensive views of advancement or profit to themselves by flattery of a foreign power. Such internal conflict naturally tightened the bands of conservatism, which needed to be strong if it were to rescue the sacred ark, the vital spirit of a small nation—"the smallest of the nations"[9]— whose territory lay on the highway between three continents; and when the dread and hatred of foreign sway had condensed itself into dread and hatred of the Romans, many Conservatives became Zealots, whose chief mark was that they advocated resistance to the death against the submergence of their nationality.[10] Much might be said on this point toward distinguishing the desperate struggle against a conquest which is regarded as degradation and corruption, from rash, hopeless insurrection against an established native government; and for my part (if that were of any consequence) I share the spirit of the Zealots. I take the spectacle of the Jewish people defying the Roman edict, and preferring death by starvation or the sword to the introduction of Caligula's deified statue into the temple, as a sublime type of steadfastness. But all that need be noticed here is the continuity of that national education (by outward and inward circumstance) which created in the Jews a feeling of race, a sense of corporate existence, unique in its intensity.

But not, before the dispersion, unique in essential qualities. There is more likeness than contrast between the way we English got our island and the way the Israelites got Canaan. We have not been noted for forming a low estimate of ourselves in comparison with foreigners, or for admitting that our institutions are equalled by those of any other people under the sun. Many of us have thought that our sea-wall is a specially divine arrangement to make and keep us a nation of sea-kings after the manner of our forefathers, secure against invasion and able to invade other lands when we need them, though they may lie on the other side of the ocean. Again, it has been held that we have a peculiar destiny as a Protestant people, not only able to bruise the head of an idolatrous Christianity in the midst of us, but fitted as possessors of the most truth and the most tonnage to carry our purer religion over the world and convert mankind to our way of thinking. The Puritans, asserting their liberty to restrain tyrants, found the Hebrew history closely symbolical of their feelings and purpose; and it can hardly be correct to cast the blame of their less laudable doings on the writings they invoked, since their opponents made use of the same writings for different ends, finding there a strong warrant for the Divine right of kings and the denunciation of those who, like Korah, Dathan, and Abiram, took on themselves the office of the priesthood which belonged of right solely to Aaron and his sons, or, in other words, to men ordained by the English bishops.[11] We must rather refer the passionate use of the Hebrew writings to affinities of disposition between our own race and the Jewish. Is it true that the arrogance of a Jew was so immeasurably beyond that of a Calvinist? And the just sympathy and admiration which we give to the ancestors who resisted the oppressive acts of our native kings, and by resisting rescued or won for us the best part of our civil and religious liberties—is it justly to be withheld from those brave and steadfast men of Jewish race who fought and died, or strove by wise administration to resist, the oppression and corrupting influences of foreign tyrants, and by resisting rescued the nationality which was the very hearth of our own religion? At any rate, seeing that the Jews were more specifically than any other nation educated into a sense of their supreme moral value, the chief matter of surprise is that any other nation is found to rival them in this form of self-confidence.

More exceptional—less like the course of our own history—has been their dispersion and their subsistence as a separate people through ages in which for the most part they were regarded and treated very much as beasts hunted for the sake of their skins, or of a valuable secretion peculiar to their species. The Jews showed a talent for accumulating what was an object of more immediate desire to Christians than animal oils or well-furred skins, and their cupidity and avarice were found at once particularly hateful and particularly useful: hateful when seen as a reason for punishing them by mulcting or robbery, useful when this retributive process could be successfully carried forward. Kings and emperors naturally were more alive to the usefulness of subjects who could gather and yield money; but edicts issued to protect "the King's Jews"[12] equally with the King's game from being harassed and hunted by the commonalty were only slight mitigations to the deplorable lot of a race held to be under the divine curse, and had little force after the Crusades began. As the slave-holders in the United States counted the curse on Ham a justification of negro slavery, so the curse on the Jews was counted a justification for hindering them from pursuing agriculture and handicrafts;[13] for marking them out as execrable figures by a peculiar dress; for torturing them to make them part with their gains, or for more gratuitously spitting at them and pelting them; for taking it as certain that they killed and ate babies, poisoned the wells, and took pains to spread the plague; for putting it to them whether they would be baptized or burned, and not failing to burn and massacre them when they were obstinate; but also for suspecting them of disliking the baptism when they had got it, and then burning them in punishment of their insincerity; finally, for hounding them by tens on tens of thousands from the homes where they had found shelter for centuries, and inflicting on them the horrors of a new exile and a new dispersion. All this to avenge the Saviour of mankind, or else to compel these stiff-necked people to acknowledge a Master whose Servants showed such beneficent effects of His teaching.

With a people so treated one of two issues was possible: either from being of feebler nature than their persecutors, and caring more for ease than for the sentiments and ideas which constituted their distinctive character, they would everywhere give way to pressure and get rapidly merged in the populations around them; or being endowed with uncommon tenacity, physical and mental, feeling peculiarly the ties of inheritance both in blood and faith, remembering national glories, trusting in their recovery, abhorring apostasy, able to bear all things and hope all things with a consciousness of being steadfast to spiritual obligations, the kernel of their number would harden into an inflexibility more and more insured by motive and habit. They would cherish all differences that marked them off from their hated oppressors, all memories that consoled them with a sense of virtual though unrecognized superiority; and the separateness which was made their badge of ignominy would be their inward pride, their source of fortifying defiance. Doubtless such a people would get confirmed in vices. An oppressive government and a persecuting religion, while breeding vices in those who hold power, are well known to breed answering vices in those who are powerless and suffering. What more direct plan than the course presented by European history could have been pursued in order to give the Jews a spirit of bitter isolation, of scorn for the wolfish hypocrisy that made victims of them, of triumph in prospering at the expense of the blunderers who stoned them away from the open paths of industry?—or, on the other hand, to encourage in the less defiant a lying conformity, a pretense of conversion for the sake of the social advantages attached to baptism, an outward renunciation of their hereditary ties with the lack of real love toward the society and creed which exacted this galling tribute?—or again, in the most unhappy specimens of the race to rear transcendent examples of odious vice, reckless instruments of rich men with bad propensities, unscrupulous grinders of the alien people who wanted to grind *them?*

No wonder the Jews have their vices: no wonder if it were proved (which it has not hitherto appeared to be) that some of them have a bad pre-eminence in evil, an unrivaled superfluity of naughtiness. It would be more plausible to make a wonder of the virtues which have prospered among them under the shadow of oppression. But instead of dwelling on these, or treating as admitted what any hardy or ignorant person may deny, let us found simply on the loud assertions of the hostile. The Jews, it is said, resisted the expansion of their own religion into Christianity; they were in the habit of spitting on the cross; they have held the name of Christ to be *Anathema*. Who taught them that? The men who made Christianity a curse to them; the men who made the name of Christ a symbol for the spirit of vengeance, and, what was worse, made the execution of the vengeance a pretext for satisfying their own savageness, greed and envy; the men who sanctioned with the name of Christ a barbaric and blundering copy of pagan fatalism in taking the words "His blood be upon us and on our children"[14] as a divinely appointed verbal warrant for wreaking cruelty from generation to generation on the people from whose sacred writings Christ drew His teaching. Strange retrogression in the professors of an expanded religion, boasting an illumination beyond the spiritual doctrine of Hebrew prophets! For Hebrew prophets proclaimed a God who demanded mercy rather than sacrifices. The Christians also believed that God delighted not in the blood of rams and of bulls, but they apparently conceived Him as requiring for His satisfaction the sighs and groans, the blood and roasted flesh of men whose forefathers had misunderstood the metaphorical character of prophecies which spoke of spiritual pre-eminence under the figure of a material kingdom. Was this the method by which Christ desired His title to the Messiahship to be commended to the hearts and understandings of the nation in which He was born? Many of His sayings bear the stamp of that patriotism which places fellow-countrymen in the inner circle of affection and duty. And did the words, "Father, forgive them, they know not what they do,"[15] refer only to the centurion and his band, a tacit exception being made of every Hebrew there present from the mercy of the Father and the compassion of the Son? Nay, more, of every Hebrew yet to come who remained unconverted after hearing of His claim to the Messiahship, not from His own lips or those of His native apostles, but from the lips of alien men whom cross, creed, and baptism had left cruel, rapacious, and debauched? It is more reverent to Christ to believe that He must have approved the Jewish martyrs who deliberately chose to be burned or massacred rather than be guilty of a blaspheming lie, more than He approved the rabble of crusaders who robbed and murdered them in His name.

But these remonstrances seem to have no direct application to personages who take up the attitude of philosophic thinkers and discriminating critics, professedly accepting Christianity from a rational point of view as a vehicle of the highest religious and moral truth, and condemning the Jews on the ground that they are obstinate adherents of an outworn creed, maintain themselves in moral alienation from the peoples with whom they share citizenship, and are destitute of real interest in the welfare of the community and state with which they are thus identified. These anti-Judaic advocates usually belong to a party which has felt itself glorified in winning for Jews, as well as Dissenters and Catholics, the full privileges of citizenship, laying open to them every path to distinction. At one time the voice of this party urged that differences of creed were made dangerous only by the denial of citizenship—that you must make a man a citizen before he could feel like one. At present, apparently, this confidence has been succeeded by a sense of mistake: there is a regret that no limiting clauses were insisted on, such as would have hindered the Jews from coming too far and in too large proportion along those opened pathways: and the Roumanians are thought to have shown an enviable wisdom in giving them as little chance as possible. But then, the reflection occurring that some of the most objectionable Jews are baptized Christians, it is obvious that such clauses would have been insufficient, and the doctrine that you can turn a Jew into a good Christian is emphatically retracted. But clearly, these liberal gentlemen, too late enlightened by disagreeable events, must yield the palm of wise foresight to those who argued against them long ago; and it is a striking spectacle to witness minds so panting for advancement in some directions that they are ready to force it on an unwilling society, in this instance despairingly recurring to mediæval types of thinking—insisting that the Jews are made viciously cosmopolitan by holding the world's money-bag, that for them all national interests are resolved into the algebra of loans, that they have suffered an inward degradation stamping them as morally inferior, and— "serve them right," since they rejected Christianity. All which is mirrored in an analogy, namely, that of the Irish, also a servile race, who have rejected Protestantism, though it has been repeatedly urged on them by fire and sword and penal laws, and whose place in the moral scale may be judged by our advertisements, where the clause, "No Irish need apply," parallels the sentence which for many polite persons sums up the question of Judaism—"I never *did* like the Jews."

It is certainly worth considering whether an expatriated, denationalized race, used for ages to live among antipathetic populations, must not inevitably lack some conditions of nobleness. If they drop that separateness which is made their reproach, they may be in danger of lapsing into a cosmopolitan indifference equivalent to cynicism, and of missing that inward identification with the nationality immediately around them which might make some amends for their inherited privation. No dispassionate observer can deny this danger. Why, our own countrymen who take to living abroad without purpose or function to keep up their sense of fellowship in the affairs of their own land are rarely good specimens of moral healthiness; still, the consciousness of having a native country, the birthplace of common memories and habits of mind, existing like a parental hearth quitted but beloved; the dignity of being included in a people which has a part in the comity of nations and the growing federation of the world; that sense of special belonging which is the root of human virtues, both public and private,—all these spiritual links may preserve migratory Englishmen from the worst consequences of their voluntary dispersion. Unquestionably the Jews, having been more than any other race exposed to the adverse moral influences of alienism, must, both in individuals and in groups, have suffered some corresponding moral degradation; but in fact they have escaped with less of abjectness and less of hard hostility toward the nations whose hand has been against them, than could have happened in the case of a people who had neither their adhesion to a separate religion founded on historic memories, nor their characteristic family affectionateness. Tortured, flogged, spit upon, the *corpus vile*[16] on which rage or wantonness vented themselves with impunity, their name flung at them as an opprobrium by superstition, hatred, and contempt, they have remained proud of their origin. Does any one call this an evil pride? Perhaps he belongs to that order of man who, while he has a democratic dislike to dukes and earls, wants to make believe that his father was an idle gentleman, when in fact he was an honorable artisan, or who would feel flattered to be taken for other than an Englishman. It is possible to be too arrogant about our blood or our calling, but that arrogance is virtue compared with such mean pretense. The pride which identifies us with a great historic body is a humanizing, elevating habit of mind, inspiring sacrifices of individual comfort, gain, or other selfish ambition, for the sake of that ideal whole; and no man swayed by such a sentiment can become completely abject. That a Jew of Smyrna, where a whip is carried by passengers ready to flog off the too officious specimens of his race, can still be proud to say, "I am a Jew," is surely a fact to awaken admiration in a mind capable of understanding what we may call the ideal forces in human history. And again, a varied, impartial observation of the Jews in different countries tends to the impression that they have a predominant kindliness which must have been deeply ingrained in the constitution of their race to have outlasted the ages of persecution and oppression. The concentration of their joys in domestic life has kept up in them the capacity of tenderness: the pity for the fatherless and the widow, the care for the women and the little ones, blent intimately with their religion, is a well of mercy that cannot long or widely be pent up by exclusiveness. And the kindliness of the Jew overflows the line of division between him and the Gentile. On the whole, one of the most remarkable phenomena in the history of this scattered people, made for ages "a scorn and a hissing," is, that after being subjected to this process, which might have been expected to be in every sense deteriorating and vitiating, they have come out of it (in any estimate which allows for numerical proportion) rivaling the nations of all European countries in healthiness and beauty of *physique*, in practical ability, in scientific and artistic aptitude, and in some forms of ethical value. A significant indication of their natural rank is seen in the fact that at this moment, the leader of the Liberal party in Germany is a Jew, the leader of the Republican party in France is a Jew, and the head of the Conservative ministry in England is a Jew.[17]

And here it is that we find the ground for the obvious jealousy which is now stimulating the revived expression of old antipathies. "The Jews," it is felt, "have a dangerous tendency to get the uppermost places not only in commerce but in political life. Their monetary hold on governments is tending to perpetuate in leading Jews a spirit of universal alienism (euphemistically called cosmopolitanism), even where the West has given them a full share in civil and political rights. A people with oriental sunlight in their blood, yet capable of being everywhere acclimatized, they have a force and toughness which enables them to carry off the best prizes; and their wealth is likely to put half the seats in Parliament at their disposal."

There is truth in these views of Jewish social and political relations. But it is rather too late for liberal pleaders to urge them in a merely vituperative sense. Do they propose as a remedy for the impending danger of our healthier national influences getting overridden by Jewish predominance, that we should repeal our emancipatory laws? Not all the Germanic immigrants who have been settling among us for generations, and are still pouring in to settle, are Jews, but thoroughly Teutonic and more or less Christian craftsmen, mechanicians, or skilled and erudite functionaries; and the Semitic Christians who swarm among us are dangerously like their unconverted brethren in complexion, persistence, and wealth. Then there are the Greeks who, by the help of Phœnician blood or otherwise, are objectionably strong in the city.

Some judges think that the Scotch are more numerous and prosperous here in the South than is quite for the good of us Southerners; and the early inconvenience felt under the Stuarts of being quartered upon by a hungry, hard-working people with a distinctive accent and form of religion, and higher cheek-bones than English taste requires, has not yet been quite neutralized. As for the Irish, it is felt in high quarters that we have always been too lenient toward them;—at least, if they had been harried a little more there might not have been so many of them on the English press, of which they divide the power with the Scotch, thus driving many Englishmen to honest and ineloquent labor.

So far shall we be carried if we go in search of devices to hinder people of other blood than our own from getting the advantage of dwelling among us.

Let it be admitted that it is a calamity to the English, as to any other great historic people, to undergo a premature fusion with immigrants of alien blood; that its distinctive national characteristics should be in danger of obliteration by the predominating quality of foreign settlers. I not only admit this, I am ready to unite in groaning over the threatened danger. To one who loves his native language, who would delight to keep our rich and harmonious English undefiled by foreign accent, foreign intonation, and those foreign tinctures of verbal meaning which tend to confuse all writing and discourse, it is an affliction as harassing as the climate, and that on our stage, in our studios, at our public and private gatherings, in our offices, warehouses, and workshops, we must expect to hear our beloved English with its words clipped, its vowels stretched and twisted, its phrases of acquiescence and politeness, of cordiality, dissidence or argument, delivered always in the wrong tones, like ill-rendered melodies, marred beyond recognition; that there should be a general ambition to speak every language except our mother English, which persons "of style" are not ashamed of corrupting with slang, false foreign equivalents, and a pronunciation that crushes out all color from the vowels and jams them between jostling consonants. An ancient Greek might not like to be resuscitated for the sake of hearing Homer read in our universities, still he would at least find more instructive marvels in other developments to be witnessed at those institutions; but a modern Englishman is invited from his after-dinner repose to hear Shakespeare delivered under circumstances which offer no other novelty than some novelty of false intonation, some new distribution of strong emphasis on prepositions, some new misconception of a familiar idiom. Well! it is our inertness that is in fault, our carelessness of excellence, our willing ignorance of the treasures that lie in our national heritage, while we are agape after what is foreign, though it may be only a vile imitation of what is native.

This marring of our speech, however, is a minor evil compared with what must follow from the predominance of wealth-acquiring immigrants, whose appreciation of our political and social life must often be as approximative or fatally erroneous as their delivery of our language. But take the worst issues—what can we do to hinder them? Are we to adopt the exclusiveness for which we have punished the Chinese? Are we to tear the glorious flag of hospitality which has made our freedom the world-wide blessing of the oppressed? It is not agreeable to find foreign accents and stumbling locutions passing from the piquant exception to the general rule of discourse. But to urge on that account that we should spike away the peaceful foreigner, would be a view of international relations not in the long run favorable to the interests of our fellow-countrymen; for we are at least equal to the races we call obtrusive in the disposition to settle wherever money is to be made and cheaply idle living to be found. In meeting the national evils which are brought upon us by the onward course of the world, there is often no more immediate hope or recourse than that of striving after fuller national excellence, which must consist in the moulding of more excellent individual natives. The tendency of things is toward the quicker or slower fusion of races. It is impossible to arrest this tendency: all we can do is to moderate its course so as to hinder it from degrading the moral status of societies by a too rapid effacement of those national traditions and customs which are the language of the national genius—the deep suckers of healthy sentiment. Such moderating and guidance of inevitable movement is worthy of all effort. And it is in this sense that the modern insistence on the idea of nationalities has value. That any people at once distinct and coherent enough to form a state should be held in subjection by an alien antipathetic government has been becoming more and more a ground of sympathetic indignation; and in virtue of this, at least one great State has been added to European councils. Nobody now complains of the result in this case, though far-sighted persons see the need to limit analogy by discrimination. We have to consider who are the stifled people and who the stiflers before we can be sure of our ground. The only point in this connection on which Englishmen are agreed is, that England itself shall not be subject to foreign rule. The fiery resolve to resist invasion, though with an improvised array of pitchforks, is felt to be virtuous, and to be worthy of a historic people. Why? Because there is a national life in our veins. Because there is something specifically English which we feel to be supremely worth striving for, worth dying for, rather than living to renounce it. Because we too have our share—perhaps a principal share—in that spirit of separateness which has not yet done its work in the education of mankind, which has created the varying genius of nations, and, like the Muses, is the offspring of memory.

Here, as everywhere else, the human task seems to be the discerning and adjustment of opposite claims. But the end can hardly be achieved by urging contradictory reproaches, and instead of laboring after discernment as a preliminary to intervention, letting our zeal burst forth according to a capricious selection, first determined accidentally and afterward justified by personal predilection. Not only John Gilpin and his wife, or Edwin and Angelina,[18] seem to be of opinion that their preference or dislike of Russians, Servians, or Greeks, consequent, perhaps, on hotel adventures, has something to do with the merits of the Eastern question; even in a higher range of intellect and enthusiasm we find a distribution of sympathy or pity for sufferers of different blood or votaries of differing religions, strangely unaccountable on any other ground than a fortuitous direction of study or trivial circumstances of travel. With some even admirable persons, one is never quite sure of any particular being included under a general term. A provincial physician, it is said, once ordering a lady patient not to eat salad, was asked pleadingly by the affectionate husband whether she might eat lettuce, or cresses, or radishes. The physician had too rashly believed in the comprehensiveness of the word "salad," just as we, if not enlightened by experience, might believe in the all-embracing breadth of "sympathy with the injured and oppressed." What mind can exhaust the grounds of exception which lie in each particular case? There is understood to be a peculiar odor from the negro body, and we know that some persons, too rationalistic to feel bound by the curse on Ham, used to hint very strongly that this odor determined the question on the side of negro slavery.

And this is the usual level of thinking in polite society concerning the Jews. Apart from theological purposes, it seems to be held surprising that anybody should take an interest in the history of a people whose literature has furnished all our devotional language; and if any reference is made of their past or future destinies some hearer is sure to state as a relevant fact which may assist our judgment, that she, for her part, is not fond of them, having known a Mr. Jacobson who was very unpleasant, or that he, for his part, thinks meanly of them as a race, though on inquiry you find that he is so little acquainted with their characteristics that he is astonished to learn how many persons whom he has blindly admired and applauded are Jews to the backbone. Again, men who consider themselves in the very van of modern advancement, knowing history and the latest philosophies of history, indicate their contemptuous surprise that any one should entertain the destiny of the Jews as a worthy subject, by referring to Moloch and their own agreement with the theory that the religion of Jehovah was merely a transformed Moloch-worship, while in the same breath they are glorifying "civilization" as a transformed tribal existence of which some lineaments are traceable in grim marriage customs of the native Australians.[19] Are these erudite persons prepared to insist that the name "Father" should no longer have any sanctity for us, because in their view of likelihood our Aryan ancestors were mere improvers on a state of things in which nobody knew his own father?

For less theoretic men, ambitious to be regarded as practical politicians, the value of the Hebrew race has been measured by their unfavorable opinion of a prime minister who is a Jew by lineage. But it is possible to form a very ugly opinion as to the scrupulousness of Walpole, or of Chatham;[20] and in any case I think Englishmen would refuse to accept the character and doings of those eighteenth century statesmen as the standard of value for the English people and the part they have to play in the fortunes of mankind.

If we are to consider the future of the Jews at all, it seems reasonable to take as a preliminary question: Are they destined to complete fusion with the peoples among whom they are dispersed, losing every remnant of a distinctive consciousness as Jews; or, are there in the breadth and intensity with which the feeling of separateness, or what we may call the organized memory of a national consciousness, actually exists in the world-wide Jewish communities—the seven millions scattered from east to west—and again, are there in the political relations of the world, the conditions present or approaching for the restoration of a Jewish state planted on the old ground as a centre of national feeling, a source of dignifying protection, a special channel for special energies which may contribute some added form of national genius, and an added voice in the councils of the world? They are among us everywhere; it is useless to say we are not fond of them. Perhaps we are not fond of proletaries and their tendency to form Unions, but the world is not therefore to be rid of them. If we wish to free ourselves from the inconveniences that we have to complain of, whether in proletaries or in Jews, our best course is to encourage all means of improving these neighbors who elbow us in a thickening crowd, and of sending their incommodious energies into beneficent channels. Why are we so eager for the dignity of certain populations of whom perhaps we have never seen a single specimen, and of whose history, legend or literature we have been contentedly ignorant for ages, while we sneer at the notion of a renovated national dignity for the Jews, whose ways of thinking and whose very verbal forms are on our lips in every prayer which we end with an Amen? Some of us consider this question dismissed when they have said that the wealthiest Jews have no desire to forsake their European palaces, and go to live in Jerusalem. But in a return from exile, in the restoration of a people, the question is not whether certain rich men will choose to remain behind, but whether there will be found worthy men who will choose to lead the return. Plenty of prosperous Jews remained in Babylon when Ezra marshaled his band of forty thousand and began a new glorious epoch in the history of his race, making the preparation for that epoch in the history of the world which has been held glorious enough to be dated from forevermore. The hinge of possibility is simply the existence of an adequate community of feeling as well as widespread need in the Jewish race, and the hope that among its finer specimens there may arise some men of instruction and ardent public spirit, some new Ezras, some modern Maccabees, who will know how to use all favoring outward conditions, how to triumph by heroic example over the indifference of their fellows and the scorn of their foes, and will steadfastly set their faces toward making their people once more one among the nations.

Formerly, evangelical orthodoxy was prone to dwell on the fulfillment of prophecy in the "restoration of the Jews." Such interpretation of the prophets is less in vogue now. The dominant mode is to insist on a Christianity that disowns its origin, that is not a substantial growth having a genealogy, but is a vaporous reflex of modern notions. The Christ of Matthew had the heart of a Jew—"Go ye first to the lost sheep of the house of Israel."[21] The Apostle of the Gentiles had the heart of a Jew: "For I could wish that myself were accursed from Christ for my brethren, my kinsmen according to the flesh: who are Israelites; to whom pertaineth the adoption, and the glory, and the covenants, and the giving of the law, and the service of God, and the promises; whose are the fathers, and of whom as concerning the flesh Christ came."[22] Modern apostles, extolling Christianity, are found using a different tone: they prefer the mediæval cry translated into modern phrase. But the mediæval cry, too, was in substance very ancient—more ancient than the days of Augustus. Pagans in successive ages said, "These people are unlike us, and refuse to be made like us: let us punish them." The Jews were steadfast in their separateness, and through that separateness Christianity was born. A modern book on Liberty has maintained that from the freedom of individual men to persist in idiosyncrasies the world may be enriched.[23] Why should we not apply this argument to the idiosyncrasy of a nation, and pause in our haste to hoot it down? There is still a great function for the steadfastness of the Jew: not that he should shut out the utmost illumination which knowledge can throw on his national history, but that he should cherish the store of inheritance which that history has left him. Every Jew should be conscious that he is one of a multitude possessing common objects of piety in the immortal achievements and immortal sorrows of ancestors who have transmitted to them a physical and mental type strong enough, eminent enough in faculties, pregnant enough with peculiar promise, to constitute a new beneficent individuality among the nations, and, by confuting the traditions of scorn, nobly avenge the wrongs done to their Fathers.

There is a sense in which the worthy child of a nation that has brought forth illustrious prophets, high and unique among the poets of the world, is bound by their visions.

Is bound?

Yes, for the effective bond of human action is feeling, and the worthy child of a people owning the triple name of Hebrew, Israelite, and Jew, feels his kinship with the glories and the sorrows, the degradation and the possible renovation of his national family.

Will any one teach the nullification of this feeling and call his doctrine a philosophy? He will teach a blinding superstition—the superstition that a theory of human well-being can be constructed in disregard of the influences which have made us human.

Notes

1.   "Hep! Hep! Hep!" may be derived from the initials of "Hierosolyma est perdita" (according to the OED, second edition) and was the cry of those who persecuted Jews in the nineteenth century, notably in Hamburg in 1819.
2.   Byron died of a fever in Missolonghi while attempting to advance the struggle for Greek independence.
3.   Giuseppe Mazzini (1805–72). Italian republican revolutionary, leader of the Risorgimento.
4.   Giovanni Battista Rubini (1794–1854). Italian tenor in the Romantic style of Bellini and Donizetti. Tommaso Aniello (1620–74). Leader of insurrection in Naples against the nobles in protest of a fruit tax benefitting Spain.
5.   According to Nancy Henry, this is probably John Richard Green (1837–83). Cf. the opening chapter of *Short History of the English People* (1874), enlarged in *History of the English People*, the first volume of which was published in 1877.
6.   The language recalls Mordecai's call, in *Daniel Deronda* (Ch. 42), to "revive the organic centre" by returning to the Jewish homeland and establishing "the dignity of a national life."
7.   Strauss's *Life of Jesus*, which George Eliot had translated, maintains that the Bible has value as a myth produced by a collective consciousness, regardless of its lack of literal truth.
8.   Ezra was a Jewish priest who led the return to Jerusalem of 1,500 Jews from the Babylonian exile (c. 390 B.C.E.). The Maccabees consisted of Matthias the Hasmonean and his five sons, who led the Jewish revolt against the Syrian king Antiochus Epiphanes (175–164 B.C.E.).
9.   Cf. Deuteronomy 7:7 ("the fewest of all people") and Jeremiah 49:15 ("small among the heathen").
10.   Jews who struggled to overthrow Roman rule were classified as Zealots.
11.   Korah, Dathan, and Abiram were Levites who led a rebellion against Moses and Aaron and, in punishment, were swallowed by the earth (Numbers 16; 26:9–11; Deuteronomy 11:6).
12.   Jews protected by the king because of benefits derived.
13.   Ham is cursed by his father Noah ("Cursed be Canaan") because he saw his father naked and intoxicated, and went to tell his brothers; Shem

and Jafeth, who walked backward to cover their father's nakedness, are blessed (Genesis 9:18–27).

14.   From Matthew 27:25.

15.   From Luke 23:34.

16.   A living or dead body held to be so worthless that it can be used with impunity as an expendable subject of experimentation.

17.   According to Nancy Henry, the German Liberal is Eduard Lasker (1829–84), and the French Republican is Leon Gambetta (1838–82). The English Conservative is Benjamin Disraeli (1804–81), twice Prime Minister, leader of the opposition in Commons, thrice chancellor of the exchequer, and novelist.

18.   John Gilpin is in reference to William Cowper's "The Diverting History of John Gilpin" (1785). Edwin and Angelina are from Oliver Goldsmith's "The Hermit" (1764). These became stock names for sentimental couples, such as the plaintiff and defendant in Gilbert and Sullivan's *Trial by Jury* (1875), which satirizes romantic engagements.

19.   Moloch-worship was an ancient Middle Eastern religion requiring child sacrifice to the god Moloch. Jews were forbidden to worship Moloch (Leviticus 18:21). The evil kings Ahaz and Manasseh in fact did so (II Kings 16:3, 21:6), but the virtuous king Josiah destroyed Moloch-worship (II Kings 23:10).

20.   Sir Robert Walpole (1676–1745), twice Prime Minister, secretary of war, and treasurer of the navy. He was accused of rigging elections and mishandling the war with Spain. William Pitt, first Earl of Chatham (1708–78), served as secretary of state from 1756–61.

21.   Matthew 10:6.

22.   Romans 9:3–5.

23.   John Stuart Mill's *On Liberty* (1859). Utilitarian treatise asserting the social benefit of fostering individuality.

V. Frances Power Cobbe
(1822–1904)

Frances Power Cobbe was an extremely prolific writer who directly influenced Victorians with her theories about liberal politics, theology, and practical humanitarianism. Her dozens of publications challenged thinkers on both sides of contemporary debates and offered genuine resolutions in an age anxious for compromise. Cobbe was primarily concerned with ending women's subjection and with animal vivisection. She helped found the National Anti-Vivisection Society in 1875 and was editor of *Zoophilist*. Furthermore, her promotion of the revised Matrimonial Causes Act certainly helped lead to its passage in 1878. Cobbe's philanthropic battles extended far beyond the fight for her own sex and for the lives of animals, however. She was also an instrumental force in Poor Law reform and worked directly to better conditions for the young, the sick, the uneducated, and the aged.

Cobbe descended from a family of theological intellects which included five archbishops and a bishop among its connections. She was born in Dublin on December 4, 1822, the only daughter of Frances Conway Cobbe and Charles Cobbe, a landowner and magistrate. In addition to studies at home, Cobbe attended school in Brighton for two years and learned Greek and geometry from a parish clergyman. Always interested in languages, Cobbe eventually learned several during her extensive travels throughout Europe and when serving as a foreign correspondent from Italy for a London newspaper.

Through travel and journalism, Cobbe crossed paths with some of the most influential thinkers of her day. She is mentioned by Matthew Arnold in *Essays in Criticism* (1865), and she writes in her articles of personal acquaintance with Charles Darwin, William Gladstone, Alfred, Lord Tennyson and Theodore Parker. Indeed, her friendship with Parker led to her being selected as editor for this eminent theologian's works.

When Cobbe returned from Italy in 1858, she began establishing herself as an influential philanthropist. Due to a modest inheritance and to the money she earned writing, Cobbe was able to devote herself wholeheartedly to social causes. In the late 1850s, she joined Mary Carpenter in Bristol to work at the Red Lodge Reformatory for girls, and also to assist her in working for ragged school reform. During this period, Cobbe developed a romantic attachment to Carpenter which was frustrated. As Barbara Caine notes, Carpenter wished Cobbe to be her competent subordinate. Cobbe ultimately left Carpenter, and in 1861 she became the "beloved friend" (to use their own term) of Mary Lloyd, with whom she remained until Lloyd's death in 1898.

Although clearly an assertive presence, Cobbe found herself warmly welcomed and esteemed as a benevolent force; her opinion was sought not only by suffragists and antivivisectionists, but also by legislators and numerous editors. The extensive publication and reprinting of her articles, lectures, books, and autobiography point to the popularity of this woman of letters. Certainly the range of Cobbe's writing is wider than could be competently achieved in modern times, due to the specialization of fields. Literally writing from "A" ("Allured, an Allegory," 1866) to "Z" ("Zoophily," 1882), Cobbe tackled a variety of topics: anthropology, biography, civil rights, crime, economics, education, entertainment, government, literary and art criticism, medicine, mysticism, philosophy, poverty, psychology, sadism, and theology. As both a sophisticated investigator and a popular journalist, Cobbe reached a wide audience; she wrote for more than thirty periodicals.

Cobbe created solid arguments for progressive thought. Although she was ridiculed in 1862 at the Social Science Congress for advocating women's admission to university degrees, many of her other pragmatic recommendations (as outlined in "Workhouse Sketches" and "Wife-Torture in England") were acted upon. While frequently witty, Cobbe's prose style is characterized by clear organization, frankness, and appeals to common sense. She showed little compunction about publicly chastising the elusive and flowery prose of the most respected male "sages," especially those whose reform proposals were grounded in theory rather than in reality. Her place among the great reformers and prose stylists of the nineteenth century was clearly noted by her contemporaries; the failure to acknowledge her importance falls absolutely on modern shoulders.

More can be learned about Cobbe by reading her series on faith, *Broken Lights* (1864–65) and *Light in Dark Places* (1883–89), and her autobiography, *The Life of Frances Power Cobbe* (1894). Another primary source of information is *Re-Echos* (1876), which collects fifty-two of the articles Cobbe had written for the London newspaper *Echo* in the early 1870s. Her essays appeared primarily between 1860 and 1890 in a variety of periodicals, including the *Contemporary Review*, *Fraser's*, the *Theological Review*, *Cornhill*, *Eclectic Magazine*, *Temple Bar*, *Fortnightly Review*, and *Littell's Living Age*. Surprisingly little recent scholarship exists on Cobbe; however, Barbara Caine's lengthy discussion of Cobbe's feminism in *Victorian Feminists* (1992) is a valuable, lucid examination of this activist's complicated relationship to the women's rights movement. Another important secondary source is Carol Bauer and Lawrence Ritt's "A Husband Is a Beating Animal—Frances Power Cobbe Confronts the Wife-Abuse Problem in Victorian England" (*International Journal of Women's Studies* 6 [March-April, 1983] 99–118), and "Wife Abuse, Late Victorian English Feminists, and the Legacy of Frances Power Cobbe" (*International Journal of Women's Studies* 6 [May-June, 1983] 195–207).

John Hallock,
Temple University

11. What Shall We Do with Our Old Maids?

Introduction

Frances Power Cobbe's "What Shall We Do with Our Old Maids?" first appeared in *Fraser's Magazine* in November, 1862, and is reprinted here from that periodical. With this essay, Cobbe concludes the discussion she previously initiated in "Celibacy v. Marriage" (*Fraser's*, 1862). Following a spicy introduction which celebrates the recent support of Deaconesses, the "lady guerillas of philanthropy," Cobbe calls attention to an expanding single female population. She attacks the notion that marriage is the happiest state for women, and she supports women's "free competition" in the employment market. The artistry of Cobbe's rhetoric is fully displayed in this discussion of the morality and immorality of marriage. With flawless logic, Cobbe disarms her opponents and states an eloquent case for the freedom to love whomever one is moved to love. Typical of Cobbe's foresight is her realization that both marriage partners must develop identities beyond the mere titles of "husband" and "wife." As Cobbe writes, only "a woman who has something else than making love to do and to think of will love really and deeply." Although Cobbe is careful to recognize the constraints brought on by motherhood, she does encourage women to develop interests away from their children. As with all of her women's rights essays, "What Shall We Do with Our Old Maids?" was regarded as highly controversial; nevertheless, it was noted as a chief catalyst for reforms in women's education, employment, and marital status.

What Shall We Do with Our Old Maids?

In the Convocation of Canterbury for this year of 1862, the readers of such journals as report in full the sayings and doings of that not very interesting assembly, were surprised to find the subject of Protestant Sisterhoods, or Deaconesses, discussed with an unanimity of feeling almost unique in the annals of ecclesiastic parliaments. High Churchman and Low, Broad Churchman and Hard, all seemed agreed that there was good work for women to do, and which women *were* doing all over England; and that it was extremely desirable that all these lady guerillas of philanthropy should be enrolled in the regular disciplined army of the Church, together with as many new recruits as might be enlisted. To use a more appropriate simile, Mother Church expressed herself satisfied at her daughters "coming out," but considered that her chaperonage was decidedly necessary to their decorum.

Again, at the Social Science Congress of this summer, in London, the Employment of women, the Emigration of women, the Education of women, and all the other rights and wrongs of women, were urged, if not with an unanimity equal to that of their reverend predecessors, yet with, at the very least, equal animation. It is quite evident that the subject is not to be allowed to go to sleep, and we may as well face it valiantly, and endeavour to see light through its complications, rather than attempt to lecture the female sex generally on the merits of a "golden silence," and the propriety of adorning themselves with that decoration (doubtless modestly declined, as too precious for their own use, by masculine reviewers), "the ornament of a meek and quiet spirit." In a former article ("Celibacy *v.* Marriage"— *Fraser's Magazine* for April, 1862) we treated the subject in part. We now propose to pursue it further, and investigate in particular the new phases which it has lately assumed.

The questions involved may be stated very simply.

It appears that there is a natural excess of four or five per cent. of females over the males in our population. This, then, might be assumed to be the limits within which female celibacy was normal and inevitable.

There is, however, an actual ratio of thirty per cent. of women now in England who never marry, leaving one-fourth of both sexes in a state of celibacy. This proportion further appears to be constantly on the increase. It is obvious enough that these facts call for a revision of many of our social arrangements. The old assumption that marriage was the sole destiny of woman, and that it was the business of her husband to afford her support, is brought up short by the statement that one woman in four is certain not to marry, and that three millions of women earn their own living at this moment in England. We may view the case two ways: either—

1st, We must frankly accept this new state of things, and educate women and modify trade in accordance therewith, so as to make the condition of celibacy as little injurious as possible; or—

2nd, We must set ourselves vigorously to stop the current which is leading men and women away from the natural order of Providence. We must do nothing whatever to render celibacy easy or attractive; and we must make the utmost efforts to promote marriage by emigration of women to the colonies, and all other means in our power.

The second of these views we shall in the first place consider. It may be found to colour the ideas of a vast number of writers, and to influence essentially the decisions made on many points—as the admission of women to university degrees, to the medical profession, and generally to free competition in employment. Lately it has met a powerful and not unkindly exposition in an article in a contemporary quarterly, entitled, "Why are Women Redundant?" Therein it is plainly set forth that all efforts to make celibacy easy for women are labours in a wrong direction, and are to be likened to the noxious exertions of quacks to mitigate the symptoms of disease, and allow the patient to persist in his evil courses. The root of the malady should be struck at, and marriage, the only true vocation for women, promoted at any cost, even by the most enormous schemes for the deportation of 440,000 females. Thus alone (and by the enforcing of a stricter morality on men) should the evil be touched. As to making the labours of single women remunerative, and their lives free and happy, all such mistaken philanthropy will but tend to place them in a position more and more false and unnatural. Marriage will then become to them a matter of "cold philosophic choice," and accordingly may be expected to be more and more frequently declined.

There is a great deal in this view of the case which, on the first blush approves itself to our minds, and we have not been surprised to find the article in question quoted as of the soundest common-sense. All, save ascetics and visionaries, must admit that, for the mass of mankind, marriage is the right condition, the happiest, and the most conducive to virtue. This position fairly and fully conceded, it *might* appear that the whole of the consequences deduced followed of necessity, and that the direct promotion of marriage and discountenancing of celibacy was all we had to do in the matter.

A little deeper reflection, however, discloses a very important point which has been dropped out of the argument. Marriage is, indeed, the happiest and best condition for mankind. But does any one think that all marriages are so? When we make the assertion that marriage is good and virtuous, do we mean a marriage of interest, a marriage for wealth, for position, for rank, for support? Surely nothing of the kind. Such marriages as these are the sources of misery and sin, not of happiness and virtue, nay, their moral character, to be fitly designated, would require stronger words than we care to use. There is only one kind of marriage which makes good the assertion that it is the right and happy condition for mankind, and that is a marriage founded on free choice, esteem, and affection—in one word, on love. If, then, we seek to promote the happiness and virtue of the community, our efforts must be directed to encouraging *only* marriages which are of the sort to produce them—namely, marriages founded on love. All marriages founded on interest, on the desire for position, support, or the like, we must discourage to the utmost of our power, as the sources of nothing but wretchedness. Where, now, have we reached? Is it not to the conclusion that to make it a woman's *interest* to marry, to force her, by barring out every means of self-support and all fairly remunerative labour, to look to marriage as her sole chance of competency, is precisely to drive her into one of those sinful and unhappy marriages? It is quite clear we can never drive her into *love*. That is a sentiment which poverty, friendlessness, and helplessness can by no means call out. Nor, on the contrary, can competence and freedom in any way check it. It will arise under its natural conditions, if we will but leave the matter alone. A *loving* marriage can never become a matter of "cold philosophic choice." And if *not* a loving one, then, for Heaven's sake, let us give no motive for choice at all.

Let the employments of women be raised and multiplied as much as possible, let their labour be as fairly remunerated, let their education be pushed as high, let their whole position be made as healthy and happy as possible, and there will come out once more, here as in every other department of life, the triumph of the Divine laws of our nature.

Loving marriages are (we cannot doubt) what God has designed, not marriages of interest. When we have made it *less* women's interest to marry, we shall indeed have less and fewer interested marriages, with all their train of miseries and evils. But we shall also have more *loving* ones, more marriages founded on free choice and free affection. Thus we arrive at the conclusion that for the very end of promoting marriage—that is, such marriage as it is alone desirable to promote—we should pursue a precisely opposite course to that suggested by the Reviewer or his party. Instead of leaving single women as helpless as possible, and their labour as ill-rewarded—instead of dinning into their ears from childhood that marriage is their one vocation and concern in life, and securing afterwards if they miss it that they shall find no other vocation or concern;—instead of all this, we shall act exactly on the reverse principle. We shall make single life so free and happy that they shall have not one temptation to change it save the only temptation which *ought* to determine them—namely, love. Instead of making marriage a case of "Hobson's choice" for a woman, we shall endeavour to give her such independence of all interested considerations that she may make it a choice, not indeed "cold and philosophic," but warm from the heart, and guided by heart and conscience only.

And again, in another way the same principle holds good, and marriage will be found to be best promoted by aiding and not by thwarting the efforts of single women to improve their condition. It is a topic on which we cannot speak much, but thus far may suffice. The reviewer alludes with painful truth to a class of the community whose lot is far more grievous than either celibacy or marriage. Justly he traces the unwillingness of hundreds of men to marry to the existence of these unhappy women in their present condition. He would remedy the evil by preaching marriage to such men. But does not all the world know that thousands of these poor souls, of all degrees, would never have fallen into their miserable vocation had any *other* course been open to them, and they had been enabled to acquire a competence by honest labour? Let such honest courses be opened to them, and then we shall see, as in America, the recruiting of that wretched army becoming less and less possible every year in the country. The self-supporting, and therefore self-respecting woman may indeed become a wife, and a good and happy one, but she will no longer afford any man a reason for declining to marry.

It is curious to note that while, on the one hand, we are urged to make marriage the sole vocation of women, we are simultaneously met on the other by the outpourings of ridicule and contempt on all who for themselves, or even for their children, seek ever so indirectly to attain this vocation. Only last year all England was entertained by jests concerning "Belgravian mothers;" and the wiles and devices of widows and damsels afford an unending topic of satire and amusement in private and public. Now we ask, in all seriousness, Wherefore all this ridicule and contempt? *If* marriage be indeed the one object of a woman's life— *if* to give her any other pursuit or interest be only to divert her from that one object and "palliate the symptoms while fostering a great social disease"—then, we repeat, *why* despise these match-making mothers? Are they to do nothing to help their daughters to their only true vocation, which, if they should miss, their lives *ought* to be failures, poverty-stricken and miserable? Nay; but if things be so, the most open, unblushing marketing of their daughters is the *duty* of parents, and the father or mother who leaves the matter to chance is flagrantly neglectful. Truly it is a paradox passing all limits of reason, that society should enforce marriage on woman as her only honourable life, and at the same time should stigmatize as dishonourable the efforts of her parents to settle her in marriage.

The spontaneous sentiment of mankind has hit a deeper truth than the theories of economists. It *is* in the nature of things disgraceful and abominable that marriage should be made the aim of a woman's life. It can only become what it is meant to be, the completion and crown of the life of either man or woman, when it has arisen from sentiments which can never be bespoken for the convenient fulfillment of any vocation whatsoever.

But it is urged, and not unreasonably—If it be admitted on all hands that marriage is the best condition, and that only one-fourth of the female sex do not marry, how can we expect provision to be made for this contingency of one chance in four by a girl's parents and by herself in going through an education (perhaps costly and laborious) for a trade or profession which there are three chances in four she will not long continue to exercise?

It must be admitted here is the great knot and difficulty of the higher branches of woman's employment. It does require farseeing care on the part of the parent, perseverance and resolution of no mean order on that of the daughter, to go through in youth the training which will fit her to earn her livelihood hereafter in any of the more elevated occupations. Nay, it demands that she devote to such training the precise years of life wherein the chances of marriage are commonly offered, and the difficulties of pursuing a steady course are very much enhanced by temptations of all kinds. If she wait till the years when such chances fail, and take up a pursuit at thirty merely as a *pis aller*, she must inevitably remain for ever behindhand and in an inferior position.

The trial is undoubtedly considerable, but there are symptoms that both young women and their parents will not be always unwilling to meet it, and to invest both time and money in lines of education which *may* indeed prove superfluous, but which likewise may afford the mainstay of a life which, without them, would be helpless, aimless, and miserable. The magnitude of the risk ought surely to weigh somewhat in the balance. At the lowest point of view, a woman is no worse off if she marry eventually, for having first gone through an education for some good pursuit; while if she remain single, she is wretchedly off for not having had such education. But this is in fact only a half view of the case. As we have insisted before, it is only on the standing ground of a happy and independent celibacy that a woman can really make a free choice in marriage. To secure this standing-ground, a pursuit is more needful than a pecuniary competence, for a life without aim or object is one which, more than all others, goads a woman into accepting any chance of a change. Mariana (we are privately convinced) would have eloped out of the Moated Grange not only with that particular "he" who never came, but with any other suitor who might have presented himself.[1] Only a woman who has something else than making love to do and to think of will love really and deeply. It is in *real lives*—lives devoted to actual service of father or mother, or to work of some kind for God or man—that alone spring up *real feelings*. Lives of idleness and pleasure have no depth to nourish such plants.

Again, we are very far indeed from maintaining that *during* marriage it is at all to be desired that a woman should struggle to keep up whatever pursuit she had adopted beforehand. In nine cases out of ten this will drop naturally to the ground, especially when she has children. The great and paramount duties of a mother and wife once adopted, every other interest sinks, by the beneficent laws of our nature, into a subordinate place in normally constituted minds, and the effort to perpetuate them is as false as it is usually fruitless. Where necessity and poverty compel mothers in the lower ranks to go out to work, we all know too well the evils which ensue. And in the higher classes doubtless the holding tenaciously by any pursuit interfering with home duties must produce such Mrs. Jellabys as we sometimes hear of.[2] It is not only leisure which is in question. There appear to be some occult laws in woman's nature providing against such mistakes by rendering it impossible to pursue the higher branches of art or literature or any work tasking mental exertion, while home and motherly cares have their claims. We have heard of a great artist saying that she is always obliged to leave her children for a few weeks before she can throw herself again into the artist-feeling of her youth, and we believe her experience is corroborated on all hands. No great books have been written or works achieved by women while their children were around them in infancy. No woman can lead the two lives at the same time.

But it is often strangely forgotten that there are such things as widows, left such in the prime of life, and quite as much needing occupation as if they had remained single. Thus, then, another chance must fairly be added to our one in four that a woman may need such a pursuit as we have supposed. She may never marry, or having married she may be left a childless widow, or a widow whose few children occupy but a portion of her time. Suppose, for instance, she has been a physician. How often would the possibility of returning to her early profession be an invaluable resource after her husband's death! The greatest female mathematician living, was saved from despairing sorrow in widowhood, by throwing herself afresh into the studies of her youth.

It may be a pleasantly romantic idea to some minds, that of woman growing up solely with the hope of becoming some man's devoted wife, marrying the first that offers, and when he dies, becoming a sort of moral Suttee whose heart is supposed to be henceforth dead and in ashes. But it is quite clear that Providence can never have designed any such order of things. All the infinite tenderness and devotion He has placed in women's hearts, though meant to make marriage blessed and happy, and diffusing as from a hearth of warm affections, kindness and love on all around, is yet meant to be subordinated to the great purposes of the existence of all rational souls—the approximation to God through virtue. With reverence be it spoken, GOD is the only true centre of life for us all, not any creature he has made. "To live unto God" is the law for man and woman alike. Whoever strives to do this will neither spend youth in longing for happiness which may be withheld, nor age in despair for that which may be withdrawn.

To resume. It appears that from every point of view in which we regard the subject, it is desirable that women should have other aims, pursuits, and interests in life beside matrimony, and that by possessing them they are guaranteed against being driven into unloving marriages, and rendered more fitted for loving ones; while their single life, whether in maidenhood or widowhood, is made useful and happy.

Before closing this part of the subject, we cannot but add a few words to express our amused surprise at the way in which the writers on this subject constantly concern themselves with the question of *female* celibacy, deplore it, abuse it, propose amazing remedies for it, but take little or no notice of the twenty-five per cent. old bachelors (or thereabouts) who needs must exist to match the thirty percent. old maids. *Their* moral condition seems to excite no alarm, their lonely old age no foreboding compassion, their action on the community no reprobation. Nobody scolds them very seriously, unless some stray Belgravian grandmother. All the alarm, compassion, reprobation, and scoldings are reserved for the poor old maids. But of the two, which of the parties is the chief delinquent? The *Zend Avesta*,[3] as translated by Anquetil du Perron, contains somewhere this awful denunciation:— "That damsel who having reached the age of eighteen, shall refuse to marry, must remain in hell till the Resurrection!" A severe penalty, doubtless, for the crime, and wonderful to meet in the mild creed of Zoroaster, where no greater punishment is allotted to any offence whatsoever. Were these Guebre young ladies so terribly cruel, and *mazdiesnans* (true believers) so desperately enamoured? Are we to imagine the obdurate damsels despatching whole dozens of despairing gentlemen in conical caps to join the society in the shades below—

> Hapless youths who died for love,
> Wandering in a myrtle grove!

It takes a vivid stretch of imagination in England, in the nineteenth century, to picture anything of the kind. Whatever other offences our young ladies may be guilty of, or other weaknesses our young gentlemen, obduracy on the one hand, and dying for love on the other, are rarities, at all events. Yet one would suppose that Zoroaster was needed over here, to judge of the manner in which old maids are lectured on their very improper position. "The Repression of Crime," as the benevolent Recorder of Birmingham would phrase it, seems on the point of being exercised against them, since it has been found out that their offence is on the increase, like poaching in country districts and landlord shooting in Ireland. The mildest punishment, we are told, is to be transportation, to which half a million have just been condemned, and for the terror of future evil doers, it is decreed that no single woman's work ought to be fairly remunerated, nor her position allowed to be entirely respectable, lest she exercise "a cold philosophic choice" about matrimony. No false charity to criminals! Transportation or starvation to all old maids!

Poor old maids! Will not the Reformatory, Union, or some other friends of the criminal, take their case in hand? They are too old for Miss Carpenter. Could not Sir Walter Crofton's Intermediate System be of some use?[4] There is reason to hope that many of them would be willing to adopt a more honest way of life were the chance offered them.

If the reader should have gone with us thus far, we shall be able better to follow the subject from a point of view which shall in fact unite the two leading ideas of which we made mention at starting. We shall, with the *first*, seek earnestly how the condition of single women may be most effectually improved; and with the *second*, we shall admit the promotion of marriage (*provided it be disinterested and loving*) to be the best end at which such improvements will tend.

In one point there is a practical unanimity between the schemes of the two parties, and this we should desire to notice before proceeding to consider the ways in which the condition of single women may be improved as such. This scheme is that of emigration for women to the colonies. Here we have multitudes of women offered in the first place remunerative employment beyond anything they could obtain at home; and further, the facilitation of marriage effected for large numbers, to the great benefit of both men and women. What there might appear in the plan contradictory to the principles we have laid down above, is only apparent, and not real. The woman who arrives in a colony where her labour, of head or hands, can command an ample maintenance, stands in the precise condition we have desired to make marriage—a matter of free choice. She has left "Hobson's choice" behind her with the poverty of England, and has come out to find competence and freedom, and if she choose (but *only* if she choose), marriage also.

It is needless to say that this scheme has our entire sympathy and good wishes, though we do not expect to live to see the time when our reviewer's plans will be fulfilled by the deportation of women at the rate of thirty or forty thousand a year.[5]

An important point, however, must not be overlooked. However far the emigration of women of the working classes may be carried, that of educated women must at all times remain very limited, inasmuch as the demand for them in the colonies is comparatively trifling. Now, it is of educated women that the great body of "old maids" consists; in the lower orders celibacy is rare. Thus, it should be borne in mind that emigration schemes do not essentially bear on the main point, "How shall we improve the condition of the thirty per cent. of single women in England?" The reviewer to whom we have so often alluded, does indeed dispose of the matter by observing that the transportation he fondly hopes to see effected, of 440,000 women to the colonies, will at least *relieve the market* for those who remain. We cannot but fear, however, that the governesses and other ladies so accommodated will not much profit by the large selection thus afforded them among the blacksmiths and ploughmen, deprived of their proper companions. At the least we shall have a quarter of a million of old maids *in esse* and *in posse* left on hands. What can we do for them?

For convenience we may divide them into two classes. One of them, without capital or high cultivation, needs employment suitable to a woman's powers, and yet affording better remuneration than woman's work has hitherto usually received. Here we find the efforts of Miss Faithfull, Miss Crowe, Miss Rye, and the other ladies in combination with the society founded by Miss Parkes, labouring to procure such employment for them by the Victoria Printing Press, the Law Copying Office, and other plans in action or contemplated for watchmaking, hair-dressing, and the like.[6] We may look on this class as in good hands; and as the emigration of women will actually touch it and carry away numbers of its members, we may hope that its destinies are likely henceforth to improve.

The other and higher class is that of which we desire more particularly to speak, namely, of ladies either possessed of sufficient pecuniary means to support themselves comfortably, or else of such gifts and cultivation as shall command a competence. The help these women need is not of a pecuniary nature, but a large portion of them require aid, and the removal of existing restrictions, to afford them the full exercise of their natural powers, and make their lives as useful and happy as Providence has intended. Of *all* the position is at the present moment of transition worthy of some attention, and suggestive of some curious speculations regarding the future of women. Channing remarks that when the negro races become thoroughly Christianized we shall see a development of the religion never known before. At least equally justly may we predict that when woman's gifts are at last expanded in an atmosphere of freedom and happiness, we shall find graces and powers revealed to us of which we yet have little dreamed. To the consideration, then, of the condition and prospects of women of the upper classes who remain unmarried, we shall devote the following pages.

All the pursuits of mankind, beside mere money-getting, may be fitly classed in three great orders. They are in one way or another the pursuit of the True, the Beautiful, or the Good. In a general way we may say that science, literature, and philosophy are devoted to Truth; art in all its branches (including poetic literature) to the Beautiful; and politics and philanthropy to the Good. Within certain limits, each of these lines of action are open to women; and it is in the aspect they bear as regards women's work that we are now to regard them. But before analysing them further, I would fain be allowed to make one remark which is far too often forgotten. Each of these pursuits is equally noble in itself; it is our fitness for one or the other, not its intrinsic sanctity or value, which ought to determine our choice; and we are all astray in our judgments if we come to the examination of them with prejudices for or against one or the other. In these days, when "the icy chains of custom and of prejudice" are somewhat loosened, and men and women go forth more freely than ever of old to choose and make their lives, there is too often this false measurement of our brother's choice. Each of us asks his friend in effect, if not in words—"Why not follow my calling rather than your own? Why not use such a gift? Why not adopt such a task?" The answer to these questions must not be made with the senseless pedantry of the assumption, that because to *us* art or literature, or philanthropy or politics, is the true vocation, therefore for all men and women it is the noblest; and that God meant Mozart to be a statesman, and Howard a sculptor, and Kant a teacher in a ragged school. The true, the beautiful, and the good are all revelations of the Infinite One, and therefore all holy. It is enough for a man if it be given him in his lifetime to pursue any one of them to profit—to carry a single step further the torch of humanity along either of the three roads, every one of which leads up to God. The philosopher, who studies and teaches us the laws of mind or matter—the artist, who beholds with illumined eyes the beauty of the world, and creates it afresh in poetry or painting—the statesman or philanthropist, who labours to make Right victorious, and to advance the virtue and happiness of mankind,—all these in their several ways are God's seers, God's prophets, as much the one as the other. We could afford to lose none of them, to undervalue none of them. The philosopher is not to be honoured only for the goodness or the beauty of the *truth* he has revealed. All truth is good and beautiful, but it is to be prized because it is *truth*, and not merely for its goodness or beauty. The artist is not to be honoured only for the truth or the goodness of the *beautiful* he has revealed. The beautiful is necessarily good and true, but it is to be loved because it is *beautiful*, and not merely for its truth or goodness.[7] Like the old Athanasian symbol, we may say, "The Truth is divine, the Beautiful is divine, and the Good is divine. And yet they are not three divine things, but three revelations of the One Divine Lord." If men would but feel this each in his own pursuit, and in judging of the pursuits of others, how holy and noble would all faithful work become! We are haunted yet with the Romish thought that a life of asceticism, of preaching, of prayer, of charity, is altogether on a different plane of being from a life devoted to other tasks. But it is not so. From *every* field of honest human toil there rises a ladder up into heaven. Was Kepler further from God than any Howard or Xavier when, after discovering the law of the planetary distances, he bowed his head and exclaimed in rapture, "O God, I think Thy thoughts after Thee!" Was Milton less divine than any St. Theresa locked in her stony cell, when his mighty genius had soared "upon the seraph wings of ecstasy" over the whole beautiful creation, and he poured out at last his triumphant Psalm—

> These are Thy glorious works, Parent of
> > Good—
> Almighty!

Of these three great modes of Divine manifestation, it would appear, however, that, though equal in sanctity and dignity, the pursuit of the True and of the Beautiful were designed for comparatively few among mankind. Few possess the pure abstract love of Truth in such fervour as to fit them to become the martyrs of science or the prophets of philosophy. Few also are those who are endowed with that supreme sense of the Beautiful, and power to reproduce it in form, colour, or sound, which constitute the gifts of the artist. Especially does this hold good with women. While few of them do not feel their hearts warmed with the love of goodness, and the desire to relieve the sufferings of their fellows, a mere fraction, in comparison, interest themselves to any extent in the pursuit of the abstract truths of philosophy or science, or possess any powers to reproduce the Beautiful in Art, even when they have a perception of its presence in nature. We may discuss briefly, then, here the prospects of the employment of women in the departments of Truth and Beauty, and in a future paper consider more at length the new aspect of their philanthropic labours and endeavours to do Good.

*   *   *

Till of very late years it was, we think, perfectly justifiable to doubt the possibility of women possessing any creative artistic power. Receptive faculties they have always had, ready and vivid perception of the beautiful in both nature and art, delicate discrimination and refined taste, nay, the power (especially in music and the drama) of reproducing what the genius of man had created. But to originate any work of even second-rate merit was what no woman had done. Sappho was a mere name, and between her and even such a feeble poetess as Mrs. Hemans,[8] there was hardly another to fill up the gap of the whole cycle of history. No woman has written the epics, nor the dramas, nay, nor even the national songs of her country, if we may not except Miriam's and Deborah's chants of victory. In music, nothing. In architecture, nothing. In sculpture, nothing. In painting, an Elisabetta Sirani, a Rosalba, an Angelica Kauffman—hardly exceptions enough to prove the rule. Such works as women did accomplish were all stamped with the same impress of feebleness and prettiness. As Mrs. Hemans and Joanna Baillie and Mrs. Tighe wrote poetry, so Angelica Kauffman painted pictures, and other ladies composed washy music and Minerva-press romances.[9] If Tennyson had spoken of woman's *Art*, instead of woman's passions, he would have been as right for the one as he was wrong as regards the other. It *was*

As moonlight is to sunlight
And as water is to wine.

To coin an epithet from a good type of the school—it was all "Angelical," no flesh and blood at all, but super-refined sentiments and super-elongated limbs.

But there seem symptoms extant that this state of things is to undergo a change, and the works of women become remarkable for other qualities beside softness and weakness. It may be a mere chance conjunction, but it is at least remarkable, that the same age has given us in the three greatest departments of art—poetry, painting, and sculpture—women who, whatever be their faults or merits, are pre-eminently distinguished for one quality above all others—namely, strength. *Aurora Leigh* is perhaps the least "Angelical" poem in the language,[10] and bears the relation to *Psyche* that a chiselled steel corslet does to a silk bodice with lace trimmings. The very hardness of its rhythm, its sturdy wrestlings and grapplings, one after another, with all the sternest problems of our social life—its forked-lightning revelations of character—and finally, the storm of glorified passion with which it closes in darkness (like nothing else we ever read since the mountain-tempest scene in *Childe Harold*)—all this takes us miles away from the received notion of a woman's poetry.

And for painting, let us look at Rosa Bonheur's canvas.[11] Those droves of wild Highland black cattle, those teams of tramping Norman horses—do they belong to the same school of female art as all the washed-out saints, and pensive ladies, and graceful bouquets of Mesdemoiselles and Signorine Rosee, and Rosalba, and Panzacchi, and Grebber, and Mérian, and Kauffman? We seem to have passed a frontier, and entered a new realm wherein Rosa Bonheurs are to be found.

*   *   *

Then for Sculpture. Will woman's genius ever triumph here? We confess we look to this point as to the touchstone of the whole question. Sculpture is in many respects at once the noblest art and the one which tasks highest both creative power and scientific skill. A really good and great statue is an achievement to which there must contribute more elements of power and patience than in almost any other human work, and it is, when perfected, one of the most sublime. We know generally very little of this matter in England. We possess pictures by the great masters sufficient in number and excellence to afford a fair conception (though of course an incomplete one) of the

powers of painting. But notwithstanding the antique treasures in the
Elgin and Arundel Collections, and a few fine modern statues to be
found in private houses in this country, it is, I believe, to every one a
revelation of a new agency in art when he first visits Italy and beholds
the "Laocöon," the "Apollo," the "Niobe," and the "Psyche" of
Praxiteles.[12] Hitherto sculpture has appeared to be merely the
production of beautiful forms, more or less true to nature. Now it is
perceived to be genius breathing through form, the loftiest thoughts of
human souls. "Apollo Belvidere" is not the mere figure of a perfect man
in graceful attitude, as we thought it from casts and copies in England.
It is Power itself, deified and made real before our eyes. The "Laocöon"
is not the hapless high-priest writhing in the coil of the serpent. It is
the impersonation of the will of a giant man, a Prometheus struggling
with indomitable courage against the resistless Fate in whose grasp
meaner mortals are crushed helplessly. The "Niobe" is not merely a
woman of noblest mould inspired by maternal anguish. She is glorified
MOTHERHOOD, on whose great bosom we could rest, and round
whose neck we could throw our arms. And the "Psyche" in the Museo
Borbonico?—is this a poor fragment of a form, once perhaps graceful
and fair, but now a mere ruin? No! It is the last gleam of the unknown
glory of ancient art, the one work of human hands which we forget to
admire because we learn to love it—the revelation to each of us of our
innermost ideal of friend or wife, the sweetest, purest of our dreams
made real before our eyes.

Not untruly has sculpture been named the *Ars Divinior.* A deep
and strange analogy exists between it and the highest we know of the
Supreme Artist's works. Out of the clay, cold and formless, the
sculptor slowly, patiently, with infinite care and love, moulds an image
of beauty. Long the stubborn clay seems to resist his will, and to
remain without grace or proportion, but at last the image begins,
faintly and in a far-off way, to reflect that prototype which is in the
sculptor's mind. The limbs grow into shape, and stand firmly balanced,
the countenance becomes living and radiant. And last of all, the
character of true sculpture appears; there is calm and peace over it all,
and an infinite divine repose, even when the life within seems higher
and fuller than that of mortality. The moulding is done, the statue is
perfected.

But even then, when it should seem that the sculptor's great
work is achieved, and that his image should be preserved and cherished

evermore, what does he in truth do with his clay? Return hither, oh traveller, in a few short days, and the image of clay is gone, its place knows it no more. It has returned to the earth whence it was taken, thrown by, perchance for ever, or else kneaded afresh in some new form of life. Did he make it, then, but for destruction, and mould it so carefully but to crush it out at last in dust? Look around with illumined eyes! In the great studio of the universe the Divine image is still to be found, not now moulded in clay and ready to perish, dull of hue and dead in lustre, but sculptured in eternal marble, white, and pure, and radiant; meet to stand for ever in the palaces on high.

Sculpture is the noblest of the arts; nay, it is above all others in this very thing which has been pointed at as its bane and limitation. Its aim must ever be the expression of calmness and repose. No vehement wildness of the painter's dream, no storm of the musician's harmony, no ecstasy of the poet's passion; but the stillness and the peace of which earth knows so little. To bring our souls into sympathy with a great work of sculpturesque repose, is to bring them into the serener fields of the upper air, where the storms approach not, nor any clouds ascend. We do not naturally in the earlier moral life feel in union with things calm and still like these. The struggle in our own breasts, the lordly will wrestling with the lower powers for mastery, leaves us rather able to sympathize with all nature's warfare of wind and wave, all human death-battles, than with the repose in which the saint's soul rests, loving the cloudless sky and waveless sea, and the smile of a sleeping child nestled in the long sweet grass of summer. To reach that rest of the whole nature, which is at the same time absolute repose and absolute action of every power and every faculty in perfect balance, is the "Beulah land,"

> Where blessed saints dwell ever in the light
> Of God's dear love, and earth is heaven below.
> For never doubt nor sin may cloud their sight,
> And the great PEACE OF GOD calms every human woe.

The art which is the idealizing, the perpetuation of repose is, then, the divinest art—the art to be practised only by great souls—great races of men. Egyptians and Greeks were races of sculptors; Hindoos and Mexicans stone cutters of goblins. We repeat that the sharpest test to which the question of woman's genius can be put is this one of sculpture. If she succeed here, if a school of real sculpturesses ever arise, then we think that in effect the problem is solved. The greater includes the less. They may still fall below male composers in music, though we have seen some (inedited) music of wonderful power from a female hand. They may produce no great drama—perhaps no great historical picture. Yet if really good statues come from their studios, statues showing at once power of conception and science of execution, then we say, women can be artists. It is no longer a question whether the creative faculty be granted to them.

Now, we venture to believe that there are distinct tokens that this solution is really to be given to the problem. For long centuries women never seem to have attempted sculpture at all; perhaps because it was then customary for the artist to perform much of the mechanical labour of the marble-cutter himself; perhaps because women could rarely command either the large outlay or the anatomical instructions. But in our time things are changed. The Princesse Marie d'Orleans, in her well-known Joan of Arc, accomplished a really noble work of sculpture. Others have followed and are following in her path, but most marked of all by power and skill comes Harriet Hosmer, whose Zenobia (now standing in the International Exhibition, in the same temple with Gibson's Venus) is a definite proof that a woman can make a statue of the very highest order. Whether we consider the noble conception of this majestic figure, or the science displayed in every part of it, from the perfect *pose* and accurate anatomy, to the admirable truth and finish of the drapery, we are equally satisfied. Here is what we wanted. A woman—aye, a woman with all the charms of youthful womanhood—can be a sculptor, and a great one.

Now we have arrived at a conclusion worthy of some little attention. Women a few years ago could only show a few weak and washy female poets and painter, and no sculptors at all. They can now boast of such true and powerful artists in these lines as Mrs. Browning, Rosa Bonheur, and Harriet Hosmer. What account can we give of the rise of such a new constellation? We confess ourselves unable to offer any solution, save that proposed by a gifted lady to whom we propounded our query. Female artists hitherto always started on a wrong track; being persuaded beforehand that they ought only to compose sweet verses and soft pictures, they set themselves to make them accordingly, and left us Mrs. Hemans' Works and Angelica's paintings. *Now*, women who possess any real genius, apply it to the creation of what they (and not society for them) really admire. A woman naturally admires power, force, grandeur. It is these qualities, then, which we shall see more and more appearing as the spontaneous genius of woman asserts itself.

We know not how this may be. It is at all events a curious speculation. One remark we must make before leaving this subject. This new element of *strength* in female art seems to impress spectators very differently. It cannot be concealed that while all true artists recognise it with delight, there is no inconsiderable number of men to whom it is obviously distasteful, and who turn away more or less decidedly in feeling from the display of this or any other power in women, exercised never so inoffensively. There is a feeling (tacit or expressed) "Yes, it is very clever, but somehow it is not quite feminine." Now we do not wish to use sarcastic words about sentiments of this kind, or demonstrate all their unworthiness and ungenerousness. We would rather make an appeal to a better judgment, and entreat for a resolute stop to expressions ever so remotely founded on them. The origin of them all has perhaps been the old error that clipping and fettering every faculty of body and mind was the sole method of making a woman—that as the Chinese make a lady's foot, so we should make a lady's mind; and that, in a word, the old alehouse sign was not so far wrong in depicting "The Good Woman" as a woman without any head whatsoever. Earnestly would we enforce the opposite doctrine, that as God means a woman to *be* a woman and not a man, every faculty he has given her is a woman's faculty, and the more each of them can be drawn out, trained, and perfected, the more *womanly* she will become. She will be a larger, richer, nobler woman for art, for learning, for every grace and gift she can acquire. It must indeed be a mean and miserable man who would prefer that a woman's nature should be pinched, and starved, and dwarfed to keep on his level, rather than be nurtured and trained to its loftiest capacity, to meet worthily his highest also.

Thus we quit the subject of woman's pursuit of the Beautiful, rejoicing in the new promise of its success, and wishing all prosperity to the efforts to afford female students of art that sound and solid training, the lack of which has been their greatest stumblingblock hitherto. The School of Art and Design in London is a good augury with its eight hundred and sixty-three lady pupils!

*   *   *

But for woman's devotion to the True in physics and metaphysics, woman's science and woman's learning, what shall we venture to say? The fact must be frankly admitted—women have even more rarely the powers and tastes needful to carry them in this direction than in that of art. The love of abstract truth as a real passion is probably antithetic in some measure to that vivid interest in persons which belongs to the warm sympathies and strong affections of women. Their quickness of perception militates against the slow toil of science, and their vividness of intuitive faith renders them often impatient of the discussions of philosophy. Many women love truth warmly enough, and for religious truth female martyrs have never been wanting since the mother of the Maccabees. But few women complete their love of truth by such hatred of error as shall urge them to the exertion of laboriously establishing and defining the limits of the truths they possess. These natural causes again have been reinforced by endless artificial hindrances. The want of schools and colleges, the absence of such rewards as encourage (though they cannot inspire) the pursuit of knowledge, popular and domestic prejudices rendering study disfavoured, difficult access to books or leisure from household duties, the fluctuating health fostered by the unwholesome habits of women; and lastly, the idleness and distractions of those very years of youth in which education can rise above the puerile instruction of a girl's schoolroom.

Far be it from us to wish to force all women into courses of severe study—to put (as has been well said of late) Arabian horses to the plough, and educate directly against the grain; only we desire thus much, that those women who do possess the noble love of knowledge and are willing to undergo the drudgery of its acquirement, should have every aid supplied and every stumblingblock removed from their paths. The improvements which in our time are making in these directions may be briefly stated. First, popular prejudice against well-educated women is dying away. It is found they do *not* "neglect infants for quadratic equations," nor perform in any way less conscientiously the various duties of life after reading Plato or even Kant. Secondly, the opening of ladies' colleges, such as Bedford-square and Harley-street, where really sound and solid instruction is given by first-rate teachers at a cost not equal to half that of the shallow and superficial boarding-school of twenty years ago. Thirdly, women have benefited even more than men by the general progress of the times, the facilitation of travelling (formerly impossible to them without protection), the opening of good lending-libraries, cheap books and postage. The dead sea of ennui in which so many of them live is now rippled by a hundred currents from all quarters of heaven; and we may trust that the pettiness of gossip which has been the standing reproach of the sex will disappear with the narrowness of life which supplied no wholesomer food for conversation or thought. To cramp every faculty and cut off all large interests, and then complain that a human being so treated is narrow-minded and scandal-loving, is precisely an injustice parallel to that of some Southern Americans whom we have heard detail those vices of the negroes *which slavery had produced*, as the reason why they were justified in keeping so degraded a race in such a condition. It would be indeed a miracle often if a woman manufactured on some not unpopular principles were anything else than a very poor and pitiful piece of mechanism. The further improvements which may be sought in these directions are of various kinds. The standard of ordinary female education cannot perhaps be elevated above that of the ladies' colleges already mentioned, but *this* standard will become not (as now) the high-water mark for a few, but the common tide-line for all women of the middle and higher classes supposed to be fairly educated. Above this high standard, again, facilities and encouragements may be given to women of exceptionally studious tastes to rise to the levels of any instruction attainable. One important way in which this last end may be reached—namely, the admission of women to the examinations and honours of the London University—has been lately much debated. The arguments which have determined its temporary rejection by the senate of the University (a rejection, however, only decided by the casting vote of the chairman), seem to have been all of the character discussed a few pages ago,—the supposed necessity of keeping women to their sole vocation of wives and mothers, and so on. The benefits which would accrue from the measure were urged by the present writer before the Social Science Congress,[13] and were briefly these—that women need as much or more than men a stimulus to carry their education to a high pitch of perfection and accuracy; that this stimulus has always been supplied to men by university examinations and rewards of honour; that it ought to be offered to women, as likely to produce on them the same desirable results; lastly, that the University of London requiring no collegiate residence, and having its examinations conducted in special apartments perfectly unobjectionable for women's use, it constitutes the one university in the kingdom which ought to admit women to its examinations.

Intimately connected with this matter is that of opening to women the medical profession, for which university degrees would be the first steps. The subject has been well worn of late; yet we must needs make a few remarks concerning it, and notably to put a question or two to objectors. Beloved reader (male or female, as the chance may be), did it ever happen to you to live in a household of half a dozen persons in which some woman was *not* the self-constituted family physician, to whom all the other members of the party applied for advice in ninety-nine cases out of a hundred? A cold, a cough, a rheumatism, a sprain, a cut, a burn, bile, indigestion, headaches and heartaches, are they not all submitted to her counsel, and the remedies she prescribes for them devoutly taken? Usually it is the grandmother or the housekeeper of the family who is consulted; but whichever it may chance to be, mistress or servant, it is always a *woman*. Who ever dreamed of asking his grandfather or his uncle, his butler or footman, "what he should do for this bad cold," or to "be so kind as to tie up this cut finger"? We can hardly imagine the astonishment of "Jeames" at such a request; but any woman abovestairs or below would take it as perfectly natural. Doctoring is one of the "rights of women," which albeit theoretically denied is practically conceded so universally that it is probable that all the M.D.'s in England, with the apothecaries to boot, do not order more drugs than are yearly "exhibited" by their unlicensed female domestic rivals. It is not a question whether such a state of things be desirable; it exists, and no legislation can alter it. The two differences between the authorized doctors and unauthorized doctoresses are simply these—that the first are paid and the second unpaid for their services, and the first have *some* scientific knowledge and the second none at all. It behoves us a little to consider these two distinctions. First, if patients choose to go for advice to women, and women inspire them with sufficient confidence to be consulted, it is a piece of interference quite anomalous in our day to prevent such services being rewarded, or in other words, to prevent the woman from qualifying herself legally to accept such reward. A woman may or may not be a desirable doctor, just as a dissenter may or may not be a desirable teacher; but unless we are to go back to paternal governments, we must permit patients and congregations to be the judges of what suits them best, and not any medical or ecclesiastical corporation. It is not that *women* are called on to show cause why they should be permitted to enter the medical profession and obtain remuneration for their services, but the *doctors*, who are bound to show cause why they should exclude them and deprive them of the remuneration which there are abundance of patients ready to bestow. This is the side of the rights of the doctor. But are we not still more concerned with the second point of difference, which involves the safety of the patient? As we have said, men and women *will* go continually to women for medical advice in all those thousand contingencies and minor maladies out of which three-fourths of the mortal diseases of humanity arise. There is no use scolding, and saying they *ought* to go to the apothecary or the M.D. People will *not* do so, least of all will delicate women do so when it is possible to avoid it. The only question is, whether the advice which in any case they will get from a woman will be good advice or bad advice—advice founded on some scientific knowledge, or advice derived from the wildest empiricism and crassest ignorance.

We have sometimes lamented that we have lacked the precaution of making memoranda of the wonderful remedies which have become known to us in the course of time, as applied by that class of domestic doctoresses of which we have spoken. They would have afforded a valuable storehouse of arguments to prove that, if "the little knowledge" of medicine (which we are told is all women could hope to acquire in a college) is "a dangerous thing," the utter absence of all knowledge whatever which they at present display, is a hundred times more perilous still. Well can we recal [sic], for instance, in the home of our childhood, a certain admirable old cook who was the oracle in medical matters of the whole establishment. Notwithstanding the constant visits of an excellent physician, it was to her opinion that recourse was had on all emergencies; and the results may be imagined when it is avowed that in her genius the culinary and therapeutic arts were so assimilated, that she invariably *cooked* her patients as well as their dinners. On one occasion a groom having received an immense laceration and excoriation of the leg, was treated by having the wound *rubbed with salt, and held before a hot fire!*

At the opposite end of the social scale we can remember a lady of high degree and true Lady Bountiful disposition pressing on us, in succession, the merits of Morison's pills, hydropathy, and brandy and salt; "and if none of them cure your attack, there is St. John Long's remedy, which is *quite* infallible." It would not be easy to calculate how often such practitioners might incur the same chance as a grandmother of our own, who, asking an Irish labourer his name, received the *foudroyante* reply—"Ah! and don't you know me, my lady? And didn't your ladyship give the dose to my wife, and she died the next day?—*long life to your ladyship!*"

All this folly and quackery—nay, the use of quack medicines altogether—would be vastly diminished, if not stopped, by the training of a certain number of women as regular physicians, and the instruction derived through them of females generally, in the rudiments of physiology and sanitary science. It is vain to calculate whether individual lady physicians would be as successful as the ordinary average of male doctors. To argue about an untried capacity, *à priori*, seems absurd; and such experience as America has afforded us appears wholly favourable. But the point is, not whether women will make as good doctors as men, but how the whole female sex may be better taught in a matter of vital importance, not only to themselves, but to men whose health is modified through life by their mother's treatment in infancy. As the diffusion of physiological knowledge among women *generally* must unquestionably come from the instruction of a few women *specially* educated, the exclusion of females from courses of medical study assumes the shape of a decree that the sex on whom the health of the community peculiarly depends, shall for ever remain in ignorance of the laws by which that health is to be maintained.

With the highest possible education for women in ladies' colleges, with University examinations and the medical profession opened to them, we have little doubt that a new life would enter into many, and the pursuit of knowledge become a real vocation, where it has been hitherto hardly more than an amusement. Many a field of learning will yield unexpected flowers to a woman's fresh research, and many a path of science grow firm and clear before the feet which will follow in the steps of Mrs. Somerville.[14] Already women have made for themselves a place, and a large one, in the literature of our time; and when their general instruction becomes deeper and higher, their works must become more and more valuable. Whether doctoresses are to be permitted or not, may be a question; but authoresses are already a guild, which, instead of opposition, has met kindliest welcome. It is now a real profession to women as to men, to be writers. Let any one read the list of books in a modern library, and judge how large a share of them were written by women. Mrs. Jameson, Mrs. Stowe, Miss Brontë, George Eliot, Mrs. Gaskell, Susan and Katherine Winkworth, Miss Martineau, Miss Bremer, George Sand, Mrs. Browning, Miss Procter, Miss Austen, Miss Strickland, Miss Pardoe, Miss Mulock, Mrs. Grey, Mrs. Gore, Mrs. Trollope, Miss Jewsbury, Mrs. Speir, Mrs. Gatty, Miss Blagden, Lady Georgiana Fullarton [sic], Miss Marsh, and a dozen others. There is little need to talk of literature as a field for woman's future work. She is ploughing it in all directions already. The one thing is to do it thoroughly, and let the plough go deep enough, with good thorough drainage to begin upon. Writing books ought never to be thought of slightly. In one sense, it is morally a serious thing, a power of addressing many persons at once with somewhat more weight than in common speech. We cannot without offence misuse such a power, and adorn vice, or sneer at virtue, or libel human nature as all low, and base, and selfish. We cannot without offence neglect to *use* such a power for a good end; and if to give pleasure be the object of our book, make it at least to the reader an ennobling and refining pleasure. A book ought always to be *the high water-mark* of its author—his best thoughts, his clearest faith, his loftiest aspiration. No need to taunt him, and say he is not equal to his book. His book ought not to be merely the average of his daily ebb and flow, but his flood-line—his spring-tide, jetsam of shells and corallines, and all "the treasures of the deep."

And again, writing is an Art, and as an art it should be seriously pursued. The true artist spirit which grudges no amount of preparatory study, no labour of final completion,—this belongs as much to the pen as to the pencil or the chisel. It is precisely this spirit which women have too often lacked, fondly imagining their quickness would do duty for patience, and their tact cover the defect of study. If their work is (as we hope and believe) to be a real contribution to the happiness and welfare of mankind hereafter, the first lesson to be learned is this— conscientious preparatory study, conscientious veracity of expression, conscientious labour after perfection of every kind, clearness of thought, and symmetry of form. The time will come, we doubt not, when all this will be better understood. Writing a novel or a book of travels will not be supposed to come to a lady by nature, any more than teaching children to a reduced gentlewoman. Each art needs its special study and careful cultivation; and the woman who means to pursue aright either literature or science, will consider it her business to prepare herself for so doing, *at least* as much as if she purposed to dance on the stage or make bonnets in a milliner's shop.

Then, we believe we shall find women able to carry forward the common progress of the human race along the path of the True, as well as of the Beautiful and the Good; nay, to give us those views of truth which are naturally the property of woman. For be it remembered, as in optics we need two eyes to see the roundness and fulness of objects, so in philosophy we need to behold every great truth from two standpoints; and it is scarcely a fanciful analogy to say, that these standpoints are provided for us by the different faculties and sentiments of men's and women's natures. In every question of philosophy there enters the intuitive and the experimental, the arguments *à priori* and *à posteriori*. In every question of morals there is the side of justice and the side of love. In every question of religion there is the idea of God as the Father of the world—the careful Creator, yet severe and awful Judge; and there is the idea of God as the Mother, whose tender mercies are over us all, who is grieved by our sins as our mothers were grieved by them, and in whose infinite heart is our only refuge. At the highest point all these views unite. Absolute Philosophy is both intuitive and experimental; absolute Morality is both justice and love; absolute Religion is the worship (at once full of awe and love) of the "Parent of Good, Almighty," who is both parents in One. But to reach these completed views we need each side by turns to be presented to us; and this can hardly be better effected than by the alternate action of men's and women's minds on each other.

Notes

1.   Cobbe is alluding to Alfred Tennyson's poem, "Mariana" (1830), in which Mariana waits for a lover who has deserted her.
2.   Cobbe is alluding to Mrs. Jellyby, a character from Charles Dickens's *Bleak House* (1853), whose charity work for the Africans of Borrioboola-Gha impedes on her ability to care for her house and children.
3.   *Avesta*, often called *Zend Avesta*, is the sacred book of Zoroastrianism, and contains that religion's cosmogony, law, liturgy, and teachings of Zoroaster (Zorathushtra).
4.   Mary Carpenter (1807–77) was a philanthropist who worked primarily with poor and neglected children, as well as with juvenile

delinquents. She founded several "ragged schools," and later in her life became involved with women's suffrage and education reform. For information on Walter Crofton's prison reform notions, consult Mary Carpenter's *Reformatory Prison Discipline, As Developed By the Right Honourable Sir Walter Crofton, in the Irish Conflict Prisons* (London, 1872).

5.   We rejoice to hear that Miss Maria S. Rye, who has already done so much for this cause, is on the point of sailing to Otago with one hundred female emigrants, to superintend personally the arrangements for their welfare. This is doing woman's work in working style truly. [Cobbe's note] Maria Rye (1829–1903) founded the Women's Employment Society, and the Female Middle-Class Emigration Society, which attempted to place girls as domestic servants in Australia and Canada.

6.   Emily Faithfull (1835–95) was a member of the Langham Place Circle, led by Bessie Parkes (1829–1925) and Barbara Leigh Smith Bodichon (1827–91). This organization advanced employment opportunities for women. Faithfull used her own resources, along with financial backing from G.W. Hastings, to establish the Victoria Press—operated by women employees.

7.   See Victor Cousin, *Du Vrai, du Beau, et du Bien*. [Cobbe's note]

8.   Felicia Dorothea Hemans (1793–1835). British poet known for her treatment of romantic themes, including nature, liberty, and childhood innocence.

9.   Joanna Baillie (1762–1851). British poet and dramatist known for her *Plays on the Passions* (3 vols. 1798–1812). Mary Tighe (Blachford) (1772–1810). A poet born in Dublin. Angelica Kauffmann (1740–1807). Swiss painter who is known for her 1764 portrait of Winckelmann. In London she was a foundation member of the Royal Academy. Minerva Press produced inexpensive, light romances, written chiefly by women for other women.

10.   *Aurora Leigh* (1857). A novel-poem by Elizabeth Barrett Browning which explicitly critiques bourgeois marriage and young women's oppression in a patriarchal society.

11.   Rosa Bonheur, also known as Marie-Rosalie (1822–99). French painter and sculptor known for her accurate and detailed paintings of animals.

12.   Praxiteles (ca. 350 B.C.). A Greek sculptor.

13.   *Female Education, and how it would be affected by University Education*. A Paper read before the Social Science Congress. Published by Emily Faithfull and Co., Great Coram-street. Price 2*d*. [Cobbe's note]

14.   Mary Fairfax Greig Somerville (1780–1872) was considered the "queen of nineteenth-century science." She published four scientific papers, as well as four highly regarded books, including *Physical Geography* (1848) and *On Molecular and Microscopic Science* (1868).

12. The Rights of Man and the Claims of Brutes

Introduction

Frances Power Cobbe's "The Rights of Man and the Claims of Brutes" first appeared in *Fraser's Magazine* in November, 1863, and is reprinted here from that periodical. It creatively and effectively conveys Cobbe's antivivisection stance. In this essay, Cobbe exposed the cruelties of Victorian experimentation and dissection of living animals, and she specifically attacked the philosophy of medical organizations that condoned such practices. While her main targets were French medical and veterinary colleges, Cobbe certainly intended to stir the consciences of vivisectors in Great Britain as well.

Unlike many modern-day animal rights activists, Cobbe was not a vegetarian and did not regard the use of furs as an abomination. With the type of balance often exhibited by principled liberals (those who see both sides of an issue), Cobbe compromises on the carnivorous use of animals and views them as objects of labor as well as delight. It is primarily the unnecessary pain inflicted on animals by science to which she objects.

The Rights of Man and the Claims of Brutes

There is a beautiful Eastern story to this purpose:—A mighty king of old built for himself the most magnificent city the world ever saw. The towers of the city were of marble, and the walls of eternal granite, with an hundred gates of brass; and in the centre of the city, by the side of an ever-flowing river, stood the palace of the king, which dazzled the eyes of the beholder with its beauty, and in whose garden there was a tree whose leaves were of emeralds and whose fruit of rubies.

But the king and his people, of whose power and riches there were no end, were wicked exceedingly, and given up to cruelty and iniquity. Therefore Allah sent a drought upon their land, and for seven years there rained no rain; and the river was dried up, and the fountains failed, and the cattle perished, and the women wailed in the streets, and the hearts of the young men failed them utterly. Then said the wise men and the elders unto the king: "Send now, we pray thee, unto the prophet who dwelleth in the land of Israel, in the cave under the mountain of Carmel, and behold he will procure us rain from the Lord." Then the king hearkened unto his wise men, and sent messengers with precious gifts unto the prophet, that he should send them rain. And the messengers went up out of the glorious city, and travelled even unto Carmel, and came to the cave wherein the prophet dwelt; and they fell down at his feet, and offered him gifts, saying unto him, "O, my lord, send us rain!" Then the prophet caused three great clouds to rise up out of the sea, even the sea of Tarshish, whereby he dwelt; and the first cloud was white as the fleece of the lamb, and the second cloud was red like blood, and the third cloud was black as night. And when the messengers saw the third cloud they cried with a loud voice, "O, my lord, give us the black cloud." Then the prophet said, "Be it unto you as you have desired, ye sons of Belial." And the messengers marvelled at him, and saluted him, and returned unto their king.

Then the king, and all his wise men and his mighty men, and all the city, both great and small, went out to meet the messengers; and the messengers fell down on their faces before the king and said, "O king, we have seen the prophet of Israel that dwelleth in Carmel, by the sea, and he offered unto us three clouds to go over our land—a white cloud, a red cloud, and a black cloud; and we chose the black cloud, to the end that the rain might fall, even the heavy rain, upon the earth." Then the king, and all the wise men, and the mighty men, and all the people, both small and great, shouted for joy, and said, "Ye chose well, O messengers. The black cloud—let the black cloud come over our land!"

And behold while they yet shouted, there arose afar off, from the way of the sea, a mighty cloud, and it was black even as the night when the moon shineth not nor any star; and as the cloud arose the face of the sun was hid, and the darkness overspread the earth, and the birds flew to the thick branches, and the wild beasts came forth, till the roar of the lion was heard even by the people of the mighty city. And the king, and his wise men, and his men of war, and all the multitude, both small and great, fell on their faces and lifted up their hands to the cloud and cried, "The rain! the rain!"

Then the cloud opened over the city and over all the people, and out of it came the SARSAR, the ice-cold Wind of Death; and it smote the king, and his wise men, and his men of war, and all the people, both small and great, and they died. There they died even as they lay upon the earth, with their hands lifted to the cloud, and the words in their mouths—"The rain!—give us the rain!"

And of that king and nation no man remembered anything, nor could the city be found any more; but the land became a desert, and the wild beasts made their dens in the cedar chambers, and the reeds rustled where the river had rolled, and the birds of the air lodged in the tree of emeralds, and plucked at the ruby fruit.

But there dwelt one man alone in that city—he only was left when the king, and his wise men, and his men of war, and all the people perished; and he dwelt there alone, and gave himself to prayer, and heeded not the gold, nor the marble palaces, nor the precious stones, but prayed night and day. And the years passed away, and the generations of mankind changed, and still he dwelt there alone; and his beard and hair were white as snow, and his eyes were glittering like a sword, but his strength failed not, nor lacked he anything, but prayed seven times a day and seven times every night to Allah the Gracious and Merciful for forgiveness of his sins.

Then after a thousand years, when the river had changed its course, and the granite walls of the city had fallen down, and the thick trees grew in the courts of the palaces, and the owls and the hyenas lodged in the holy places of the temple, there came a servant of God, whose eyes were opened that he might find the city, and he entered in through the broken gates of brass, and came unto the fig-tree by the fountain, where dwelt the man of prayer—the solitary man; and the solitary man lifted up his eyes, and when he saw the servant of God he fell on his face, and returned thanks that he had seen again the countenance of a man. Then the servant of God wept for pity, and said, "O my brother, how camest thou to dwell here alone?" And the solitary man, the man of prayer, answered and said, "O servant of God, in a fortunate hour art thou come unto me; and blessed be He that sent thee, for now may I die, and my sins be forgiven. Behold, I was one of the wicked men of this city, sons of Belial were we all, and thought not of God, but only of our own lusts, and our palaces, and our high feasts, and our beautiful women; and my brethren were cruel also, and scourged their slaves oftentimes, and tortured their prisoners of war, and put their cattle to death with evil treatment. And it came to pass that I saw a camel bound upon my father's grave, and left to perish with hunger; and she knew me, and looked me in the face and groaned, and strove to lick my hands. Then was I moved with compassion, and loosened her and let her go free, and drove her into the rich pastures. And for this that I showed mercy to the camel hath the Lord showed mercy unto me; and when all my brethren went down to destruction in the day of His wrath, when the Sarsar came forth out of the black cloud and slew them all, then was I saved, to the end that I might repent. Lo! a thousand years have I prayed in solitude, till the bones of my brethren are dust, and the thick trees grew in their palaces, and the roar of the lion is heard in their chambers of cedar; and no voice of man have I heard nor human face have I seen till thou hast visited me. And now know I that I have not prayed in vain, but that my sins are forgiven, and that I may die in peace. Therefore, I pray thee, lay thine hand upon me, and let me feel the hand of a man, and say for me the prayer of departure, and let me die." And the servant of God did as the solitary man desired, and blessed him; and the shadows of death came over him like the twilight, and his eyes ceased to shine brightly, and he laid him down with his hand on the breast of the servant of God, and blessed God with a few words, and died in peace. And the servant of God buried him there under the fig-tree by the fountain, and wept over him, and went out of the city through the broken gates of brass, and returned not, neither looked back. And no man from that day forth has beheld it, neither entered there, nor knoweth any man where that city is to be found; but the wilderness hath swallowed it up, and the wild beasts have made it their home, because of the wickedness of the people and their oppressions upon man and upon beast in the sight of the Lord.

*   *   *

There is a Western story, not quite so beautiful, and with a somewhat different moral—a story which may be found by the diligent reader in the *Times* and other journals for the months of July and August, in this year of grace one thousand eight hundred and sixty-three. This Western apologue runs somewhat to the following purpose:—

There was a certain great and lordly city whose prince was among the powerful of the earth, and for whose nod whole nations waited obediently; and this city, which aforetime had been a great and vast city, was by this prince still further exalted and adorned, till it was wonderful to behold. And there were in that city royal palaces, with pictures and statues innumerable, and gardens wherein were all manner of beasts of the field and fowls of the air; and temples were there, all bedaubed with gold, whereof the chief were dedicated, not to Allah the Gracious, the Merciful, but to two women, whose names were Miriam of Nazareth and Miriam of Magdala. And of the streets of that great city there were no end, for they were all made by the power of the prince; and every poor man's house was pulled down, and every rich man's house destroyed, so that those great streets might traverse the city, which became even as the cities of old under their tyrants—like unto Babylon, and unto Persepolis, and Tadmor of the Waste. Then men boasted of that great and wonderful city, and said it was the centre of the world, and that the buildings thereof were all on one great plan, even as the world which Allah has made. But they who made this boast were blind and fallible; for in the world of Allah nought is uniform or monotonous, nor does one tree resemble another tree, nor one mountain another mountain, but the great plan of them all is endless variety, and the unity thereof is the opposite of uniformity. But the works of men, the tyrants of the false priests, who have built cities and temples, and made laws, and established religions, these all have wrought to produce uniformity without variety; and these are they whose labours this great city resembles, rather than the blessed creations of Allah. And in this city dwelt many wise men and learned among the most learned of the earth; and there were delicate women, and men who wore soft raiment, and fared sumptuously every day. And all the people of the city believed that they were the most learned, and delicate, and refined people in all the world; and that elsewhere men were brutal and stupid, and women coarse and evil entreated, and that save in their city there was no civilization.

Now it came to pass that in that city a strange thing was found. Amid all the proud palaces, and delicious gardens, and halls for feasting, and places for singing men and singing women, and for dancing and all manner of luxurious delights—and among the gilded temples dedicated to Miriam of Nazareth and Miriam of Magdala—among all these places there were certain buildings set apart for a purpose of another kind. Many wise men assembled there, and many learned men, and men adorned with tokens of the favour of the great prince, and with the ensigns of a noble order called that of Honour; and these men, with their disciples (who also were youths of the better sort, and habited ever in well-ordered garments), employed themselves in these public buildings[1] at frequent intervals, week after week, and year after year, in the form and manner following: They took a number of tame and inoffensive animals—but principally those noblest and most sensitive animals, horses—and having bound them carefully for their own safety, proceeded to cut, hew, saw, gouge, bore, and lacerate the flesh, bones, marrow, heart, and brains of the creatures groaning helpless at their feet. And in so orderly and perfect a fashion was this accomplished, that these wise men, and learned men, and honourable men discovered that a horse could be made to suffer for ten hours, and to undergo sixty-four different modes of torture before he died. Wherefore to this uttermost limit permitted by the creature did they regularly push their cutting and hacking, delivering each horse into the hands of eight inexperienced students to practise upon him in turn during the ten hours.[2] This, therefore, they did in that great city, not deigning to relieve the pains they were inflicting by the beneficial fluid whereby all suffering may be alleviated, and not even heeding to put out of their agonies at the last the poor mangled remnants of creatures on which they had expended their tortures three score and four.

And the people of this city still boasted and said, "Behold, we are the most wise, and the most brave, and the most polished people on the face of the earth, and our city is the centre of civilization and of humanity."

*   *   *

These Eastern and Western tales have a strangely-different character assuredly. The state of men's minds, when they could imagine that a single act of mercy to a brute would procure the salvation of the doer in the midst of the destruction of his city, is curiously contrasted with that other state when they can calmly contemplate hideous tortures perpetrated regularly, and as a matter of business, upon hundreds of animals every year, and continue to uphold the tortures in esteem, and in high public functions, as the instructors of youth. We do not seem to have advanced much over the Moslem by our eighteen centuries of Christianity, so far as this matter is concerned.

The question, however, of cruelty to the brutes is one not to be hastily dismissed, nor can the recital of any barbarities be admitted to determine it in all its bearings. In quoting the above Eastern apologue, and recording the terrible fact of contemporary Parisian manners, we beg to disclaim all intention of treating the subject by that method of mere appeal to the feelings by which nearly every question of morals can be distorted and prejudiced. The infliction of pain is a thing naturally so revolting to the cultivated mind, that any description of it inevitably arouses strong sentiments of dislike, if not of horror; and were we to proceed no further to explain the motives and causes of such inflictions, vivid pictures of all penal, and even of all surgical treatment, might easily be drawn, so as to call forth reprobation upon the heads of the greatest benefactors of humanity. In the following pages we shall endeavour to reach the ground of the whole controversy by arriving at some answer to the fundamental question, "What *is* cruelty to animals? What are the duties of man as regards the welfare of the brutes, and how are they to be ranked in comparison with the duties he owes to his human fellow-creatures?" The search for the solution of these problems will fortunately absolve us from the painful task of entering into any description of the cruelties committed against animals either in France or England, or discussing special acts of public lecturers or private students of physiology. In all such cases it is the vagueness of popular moral opinion in which evil finds its great defence; and so long as cruel experiments are only rebuked by the denunciations of excited sentiment, so long will the perpetrators pass by contemptuously the ignorant blame of those who "understand nothing of the necessities of the case, or the interests of science," or (at the best) will draw a veil of secresy over the disgusting mysteries of their operating tables. A different result would be obtained if society in general could be brought to form a sound and clear opinion of the limits wherein the sufferings of animals may lawfully be inflicted for the benefit of mankind, and could then pronounce with calm and dispassionate judgment its severest censure and condemnation upon every act which should transgress these limits, and therefore deserve the opprobrium of "cruelty."

The world owes to Bishop Butler the exposition of that ultimate ground of moral obligation on whose broad basis stand our duties to all living beings, rational and irrational. He says that if any creature be *sentient*—*i.e.*, capable of suffering pain or enjoying pleasure—it is cause sufficient why we should refrain from inflicting pain, and should bestow on it pleasure when we may. That is enough. We need go no further to seek for a primary ground of obligation for mercy and kindness. Many other motives may, and do, come in to enhance and modify this obligation; but, standing by itself, it is sufficient. If we could divest ourselves of every other idea, and even admit the dreadful hypothesis that neither man nor brute had any Creator, but came into existence by some concourse of unconscious forces; yet even then—in a sunless, hopeless, fatherless world—there would still remain the same duty, if the creature *could* feel pain, to avoid inflicting it; if it could feel pleasure, to bestow it. We cannot get below this principle. It is an ultimate canon of natural law—a *necessary* moral law (in metaphysical parlance)—since we cannot even conceive the contrary, nor figure to our imaginations a world or a condition of things wherein the obligation could be suspended or reversed.

Let us endeavour to arrive at a clear analysis of such natural obligations:—

First. In the case of rational, moral beings—what are our necessary obligations towards them? We have seen that as they are *sentient* beings we are bound to avoid their pain and seek their pleasure; but as they are more than sentient, and also rational and moral beings, other and higher obligations are added to those which concern their pain and pleasure. The highest end of a merely sentient being is enjoyment of pleasure and freedom from pain, *i.e.*, happiness; but the highest end of a rational and moral being is virtue. Thus, as we are bound to seek the sentient being's happiness because he is capable of happiness, so we are bound to seek the moral being's virtue because he is capable of virtue. Here, also, we have reached an ultimate obligation. And inasmuch as virtue immeasurably transcends happiness, so must moral interests transcend sentient interests; and the being who is both moral and sentient, demands that his moral interests be primarily consulted, and his sentient interests secondarily; and the being who is only sentient and not moral is placed altogether subordinately, and can only claim that his interests be regarded after those of the moral being have been fulfilled. To this simple ground of obligation, to seek the virtue of all beings capable of virtue, there are, of course, added many religious and fraternal motives of the greatest force and sanctity in enhancing our duty of aiding our fellow men. But the original ground (as in the former case) is sufficient of itself. Were there no Divine Author of virtue, no immortality of blessedness for the virtuous soul, yet still the fact that a being could attain to virtue would constitute an obligation to seek his virtue.

The great ends, then, of the obligation of man to his rational fellow-creature is, in the first place, to seek his virtue, and in the second place his happiness. To the virtue he can *conduce*, and the happiness he can *produce* —both in limited degrees, which degrees are the sole bounds (theoretically) of his obligations.

But, practically, the power of any human being, either to conduce to the virtue, or produce the happiness of mankind are limited, not only by the influence he can exercise on any one, but by the numbers on whom he can, in his narrow sphere, exercise any influence at all. Secondary moral obligations here come into play, requiring that in that necessarily narrow sphere of his labours there shall be *precedence* in his benevolence given to certain persons above others. If a man's powers permitted him to aid the virtue and happiness of all mankind—of all equally—he would be bound to do so. As this is impossible, he must partition his benevolent cares on certain obvious principles of selection—propinquity of blood, contract of marriage, debts of gratitude, &c. Roughly speaking, these secondary obligations may be described as regulating that benevolence be first shown to those nearest to us, and afterwards to those more remote. They cannot be lawfully interpreted to *abolish* the claims of more remote objects of benevolence, but only to *subordinate* them; that is, when any degree of equality exists between the wants of the nearer and further claimants, the nearer has the precedence and preference. But when the want of the nearest claimant is altogether trifling, and the want of the remoter claimant urgent and vital, the prior claims of the first cannot be held to supersede those of the second, which would in effect amount to their entire abolition.

These (we fear, somewhat tedious) analyses of principles lead us to the right point for considering the obligations owed by man to the lower animals. The brutes are sentient, but not moral creatures, therefore our concern is solely with their happiness. To what does this claim amount? If we had absolute power we should desire to relieve all animals from all pain and want, and we should bestow on them such pleasures as their humble natures can receive. Obviously we can practically do little more than meet these obligations towards the animals with whom we come in contact by refraining from causing them suffering, and supplying those which belong to us with proper food and shelter. The life of a brute, having no moral purpose, can best be understood ethically as representing the sum of its *pleasures*; and the obligation, therefore, of producing the pleasures of sentient creatures must be reduced, in their case, to the abstinence from unnecessary destruction of life. Such, then, are our duties towards the brute, simply considered, without reference to the human race.

But the claims of the brutes on us for happiness must necessarily be subordinated not only to human claims for moral aid, but for human claims for happiness also. First, the happiness of animals is of a vastly lower and smaller thing than the happiness of man; secondly, all the interests of man touch upon moral grounds, assume higher importance than those of un-moral beings; and lastly, because that race of man to which we belong must have over us claims of precedence superior to any other race, were it even angelic, which should be more remote. So clear and so wide is this line of demarcation between our duties to man and to the brutes that it appears almost an impertinence thus to analyze it; and we may doubtless safely proceed in our argument, assuming it as granted on all hands that there is an *absolute* subordination between the claims of the animal and those of man. The whole lower creation is for ever and utterly subordinated to the higher.

What then remains of the obligation to consider the pain and pleasure of the sentient but un-moral animals? Is there any space left for it in the crowd of human duties? Surely there is a little space. Claims which are *subordinated* to higher claims are not (as we have already said) therefore *abolished*. Here is an error common both to our views of the relative claims of different human beings, and of the relative claims of brutes and men. There is in both cases a point where the rights of the secondary claimant come into the field, else were there in morals the anomaly of moral obligations which should never oblige any one. Where is this point to be found?

We have already said that in regulating the precedency of human claims, the point is found where there ceases to be any kind of equality between the wants of the two claimants. Where the wants are equal (or anything like equal) the nearest comes first, the remoter afterwards. If a father need bread to save him from starvation, and a friend need it also for the same purpose, the father's claims must come first. But if the father need it only to amuse himself by throwing it to fowls on the river, and the friend need it to save him from death, then the father's claims go to the ground, and the friend's become paramount. This principle is continually neglected in human affairs, and the neglect causes great moral errors. The parent, husband, wife, or child whom affection and duty both direct to make their nearest and dearest the object of their "precedency of benevolence," continually fall under the temptation to make them their *exclusive* objects, and evade other obligations under the delusion that they are all merged in the one primary obligation. The same thing takes place in the case of animals. Men say, "Human obligations come before all obligations to the brutes. Let us wait till all human beings are virtuous and happy, and then it will be time to attend to the brutes." But we are no more morally justified in the one case than in the other, neither in merging all human duties in duties to one individual, nor in waiting to consider our obligations to the animals to those Greek kalends when all human wants will be abundantly supplied.

The point where the inferior claim of the brute, as of the man, must come into the field, can only be in each case where there ceases to be any kind of equality between the superior and inferior claims. We must consider carefully what can constitute the relative claims of beings of such different rank. Passing below the last human claimant on our benevolence, we find "a great gulf fixed." With the rationality and moral freedom of the agent, life itself has so far altered its value that we no longer recognize in it any of the sanctity which pertained to the life of a man; nor can the creature's comfort or enjoyment of any kind be put in the balance. We can in no case say that the claim of life for the brute is the same thing as the claim of life for a man; nay, even of security, or food, or comfort of any kind for the man. Everything which could fairly interpreted to *be* a want for the man must have precedence over even the

life of the animal, but here we must stop. Those cruel impulses of
destruction, which we may call *wantonness* in a man, have no claims
to be weighed against the brute's life and welfare. His gluttonous tastes,
his caprices, his indolence, have no claims. Here the claims of the brute
come on the field. Our obligations to consider its humble happiness
must appear here or nowhere. They are postponed utterly to man's
wants. They stand good against his *wantonness*. Practically, where
does the principle lead us? Simply to this—that we may slay cattle for
food, and take the fowls of the air and the fish of the sea to supply our
table; but that we may not (for example) torture calves to produce white
meat, nor slash living salmon to make them more delicate, nor nail
fowls to the fireside to give them diseased livers. We may use horses
and asses in our ploughs and our carriages, but we have no right to
starve and torture our poor brute servants for our avarice or malignity.
We may clear every inhabited country of wild beasts and noxious
reptiles and insects whose existence would imperil our security or
militate against our health or cleanliness, or who would devour our own
proper food; but we have no right to go into untrodden deserts to take
away the lives of creatures who there have their proper home, nor to
kill in our own country harmless things like seagulls and frogs for the
mere gratification of our destructive propensities.

And further. Beside these limits to the taking of life, there are
limits to the infliction of gain. Here, again, *if* the pain be *necessary*, if
the life demanded by human wants cannot be taken without the
infliction of some degree of pain; or if (without killing a brute) we are
obliged to put it to some suffering, to fetter it for our security, or for
any similar reason, here, also, we may be justified. But though we may
thus inflict pain for our *want*, we are no more justified in inflicting it
than in taking life for our *wantonness*. If from the odious delight in
witnessing suffering, or from furious tempers, or parsimony, or idle
curiosity, we put an animal to needless torture, we stand condemned; we
have offended against the law requiring us to refrain from inflicting pain
on any being which, by its sentient nature, is sensible to pain.

These views are surely almost self-evident. To affirm the
contrary and maintain that we have a right to take animal life in mere
wantonness, or to inflict needless torture upon animals, is to deny that
a sentient being has any claims whatever, or that his capacity for
suffering pain and enjoying pleasure ought to determine in any way our
conduct towards him. For if that capacity for enjoyment is not to

protect his life (*i.e.*, the whole sum of his pleasures) against our wanton destruction, nor his capacity for pain protect his nervous frame from our infliction of needless torture, there is nothing left to be imagined of occasion wherein his claims could be valid.

The line then which we are seeking must be drawn here or nowhere. *Animals' lives (i.e., their whole sum of pleasures) may be taken for man's wants, even if those wants be ever so small, but not for his wantonness; nor may they be taken in any case with needless infliction of pain.*

We shall assume that the reader will concede this principle. It remains to test its application to the controversy which concerns us at present—the right of men to put animals to torture for the sake of (what they claim to be) the interests of science. We must endeavour to discuss this question very calmly, and not allow ourselves to be carried away by the natural indignation caused by pictures of agony. Almost similar pictures of human agony might be drawn from the scenes in any military hospital, and yet would argue nothing against the goodness of the operation.

"Science" is a great and sacred word. When we are called on to consider its "interests" we are considering the cause of that truth which is one of the three great portals whereby man may enter the temple of God. Physical science, the knowledge of God's material creation, is in its highest sense a holy thing—the revelation of God's power, wisdom, love, through the universe of inorganic matter and organic life. The love of truth for its own sake, irrespective of the utility of its applications, has here one of its noblest fields; and no love of the beautiful by the artist, nor of the good by the philanthropist, can surpass it in sanctity, or claim, on moral grounds, a larger liberty.

Where then are we to rank "the interests of science," among human wants or wantonnesses? Surely among the wants deserving of fullest privilege. Man, in his highest capacity as a rational being, hungers for truth as the food of his soul, even as he hungers for meat for his body; and the wants of the soul must ever be placed in higher rank than those of the body. He has a right to seek truth as he has a right to seek natural food, and may obtain it equally lawfully by the same measures. Thus we arrive at the conclusion that man has a right to take animal life for the purposes of science as he would take it for food, or security, or health. And this, be it remembered, is strictly for science, *as* science, apart from the contingent utility which may result from any discovered truths. When men go about explaining the probable *use* which may be derived from a scientific experiment, they are employing supererogatory argument. The scientific truth, *as a truth*, is an end in itself: the derivable utility affords another and supplementary argument.

Of course, when it happens, as in the case of anatomical researches, that every discovered truth is likely in a high degree to contribute to the restoration of human health and the salvation of human life, then the supplementary argument hence derived for the prosecution of such researches is proportioned to the whole value of human health and life, and deserves the highest recognition. For all purposes of reasoning, however, we may carry with us the full admission that the interests of science alone, *as science*, are enough to justify a man in taking away the life of any animal. We may take animal life (that is, the whole sum of the animal's pleasures) for the interests of science; but we must take it with "no needless infliction of pain." Now, unhappily, until lately, nearly all experiments of science were inevitably accompanied by the infliction of torture. It was not so much the creature's life which the experimenter required as its endurance of all manner of lacerations and "vivisections." It must be owned that here was a trying problem. Should science (it was asked) turn aside in her royal progress and forego her claims for the sake of some miserable brute or reptile—say of the frog, which Marshall Hall dared to call "God's gift to the physiologist?" Or should the torture of a thousand animals be held as nothing in the balance against the supreme interests of man? It would seem that in such a conflict, such an antinomy of duties, as Kant would have named it, our sympathies would have been with the man who relinquished his experiment at the instigations of mercy; but that, at the same time, we could not presume to censure the man who pursued it unrelentingly.

Be it remembered, however, that here and everywhere it can only be in the *true* interests of science that such sacrifices can be justified at all. Of this we shall say more anon. But this whole phase of the question may now be put aside for ever. The most beneficent discovery of ages—the discovery for which the sages of old would have offered hecatombs, and yet for which no *Te Deum* has ascended from the churches of Christendom as for many a bloody victory—the great discovery of perfect anæsthetics, has altered the whole condition of the case between the man of science and the brutes. It is at the option of the physiologist, by the use of chloroform, to perform nearly every experiment he can desire without the infliction of any pain whatever. With trifling exceptions of a few prolonged experiments of doubtful value, he can test at will any scientific truth at the cost, perhaps, of life, but never of torture.

How stands the case now? Surely that such experiments as may be required by science at the cost of animal life may be freely made at such cost; and that the experiments which require processes naturally involving torture, may be freely performed with the use of anæsthetics and consequent avoidance of torture, *but not otherwise*. Here is the line which Providence has drawn for us in these latter days as clear as daylight. There is in our hands the means of obviating the torture while reserving the interests of science; and we are inexcusable if from indolence, parsimony, or any other motive, we fail to use it. The experiment then becomes unlawful to us and falls under the condemnation of wanton cruelty. Let us see precisely what these two conditions involve: firstly, that the *life* we are going to take is really demanded by science; secondly, that the *pain* of the experiment shall be removed by anæsthetics.

For animal life to be really demanded by science we must conclude that it is wanted firstly, for the discovery of some new truth; secondly, for the establishment of some questionable fact; thirdly, for general instruction. Thus an anatomist may kill a bird or beast to discover or ascertain the facts of its structure, and the natural historian may kill it to affix its place in zoology or ornithology, or the toxicologist may kill it to preserve it in a museum for general instruction. All these reasons for taking the lives of animals must be held valid. But, where there is no anticipation of discovering a new truth, where there is no questionable fact to be ascertained, and where general instruction can be obtained perfectly without the sacrifice of fresh life, then there remains no justification for the act. It passes under the censure of wanton destruction.

Secondly, that we may consider the conditions for the justification of torturing experiments fulfilled, we must demand that in every case in which the production of severe pain is involved, the experimenter is bound to employ chloroform or some other anæsthetic with such sufficient care as to obviate the pain. No excuse of trouble or expense can be admitted; for if the individual society be unwilling or unable to undergo such needful trouble and expense, they are disqualified from undertaking experiments which cannot lawfully be performed save under such conditions. Here then stands the case against the vivisectionists. Have they done that which in itself is lawful under lawful conditions? Have they taken the lives of brutes only when the interests of science really demanded them? and have they performed painful experiments always under the influence of anæsthetics? If they have observed these conditions they must stand morally exempt from blame, and the popular outcry against them deserves to be disregarded as ignorant and futile. If they have transgressed these conditions, then they must stand morally convicted of the heinous offence of cruelty, and the indignation and disgust of mankind would be amply justified against them.

We cannot pretend to bring forward evidence of the infraction of these conditions by the societies and individuals who have been accused of cruelty in vivisection. The subject has been discussed in all the leading journals of the country, and facts have been alleged of sufficient gravity and supported by ample authority to justify in full the anxious investigation of the case by men of humanity. Viewing the evidence before us, it appears impossible to doubt that in France, for years back, a vast number of horses and dogs have been dissected alive and submitted to every conceivable operation for the instruction of pupils in anatomy and veterinary surgery, and that no chloroform has been in use on these occasions. On the other hand, in England, it is affirmed, seemingly on good authority, that vivisections are comparatively rare, and are performed only by scientific men for the ascertainment of physiologic facts, and usually with the exhibition of chloroform.

If these facts be so, it appears beyond question that the French system has terribly transgressed the limits of morality in this matter. Dead horses and dogs would have served the purpose of instruction to the pupils in anatomy as well as living ones; and the whole mass of torture involved in their living dissection might have been spared. If for the purpose of instructing their pupils in the surgery of the living fibre, it may have been necessary to perform some operations on animals before death, yet of those actually performed daily at Allfort (sixty-four on each horse) the great majority were (like the removal of the hoof) wholly useless, and present no kind of compensating benefit for the acute torture they inflict, inasmuch as the operations cannot be copied in the human subject, nor would they ever be used by any owner in the case of a horse. As to the primary motives justifying such taking of life for purposes of science, they cannot be alleged in the case at all; for there is no attempt at discovering any new fact, or ascertaining any doubtful one, ever propounded. These points have been clearly demonstrated in the French Academy; and in the *Séance* of August 25 of the present year, M. Dubois proposed a motion, whereby the evils in question would have henceforth been forbidden, the pupils instructed on dead bodies, and the dissection of living animals confined to special cases of the discovery or verification of new facts. He proposed that three replies should be made to the questions asked by Government on the subject, to the following effect:—

1. The Academy, without dwelling on the injurious form of the documents that have been submitted to it, acknowledges that abuses have been introduced into the practice of vivisection.
2. To prevent these abuses, the Academy expresses the wish that, henceforward, vivisections may be exclusively reserved to the research of new facts or the verification of doubtful ones; and that, consequently, they may be no more practised in the public or private courses (of lectures) for the demonstration of facts already established by science.
3. The Academy equally expresses the wish that the pupils at the schools of veterinary medicine may henceforward be exercised in the practice of operations on dead bodies, and no more on living horses.

As this report was negatived by a majority in the Academy, and the report actually adopted evaded the questions presented, and left the whole matter in its original condition, we are under the painful necessity of still leaving at the door of the men of science in France the terrible charge of perpetrating and sanctioning the agonizing deaths of multitudes of highly sensitive animals, wholly without justification from the real interests of science.

Further, the condition on which painful experiments can be lawfully made, namely, the use of anæsthetics, being to all appearance altogether rejected in the case of the French vivisections, the last justification is withdrawn, and the case stands as an exemplification of the greatest possible offence to be committed towards the animals, without any extenuating circumstances. The most highly organized and most friendly creatures are put to the death of uttermost and most prolonged agony, entirely without justification, and with the habitual neglect of that precaution by which all their sufferings might have been obviated. When we say that this great moral offence has been committed for years, and is still committed, in defiance of remonstrance, by the splendidly-endowed scientific associations of one of the most civilized countries in the world, we seem to have reached the last term of condemnation which useless, wanton, deliberate, and exquisite cruelty can incur.

*   *   *

In the preceding pages we have endeavored to examine this question from the purely moral side, and as a problem of ethics separable from religious considerations, or natural sentiments of pity or disgust. Solely as a matter of moral duty imperative on us as rational free agents, we have (it is hoped) demonstrated that the claims of animals must be regarded so far as to cause us to respect their lives when no human want, but only wantonness, asks their destruction; and also that the infliction of torturing experiments upon them can only be justified when accompanied by the use of anæsthetics. Offences against these principles we have condemned on purely ethical grounds, and as infractions of the immutable laws of morality.

But it is impossible to regard a subject of this kind solely from the bare stand-point of ethics. Man is something else beside the agent of a "categoric imperative." He is also a creature of affections and sympathies; and, above all, he is a religious being, whose acts and feelings bear a certain relation to his Creator.

Now, as to the affections and sympathies of man, there are many species of animals on which they are naturally bestowed in a greater or less degree, and to kill or torture such animals is not only an offence against the laws of morality, but against the instincts of humanity and the feelings of the heart. So strongly has this been felt, that a great philosopher has actually asserted that the ground of our duty of mercy to the animals was not founded on their sentient nature but on our sensibilities; and that cruelty was forbidden, not because it tortured the animal, but because it brutalized the man.[3] Here, however, he committed (as Bentham well showed) an enormous error, and ignored the true principle laid down by Butler. Such a doctrine, if admitted, would introduce the same hateful system of morals towards the brutes as that which too often polluted human charity, causing it to be performed, not for the benefit of the receiver, but the moral and spiritual interest of the giver. Each duty must be done for its own sake, not for the sake of any other object, however desirable; nay, in truth, no duty can be fulfilled truly (in both sentiment and action) save disinterestedly. The attempt to produce our own moral culture out of our humanity or beneficence is, *by the hypothesis,* absurd. Only disinterested and single-hearted actions really warm and enlarge the soul, not self-regardful ones. We are bound to consider the welfare of the brutes for their sakes, not ours, because they are so constituted as to suffer and enjoy. That is the *moral* principle of the case.

Humane feelings, however, towards the brutes, though not the ground of our obligations towards them, form a natural tie which cannot be rudely broken without doing violence to many of the finer attributes of our nature. If a man be condemned in the court of morality for selling a faithful horse or dog to the vivisectionists, he would surely also be condemned for that act in the sentiments of every man of refined feelings. There is a story extant, so hideous that we hesitate to tell it, of a certain man of science who performed on his dog what he was pleased to term *une experience morale.* He tortured it for days in a peculiarly horrible manner, to try when the animal's affection would be overcome by his cruelty. The result proved that the dog died without ceasing to show his humble devotion to the man (or *monster,* we should say) who put him to such a test. The indignation which this fiendish act arouses in our minds is not solely a moral reprobation: it partakes also of the bitterness provoked by an outrage upon the affections.

The sentiment of tenderness to the brutes is of course but only inferior in sacredness to the moral principle, but also unlike it in being a very variable matter. Different nations and different individuals have it in very diverse degrees. The inquiry into its extent and influence would doubtless afford an interesting chapter in the study of human nature: we should find, as a rule, the more highly cultivated nations feeling the sentiment most vividly; but to this rule there would be many exceptions. The Arab's care for horses, the Turk's care for cats, are probably unparalleled elsewhere. But on the other hand, we find the Greeks, even in Homer's time, able to relish the sweet tale of Argus; while the whole magnificent literature of the Hebrews contains no passage, save in the story of Tobit, to imply any friendly feelings towards the animals. The singular commands in the Pentateuch, not to

"muzzle the ox which treadeth out the corn," and not to "seethe a kid in
its mother's milk," suggests rather the design of the legislator to soften
the hard natures of the Israelites than to protect the animals from
suffering, inasmuch as neither of the acts forbidden involved any real
cruelty. In Hindoo literature, again, there appear to be perpetual tender
references to the lower creatures. In the *Mahabharata*, in particular,
there is an exquisite story of the hero who insisted on the admission of
his faithful dog along with himself into heaven, and refused to accept
the offers of Ludra to conduct him there without it. At last the dog
transforms himself into Yamen, god of Death, who has followed the
hero's steps through the world, and now leaves him with a blessing to
enter Paradise, free from the penalty of mortality.[4] As might naturally
be expected, the condition of animals is much modified in countries
where they are either supposed to be inhabited by Divine beings, or else
the abodes of human souls undergoing metempsychosis. This latter
doctrine, involving such low and ludicrous circumstances as the
transmigration represented in the Theban tomb of the gluttonous man
into the pig, has perhaps met on that account with more contempt
among us than its *moral* character deserves. Among the multitudinous
superstitions of mankind, and fantastic dreams concerning the
"undiscovered country, from whose bourne no traveller returns," not by
any means the worst is that which would represent the future
punishment for sinking our human nature in cruelty, sensuality, or
sloth, to be the *loss* of that human nature for a time, and the
incarnation of the sinful soul in some cruel, or sensual, or slothful
brute. Between this idea (combined as it always is, with the prospect of
final restoration) and the doctrine of a burning cave of everlasting
blasphemy and despair, it may be thought that the notions of
Pythagoras and the originators of the Egyptian and Hindoo theologies
were not unworthy of comparison. Probably, however, the results of
neither doctrine concerning the future would have essentially conduced
to human virtue; and as to the influence of that of the metempsychosis
on the conduct of men towards the brutes, its humanizing effects have
doubtless been counterbalanced by the introduction of vegetarian errors,
and consequent discouragement of animal life; and also by inducing a
degree of care for some favoured brutes, infringing monstrously upon
the rights of mankind. The writer's father was witness, during the old
Mahratta wars, of various revolting scenes of famine, wherein the sacred
cows of the Hindoo temples were standing gorged to repletion beside

huge vessels of rice devoted to their use, while the starving population lay dying and dead of hunger all around.

Turning from nations to classes, we should find as a rule that the most cultivated are the most merciful. But here also there are exceptions. In England it is the half-brutalized and sottish carter, or the degraded and filthy dealer in "marine stores,"[5] who is brought up before the magistrate for furiously flogging his stubborn horse, or skinning alive some miserable cat. In France, alas! it is men of science—men belonging to the learned professions—who disembowel living horses and open the brains of dogs. In the case of individuals, the presence or absence of tenderness for animals appears to constitute a very curious test of character. Its connexion with benevolence towards mankind is of the inverse kind in too many instances. Few earnest philanthropists care at all for animals, or have any special sympathies with favourite dogs, horses, or birds; and they often seem to resent the care of others for such creatures as a defrauding of human claims. When the proposal was made for opening that very unassuming little institution in Islington for the shelter of lost dogs, the outcry raised on the part of human charity was greater than has ever greeted the erection of one of the gin-palaces or casinos, or other conservatories of vice in the kingdom. The objectors did not recognize the great law of human nature by which mercy begets mercy, even as "revenge and wrong bring forth their kind," and that the "merciful man" may not seldom have *become* merciful by beginning with mercy to "his beast." If it had no result whatever on human feelings, it would be hard to say that keeping a kennel for a few starving brutes was a much worse expenditure of money than sundry others with which the rich gentlemen of England indulge themselves.

But if the strong feelings of philanthropists for human claimants are somewhat chill as regards the animals, there is, on the other hand, a more deplorable inclination among all who have a tendency to misanthropy to bestow on animals an amount of affection very visibly distorted from its rightful human channels. Every Timon in the world has his dog, every embittered old maid her cat or parrot. They do not love these creatures so much because the dog, cat, or parrot fills up the measure of their affections, as because they have withdrawn their affections from humanity, and pour them out on the brutes in the place of better objects. This kind of love for animals has in it somewhat truly painful to witness. It cannot be defended in any manner, yet our pity may fairly be given to a condition of heart which reveals a past of intense suffering, and is in itself a state of disease of the affections. We are inclined to feel contemptuous, or perhaps a little resentful, when, in a world full of human woes and wants, a vast amount of tenderness and compassion is lavished upon some overfed spaniel, dying of the results of excessive indulgence, or a legacy, which might have afforded education to a child, is devoted to the maintenance of a parrot. We are disgusted when we hear of a lady comforting a mother on the death of her only daughter, by saying, "I felt just the same when my Fido died." But resentment and contempt are no right sentiments for such sorrowful exhibitions of moral malady any more than for the depraved appetite of physical disease. Probably the worst form of this distortion of the affections, and one for which no excuse can be made, is to be found when the pride of the over-indulged men and women of wealth and rank keeps them aloof from their human fellow-creatures, and leads them to lavish on their animal favourites the care and tenderness they would disdain to display to a human being. The lady of fashion, who leaves her child unvisited for days in its nursery, under the care of menials, while she watches the feeding of her spaniel, and covers it with caresses, is about as odious a specimen of humanity as may easily be found.

On the other hand, there are cases of intense love for animals in persons *necessarily* of a solitary life which are among the most affecting incidents in the world. In Le Maitre's beautiful story of Le Lépreux de la Citè [sic] d'Aoste (founded entirely on facts verified on the spot to the present day), the outcast leper and his sister are recorded to have dwelt in the ruined tower outside the city for many years of their suffering lives, utterly cut off from human intercourse. One day a poor little cur, starving and homeless, wandered into their secluded garden. They received it with delight, and the sister fed it, and made it her constant companion and favourite. After some years the sister died, and the leper was left utterly and for ever alone, save for the presence of the little dog, which gave him the only semblance of affection left for him to hope for in the world; and by its caresses and intelligence served a little to beguile his days and nights of ceaseless suffering. One day the poor animal strayed out of his garden towards the town. It was recognized as the leper's dog and the people were seized with the alarm that it would carry the infection of his disease into the town. Fear is the most cruel of all things. They stoned and beat the poor creature till it only escaped from them at last to crawl back to its master and expire at his feet. He who would not sympathize with the leper's grief, must have a heart hardened indeed.

Again, there is a most remarkable story (recorded, we believe, a few years ago, in a paper in the *Quarterly Review*) of a French convict who was long the terror of the prison authorities by his violence and audacity. Time after time he had broken out and made savage assaults on his jailers. Stripes and chains had been multiplied year after year; and he was habitually confined in an underground cell, from whence he was only taken to work with his fellow convicts in the prison yard: but his ferocity long remained untamed. At last it was observed that he grew rather more calm and docile, without apparent cause for the change, till one day, when he was working with his comrades, a large rat suddenly leaped from the breast of his coat and ran across the yard. Naturally the cry was raised to kill the rat, and the men were preparing to throw stones at it, when the convict, hitherto so ferocious, with a sudden outburst of feeling implored them to desist, and allow him to recover his strange favourite. The prison officials for once were guided by a happy compassion, and suffered him to call back his rat, which came to his voice, and nestled back in his dress. The convict's gratitude was as strong as his rebellious disposition had hitherto proved, and from that day he proved submissive and orderly. After some years he became the trusted assistant of the jailers, and finally the poor fellow was killed in defending them against a mutiny of the other convicts. The love of that humblest creature finding a place in his rough heart had changed his whole character. Who shall limit the miracles to be wrought by affection, when the love of a *rat* could transform a man?

But whatever result a general review might give us of the amount of tenderness of nations and classes of men for animals, there can be little doubt that it would prove to be a *real* characteristic of humanity, and possessed of a definite place among the sentiments of our nature. On the other hand, the affection and devotion of many species of animals for man are matters of too great notoriety to need more than passing reference. The dog, horse, elephant, cat, seal, and many species of birds, show these feelings in the most unmistakable manner; in some cases marking their love by truly heroic self-sacrifice, or by dying of grief for the loss of their masters. Probably many other species of beasts and birds would prove capable, on experiment, of similar attachment. The tie established in such instances between a man

and the brute who gives him his unbounded devotion, is unquestionably
one of great tenderness. The poor dog's love is a thing so beautiful that
to despise it is to do violence to every softer instinct. The man is in so
far below the brute if the brute can give him a pure, disinterested,
devoted love, and he can give back no tenderness and pity in return.
Cowper said well—

> I would not have that man to be my friend,
> Who needlessly sets foot upon a worm.

The human affections of one who could feel no emotions of pity
for the animal which attached itself to him must be of little worth, and
partake largely of egotism or mere selfish passion. Woe to the woman
or the child who should depend on such a man.

To choose for objects of cruel experiments animals endowed with
the wondrous power of *love*, is not then only a moral offence, viewed
in the light of a needless torture of sentient creatures; it is also a sin
against all the instincts of tenderness and pure sentiment. We are
justified not only in condemning it on moral grounds, but in revolting
against it in the name of the common heart of humanity.

There remains one grave and solemn side of this question which
we have some hesitation in approaching. Man and brutes are not mere
creatures of chance. Sentiment[s] of pity are not matters of arbitrary
taste. Moral laws do not alone bind us with a sacred obligation of
mercy. The MAKER of man is also the Maker of all the tribes of earth
and air and waters. Our Lord is their Lord also. We rule the animal
creation, not as irresponsible sovereigns, but as the vicegerents of God.

The position of the brutes in the scale of creation would appear
to be that of the complement of the mighty whole. We cannot suppose
that the material universe of suns and planets was created for irrational
and immoral beings, but rather to be the habitation of various orders of
intelligences endowed with that moral freedom by which they may
attain to virtue and approach to God in ever-growing likeness and love.
If we may presume to speculate on the awful designs of the Supreme
Architect, we almost inevitably come to this conclusion, that these
world-houses were all built to be, sooner or later, in the million
millenniums of their existence, the abodes of living souls. Be this as it
may regarding the other worlds in the universe, we must at least believe
that here (where such beings actually exist) their palace-home of plains
and hills and woods and waters, with all its libraries of wisdom, its

galleries of beauty, has been built for *them*, and not for their humble fellow-lodgers, the brutes and the fowls, the insects and the fish. They are, we must conclude, the complement and filling-up of the great design. Some of them are the servants appointed for our use; all of them are made to be happy—to fill the world with their innocent delight. We cannot think that any of them, any sentient creature, was made primarily for another creature's benefit, but first for its own happiness, and then afterwards to "second too some other use." Thus we believe the world was made for man, the end of whose creation is virtue and eternal union with God; and the complement of the plan are the brutes, whose end is such happiness as their natures may permit.

If this be so, our relation to the whole animal creation is simply that of *fellow-creatures*, of a rank so much higher, that our interests must always have precedence. But to some orders of animals we are in a much nearer relation, for these are the servants given us expressly by God, and fitted with powers and instincts precisely suiting them to meet our wants. The camel, horse, ass, elephant, the cow, sheep, goat, dog, cat, and many species of fowls, are all so constituted as to supply us with what we need in the way of services, food, clothing, and protection. Our use or misuse of these servants is a matter in which it it impossible to conceive that we are irresponsible, or that we do not offend the merciful Creator when, instead of profiting by His gifts, we use our superior power to torture and destroy the creatures He has made to serve us, and to be happy also. If there be one moral offence which more than another seems directly an offence against God, it is this wanton infliction of pain upon His creatures. He, the Good One, has made them to be happy, but leaves us our awful gift of freedom to use or to misuse towards them. In a word, He places them absolutely in our charge. If we break this trust, and torture them, what is our posture towards Him? Surely as sins of the flesh sink man below humanity, so sins of cruelty throw him into the very converse and antagonism of Deity; he becomes not a mere brute, but a *fiend*.

These would seem to be the simple facts of our relation to the animals, viewed from the religious point of view, on the hypothesis that our usual ideas concerning the lower creation are correct, that brutes have no germ of a moral nature, no prospect of immortality, and that between us and them there are no other ties but those of fellow-creaturehood. It may be that a more advanced mental philosophy, and further researches in science, may modify these ideas. It may be that we shall come to see that sentient life and consciousness and self-consciousness are mysterious powers working upward through all the orders of organic existence; that there are rudiments in the sagacious elephant and the affectionate dog of moral faculties which we need not consign hopelessly to annihilation. It may be that we shall find that man himself, in all the glory of his reason, has sprung, in the far-off eyes of the primeval world, not from the "clod of the valley" any more than from Deucalion's stones, but from some yet-undiscovered creature which once roamed the forests of the elder world, and through whom he stands allied in blood to all the beasts of the field. It may be we shall find all these things; and finding them we shall not degrade man, but only elevate the brute. By such ideas, should science ever ratify them, we shall certainly arrive at new and vivid interests in the animal creation, and the brutes will receive at our hands (we must needs believe) some more tender consideration. But these are, as yet, all doubtful speculations, and we do not need to rest a feather's weight of argument upon them to prove that as religious beings we are bound to show mercy to all God's creatures. God has made all the domestic animals with special adaptations to our use. But there is one species whose purpose is manifestly so peculiarly beneficent, that we cannot pass over it in forming an estimate of our relation to the lower creatures. Many beasts and birds are capable of attaching themselves to man, but the dog is endowed with a capacity for loving his master with a devotion whose parallel we must seek only in the records of the purest human friendship. There is no phenomenon in all the wondrous field of natural history more marvellous than this; and the beaver's architecture, the bee's geometry, may justly be ranked second to the exquisite instinct by which the dog has been rendered capable of such quick and vivid sympathy, such disinterested and self-sacrificing devotion. Nowhere, would it seem, do we come on clearer traces of the tender mercies of the Universal Father, and of His thoughtful provision (if we may so express it) for his children's wants, than in these instincts given to the dog to make him the friend of man, and enable his humble companionship to soothe the aching and cheer the solitary heart. In the various vicissitudes of human life, Providence has found it needful to allot to thousands years of loneliness, and days filled with the anguish of bereaved, or separated, or deceived affection. At the best, numbers of us must lack (amid, perhaps, much true friendship) that special tenderness of *unquestioning* and caressing love which children might supply. But even here that same Providence has, in a measure, supplied and forestalled the want of our hearts, even as it supplies the wants of our physical nature for food and rest. As a mother might give to her child a toy to replace some unsuitable companion, so has the dog been given to us, and fitted to be our gentle playfellow. How does he so marvellously understand our happy moods, and bound beside us with his joyful gambols? And how does he, in a moment, comprehend when we are sad—he who sheds no tears, nor shows any of our marks of grief—and try to lick the listless hand, and nestle to our side, as if to prove to us that his humble devotion will never fail us? How does it come to pass that his affection for his own species, and attachment to his home, and care for his food and safety, are all secondary with him to the love of his master; and that he leaves his companions and his abode without a sign of regret, and flings himself into any danger of robbers, or angry seas, to save him; and, finally, will often refuse all food, and die of starvation upon his grave? These are *wondrous* instincts—wondrous powers of pure disinterested love, whose existence in a creature so suitable in other ways to be the companion and guardian of man, is surely as much an evidence of the Creator's goodness as almost any other in the range of natural theology.

Nor is it some costly animal, whose support only the rich man could afford, or some delicate one, unable to live in different climates, to which such instincts have been given. Over all the globe, from north to south, the canine race can live, from Esquimaux's hut to the kraal of the Hottentot; nor are there many so poor but that they may enjoy its possession. From the king who distrusts the friendship of his venal courtiers, to the blind beggar in his uttermost desolation, there are few whose deceived or lonely hearts cannot find some humble comfort in the true attachment of a dog.

Nay, may we go yet a step further? May we say that in these dumb companions God has placed beside us, in some sense, the emblems of what our own devotion might be to Him who is *our* Master; on whom we depend for all things, and from whose hand we also ought to take our joys and chastisement with the same unwavering faith and grateful love? It may be so; and we, the oft-offending children of that great Father, may look on the blameless and loving servants He has given us—servants who obey us so readily, and trust us so unreservedly—and find in them more than companions, even monitors also.

But we must not pursue these themes. Still less can we turn now to argue as to the *right* of men to subject creatures like these to hideous experiments and agonizing tortures. God help us not only to have mercy on His creatures, but to love them also in their place, and bless Him for their service to us, and for the happiness which He, the Lord of all, has not disdained to bestow upon them. We shall be the nearer to him for doing so; for well did Coleridge say:—

> He prayeth well who loveth well
> Both man, and bird, and beast;
> He prayeth best who loveth best
> All creatures great and small;
> For the dear God who loveth us,
> He makes and loves them all.

Notes

1.   The School of Medicine, the College of France, the Faculty of Sciences, and the Veterinary College of Allfort. [Cobbe's note]

2.   The *Times*, Sept. 5th (or 6th). [Cobbe's note]

3.   This sentence is a paraphrase of Macaulay's excellent epigram that the Puritans forbade bear-baiting, not because it caused pain to the brute, but because it caused pleasure to the man. [Cobbe's note]

4.   See the résumé of the poem in Mrs. Spiers' (now Mrs. Manning's) admirable book, *Ancient India*. [Cobbe's note]

5.   Marine store shops were similar to rag-and-bone shops, but also traded in marine goods, due to their location in waterfront areas.

13. Wife-Torture in England

Introduction

If one article by Frances Power Cobbe could capture the essence of her prose, "Wife-Torture in England," published in the *Contemporary Review* in April, 1878, and reprinted here from that periodical, would be it. The article represents Cobbe in the middle years of her productivity and endures as a powerful accomplishment even to modern readers. Cobbe was appalled by the humorous treatment of violence as it frequently befell wives, both of the upper and middle classes (in secrecy) and the lower classes (more publicly). Cobbe equates the relationships between men and women with those of masters and slaves. She then moves to listing both the political defenders and opponents of "[a]n Act for the Protection of Wives whose Husbands have been convicted of assaults upon them." A copy of the bill precedes her closing section, with recommendations for divorce law amendments. While the far-reaching effect of this article cannot be assessed absolutely, it clearly helped move a nation towards reckoning with the epidemic of wife abuse. Cobbe's closing call for the men of England to step forward and remedy the crisis was heeded and legislation enacted.

Wife-Torture in England

It once happened to me to ask an elderly French gentleman of the most exquisite manners to pay any attention she might need to a charming young lady who was intending to travel by the same train from London to Paris. M. de _____ wrote such a brilliant little note in reply that I was tempted to preserve it as an autograph; and I observe that, after a profusion of thanks, he assured me he should be "trop heureux de se mettre au service"[1] of my young friend. Practically, as I afterwards learned, M. de _____ did make himself quite delightful, till, unluckily, on arriving at Boulogne, it appeared that there was some *imbroglio* about Miss _____'s luggage and she was in a serious difficulty. Needless to say, on such an occasion the intervention of a French gentleman with a ribbon at his button-hole would have been of the greatest possible service; but to render it M. de _____ would have been obliged to miss the train to Paris; and this was a sacrifice for which his politeness was by no means prepared. Expressing himself as utterly *au désespoir*, he took his seat, and was whirled away, leaving my poor young friend alone on the platform to fight her battles as best she might with the impracticable officials. The results might have been annoying had not a homely English stranger stepped in and proffered his aid; and, having recovered the missing property, simply lifted his hat and escaped from the lady's expressions of gratitude.

In this little anecdote I think lies a compendium of the experience of hundreds of ladies on their travels. The genuine and self-sacrificing kindness of English and American gentlemen towards women affords almost a ludicrous contrast to the florid politeness, compatible with every degree of selfishness, usually exhibited by men of other European nations. The reflection then is a puzzling one—How does it come to pass that while the better sort of Englishmen are thus exceptionally humane and considerate to women, the men of the lower class of the same nation are proverbial for their unparalleled brutality, till wife-beating, wife-torture, and wife-murder have bec me the opprobrium of the land? How does it happen (still more strange to note!) that the same generous-hearted gentlemen, who would themselves fly to render succour to a lady in distress, yet read of the beatings, burnings, kickings, and "cloggings" of poor *women* well-nigh every morning in their newspapers without once setting their teeth, and saying, "This must be stopped! We can stand it no longer?"

The paradox truly seems worthy of a little investigation. What reason can be alleged, in the first place, why the male of the human species, and particularly the male of the finest variety of that species, should be the only animal in creation which maltreats its mate, or any female of its own kind?[2]

To get to the bottom of the mystery we must discriminate between assaults of men on other men; assaults of men on women who are not their wives; and assaults of men on their wives. I do not think I err much if I affirm that, in common sentiment, the first of these offences is considerably more heinous than the second—being committed against a more worthy person (as the Latin grammar itself instructs boys to think); and lastly that the assault on a woman who is *not* a man's wife is worse than the assault on a wife by her husband. Towards this last or *minimum* offence a particular kind of indulgence is indeed extended by public opinion.[3] The proceeding seems to be surrounded by a certain halo of jocosity which inclines people to smile whenever they hear of a case of it (terminating anywhere short of actual murder), and causes the mention of the subject to conduce rather than otherwise to the hilarity of a dinner party. The occult fun thus connected with wife-beating forms by no means indeed the least curious part of the subject. Certainly in view of the state of things revealed by our criminal statistics there is something ominous in the circumstance that "Punch" should have been our national English street-drama for more than two centuries.[4] Whether, as some antiquarians tell us, Judas Iscariot was the archetypal Policinello, who, like Faust and Don Juan, finally meets the reward of his crimes by Satanic intervention, or whether, as other learned gentlemen say, the quaint visage and humour of the Neapolitan vintager Puccio d'Aniello, originated the jest which has amused ten generations, it is equally remarkable that so much of the enjoyment should concentrate about the thwacking of poor Judy, and the flinging of the baby out of the window. Questioned seriously whether he think that the behaviour of Punch as a citizen and *père de famille* be in itself a good joke, the British gentleman would probably reply that it was not more facetious than watching a carter flogging a horse. But invested with the drollery of a marionette's behaviour, and accompanied by the screeches of the man with the Pan-pipe, the scene is irresistible, and the popularity of the hero rises with every bang he bestows on the wife of his bosom and on the representative of the law.

The 'same sort of half-jocular sympathy unquestionably accompanies the whole class of characters of whom Mr. Punch is the type. Very good and kind-hearted men may be frequently heard speaking of horrid scenes of mutual abuse and violence between husbands and wives, as if they were rather ridiculous than disgusting. The "Taming of the Shrew" still holds its place as one of the most popular of Shakespeare's comedies; and even the genial Ingoldsby conceived he added a point to his inimitable legend of "Odille," by inserting after the advice to "succumb to our she-saints, videlicet wives," the parenthesis, "that is, if one has not a 'good bunch of fives.'"[5] Where is the hidden fun of this and scores of similar allusions, which sound like the cracking of whips over the cowering dogs in a kennel?

I imagine it lies in the sense, so pleasant to the owners of superior physical strength, that after all, if reason and eloquence should fail, there is always an *ultima ratio*, and that that final appeal lies in their hands. The sparring may be all very well for a time, and may be counted entirely satisfactory *if they get the better*. But then, if by any mischance the unaccountably sharp wits of the weaker creature should prove dangerous weapons, there is always the club of brute force ready to hand in the corner. The listener is amused, as in reading a fairy tale, wherein the hero, when apparently completely vanquished, pulls out a talisman given him by an Afreet, and lo! his enemies fall flat on the ground and are turned into rats.

Thus it comes to pass, I suppose, that the abstract idea of a strong man hitting or kicking a weak woman—*per se*, so revolting— has somehow got softened into a jovial kind of domestic lynching, the grosser features of the case being swept out of sight, just as people make endless jests on tipsiness, forgetting how loathsome a thing is a drunkard. A "jolly companions" chorus seems to accompany both kinds of exploits. This, and the prevalent idea (which I shall analyze by-and-by) that the woman has generally deserved the blows she receives, keep up, I believe, the indifference of the public on the subject.

Probably the sense that they must carry with them a good deal of tacit sympathy on the part of other men has something to do in encouraging wife-beaters, just as the fatal notion of the good fellowship of drink has made thousands of sots. But the immediate causes of the offence of brutal violence are of course very various, and need to be better understood than they commonly are if we would find a remedy for them. First, there are to be considered the class of people and conditions of life wherein the practice prevails; then the character of the men who beat their wives; next that of the wives who are beaten and kicked; and finally, the possible remedy.

Wife-beating exists in the upper and middle classes rather more, I *diff.* fear, than is generally recognized; but it rarely extends to anything *in* beyond an occasional blow or two of a not dangerous kind. In his *class* apparently most ungovernable rage, the gentleman or tradesman somehow manages to bear in mind the disgrace he will incur if his outbreak be betrayed by his wife's black eye or broken arm, and he regulates his cuffs or kicks accordingly. The dangerous wife-beater belongs almost exclusively to the artisan and labouring classes. Colliers, "puddlers," and weavers have long earned for themselves in this matter a bad reputation, and among a long list of cases before me, I reckon shoemakers, stonemasons, butchers, smiths, tailors, a printer, a clerk, a bird-catcher, and a large number of labourers. In the worst districts of London (as I have been informed by one of the most experienced magistrates) four-fifths of the wife-beating cases are among the lowest class of Irish labourers—a fact worthy of more than passing notice, had we time to bestow upon it, seeing that in their own country Irishmen of all classes are proverbially kind and even chivalrous towards women.

There are also various degrees of wife-beating in the different localities. In London it seldom goes beyond a severe "thrashing" with the fist—a sufficiently dreadful punishment, it is true, when inflicted by a strong man on a woman; but mild in comparison of the kickings and tramplings and "purrings" with hob-nailed shoes and clogs of what we can scarcely, in this connection, call the "dark and true and *tender* North." As Mr. Sergeant Pulling remarks,[6] "Nowhere is the ill-usage of woman so systematic as in Liverpool, and so little hindered by the strong arm of the law; making the lot of a married woman, whose locality is the 'kicking district' of Liverpool, simply a duration of suffering and subjection to injury and savage treatment, far worse than that to which the wives of mere savages are used." It is in the centres of dense mercantile and manufacturing populations that this offence reaches its climax. In London the largest return for one year (in the Parliamentary Report on Brutal Assaults) of brutal assaults on women was 351. In Lancashire, with a population of almost two millions and a-half, the largest number was 194. In Stafford, with a population of three-quarters of a million, there were 113 cases. In the West Riding, with a million and a-half, 152; and in Durham, with 508,666, no less than 267. Thus, roughly speaking, there are nearly five times as many wife-beaters of the more brutal kind, in proportion to the population, in Durham as in London. What are the conditions of life among the working classes in those great "hives of industry" of which we talk so proudly? It is but justice that we should picture the existence of the men and women in such places before we pass to discuss the deeds which darken it.

They are lives out of which almost every softening and ennobling element has been withdrawn, and into which enter brutalizing influences almost unknown elsewhere. They are lives of hard, ugly, mechanical toil in dark pits and hideous factories, amid the grinding and clanging of engines and the fierce heat of furnaces, in that Black Country where the green sod of earth is replaced by mounds of slag and shale, where no flower grows, no fruit ripens, scarcely a bird sings; where the morning has no freshness, the evening no dews; where the spring sunshine cannot pierce the foul curtain of smoke which overhangs these modern Cities of the Plain, and where the very streams and rivers run discoloured and steaming with stench, like Styx and Phlegethon, through their banks of ashes. If "God made the country and man made the town,"we might deem that Ahrimanes devised this Tartarus of toil, and that here we had at last found the spot where the Psalmist might seek in vain for the handiwork of the Lord.[7]

As we now and then, many of us, whirl through this land of darkness in express trains, and draw up our carriage windows that we may be spared the smoke and dismal scene, we have often reflected that the wonder is, *not* that the dwellers there should lose some of the finer poetry of life, the more delicate courtesies of humanity, but that they should remain so much like other men, and should so often rise to noble excellence and intelligence, rather than have developed, as would have seemed more natural, into a race of beings relentless, hard, and grim as their own iron machines—beings of whom the Cyclops of the Greek and the Gnomes of the Teuton imaginations were the foreshadowings. Of innocent pleasure in such lives there can, alas! be very little; and the hunger of nature for enjoyment must inevitably be supplied (among all save the few to whom intellectual pursuits may suffice) by the grosser gratification of the senses. Writers who have never attempted to realize what it must be to hear ugly sounds and smell nauseous odours and see hideous sights, all day long, from year's end to year's end, are angry with these Black Country artisans for spending largely of their earnings in buying delicate food—poultry and salmon, and peas and strawberries. For my part, I am inclined to rejoice if they can content themselves with such harmless gratifications of the palate, instead of the deadly stimulants of drink, cruelty, and vice.

These, then, are the localities wherein Wife-torture flourishes in England; where a dense population is crowded into a hideous manufacturing or mining or mercantile district. Wages are usually high though fluctuating. Facilities for drink and vice abound, but those for cleanliness and decency are scarcely attainable. The men are rude, coarse, and brutal in their manners and habits, and the women devoid, in an extraordinary degree, of all the higher natural attractions and influences of their sex. Poor drudges of the factory, or of the crowded and sordid lodging-house, they lose, before youth is past, the freshness, neatness, and gentleness, perhaps even the modesty of a woman, and present, when their miserable cases come up before the magistrate, an aspect so sordid and forbidding that it is no doubt with difficulty he affords his sympathy to them rather than to the husband chained to so wretched a consort. Throughout the whole of this inquiry I think it very necessary, in justice to all parties, and in mitigation of too vehement judgment of cases only known from printed reports, to bear in mind that the women of the class concerned are, some of them wofully [sic] unwomanly, slatternly, coarse, foul-mouthed—sometimes loose in behaviour, sometimes madly addicted to drink. There ought to be no idealizing of them, *as a class*, into refined and suffering angels if we wish to be just. The home of a Lancashire operative, alas! is not a garden wherein the plants of refinement or sensitiveness are very likely to spring up or thrive.

Given this direful *milieu*, and its population, male and female, we next ask, What are the immediate incitements to the men to maltreat the women? They are of two kinds, I think,—general and particular.

First, the whole relation between the sexes in the class we are considering is very little better than one of master and slave. I have always abjured the use of this familiar comparison in speaking generally of English husbands and wives, because as regards the upper orders of society it is ridiculously overstrained and untrue. But in the "kicking districts," among the lowest labouring classes, Legree himself might find a dozen prototypes, and the condition of the women be most accurately matched by that of the negroes on a Southern plantation before the war struck off their fetters.[8] To a certain extent this marital tyranny among the lower classes is beyond the reach of law, and can only be remedied by the slow elevation and civilization of both sexes. But it is also in an appreciable degree, I am convinced, enhanced by the law even as it now stands, and was still more so by the law as it stood before the Married Women's Property Act put a stop to the chartered robbery by husbands of their wives' earnings. At the present time, though things are improving year by year, thanks to the generous and far-seeing statesmen who are contending for justice to women inside and out of the House of Commons, the position of a woman before the law as wife, mother, and citizen, remains so much below that of a man as husband, father, and citizen, that it is a matter of course that she must be regarded by him as an inferior, and fail to obtain from him such a modicum of respect as her mental and moral qualities might win did he see her placed by the State on an equal footing.

I have no intention in this paper to discuss the vexed subject of women's political and civil rights, but I cannot pass to the consideration of the incidental and minor causes of the outrages upon them, without recording my conviction that the political disabilities under which the whole sex still labours, though apparently a light burden on the higher and happier ranks, presses down more and more heavily through the lower strata of society in growing deconsideration and contempt, unrelieved (as it is at higher levels) by other influences on opinion. Finally at the lowest grade of all it exposes women to an order of insults and wrongs which are never inflicted by equals upon an equal, and can only be paralleled by the oppressions of a dominant caste or race over their helots. In this as in many other things the educating influence of law immeasurably outstrips its direct action; and such as is the spirit of our laws, such will inevitably be the spirit of our people. Human beings no longer live like animals in a condition wherein the natural sentiments between the sexes suffice to guard the weak, where the male brute is kind and forbearing to the female, and where no Court of Chancery interferes with the mother's most dear and sacred charge of her little ones. Man alone claims to hold his mate in subjection, and to have the right while he lives, and even after he dies, to rob a mother of her child; and man, who has lost the spontaneous chivalry of the lion and the dog, needs to be provided with laws which may do whatever it lies [sic] with laws to effect to form a substitute for such chivalry. Alas! instead of such, he has only made for himself laws which add legal to natural disabilities, and give artificial strength to ready-constituted prepotence.

I consider that it is a very great misfortune to both sexes that women should be thus depreciated in the opinion of that very class of men whom it would be most desirable to impress with respect and tenderness for them; who are most prone to despise physical infirmity and to undervalue the moral qualities wherein women excel. All the softening and refining influences which women exert in happier conditions are thus lost to those who most need them,—to their husbands and still more emphatically to their children; and the women themselves are degraded and brutified in their own eyes by the contempt of their companions. When I read all the fine-sounding phrases perpetually repeated about the invaluable influence of a good mother over her son,—how the worst criminals are admitted to be reclaimable if they have ever enjoyed it,—and how the virtues of the best and noblest men are attributed to it, as a commonplace of biography,—I often ask myself, "Why, then, is not something done to lift and increase, instead of to depreciate and lower, that sacred influence? Why are not mothers allowed to respect themselves, that they may fitly claim the respect of their sons? How is a lad to learn to reverence a woman whom he sees daily scoffed at, beaten, and abused, and when he knows that the laws of his country forbid her, ever and under any circumstances, to exercise the rights of citizenship; nay, which deny to her the guardianship of *himself*—of the very child of her bosom—should her husband choose to hand him over to her rival out of the street?"

The general depreciation of women *as a sex* is bad enough, but in the matter we are considering, the special depreciation of *wives* is more directly responsible for the outrages they endure. The notion that a man's wife is his PROPERTY, in the sense in which a horse is his property (descended to us rather through the Roman law than through the customs of our Teuton ancestors), is the fatal root of incalculable evil and misery. Every brutal-minded man, and many a man who in other relations of life is not brutal, entertains more or less vaguely the notion that his wife is his *thing*, and is ready to ask with indignation (as we read again and again in the police reports), of any one who interferes with his treatment of her, "May I not do what I will *with my own?*" It is even sometimes pleaded on behalf of poor men, that they possess *nothing else* but their wives, and that, consequently, it seems doubly hard to meddle with the exercise of their power in that narrow sphere![9]

I am not intending to discuss the question of the true relation between husbands and wives which we may hope to see realized when

> Springs the happier race of human kind

from parents "equal and free"—any more than the political and social rights of women generally. But it is impossible, in treating of the typical case wherein the misuse of wives reaches its climax in Wife-beating and Wife-torture, to avoid marking out with a firm line where lies the underground spring of the mischief. As one of the many results of this *proton pseudos*, must be noted the fact (very important in its bearing on our subject) that not only is an offence against a wife condoned as of inferior guilt, but any offence of the wife against her husband is regarded as a sort of *Petty Treason.* For her, as for the poor ass in the fable, it is more heinous to nibble a blade of grass than for the wolf to devour both the lamb and the shepherd. Should she be guilty of "nagging" or scolding, or of being a slattern, or of getting intoxicated, she finds usually a short shrift and no favour—and even humane persons talk of her offence as constituting, if not a justification for her murder, yet an explanation of it. She is, in short, liable to capital punishment without judge or jury for transgressions which in the case of a man would never be punished at all, or be expiated by a fine of five shillings.[10]

Nay, in her case there is a readiness even to pardon the omission of the ordinary forms of law as needlessly cumbersome. In no other instance save that of the Wife-beater is excuse made for a man taking the law into his own hands. We are accustomed to accept it as a principle that "lynching" cannot be authorized in a civilized country, and that the first lesson of orderly citizenship is that no man shall be judge, jury, and executioner in his own cause. But when a wife's offences are in question this salutary rule is overlooked, and men otherwise just-minded, refer cheerfully to the *circonstance atténuante*[11] of the wife's drunkenness or bad language, as if it not only furnished an excuse for outrage upon her, but made it quite fit and proper for the Queen's peace to be broken and the woman's bones along with it.

This underlying public opinion is fortunately no new thing. On the contrary, it is an idea of immemorial antiquity which has been embodied in the laws of many nations, and notably, as derived from the old Roman *Patria Potestas*, in our own. It was only in 1829, in the 9th George IV., that the Act of Charles II., which embodied the old Common Law, and authorized a man "to chastise his wife with any reasonable instrument," was erased from our Statute-Book. Our position is not retrograde, but advancing, albeit too slowly. It is not as in the case of the Vivisection of Animals, that a new passion of cruelty is arising, but only that an old one, having its origin in the remotest epochs of barbarian wife-capture and polygamy, yet lingers in the dark places of the land. By degrees, if our statesmen will but bring the educational influence of law to bear upon the matter, it will surely die out and become a thing of the past, like cannibalism,—than which it is no better fitted for a Christian nation.

Of course the ideas of the suffering wives are cast in the same mould as those of their companions. They take it for granted that a Husband is a Beating Animal, and may be heard to remark when extraordinarily ill-treated by a stranger,—that they "never were so badly used, no not by their own 'usbands." Their wretched proverbial similarity to spaniels and walnut-trees, the readiness with which they sometimes turn round and snap at a bystander who has interfered on their behalf, of course affords to cowardly people a welcome excuse for the "policy of non-intervention," and forms the culminating proof of how far the iron of their fetters has eaten into their souls. A specially experienced gentleman writes from Liverpool: "The women of Lancashire are *awfully fond* of bad husbands. It has become quite a truism that our women are like dogs, the more you beat them the more they love you." Surely if a bruised and trampled woman be a pitiful object, a woman who has been brought down by fear, or by her own gross passions, so low as to fawn on the beast who strikes her, is one to make angels weep?[12]

To close this part of the subject, I conceive then, that the common idea of the inferiority of women, and the special notion of the rights of husbands, form the undercurrent of feeling which induces a man, when for any reason he is infuriated, to wreak his violence on his wife. She is, in his opinion, his natural *souffre-douleur*.[13]

It remains to be noted what are the principal incitements to such outbursts of savage fury among the classes wherein Wife-beating prevails. They are not far to seek. The first is undoubtedly *Drink*—poisoned drink. The seas of brandy and gin, and the oceans of beer, imbibed annually in England, would be bad enough, if taken pure and simple,[14] but it is the vile adulterations introduced into them which make them the infuriating poisons which they are—which literally *sting* the wretched drinkers into cruelty, perhaps quite foreign to their natural temperaments. As an experienced minister in these districts writes to me, "I have known men almost as bad as those you quote (a dozen wife-murderers) made into most kind and considerate husbands by total abstinence." If the English people will go on swallowing millions' worth yearly of brain poison, what can we expect but brutality the most hideous and grotesque? Assuredly the makers and vendors of these devil's philtres are responsible for an amount of crime and ruin which some of the worst tyrants in history might have trembled to bear on their consciences; nor can the national legislature be absolved for suffering the great Drink interest thus foully to tamper with the health—nay, with the very souls of our countrymen. What is the occult influence which prevents the Excise from performing its duty as regards these frauds on the revenue?

2. Next to drunkenness as a cause of violence to women, follows the other "great sin of great cities," of which it is unnecessary here to speak. The storms of jealousy thence arising, the hideous alternative *possession* of the man by the twin demons of cruelty and lust—one of whom is never very far from the other—are familiar elements in the police-court tragedies.

3. Another source of the evil may be found in that terrible, though little recognized passion, which rude men and savages share with many animals, and which is the precise converse of sympathy, for it consists in anger and cruelty, excited by the signs of pain; an impulse to hurt and destroy any suffering creature, rather than to relieve or help it. Of the widespread influence of this passion (which I have ventured elsewhere to name *Heteropathy*), a passion only slowly dying out as civilization advances, there can, I think, be no doubt at all. It is a hideous mystery of human nature that such feelings should lie latent in it, and that cruelty should grow by what it feeds on; that the more the tyrant causes the victim to suffer the more he hates him, and desires to heap on him fresh sufferings. Among the lower classes the emotion of

Heteropathy unmistakably finds vent in the cruelty of parents and step-parents to unfortunate children who happen to be weaker or more stupid than others, or to have been once excessively punished, and whose joyless little faces and timid crouching demeanour, instead of appeals for pity, prove provocations to fresh outrage. The group of his shivering and starving children and weeping wife is the sad sight which, greeting the eyes of the husband and father reeling home from the gin-shop, somehow kindles his fury. If the baby cry in the cradle, he stamps on it. If his wife wring her hands in despair, he fells her to the ground.[15]

_4._ After these I should be inclined to reckon, as a cause of brutal outbreaks, the impatience and irritation which must often be caused in the homes of the working classes by sheer *friction*. While such people, when they get tired of each other or feel irritable, are enabled to recover their tempers in the ample space afforded by a comfortable house, the poor are huddled together in such close quarters that the sweetest tempers and most tender affections must sometimes feel the trial. Many of us have shuddered at Miss Octavia Hill's all-too-graphic description of a hot, noisome court in the heart of London on a fine summer evening, with men, women, and children "pullulating," as the French say, on the steps, at the windows, on the pavement, all dirty, hot, and tired, and scarcely able to find standing or sitting room.[16] It is true the poor are happily more gregarious than the rich. Paradoxical as it sounds, it takes a good deal of civilization to make a man love savage scenery, and a highly cultivated mind to find any "pleasure in the pathless woods" or "rapture in the lonely shore." Nevertheless, for moral health as much as for physical, a certain number of cubic inches of space are needed for every living being.

It is their interminable, inevitable propinquity which in the lower classes makes the nagging, wrangling, worrying women so intolerably trying. As millers get accustomed, it is said, to the clapping of their mill, so may some poor husbands become deaf to their wives' tongues; but the preliminary experience must be severe indeed.

These, then, are the incentives to Wife-beating and Wife-torture. What are the men on whom they exert their evil influence?

Obviously, by the hypothesis, they are chiefly the drunken, idle, ruffianly fellows who lounge about the public-houses instead of working for their families. Without pretending to affirm that there are no sober, industrious husbands goaded to strike their wives through jealousy or irritation, the presumption is enormous against the character of any man convicted of such an assault. The cases in which the police reports of them add, "He had been bound over to keep the peace several times previously," or "He had been often fined for drunkenness and disorderly behaviour," are quite countless. Sometimes it approaches the ludicrous to read how helplessly the law has been attempting to deal with the scoundrel, as, for example, in the case of William Owen, whom his wife said she "met for the first time beside Ned Wright's Bible-barrow," and who told the poor fool he had been "converted." He was known to Constable 47 K as having been convicted *over sixty times* for drunkenness and violent assaults; and the moment he left the church he began to abuse his wife.

The pitilessness and ferocity of these men sometimes looks like madness. Alfred Stone, for example, coming home in a bad temper, took his wife's parrot out of its cage, stamped on it, and threw it on the fire, observing, "Jane! it is the last thing you have got belonging to your father!" In the hands of such a man a woman's heart must be crushed, like the poor bird under his heel.

Turn we now from the beaters to the beaten. I have already said that we must not idealize the women of the "kicking districts." They are, mostly, poor souls, very coarse, very unwomanly. Some of them drink whenever they can procure drink. Some are bad and cruel mothers (we cannot forget the awful stories of the Burial Clubs); many are hopelessly depraved, and lead as loose lives as their male companions. Many keep their houses in a miserable state of dirt and disorder, neglect their children, and sell their clothes and furniture for gin. Not seldom will one of these reckless creatures pursue her husband in the streets with screams of abuse and jeers. The man knows not where to turn to escape from the fury. When he comes home at night, he probably finds her lying dead drunk on the bed, and his children crying for their supper. Again, in a lesser degree, women make their homes into purgatories by their bad tempers. There was in old times a creature recognized by law as a "Common Scold," for whom the punishment of ducking in the village horse-pond was formally provided. It is to be feared her species is by no means to be reckoned among the "Extinct Mammalia." Then comes the "nagging" wife, immortalized as "Mrs. Caudle;" the worrying, peevish kill-joy, whose presence is a wet blanket—nay, a wet blanket stuck full of pins; the argumentative woman, with a voice like a file and a face like a ferret, who bores on, night and day, till life is a burden.[17]

These are terrible harpies. But it is scarcely fair to assume that every woman who is accused of "nagging" necessarily belongs to their order. I have no doubt that every husband who comes home with empty pockets, and from whom his wife needs to beg repeatedly for money to feed herself and her children, considers that she "nags" him. I have no doubt that when a wife reproaches such a husband with squandering his wages in the public-house, or on some wretched rival, while she and her children are starving, he accuses her to all his friends of intolerable "nagging," and that, not seldom having acquired from him the reputation of this kind of thing, the verdict of "Serve her Right" is generally passed upon her by public opinion when her "nagging" is capitally punished by a broken head.

But *all* women of the humblest class are not those terrible creatures, drunken, depraved, or ill-tempered; or even addicted to "nagging." On the contrary, I can affirm from my own experience, as well, I believe, as that of all who have had much to do with the poor of great cities, there are among them at least as many good women as bad—as many who are sober, honest, chaste, and industrious, as are the contrary. There is a type which every clergyman, and magistrate, and district visitor will recognize in a moment as very common: a woman generally small and slight of person, but alert, intelligent, active morning, noon, and night, doing the best her strength allows to keep her home tidy, and her children neat and well fed, and to supply her husband's wants. Her face was, perhaps, pretty at eighteen: by the time she is eight-and-twenty, toil and drudgery and many children have reduced her to a mere rag, and only her eyes retain a little pathetic relic of beauty. This woman expresses herself well and simply: it is a special "note" of her character that she uses no violent words, even in describing the worst injuries. There is nothing "loud" about her voice, dress, or manners. She is emphatically a "*decent*," respectable woman. Her only fault, if fault it be, is that she will insist on obtaining food and clothing for her children, and that when she is refused them she becomes that depressed, broken-spirited creature whose mute, reproachful looks act as a goad, as I have said, to the passions of her oppressor. We shall see presently what part this class of woman plays in the horrible domestic tragedies of England.

We have now glanced at the conditions under which Wife-beating takes place, at the incentives immediately leading to it, the men who beat, and the women who are beaten. Turn we now to examine more closely the thing itself.

There are two kinds of Wife-beating which I am anxious the reader should keep clearly apart in his mind. There is what may be called *Wife-beating by Combat*, and there is Wife-beating properly so called, which is only wife, and not wife-and-husband beating. In the first, both parties have an equal share. Bad words are exchanged, then blows. The man hits, the woman perhaps scratches and tears. If the woman generally gets much the worst of it, it is simply because cats are weaker than dogs. The man cannot so justly be said to have "beaten" his wife as to have vanquished her in a boxing-match. Almost without exception in these cases it is mentioned that "both parties were the worse for liquor." It is in this way the drunken woman is beaten, *by the drunken man*, not by the ideal sober and industrious husband, who has a right to be disgusted by her intoxication. It is nearly exclusively, I think, in such drunken quarrels that the hateful virago gets beaten at all. As a general rule she commands too much fear, and is so ready to give back curse for curse and blow for blow, that, in cold blood, nobody meddles with her. Such a termagant is often the tyrant of her husband, nay, of the whole court or lane in which she lives; and the sentiments she excites are the reverse of those which bring down the fist and the clogs of the ruffian husband on the timid and meek-faced woman who tries, too often unsuccessfully, the supposed magic of a soft answer to turn away the wrath of such a wild beast as he.

One word, however, must be said, before we leave this revolting picture, even for that universally condemned creature, the drunken wife. Does any save one, the Great Judge above, ever count how many of such doubly-degraded beings have been *driven* to intemperance by sheer misery? How many have been lured to drink by companionship with their drunken husbands? How many have sunk into the habit because, worn out in body by toil and child-bearing, degraded in soul by contempt and abuse, they have not left in them one spark of that self-respect which enables a human being to resist the temptation to drown care and remembrance in the dread forgetfulness of strong drink?

The second kind of Wife-beating is when the man alone is the striker and the woman the stricken. These are the cases which specially challenge our attention, and for which it may be hoped some palliative may be found. In these, the husband usually comes home "the worse for liquor," and commences, sometimes without any provocation at all, to attack his wife, or drag her out of the bed where she is asleep, or has just been confined. (See cases p. 74.) Sometimes there is preliminary altercation, the wife imploring him to give her some money to buy necessaries, or reproaching him for drinking all he has earned. In either case the wife is passive so far as blows are concerned, unless at the last, in self-defence, she lays her hand on some weapon to protect her life—a fact which is always cited against her as a terrible delinquency.[18]

Such are the two orders of Wife-beating with which a tolerably extensive study of the subject has made me familiar. It will be observed that neither includes that ideal Wife-beater of whom we hear so much, the sober, industrious man goaded to frenzy by his wife's temper or drunkenness. I will not venture to affirm that that Ideal Wife-beater is as mythical as the griffin or the sphinx, but I will affirm that in all my inquiries I have never yet come on his track.

I have insisted much on this point, because I think it has been strangely overlooked, and that it ought to form a most important factor in making up our judgment of the whole matter and of the proper remedies. It will be found, I believe, on inquiry that it is actually surprising how very seldom there is anything at all alleged by the husband against the wife in the worst cases of wife-torture—except the "provocation" and "nagging" of asking him for money; or, as in the case of poor Ellen Harlow, of refusing him twopence out of her own earnings when he had been drinking all day and she had been working.[19] In thirty-eight cases taken at random, five were of the class of drunken combats; and in thirty nothing was reported as alleged against the victims. In many cases strong testimony was given of their good conduct and industry: *e.g.* the wife of William White, who was burnt to death by the help of his paraffin lamp, was a "hard-working industrious woman." The wife of James Lawrence, whose face bore in court tokens of the most dreadful violence, "said that her husband had for years done nothing for his livelihood, while she had bought a shop, and stocked it out of her own earnings." The wife of Richard Mountain had "supported herself and her children." The wife of Alfred Etherington, who has been dangerously injured by her husband kicking and jumping on her, had been supporting him and their children. The wife of James Styles, who was beaten by her husband till she became insensible, had long provided for him and herself by charwork; and so on.

Regarding the extent of the evil it is difficult to arrive at a just calculation. Speaking of those cases only which come before the courts,—probably, of course, not a third of the whole number,—the elements for forming an opinion are the following:—

In the Judicial Statistics for England and Wales, issued in 1877 for 1876, we find that of Aggravated Assaults on Women and Children of the class which since 1853 have been brought under Summary Jurisdiction there were reported,

In 1876	—	—	—	—	—	2,737
In 1875	—	—	—	—	—	3,106
In 1874	—	—	—	—	—	2,841

How many of these were assaults made by husbands on wives there is no means of distinguishing, but, judging from other sources,[20] I should imagine they formed about four-fifths of the whole.

Among the worst cases, when the accused persons were committed for trial or bailed for appearance at Assizes or Sessions (coming under the head of Criminal Proceedings), the classification adopted in the Parliamentary Return does not permit of identifying the cases which concerned women only. Some rough guess on the matter may perhaps be formed from the preponderance of male criminals in all classes of violent crime. Out of 67 persons charged with Murder in 1876, 49 were men. Of 41 charged with Attempt to Murder, 35 were males. Of 157 charged with Shooting, Stabbing, &c., 146 were men. Of 232 charged with Manslaughter, 185 were men; and of 1,020 charged with Assault inflicting bodily harm, 857 were men. In short, out of 1,517 persons charged with crimes of cruelty and violence, more than five-sixths were males, and only 235 females. Of course the men's offences include a variety of crimes besides Wife-beating and Wife-torture.

The details of the crimes for which twenty-two men who were capitally convicted in 1876 suffered death are noteworthy on this head. (Criminal Statistics p. xxix.) Of these:—

Edward Deacon, shoemaker, murdered his wife by cutting her head with a chopper.

John Thomas Green, painter, shot his wife with a pistol.

John Eblethrift, labourer, murdered his wife by
stabbing.

Charles O'Donnell, labourer, murdered his wife by
beating.

Henry Webster, labourer, murdered his wife by cutting
her throat.

Beside these, five others murdered women with whom they were
living in vicious relations, and three others (including the monster
William Fish) murdered children. In all, more than half the convicted
persons executed that year were guilty of wife-murder,—or of what we
may term *quasi*-wife-murder.

A source of more accurate information is to be found in the
abstracts of the Reports of Chief Constables for the years 1870–1–2–3–
4, presented to the Home Secretary, and published in the "Report on
Brutal Assaults" (p. 169, et seq.). In this instructive table Brutal
Assaults on Women are discriminated from those on men, and the total
number of convictions for such assaults for the whole five years is
6,029; or at the average of 1,205 per annum. This is, however,
obviously an imperfect return. In Nottinghamshire, where such offences
were notoriously common, the doings of the "Lambs" have somehow
escaped enumeration. "The Chief Constable states that he is unable to
furnish a correct return." From Merionethshire no report was received in
reply to the Home Office Circular; and from Rutland, Salop, Radnor,
and Cardiganshire, the Chief Constables returned the reply that there
were no brutal assaults in those counties during the five years in
question,—a statement suggesting that some different classification of
offences must prevail in those localities, since the immunity of
Cardiganshire and Salop for five years from such crimes of violence
would be little short of miraculous, while Flint alone had sixteen
convictions. Thus I conceive that we may fairly estimate the number of
brutal assaults (*brutal* be it remembered, not ordinary) committed on
women in England and Wales and actually brought to justice at about
1,500 a year, or more than four *per diem*; and of these the great
majority are of husbands on wives.

Let us now proceed from the number to the nature of the offences
in question. I have called this paper English *Wife-torture* because I
wish to impress my readers with the fact that the familiar term "wife-
beating" conveys about as remote a notion of the extremity of the
cruelty indicated as when candid and ingenuous vivisectors talk of

"scratching a newt's tail" when they refer to burning alive, or dissecting out the nerves of living dogs, or torturing ninety cats in one series of experiments.

Wife-*beating* is the mere preliminary canter before the race,—the preface to the serious matter which is to follow. Sometimes, it is true, there are men of comparatively mild dispositions who are content to go on beating their wives year after year, giving them occasional black-eyes and bruises, or tearing out of a few locks of their hair and spitting in their faces, or bestowing an ugly print of their iron fingers on the woman's soft arm, but not proceeding beyond these minor injuries to anything perilous. Among the lower classes, unhappily, this rude treatment is understood to mean very little more than that the man uses his weapon—the fists—as the woman uses hers—the tongue—and neither are very much hurt or offended by what is either done by one or said by the other. The whole state of manners is what is to be deplored, and our hope must be to change the bear-garden into the semblance of a civilized community, rather than by any direct effort to correct the special offence. Foul words, gross acts, drink, dirt, and vice, oaths, curses, and blows, it is all, alas! *in keeping*—nor can we hope to cure one evil without the rest. But the unendurable mischief, the discovery of which has driven me to try to call public attention to the whole matter, is this—Wife-*beating* in process of time, and in numberless cases, advances to Wife-*torture*, and the Wife-torture usually ends in Wife-maiming, Wife-blinding, or Wife-murder. A man who has "thrashed" his wife with his fists half-a-dozen times, becomes satiated with such enjoyment as that performance brings, and next time he is angry he kicks her with his hob-nailed shoes. When he has kicked her a few times standing or sitting, he kicks her down and stamps on her stomach, her breast, or her face. If he does not wear clogs or hob-nailed shoes, he takes up some other weapon, a knife, a poker, a hammer, a bottle of vitriol, or a lighted lamp, and strikes her with it, or sets her on fire;—and then, and then only, the hapless creature's sufferings are at an end.

*   *   *

I desire specially to avoid making this paper more painful than can be helped, but it is indispensable that some specimens of the tortures to which I refer should be brought before the reader's eye. I shall take them exclusively from cases reported during the last three or four months. Were I to go further back for a year or two, it would be easy to find some more "sensational," as, for example, of Michael Copeland, who threw his wife on a blazing fire; of George Ellis, who murdered his wife by pitching her out of window; of Ashton Keefe, who beat his wife and thrust a box of lighted matches into his little daughter's breast when she was too slow in bringing his beer; and of Charles Bradley, who, according to the report in the *Manchester Examiner*, "came home, and after locking the door, told his wife he would murder her. He immediately set a large bulldog at her, and the dog, after flying at the upper part of her body, seized hold of the woman's right arm, which she lifted to protect herself, and tore pieces out. The prisoner in the meantime kept striking her in the face, and inciting the brute to worry her. The dog dragged her up and down, biting pieces out of her arms, and the prisoner then got on the sofa and hit and kicked her on the breast."

But the instances of the last three or four months—from September to the end of January—are more than enough to establish all I want to prove; and I beg here to return my thanks for a collection of them, and for many very useful observations and tabulations of them, to Miss A. Shore, who has been good enough to place them at my disposal.

It is needful to bear in mind in reading them, that the reports of such cases which appear in newspapers are by no means always reliable, or calculated to convey the same impressions as the sight of the actual trial. In some of the following instances, also, I have only been able to obtain the first announcement of the offence, without means of checking it by the subsequent proceedings in court. *Per contra*, it should be remembered that if a few of these cases may possibly have been exaggerated or trumped up (as I believe the story of the man pouring Chili vinegar into his wife's eyes proved to have been), there are, for every one of these *published* horrors, at least three or four which *never are reported at all*, and where the poor victim dies quietly of her injuries like a wounded animal, without seeking the mockery of redress offered her by the law.

James Mills cut his wife's throat as she lay in bed. He was quite sober at the time. On a previous occasion he had nearly torn away her left breast.

J. Coleman returned home early in the morning, and, finding his wife asleep, took up a heavy piece of wood and struck her on the head and arm, bruising her arm. On a previous occasion he had fractured her ribs.

John Mills poured out vitriol deliberately, and threw it in his wife's face, because she asked him to give her some of his wages. He had said previously that he would blind her.

James Lawrence, who had been frequently bound over to keep the peace, and who had been supported by his wife's industry for years, struck her on the face with a poker, leaving traces of the most dreadful kind when she appeared in court.

Frederick Knight jumped on the face of his wife (who had only been confined a month) with a pair of boots studded with hobnails.

Richard Mountain beat his wife on the back and mouth, and turned her out of her bed and out of their room one hour after she had been confined.

Alfred Roberts felled his wife to the floor, with a child in her arms; knelt on her, and grasped her throat. She had previously taken out three summonses against him, but had never attended.

John Harris, a shoemaker, at Sheffield, found his wife and children in bed, dragged her out, and, after vainly attempting to force her into the oven, tore off her night-dress and turned her round before the fire "like a piece of beef," while the children stood on the stairs listening to their mother's agonized screams.

Richard Scully knocked in the frontal bone of his wife's forehead.

William White, stonemason, threw a burning paraffin lamp at his wife, and stood quietly watching her enveloped in flames, from the effects of which she died.

William Hussell, a butcher, ran a knife into his wife several times and killed her. Had threatened to do so often before.

Robert Kelly, engine-driver, bit a piece out of his wife's cheek.

William James, an operative boilermaker, stabbed his wife badly in the arm and mouth, observing afterwards, "I am sorry I did not kill both" (his wife and her mother).

Thomas Richards, a smith, threw his wife down a flight of fourteen steps, when she came to entreat him to give her some money for her maintenance. He was living with another woman—the nurse at a hospital where he had been ill.

James Frickett, a ratcatcher. His wife was found dying with broken ribs and cut and bruised face, a walking-stick with blood on it lying by. Frickett remarked, "If I am going to be hanged for you, I love you."

James Styles beat his wife about the head when he met her in the City Road. She had supported him for years by char-work, and during the whole time he had been in the habit of beating her, and on one occasion so assaulted her that the sight of one of her eyes was destroyed. He got drunk habitually with the money she earned.

John Harley, a compositor, committed for trial for cutting and wounding his wife with intent to murder.

Joseph Moore, labourer, committed for trial for causing the death of his wife by striking her with an iron instrument on the head.

George Ralph Smith, oilman, cut his wife, as the doctor expressed it, "to pieces," with a hatchet, in their back parlour. She died afterwards, but he was found Not Guilty, as it was not certain that her death resulted from the wounds.

Fletcher Bisley, a clerk, struck his wife violently on the head with a poker, after having tried to throw a saucepan of boiling soup at her son. Both had just returned home and found Bisley in bed.

Alfred Cummins, tailor, struck his wife so as to deprive her of the sight of an eye.

Thomas Paget, laundryman, knocked down his wife in the street and kicked her till she became insensible, because she refused to give him money to get drink.

Alfred Etherington, shoemaker, kicked his wife in a dangerous way, and a week later dragged her out of bed, jumped on her, and struck her. He said he would have her life and the lives of all her children. He gave no money for the support of his family (six children), and he prevented her from keeping the situations she had obtained for their maintenance. She had summoned him six or seven times.

Jeremiah Fitzgerald, labourer, knocked down his wife and kicked her heavily in the forehead. He had been twice convicted before. The woman appeared in court with her face strapped up.

Patrick Flynn, violently kicked his wife after he had knocked her down, and then kicked a man who interfered to

save her. Had already undergone six months' hard labour for
assaulting his wife.

Here is a case recorded from personal observation by a magistrate's
clerk:—

> I attended a dying woman to take her deposition in a
> drunkard's dwelling. The husband was present in charge of the
> police. The poor wretched wife lay with many ribs broken,
> and her shoulder and one arm broken, and her head so smashed
> that you could scarcely recognize a feature of a woman. She,
> in her last agony, said that her husband had smashed her with
> a wooden bed-post. He, blubbering, said, 'Yes, it is true, but I
> was in drink, or would not have done it.'

And here is one that has come in while I have been writing:—

> At the Blackburn police-court, yesterday, John
> Charnock was committed for trial on a charge of attempted
> murder. It was stated that he had fastened his wife's head in a
> cupboard and kicked her with his iron clogs, and that he had
> deliberately broken her arm. (Feb. 3, 1878.)

And here another (reported in the *Manchester Courier*, February 5th)
so instructive in its details of the motives for Wife-murder, the sort of
woman who is murdered, the man who kills, and the sentiment of juries
as to what constitutes "provocation" on the part of a wife, that I shall
extract it at length:—

MANSLAUGHTER AT DUKINFIELD.

> Thomas Harlow, 39, striker, Dukinfield, was indicted
> for the manslaughter of his wife, Ellen Harlow, 45 years old,
> at Dukinfield, on 30th November, 1877. The prisoner was
> committed by the magistrates on the charge of wilful murder,
> but the grand jury reduced the indictment to that of
> manslaughter. Mr. Marshall prosecuted; and the prisoner,
> who was undefended by counsel, stated, in his plea, that he
> had no intention of killing his wife when he struck her.
>   The prisoner, who was employed in and about
> Dukinfield, lived with his wife and three children in Waterloo
> Street, in that town. On the morning of the 30th November

the deceased went out hawking as usual, and returned shortly after twelve o'clock. During the time she was away the prisoner remained in the house sitting by the fire, and for the most part drinking beer. When she returned she busied herself in preparing dinner, and the prisoner went out for a short time. In the afternoon the prisoner laid himself down, and slept for two or three hours. About five o'clock the deceased, and a lodger named Margaret Daley, and several others, were sitting in the house, when the prisoner came in and asked his wife for twopence. She replied that she had not twopence, and that she had had trouble enough with being out hawking all day in the rain and hungry. He then began to abuse her, and asked her for something to eat. She gave him some potatoes and bacon; after eating the greater part of which he again began to abuse her. He once more asked her for twopence, and Margaret Daley, seeing there was likely to be a disturbance, gave him the twopence, and told him he had better get a pint of beer. Instead of getting beer, however, he sent a little girl to purchase a quantity of coal, and then recommenced abusing his wife. Shortly afterwards he was heard to exclaim, 'There will be a life less to-night, and I will take it.' At this time the persons who were sitting in the house when the prisoner came in went out, leaving Harlow, his wife, and their son Thomas, and Daley together. The prisoner had some further altercation with his wife, which ended with him striking her a violent blow under the right ear, felling her to the floor. She died in a few minutes afterwards, the cause of death being concussion of the brain. The prisoner subsequently gave himself into custody, and made a statement attributing his conduct to the provocation his wife had given him.

The jury found the prisoner guilty, and recommended him to mercy *on account of the provocation* he received. Sentence was deferred.

I think I may now safely ask the reader to draw breath after all these horrors, and agree with me that they cannot, *must* not, be allowed to go on unchecked, without some effort to stop them, and save these perishing and miserable creatures. Poor, stupid, ignorant women as most of them are, worn out with life-long drudgery, burdened with all the pangs and cares of many children, poorly fed and poorly clothed, with no pleasures and many pains, there is an enormous excuse to be made for them even if they do sometimes seek in drink the oblivion of

their misery—a brief dream of unreal joy, where real natural happiness
is so far away.[21] But for those who rise above these temptations, who
are sober where intoxication holds out their only chance of pleasure;
chaste in the midst of foulness; tender mothers when their devotion
calls for toilsome days and sleepless nights,—for these good,
industrious, struggling women who, I have shown, are the chief
victims of all this cruelty,—is it to be borne that we should sit
patiently by and allow their lives to be trampled out in agony?

What ought to be done?

First, what has been done, or has been proposed to be done, in
the matter?

In June, 1853, an Act was passed (16th Victoria, c. 30) entitled
"An Act for the Better Prevention and Punishment of Aggravated
Assaults upon Women and Children, and for Preventing Delay and
Expense in the Administration of the Criminal Law." In the preamble
to this Act it is stated that "the present law has been found insufficient
for the protection of women and children from violent assaults;" and the
measure provides that assaults upon any female or any male child—
occasioning actual bodily harm —may be punished by summary
conviction before two Justices of the Peace in Petty Sessions, or before
any Police or Stipendiary Magistrate. The penalty to be inflicted is not
to exceed imprisonment for six months with or without hard labour, or
a fine not exceeding £20. The offender may also be bound to keep the
peace for any period not exceeding six months from the expiration of
his sentence. Failing to enter into recognizances, the offender may be
kept in prison for a period not exceeding twelve months.

Since this Act was passed twenty-five years ago, no further
legislation has taken place on the subject except the Consolidating Act
(24 and 25 Vict. c. 100), which simply re-enacts the Act as above
stated.

Beside this Act on their behalf, wives are able to obtain relief in
certain cases, under the Divorce Act. That is to say, those women who
are able to apply to the Divorce Court may obtain, under section 16 of
the Act (20th and 21st Vict. c. 85), on proof of cruelty, a sentence of
Judicial Separation, which shall have the effect of a divorce *à mensâ et
thoro*.[22]

In the case of the ignorant, friendless, and penniless women, who
are the chief victims of Wife-torture, such relief as this court affords is
practically unattainable; but another clause of the same Act (the twenty-

first) is of great value to them. It provides that a wife deserted by her husband may, at any time after such desertion, apply to a Police Magistrate in the metropolitan district, or to Justices in Petty Sessions if in the country, for an order to protect any money or property she may acquire; and if any such Protection Order be made, the wife shall, during its continuance, "be in all respects in the same position, with regard to property and contracts, and suing and being sued, as she would have been under the Act if she had obtained a decree of Judicial Separation."

For reasons to be hereafter noticed, this clause in the Divorce Act is of the utmost importance in establishing the principle that a Police Magistrate, or two Justices of the Peace in Session, may pronounce, on proof of the minor offence of desertion by the husband, a sentence which is tantamount, so far as property is concerned, to a Judicial Separation. The clause is, I am informed, brought very frequently indeed into action, and the magistrates not unfrequently interpret "desertion" to signify an absence of three months without cause, albeit in the Divorce Court such absence must exceed two years to enable the wife to obtain a judicial separation.

It was doubtless believed by the benevolent promoters of these Acts that their provisions would have done a good deal to check the ill-usage of wives. But the offence appears to have diminished very little, if at all, during the twenty years which have since intervened, and at last one well-meaning, though somewhat eccentric member of the House of Commons felt himself moved to speak on this subject.

On the 18th May, 1874, Colonel Egerton Leigh made a vehement appeal for some increased punishment for aggravated assaults on women. He said that England had been called the Paradise of Women, and he brought forward his motion to prevent it from becoming a Hell of Women. After a speech, in which Colonel Leigh appeared overcome by emotion, he ended by saying that he "was sure the women of England would not appeal in vain to the House of Commons," and Mr. Disraeli answered him in the same vein of cheerful confidence which that Honourable House always expresses in its own eagerness to do justice to women. The House "must have sympathized," he said, "with Colonel Leigh, for it was a subject on which there could not be any differences of opinion." He hoped "his honourable and gallant friend would feel he has accomplished his object in directing the attention of the country to the subject, and that he would allow his right honourable friend, the Secretary of State for the Home

Department, whose mind is now occupied with this and similar subjects, time to reflect as to the practical mode in which the feeling of the country can be carried out." Colonel Leigh was requested to be "satisfied that after the address he has made, Her Majesty's Government will bear in mind what is evidently the opinion of the House;" and, of course, Colonel Leigh expressed himself as perfectly satisfied, and withdrew his amendment (authorizing flogging) with one of the jokes, which are so inexpressibly sickening in connection with this subject about "fair play for the fairer sex."[23]

On the 15th October, 1874, six months after Colonel Leigh had thus broken a lance in defence of the tortured women, the Home Office issued a Circular inquiring the opinion of the Judges, Chairmen of Quarter Sessions, Recorders, Stipendiary Magistrates of Metropolitan Police Courts, and Sheriffs of Scotch Counties, respecting five points connected with brutal assaults, the principal being whether the existing law was sufficiently stringent, and whether flogging should be authorized, "especially in cases of assaults on women and children."

The replies to these questions were published in a Parliamentary Blue Book entitled "Reports on the State of the Law relating to Brutal Assaults," in 1875, and the following is a summary of the results:—

There was a large consensus of opinion that the law as it now stands is insufficient to effect its purpose. Lord Chief Justice Cockburn says, "In my opinion the present law against assaults of brutal violence is not sufficiently stringent" (p. 5), and Mr. Justice Lush, Mr. Justice Mellor, Lord Chief Baron Kelly, Baron Bramwell, Baron Pigott, and Baron Pollock, express the same judgment in almost the same words (pp. 7–19).

Several of these, and also other judges, who do not directly say that they consider the present law insufficient, manifest their opinion that it is so by recommending that (under various safeguards) the penalty of flogging be added thereto. The agreement of opinion of these great authorities on this point appears (to the uninitiated) as if it must have been sufficient to carry with it any measure which had such weighty recommendation.

The following are the opinions in favour of flogging offenders in cases of brutal assault:—

Lord Chief Justice Cockburn, Mr. Justice Blackburn, Mr. Justice Mellor, Mr. Justice Lush, Mr. Justice Quain, Mr. Justice Archibald, Mr. Justice Brett, Mr. Justice Grove, Lord Chief Baron Kelly, Baron

Bramwell, Baron Pigott, Baron Pollock, Baron Cleasby, and Baron Amphlett. The opinions of Lord Coleridge and Mr. Justice Denman were hesitating, and the only decided opponent of flogging at that time on the judicial bench in England was Mr. Justice Keating.

The Chairmen of Quarter Sessions and magistrates in Sessions were in *sixty-four* cases out of the sixty-eight from whence responses came to the Home Office, in favour of flogging:—Leftwich, Oxford (county), Stafford (county), and the North Riding being the only exceptions.

The Recorders of *forty-one* towns were likewise in favour of flogging, and only those of Lincoln, Nottingham, and Wolverhampton were opposed to it. The Recorders of Folkstone and of Newcastle-on-Tyne added the recommendation that a husband who had been flogged for a brutal assault on his wife should be divorced from her.

On reading this summary it will doubtless to many persons appear inexplicable that three years should have elapsed since so important a testimony was collected at the public expense, and at the trouble of so many eminent gentlemen whose time was of infinite value; and that, so far as can be ascertained, absolutely nothing has been done in the way of making practical use of it. During the interval scores of Bills, on every sort and kind of question *interesting to the represented sex*, have passed through Parliament; but *this* question, on which the lives of women literally hang, has never been even mooted since Lord Beaconsfield so complacently assured its solitary champion that "Her Majesty's Government would bear in mind the evident feeling of the House on the subject." Something like 6,000 women, judging by the judicial statistics, have been in the intervening years "brutally assaulted"—that is, maimed, blinded, trampled, burned, and in no inconsiderable number of instances murdered outright—and several thousand children have been brought up to witness scenes which might, as Colonel Leigh said, "infernalize a whole generation." Nevertheless, the newspapers go on boasting of elementary education, and Parliament busies itself in its celebrated elephant's trunk fashion, alternately rending oaks and picking up sixpences; but *this* evil remains untouched!

The fault does not lie with the Home Office—scarcely even with Parliament, except so far as Parliament persists in refusing to half the nation those political rights which alone can, under our present order of things, secure attention to any claims. We live in these days under *Government by Pressure*, and the Home Office *must* attend first to the claims which are backed by political pressure; and Members of Parliament *must* attend to the subjects pressed by their constituents and the claims and subjects which are not supported by such political pressure *must* go to the wall.

Nevertheless, when we women of the upper ranks,— constitutionally qualified by the possession of property (and, I may be permitted to add, naturally qualified by education and intelligence at least up to the level of those of the "illiterate" order of voters), to exercise through the suffrage that pressure on Parliament,—are refused that privilege, and told year after year by smiling senators that we have no need whatever for it, that we form no "class," and that we may absolutely and always rely on men to prove the deepest and tenderest concern for everything which concerns the welfare of women, shall we not point to these long-neglected wrongs of our trampled sisters, and denounce that boast of the equal concern of men for women as a falsehood?

Were women to obtain the franchise to-morrow, it is morally certain that a Bill for the Protection of Wives would pass through the legislature before a Session was over. I have yet hopes that even before that event takes place, some attention may be directed to the miserable subject, and that it may be possible to obtain some measure, holding out a prospect of relief to the wretched victims—if not of repression of the crime of Wife-torture. What measure ought we to ask for the purpose?

Of the desirability that any step should be taken in the direction of inflicting the lash for aggravated assaults on women, I shall not presume in the face of such authorities as have been cited above, to offer any opinion whatever.

One thing is manifest at all events. It is, that if flogging were added to the present penalties of wife-beating, the great difficulty which meets all efforts to stop the practice would be doubled. That difficulty is the inducing of the women (whose evidence is in most instances indispensable) to bear testimony against their husbands. It is hard enough to lead them to do so when the results will be an imprisonment to end in one month or in six, after which the husband will return to them full of fresh and more vindictive cruelty, and when in short, bringing him "up" means abandoning the last ray of hope of ever making a happy home. This sentiment, half prudence, half perhaps in some cases lingering affection, cannot be overcome (even were it desirable to do so), as the law now stands, and causes endless failures of justice and perplexity to the always well-meaning magistrates. As a general rule it is said the wives will often tell their stories to the constables at the moment of the arrest, and can frequently be induced to attend in court the day or two after their injuries and while still smarting from their blows, and kicks, and "cloggings." But if a week be allowed to elapse, still more if the case be referred to the Quarter Sessions or Assizes, the wife is almost certain in the interval to have relented, or to have learned to dread the consequence of bearing testimony, and, instead of telling her true story, is constantly found to narrate some poor little fable, whereby the husband is quite exonerated, and, perhaps the blame taken on herself, as in the pitifully ludicrous case cited by Colonel Egerton Leigh in the House of Commons—of the woman who appeared without a nose, and told the magistrate she had *bitten it off herself!* On this subject, and on the defects of our whole procedure in such cases, some just remarks were bade by Mr. Serjeant Pulling in a paper read before the Social Science Congress at Liverpool, published in the Transactions for 1876, p. 345. He says—

> No one who has gained experience of wife-beating cases, can doubt that our present system of procedure seems as if it were designed not to repress crime, but to discourage complaints. A woman after being brutally assaulted by her husband, and receiving a sufficient number of kicks and blows to make her think she is being murdered, calls out for the aid of the police; and if her statements were there and then authentically recorded, and afterwards, on the commitment and trial of the aggressor, allowed to form part of the formal proof against him (subject of course to the right of the accused to refute it by cross-examination), there can be little doubt that the ends of justice would oftener be attained. In practice, however, the course is for the police to hear the loose statements of the scared victim and bystanders; and the subsequent proceedings are left very much to depend on the influences brought to bear on the poor wife in the interim (before the trial). She may relent before morning comes, or be subjected to so much sinister influence on the part of the husband and his friends as to be effectually prevented from disclosing the whole truth at all; or if doing so in the first stage of the proceedings she may be easily made so completely to neutralize its effect, that conviction becomes

impracticable. The lesson taught to the ruffian is that if he ill-uses his dog or his donkey he stands a fair chance of being duly prosecuted, convicted, and punished; but that if the ill-usage is merely practised on his wife, the odds are in favour of his own entire immunity, and of his victim getting worse treatment if she dare appear against him.

To avoid these failures of justice, and the consequent triumph of the callous offenders, magistrates are generally very anxious to have these cases summarily disposed of, and to strike while the iron is hot. But of course there hence arises another evil, namely, that the greater offences, which ought to be tried in the higher courts, and were intended to receive the heaviest penalty which the law allows, are punished only to the extent of the powers of the summary jurisdiction, of which the maximum is six months' imprisonment. Occasionally there is reason to believe the magistrates mend matters a little by the not unfair device of ordering the offender to find security for good behaviour, which, as he is generally unable to discover anybody foolish enough to give it for him, involves his incarceration in jail, possibly for a year. And, again, magistrates kindly endeavour to make the period of detention serve the process of reclaiming the man to better feelings about his wife, by allowing her entreaty to weigh importantly in any application to curtail his sentence, and letting him know that any repetition of offence will be closely watched and doubly severely punished.[24] But all these humane devices, though sometimes, it is to be hoped, successful, yet leave the mournful fact patent to observation that the existing law, even worked with the extremest care and kindness, cannot and does not prevent the repetition, year after year, of all the frightful cruelties, beating, burnings, cloggings, and tramplings of which we have given some pages back a few awful samples.

The relief which I most earnestly desire to see extended to these women, and from which I would confidently hope for *some* alleviation of their wretched condition, though its entire cure is beyond hope, is of a very different sort. It is this. A Bill should, I think, be passed, *affording to these poor women, by means easily within their reach, the same redress which women of the richer classes obtain through the Divorce Court.* They should be enabled to obtain from the Court which sentences their husbands a Protection Order, which should in their case have the same validity as a judicial separation. In addition to this, the *Custody of the Children should be given to the wife,* and an order

should be made for *the husband to pay to the wife such weekly sum for her own and her children's maintenance as the Court may see fit.*
The following are the chief clauses in a Bill, which has been prepared by Alfred D. Hill, Esq., J.P., of Birmingham, and the principle of which has been approved by many eminent legal authorities:—

BILL

Intituled *An Act for the Protection of Wives whose Husbands have been convicted of assaults upon them.*

Whereas it is desirable to make provision for the protection of wives whose husbands have been convicted of assaults upon them: Be it enacted by the Queen's Most Excellent Majesty, by and with the advice and consent of the Lords Spiritual and Temporal and of the Commons in this present Parliament assembled, and by the authority of the same, as follows:—

1. In any case where a husband has been convicted summarily or otherwise of an assault upon his wife, and has been sentenced to imprisonment therefor without the option of a fine in lieu of such imprisonment, it shall be competent for the Court by which such sentence has been pronounced, either at the time of such conviction or at any time afterwards, upon proof thereof, to make and give to the wife upon her application an order protecting her earnings and property acquired since the date of such order from her husband and all creditors and persons claiming under him; and such earnings and property shall belong to the wife as if she were a *feme sole*; and if any such order of protection be made, the wife shall, during the continuance thereof, be and be deemed to be in the like position in all respects with regard to property and contracts, and suing and being sued, as she would be if she had obtained a decree of judicial separation from the Court for Divorce and Matrimonial Causes.

2. The police magistrate or justices shall include in such order as aforesaid an injunction restraining the husband from going to or visiting the wife without her consent; and if any husband against whom any such injunction shall be made shall commit any act of disobedience thereto, such act shall be deemed to be a misdemeanour, upon due proof of which any Court which would have been competent to make such order and injunction may commit him to the common gaol or house of correction of the city, borough, or county within the

jurisdiction of such Court for any period not exceeding three
months with or without hard labour.

3. And any Court which would have been competent to
make such order as aforesaid may further include in such order
a provision that the wife shall have the legal custody of the
children of her husband and herself. And the same Court which
would have been competent to make such order may further
include in such order a provision directing that the husband
shall pay to the wife a weekly sum not exceeding ____
shillings per week for the maintenance of herself and of such
children, which provisions of the order shall, if the payments
required by it be in arrear, be enforced in the manner
prescribed by the Act of the 11th and 12th Vict. c. 43, for the
enforcing of orders of justices requiring the payment of a sum
of money.

4. Every such order as aforesaid shall, within ten days
after the making thereof, be entered with the registrar of the
county court within whose jurisdiction the wife is resident,
and a copy of such order shall, within such ten days, or within
a reasonable time in that behalf, be served upon the husband.
And it shall be lawful for the husband to apply to the Court for
Divorce and Matrimonial Causes, or to the magistrate or
justices by whom such order was bade, for the discharge
thereof, and they may (if they think fit) discharge the same.
And the said Court for Divorce and Matrimonial Causes, or
magistrate, or justices, is or are hereby authorized to
discharge such order if it, he, or they shall deem fit.

(Here follows Schedule.)

The reasons which may be urged on behalf of this measure are
manifold. They rest at all points on admitted principles of legislation.

In the first place, the Divorce Laws offering to women *who can
avail themselves of them* the remedy of Judicial Separation in cases of
the cruelty of their husbands, it is a matter of simple justice that the
same remedy should be placed within the reach of those poor women
who are subjected to tenfold greater cruelties than those which the court
always rules to constitute a ground for such separation. It is impossible
to imagine a matter in which the existence of "one law for the rich and
another for the poor" is more unrighteous and intolerable than this. At
the same time, except by some such machinery as has been
suggested,—namely, that the police magistrate or petty sessions court
should be given the power to pronounce the separation,—it is difficult

to conceive of any way in which the very humble and ignorant class of women, with whom we are concerned, could ever obtain the decree which is *in principle* at present their *right*.

A second reason for such a measure is that, as above stated, Magistrates are already empowered, in cases of *desertion*, to give Protection Orders which are expressly stated to be (so far as property is concerned) equivalent to a Judicial Separation—and which (very frequently given as they are) practically act as Judicial Separations in all respects. The objection which has been raised by some hasty readers of the Bill, that it proposes to give an unheard-of power to one or two Magistrates, thus falls to the ground. They already practically exercise the same power every day in the minor case of desertion. The husband is also afforded by the Bill every facility for obtaining a discharge of the Order should it appear to have been unjustly given.

Finally, a most important reason for adopting such a measure is that it —or something like it—is indispensable to induce the victim of such outrages to apply for legal redress.[25] The great failure of justice which has so long gone on in this matter, is chiefly due, as I have said before, to the fact that the existing law *discourages* such applications,—and in like manner must every projected law do so which merely adds penalties to the husband's offence without providing the suffering wife with any protection from his renewed violence when that penalty has been endured. Under the Wives Protection Bill, should it become law, the injured wife would have the *very thing she really wants*, namely, security against further violence, coupled with the indispensable custody of her children (without which, no protection of herself would offer a temptation to the better sort of women), and some small (though probably precarious) contribution to their maintenance and her own. With this real relief held out to them by the law, I should have little doubt that we should find the victims of brutal assaults and of repeated aggravated assaults very generally coming forward to bear testimony and claim their release, and the greatest difficulty attendant on the case would be at an end.

Even were there but a few who availed themselves of the boon, I still think it would be fitting and right that the law should hold it out to them. In many instances no doubt the mere fact that the wife had such a resource open to her would act very effectually on the husband as a deterrent to violence.

As to the justice and expediency of giving the custody of the children (both boys and girls of all ages) to the wife, there can be, I should think, little hesitation. The man who is, *ex hypothesi*, capable of kicking, maiming, and mutilating his wife, is even less fit to be the guardian of the bodies and souls of children than the lord and master of a woman. They are no more safe under his roof than in the cage of a wild beast, and the guilt of leaving them in the one place is little less than that of placing them in the other. When a child is killed by one of these drunken savages,—as the illegitimate child of George Hill, whom he knocked on the head with a hammer in revenge for having an affiliation order made on him; or as the child of six years old whom James Parris murdered because its mother failed to keep an appointment,—or when a child is cruelly injured, as the poor little girl into whose breast Ashton Keefe thrust a box full of ignited matches because she had been slow in fetching his beer,—when these outrages occur we are indignant enough with the offenders; but, if they had previously betrayed their tiger instincts, is there no guilt attaching to those who *left* these defenceless creatures in their dens? For both the children's sakes and the mothers' this clause of the Bill; then, appears of paramount importance—in fact, a *sine quâ non* of any measure possessing practical value.

Lastly, as regards the alimony for the wife, and the maintenance for the children, to be paid by the husband after the term of his imprisonment, I presume the justice of the provision will not be disputed. The man obviously cannot wipe away his natural obligations by the commission of a deed of cruel violence, and it would be a most dangerous lesson to let him think he could do so. The difficulty of course lies in enforcing such an order in the case of those lowest classes of artisans and labourers who can move freely from place to place, obtaining employment anywhere with the help of a bag of tools, or tramping the country from workhouse to workhouse. In the case of affiliation orders it is, I understand, found pretty uniformly that the small tradesmen, and men having a fixed business, pay their weekly dole fairly regularly, thereby minimizing the scandal; but the lower and looser sort of men decamp, and are lost sight of sooner or later, the Poor-law authorities rarely troubling themselves to look after them. The same resource of escape will undoubtedly be sought by not a few separated husbands should the Bill before us become law. The evil is serious, but perhaps not so serious or irremediable as it may appear. In the first place the Poor-law authorities or the police might surely be stirred to put in motion the machinery which lies ready to hand in case of greater crimes. A man was whipped last January by order of the Recorder of Hereford, under the Act 5 George IV., c. 83, for leaving his wife and children four times, and throwing them on the Union. It would be a useful lesson to impress pretty generally the fact that such legal responsibilities cannot be shirked in England with impunity.[26]

Secondly, there are few of these beaten wives who would not be far better off separated from their husbands *even if they never received a farthing of maintenance* than they are under their present condition, or would be under liability to their occasional raids and incursions. Such women (as I have maintained so often) are nearly always the bread-winners of the family. They have usually been for months or years earning their children's subsistence and their own, and very often that of their husbands beside. The withdrawal of this supposed conjugal "support" accordingly means the withdrawal of a minus quantity. They will find themselves where they were, with this difference, that they will not see their husbands reeling home to empty their scanty cupboards—chartered robbers, as scores of such husbands are. It is true the sole charge of their children will devolve on them, but (and this is a reflection which goes far further into the matter than I can pursue it) they will have no *more* children than those already born. Women never reach the bottom of the abyss of their misery save when the pangs and weaknesses of child-bearing and child-nursing are added to their burdens, and when to the outrage of their tyrant's blows is joined the deeper degradation of bearing him children year by year, to furnish fresh victims of his cruelty, and to rivet their chains. The subject is too revolting to be dwelt upon here.

Of course it is not difficult to find objections to the proposed measure. I have already referred to, and I hope satisfactorily answered, that which rests on the supposed difficulty of entrusting a single Police Magistrate or Justices in Petty Sessions with such powers as are given them in the Bill. As no complaints have ever been published of their frequent use of analogous power in cases of Desertion, I know not why we should anticipate them in those of Brutal Assault.

Again, objections have been taken to the Bill on the ground that cases of collusion might occur under its provision. It has been suggested, for example, that a wife desiring to get rid of her husband might designedly provoke him to beat her, and that she might prefer taking the beating, and so obtaining both his money and release from his presence. Or again, it is said that a wife who had given a man cause for jealousy, and had been beaten by him in consequence, would thus obtain her object of separation and freedom to live with her paramour. Or again, that a wife who drank and "sold up" her husband's goods might have practically done him much more grievous injury than he has done her by the thrashing he gives her, and yet, under such an Act as is proposed, the husband would be compelled to give a share of his wages to her, and to see his children in her custody possibly starving and ill-treated. To all these hypothetical cases I have only to reply that, should they ever be realized, they would certainly form a failure of justice, and that I should sincerely regret that any man, even a wife-beater, should suffer wrongfully, or a jot more than he deserves. But I confess I am more concerned to protect the *certainly* beaten wives than their hypothetically ill-used beaters; and that most of the suggestions above named appear to me exceedingly far-fetched, and unlikely ever to be verified.

The real and valid objection to the Bill—which I cannot blink—is the same which necessarily adheres to every severance of married couples which does not sanction their marrying again—in short, to every divorce *à mensâ et thoro*, which is not a divorce *à vinculo*. The latter kind of divorce—though we have the opinion of Mr. Lonsdale and Mr. Digby Seymour that it ought to be given to the wife in such cases of brutal assault—seems too dangerous a resource, seeing that it might often act as an incentive to commit the assault in the case of a husband, and an incentive to provoke one in the case of the wife. The *quasi*-judicial separation, on the other hand, which is all the Bill proposes, of course leaves the separated man and woman liable each to fall into vicious courses since marriage is closed to them, and thus to contribute to the disorder of the community. The evil, I think, must be fairly weighed against the benefits anticipated from the measure; but the reflection that the wife-beater is almost always *already* a man of loose and disorderly life will tend to diminish our estimate of that evil's extent. The decent respectable wife, such as I hope I have shown a large class of beaten wives to be, would of course live like a well-conducted widow.

*   *   *

I entreat my readers not to turn away and forget this wretched subject. I entreat the gentlemen of England,—the bravest, humanest, and most generous in the world,—not to leave these helpless women to be trampled to death under their very eyes. I entreat English ladies, who, like myself, have never received from the men with whom we associate anything but kindness and consideration, and who are prone to think that the lot of others is smooth and happy as our own, to take to heart the wrongs and agonies of our miserable sisters, and to lift up on their behalf a cry which must make Parliament either hasten to deal with the matter, or renounce for very shame the vain pretence that it takes care of the interest of women.

Notes

1.   French for "more than happy to be of service."
2.   With the exception, perhaps, of the Seal. Mr. Darwin gives a sad picture of amphibious conjugal life: "As soon as a female reaches the shore ('comes out,' as we should say in 'society'), the nearest male goes down to meet her, making meanwhile a noise like the clucking of a hen to her chickens. He bows to her and coaxes her, until he gets between her and the water so that she cannot escape him. Then his manner changes, and with a harsh growl he drives her to a place in his harem."—*Descent of Man*, vol. ii. p. 269. What an "o'er true tale" is this of many a human wooing and of what comes later; the "bowing and coaxing" first, and the "harsh growl" afterwards! I am surprised Mr. Darwin did not derive from it an argument for the Descent of Man from the Seal.

It is very instructive to watch the behaviour of a big male dog undergoing the experience which is understood to surpass the limits of a man's endurance; namely, being "nagged" by a little vixen who stands opposite to him in an attitude exactly corresponding to the "arms akimbo" of her human prototype, and pours out volleys of barking which would, obviously, in the police courts be reported as "abusive language." The much-tried dog—let us say a Retriever or Newfoundland—who could annihilate his little female assailant—a toy Terrier or Pomeranian, perhaps—in two mouthfuls, and who *would* do so in the case of an enemy of his own sex—always on these occasions starts aside with well-feigned surprise, as if astonished at the reception of his advances; lifts his ears as a gentleman raises his hat, and presently bounds away, lightly: "I beg your pardon, madam! I am the last dog in the world, I assure you, to offend a lady!" Be it noted that if that dog had retreated before the bullying of another male dog, he would have slunk off with his tail between his legs, ashamed of his own poltroonery. But from the female termagant he retires with all the honours of war, and with his tail held aloft like a standard; quite conscious that he is acting as becomes a dog and a gentleman. [Cobbe's note]

    3.   Not universally I am glad to hear. In Yorkshire and several other counties a very old custom exists, or did exist as late as 1862, called "Riding the Stang" or "Rough Music," which consists in giving a serenade with cows' horns, and warming-pans, and tea-kettles to a man known to have beaten his wife or been unfaithful to her. See a very curious account of it and of its good effects, in Chambers' Book of Days, vol. ii. p. 510. A correspondent kindly sends further details, from which it appears that there is always a sort of herald or orator on the occasion, who, when the procession halts before the delinquent's house, recites verses in this style:—

                          "There is a man in this place,
    (*piano*)   Has beat his wife [a pause]
    (*fortissimo*)   Has beat his wife!!

    "'Tis a very great shame and disgrace
    To all who live in the place," &c.

The custom derives its name from the old Scottish "Stange"—a long pole on which the culprit is sometimes made to take a very disagreeable ride. [Cobbe's note]

    4.   Punch and Judy were husband and wife characters who appeared frequently in puppet shows in Great Britain. Punch, who has a fierce temper, regularly beats Judy and their baby with his stick.

    5.   Cobbe is referring to author Thomas Ingoldsby (1788–1845).

    6.   Transactions Social Science Association, 1876, p. 345. [Cobbe's note]

    7.   Styx and Phlegethon are two of the five rivers of hell. Ahrimanes was an evil spirit in Zoroastrianism who rebelled against his creator and became the instigator of all evil on earth.

    8.   Let it be noted that while they *were* slaves, these negroes were daily subjected to outrages and cruelties of which it thrilled our blood to hear. Since they have been emancipated their white neighbours have learned at least so far to recognize them as human beings, that these *tortures* have become comparatively rare. [Cobbe's note]

    Cobbe is referring to Simon Legree, the sadistic plantation owner in Harriet Beecher Stowe's *Uncle Tom's Cabin* (1852).

    9.   Stripped of the euphemisms of courtesy wherewith we generally wrap them up, it cannot be denied that the sentiments of a very large number of men towards women consist of a wretched alternation of exaggerated and

silly homage, and of no less exaggerated and foolish contempt. One moment on a pedestal, the next in the mire; the woman is adored while she gives pleasure, despised the moment she ceases to do so. The proverbial difficulty of introducing a joke into the skull of a Scotchman is nothing to that of getting into the mind of such men that a woman is a *human being*—however humble—not a mere adjunct and appendage of humanity; and that she must have been created, and has a right to live for ends of her own; not for the ends of another; that she was made, as the old Westminster Catechism says, "to glorify God and enjoy Him for ever," not primarily or expressly to be John Smith's wife and James Smith's mother. We laugh at the great engineer who gave as his opinion before a Royal Commission that rivers were created to feed navigable canals; and a farmer would certainly be treated as betraying the "bucolic mind" who avowed that he thought his horse was made to carry him to market, and his cat to eat his mice and spare his cheese; yet where women are concerned—beings who are understood to be at least *quasi*-rational, and to whom their religion promises an immortal life hereafter of good and glory—the notion that the Final Cause of Woman is Man seems never to strike them as supremely ridiculous. [Cobbe's note]

    10.   Old English legislation embodied this view so far as to inflict the cruelest of all punishments—burning to death—on a woman guilty of *petty treason, i.e.*, the murder of her husband, while the husband was only liable to hanging for murdering his wife. A woman was burned to death under this atrocious law at Chester, in 1760, for poisoning her husband. The wretched creature was made to linger four months in jail under her awful sentence before it was executed. [Cobbe's note]

    11.   French for extenuating circumstance.

    12.   And there are gentlemen who think there is something beautiful in this! The Rev. F.W. Harper, writing to the *Spectator* of January 26, says, "I make bold to believe that if ever I should turn into a wife I shall choose to be beaten by my husband to any extent (short of being slain outright), rather than it should be said a stranger came between us." After thus bringing to our minds the beatings, and kickings, and blindings, and burnings, and "cloggings," which sicken us, he bids us remember that the true idea of marriage is "the relation of Christ to his Church!" It is not for me to speak on this subject, but I should have expected that a minister of the Christian religion would have shuddered at the possibility of suggesting such a connection of ideas as these notions involve. Heaven help the poor women of Durham and Lancashire if their clergy lead them to picture a Christ resembling their husbands! [Cobbe's note]

    13.   French for scapegoat, whipping "boy."

    14.   I doubt that, even if reduced to bestial helplessness by these drinks in a pure state, men would ever be goaded by them to the class of passions excited by the adulterated ones. I have myself seen in Savoy whole crowds of men returning from market, all more or less tipsy from the free use of the excellent Vin de Seychelles, but instead of quarrelling or fighting, or

beating their horses and pigs, their demeanour was ludicrously good-humoured and affectionate. [Cobbe's note]

15.   Hope of the Human Race, p. 172 (The Evolution of the Social Sentiment). By Frances Power Cobbe. Williams and Norgate. [Cobbe's note]

16.   Octavia Hill (1838–1912) was a philanthropist who worked in housing reform.

17.   I have seen a woman like this tormenting a great, good-natured hobbledehoy, who unhappily belonged to Carlyle's order of "Inarticulate ones," and found it impossible to avoid being caught every five minutes in the Socratic *elenchus*, which she set for him like a trap whenever he opened his mouth. At length when this had lasted the larger part of a rainy day, the poor boy who had seemed for some time on the verge of explosion, suddenly sprang from his chair, seized the little woman firmly though gently round the waist, carried her out into the hall, and came back to his seat, making no remark on the transaction. Who could blame him? [Cobbe's note]

18.   Such was the case of Susannah Palmer, a few years ago, whose husband had beaten her, and sold up her furniture again and again, blackened her eyes, and knocked our her five front teeth. At last on one occasion, with the knife with which she was cutting her children's supper, she somehow inflicted a slight cut on the man while he was knocking her about the head. He immediately summoned her for "cutting and wounding him," and she was sent to Newgate. I found her there, and afterwards received the very best possible character of her from several respectable tradespeople in whose houses she had worked as a charwoman for years. Friends subscribed to help her, and the admirable chaplain of Newgate interested himself warmly in her case and placed her in safety. [Cobbe's note]

19.   This, however, was a "provocation" on which a Chester jury founded a recommendation to mercy when they found him guilty of manslaughter. See p. 75. [Cobbe's note]

20.   *E.g.* the Report of the Society for the Protection of Women and Children, which has this significant passage: "Some of the cases of assaults were of a brutal and aggravated character, . . . thirty-three by husbands on wives, five by fathers, and four by mothers on their children." [Cobbe's note]

21.   Few people reflect how utterly devoid of pleasures are the lives of the women of the working classes. An excellent woman, living near Bristol, having opened a Mothers' Meeting, was surprised to find that not more than one out of forty of her poor friends had ever seen the sea, and not more than three had travelled on the railway. Of course their fathers, husbands, brothers, and sons had all seen these wonders, but they—never. That good woman accordingly took the whole party one summer's day to the beach at Weston-super-Mare, and the sight of their enjoyment drew the tears from her eyes,—and from mine when she described it. [Cobbe's note]

22. Latin for "From Table and Bed." A separation granted by a court, whereby a husband and wife, although still married, are no longer required to live together.

23. Hansard, vol. ccxix. p. 396. [Cobbe's note]

24. I have before me a letter written by a man under these circumstances from Clerkenwell House of Detention to his wife. The writer (who was sent to jail for beating the aforesaid poor woman very cruelly) is wonderfully civil, and even condescends to coax. He regrets that it is long since he heard from her, but adds, "I hope you will not forget to try and get me out. If you will go to the magistrate, Mr. ***, i [sic] mean, it is very likely you can get my time reduced. I hope you will do all you can for me. I have quiet (*sic*) made up my mind to do what is right to everybody, more especially to you. I hope you will not be angery [sic] with me writing. I do hope and pray that you will do all you can for me. So good-bye, hopeing [sic] to see and hear from you soon, and with your kind assistance to soon be out. So no more at present from your poor Petitioner, ***." The intelligent reader will perceive that there is not a single word of regret for his cruelty in this epistle. Still it is a good point when the tyrant can be brought thus to sue his victim. All honour to the wise and kindly magistrate who brought it about. [Cobbe's note]

25. Mr. W. Digby Seymour, Recorder of Newcastle-on-Tyne, in giving in his opinion on the desirability of adding flogging to the penalties of wife-beating, says—"If you flog the husband you will for ever degrade him as a married man. Let him be flogged by all means; but why not amend the laws of divorce, and in cases of a conviction for 'brutal violence,' entitle the wife, on simple proof of conviction, to a divorce *à vinculo?*"— Returns, p. 90.

Mr. Lonsdale, Recorder of Folkestone, says practically the same: "I would not authorize flogging in cases of assaults upon wives unless that punishment were allowed to have the effect of a judicial separation."—Ibid. p. 82. [Cobbe's note]

26. Perhaps the best plan as regards the maintenance for a wife would be (as suggested by an experienced magistrate) that the money should be paid through, and recoverable by, the Relieving Officer of the parish. This would afford her much greater security, and obviate the chance of collision with the husband. [Cobbe's note]

---

14. Schadenfreude

Introduction

Frances Power Cobbe's "Schadenfreude" first appeared in the *Contemporary Review* in 1902, and is reprinted here from that periodical. If alive today, Cobbe might have renamed "Schadenfreude" "Sadism." Because the English term did not yet exist, Cobbe used the German word for "pleasure in the pain of others." In a sense, the theme of this article ties all of Cobbe's work together, as her liberal disdain for intolerance and her crusade against cruelty to animals, women, and the poor unite the core body of her literary output. Cobbe's concern here, however, is with the sadist, rather than with the object of sadism, and she explores the issue with reserved fascination. "Schadenfreude" was written towards the end of Cobbe's life, and the evolution in her language is evident. Certainly this essay is a testament to Cobbe's ever-sharpening pen. More importantly, it reflects a woman who possesses a deep sense of satisfaction in the redefinition of a society she touched deeply.

Schadenfreude

Pleasure *in the Pain of others* is an emotion for which the
English language has no proper name. Archbishop Trench, in his
charming book on the *Study of Words* (p. 76), innocently remarks
"What a fearful thing it is that any language should possess a word to
express the pleasure which men feel at the calamities of others; for the
existence of the word bears testimony to the existence of the thing! And
yet such in more languages than one may be found!" In the Greek the
word is epicairekakia, and in German we have Schadenfreude,
Schadenlust, and Schadenfroheit, all meaning the same thing; "Pleasure
in the misfortunes of others," "Malignant Joy."

Nevertheless, though neither we English nor the French or
Italians have any name for it, we have the *thing*; for it is common to all
races of men in all ages, and to the followers of all religions, by no
means excepting the Christian. Nay, the truth seems to be that there is
scarcely one of us who on reflection can boast that such abominable
pleasure is wholly foreign to his own experience, or that he has not
again and again witnessed its unquestionable manifestations amongst
his fellows. Nor is it to be granted that (as we might all wish to think,
and perhaps actually have hitherto thought), this odious pleasure is only
felt when revenge or hatred creates the desire to "render evil for evil" or
to defeat an enemy. Still less can it often be excused as righteous
acquiescence in retributive justice. It may, of course, now and then arise
from one or other of these sources, but far more frequently it springs
from a much broader one: a common instinct of *Heteropathy*, which
undoubtedly is natural to man and to most animals, causing the sight of
suffering in others to call forth emotions the exact opposites of
sympathy. It is the earliest—shall we say, the normal?—sentiment of
brute and child and savage, and only by slow degrees does it dwindle to
Aversion, and at last undergo the blessed transformation into genuine
Sympathy. I shall now endeavour, by familiar examples, to substantiate
this terrible charge against human nature; and then turn to the pleasant
task of pointing out the many ways in which it would appear that it is
at last dying out, and in which we may all help to extinguish it. Of
course, in selecting examples of *Schadenfreude* we are bound to
exclude all cases in which the *duty* of giving pain may fairly be

predicated, and the pain-giver may be charitably credited with acting under moral pressure.

Let us begin by tracing *Schadenfreude* in the least coarse, if not always the least cruel form of its manifestations—a form which may be studied in all ranks of society, even in the highest, and in nine family circles out of ten. That form is Pleasure in the *mental* pain of others. Words which are stings, words which are lashes beneath which the victim shrinks and winces, innocent pride is wounded, harmless *amour propre* mortified to the quick, hope which was brightening a dull life quenched in disappointment—alas! alas! who has not heard such words uttered over and over again from parent to child, or brother to sister, or wife to husband? Was there no *pleasure* to the speaker in his verbal blow or sting? We commonly slur over such word-cruelties as excusable on the score of an "irritable temper," or a "sharp tongue," or "the knack of saying unpleasant things." But the temper and tongue and knack are all due to *Schadenfreude*; and the proof is, that when the unkind speeches fall flat before the imperturbable self-complacency of their object they cease to be repeated. No pain to the victim means no pleasure to the aggressor. On the other hand, the betrayal of extreme sensitiveness to such wounds is a provocation to merciless repetition of the cruelty, as may be often seen in the deplorable case of the unhappy butt of a family.

Nearly akin to this Verbal Cruelty is Literary Satire. Hobbes' idea of the nature of laughter as "a sudden sense of our own superiority" (a theory which proves the holder never to have laughed one honest, joyous laugh at genuine humour in his life), seems to be verified in the sardonic pleasure taken in those satires which present the men and women whom they attack as contemptible or ridiculous so that the reader chuckles in his own superiority over, and insight into, their weaknesses and absurdities. That a great deal in the satires of Molière, Boileau and Voltaire, of Dryden, Pope and Swift was carefully designed to inflict the keenest pain possible, no reader can doubt (*e.g.*, as a sample, Pope's address to Lady Mary Wortley Montagu, *Though Artemisia talks by fits*, etc.). And in proportion as this effort was successful did the readers enjoy their *Schadenfreude* over the stabs and stings. Tennyson's ideal poet who is

Dowered with the Hate of Hate,
The Scorn of Scorn.

was not yet born or thought of. Poetry descended to pin-pricks. But the satirists of the Eighteenth century were isolated archers, shooting their poisoned arrows from their private windows. The beginning of the Nineteenth century saw bands of literary ruffians marshalled in order for each of the two parties in politics, and prepared to shoot down, scatter and trample upon all who presumed to hold other views of politics or religion than their own. The *Quarterly* and *Edinburgh* Reviews, in the first decades of the century, were, to the authors of the period, very much what the scalping Indian tribes of Sioux or Choctaws were to the New England settlers. Justice to an author's literary merits, or a fair estimate of his work while condemning his opinions, were obviously never so much as contemplated. To read their reviews of the poems of Keats, of Shelley, or of Byron, or even their remarks on the humane appeals of the men who were then striving to carry the first measures in favour of prevention of cruelty to animals, is to pass back into another age from ours. They caught a Tartar, indeed, when they attacked Byron and he retorted in *English Bards and Scotch Reviewers*,[1] but Shelley's sweet soul replying to their insults in his *Lines to a Critic* proved that, Atheist as they called him, his spirit was far more Christian than theirs:—

> Honey from silk worms who can gather?
>   Or silk from the yellow bee?
> The grass may grow in wintry weather,
>   As soon as hate in me.
>   •   •   •   •
> The passion like the one I prove
>   Cannot divided be;
> I hate thy want of truth and love,
>   How should I then hate thee?[2]

There must of course have been thousands of readers of the upper classes who enjoyed their *Schadenfreude* over the savage scourging of a poet like this and of Keats, or those Reviews could not have flourished and survived to better times. But again, only thirty years ago, there were published many bitterly and coarsely satirical papers, such as would have no popularity now in England. The foremost among them was the *Saturday Review*. This journal attained the climax of success by holding up on prongs of ridicule—and not without frequent misrepresentation—every book, or practice, or rising effort which its conductors disliked or had no particular interest in praising. Very few of its articles could claim attention on the score of fine critical acumen or sound judgment, but the public of that day, especially that of the London clubs, enjoyed their *Schadenfreude* mightily over its saturnine columns. On women, in particular, and their then new-born hopes of freedom and culture, the *Saturday Review* squirted its venom every week like a toad by the roadside. What feelings, save *Schadenfreude*, could have caused anybody to enjoy reading these acrid columns?[3]

The subject of enjoyment in cruel Speeches and cruel Writings leads us on to the still more frightful topic of enjoyment in Physical cruelty—in the infliction, or sight, of the bodily pain of human or animal sufferers.

Whosoever was the author of the Book of Proverbs he remains responsible for having supplied innumerable parents with Scriptural warrant for enjoying their *Schadenfreude*, by not "sparing the rod." With his support, for three thousand years fathers and schoolmasters, and alas! often mothers and schoolmistresses went on, to the verge of our own times, inflicting on children every variety of cruel castigation for infantine and boyish faults. Merely to name all the instruments of such penal severity,—the "cane," the "tawse," the "birch," the "horsewhip," the "cat," the "rod," the "rope's end,"—is to remind ourselves of the multifarious cruelties of days happily nearly bygone. "Boxes" on the ears (often creating deafness), "pandies" on the little trembling hands, seclusion in a dark room or tied to a bed-post, bread and water diet—these and a score of other evil inventions were continually used for the most childish transgressions or stupidity. Does the reader seriously question whether there were not a great measure of *Schadenfreude* in the infliction of all this misery? That odious and abominable Rod, with its double sting of pain and shame, what a curse it has been to humanity all down the ages! If it had given no more pleasure to parents and teachers to flog a boy or girl than to dust a bookshelf, and if no hidden abominable gusto accompanied the indecent and cruel act, it is certain there would not have been one whipping for ten thousand which have been actually inflicted.[4]

Let us now turn to the treatment of Animals and estimate, if it be possible, what frightful *Schadenfreude* must have prompted all the cruelties to horses, asses, cattle, sheep, cats, dogs and fowl, of which 5000 cases are, on an average, brought to punishment in England every year by the Royal Society for the Prevention of Cruelty to Animals.

What are the numbers and what the heinousness of such cruelties which are never exposed or brought to justice, even in this country, and how many more there are and how much worse in Southern Europe God alone can know. That there is "pleasure in the pain" of the beaten horse and ass and dog, no one can pretend to doubt. There is also pleasure, undoubtedly, in many other more elaborate cruelties of this class. Pouring paraffin over a dog and setting it on fire; shutting up a cat in an oven; throwing animals down wells to starve; these and a hundred similar atrocities, recorded every year in the courts of justice, mean that so many men and boys, women and girls, have found pleasure in inflicting such pain on harmless and helpless creatures. In Southern Italy there are half a dozen instruments of torture in the way of iron bits and mouthpieces and whips, of which several thousands have been confiscated, and may be now seen in the office of the excellent Neapolitan Society for Protection of Animals in the Piazza della Borsa.

But these cruelties and the *Schadenfreude* taken in them by brutal and brutalised peasants and carters are now regarded with disgust by all persons claiming any share of refinement of feeling. The English Act of 1822, which first in history punished cruelty to animals, has fulfilled amply the prophecy of Lord Erskine. It has proved "an honour to the Parliament of England and an era in the civilisation of the world." It has been a vast educational influence in Britain; and the laws which have since been framed on the model of it in all other civilised countries (with the exception, I believe, of Spain), have in their measure taught lessons of humanity; even where Roman Catholic casuists teach that animals have no rights any more than stocks and stones. (See Father Rickaby of Stonyhurst's "Moral Philosophy," p. 250). But now, what are we to say as to the *Schadenfreude* found by men of a totally different order in Field Sports? Is there here anything to be described truly as Pleasure in Pain?

I do not deny the right of man to place himself at the head of the carnivora and take the lives of animals for his food. Nor do I question that a score of pleasures, some elevated and all harmless—pleasure in scenery of wood or river or moor, wholesome exercise, fresh air, and sympathy with horses and dogs in their delight—mingle with and form the larger part of the enjoyments of the chase. But when all is said in its defence, it remains assuredly a singular fact that the Hunting Instinct of prehistoric times (when it had, of course, its proper place and use) should survive unquenched among so many men, and not a few women, into the twentieth century; and that the word "SPORT" should be applied *par excellence* to the killing of deer, foxes, hares, grouse, pheasants, partridges, salmon and trout! People who feel *pain* (not pleasure) at the piteous sight of a dying stag or wounded pheasant, can no more enjoy such sport as a hunt or a *battue* offers than they can frisk and dance on a floor full of upturned nails. The pain of the spectacle at the close of each run or successful shot much more than outweighs the pleasure of the surrounding conditions. We are driven to conclude that if others do not feel any Pleasure in the sight of the bleeding, dying creature (as we would willingly believe), yet at least they feel so little Pain that it forms no recognisable deduction from the pleasures of "sport." As to the women who frequent otter-hunts in their gala uniforms of red and blue, and stand by to see the intelligent, sensitive creatures impaled on a spear or torn to pieces alive by the hounds, such women must experience *Schadenfreude* in almost an ecstatic form. Eighteen centuries ago they would have sat in the Colosseum, in the latest fashions of that time, and have enjoyed no less enthusiastically,— perhaps even more so,—the spectacle of their Christian fellow-citizens devoured by the lions.

How much of the hideous joy in pain may mingle with the passions of the Battlefield it would be impossible to estimate. A gentleman who commanded a regiment through the whole American War of North and South told me that in no single battle did the opposing forces come sufficiently near for the soldiers to see each other's faces; and he very justly counted it a great advantage that so it had been; and that no personal feelings of animosity had any chance of arising. But when a *mêlée* takes place, and the horsemen or infantry charge at the point of the bayonet or with drawn swords, it must be a fearful stimulus to whatever ferocity or "Pleasure in Pain" lurks in any breast. Quite apart from this "fierce joy" of actual battle, War has unquestionably a tendency on a gigantic scale to harden the heart, not only of the actual combatants, but of the nations which have to share the dreadful excitement and to triumph over tender feelings of numberless kinds. It has seemed to me that since this ever-to-be-deplored South African War has been going on, there has been a new undercurrent of ferocity dimly discernible through the whole spirit of the nation.[5]

The last and most dreadful form of *Schadenfreude* has, of course, been the fiendish revelling in inventions of cruelty used as

Punishments on captives, criminals, heretics and revolted slaves. When we recall the burnings, the impalings, the flayings, the stonings, the poundings in mortars, the boiling in cauldrons of oil, the breaking on the wheel, of which, and of scores of similar horrors, History ancient and modern is full of records, we obtain an astounding view of the inconceivable savagery of the *Schadenfreude* wherein tyrants, executioners and populace indulged together. Let the reader whose imagination in such matters may be dull turn over the eighteen fine engravings in the old folio edition of Calmet's *Dictionary of the Bible* and judge how large must have been the amount of Pleasure in Pain taken by those ancient people, whom we are wont to look upon as superior to all the heathen round them. The stonings alone (as I realised once very vividly, standing on the scene of Stephen's martyrdom) could only have been carried out by men in whom every touch of pity had vanished, who could behold a fellow-creature crushed and mangled, blinded, bleeding and helpless on the ground, and could then *take up another stone* and fling it at him! It would seem as if the ancient Persians were even more cruel still; for some of their devices—notably that of the Boat—haunt one, when once read of, for the rest of life. For this reason I will not detail it. The Assyrians must have taken pleasure in the spectacle of their impaled prisoners or they would never have perpetuated the ghastly scene on their monuments which have recorded it for 3,000 years. The Romans—but what can be said to fit those men and women of old Rome—the contemporaries, be it remembered, of Cicero and Horace, of Virgil and Seneca,—who crowded the arenas to witness what happened there to the Gladiators and to the martyrs? After the Servile War 5,000 crosses stood beside the Appian Way, each sustaining, no doubt *for several days*, a crucified slave.[6] Let it be remembered, if we need to realise the full horrors of that familiar Way, that each of these was a white man who had revolted from the intolerable cruelty of his Roman Masters and had fought bravely for liberty. It is surprising that this scene (surely one of the most ghastly recorded in all history?) has hardly left any impression, so that few readers remember it, even while the agonies of crucifixion are for ever being brought to our imagination in connection with the (comparatively short) sufferings of Christ.

Then, passing from the ancient world to Christendom in the Middle and later Ages, what inventions of cruelty meet us on all sides—the stake at the *Auto da Fé*,[7] and in our own Smithfield, the

Rack, the Maiden, the *peine forte et dure*, the *In Paces*, the awful Wheel on which men were broken even late in the eighteenth century! Does anyone presume to doubt that the inventors of these devilish things took *pleasure* in their work? Nay, that the mass of the population in those cruel days found enjoyment in it? So long as punishments were public, so long crowds of men and women pushed forward to witness them. Even within the memory of living persons this was the case when men were "flogged at the cart's tail," or hanged at Newgate. That the pleasure was taken, not in any justifiable sense of sternly accomplished justice for some cruel crime, but simply *in the suffering*, whether just or unjust, is proved by the triviality of the offences (such as sheep stealing) for which men were then hanged or flogged. The pleasure of the spectacle, the *Schadenfreude* of the populace, was irrespective of the victim's guilt. Retributive Justice concerned the Judge very little, and the howling, yelling, laughing mob not at all.

Beyond these barbarities to men, and surviving still, when the torture of the most heinous murderer would no more be permitted in Europe,—the harmless brutes are now subjected to the most prolonged and acute agonies in hundreds of physiological and pathological laboratories in England, France, Germany and America. This anomaly, we are (in England) assured, is permitted in the interests of *human bodies*, for the diseases of which it is supposed to seek remedies; just as *Autos da Fé* were sanctioned in the interests of human Souls to prevent the spreading of perilous heresy. By the more honest Continental physiologists it is avowed that the experiments are carried on simply in the interests of Science. To keep the discussion to our present argument, I would here entreat the reader to turn over for himself the great works of Cyon, Claude Bernard and the other chief vivisectors, and judge what are the real springs of interest which bring them to work over the torture-trough. The conclusion which I, for my part, have reached after a quarter of a century of such painful study, is that we have done vivisectors more than justice heretofore when we have credited them with either a burning zeal for therapeutic discoveries or for the advance of Science; and have merely blamed them for *disregarding* the claims of humanity in view of such high aims. I am persuaded that what (no doubt by a slip of undesigned candour) is described in the recent *Life of Claude Bernard* by an eminent English physiologist as the "JOYS of the Laboratory," are very real "joys" to the vivisector; that is, *Schadenfreude*,—Pleasure in the Pain he witnesses and creates.

Having now glanced over several fields wherein Pleasure is taken in the Pain of men or of animals, it may be well to define the sentiment a little more exactly, and try to apportion its proper place in morals.

Cruelty, subjectively considered, is of many kinds:—

1. *Ignorant cruelty;* the person who causes suffering not knowing he does so.
2. *Careless cruelty;* the agent being indifferent to the pain he causes.
3. *Interested cruelty;* the agent causing the suffering, either reluctantly or indifferently, for ulterior purposes of his own, or of third parties.
4. *Malicious cruelty;* the agent causing the suffering for the sake of his own pleasure therein.

This last is the cruelty for which alone *Schadenfreude* is answerable; and though it may be doubtful whether (in these days at all events) it actually causes as much suffering as *Interested Cruelty*, it has in the past been a most prolific source of woes unnumbered and untold. Nor is it only on account of the evils it has produced and still produces every day that *Schadenfreude* must be pronounced morally wrong and wicked. The sentiment itself, even when it is only entertained by a silent and inactive spectator of cruelty, is itself diabolical and to the last degree un-Christian. Yet here we are met by one of the most surprising facts in the history of ethics. This abominable sentiment, and all the cruelty to man and brute of which it has been the prompter, remains after twenty centuries of Christianity almost unnoticed by the Churches of Christ. No moralist—so far as my small knowledge extends, whether Catholic or Protestant—no Father, no Schoolman, no Casuist of later times, no Protestant preachers have denounced Cruelty and the Pleasure in Pain with anything approaching to the measure of its moral delinquency.

Yet if there be one lesson which may claim to be supremely Christian—the lesson which differentiates Christ's morality from the morality of Judaism and of all heathen systems except Buddhism,—it is the sublime teaching of the Sermon on the Mount to love not only our neighbours but our enemies; to return good for evil; to forgive to seventy times seven. St. Paul accepted and repeated the Divine doctrine with all imaginable force, and proclaimed that all other gifts and graces are valueless without Love and the Charity which is "*kind.*" Yet, while these are admitted on all hands to be supreme virtues in the estimate of the Christian Religion, how has it come to pass that little or no notice is taken commonly of the Vice which is the very antithesis of this Virtue—the Nadir to this Zenith of goodness and holiness? If we really accepted the precept of Love to all and under all conditions as the supreme Divine law, should we not regard the sin of positively torturing and taking pleasure in the sight of torture, as the very last and worst of offences? Should not the early Christian teachers, when they mapped out the Seven Deadly Sins, have placed Cruelty the very first on the list? What were they doing, and what has the Church of Rome been doing ever since, to tell us that Sloth, Covetousness, Lust, Anger, Envy, Pride, and even Gluttony are mortal sins, and say not one word about Cruelty to man or beast?

Again, these Christian teachers of old devised a whole legion of Devils to preside over various departments of human life and to terrify mankind with Dantesque horrors. They told us of Lucifer, Mammon, Belphegor, Zamiel, Asmodeus, Abaddon, Samael, Apollyon, Belial, Beelzebub, and for aught I know many others. But not one of them is a Devil of Cruelty! Even now our English minds (through whole regions of which the old Roman theology and morals still unconsciously dribble), rarely take in the idea that the supreme Vice is Cruelty, that while all other Vices degrade man to the level of the beast, Cruelty sinks him to that of the fiend. When we speak of Vice, commonly, we think of sexual vice or of intemperance. We do not think of that Vice of which—so it seems to me—we must, if guilty, repent through all the cycles of our immortality.[8]

But (let us thank God for it!) better days are slowly dawning on mankind. Christians and non-Christians alike begin to recognise that "Love is the fulfilling of the Law;" and the new sympathy with our humbler fellow-creatures which men are exhibiting all over the world seems truly to reveal a new Lesson of Mercy, spoken by the Divine Spirit in thousands of human souls.

I shall, with thankfulness, now note some marks of such real progress of humanity which have become visible in my long lifetime.

To begin where we began. Bitter words and personalities are now distinctly condemned as in bad taste. The tone of the highest society has become, not so much elaborately and formally polite, as in the eighteenth century, as affectionate and sympathetic almost to excess. Among very well-bred women, in particular, it is the habit to use endearing expressions and exhibit a cordiality towards acquaintances far removed from the distant courtesy of our grandparents. Most noteworthy is the change which has taken place in regard to the treatment of personal defects. A comedy has lately been produced in London of which the special gist consisted in the disfigurement of a lady's nose! That play was a failure. Nobody saw a joke in a disfigured nose; while very lately another play was highly successful wherein the hero's ugly nose constituted his claim to sympathy.[9] These straws show how the wind blows. A Scotch lady of good birth once told me that about sixty years ago she could not walk in the streets of Edinburgh without being jeered at because one of her legs was slightly shorter than the other. Nothing of the kind would occur now in Great Britain; though it does so still in Italy, as I have experienced when I once ventured to take a solitary walk on the Lido in deep English mourning. The just-published report of the excellent Sicilian Society for Humane Education at Palermo states that in 1901 "The Society had six people prosecuted for cruelty to children, and *forty-two* for cruelty to and *derision* of the old"! Very soon we may hope that neither lunacy nor idiocy, neither blindness nor lameness, nor deafness, nor disfigurement, nor old age, will be found objects for cruel laughter, but rather for sincere pity and sympathy. Neither shall we laugh any more with Cervantes and a thousand of his successors at that most pitiful spectacle, a *Rosinante*,—a poor, starved, overworked, broken-down horse; the victim of man's tyranny and cruelty. A worthy subject, indeed, for a perennial jest!

Again, the gall has gone, or nearly gone, out of the ink of our literature. There are no more great satirical poems, and the tone of the Reviews, great and small, has changed infinitely for the better. To read, for example, in the *Quarterly Review* for January this year the article on Women, and realise how the same subject would have been treated in that same Review forty or fifty years ago, is to measure a long step in true progress. Nor would the *Saturday Review* of thirty years ago be popular now; much less be allowed to ride roughshod and domineer over the whole field of letters.

There is no need to remark on the great mitigation of the Punishments of children. Another twenty years will, I trust, see canes and birches hung up in museums of ethnology, along with thumbscrews.

I am not in a position to judge how much less Pleasure in Pain is taken in Field Sports now than formerly; but at least the dogs which take part in them are, I understand, no longer flogged in the barbarous manner and with the cruel dog-whips of fifty years ago. I hope, also (though not very confidently, in view of the failure of the good Bishop of Hereford's Bill against Spurious Sports) that greater care is taken than heretofore to put wounded birds out of misery. Only in the practice of Vivisection is there a dreadful backwater in the tide of advance in humanity; and the recurrence to the systematic indulgence—if not of actual Pleasure in Pain,—yet at least of such utter indifference to the infliction of pain as arrives at the same result so far as the victims are concerned.

Lastly, a very noteworthy and interesting evidence of the decline of *Schadenfreude* among thoughtful persons is the growing unwillingness to believe in an eternal Hell; or, at all events, to face that tremendous dogma with the coolness of our fathers. The conviction has at last come home to us that there can be no Heaven for Saints if there be any Hell for Sinners. Lazarus can have no rest in Abraham's bosom if he sees Dives pining for a drop of water. The way in which the doctrine of the enduring misery of lost souls has sunk down into obscurity and into something very like contempt, even within the recollection of living persons, is surprising. A hundred years ago there was beginning to be felt some repugnance to the famous outburst of Tertullian's feelings on the subject: "You are fond of spectacles? Expect the greatest of all spectacles, the last eternal judgment of the universe! How shall I admire, how laugh, *how rejoice, how exult* when I behold so many monarchs groaning in the abyss, so many philosophers blushing in red-hot flames with their deluded scholars! so many celebrated poets! and tragedians! and dancers"![10] and so on, and so on. In short, by his own account, this great Father of the Church (of whom St. Cyprian always spoke as his "Master"), frankly anticipated an eternity of *Schadenfreude* and called it "Heaven"! Long after him Baxter's *Saints' Rest* presented the same idea of a Paradise, with the torments of the Damned for stimulus of satisfaction. The stern New England Puritans sang hideous hymns wherein they anticipated without regret the eternal separation of husbands and wives, parents and children. Every effort, down to the first half of the last century, was made even by comparatively wide-minded and Arminian fathers and mothers to impress the imagination of the young with the ghastly idea of the Eternity of Woe as the grand incentive to a holy life. I can myself vividly recall sitting (an unusually happy child) among beautiful sandhills on a summer's day, and endeavouring, as a matter of religious duty, to realise what it would be to be burning for a hundred years for every grain of sand in those hills, and at the end to be no nearer to release. The Blessed were, in fact, supposed to be souls in which every spark of pity was for ever extinct, and in which *Schadenfreude* should be the universal sentiment! Surely the unquestionable loss of popularity (to say nothing more) of this view of the Future World, is a cogent testimony to the advance of our race in true Christianity,—the Christianity of the Sermon on the Mount?

But in a still larger and deeper way the change is manifest. We no longer feel we *could* worship as our God a Being capable of maintaining in His universe an Eternal Hell. To Dante it seemed quite fit that on the Infernal Gate of the Hopeless should be inscribed—

> Dinanzi a me non fur cose create,
> Se non eterne, ed io eterno duro,[11]

so that before man existed, or had sinned, the hideous Torture-chambers of Dante's imagination were ready built for him by One who, by colossal paradox, was called "*Il primo Amore*"! But the seven centuries which have elapsed since the great poet's time have left us (thank God!) with other beliefs. We may indeed "lift lame hands of faith," but at least we "*trust*"

> That somehow good
> Shall be the final goal of ill.

and that

> Not a life shall be destroyed,
> Or cast as rubbish to the void,
> When God shall make the pile complete.

We recognise that the hope and desire for such universal mercy and restitution is what we have

The likest God within the soul.[12]

To love the Lord of Hell was perhaps possible—indeed, it seems to have been somehow accomplished by men and women, otherwise sane and kindly-hearted—in 1800. It is scarcely possible in 1900. And so we have come to think of God only as our FATHER IN HEAVEN, and Hell has vanished almost as a nightmare of the past. Be it noted that it is not only, or chiefly, to escape the dread of perdition *on our own account*, that we have swept the terror away, but because we have felt that, if we are to love God, we must believe in His love for all men; and if we are to be happy in any world hereafter we must know there is no place anywhere of hopeless and unending sin and suffering, to spoil for us all the joys of Heaven.

Notes

1.   *English Bards and Scotch Reviewers*, written in March, 1809, was a satirical poem aimed at the *Edinburgh Review* who had written scathingly of Byron's 1807 volume of poetry, *Hours of Idleness*.

2.   "Lines to a Critic" (published posthumously in 1824). The critic is probably Robert Southey whom Shelley (incorrectly) thought to be the author of a personalized attack on his character in the *Quarterly Review* in 1819.

3.   After the long lapse of years I may amuse the reader by narrating how the editor first published a bitter review of one of my books and then very shortly after invited me, through my publishers, to join his staff. My message in reply was:—"Tell Mr. Cook that if his review of my 'Studies' was a fair and just one I am not good enough to be his contributor. If it was unfair and unjust, his Review is not good enough for me." [Cobbe's note]

4.   A ludicrous example of unintentional confession of the real feelings of the whipper occurred some years ago in Dublin. A lady told me that she had reason to believe that her little girl was threatened with a whipping at the school which she attended. The lady accordingly wrote to the schoolmistress forbidding the punishment. She received in reply a letter in which the mistress sadly complained that she had "snatched the cup of pleasure from her lips!" [Cobbe's note]

5. Cobbe is referring to the Boer War, a war between British and Dutch settlers in South Africa, which lasted from 1899 to 1902.

6. The Servile Wars were three slave uprisings against Roman rule which occurred in c.134–132 BC, c.102–99 BC, and 73–71 BC.

7. The place where public announcement was made of sentences imposed during the Spanish Inquisition.

8. How far apart in such matters are Intuitive and Utilitarian morality may be noted from the tone taken by Bentham in speaking of the subject of this paper. He says: "There is no such thing as any sort of motive that is in itself a bad one. Let a man's motive be ill-will, call it even malice, envy, cruelty, it is still a kind of pleasure that is his motive—the pleasure he takes in the thought of the pain which he sees his adversary undergo. Now even this wretched pleasure taken by itself is good." Introduction to his "Principles of Morals," by Jeremy Bentham, p. 169. [Cobbe's note]

9. Edmond Rostand's poetic drama, Cyrano de Bergerac had appeared in 1897.

10. Tertullian *de Spectaculis*, C. 30, quoted by Gibbon. [Cobbe's note]

11. Canto III, ll. 7–8 of Dante's *The Divine Comedy*, Inferno [Hell]. Translated by Henry F. Cary as: "Before me things create were none, save things / Eternal, and eternal I endure."

12. Cobbe is quoting from Alfred Tennyson's *In Memoriam*, lyrics 54 and 55. The lines in lyric 54 should read: "O, yet we trust that somehow good / Will be the final goal of ill, / To pangs of nature, sins of will, / Defects of doubt, and taints of blood; / That nothing walks with aimless feet; / That not one life shall be destroyed, / Or cast as rubbish to the void / When God hath made the pile complete; . . .".

VI. Eliza Lynn Linton

(1822–1898)

To Victorian readers and current critics alike, Eliza Lynn Linton
was a fierce opponent of her sex, and her voluminous body of works
attacks the Victorian woman's desire for marital, educational, domestic,
political, and occupational liberation. However, Lynn Linton's
criticism of women is complex and conflicted: her works are riddled
with ruptures, ambiguities, and inconsistencies which reveal her
unresolved struggles with feminism. In her essays, Lynn Linton
sometimes employs a male-identified antifeminist or misogynistic
persona in order to write "like a man" and establish her authority as a
social critic in a patriarchal culture. In her antifeminism, she opposed
social and political rights for women equal to men; in her misogyny
she evinces a blunt dislike for "femaleness" or the stereotypical
woman's character. Although her misogyny distressed both women's
rights activists and the traditional chivalric men of her day, her literary
talent was nevertheless admired and encouraged by many, including
Algernon Charles Swinburne, Charles Dickens, and Walter Savage
Landor. But unlike numerous other women who spoke out against
increased women's rights, Lynn Linton, by both nineteenth- and
twentieth-century standards, lived a "feminist" lifestyle.

Born on February 10, 1822, the twelfth child of Charlotte
Goodenough and Reverend James Lynn, Eliza was five months old
when her mother died. After her mother's death, she and her siblings
were raised by Reverend Lynn, whose philosophy of parenting entailed
inculcating strong religious conviction into his children while, at the
same time, neglecting to educate formally the youngest members of his
family. In her teen years, Lynn Linton sought to make up for her
educational deficiencies by teaching herself French, Italian, German,

Spanish, and some Latin and Greek; she also read extensively in history and philosophy, classical and modern literature. At age fifteen, Lynn Linton began secretly corresponding with Richard Bentley, publisher of *Bentley's Miscellany*. Aspiring to become a writer, and aware that her father would vehemently object to her goal, she sought the guidance of Bentley, whom she considered a less antagonistic, more fatherly, judge of her ability. Although he did not publish her stories, his decision to read her work gave Lynn Linton the encouragement she needed to continue writing.

After William Ainsworth published two of Lynn Linton's poems in 1844, she found the courage to tell her father that she was intent on pursuing a writing career. Four years later, Lynn Linton became the first woman journalist in England to draw a fixed salary when John Douglas Cook hired her as a staff writer for the *Morning Chronicle*. Around this time, she met George Eliot, toward whom she harbored a lifelong envy. Lynn Linton begrudged Eliot her celebrity and acceptance by great intellectuals—a fame Eliot achieved despite her adulterous relationship with George Henry Lewes. Placing herself in the shadow of the great novelist, Lynn Linton struggled to accept the limitations of her own popularity and influence.

In 1858 at the age of thirty-six, Eliza Lynn married William James Linton. Determined to keep her own property in defiance to the law, she had her husband sign a contract stating that she would maintain control of her inheritance and earnings after their marriage. The marriage did not last long: they separated in 1864, and soon after William Linton emigrated to America. Lynn Linton spent the rest of her life writing essays and novels, as well as traveling with close female friends.

Lynn Linton had begun her intellectual life as a political radical, free thinker, and proponent of free love. In 1854 she wrote an essay for William Linton's *English Republic* which praised Mary Wollstonecraft's *A Vindication of the Rights of Woman*. Although Lynn Linton's initial enthusiasm for women's rights quickly gave way to a more blatant antifeminism, she never completely relinquished all of her feminist beliefs. For instance, to her the New Woman was a boisterous, unladylike, "wild woman" or a coarse, vocal member of the "shrieking sisterhood," but she importunes them: "There is very little which [women] may not do if they like—and can." While she warns against "over-study in girls who are one day to be mothers," she believed in the higher education of women to an extent. In discussing marriage, Lynn Linton was the most overtly progressive. She believed that the divorce laws were oppressive for men and women and should be extended to include madness, drunkenness, and felony as just causes for divorce. Further, she argued that women must be allowed to keep their property after marriage, and, in the case of divorce, mothers must have rights to their children equal to those of fathers. While Lynn Linton's opinion regarding the extent and kind of freedoms and privileges women should enjoy outside the home varied, as long as women chose to accept their "duty" in the domestic sphere, she was willing to fight for most of their rights.

Between 1844 and her death in 1898, Lynn Linton produced a continual flow of essays, the majority of which focused on women's issues. She published in over twenty periodicals, but most extensively in the *Saturday Review*, *Temple Bar*, the *Fortnightly Review*, the *New Review*, and the *Nineteenth Century*. Her *Saturday Review* articles gained her the most recognition, especially "The Girl of the Period," which was published on March 14, 1868. This essay achieved instant notoriety: the issue sold out, the essay was later circulated as a pamphlet, and "girl of the period" became a catch phrase to describe the modern, middle-class young woman. Although she never again equalled the success she had with this essay, Lynn Linton continued publishing pejorative, descriptive bimonthly essays about women in the *Saturday Review* for ten years. Unfortunately, Lynn Linton's *Saturday Review* essays are unsigned; aside from Merle Mowbray Bevington's incomplete bibliography of her essays in *The Saturday Review, 1855–1868* (1941), scholars have little to go on when determining which essays are hers and which are those of imitators. However, several of Lynn Linton's *Saturday Review* essays were periodically collected and reprinted in such anthologies as *Modern Women and What Is Said of Them* (1868), and *The Girl of the Period and Other Social Essays* (1883). Lynn Linton's wit and satirical ingenuity, manifested in these popular essays, gained her recognition from both amused and angry audiences.

Given Lynn Linton's infamy as a writer, it is no wonder she has been excluded from the canon. Her popularity in her own time was unstable; as a writer, her literary voice is unenlightened and irascible; and many critics now dismiss her as an antifeminist. On the other hand, a close reading of her essays reveals her flair with language, her ability to manipulate the rhetoric and conventions of the essay form, and her ideological complexity. Lynn Linton can be appreciated as a writer who exhibits artistic self-consciousness in her ability to create a distinct literary persona and literary complexity as she weaves incisive subtexts into her essays.

Despite the exclusion of her works from the canon, Lynn Linton's life has drawn a considerable amount of interest from biographers. Shortly after her death, her friend George Somes Layard wrote *Mrs. Lynn Linton: Her Life, Letters and Opinions* (1901), a reconstruction of her life based largely on her own letters and his intimate association with her. In *Eliza Lynn Linton: The Girl of the Period* (1979), Herbert Van Thal depicts Lynn Linton as a noteworthy Victorian figure. Nancy Fix Anderson's psychological portrait of this complex woman in *Woman Against Women in Victorian England: A Life of Eliza Lynn Linton* (1987), is the most contemporary and full account of Lynn Linton's life. Besides the essays included in this anthology, other representative works by Lynn Linton include *The Autobiography of Christopher Kirkland* (1885)—which is, in fact, an autobiography of Lynn Linton—and *My Literary Life: Reminiscences of Dickens, Thackeray, and George Eliot* (1889).

Noreen Groover Lape,
Temple University

15. The Girl of the Period

Introduction

Eliza Lynn Linton's "The Girl of the Period" appeared on March 14, 1868, in the *Saturday Review*, and is reprinted here from that periodical. The article caused an immediate uproar among supporters of the women's rights movement, as well as among more traditional, chivalric defenders of Womanhood. In an extended satirical caricature, Lynn Linton mourns the loss of the "ideal" woman and chastises the "girl of the period" who has taken her place. After the publication of the essay, the term "girl of the period," or "G.O.P.," entered the Victorian vocabulary, becoming a catch phrase used by social critics to describe what had before been known as the "fast young girl." Because of its notoriety, "The Girl of the Period" was reissued as a pamphlet in 1868. It was also reprinted in various anthologies of Lynn Linton's work, including *Modern Women and What Is Said of Them* (1868) and *The Girl of the Period and Other Social Essays* (1883).

The Girl of the Period

Time was when the stereotyped phrase, "a fair young English girl," meant the ideal of womanhood; to us, at least, of home birth and breeding. It meant a creature generous, capable, and modest; something franker than a Frenchwoman, more to be trusted than an Italian, as brave as an American but more refined, as domestic as a German and more graceful. It meant a girl who could be trusted alone if need be, because of the innate purity and dignity of her nature, but who was neither bold in bearing nor masculine in mind; a girl who, when she married, would be her husband's friend and companion, but never his rival; one who would consider their interests identical, and not hold him as just so much fair game for spoil; who would make his house his true home and place of rest, not a mere passage-place for vanity and ostentation to go through; a tender mother, an industrious housekeeper, a judicious mistress. We prided ourselves as a nation on our women. We thought we had the pick of creation in this fair young English girl of ours, and envied no other men their own. We admired the languid grace and subtle fire of the South; the docility and childlike affectionateness of the East seemed to us sweet and simple and restful; the vivacious sparkle of the trim and sprightly Parisienne was a pleasant little excitement when we met with it in its own domain; but our allegiance never wandered from our brown-haired girls at home, and our hearts were less vagrant than our fancies. This was in the old time, and when English girls were content to be what God and nature had made them. Of late years we have changed the pattern, and have given to the world a race of women as utterly unlike the old insular ideal as if we had created another nation altogether. The girl of the period, and the fair young English girl of the past, have nothing in common save ancestry and their mother-tongue; and even of this last the modern version makes almost a new language, through the copious additions it has received from the current slang of the day.

The girl of the period is a creature who dyes her hair and paints her face, as the first articles of her personal religion; whose sole idea of life is plenty of fun and luxury; and whose dress is the object of such thought and intellect as she possesses. Her main endeavour in this is to outvie her neighbours in the extravagance of fashion. No matter whether, as in the time of crinolines, she sacrificed decency, or, as now, in the time of trains, she sacrifices cleanliness; no matter either, whether she makes herself a nuisance and an inconvenience to every one she meets. The girl of the period has done away with such moral muffishness as consideration for others, or regard for counsel and rebuke. It was all very well in old-fashioned times, when fathers and mothers had some authority and were treated with respect, to be tutored and made to obey, but she is far too fast and flourishing to be stopped in mid-career by these slow old morals; and as she dresses to please herself, she does not care if she displeases every one else. Nothing is too extraordinary and nothing too exaggerated for her vitiated taste; and things which in themselves would be useful reforms if let alone become monstrosities worse than those which they have displaced so soon as she begins to manipulate and improve. If a sensible fashion lifts the gown out of the mud, she raises hers midway to her knee. If the absurd structure of wire and buckram, once called a bonnet, is modified to something that shall protect the wearer's face without putting out the eyes of her companion, she cuts hers down to four straws and a rosebud, or a tag of lace and a bunch of glass beads. If there is a reaction against an excess of Rowland's Macassar, and hair shiny and sticky with grease is thought less nice than if left clean and healthily crisp, she dries and frizzes and sticks hers out on end like certain savages in Africa, or lets it wander down her back like Madge Wildfire's,[1] and thinks herself all the more beautiful the nearer she approaches in look to a maniac or a negress. With purity of taste she has lost also that far more precious purity and delicacy of perception which sometimes mean more than appears on the surface. What the *demi-monde* [2] does in its frantic efforts to excite attention, she also does in imitation. If some fashionable *dévergondée en evidence* [3] is reported to have come out with her dress below her shoulder-blades, and a gold strap for all the sleeve thought necessary, the girl of the period follows suit next day; and then wonders that men sometimes mistake her for her prototype, or that mothers of girls not quite so far gone as herself refuse her as a companion for their daughters. She has blunted the fine edges of feeling so much that she cannot understand why she should be condemned for an imitation of form which does not include imitation of fact; she cannot be made to see that modesty of appearance and virtue ought to be inseparable, and that no good girl can afford to appear bad, under penalty of receiving the contempt awarded to the bad.

This imitation of the *demi-monde* in dress leads to something in manner and feeling, not quite so pronounced perhaps, but far too like to be honourable to herself or satisfactory to her friends. It leads to slang, bold talk, and fastness; to the love of pleasure and indifference to duty; to the desire of money before either love or happiness; to uselessness at home, dissatisfaction with the monotony of ordinary life, and horror of all useful work; in a word, to the worst forms of luxury and selfishness, to the most fatal effects arising from want of high principle and absence of tender feeling. The girl of the period envies the queens of the *demi-monde* far more than she abhors them. She sees them gorgeously attired and sumptuously appointed, and she knows them to be flattered, fêted, and courted with a certain disdainful admiration of which she catches only the admiration while she ignores the disdain. They have all for which her soul is hungering, and she never stops to reflect at what a price they have bought their gains, and what fearful moral penalties they pay for their sensuous pleasures. She sees only the coarse gilding on the base token, and shuts her eyes to the hideous figure in the midst, and the foul legend written round the edge. It is this envy of the pleasures, and indifference to the sins, of these women of the *demi-monde* which is doing such infinite mischief to the modern girl. They brush too closely by each other, if not in actual deeds, yet in aims and feelings; for the luxury which is brought by vice with the one is the thing of all in life most passionately desired by the other, though she is not yet prepared to pay quite the same price. Unfortunately, she has already paid too much—all that once gave her distinctive national character. No one can say of the modern English girl that she is tender, loving, retiring, or domestic. The old fault so often found by keen-sighted Frenchwomen, that she was so fatally *romanesque*, so prone to sacrifice appearances and social advantages for love, will never be set down to the girl of the period. Love indeed is the last thing she thinks of, and the least of the dangers besetting her. Love in a cottage, that seductive dream which used to vex the heart and disturb the calculations of prudent mothers, is now a myth of past ages. The legal barter of herself for so much money, representing so much dash, so much luxury and pleasure—that is her idea of marriage; the only idea worth entertaining. For all seriousness of thought respecting the duties or the consequences of marriage, she has not a trace. If children come, they find but a stepmother's cold welcome from her; and if her husband thinks that he has married anything that is to belong to him—a *tacens et placens uxor* pledged to make him happy—the sooner he wakes from his hallucination and understands that he has simply married some one who will condescend to spend his money on herself, and who will shelter her indiscretions behind the shield of his name, the less severe will be his disappointment. She has married his house, his carriage, his balance at the banker's, his title; and he himself is just the inevitable condition clogging the wheel of her fortune; at best an adjunct, to be tolerated with more or less patience as may chance. For it is only the old-fashioned sort, not girls of the period *pur sang*, that marry for love, or put the husband before the banker. But she does not marry easily. Men are afraid of her; and with reason. They may amuse themselves with her for an evening, but they do not take her readily for life. Besides, after all her efforts, she is only a poor copy of the real thing; and the real thing is far more amusing than the copy, because it is real. Men can get that whenever they like; and when they go into their mothers' drawing-rooms, to see their sisters and their sisters' friends, they want something of quite different flavour. *Toujours perdrix* [4] is bad providing all the world over; but a continual weak imitation of *toujours perdrix* is worse. If we must have only one kind of thing, let us have it genuine; and the queens of St. John's Wood in their unblushing honesty, rather than their imitators and make-believes in Bayswater and Belgravia. For, at whatever cost of shocked self-love or pained modesty it may be, it cannot be too plainly told to the modern English girl that the net result of her present manner of life is to assimilate her as nearly as possible to a class of women whom we must not call by their proper—or improper—name. And we are willing to believe that she has still some modesty of soul left hidden under all this effrontery of fashion, and that, if she could be made to see herself as she appears to the eyes of men, she would mend her ways before too late.

It is terribly significant of the present state of things when men are free to write as they do of the women of their own nation. Every word of censure flung against them is two-edged, and wounds those who condemn as much as those who are condemned; for surely it need hardly be said that men hold nothing so dear as the honour of their women, and that no one living would willingly lower the repute of his mother or his sisters. It is only when these have placed themselves beyond the pale of masculine respect that such things could be written as are written now; when they become again what they were once they will gather round them the love and homage and chivalrous devotion which were then an Englishwoman's natural inheritance. The marvel, in the present fashion of life among women, is how it holds its ground in spite of the disapprobation of men. It used to be an old-time notion that the sexes were made for each other, and that it was only natural for them to please each other, and to set themselves out for that end. But the girl of the period does not please men. She pleases them as little as she elevates them; and how little she does that, the class of women she has taken as her models of itself testifies. All men whose opinion is worth having prefer the simple and genuine girl of the past, with her tender little ways and pretty bashful modesties, to this loud and rampant modernization, with her false red hair and painted skin, talking slang as glibly as a man, and by preference leading the conversation to doubtful subjects. She thinks she is piquante and exciting when she thus makes herself the bad copy of a worse original; and she will not see that though men laugh with her they do not respect her, though they flirt with her they do not marry her; she will not believe that she is not the kind of thing they want, and that she is acting against nature and her own interests when she disregards their advice and offends their taste. We do not see how she makes out her account, viewing her life from any side; but all we can do is to wait patiently until the national madness has passed, and our women have come back again to the old English ideal, once the most beautiful, the most modest, the most essentially womanly in the world.

Notes

1.   Madge Murdockson (Madge Wildfire) is a character in Scott's *The Heart of Midlothian* (1818).
2.   French for the class of women who have lost their social standing, usually because of their real or imagined promiscuous and indiscreet behavior.
3.   French for a conspicuously shameless or profligate woman.
4.   "toujours perdrix," in French, translates as "always partridge."

16. George Eliot

Introduction

Eliza Lynn Linton's "George Eliot," which appeared anonymously in *Temple Bar* in April, 1885, and which is reprinted here from that periodical, is a review of *The Life of George Eliot*, by John Cross. Like a great many Victorian writers, Lynn Linton uses the book under review as a springboard to launch her own polemic—in this case, an attack on the life and works of Eliot. She criticizes Eliot's fictional characters, her adulterous relationship with George Lewes, and her "protoplastic" and "chameleon-like" demeanor. A testament to the freedom derived from anonymity, this essay reveals Lynn Linton's masterly use of irony as she repeatedly turns her compliments into criticisms of the great writer.

George Eliot

We have let the rush of criticism pass by before entering on this "Life of George Eliot," in praise of which so high a note has been struck;—if we were not afraid of being considered one of the sons of Belial, we should say too high a note. For though, naturally enough, supremely interesting to the intimate friends who have supplied the materials and are carried along to vicarious fame in her skirts, this "Life" of our great novelist is in a great measure disappointing to the outside public, and, as a whole, is both meagre and tedious. It is almost entirely bare of those pictorial incidents and dramatic presentations which make an interesting picture and a solid, round and tangible history, and we never get a fair hold of facts. This bareness is due to the method adopted by Mr. Cross of letting George Eliot tell her own life, by piecing together fragments of her letters into one continuous whole, and adding next to nothing from the outside. Thus we get only her own version of the events in which she was the chief actor; and by this version we have but the slenderest scantling of things as they were; while we are deluged with reflections and aphorisms, and records of trivial matters which could well be spared. We never see the person objectively nor stereoscopically; and the almost god-like faultlessness of the character, as it is indicated, is matched only by the vagueness of the drawing and the indefiniteness of the features.

We confess the tender care and skilful manipulation shown by Mr. Cross in this delicate and difficult task. There is no break of gauge and no sense of confusion; the dovetailings are so smooth as to be practically invisible, and the whole thing runs as easily together as if all these diverse constituents had been originally poured into the same mould. But this does not redeem the result from tedium, nor make the picture stereoscopic. The book is fully half too long; and there are the wearisome repetitions and the monotony of theme inseparable from letters written at the same time to various friends. Also we have far too much of passing moods and not enough of characteristic actions; and more is omitted than is told. Those who knew George Eliot in her unfledged condition when she was only a tentative beginner, and before she had culminated and set into her final form, will remember one or two episodes which showed the dominant characteristic of her moral nature with more sincerity than anything to be found in this "Life;" and the curious slurring over of names which in their time were important landmarks in her history, gives to those who know something of the *dessous des cartes*[1] a certain feeling of suppression and nebulosity which makes this life not so much genuine history, as a trimmed, erased and amended protocol. In a word, the book has been written to embalm and preserve the image of the Ideal George Eliot, as success made her appear, and as the world accepted for reality.

Of her early life the account is singularly insufficient; and her girlhood leaves on the reader a grey and colourless impression, to the last degree depressing. Her letters to Miss Lewis are the letters of a melancholy, clever, but crudely pedantic, morbidly introspective and egotistical girl, with whom religious speculation is only another word for ennui, and whose blank despair springs from unfulfilled desires and monotony of life. "A young girl with a full passionate nature and hungry intellect, shut up in a farmhouse in the remote country" must needs have many bitter hours and anxious lookings for the Shiloh who is to deliver her. And Marian Evans suffered from this narrowness of horizon and poverty of pasture, as so many have suffered before her, and so many will suffer in days yet to come. Her emancipation was brought about by a wider intercourse with the world outside, and by new friendships made with people such as the Brays and Hennells and Brabants—people of larger minds, more cultivated intellects, and freer views than were to be found in her inherited surroundings. But so much went to the good of her account:—lonely she might be, but she was never cold-shouldered at her own home, never snubbed nor suppressed nor made to feel that her exceptional gifts were exceptional defects. She was always admired, believed in, sympathised with, helped forward; and she did not lose her time by the arduous process and inevitable mistakes of self-education. Certainly, when she threw off some of her early mental wrappings and grew to be so far unorthodox as to refuse to go to church—the sole bit of aggressive conscientiousness recorded of her— she came into temporary collision with her father; and the shock of the conflict did for a time strain and fray the home bond. But things eventually came right by her own submission, and henceforth her life was lapped in love and cradled in care. In her education, both in that which was early and formal and in that which was mature and adventitious, she was never left unguided in her studies nor unassisted in her mental development. She was essentially and at all times helped forward, as we have said; and with an unhappy and morbid, anxious and worrying temperament, she was singularly blessed in her affections and fortunate in her life. Of this singular grace of good fortune we shall speak again.

Despondent as these girlish letters are, with their exaggerated sense of sin and estimate of sorrow, they show the marvellous power of assimilation which made George Eliot what she was. No modern intelligence known to us was so plastic, or rather so protoplastic as hers. Mr. Cross calls her chameleon-like. She was not an original thinker; and partly for want of initiative mental power, partly for want of physical energy, she does not seem to have tried her hand at any of those rough-hewn efforts which are usually the first efforts of unformed genius. But she read and studied with heroic force; and she grew to be a learned woman of rare solidity and thoroughness. Her nature, at once earnest and far-reaching, allowed of no shams in knowledge, no superficiality in study. She put herself fairly outside her subject, and absorbed it all, from end to end. This thoroughness of study was one of her grandest mental characteristics; and this gave her that special flavour of ripeness, of matured thought, of breadth of view and depth of insight, which made her so eminently delightful as a conversationalist, when she took pains to please—and she generally did take pains,—and so valuable as an intellectual companion and helper. She was the most magnificent kind of Papin's digester; and all that she had learned in her youth and added to in her maturity she reproduced with so much vital power as to be in itself genius. Yet she was eminently the result of other men's teachings; and throughout her life she bore the impress now of one, now of the other, of her various masters. Her web was woven from threads supplied from without, and she was neither a constructive philosopher, as her admirers claimed for her, nor even a creator of literary and enduring types. She was one instance the more, to be added to the many existing, of the want of the originative faculty in women. Had a man possessed her weight of brain, her education, her mental capacity generally, he would have been the founder of a new school or in philosophy or in literature—adding to the power common to both sexes the gift of construction special to his own.

George Eliot created no literary types. She drew with the hand of a master living, breathing men and women; but they are individual not generic. They are too complex and self-conscious, and lack too much the unity of conception, the simplicity of presentation which makes a character take rank as a true type. They are not the embodiments of certain dominant qualities common to a whole class which henceforth may be gathered under that one distinctive cloak—such as we have in Tartuffe or even his younger bother Pecksniff; in Becky Sharp or my Uncle Toby; in Robert Macaire or Manon Lescaut—of whom however there is an echo in Hetty.[2] But then Hetty was drawn from one who was the living reproduction of Manon. Tito, weak, self-indulgent, pleasure-seeking, beauty-loving, slippery and wholly unconscientious, who by the very fact of moral weakness could drift into the commission of a strong man's crime, approaches nearest to a type of any of her characters, and is most of a true creation. For Mrs. Poyser herself is not an original creation.[3] George Eliot certainly disclaims "the mistake of supposing that Mrs. Poyser's original sayings are remembered proverbs." "I have no stock of proverbs in my memory," she says, "and there is nothing put into Mrs. Poyser's mouth which is not fresh from my own mint." People in the country however, where Mrs. Poyser's prototype lived, have a different version. They will tell you that they recognised her chief sayings and knew the best of them already by heart, when they appeared embalmed in the matchless amber of George Eliot's style. We could not say of any of her characters what we all said of Becky Sharp: "We know her—she is so and so;" each finding her in his own acquaintance because of that suggestive while simple, that faceted while spherical, quality of the type, which enables each reader to recognise and translate, according to his own view. We know George Eliot's people as they live in her pages; but, unlike Miss Austen's, we do not know them out of those pages. We hear them, see them, shake hands with them, laugh and weep with them, within the covers; but we do not meet them in our friends' drawing-rooms. They are solid and alive in their own sphere, but they are essentially portraits modified and redraped; and those who knew the ground could always individualise the more prominent characters. With all her scientific knowledge, George Eliot never created anything which touched Zola's wonderful conception of heredity and variation in the Rougon-Macquart series; and, psychological and analytical as she is, she is not up to Balzac's height, nor is her definition so fine, nor her penetration so subtle, as his. This individualism and want of typical comprehensiveness in her characters, unlike Miss Austen, is on the same lines as those on which Sir Walter Scott worked. The genius which drew Maggie Tulliver and Hetty, Mrs. Poyser and Silas Marner, Dorothea and Rosamond, and all the rest, was akin to that which reproduced the deathless lineaments of Edie Ochiltree and the Antiquary, Meg Merilees and Dominie Sampson, Mause Headrigg and Bailie Nicol Jarvie.[4] Thus, neither of these great masters of the art of fiction has given a new literary signpost to the language— like Quixotic, for example, Shandean, Pantagruelistic, Mephistophilean, or even Pecksniffian.[5] *En revanche*,[6] George Eliot gave us a new scientific term in "meliorism;" which perhaps is more to the purpose.

The chameleon-like quality of her mind, and her marvellous power of assimilation, made George Eliot able to profit by outside advantages as those of a more original and independent nature cannot. Her protoplastic nature gave her the greatest part of her power and all her personal influence. It was indeed her chief personal charm, but it altered her own shape for so long as the flexible time of her life lasted. It is interesting to trace the modifications of thought and the changes in her points of view, which were the results of this man's influence or of that. Though more remains behind than is brought to the front in this book, which says so much and tells so little, this fact is tolerably clear. And in the disastrous overlay of art by science which spoilt her last novels, the hand of George Lewes and the colour of her habitual environment are evident enough. Certainly her own early tendencies were always more or less scientific; and what came after but increased and developed, and did not create that tendency. But it increased it to a disastrous amount, developed it to a ruinous extent, and art was crushed beneath the ponderous pedantry which, in the beginning and when sparingly used, had been like salt to the roast, or a point of colour in a picture. Her first novels are free from the defects which marred the beauty of the last. They are the most artistic, the most spontaneous, the least conscious and the least introspective. "Romola" marks the point of departure, and is the watershed between the two regions of art and science—fiction and metaphysics. For all its beauty and nobleness it is more laboured than its predecessors, and is touched with that fatal defect of heaviness which spoilt "Middlemarch" and destroyed "Daniel Deronda." Of this last indeed, when we come to such monstrosities as the "dynamic glance" of an eye and the "epidermis" showing through a rent in a garment, used in serious fiction and not as a comic exaggeration, we have come to a decadence which nothing but fanaticism refuses to admit.

The letters out of which this "Life" is framed, are singularly— perhaps necessarily, but nevertheless unpleasantly—egotistical. George

Eliot's friends would, naturally enough, be interested in the record of her passing emotions, her temporary ailments, her skin-deep discomforts. To the public they are unimportant. Frankly, to know that she more than any other mortal man or woman did on such and such a date some thirty years ago, suffer from a week's *malaise*, or go to bed with a headache and get up without it, cannot interest people to whom yet her work is deservedly dear. Those who accept her as a quasi-revelation, and who devour all her utterances as the texts of a new gospel, will not be displeased. But these are the minority. Every now and then however a fine sentiment breaks through the duller record and narrower circle.

> 'Tell me not that I am a mere prater,' she says in a letter to Miss Sara Hennell; 'that feeling never talks. I will talk, and caress, and look lovingly until death makes me as stony as the Gorgon-heads of all the judicious people I know. What is anything worth until it is uttered? Is not the universe one great utterance? Utterance there must be in word or deed to make life of any worth. Every true pentecost is a gift of utterance.'

It would be hard to match the truth and loveliness of that extract, written too as it is from a full heart as well as a nobly conditioned brain!

Again, she says finely and with true insight, but with insight only, not personal adoption:

> 'I love the souls that rush along to their goal with a full stream of sentiment—that have too much of the positive to be harassed by the perpetual negatives, which, after all, are but the disease of the soul to be expelled by fortifying the principle of vitality.'

Again:

> 'If I had children I would make them carpenters and shoemakers; that is the way to make them Messiahs and Jacob Boehms. As for us, who are dependent on carpets and easy-chairs, we are reprobates, and shall never enter into the kingdom of heaven.'

Her pen-and-ink silhouettes too are good. Perhaps the best—
because containing a touch of humour, in which her letters are so sadly
deficient—is that of Liebig, "in his laboratory, with his velvet cap on,
holding little phials in his hand and talking of Kreatine and Kreatinine
in the same easy way that well-bred ladies talk scandal." "Melchior
Meyr, a maker of novels and tragedies, otherwise an ineffectual person,"
has a certain Carlylese ring in it; but, "King Max, who seems to be
really a sensible man among kings"; "Heyse, like a painter's poet,
ideally beautiful, rather brilliant in his talk, and altogether pleasing";
"Geibel, a man of rather coarse texture, with a voice like a kettledrum,
and a steady determination to deliver his opinions on every subject that
turned up," are touches of her own, though not specially pictorial nor
graphic.

Her letters as literature, in their descriptions of both places and
people, are in no way superior to those of any intelligent woman who
goes to Germany and Italy for the first time and enjoys what she sees.
Wearisomely long extracts are given from her journals to tell the world
what George Eliot thought of the picture galleries and the artists of
Dresden and Munich, Florence and Rome. Out of the whole amount
there are not half-a-dozen sentences worth preserving. Here is one of the
most characteristic:

> The most popular Murillo, and apparently one of the
> most popular Madonnas in the (Dresden) gallery, is the
> simple, sad mother with her child, without the least divinity
> in it, suggesting a dead or sick father, and imperfect
> nourishment in a garret.

George Eliot was a painful worker, laborious, careful,
conscientious, and bringing forth her books with much travail of the
soul and sorrow to the body. It is tragic to read of her sufferings in the
production of her stories—sufferings just a grade below those which
afflicted Carlyle. She has none of that joyous, free, Greek-like
spontaneity which makes artistic work a divine delight. She brought
forth gods, but she brought them forth with anguish; and each
succeeding book cost her yet more and more distress. Impelled by the
force of circumstances to active labour, she was obliged to use her
powers, which, had she been a rich woman, would never have been used
save for the acquirement of knowledge. "My idle brain wants lashing to
work like a negro, and will do nothing under a slighter stimulus," she

says pathetically; and this was too truly the case. Without the encouragement given her by Mr. Lewes she would probably never have found the genius that had lain so long dormant within her. A translator of the first strength, a clear and searching critic, a scholar and a student of rare thoroughness, she had never yet done more than dream of some day writing a novel, which should embody the, as she believed, small amount of dramatic and poetic power she had. She had written merely "the introductory chapter, describing a Staffordshire village, and the life of the neighbouring farmhouses;" and this chapter something led her to read one evening at Berlin to Mr. Lewes. "He was struck with it as a bit of concrete description," she says; "and it suggested to him the possibility of my being able to write a novel, though he distrusted, indeed disbelieved in, my possession of any dramatic power." However, some time after, at Tenby, where they had gone for the hunting of zoophytes—of which Mr. Lewes made such good use in his charming book "Sea-side Studies"—the spell was broken, the prison doors were thrown open, and the "Sad Fortunes of the Reverend Amos Barton" rose like a star in the sky. Mr. Blackwood saw the value of his new contributor; and the incognito of the writer added the zest of curiosity to admiration.[7] The "Scenes of Clerical Life" gained universal and deserved success; and henceforth George Eliot won all along the line. She made the royal reputation of one who could do no wrong; and fame put to silence criticism. Nothing in the whole "Life" is so fresh, so animated, as this part which treats of her first success. For the time all the haunting melancholy, the brooding self-distrust, the egotistical introspection, the perpetual worrying over thoughts, facts and feelings—over the pain of the day and the dread of the morrow—the morbid self-made unhappiness which marred the enjoyment of life for her, sank into the background; and we see her as frankly delighting in, and delightful by reason of, her new-found power, as well as because of the fuller measure of grist to the not over-richly provided mill of their joint fortunes which her work brought the united pair.

But there is one thing which, to our way of thinking, was both dishonouring to her craft and humiliating to herself. This was the strange lapse of dignity and good taste recorded in the following extract. "I ordered copies ('Scenes of Clerical Life') to be sent to the following persons—Froude, Dickens, Thackeray, Tennyson, Ruskin, Faraday, the author of 'Companions of my Solitude,' Albert Smith, Mrs. Carlyle." We know of no other instance where a self-respecting writer has done this—remembering that most of these people, if not all, were unknown celebrities, not personal friends; and that she, George Eliot herself, was as yet both obscure and untried, and quite uncertain how her book would be received by the public. She lived in a state of undignified ferment and anxiety about reviews, subscriptions, sale, payments, and what the world said; so that she did not offer the homage of a new success to assured greatness. It was simply a piece of personal touting, of *réclame*, in all ways unworthy of her. This undignified ferment of her first experience was strangely unlike the attitude afterwards assumed when she had found her fame and henceforth was free from fear.

"Don't think about reading 'Silas Marner,' just because it is come out," she writes to one of her earliest and best friends—one who would be certain to read every line she might write. "I hate *obligato* reading and *obligato* talk about my books. *I never send them to any one,* (sic) and never wish to be spoken to about them, except by an unpremeditated and spontaneous prompting."

This was the second phase—the phase which came upon success. In the beginning, there was none of that great-hearted superiority to criticism—that grand, calm way of doing the best possible to one's powers, and letting the issue take care of itself—which is the noblest but perhaps not the most profitable way of dealing with the world. And this greedy desire for appreciation—for news of what the reviews said and the public thought—this singular absence of nobility in her attitude as well as the money-hunger underlying her business transactions, filling the canvas of this earlier time—contrast strangely with the later presentation which gives us George Eliot with the calm dignity of an Egyptian goddess shot through with the tender grace of a Madonna— elevated beyond all the frivolities of life, superior to all its littlenesses, and as impervious to the shafts of an angry Apollo as she was deaf to the barking of yelping curs.

In point of fact, George Eliot had none of that proud independence which comes from self-reliance and strength of character. She had no strength of character. She had a masterly intellect—a superb intelligence; but her nature was of that hot-house kind which is dependent on circumstance for its own condition—which cannot live in the cold shade of neglect and which must have the help of sympathy to live at all. Her letters echo and re-echo that one cry: "Give me sympathy;" and are penetrated through and through with the hungry longing for love. Without sympathy from many her gifts of mind were of no avail; and the love of one was essential to her very existence. As time went on adulation grew to be as essential as love; and as little as she could live without the personal companionship of a lover to minister to her needs and devote himself to her care, so little could she live without the adulation to which she had grown accustomed. Had Mr. Lewes been a different man—had he had one touch of delicacy of conscience, of sensitiveness of fibre—had he failed a hair's breadth in his resolute determination to get what he wanted, to make the best job of life possible, and to play his part like the finished actor he was—she would not have had strength of character on her side to have taken the step she did. This step however was not so momentous in her unknown days as it would have been later, when she had come to her fame. Then, in all probability, she would not have taken it at all. But when they went away to Germany together, neither she nor Mr. Lewes gave up what the world calls social position, because the one had none to give up, and the other had lost what he once had; and both gained in personal advantage by the association. He had a helpmate whose intellect and its earnings were to his good; and she had the devotion of a man whose love had in it that element of adoration and self-suppression which is dearest of all to a woman like George Eliot, at once jealous and dependent, demanding exclusive devotion and needing incessant care— but ready to give all she had in return. This power of self-suppression for the sake of a woman had been already shown in Mr. Lewes's conduct to his wife—the true history of which will never now be written. Falling in love with Marian Evans, he grew tired of the singular part he had voluntarily played for some years; and so swept the board clear. And through the twenty years of their union this self-suppression again was the main feature in this singular man's contradictory career. His own works, his own fame, his own individuality were all merged in his companion's; and his life was one long act of devotion to her and their joint interest—to making her as happy, and keeping her mind as tranquil, as her morbid temperament and frail health permitted; protecting her from every annoyance— making himself the fender to keep her free from the slightest shock or abrasion—surrounding her with a certain halo of almost sacred mystery—keeping her in a state of almost regal exclusiveness—and employing all his histrionic powers to perfecting the *mise en scène* and the attitude to be taken on the boards. This devotion was a curious interlacing of selfishness and unselfishness. He made his own account by it, both pecuniarily and socially; but it shows the lovable side of the man as well as the more ignoble. It is however pure fiction to talk of this union as an act of heroic self-sacrifice on the part of Marian Evans for the sake of redeeming a wasted life—restoring a ruined home. Whatever had gone on within the four walls of that dislocated home, had gone on with Mr. Lewes's express permission and sympathetic sanction; and the whole story was as well known to Miss Evans as to others. That sermon of eulogistic forgiveness of her own informal connection, preached on the text of this sublime self-sacrifice, which the world repeated at all street corners to the glory of George Eliot, was a sermon preached in the air. In the beginning of things the connection, which her fame exalted into an epic poem, was a very simple, natural, and commonplace arrangement between two people who loved each other and who could not marry by any law of any land. Afterwards all sorts of myths grew about the bond; and those respectabilities who crowded her drawing-room, yet did not like to countenance adultery to the world at large, did their best to salve over their consciences by pretending that there had been some kind of ceremony which sanctified and redeemed the union. They went so far as to say that the real wife was dead, that the whole affair had therefore been legalised, and that what had been at the first informal was now made straight and sure. That too was one of the fictions of the hour.

This step—this life—would have ruined any one save herself; but George Eliot, as we have said, was one of the most fortunate women on record. Everything worked for her good; and where others would have been crushed she came out with not so much as a scratch. She lived as his wife with a man whose name she bore, whose children called her mother, and whose wife, the mother of those children, was living almost within a stone's throw of her own home. Yet she wrote the most eloquent defence of marriage in our language, and vaunted its sacredness and quasi-indissolubility in terms which would have satisfied a Roman Catholic. And, living thus, she was courted by the chief and most responsible men of the time, and by the best and most straitlaced women—those who would have denied to others every kind of relief from hopeless madness say, from moral brutality, or from that dissension born of incompatibility which destroys all the sweetness of life, and takes from it all its dignity. She was unorthodox and coquetted with various forms of unchristianised philosophy; but she writes to a friend this comprehensive disclaimer which could sweep into its net an archbishop himself:

> Pray don't ever ask me again not to rob a man of his religious belief, as if you thought my mind tended to such robbery. I have too profound a conviction of the efficacy that lies in all sincere faith, and the spiritual blight that comes with no-faith, to have any negative propagandism in me. In fact, I have very little sympathy with Freethinkers as a class, and have lost all interest in mere antagonism to religious doctrines. I care only to know, if possible, the lasting meaning that lies in all religious doctrines from the beginning till now.

She kept as her friends people of the most diverse opinions and those of the most pronounced views—with which she did not openly connect herself—and she offended no one. She had no passion of conviction, no aggressive flag of faith that carried her into battle and caused her to be pilloried by her opponents. Soft in speech and manner, full of sympathy and protoplastic quality—like an amœba enveloping the mind and soul of another and drawing it out into herself—she had the most wonderful power of attracting love and keeping it. Plain in feature and singularly artificial in bearing, with what would have been in any one else an irritating slowness of speech and ponderosity of diction—a *poseuse* of colossal pretensions—she was loved by all men and passionately regarded by many. She might have changed her partner when she would, during Mr. Lewes's life-time; and if, after his death, she had not married Mr. Cross, she might have married others. Her good fortune accompanied her in her marriage as it had in her informal union. To the mere worldly reasoner on the ethics of social conduct it would seem that this marriage would have stultified her whole former career, and would have reduced again to concubinage that which, by dignity of attitude and depth of love, by the halo of success and the sanctifying touch of time, by the homage of the world and the countenance of respectability, had taken rank as a true marriage; it would seem that she would have embodied the strange paradox of making her reputation as the mistress of one man and losing it as the wife of another. It was none of all this. People condoned the want of constancy and good taste which should have kept her in perpetual widowhood—which should have made her carry on to the grave the sacredness of her first mistake—as they had already condoned that mistake and created it into a virtue. And her marriage in less than a year and a half after the death of her life's great love, with a man many years her junior, had nothing in it to her admirers of desecration nor of fatuity.

The hot-house quality of her nature as well as other temperamental characteristics was shown in that marriage, and comes out in the letters of naïve delight in her new possession. Old as she was, past sixty, she could not live without a lover, a husband. She had not strength to bear the burden of loss and loneliness, and she does not seem to have transformed into maternal affection the burning passion and wealth of love with which she was weighted. For all that, in one place she says: "The highest calling and election *is to do without opium*, and live through all our pain with conscious clear-eyed endeavour"—she could not live through hers, poor soul! but took refuge in the opiate of another love to deaden her grief for that which she had lost. And the world, which had made an epic of her informal union with Mr. Lewes, now made an idyl of her marriage with Mr. Cross.[8]

When the glamour now round her name has a little faded away—when the charm of her personal intercourse has passed into tradition and the effulgence of her fame has become dimmed and lessened by time—then George Eliot's Life and Works will take their proper place in history and literature. When no longer men, penetrated with admiration for her genius and love for her person, and eager to exalt her to the highest point of the highest kind of honour, quote Kant and the author of "Middlemarch" as equals, support Mill by her authority, and pat Spinoza on the back by her hand—then the worth of her philosophy will be more fairly judged than it can be now when the echo of those silver trumpets which so loudly proclaimed her glorious deserving still vibrates in the air. Then it will be seen and confessed that, in view of the great ethical teacher she posed for—to be accepted as she posed—in view of the weight she gave to moral responsibility and the example set by her action—her life was a contradiction; that, if her first works were mountains of light, her last were monuments of dulness; and that her philosophy, more nebulous than concrete matured no system, mastered no difficulties, and was neither distinctly constructive on the one hand nor boldly negative on the other. She is full of large-lined, eloquent sayings which have the power of touching all hearts alike. When reduced to their essence they leave nothing that we can really hold. They are protoplasm without grit or fibre—chameleons, now green and now red according to the base on which they rest. What there was of noble in her intellect and powerful in her genius will live; but the inflation of the moment will collapse, and that portion of her fame which is factitious because it was personal will die with the men who created it. Her union with Mr. Lewes will be robbed of its exaggerated assumptions of holiness and sacrifice, and will be taken for what it was worth; but the thread which ran through the web of her life's history will never be truly told—for those who know it keep silent, and those who do not know it would deny it if they were told.

Notes

1. "dessous des cartes." French. To know something of the hidden side of the cards; to have inside information.
2. References to Molière's play *Tartuffe* (1664), and to W.M. Thackeray's *Vanity Fair* (1847–48), whose protagonist Becky Sharp is both wily and charming. Robert Macaire, immortalized by the French cartoonist Daumier, is a cad. With his companion Bertrand, he manipulates the unsuspecting. The pair were originally the villains in *L'Auberge des Adrets* (1823), a melodrama by Benjamin Antier. Most likely, Lynn Linton is referring to Manon Lescaut, the protagonist of the abbé Prévost's *Manon Lescaut, Histoire du Chevalier des Grieux et du* (1731), who falls madly in love with a woman—in spite of her infidelity. Hetty Sorrel is a main character in George Eliot's *Adam Bede* (1859).
3. Tito Melma is the scheming central character in Eliot's historical novel *Romola* (1863). Mrs. Poyser is a character in Eliot's *Adam Bede* (1859).
4. Maggie Tulliver is the protagonist of Eliot's *Mill on the Floss* (1860); Dorothea Brooke and Rosamond Vincy are characters in Eliot's *Middlemarch* (1871–2); Silas Marner is the protagonist of Eliot's novel of the same name (1861); Edie Ochiltree is a character in Sir Walter Scott's *The Antiquary* (1816); Meg Merrilees (Merriles) is a character from Scott's *Guy Mannering* (1815); Mause Headrigg is a character from Scott's *Old Mortality* (1816); Dominie Sampson is a character from Scott's *Guy Mannering*; Bailie Nicol Jarvie is a character from Scott's *Rob Roy* (1818).
5. Quixotic, from Cervante's *Don Quixote* (1615), refers to one who is highly idealistic and impulsive; Shandean, from Sterne's *Tristam Shandy*, is derived from "Shandy," meaning half-crazy or crack-brained;

Pantagruelistic, from F. Rabelais's *Pantagruel* (1532 or 1533), refers to one of giant proportions, one who parades exuberance; Mephistophilean, from Goethe's *Faust,* pertains to cruel, diabolical behavior; Pecksniffian, from Dickens's *Martin   Chuzzlewit* (1844), refers to one who is hypocritical.

6.   Literally translated as "by revenge" in French.

7.   John Blackwood was George Eliot's publisher.

8.   Eliot had lived for years in an adulterous relationship with George Lewes. After he died, Eliot married a much younger man, John Cross. Lynn Linton always resented Eliot's acceptance by the same society which spurned Lynn Linton after she separated from her husband.

17. Nearing the Rapids

Introduction

Eliza Lynn Linton's "Nearing the Rapids" appeared in March, 1894, in the *New Review*, and is reprinted here from that periodical. Published the same year that the Local Government Act guaranteed local franchise to married women, and the year that women were for the first time placed on a Royal Commission for Secondary Education, this essay bemoans such measures as marking the beginning of England's decline. Drawing from Thomas Carlyle's essay, "Shooting Niagara and After?" (1867), which protested the passing of the Second Reform Bill, Lynn Linton argues that traditional England is "nearing the rapids" as women's rights activists achieve suffrage and success in politics. In the article's conclusion, Lynn Linton conflates women's initiation into politics with the loss of the "real womanly ideal." In contrast to her more ambiguous opinions on women and divorce or women and education, Lynn Linton was always vehemently opposed to women becoming involved in politics.

Nearing the Rapids

Those rash pilots, the Woman's Rights men and women, bent on shooting Niagara and wrecking the old-time womanly ideal, have come appreciably nearer their object. A seat in the County Council is a good stretch onward to a vote in the House of Commons; and even illogical England cannot deny the conclusions of its own premises. It seems now as if it has to come—the warnings of common-sense notwithstanding; for even the House of Lords, which has protected us from certain other dangers, is not sound on this point, and the Conservatives, who have saved the Union, cannot be depended on to save the home, society, and our national dignity.[1]

Many reasons make the admission of women into the region of active politics a national danger and a national disgrace. As things are, by the mere fact of sex and its functions, women have already an overwhelming influence over men. As mothers they build up the body and give the first impress to the mind of the child. What they are in health and morality, reacts on the health and morality of their offspring; and the rule of the nursery by its food, its teaching, its governance, lays the foundations of a man's wholesome physique or unserviceable nerves. As the first love of the adolescent they set the pattern of the womanly ideal. As the first mistress they make or mar a man's life, and shape his very soul for good or evil. As the wife they are for the most part the supreme authority in the home where the husband is only the paying lodger—tyrants or benevolent despots as their character determines, but always despots on whom mainly depends the happiness or the unhappiness of the marriage, the comfort or distress of the household. As the queens of society they fashion the manners and decide the standard of morality of that society, and from the cut of a sleeve to the subjects permitted to be discussed at the five o'clock tea—from the amount of countenance given to vice to the conventional shibboleth and the conventional gesture—they and they alone are responsible. Everywhere their power is felt; everywhere their sex is predominant. What they disallow cannot exist; and the most influential statesman, the bravest soldier, is a mere cipher where "tone" is concerned. To add to this tremendous influence already existing, the direct power of a preponderating vote will be to shift the balance entirely to the feminine side;—which will surely be a disadvantage to the nation at large.

Hitherto we have been one of the most masculine people in Europe, as masculine as were ever the old Romans; free from hysterics, from the histrionic element, from vapourings, from silly vanities. When the rule of woman has begun, and the men have to tail off behind the petticoat, we shall be more French than the French themselves, with irresponsible empresses pressing on disastrous wars, and peripatetic Louise Michels advocating loot and insurrection.

There is a certain class of women whom the Liberals, the originators of the Woman's Rights movement, will not suffer to be registered nor segregated. Many of the more prosperous of these live in lodgings of a quiet and quasi-respectable character, and if they are sober, relatively well-conducted, and careful of appearances, their holding is not disturbed, though their calling is known. These women will be eligible for the lodger franchise; and this will be the first and only instance known to modern Christianity, or, so far as I know, to any form of civilised heathendom, where the politics and government of a country will be directly influenced by its public prostitutes. Less revolting than this, but in its own way as humiliating, will be the voting power of that large class of futile spinsters and widows, rife in country towns—women who have not one single idea in their heads save what they pick up in crumbs from the curate and the paid missionary—women whose view of the universe is bounded by their own local gossip—who believe in ghosts and the sea-serpent, and swallow all they hear without the smallest pinch of salted scepticism. These women, and the still lower stratum of rated rent-paying village shopkeepers and charwomen, will have votes whereby the maintenance of our naval power, or the destruction of our Imperial prestige, will be determined. We have on the register already a crowd of unfit electors. Why add another and yet larger crowd still more unfit? What good will it do us to pile the Pelion of weak and silly womanhood on the Ossa of rough and ignorant manhood? How much nearer shall we be to the perfection of good government when folly wriggles where brutality shoulders, and neither folly nor brutality understands the merits of the principles each undertakes to destroy or to establish? When people talk of the woman's vote, they think only of the educated landed proprietor—the keen-witted widow left in charge of grave interests; and they contrast these unenfranchised Cornelias with their half-educated gardeners, their drunken tenantry, their ignorant coachmen and butlers, and think what a monstrous miscarriage of justice this inequality is!

They do not remember the fringe of upper-class prostitutes; the serried mass of foolish, futile little shopkeepers and the like in small country towns; the spinsters who know absolutely nothing of men or life or human nature anyhow; the widows who judge the whole world according to the pattern of the late-lamented, than whom was never a better man born, or the undesired well rid of. Even men who have taken their stand on the question, have let themselves be swayed solely by the vision of the unenfranchised lady of education and sense of responsibility, and have not seen that, through the same opened door as allows her to enter into the world of active and influential politics, will troop the world of the backboneless, the ignorant, the impulsive, and the immoral, all eligible for a turn at the scales wherein the safety and the dignity of the empire are balanced against private fads and ineffectual voters.

This movement among women, like so much else, is due to the new conditions of society and domestic economy, whereby restlessness has been created and the home occupations which once absorbed the sex have been superseded by general and special providers. In the days when things were done at home which now are brought in from the outside, the lives of women were filled to the brim with duties which few were shameless enough to neglect. The very term of good housewife was contrasted with that of slut, slattern, Dorothy Dolittle, and what not; and well-born ladies themselves, like Mrs. Delaney and her compeers, found their honour in the perfect management of their households and the fine apportionment of expenditure. Now, however, with everything done out of the home, the time once occupied within the four walls is left vacant and disused, and Satan vindicates his old claim to be considered the most indefatigable taskmaster we have.

With this loss of domestic duties and the cessation of domestic activities the home naturally becomes monotonous, and the girls refuse to stay in it if they can in any way escape, while the married women delegate their dwindled duties to the servants, and stream out to the club and the shops, their friends and the office, for the excitement home cannot afford them. Anything for a change! If familiarity breeds contempt, sameness creates satiety; and a change from even good to bad is preferable to an unbroken round of good.

This dislike of monotony and consequent feverish desire for novelty, lie at the root of much in this new Woman's Movement. It is not that the thing desired is in any way better than the thing rejected;

but it is different. A woman will gladly enter a chemist's shop and find her pleasure in manipulating evil-smelling drugs for less wages than a servant at home costs her; but she will despise cooking and bread-baking and the saving of that extra servant by her own labour. In manufacturing towns the married women who are "hands" spend more on a caretaker to look after their children in their absence, than they earn in the factory. But the factory is eagerly sought after and the home is deserted. So, women will endure the hardships of an African expedition, and run the dangers of tiger-shooting and buffalo-hunting, who shudder at the risks of childbearing, and hold the apportionment of dangers made by nature herself as the last expression of injustice.

As to this apportionment of work, duties, dangers, the women who cry out the loudest against things as they are, cry out in two languages. On the one side they fall foul of the work that falls to the lot of the sex, the housekeeping, the childbearing and subsequent care of the children, without which life could not go on at all, nor society hold together. On the other, they demand to share in all the occupations and pursuits of men, and hold the barriers which would keep them from pushing those men from their stools as iniquitous. One gets up and complains of the hardships endured by domestic servants, and how the poor, frail, nervous sisterhood in cap and apron merits active pity and slacker thongs. Another shrieks for leave to compete with men, even in the barrack-yard and on the cross-trees if she wishes; and when amiable philanthropists banish her from the pits where men work nearly naked, and the presence of the sex creates a very pandemonium tenanted by more demons than one, she howls to the world at large, and calls the very gods to witness to her wrongs. So that really, between sobs over the magnitude of the work they have to do, and shrieks over that, much bigger and harder, which they demand to do, the sane and quiet bystander is somewhat puzzled to know what the malcontents would be at and where the shoe really pinches.

When they get the vote, however, all this will be rectified, and the Utopia promised so far back as the days of Aristophanes will be a living fact. When they get the vote! Does any one ever think of the absurd anomaly involved in this gift of supremacy to the sex, which among its own members denies the simplest right of personal freedom—when it can? Mind! I do not say that the house-mistress is wrong in keeping a strict hand over her maids; but we must remember that in the person of her mature servants she has potential electors whose votes would go towards determining the destinies of the empire, were they not in service; but being just the same creatures they are now, were paying rates, rent, and taxes. And these women she does not think capable of taking care of themselves after ten o'clock at night. These same potential voters, whose views on peace or war, the budget, bi-metallism, our Indian Empire, our Colonies, Ireland, free trade, and the like, would be of so much and so much weight, may not have their young men to see them, and may not have young men at all in anything like evidence, and are supposed to be kept straight only by leading-strings. Side by side with this view runs that other, so fashionable with some, which makes the virtue of a woman not her own affair so much as man's, and holds her to be not responsible for her own fall so much as is the man. She may influence Imperial politics, but that one precious possession which all ages have agreed to give into her own keeping, with punishment to her primarily and chiefly when she loses it, is now handed over to men, and they are in fault while she is exonerated. And no one has the courage to say that more men, ten times over, are ruined by women than there are women ruined by men. The flabby philanthropists who vapour about the "poor dear harlots" of the streets, and call them temples of the Holy Ghost, soiled doves, and the like, never think of the young boys who are ruined for life by some specious, smiling vampire—the weak and passionate men who go down to the grave dishonoured, destroyed by some splendid harpy who, for their mad love gave cruel calculation—for their sincerity, blind, fatuous, suicidal as it might have been, gave falsehood as deep as hell and treachery as infamous as that Judas' kiss in the Garden. All the sympathy of pitiful hearts goes out to the lost woman—none is kept for the ruined man. And the only piece of legislation directly traceable to woman's influence is one which confirms and protects the power of these lost women to destroy for all time innocent boys and youths built up of ordinary flesh and blood, and imbued with ordinary masculine instincts.[2]

By nature, education, and function, women are both interfering and arbitrary. Almost all are penetrated with the desire to set things and people to rights. What they are not in themselves they will not allow others to be, if they can in any way prevent it; and to pluck brands from the burning, reclaim sinners, and reduce the whole world to their own pattern, rank as virtues with the average woman who does not understand her own instincts. From the afternoon costume of a maid servant to the routing out of the Hindu Zenana, and the public "discovery" of the purdah woman, the sex, which hates monotony in its individual person, demands uniformity from others. Where they can, they clip the men's lives into as near a likeness to their own as they can manage. Where they cannot, they copy the thing which else they would have forbidden. In America they raid an obnoxious ginshop—in England they walk with the guns and shoot big game in Africa, smoke in public carriages and dress so like their brothers as to be undistinguishable from the waist upwards. When we have added the perilous arm of political power to the restless love of interference—or, failing this, of assimilation to the stronger sex, which now characterises the weaker—we shall pass under a despotism greater than any the world has ever seen since old Egypt gave the reins to women, and she transferred them to the priesthood. For how tyrannical women are we can see for ourselves any day in the week. See them as paid housekeepers, or matrons, or upper servants, as commanders in any class of life, and their tyranny is infinitely greater than that of men over one another. This is explicable enough. Men have muscles, and an obnoxious "boss" can be knocked down and kicked. Women have only nails; and do not often use them. But whatever the explanation, the fact remains the same—women use authority more unscrupulously than men, and the spindle lies heavier than the spear. The modern craze for dispossessing men in favour of women is among those ideas which, like the primeval tortoise, stand on nothing. It is a vicious circle, and the evil of the whole thing increases with use. The more women are employed where men used to be the sole wage-earners, the fewer marriages there will be, and the yet more and more number of women will be left unprovided for. Women work for less than men, and undercut wages all round. Their employment necessitates the exodus of the stronger sex; and so the vicious circle goes, ever increasing in evil consequences to society. And the worst of it all is, it is not only the necessitous women who leave home and seek employment, for which they will take just as little remuneration as will keep body and soul together—well-endowed women are eager to do work for any or no payment, simply for the sake of occupation; or if they stand out for the market-value of their services, they literally take the bread out of the mouths of their hungry sisters, and in either case they add to the congestion of the already-overstocked labour market. It is a pitiful sight! Women of wealth and standing lay aside their inherited pride, their dignity, their delicacy, and come down among the coarse throngs of the market-place, eager to jostle, callous to insult, and hardened against the natural promptings of female shame and delicacy. They will not see the degradation of this competition with their poorer sisters as they will not see the folly of their unequal competition with men. That œstrum of unrest—the very tsetse fly of modern life—has stung them, and anywhere, anywhere out in the world, and out of the home!

And what is the truth in this competition with men? As a race women are not equal to men in strength, in endurance, in ability to accept responsibility, in staying power. The strongest woman is not equal to the strongest man; the most neurotic and hysterical man is not so neurotic and hysterical as his congenital sister. Of course a strong and purposeful woman beats an effeminate man—is far and away ahead of him in all things, mental and physical; but range the sexes according to degree, and the men are relatively superior to the women. All parallels are in favour of the greater strength of men; but the advocates of the new movement contrast an Amazonian woman with a miserable abortive little mannikin, and then say, "Ha! ha! who is the strongest here?" This is the kind of logic that holds good with the multitude, and the demurrers are assailed with full-flavoured epithets less nice than suggestive.

With the new school of thought, and the new class of woman it has bred, we have lost both the grace and the sweetness—both the delicacy and the virtues—of the real womanly ideal. The manners of the day are coarser, rougher, more unbraced than they used to be when girls were kept nearer to their mothers, and their mothers themselves bided more at home and held a stricter rule than they do now. Think of the advice to his daughters given by the Knight of Landry!—think of Ischomachus and his young wife!—nay, even of that reproach in the last century made against the mothers who, "instead of the bashful posture of stooping and hanging down the head, taught their daughters the comparative boldness of tossing and bridling!" As if we would submit to those effete coquetries of tossing and bridling, we who hail our young men as "chappies" and "Johnnies," and who find Dodo the exact representative of a certain class of girls, as, indeed, she is. That sweet and subtle quality of maidenly modesty, which used to be one of the most marked characteristics of English girls; that delicate innocence and ignorance of evil, has gone by the board; and, though less hoydenish, our modern young ladies of the new school are not a whit

more delicate than was "Miss." Yet, God be thanked! we have still
some left who are as lovely and pure as the most careful guardian of the
old time womanly ideal would have them—girls and women who are
not ashamed of the virtues belonging to that old-time ideal—the virtues
which Paul taught and Jesus loved,—nor averse from the old-time
restrictions with which these special virtues were bound up. But, alas!
with these, the sweet and trusty Loyalists, we have crowds and crowds
of those others for whom shame, restriction, modesty, and specialised
qualities of sex do not exist, and are despised in the very roll-call.
Submission? patience? forbearance? self-sacrifice? Faugh! where is the
translated squaw who will advocate these? The virile woman shoulders
the fast girl, and the contrast is displeasing on both sides alike. On the
top of omnibuses, down the river, in the stubble-field, and in the
smoking-room, wherever men go, there go too these loud-voiced, Wild
Women with their slang and petty oaths, their bold eyes, swinging gait,
and doubtful conversation. And the favourite boast among them is that
they are no longer the complements but the rivals, the equals, the
superiors of man. And women, mothers themselves, advocate even
wider licence still, and the key of all fields free of the restraint of
chaperonage. The one grand distinction between carefully brought-up
lady-girls, and the wastrels of the streets and lanes—their ignorance of
certain things while young and inexperienced—their unsullied purity of
mind—this distinction it is now seriously proposed to destroy; and the
premature initiation of young unmarried women into the knowledge of
the mysteries as of the vices of life, is one of the clauses in the charter
of the New Revolt. It is said this knowledge will preserve the girls
from harm. Do we find this so with the servant and peasant class who
know all things from the age of twelve onwards?

   All this is disastrous to the nation on every side. What society
wants in its women is a race of beings to supplement the shortcomings
of the men, each sex being the complement of the other. What the
nation wants is a race of women primarily fitted to be good mothers.
The wealth of a country is its population; and the finer and healthier the
children of to-day, the stronger and nobler will be the men of to-morrow
and the grander the destinies of the empire. Whether the new woman,
with her unhomed habits and manly ambitions, her overtaxing Higher
Education and that deadly spirit of rivalry to men can fulfil either of
these great duties of her sex, as hitherto they have been fulfilled,
remains to be seen. Many things are hidden in the closed hand of Time,

many questions lie unanswered on the knees of the gods. The ultimate and practical outcome of this mad desire to shoot Niagara and try conclusions with the whirlpool at the end of the fall, is one of them. And whether the modern woman can travesty Nature, upset all old-established distinctions and come out of the flurry with safety to herself and good to the race at large is as yet a problem to which Œdipus himself would have no answer, nor through the difficulties of which could the Master Thief find safe issue.

Notes

1.   Lynn Linton is alluding to the Conservatives' defeat of an Ireland Home Rule bill, which came before Parliament in 1893.
2.   Most likely, Linton is referring to the repeal of the Contagious Diseases Acts in 1886. Prostitutes could no longer be forcibly examined for venereal disease.

VII. Margaret Oliphant
(1828–1897)

Noted primarily for her successes as a novelist and biographer, Margaret Oliphant was also an astonishingly prolific critic and essayist who wrote for some of the most widely read and highly regarded literary periodicals of the Victorian age, including the *Edinburgh Review*, *Macmillan's*, *Fraser's*, and especially *Blackwood's Edinburgh Magazine* (*Maga*). Oliphant's essays and reviews frequently present conservative social and literary opinions. While she personally supported many progressive ideas, including women's voting and property rights, Oliphant generally did not use her professional position to advocate political changes on behalf of women. Her literary criticism was similarly conservative: she remained committed to the ideal of domestic realism evident in her own fiction, and against such innovations as sensation and modernism. Because of her long association with *Maga*, she wielded much influence as a critic, an influence that evoked both resistance and admiration. Henry James complained of her, "I should almost suppose in fact that no woman had ever, for half a century, had a personal 'say' so publicly and irresponsibly"; while her publisher William Blackwood declared, "Mrs. Oliphant has been to the England of letters what the Queen has been to society as a whole."

Margaret Oliphant Wilson, born in Wallyford, Scotland, on April 4, 1828, was the daughter of Margaret Oliphant and Francis Wilson. She grew up in northern England. Educated largely at home, she began writing in her teens to occupy herself by her mother's sickbed. Her first novel, *Margaret Maitland*, was published in 1849, and the £150 she received was a significant addition to her family's income; her father, a clerk, had difficulty maintaining the family, which included an alcoholic older brother. In 1852, Margaret married her cousin Francis (Frank) Oliphant, a stained glass designer whose death in 1859 left her stranded in Italy with small children and encumbered with debt. From that point on, she wrote constantly to support herself, her children, and eventually her brothers and one brother's family as well. Oliphant wrote over ninety novels, including her best-known series, the Chronicles of Carlingford; nearly thirty nonfiction books, including *Historical Sketches of the Reign of George Second* (2 vols., 1869) and *The Literary History of England* (3 vols., 1882), and scores of essays and articles. Her half-century career culminated in her powerful *Autobiography*, published posthumously in 1898.

Oliphant was ambiguous about her literary life. Despite being surrounded by men who failed to meet societal expectations and provide for their families, Oliphant seems initially to have remained invested in the notion of separate spheres. In her *Autobiography*, she emphasizes that she had "no particular purpose"—no vocation—when she began writing, and that any effort to remove herself from daily responsibilities—the "(feminine) life of the house"—would have made her work "unnatural," both in her own eyes and in those of the people around her. Yet she was proud of supporting her family, and wondered how being kept "in a mental greenhouse" like George Eliot might have fostered her own art. In the 1850s she began her reviewing career somewhat tentatively, glad that anonymous publishing practices concealed her age and sex. Her desire not to be seen as an "unnatural" woman seems to have undermined her business sense, so that despite the volume of work she produced—especially for Blackwood's—she wrote virtually everything on speculation and relied on personal relations to ensure further employment. However, as she gained greater experience and her family responsibilities lessened, Oliphant became much more confident and self-assertive in her professional life. After her quarter-century anniversary with Blackwood's, she pressed for a more businesslike arrangement with the firm, and from 1886 on, she wrote commissioned columns; "The Old Saloon" (1887–1892) featured literary reviews, and "The Looker-On" (1894–1896) featured social commentary.

Despite the volume and overall quality of her work, Oliphant's reviews and essays have seldom appeared in critical anthologies. This is certainly due in part to the self-deprecating persona she presents in the original edition of her *Autobiography*, until recently the only edition available. Through well-intentioned but misguided editing, Oliphant was depicted as writing merely out of necessity and with no particular talent; readers as insightful as Virginia Woolf and Elaine Showalter accepted Oliphant's word that she was a failure. Oliphant's reputation also has not been helped by her perceived conservatism: feminist scholars have been slower to recover women authors who seem to be antifeminist. Furthermore, contemporary responses to her critical work were mixed. George Augustus Sala accused her of forgetting that "novels are written for grown people and not for babes and sucklings" and referred to one of her *Maga* reviews as representative of the "cant of modern criticism"; Thomas Hardy, complaining of her review of *Jude the Obscure*, denounced her as "propriety and primness incarnate." Yet, the sharpness of these responses suggests how deeply her critical pronouncements were felt. Responses to her fiction were less divided: *Englishwoman's Review* editor Helen Blackburn included her in a list of notable women authors, and she was reported to be Queen Victoria's favorite novelist. Recent scholars have urged a reconsideration of both Oliphant's fiction and her criticism. Certainly her central role in one of the major publishing firms of the period and the consequent wide circulation of her judgments on literature, history, and contemporary society merit greater critical examination.

Oliphant's critical essays vary widely in subject matter. Ones that may be of interest to readers of this volume include the following: "The Condition of Women" (1858), "Sensation Novels" (1862), "Novels" (1867), her "Century of Great Poets" series (1871–1873), and "'Tis Sixty Years Since" (1897), all in *Maga*; and "The Grievances of Women" (1880) in *Fraser's*. The classic Oliphant biography is Vineta and Robert Colby's *The Equivocal Virtue: Mrs. Oliphant and the Victorian Literary Market Place* (1966). Merryn Williams's *Margaret Oliphant: A Critical Biography* (1986) updates and augments the earlier work; an especially helpful addition is Williams's exhaustive bibliography. The 1899 *Autobiography and Letters* is still a valuable resource for Oliphant's correspondence, but readers should be sure to consult Elisabeth Jay's "Complete Text" edition of the *Autobiography* (1990), which restores both deleted passages and the original structure of the text. Recent reappraisals of Oliphant include Joseph H. O'Mealy's study of *Miss Marjoribanks* in *Victorian Newsletter* (1992), and examinations of her criticism by J. Haythornthwaite (*Publishing History*, 1990) and D.J. Trela (*George Eliot-George Henry*

Lewes Studies, 1993). Oliphant is also the focus of a volume edited by Trela entitled *Margaret Oliphant: Critical Essays on a Gentle Subversive* (1995), which brings together many essays on Oliphant's fiction and social and literary criticism.

Solveig Robinson,
University of Puget Sound

18. The Literature of the Last Fifty Years

Introduction

Margaret Oliphant's "The Literature of the Last Fifty Years" appeared in *Blackwood's Magazine* in June, 1887, and is reprinted here from that periodical. Inspired by Queen Victoria's Golden Jubilee, Oliphant evaluates in this article the art and influence of numerous individuals working in a variety of genres, and considers which of her contemporaries will stand the test of time. Oliphant's canon, like the canons of other Victorian critics grappling with the same sense of the moment, includes many of the expected names: poets Tennyson and Robert and Elizabeth Barrett Browning, historians Macaulay and Carlyle, philosophers Mill and Spencer, scientists Darwin and Huxley, and novelists Dickens, Thackeray, and Eliot. But her essay also mentions many less familiar names. In justifying which writers deserve to be listed among those "who will hereafter be known in universal history as of the age of Victoria," Oliphant reveals her critical conservatism, as well as her concern for how writers and readers connect.

"The Literature of the Last Fifty Years" was written late in Oliphant's career and appeared in her "Old Saloon" series; it reveals her most mature and self-confident critical voice. Despite some nostalgia for the standards of the early years of Victoria's reign, Oliphant nevertheless celebrates the progress of her age, including the fact that for the first time at least two women (Eliot and Barrett Browning) have achieved the "highest place in literature."

The Literature of the Last Fifty Years

It is in the nature of human things that the ear should grow weary of hearing, and the mind of following the thousand devices and schemes, the rhapsodies and the commonplaces, the designs of self-glorification hidden under a cloak of loyalty, with which this year has resounded, and which, in this particular month, will make the welkin ring. The object of all these honours, could we penetrate the depths of the august solitude in which the Majesty of England dwells, will no doubt be more glad than any one to hear the last of the Jubilee. But at the same time there is something picturesque and striking in every such climax of national life. We pause, by natural impulse, at the milestones of the uncommemorated years as we pass them by, making our little personal record of events and changes—sometimes of revolutions unknown to fame, which alter the currents of our lives—sometimes of nothing more important than that chronicle of small beer, which fortunately is commoner than the revolutions; but even in the placid tenor of a private existence, the golden, nay, even the silver wedding, is a moment at which a general review of life is the most natural occupation of the mind. Rare are the individuals to whose lot it falls to celebrate the greatest of these anniversaries. When such an occurrence happens, the man, however insignificant his position, is a living chronicle. Though he may have taken a notable part in none of them, he has at least seen a hundred changes, some which make epochs, all making history. He has seen the great shuttle moving through the loom of time. And if he has a mind to think or a voice to speak, what a crowd of incidents, what wonderful developments, what secrets new and old, are his to tell! The fifty years that are now accomplished are to us more impersonal. The great Lady who was, so to speak, the Bride of fifty years ago, having begun her reign in such early bloom of youth, is fortunately scarcely yet to be called old, though experienced in her august profession beyond all competitors, and learned in the course of events and all the hidden strings and mechanism of State which sway the world, as perhaps only a sovereign, who is never out of office, can be. But with that great sphere we have no pretension to intermeddle. For all so great as Queen Victoria is, and for all so splendid as is her kingdom, did there happen to fail in her realm one little implement called a pen, the glory and the greatness would be dim to future ages, and our grandsons who come after us would but guess faintly at our strength and power, and of our familiar features, and our human ways, and how we succeeded to our fathers, as they to us, would know nothing. The character of the great, the meaning of the humble, the vesture and costume of humanity, and all its records of the heart, depend absolutely upon that little implement. In the past ages the man who stands up like a mountain, or shines like a light across the plains of oblivion, is the man who has had a historian worthy of him. The annalists, the minstrels, the story-tellers, are to the past what the sovereign is to the present—the fountain of honour. Without these there is no memorial. Without their successors in the modern world, there would, beyond the limit of a generation, and often not even in that, be little mental appreciation and no fame.

It would be curious to inquire how the succeeding age would make out to itself an image of this without the help of literature. How profoundly puzzled it would be with many things upon which at present we rather plume ourselves! No doubt the next century will be so much superior to ourselves in all the inventions of practical science, that our attempts at railways, telegraphs, &c., will amuse it as rudimentary efforts. It will perhaps wonder, while recognising the energy of life which found expression in this network of intercommunication, how grown men should be so infantile in their adaptation of half-developed forces, and how it was that the human intellect so much vaunted should not have leaped at once to the extended use of these forces, which, mounted on our shoulders and seeing over our heads, has become easy to them. They will contemplate, we hope with admiration, certainly with wonder, our magnificent Houses of Parliament and Courts of Law, grand buildings in which to lodge the makers of our laws and the administrators thereof, so majestic, so splendid[1]—yet without the faintest stirring of an individual impulse, art whimsically *aux prises*[2] with science, and knocking its head in blind obedience to the rules of the past against the necessities of the present, the comforts, only half understood as our impertinent descendants will think, imperiously demanded by an advancing civilisation. All these things our successors would have to puzzle out with much confusion, with much merry-making, probably, over an age which thought itself so wise and was so fatuous. And how strangely then would loom through the distance the great figures, growing dim and shadowy among the mists, indistinct, as of that woman clothed with the sun in the Revelations stretching out maternal arms, the sceptre of mercy, the orb of justice over half a world—or of that dim-eyed old magician who is the favourite of all folk-lore, whose spells go so far to wreck the nations. And all this for want of the literary person whose office is but lightly thought of by the generations, though it is he only who has made them known and comprehensible to each other from the beginning of time.

At the end of this long vista of fifty years, it will not be inappropriate to place before the reader a brief survey of those writers who will hereafter be known in universal history as of the age of Victoria. It is pleasant, and gives occasion to a graceful nomenclature, that so many of the greatest periods in our literary history should coincide with the reigns of female sovereigns. It is not, we fear, because these royal ladies have specially patronised the arts. The age of Anne was the one in which men of letters were most in the way of promotion; but that was not from the patronage of the Queen, or perhaps from any other reason but the natural fitness of things—the statesmen of the period specially requiring aid, and the literary men of the period being, as it happened, capable of giving it in a marked and remarkable way. In our time no ode of Lord Tennyson or any other poet would be at all likely to affect the country as Addison's "Campaign" did;[3] though Addison, in comparison with Lord Tennyson, is not to be named as a poet, and his work was turgid and artificial, held aloft only by the power of two or three fine lines. Even in that time, however, except that Addison was made an (indifferent) Secretary of State, and Prior an (insignificant) ambassador,[4] the general mass of literary workers had no distinction (except the pillory now and then) any more than they have now. Grub Street was a place of evil fame even when Johnson was autocrat, and had the privilege of being rude to the finest people in London. And though literature has now become highly respectable, it has not come any nearer to those honours and rewards which show the public gratitude for public services. We do not for our part see why there might not be a bit of ribbon, a cross of honour, for the literary man if he would like it (and no doubt he would like it), in the distributions of distinctions which will abound during this year. As it is, all that Great Britain ever awards to her instructors in literature is a pension on the Civil List, which some people consider as rather a concession to poverty than a title of honour. Lord Tennyson's peerage, to be sure, is a great exception: but peerages are prodigious prizes and a little alarming. Should her Majesty be disposed to admit her faithful servants of the year into the ranks of the Rewarded, we should with humility suggest a much milder decoration. As we do not, however, delude ourselves with the hope that our advice will be asked in the matter, we may take comfort on the other hand in the fact that the absence of such acknowledgments has never at any period done our robust literature any harm.

And we may add with all modesty that we do not think we need fear for the Victorian age in literature in comparison with most of its predecessors. Within her Majesty's reign is contained the beginning and the end of much great literary work. We do not purpose to enter here into any discussion of the crowd of living authors whose place has not yet been ascertained by that calmer judgment which only comes when work is ended. Yet it would be impossible to review the literature of Queen Victoria's reign without referring to the two poets, still happily spared to us, who are its glory and its pride. We will avow, to begin with, a bold opinion. With every hope and prayer that Lord Tennyson and Mr Browning may live and enjoy life till they have reached the utmost possible bounds of living, we should support by all means in our power a Bill in Parliament which should ordain to those two poets silence—for the remainder of their honoured days. Is it with this intention, we wonder, that so many poets, according to the wise regulations of Providence, have died young? that no bondage of repetition, no horrible compulsion of the expected, should wring from their lips songs no longer voluntary, utterances not demanded by nature, the result of a conventional necessity or of the mistaken desire to keep a place which requires from them no such effort? We are at liberty, at all events, to consider Tennyson and Browning as men who have accomplished their day's work, and to whom it is both permitted and desirable that they should repose upon their laurels. When the Queen came to the throne fifty years ago, Alfred Tennyson was the youngest of the singers who had from the beginning of the century abounded in the land. To come after one of the greatest waves of poetical inspiration which England has ever known, while the music of Shelley's exquisite verse still lingered in the nation's ear, and Byron all aglow with fire and eloquence had left the flush of an early sunset still on all the hills— while Wordsworth still stood like a mountain-peak unimpaired by years, though silent like that same mountain, and apt to quench lesser lights in his great shadow—was a terrible ordeal for a young poet; besides that, in the natural sequences of time, a pause has generally followed at the close of a great poetical epoch, giving time for the general public, not able for too much stimulation in this way, to draw breath. Notwithstanding all that was thus against him, there are many of the poems in the first collection of verses published by young Tennyson more than fifty years ago which remain among those which are now universally acknowledged as his finest utterances. Nothing in the "Idylls of the King" is more beautiful than the poem which now occupies its fit place among them, and in which the first suggestion of that noble series is contained, the "Morte d'Arthur." Its new and strange music, conveying an accent of its own—a cadence unaccustomed, fine, pensive, penetrating—startled at first the general ear, and added to the force of that natural resistance with which we all make a stand against every new pretender to the rank of poet. But that opposition was factitious and short-lived: and Tennyson's first publication forms an admirable and unmistakable foundation for his fame. He has perhaps never done anything finer in the profounder intellectual regions of poetry than the "Two Voices," nothing more vivid and splendid in its power of vision than the "Dream of Fair Women."[5] His after-work has developed during the progress of these years into as noble and as pure a collection of poetry, we make bold to say, as belongs to any English name. Comparisons with Shakespeare are absurd. There is but one of that name, and there is nothing that is Shakespearian in Tennyson. Comparisons with Milton, also, are to a great extent out of the question. Other poets may emulate his music, but no one has reached that fine diapason of sound, those organ-notes which at their lightest have something of the sacred in them. Our Laureate does not touch so large or so solemn a scale. He gathers up rather from an older original the tale that is dear to English ears. The "very parfitt gentil knyghte," the young squire who was "as fresche as are the flouris in Maye,"[6] come back to us with a difference out of that pilgrimage which our poet would never have drawn so broadly or with such variety and human tolerance, yet in which he might have ridden with Chaucer among the gentle people at the front, marking with luminous eyes their antique courteous fashions, and gliding unawares, though with so many modern thoughts, into the place of him

> Who left half told
> The story of Cambuscan bold.[7]

The modern thoughts come strangely in, yet add a not discordant note. Perhaps they go a trifle too far when they come to the flippant maiden of one of the later idyls, with her much-quoted impertinent little nose, "tiptilted like the petal of a flower," the *minois chiffonné* of a French *soubrette*, rather than the piquant irregularity of feature which belongs to an English girl.[8] It is perhaps, however, this touch of modern delicacy of thought in Lancelot which has made him so completely the ideal knight of our modern imagination. He muses, as his original would not have mused, without the passion which carried that paladin astray, with a sobered and tragic faithfulness which Chaucer's audience would have failed to appreciate, but which has touched the very heart of the Victorian age. His grave superiority to all blandishments and delusions, his love which has been subdued into a great, all-pardoning, all-enduring fidelity, the mournful force of that faith unfaithful which has kept him falsely true, are neither medieval nor legendary; they are of the nineteenth century, belonging to a being whose reason has got the upper hand of passion, whose imagination is under subjection to his love, not in the way of picturing its charms and raptures, but of representing the impossibility of an end to such a bond, the supreme necessity of constancy. It is the Lancelot of middle age, the knight who has outgrown illusion—a character in which the highest spiritual nobleness and devotion develops out of hasty passion and guilt. No such knight ever sat at the Round Table, we may be sure; and it is possible, if a profane impulse seized the critic, to imagine Queen Guinevere, a passionate Celtic princess, to have fiercely resented the philosophy of the thoughtful lover. But with his modern heart in his mail-clad bosom, what image more noble has this century produced than that of Lancelot? It may be a little dangerous in morals to suggest that he never could have been so perfect a knight had he not been a great sinner to begin with; but that is quite irrelevant to the question.

Lord Tennyson has made one other supreme addition to poetry, which even in this brief summary must be noted. "In Memoriam" came to the world with all the tenderest prejudices of the generation in its favour; but its effect at first was not perhaps what might be thought. There were (and are) in fact harsh verses in it, break-jaw passages about fixing the limits of knowledge, about nature, red in tooth and claw, and other matters as little poetical. And the critics objected that sorrow does not speak in so long a strain nor with such breaks of philosophy and argument and such pauses for discussion, in all of which objections there was a certain truth. But, notwithstanding, "In Memoriam" has grown into the popular heart. We can find nothing in the language to place beside it. "Lycidas" and "Adonaïs" are elegies,[9] lamentations over the dead made glorious by his ending, whose going away has filled the earth with sorrow, whose disappearance is as the failing of the sun from the day or the heavenly stars from the night. But Tennyson's inspiration is a different one. It is the reverie of a bereaved and stricken soul, which he puts into a music most tender, most melancholy, the very voice of that grief which cannot exhaust itself in any passion or storm of mourning, but which is the chief occupation, the prevailing sentiment of the mind. The soft cadences of the verse wander from earth to heaven, from heaven to earth, like the wild and wandering thoughts which have one centre to which they always return. Sick fancies come and go, and now the mind will follow one suggestion, now another, interrogating the spheres, questioning with itself, soaring like a bird almost out of sight of its trouble, dropping down again low to the grasses of the grave, always returning to the one predominant memory, the loss which never can be forgotten, the pang that will not be stilled. In this way it is the poem of all others in English, or so far as we are aware in any language, which gives a voice and utterance to the varying moods, the passion and the calm of grief, the longing memories that mingle themselves with a thousand new currents of thought, yet return and return, like the circles of the lark, to the lowly bed in which all centre. To have done this, in poetry which is almost always beautiful and often most touching in its pathos and profound humanity, is glory enough for a man, and the world was so much the poorer when her Majesty began to reign, that there was as yet no such litany and ritual of grief. Other men have raised monuments, and precious ones, to those they have lost; Tennyson alone has embodied the endless vicissitudes of the sorrowing heart, the world-wide atmosphere through which our individual loss breathes a chill and penetrating sense of vacancy which all the universe cannot fill up. There are some critics who affect to despise the sane and wholesome limits within which this great poet has seen it meet to confine himself, who call his high reticence and moral purity feminine, and accuse him of bringing down the issues of life to the atmosphere of the drawing-rooms. But Tennyson's poetry will remain, we do not doubt, the highest expression of the mind of his age—an age which, unfortunately, is no longer quite this age, the happier simpler period of the reign, when for a time the standard of society seemed altogether higher and purer, when the scandals of the past seemed to have died away in a clearer moral atmosphere, wherein noxious things could not live. It is no reproach either to the Laureate or the Queen if that fine moment did not last. And poetry, like society, when less lofty, more sensual and earthly, is apt to claim for itself the credit of a stronger manhood—a claim as unfounded as it is derogatory both to human nature and to art. Mr Swinburne has carried into more luscious sweetness the melody of words; but that broader and larger nature which stretches far beyond the monotone of passion has little place in the sweetness, long drawn out, of his newer fashion.

It is more difficult to characterise Mr Browning's poetry than that of his illustrious contemporary. He has had the misfortune, a little from his excellences, but still more from his peculiarities which are not excellent, to attract to himself the mystical worship of a sect which goes far at present to make the poet ridiculous. But he is not to blame if the difficulties of his enunciation have produced a *bizarre* worship which is to the glorification of the worshippers rather than that of their idol. We can only regret that these uncouth rites have beguiled him into continuing a series of metaphysical studies which discourage the true lover of poetry, and intensify the veil which hangs between so admirable a poet and the appreciation of the reasonable world. It is unnecessary to speak of "Sordello" or even of "Paracelsus," or these finely poetical but impracticable dramas which cannot even by the enthusiasm of the *illuminati* be buoyed into life.[10] Perhaps Mr Browning is at his greatest in the "Men and Women," which stand in the middle of his poetical career, when his faculties were at their finest, and his powers least hampered by the inadequacy of words.[11] There is nothing finer in the language than some of these poems, especially those in which he has confined the redundancy into which his laboured utterance leads him, the necessity of explaining, elucidating, and repeating everything he has to say. The defect is invisible in the wonderfully pathetic picture of Andrea del Sarto, in the fine, keen, clear physiognomy of the Greek Cleon, and in some of the other wonderful studies of human thought and meaning which are in this fine collection. The poet throws himself back into the being of his temporary hero with an insight and comprehension, a visible force and vividness, which give singular reality to the picture—a mode of treatment new to poetry, and as effective as it is original. It is always the most exacting and difficult of literary studies to set forth a man in his own language, in a portion of his own existence, not acting even but thinking, disclosing the secrets of his own being, and, above all, to do this within a limited space, which gives no licence for external description, nor any accumulation of accessories. The highest gifts of the historian are sometimes occupied in the accomplishment from without of such portraits, and there can be little doubt that the habit and power of doing this has added a wonderful attraction and grace to history. But such characterisations are little known in poetry. They have hitherto been confined to the drama, where indeed it is only by his own interpretation that we understand the hero; but where he has at least the events of a highly wrought episode, an exciting series of incidents, to make his revelation by. Mr Browning has put aside all such aids in those wonderful little pieces of work. The melancholy painter in his evening talk, half musing, half speech, with the sense of his failure aching at his heart, and the still more miserable consciousness of what he might have been and done—subdued to pathetic calm by that quiet despair and sense of the conclusion of all possibilities—is such a perfect picture as no other art could make, and overwhelms us with the pathos of a self-portraiture from which all self-deceptions have died away. The completeness of the mournful vision, which is not without a smile at itself and at all the delusions that are over, and that profound consciousness of defeat which has so few expositors, yet which is perhaps the most deeply moving of all the experiences of existence, convey to our minds a pang of pity and sympathy. Quite different on the very opposite edge of life, is the experience of the poet, the all-accomplished, all-fortunate Greek, to whose dignified retirement the offerings and the adoration of princely admirers come, and who is surrounded by everything beautiful and rare, and the consciousness of having done all that genius and good fortune can—yet whose sigh out of his old age and that one inevitable failure of waning life which makes the great poet in his greatness less than the vigorous manhood of the slave whose muscles he casts a passing, admiring, half-contemptuous, half-envious glance at, as he raises his head from his tablets—is little less sad than that of the painter. The reader, whose verdict after all is that of final fame—he who pretends to no profounder insight, but judges the highest poetry as well as the commonest prose by the light of reason and nature—will find in this fine series nothing to alarm him or unduly tax his understanding, and much that he will find nowhere else,—the workings of a very powerful and philosophical mind, combined with a poetical genius of the highest strain. Once again we disavow all ideas of competition with Shakespeare. Mr Browning's mind is not Shakespearian in any sense of the word. But it is not necessary to be of the stature of Jove, in order to stand high among the gods. In the persons of Lord Tennyson and Mr Browning, our half-century need not fear to hold up its head in the company of the ages.

We will not discuss the younger band, whose position is yet not wholly ascertained. Mr Swinburne, indeed, has made his mark; and posterity is not likely to reverse the decision with which his own generation has crowned this master of exquisite words and all the music that can be put into verse—all the music, but perhaps less than the due amount of meaning. Rossetti, to whom the completeness of the preterite has come, has his own niche in the Temple of Fame—a conspicuous one, yet never, we think, to be a centre of that universal consent of love and interest which is the meed of a great poet. He is a poet who never ceases to be a painter; nor does he in his most exalted moments of mystic spiritualism ever break that bond of flesh and circumstance which is necessary to his original art. His Blessed Damozel is as ready as any large-eyed model to be reproduced on canvas.[12] No man can paint a soul; therefore it is entirely comprehensible that the heavenly vision, as revealed to a painter's eyes, should warm with the pressure of her bosom the bar upon which she leans, looking out for her lover. But it is not celestial; nor is it thus that the great poets realise the unseen. Mr Matthew Arnold is a most accomplished and distinguished writer; but our own mind is not made up about his poetry, though it has, no doubt, reached a large degree of appreciation, especially among the cultivated classes. So has Mr William Morris. In our present undecided frame of mind, we are disposed to think that the fare provided by both these poets is of the nature of luxury—a something above and beyond the necessities of living. Perhaps some readers will think all poetry partakes of this character. We are not, however, of that opinion. Great poetry is daily bread.

It would be at once unjust and untender to pass over, in the record of these fifty years of poetry, the name of Elizabeth Barrett Browning, who is perhaps, taken all in all, the greatest Woman-poet whom England has known. No woman, so far as we know, has ever been a great poet, or attained the level of the highest. But among those who have at all approached that level, Mrs Browning holds the first place. Some of her sonnets (so called) from the Portuguese are exquisite in their tenderness and beauty; and her only sustained effort, "Aurora Leigh," has much power and sweetness, and a force of subdued but sustained enthusiasm which is very impressive.[13] Although it touches upon a loathsome subject, with that curious attraction in repulsion which seems to move the feminine mind towards what it most hates, the poem is full of the finest thought and of that love of love and all things lovely which gives one of its deepest charms to poetry. The fresh and peaceful English landscape, the "old miraculous mountains heaving forth," as Italy, almost more beloved than England, comes in sight—and the corresponding pictures of life and thought, the glow of feeling in the young enthusiasts who feel it their mission to reclaim the world, and the profounder passion of maternal love which conquers shame—are very fine and true. This poem has fallen a little out of sight amid the crowds of modern competition, as everything does; but it must always find an honourable place in the literary records of Queen Victoria's reign.

In the dignified realm of history during those fifty years, we have the growth of a new and brilliant school to record. History was more serious than entertaining fifty years ago. It aimed at an authoritative standing, and to fix the canon of what was and what was not to be believed. In those days Hallam was in the front of literature, with his grave and deeply considered record of the English constitution[14]—one of those unique and final books which may originate an entire school, but are never themselves put out of date; and we had the brilliant military pictures of Sir William Napier to carry on the existing recollection, which had not yet died out of men's minds, of the great wars which England hoped had pacified the world.[15] And Sir Archibald Alison had begun that great history of Europe—great in volume and in subject— which so many years were necessary to complete.[16] But in these great works the subjects were approached from the point of view of a scientific perspective, and the writers did not propose to themselves to rival the most vivid romancer in imaginative realisation and reproduction. Napier, it is true, was always vivid, always brilliant, with the energetic genius of his race—a soldier even when a historian. But the muse of History, in all her seriousness, still led the serious footsteps of her servants through the straight road, the king's highway of important events. The first historian of her Majesty's reign, Lord Mahon, continued in the same traditions, in his precise, correct, and not inelegant history of the eighteenth century,[17] which continues to hold its place as a trustworthy and impartial narrative of an age full of important decisions, more picturesque than our own, and in many respects the turning-point of national life. The first of the Victorian historians was not a brilliant writer, nor was there much that was novel or striking in his views; but he did his work with great accuracy and care, and at one portion of his narrative, that in which the unhappy house of Stuart made its last romantic attempt to recover the throne, and underwent the last disastrous catastrophe, almost rises into the heroic style which becomes so tragic a subject. But eloquence was not the characteristic of the book, which, in general, was very calm, regular, and systematic—a duty and necessity, rather than a pleasure, to read.

This work however was, at the moment of its appearance, and as a matter of literature, far less important than the great outburst of a new style and school, the brilliant and dazzling volumes in which a writer already known, who had leapt into the literary field, with a style singularly formed and polished, in the very heat of youth, now took the world by storm. Macaulay had already gained an important reputation in various fields.[18] He had made his mark in Parliament, he had done excellent work in India, he had contributed many striking essays to the "Edinburgh Review." But the public was scarcely prepared for a work which was as enthralling in its interest as any romance, and carried its readers breathless through even the survey and estimate of the condition of the country at the great Revolution, which in almost any other hands would have been a chapter of reference, to be followed to its end only by the plodding reader or careful student. This book, we may venture to say, changed the fashion of historical writing, and was in itself a literary revolution. It was not an impartial history. There are those who affirm that it is not even trustworthy in many details; that its view throughout is a Whig view; that its author carried his party prejudices with him, and darkened the shadows and heightened the lights in a manner which added relief and animation to the picture as well as splendour to the achievements of his hero; but which was anything but that calm balance and judicial estimate which had been expected from history. No doubt there was a certain foundation for those complaints; but this new impulse has been carried so much further since then, and has found its issue in so many partisan records and highly coloured narratives, that we turn back to Macaulay with relief, feeling that the malicious pleasure he perhaps felt in lightly impaling a Quaker courtier was at least pardonable, and that the careless contempt with which he sometimes sweeps aside explanations and motives which on the other side he gives the utmost force of his skill to elaborate and set forth, was, on the whole, less wilfully injurious to the opposite party than naturally favourable to his own. It is one thing to incline with a higher appreciation to those views and leaders on whom one's eyes have been bent by all the traditions of breeding and party, and another to fix with a keen personal prejudice and enmity upon a historical figure far removed from the present scene, and pursue an unfortunate race with posthumous virulence. Macaulay has, perhaps, been guilty of the first and milder injustice: he can scarcely be accused of the second. William of Orange had never been a popular hero, nor is he, now that his historian has done all that man could do for him; but it is a not ungenerous office to concentrate the most favourable light upon the head of a man who filled a thankless position, and occupied a necessary place with much stoical and unappreciated self-sacrifice, though also with much addition to his outward rank and greatness. The fine pictorial background, the brilliant individual portraits, the life and vivid embodiment of the age in all its struggles and endless intrigues, were all novel and delightful to the readers of this splendid piece of historical work. It made an epoch in literature, to use the phrase of the time. No book, we suppose, of modern (and consequently none of ancient) times has ever had so vast a circulation. Neither the circulation nor the almost fabulous remuneration is an absolute test of excellence, it is needless to say. But the universal admiration, interest, and delight with which the book was received are more trustworthy evidences, and these were never so entirely the recompense of any English history up to this day. The first volumes were published in the year 1848, when the Continent was all aflame with revolutions, none of which were so lasting or so momentous as that of which our historian treated. The story of literature contains no greater sensation, and few more important events.

    Another historical work of a still more remarkable but very different kind—one which has taken its place among the greatest works of literature without ever approaching near the popular acceptance of Macaulay—had come into being ten years before, at the very beginning of her Majesty's reign—"The History of the French Revolution," by Thomas Carlyle.[19] This is not the place for discussions of character or individual arguments, since it is books we have to deal with and not men; but it is difficult to mention that great and much-traduced name without a protest against the cruel and false estimate of our illustrious countryman—a man never apt to study the light in which he should present himself to posterity, or to take thought of the manner in which his mantle was wrapped about him when he fell—which it seems probable will be accepted as final by the world. Whether he is ever likely to be placed in a more true light before a generation which has no other way of knowing him than that afforded by his trusted biographer,[20] we mournfully doubt. The question is too painful a one to be entered into here. "The History of the French Revolution" has nothing of the brilliant ease and sparkling lights of that which we have just been discussing. Macaulay's smooth and accomplished grasp of his period is like the touch of a white-gloved demonstrator in a drawing-room, or at least in the most refined of lecture-rooms, beside the giant's grip with which Carlyle takes hold of that wild scene—the one mad and horrible moment of modern history in which all that was permitted to the ancient drama, the pity and terror of solemn fate, is overpassed in the horror of that tragedy of real life which knows no limits. Carlyle is no *raconteur*; he is a spectator, looking on while those confused yet tragic combinations roll up, form, and disperse, breaking away again into fragments, like the storm-clouds upon the sky, and while the torrents of blood burst forth, and the demons rave, and carnage fills the streets. He sees, what no mere historian can see, the murderers of September at their horrible work in one corner of the great and terrible city,[21] while in another the children play and the women chatter, and humble life goes on as if such things could never be. Sometimes a tone of heart-breaking pathos comes in, sometimes that laugh which is more terrible than tears. The pathetic groups in the prisons, the livid fanatic at the head of affairs, the theorists, the avengers, the little human vanities all in flower upon the very edge of the scaffold, are in movement before our eyes, the terrible panorama opening out in scene after scene. There may be some upon whom the grim humour will jar, and some to whom the confusion of the tragic scene will be increased by the peculiarities of the diction, the rolling clouds of words heaped upon each other in vaporous stormy sentences, altogether unlike the polished calm of a restrained and dignified historical style. But no one can deny the force and splendour of the picture, or the supreme and shuddering interest with which the reader is made to enter into sight and hearing of this terrible world-convulsion and crisis of national existence.

The history of Oliver Cromwell and his period, which followed from the same hand, at a considerable interval of years, was of a nature to excite greater discussion and a warmer criticism. But there can be little doubt that it modified to a very great degree the common opinion upon that great figure in English history, and to a large extent vindicated the Protector from those imputations of hypocrisy and selfish ambition which had become the commonplaces of history. It is not necessary to paint everything concerning a great actor in history in the most odious colours, in order to emphasise our disagreement with him, or even moral disapproval of the part he had taken; but this was what preceding historians, with almost one accord, had done. Apart from Carlyle's success in this respect—if anything in the book can be considered apart from the one great image which fills it—the picture of the time is as vivid as that of the French Revolution, and made in a similar way, as by the hand of a spectator, more actively engaged than in the former case—himself almost acting, expounding, elucidating all that passes before his eyes, with a sentiment much stronger, identifying himself with all that takes place. Indeed Carlyle is as present as Cromwell, interpreting in the strong medium of his natural Scotch Calvinism and religionism, deeply tinctured by the Old Testament, the other rugged personality, the Puritan, in which so many predominating principles were the same. We cannot but feel that the choice of Frederick as the hero of Carlyle's later life was something of a mistake; for there was no such point of contact by which the biographer could enter into the most intimate relations with his subject: and that wonderful mass of learning and research, which was the burden of his own life for years, has not succeeded in impressing upon the general mind anything like so remarkable an apprehension of the questionable hero and his time as was conveyed to us by the other two great historical studies. The work perhaps was too great, the material too immense, the details too minute and voluminous. There was less unity in the interest, and consequently less force in the picture. The comparatively brief narrative of the Abbot Samson and his surroundings in "Past and Present,"[22] perhaps the most completely lovable and delightful of all Carlyle's work, shows his power of throwing himself into the scene he depicts, and his wonderful sympathetic realisation of character and power of poetic vision at their very best.

To make a list of all the remarkable historical works which have distinguished our age, would be of itself a laborious undertaking. Chief among them are the highly coloured, and in many respects most effective and picturesque, studies of Mr Froude, in which the strong *parti pris*,[23] the incapacity for regarding almost any event or character simply, and on its own merits, do not hinder—nay, perhaps rather help to secure—the absorbed attention of the reader. Nor does the singular heat of hostile feeling with which he pursues not only certain favourite personages, but even such a great institution as the Church of England for example—or the remarkable peculiarity of moral vision, which raises so many grievances along his path wherever that distinguished writer has passed—detract from the interest. The reader, who cannot fail to have been impressed and stirred by his vivid pictures, will yet remember with what relentless hatred he pursued Mary Stuart to the block and the grave, untouched by even that natural sentiment which is impressed by every courageous and dignified death-scene, whoever the sufferer may be. But indeed this historian's love is as much to be dreaded as his hatred—as his recent works have proved. The picturesque and vivid workmanship of Mr Kinglake, the epic of a great campaign; the valuable labours of Dr Stubbs, of Mr Freeman,[24] and of other well-known living writers, who still continue to enrich our records, and whose work we hope will not yet for a long time be recognisable as complete, do not require more than a mention. There is now a great school of historical investigation, bringing to the elucidation of our national records much fine understanding and manly work, a few crotchets, and a great deal of admirable talent and skill. Instead of long silence, broken now and then by a chapter of classical history, or a learned prelection on some distant and unattractive theme, we have a crowd of energetic workers, clearing the very springs of history, and spreading enlightenment and knowledge round. In Scotland, too, a group of devoted patriotic students have given their best efforts to the authentication of our ancient history, among whose names that of the late John Hill Burton—whose excellent and valuable "History of Scotland" is scarcely less remarkable than the delightful "Book-Hunter," which has originated quite a little school of its own—was for a long time the first.[25] And a corresponding group in Ireland has been labouring, unmoved by all external clamour, upon the primitive records of the Isle of Saints. The great popular acceptance of the brilliant little History for the People of the late Rev. J.R. Green,[26] did that ingenious riter wrong; for it forced into the position of an independent work of personal research and thought what was intended only for a more lucid and attractive statement of the work done by others; and thus perhaps wore out more quickly than otherwise might have been, the strength and life of the writer, whose forces were unequal, and whose time was too short for such a task.

We have spoken (with the one exception of Carlyle) only of works of English history. But the historical writers of the half-century have not been confined to this subject. The great work of Grote upon ancient Greece[27] has for a long time put every competitor out of the field, and become in its weighty conscientiousness and power the chief authority upon that ever-interesting theme. We have already referred to the most prodigious piece of work of all, a History which has been perhaps more popular than any big book of its dimensions ever was, and which was for a long time almost as productive as an estate, a most valuable piece of literary property, Sir Archibald Alison's "History of Europe." The "History of Civilisation" of the late Mr Buckle was still greater in its conception,[28] and could it ever have been carried out, would no doubt have reached to some prodigious number of volumes, worthy of the huge collection of books in which its author had built himself up with a curious symbolical fitness. For though his theme was mankind, his knowledge was of books alone, and his work is full of those strange ignorances and clever mistakes to which a mind trained in the atmosphere of a literary hothouse, out of reach of all practical contact with the nature he attempted to define and chronicle, is naturally subject. The appearance of his first volume, however, the introduction to his vast subject, created a great sensation in the literary world, and the amiable recluse found himself famous to his great surprise and considerable embarrassment. However, he took his fame with much seriousness, and without any misgivings as to the result. Buckle was one of the first of the band of philosophical thinkers rejecting the creed of Christianity and even of Theism, which have made so great an appearance in our day; and his name naturally leads us to those of others in many respects more remarkable than his own, who have given to our philosophical literature a new development, and who have established Natural Science, with all the philosophies dependent on it, as one of the greatest subjects and most intimate occupations of the time.

We have again to recur to the name of Carlyle when we enter, or rather before we enter, this field. His historical works, though so remarkable, perhaps scarcely took so strong a hold upon the mind of his generation as those which for want of a better title we must call philosophical. He had no system of philosophy, however, to set forth, but rather the mind and thoughts upon all things in heaven and earth of one of the most remarkable of human beings, a man half prophet, half iconoclast, in whom a devout heart, instinct with all the lore of a cottage-taught religion, and the austere morality and rustic intolerance of a Scotch peasant, were linked with a spirit which had caught fire at that of Goethe, and had thrown off all allegiance of faith—a spirit full of sardonic humour and powers of mockery and vituperation unrivalled, fiercely unsympathetic with all that was uncongenial to his nature, while tender to every touch of feeling within its own intense but limited range. The problem of this curiously mingled nature, so open to malign interpretations, yet so attractive to all the enthusiasms, puzzled yet delighted the world as it revealed itself in the often grand and sometimes chaotic literary utterance, a style which was in reality the sublimated but most genuine style of a Scotch peasant of genius, full of reflections from the Hebrew eloquence of the Old Testament, and from that prodigious gigantic ancient German, which were perhaps the two things nearest to his own heroic old Saxon-Scotch. Perhaps it needs an acquaintance with that ponderous and solemn speech of the old shepherds and ploughmen, slow and grandiose in unintended solemnity, "such as grave livers do in Scotland use," to comprehend the naturalness and simplicity of Carlyle's often contorted and sometimes convulsive utterance. And it certainly requires a knowledge no longer at all general of the primitive moorland peasant of the beginning of the century to understand the fashion of a man, all astray among fine English literary folks in Queen Victoria's reign. These curious contradictions and incomprehensibilities will make him always a most interesting figure in literary history, even under the shadow which has been thrown over his name, and nothing can impair the splendour of his contributions to literature. Such works as "Sartor Resartus" stand detached like great poems from all surroundings, and are indeed more rare than the greatest of poems. It would be difficult to apportion to Carlyle his place in any literature. He stands apart like a great lonely peak in a world of mountains, not loftier perhaps than the great forms about him veiled in summer verdure or eternal snow—but more conspicuous in solitary grandeur, with crags and precipices and heaven-pointing needles, sometimes resplendent in the glory of setting suns, sometimes clad in

greys and purples of distance, to which neither verdure nor snows
cling.

A very different apparition is that of the philosopher whose
act with Carlyle has afforded a curious anecdote to literary history,
a still more curious contrast between two men as unlike as any two
could be got together at random in any thoroughfare, though both
influential in their different ways and so remarkable. Everybody
knows the tragic incident of the destruction of Carlyle's precious
manuscript, the first volume of the "French Revolution," upon which
all his hopes of fame and even of daily bread hung, by horrible
misadventure or carelessness, in the hands of John Stuart Mill; and that
memorable scene when the pair of penniless people in London, hearing
suddenly of this tremendous misfortune, could not by more than a look
communicate to each other their despair, so necessary was it to console
the misery of the destroyer, who, "deadly pale," came to tell them of
what had happened.[29] What a curious picture! The culprit, rich and at
his ease, to whom a hundred or even a thousand pounds was nothing,
could that make up for this thing which was irremediable, pale and
trembling, before that proud, passionate, eloquent, fiery pair, either of
whom could have annihilated with desperate, vehement words any
offender. What lava-torrents of indignation and despair ought to have
covered him as he stood, turning him to a cinder! As a matter of fact,
they were the consolers of his despair, not he of theirs. And everybody
knows also the strange training of Mill as disclosed in his
Autobiography, and the amiable, benevolent, gentle nature of the man
thus twisted and tortured out of humanity, and how he took refuge in
woman-worship and learned a wistful hope in immortality out of the
intolerable pang of bereavement.[30] His great work on "Logic" is
another of the books which make a distinct epoch and new beginning;
and we perhaps can scarcely estimate how much the general public has
derived its present conceptions of individual right and social
responsibility from the famous "Essay on Liberty," which has
stimulated so many minds, and grown into the common code so
completely that thousands recognise its tenets as born with their birth,
without any consciousness from whence they came. His other works on
Political Economy, the Utilitarian system, and other cognate subjects,
are all important and interesting. These were hereditary tenets and
occupations, for he was brought up under the shadow of Jeremy
Bentham, and was in a great degree the expositor and prophet of his

father James Mill, another stern Scotch dogmatist and theorist,[31] into whose immovable mould the gentler, more sensitive, and impressionable nature of the son was compressed with very curious effects. The strange little book on the "Subjection of Woman [sic]" belongs to a very different phase of his character, to the much-repressed emotional side, which only got vent under the feminine influence which to him seemed all but divine in the latter part of his life. His books, excepting the highly popular "Essay on Liberty," are chiefly for the student; and have had an immense influence upon the teaching of Mental Science; but the image of the man as revealed in his own story is of the greatest interest to all.

The philosophers who have followed Mill in this field—his contemporaries, yet successors—are too many and too important to be dealt with here. Mr Herbert Spencer, who is a host in himself, is fortunately still with us; and so are, a band almost uncountable, the school of English writers, many of them most accomplished and eloquent, to whom the philosophy of Comte is more attractive than that of the Gospel.[32] There have never perhaps been so many attractive and charming unbelievers in the field; yet we do not entertain the apprehensions expressed by many for the permanence of the older faith.

It is difficult to dissociate the two men above considered, Carlyle and Mill, in their very different developments, from their productions; but when we turn to Charles Darwin, who perhaps is the most influential of all the scientific writers of our epoch, we associate no personality with his work, and feel no temptation to inquire what manner of man he was. This is one drawback which attaches to wealth, comfort, and a quiet life, that there is little attraction for human sympathy in them. But the importance of Darwin in the literary and scientific history of his time is not to be mistaken. His works have been read according to a very usual formula not so applicable now as in former days—like novels. It would perhaps be a truer form of applause to say of a successful novel that it has been read like Darwin. His works have been discussed in every drawing-room as well as studied in every scientific retirement; but this, we are disposed to believe, as has been the case with many other of the scientific works of the period, rather because of the lucidity and interest of the style and the manner of putting these wonderful new doctrines—from their character as literature, in short—than from interest in their subjects or conviction of their truth. It is harder than any philosopher has ever conceived to make ordinary men and women consider in any other light than that of a piquant pleasantry, touching upon the burlesque, the idea that they are themselves the offspring of jellyfish. Notwithstanding this, there can be no doubt that the doctrine of Evolution has had the greatest effect in science, has exercised a considerable influence upon the religious polemics or apologetics of the time, and has been very startling to many minds and very stimulating to many others. Whether the problem of human existence is thus simply solved, and whether the scientific reasoner is at liberty to believe that he may jump the vast gap which exists between the evolution of the highest animal and that wonderfully different creature, the speaking, thinking, inventing, creative being man, we are not called upon to decide. It may be taken as an example of humility more striking than any ever exacted from a monk in the elder ages, that such a man as Darwin is able to conceive of himself as sufficiently accounted for by the processes he describes, and on which he founds his theory of the succession of the races, taking the tremendous athletic exercise of that last great leap as possible and permissible without danger to life or limb. His works on the "Origin of Species," his theories of the survival of the fittest, and of those developments which he considered owing to the desire of one sex to please the other (a desire, alas! singularly inoperative in adding to the beauty of the human species nowadays), took the scientific world by storm, and have since shaped more or less almost all thinkings on these subjects. To undervalue the weight and importance of these works because we are personally unable to be convinced by them, or to consider them otherwise than as largely founded on the conjectures of a remarkable imagination, backed up by equally remarkable powers of reasoning—would be an unworthy attempt. Darwin's work has the peculiarity that it is unpolemical; his conclusions are worked out with all the calm of scientific research, with none of that lively pleasure in flinging a challenge to the upholders of religious systems, whose theory of the origin of man is that he was developed from above and not from below, which actuates, for instance, the writings and utterances of Professors Huxley and Tyndall,[33] and other philosophers of their class. It pleased Darwin's observant genius to watch the labours of the earthworms, the subjects of his latest work, throwing up their little inequalities on the earth's surface, and to calculate how by these unnoticed means the outer husk of the great globe itself was sustaining continual modifications—better than to shake his demonstrative fist in the face of the world. And in these later observations he had the inestimable advantage of being on the spot, which he unfortunately was not during any one of the greater developments by which, according to his theory, the naked savage came out of the loins of La Bête, as M. Cherbuliez has called it, to develop somehow—how? by an evolution quite miraculous and incomprehensible—into Charles Darwin and other eloquent philosophers of his kind.

The extraordinary growth of this new branch of literature, and the change it has made even in the very nomenclature of things, and the interest it has aroused among readers of all classes, is one of the most striking facts in our half-century. We are disposed to believe, as we have already said, that in a great many cases its effect is one of a purely literary kind, and largely dependent upon the remarkable excellence as writers of the chief expounders of the new theories, whose writings are rarely dull, often full of epigram and wit, and graces of the imagination—gifts and qualities which are new to the exponents of abstract science. Never before perhaps has philosophy, concerned with such fundamental matters, found for itself so attractive a form, or spoken with a voice so harmonious and adapted to charm and enthral. An age full of mental curiosity, and delighted, as all the generations are, with everything that is new, would be stoical indeed if it could shut its ears to the voice of the charmer when it charms so wisely. It is less easy here, as in other regions of literature, to deal with the work of living authors than with those which are rounded into completeness by death; but the names which we have already mentioned of Huxley and Tyndall may stand as the greatest representatives of those contemporary writers who give unquestionable brilliancy of style and a fine force of rhetoric, often of eloquence, to the support of the new philosophy of Nature.

It is with a little relief that we escape from the consideration of matters which we find too high for us, to another more familiar branch of literature which has had the most wonderful growth and development in Queen Victoria's reign. In whatever way we may be surpassed by our predecessors, no age that has gone before us is likely to challenge the importance of these fifty years in the development of Fiction. This age has seen at least three novelists of the highest rank develop and conclude their work. Dickens had indeed begun the publication of "Pickwick," which has not yielded in popularity to any of his books, when her Majesty ascended the throne, and Thackeray was already making essays which—it is impossible to divine why, since his great rival's fortune had at once been made by the "Sketches by Boz"[34]—did not at once open to him the doors of literary triumph. Both these great writers belong, however, by every law to Queen Victoria's reign. They were so exactly contemporary in age, in production, and ultimately in fame, that it is almost impossible not to place them more or less in competition with each other; and there was in their day a very marked division between the partisans of Dickens and those of Thackeray. The former had most simple-minded readers on his side. He had the world of the *bourgeoisie*—a word which we cannot attempt to translate— entirely for him. The strongly formed impression that Thackeray was a cynic, that he attributed ignoble motives even to good actions, and laughed, even though the laugh might be kind, at humble virtue, and found no goodness without alloy, sounds strange now when we remember that it is the creator of Colonel Newcome, of Mrs Pendennis, and of Esmond,[35] of whom these things were said. But it was the general belief, and one to which perhaps "Vanity Fair," with all its wonderful wealth of human character, gave some countenance: and this as much as anything perhaps made him somewhat doubted and feared by that gentle public which wept over little Nell, and found pathos in the story of Smike—which was never the public of the critic, yet was that to which Dickens owed much of his first acceptance. Curiously enough, as has been remarked elsewhere, it is this sentimental side of him—his sugary domesticities, his Tiny Tims,[36] his gushing showmen and acrobats—which seems to have impressed our neighbours in France, and originated among them what might almost be called a Dickens school. But in his own world of humorous delineation—that to which the groups of Wellers, Gamps, the inimitable figures of Micawber and Dick Swiveller, of Mark Tapley and Peggotty,[37] and a hundred more belong—Dickens stands above all competition. These are not illustrations of ordinary humanity, persons whom we might encounter any day, according to the formula by which we applaud other studies of life and manners. Rarely have any of us the good fortune to meet with Mr Micawber, and Sam Weller is as pure fiction as Figaro;[38] but the delightful exaggeration and tenderly absurd ideality make a being more real than any portrait. The Cockney clerk is not a personage on the face of him who attracts the imaginative spectator; but over Dick in his dismal office, gravely respectful of his Marchioness,[39] who has not laughed and cried? Mr Micawber, in his gentility, his certainty of something turning up, his shabbiness, his light-heartedness, and all the illusions which are so real to him, is worth a thousand respectable literary impersonations of better men. There are very few creations of poetry or fiction whom we should be less willing to give up. He is always a delight, with his wife, who never will be separated from Mr Micawber, whatever her family may do or say, and all their shifts, and their fine convictions of ultimate prosperity, and even his gaiters, and his collars, and his eyeglass, and his jaunty air. Mrs Gamp is almost, if possible, a more perfect creation, though nothing could make her dear to us like Mr Micawber. The extraordinary power with which Dickens threw himself into the confused brain of a woman of this class, following out the queer sequence of thoughts, the droll little thread of fanciful invention in the person of that familiar spirit Mrs Harris, her dæmon, and the author of some of her best sayings,[40] with all the peculiar lights that fall upon society and general human affairs from her professional lantern, is greater than if the subject had been more congenial. "Pickwick," "Nicholas Nickleby," "Martin Chuzzlewit," "David Copperfield," are works which, in their way, are not to be surpassed, and which contain, with a great deal of mannerism, much stilted writing, and many melodramatic incidents of a very inferior character, such whimsical creations, and ever humorous, ever entertaining embodiments of character, as any age might be proud to have produced. The latter works, we think, stand on a lower level, but still contain enough to make the fortune of a dozen writers. And though we do not allow Dickens's pathetic scenes, though he evidently liked them much himself, any particular excellence, yet the narrative of the childhood of David Copperfield, and his boyish miseries, and the journey to his aunt's house, is almost as good in its reflection of childish pain and suffering as could be; and the humour of his boyish courtship, and a great part of the episode of Dora,[41] is delightful. It is, however, upon such creations as Micawber that the supremacy of Dickens's genius rests.

Thackeray's humour is far more pervasive, delicate, and human. His mind was a much more highly cultivated mind, and free from those associations and deprivations which make Dickens always at his least best (to use no stronger words) in the society of ladies and gentlemen. Thackeray was perfectly at home there, and required nothing extraordinary, no eccentricity nor absurdity of circumstance, to open up to him all that was humorous and strange in human life. He needed no more than a handful of the most ordinary figures, going about the most usual occupations, to find comedy and tragedy and all those intricacies of motive and feeling which make human creatures pitiful and laughable, and yet sometimes sublime and great. He preferred, perhaps, to show them in the former light, to turn them outside in, and reveal what they were thinking at the moment of their first appearance, and to open out with the grin of a delighted discoverer those pretences in which they had wrapped themselves about. But when he encountered among the creations of his genius (for it was Thackeray, we think, who was the first to say that the men and women in a book had a will of their own, and developed themselves, instead of allowing themselves to be manipulated, as the world believes, by the hand of their maker) one who was of nobler mettle, what a perfect tenderhearted gentleman, what an ideal man it was who rose under this cynic's touch! Henry Esmond and Colonel Newcome are men to ennoble a generation. He who professed to write a novel without a hero because the being was impracticable, produced these two at least, to prove how completely and with what supreme naturalness and truth the thing was to be done. He has not been so happy in his women, perhaps because his imagination did not require so much for the feminine ideal; but his work throughout is so perfect, his characters so living, with such distinctness of atmosphere about them, crowded though every scene is, that this point of weakness tells the less. It is only the ideal women who are weak. Becky the inimitable, whom amid all her wrongdoings we cannot succeed in disliking, the wonderful old Lady Kew, Beatrix Esmond in her splendid youth and in her frightful age, are amazing in their force and vivid power.[42]

These two great humorists, fictionists, creators, to whom it is scarcely just to give the commoner title of novelists, since their art was something distinct from the craft of the *raconteur*, were perhaps the most perfect artists of any who have arisen in this age.

The great female writer of the Victorian period is equally remarkable, perhaps even more so, as being the only woman who has yet attained the highest place in literature. The position of George Eliot is unique. Her books have been the object of a kind of worship, as she herself was while she lived; but that of its very nature is evanescent, and they have now to stand before a more difficult tribunal—a tribunal which has not yet given forth its last word on the subject. We, however, who are of her generation, have little doubt that the verdict will remain unchanged, at least in respect to her earlier works. The very first of these, produced without any previous indication of power in the maturity of her years, affected the world at once to enthusiasm, and she never struck a stronger or a deeper note than in the simple story of Amos, or rather of Milly Barton,[43] the poor curate's mild and lovely wife, the mother of many children, the smiling domestic martyr, whose little tragedy has taken a place among our most cherished recollections as completely as if we had been members of the little rural parliament which discussed her simple story. The power and the pathos of this most remarkable beginning, and its heart-breaking catastrophe, does not prevent it from being at the same time full of all the humours of a fresh and unexplored country, delightful in indications of rustic character, and in those wise sayings of village sages which afterwards rose in Mrs Poyser[44] to the climax of proverbial wisdom. The books which followed this in succession—"Adam Bede," "The Mill on the Floss," and "Silas Marner"—raised George Eliot's name to the very highest level of English writers. It is needless to dwell upon books which everybody knows so well. They are full of power and insight, of unfailing humour, and at the same time of the deepest pathos, sometimes rising to the height of tragedy. In this vein, we know of nothing more powerful than the journey of Hetty Sorrel[45] in quest of her lover and betrayer, and the return home of the miserable girl, dazed with suffering and shame and weariness, and the dull despair of absolute helplessness and ignorance. There is nothing more impressive or more tragic in the language. The latter works of this great writer are, to our mind, injured by too much philosophy and the consciousness of being considered a public instructor; but there are very fine and original creations of character in them all. Rosamond in "Middlemarch," and Gwendoline in "Daniel Deronda," are exceedingly powerful conceptions, as is, perhaps the greatest of all, the wonderful Tito of the great Italian romance "Romola,"[46] where there is somewhat too much of the dry bones of archæological research, but where the character of the handsome, poetic, crafty, and self-seeking Greek is extraordinary in its relentless power.

    Another woman who has been set up by some writers on a pedestal almost as high—Charlotte Brontë, the author of "Jane Eyre"—lived and died before George Eliot was heard of. Any comparison between the two would be a mistake. The three books upon which Charlotte Brontë's fame is founded were passionate narratives of a woman's mind and heart, pent up without outlet or companionship—reflections of an individual being, extremely vivid and forcible, but in no way, we think, to be compared with the far stronger, higher, and broader work which we have just discussed. There is but one strain of intense sentiment in these books—the desire of a lonely creature longing for its mate, an all-engrossing thought which does not prevent the heroine from seeing everything around with wonderfully vivid perceptions, the eyes of genius, but which intensifies the sensations of solitude, and the vacancy of the heart, into a force of passion with which perhaps no woman, either before or since, has expressed that yearning of the woman towards the man which formed part of the primeval curse, and which indeed has produced the greater part of all distinctively feminine distresses. The inevitable failure in dignity involved in this impassioned revelation has been forgiven to her on account of the force which it gives to her very remarkable books—which, it is only just to say, made an epoch among English works of fiction, more than did the works of George Eliot, though the latter were in every way greater. Emily and Anne Brontë have to some considerable extent shared their sister's fame—one with some reason, as the writer of the extraordinary and feverish romance "Wuthering Heights," which in very painfulness and horror made an impression upon the mind of the public, greater perhaps than its intrinsic merits justify. Perhaps, however, it was as much the remarkable biography of Charlotte Brontë, involving those of her sisters, written by Mrs Gaskell, with a frankness of revelation new to the time, though sufficiently practised since, which brought this remarkable family under the observation of the world, and heightened the effect of all their literary performances, raising the two secondary figures to something of the same level as Charlotte. Mrs Gaskell herself was also well worthy of note as a novelist, and, like the Brontës, belongs altogether, beginning and end, to the Victorian period. Their lives and works take up but a short part of these fifty years, but already Mrs Gaskell has fallen into that respectful oblivion which is the fate of a writer who reaches a sort of secondary classical rank, and survives, but not effectually, as the greater classics do. Even for "Jane Eyre," though it has a much stronger power of survival than "Mary Barton,"[47] it is necessary now to look in private libraries, or in the old-fashioned circulating libraries of our youth, where such last. And indeed it would be a very profitable exercise for the gentle reader, when the moment comes when he (or she) goes to the seaside or any watering-place, to take along with his waters or his baths a course of the novels which belong to the happy days of the Victorian era—those days when society was purer and manners better—when the Queen was at the head of everything in her kingdom, its pleasures and its social habits, as well as more serious things, and when her Majesty's potent example tempered everything, and kept the atmosphere more clear than it has been since. Circulating libraries in watering-places where Mudie[48] is not yet supreme, and where books remain and accumulate, are the places to make sure of Mrs Gaskell, and even to bring one's self once more under the more powerful spell of Lucy Snowe[49] and Jane Eyre.

We will not touch upon the living professors of this branch of literature, though their name is legion. But there are two who have also passed away into silence, who cannot, in presence of Dickens, Thackeray, and George Eliot, be put in the first class of writers of fiction, but who are wronged by that overshadowing greatness, and have a right to a first class of their own. Anthony Trollope and Charles Reade[50] are enough, indeed, to have made a generation happy. This is one of the evils of a too great wealth of genius pouring upon us, as that fitful inspiration does, not in proportion to the time, but like that wind of greater inspiration still, which bloweth where it listeth, and in defiance of all laws of evolution. It is but the other day that Trollope was among us, telling us those stories of ourselves and our neighbours which, if never reaching any supreme point of insight like Thackeray's, are so entirely like life, and the people we encounter, that we all found in his books a new circle of acquaintance, only so much more entertaining than those of flesh and blood, that we had their story presented concisely, and had not to follow it out in fragments through the years, and that their minds were as open to us as their acts, and more interesting. Amid all his groups of clerical people, what excellent company! The Grantleys in ordinary life would not admit us to all their conferences as that pair do, with their anxieties for their family, and desire to see everybody belonging to them well established and comfortable, their little mutual disapprovals and criticisms, and impatience with the foolish other people who will always take their own way,—the old Warden, so gentle, so persuadable, so immovable; and Elinor, almost as troublesome as he. Mrs Proudie belongs to heroic regions; she is a figure for all time: and there are touches in the tragic history of Mr Crawley, that martyr of poverty and mischance, and in Lady Mason's strange unexpected crime; and on the burlesque side, in that ludicrous tragedy of the unfaithful Crosbie, and his lady Alexandrina,[51] which go to the very height of imaginative portraiture. When our grandchildren want to see us, as they surely will, in our habit as we lived, they will find the England of Queen Victoria's reign in Anthony Trollope's books with an admirable distinctness and reality which perhaps they will find nowhere else: for he takes no uncommon types, develops no unknown lines of living, but is all for the common strain of his generation, and draws it as it lived. Amid such a crowd of persons there must be some less well executed than the others; and it is not to be asserted that the strain of a life's work, which was never the work of a student, but done with a continual accompaniment of energetic living on his own part, was not sometimes felt. But the entertainment, the honest pleasure, the relief in hours of weariness, to be got out of Anthony Trollope's novels is endless, and their picture of society always animated and true.

Charles Reade is at once less and more than his contemporary. The spice of adventure, of excitement, and of extravagance in him belongs to a much higher imaginative level, but there is a corresponding failure in the commonplaces wherein Trollope's strength lies. Charles Reade is a little impatient of that everyday level. He loves to tell an exciting story, to blow a pleasure-yacht out to sea in the midst of the quietest social arrangements, and to interpolate a thrilling event between two discussions of toilet, in the midst of a young lady's difficulties of choice between two lovers. Sometimes he carries us away altogether to a desert island, and plays all kinds of pranks like a science-professor gone mad, yet keeps us breathless all the same. The "Cloister and the Hearth" is like a piece of medieval life transported bodily into the midst of us. It is in literature what Nuremberg is in art, a thing as real as the old city. We hear that his biographers have foolishly tried to enhance the glory of a writer never sufficiently appreciated, by the suggestion that "Romola" was more or less a plagiarism from this wonderful book, than which surely there could be no more extraordinary mistake. It needs no such enhancement of interest. We should say, putting aside Sir Walter and "Notre Dame,"[52] that there is no other such historical novel. To open Reade's masterpiece is to walk into a world of living folk, not in fictitious costume or charged with archæological detail, but at home among their natural surroundings, all individual, unconscious of our observation. His other works are full everywhere of the same easy grasp and power. He is a painter's painter, if we may use the words, or rather a writer's writer. The members of his own craft look on in delighted wonder when he takes his subject in hand. He treats it as it pleases him, not as we others would treat it, but always with a grasp and easy power which of itself gives a keen pleasure. And this wilful strength makes him somewhat difficult to characterise; it is quite as likely at any moment that it may turn to the fantastic as to the reasonable side, and it is even a little impatient of the intricacies of character-painting. We look back to the personages of his dramas without any warm individual feeling. We are deeply interested in them so long as they are in his hands, but they have no separate life, except, perhaps, in the case of David Dodd,[53] the simple, faithful, generous sailor, whose beauty of nature makes even his impatient creator pause. To our own thinking, the story, one of his briefest, "Love me Little, Love me Long," is one of the finest of Charles Reade's productions; but we do not think that the public has confirmed that opinion.

One great name the reader will perceive has been omitted, that of the late Lord Lytton,[54] whose fame had risen before the beginning of these fifty years, although indeed the finest manifestation of his powers, the new beginning, inaugurated in this Magazine, which produced "The Caxtons," "My Novel," and their successors, are all to the good and glory of the Victorian age.

We cannot enter into any discussion, which might be invidious, of the existing novelists of the day. The above have all concluded their work. They are from beginning to end of Queen Victoria's reign, and their fame is of her day.

One other development of literature we must mention ere we close. It is that of criticism, especially the criticism of art, and most especially the criticism of one who will interest posterity perhaps as much as any of the greatest writers we have mentioned—to wit, John Ruskin. He is one of those who can never be dissociated from his works, or rather his works from him. They are all pervaded with a delicate personality—fastidious, generous, querulous, tender, cruel—the very soul of an imaginative and susceptible being seeing everything through a glamour of genius and feeling, prejudice and prepossession. We cannot enter into his principles of art, which are too absolute and too capricious to have had much living effect upon the art of his period, and in which he has mingled so much extravagance that the sober-minded have been as often revolted as the enthusiastic have been impressed. It is no doubt owing in some degree to Mr Ruskin's

continued and eloquent partisanship that Turner's[55] great merits have
been so universally and promptly acknowledged; but on the other hand,
it is perhaps equally owing to him that other artists, following the
school once called pre-Raphaelite, over the creation of which he
presided,[56] have lessened their own fame by mannerisms and
monotonies, which are not to be desired in Art, as they do not exist in
Nature. But when that little has been said, there remains no name in
modern English literature which we could less dispense with. One of
the greatest masters of style who has ever employed English speech,
and who has employed it beautifully, worthily, with a thousand touches
that go to the heart, though with some which tempt a smile, and some
which have the gift to enrage the adversary, he is still exercising that
gift, with perhaps something of an old man's garrulity, and an extreme
of gentle egotism which requires much tenderness on the part of the
reader. But the tenderness happily exists, and this most fanciful of old
men eloquent does not appeal to it in vain.

Space fails us to record as we ought the wonderful development
of journalism and periodical writing of all kinds which has taken place
within these fifty years. The petty newspaper of the provincial town,
which Dickens made fun of at the beginning of the half-century, has
dropped away into the obscurest regions, and half-a-dozen ambitious and
influential organs of opinion have sprung up into its place. In London
itself what a difference! Those correspondents that dart across the world
at a moment's notice to supply our breakfast-tables with the latest
intelligence, sometimes by incredible feats of horsemanship, sometimes
at the risk of their lives, had no existence in those peaceful days—in
which, by the way, there existed no telegraph to convey their messages;
and, we might add—which is for us a less cheerful aspect of the
subject—no wars to report upon! The development of the newspaper,
and of the profession of journalism, is indeed subject enough for as
many pages as we have to devote to literature in general. And it is
possible that, did we enter into the subject, we should have something
more to say than admiration and wonder. It is a very responsible and
dangerous business to prepare in haste, as must be done, a facile
literature of every day, so abundant in quantity as to make a
recognisable claim upon the time of those who feel bound to keep up
with the opinions and sentiments of the day. To many such it becomes
more and more all the literature they can attain, and this is not a very
comfortable outlook. But the level of good writing in the newspapers is

on the whole high, and represents a large amount of fine intellect and good training, somewhat sacrificed for an inadequate end.

And in her Majesty's reign there has arisen a genial power, a merry moralist who has whipped us many a rascal off the scene, and laughed down many a folly, and jeered impartially at all political parties, and at the pets of fashion, and at the heroes of the crowd—but never failed, amid all its quips and jests, to give honour to the worthy, and never at the noisiest of its mirth mocked at goodness, or suggested any unclean thing or thought. We are proud to think that though he has had many imitators, and every foreign capital has something after his model, only within our own island could Mr Punch[57] be what he is.

We have crowded into these pages as complete a survey as possible of the literature of Queen Victoria's reign. Our Royal Mistress has as much honour of her subjects in this way as any monarch that ever sat on the throne of Great Britain before her. And let us not forget that to this abundant and noble literature the Queen has added certain sketches of her own which will not be the least sought after by posterity,[58] and upon which some historian of the future will no doubt seize with enthusiasm, making out from them, like a new Macaulay, a portrait which will be very delightful to the imagination,—the portrait of an ingenuous and charming sensibility and womanly sweetness, which with all the force of contrast will shine the more from amid the splendour of a throne; but which will not, as we know, do justice to the admirable good sense, the great experience, and all the statesmanlike endowments which fifty years of devoted work and ceaseless interest in all the concerns of her people have refined and developed in our Queen.

Notes

1. Destroyed by fire in 1834, the Houses of Parliament were rebuilt between 1840 and 1867; the Law Courts were designed in 1866 and completed in 1874–82. Both buildings are notable examples of Victorian Gothic Revival architecture.
2. French for "grappling with."
3. Poem celebrating the 1704 English victory over the French at Blenheim, in the War of Spanish Succession.
4. Matthew Prior (1664–1721). Poet and ambassadorial secretary to the Netherlands.

5. Two works included in Tennyson's 1833 *Poems*.
6. Descriptions of the Knight and his Squire in the *Prologue* to Chaucer's *Canterbury Tales*.
7. Reference in Milton's *Il Penseroso* (1631) to Chaucer's *Squire's Tale*.
8. Reference to Lynette in "Gareth and Lynette" from the *Idylls*. Oliphant describes her as having the pouting, childish face of a French maid.
9. Two of the most highly regarded elegies in English. "Lycidas" (1637) is Milton's elegy on fellow student Edward King; "Adonaïs" (1821) is P.B. Shelley's elegy on fellow poet John Keats.
10. "Sordello" (1840), a narrative poem based on the life of an Italian troubadour poet, examines issues of self-discovery and expression; "Paracelsus" (1835), a dramatic poem based on the life of a Swiss alchemist, is concerned with the conflict between love and knowledge; the final reference is to Browning's plays published between 1837 and 1846. None of these works were popular successes.
11. The 1855 volumes that confirmed Browning's career; they included the poems "Andrea del Sarto" and "Cleon," which Oliphant discusses below.
12. D.G. Rossetti's poem by this name was first published in 1850; he also created numerous versions of a painting by the same title.
13. *Sonnets from the Portuguese* was published in 1850; the long verse-novel *Aurora Leigh*, which includes a sympathetic depiction of an unwed mother, was published in 1857.
14. Henry Hallam (1777–1859). Historian, whose best-known work was his *Constitutional History of England* (1827).
15. Sir William Napier (1785–1860). Military historian noted for his *History of the War in the Peninsula* (1828–40) and *The Conquest of Scinde* (1845).
16. Sir Archibald Alison (1792–1867). While his best-known work was his *History of Europe during the French Revolution* (1833–42), he also wrote legal treatises and a noted autobiography.
17. Philip Henry Stanhope, Lord Mahon (1805–75). President of the Society of Antiquaries, and noted for his *History of England from the Peace of Utrecht to the Peace of Versailles* (1836–54).
18. Thomas Babington Macaulay (1800–59). His *History of England* (1849–55) was a bestseller throughout the nineteenth century and was a model for modern historical writing.
19. *History of the French Revolution* (1837) established Carlyle's reputation as a writer of great narrative and descriptive power. Oliphant discusses a number of other works by Carlyle, including: *Oliver Cromwell's Letters and Speeches* (1845), *The History of Frederick II of Prussia* (1858–

65), *Past and Present* (1843), his translations of Goethe (1820s), and *Sartor Resartus* (1833–34).

20. J.A. Froude (1818–94). Historian (discussed below) and friend of the Carlyles; his biographies of the Carlyles broke social codes by revealing their marital difficulties.

21. Reference to the 1793 massacres in various Paris prisons.

22. Abbot Samson, a medieval English religious leader, is depicted as the model of a communal leadership style that Carlyle contrasts starkly with the leadership style of nineteenth-century industrialists.

23. French for "prejudice, bias." In the following passage, Oliphant alludes to Froude's *Nemesis of Faith* (1849) and *History of England from the Death of Cardinal Wolsey to the Defeat of the Spanish Armada* (1856–70).

24. Alexander Kinglake (1809–91) was noted for his *Invasion of the Crimea* (1863–87); Dr. William Stubbs (1825–1901) was Regius professor of modern history at Oxford and best known for his works on constitutional history (*Select Charters and Other Illustrations of English Constitutional History*, published in 1870, and *Constitutional History of England*, published 1874–78); E.A. Freeman (1823–92) was noted for his *History of the Norman Conquest* (1867–79) and *Reign of William Rufus* (1882).

25. John Hill Burton (1809–81). A Scottish historian who published *History of Scotland* in 1853 and *Bookhunter* in 1860.

26. Rev. J.R. Green (1837–83). His *Short History of the English People* was noted for its simple style and broad approach and was later expanded into *The History of the English People* (1877–80).

27. George Grote (1794–1871). Historian and London MP whose *History of Greece* was published 1846–56.

28. Henry Thomas Buckle (1821–62) is noted for his *History of Civilization in England* (1857–61).

29. The first draft of Carlyle's manuscript was accidentally burned, according to Michael St. John Packe, "while in J.S. Mill's charge." Thomas and Jane Welsh Carlyle were put in the odd position of consoling Mill for the mishap.

30. Mill's 1873 *Autobiography* describes his upbringing according to utilitarian principles and the nervous breakdown and reaction that ensued from a childhood in which imagination and play were restricted. As political theorist, editor, and MP, he was an ardent defendant of progressive thought. Other works of his that Oliphant discusses include: *System of Logic* (1843), *On Liberty* (1859), *Utilitarianism* (1861), *Principles of Political Economy* (1848), and *The Subjection of Women* (1869).

31. Jeremy Bentham (1748–1832). Philosopher and founder of the principle of utilitarianism. James Mill (1773–1836). Philosopher and disciple of Bentham's principles.

32. Herbert Spencer (1820–1903). A founder of evolutionary philosophy and of modern sociology who was influenced by the work of

French philosopher Auguste Comte (1798–1857), who originated the theory of Positivism.

33.   T.H. Huxley (1825–95) was a surgeon and supporter of many of Darwin's theories. John Tyndall (1820–93) was a professor of natural history at the Royal Institution and a popularizer of science, including Darwin's theories.

34.   *Sketches by Boz* (1836–37), was Dickens's first publication. Oliphant also discusses the following works by Dickens: *Pickwick Papers* (1837), *Nicholas Nickleby* (1838–39), *The Old Curiosity Shop* (1840–41), *A Christmas Carol* (1843), *Martin Chuzzlewit* (1843–44), and *David Copperfield* (1849–50).

35.   Characters, respectively, from Thackerey's *The Newcomes* (1853–55), *Pendennis* (1848–50), and *The History of Henry Esmond* (1852).

36.   Representative pathetic children in Dickens's works: Little Nell is the heroine of *The Old Curiosity Shop*; Smike is Nicholas Nickleby's companion; Tiny Tim is the frail lame boy in *A Christmas Carol*.

37.   Strongly drawn comic characters in Dickens's fiction: Sam Weller is Pickwick's Cockney servant; Sarah Gamp is a drunken nurse-midwife in *Martin Chuzzlewit*; Mr. Micawber is a chronic debtor and foster father to David Copperfield; Dick Swiveller is a clerk in the Brass law firm in *The Old Curiosity Shop*; Mark Tapley is Martin Chuzzelwit's companion in America; Peggotty is David Copperfield's nurse.

38.   Character in the *Barber of Seville*, a type of the resourceful servant.

39.   Kitchen drudge in *The Old Curiosity Shop*.

40.   Sarah Gamp's imaginary friend in *Martin Chuzzlewit*.

41.   David Copperfield's child-bride.

42.   Characters in Thackeray's novels: Becky Sharp is the antiheroine of *Vanity Fair* (1847–48); Lady Kew is the heroine's domineering grandmother in *The Newcomes*; Beatrix Esmond is the headstrong cousin and sometime love interest of Henry Esmond.

43.   Characters in Eliot's first work of fiction, *Scenes from Clerical Life* (1857).

44.   Outspoken farm wife in *Adam Bede* (1859).

45.   One of the two heroines in *Adam Bede*.

46.   Rosamond is the spoiled wife of Lydgate in *Middlemarch* (1871–72); Gwendolen (misspelled by Oliphant) is the heroine of *Daniel Deronda* (1874–76); and Tito Melma is the scheming central character in Eliot's historical novel *Romola* (1863).

47.   Gaskell's first novel, published in 1848.

48.   The largest of the circulating libraries, based in London.

49.   Heroine in Charlotte Brontë's *Villette* (1853).

50. Charles Reade (1814–84), popular novelist; his best-known and most admired work was *The Cloister and the Hearth* (1861).

51. Characters in Trollope's series of Barsetshire Novels—*The Warden*, *Barchester Towers*, *Framley Parsonage*, *The Small House at Allington*, *The Last Chronicle of Barset* (1855–67).

52. The novels of Sir Walter Scott; *Notre Dame de Paris* (1831) by French novelist Victor Hugo.

53. Character in Reade's novels *Love Me Little, Love Me Long* (1859) and *Hard Cash* (1863).

54. Edward Bulwer-Lytton (1803–73). Novelist and politician; Oliphant mentions his novels *The Caxtons* (1849) and *My Novel* (1853).

55. J.M.W. Turner (1775–1851) was an English landscape painter.

56. The Pre-Raphaelite Brotherhood, a group of artists and poets founded in 1848 by John Millais, D.G. Rossetti, and William Holman Hunt and soon disbanded; Ruskin defended the painters' style and supported their work.

57. Fictional namesake of the popular illustrated paper.

58. *Leaves from a Journal of Our Life in the Highlands 1848–61* (1868).

VIII. Isabella Bird Bishop
(1831–1904)

One of Victorian Britain's most celebrated women travelers, Isabella Bird Bishop published a wide range of travel books and periodical articles based on her experiences abroad. Unlike many Victorian travel writers who sought to identify themselves with a specific region of the wider world, Bird Bishop wrote about her experiences in places as varied as North America, Hawaii, Asia and Northern Africa, and her works are characterized by their imaginative combination of personal narrative and ethnographic interest. The determination with which she pursued her travels and the success of her accounts can be measured in part by her acceptance in 1891 into the Royal Scottish Geographical Society and her subsequent admittance as the first woman fellow of the highly prestigious Royal Geographical Society. While her writing helped to satisfy the Victorian thirst for information about regions of the world considered remote from Great Britain, it also enabled her to establish considerable intellectual credibility. This in turn facilitated her efforts to publish periodical articles and give public lectures on social and political topics that in Victorian society might otherwise have been considered beyond the purview of a woman.

Bird Bishop was born on October 15, 1831, the daughter of Dora Lawson and the middle-class clergyman Edward Bird. She grew up first in Tattenhall, Cheshire, and her country parsonage roots nurtured an interest in religion and hymnology that she sustained throughout her life. Although she received no formal schooling, she read widely as an adolescent in areas ranging from literature and history, to biology, chemistry and botany. Encouraged in practical Christian philanthropic pursuits, she became, like other middle-class women, active in several charitable causes. In 1860, after her father died, she moved to Edinburgh, where she lived with her mother and younger sister Henrietta. Bird Bishop's achievements as a traveler—most of which occurred after this point in her life—are especially remarkable in light of her health history. She suffered from a debilitating spinal ailment throughout her life, and her travels were initially undertaken on the advice of a doctor who thought the change of scenery would speed her recovery from an unsuccessful operation. Although she was married briefly (her husband, Dr. John Bishop, died just five years after their 1881 marriage), Bird Bishop usually traveled alone, and her status as a single-woman traveler made some of her destinations (e.g., the western regions of the United States, China, Japan, Tibet, and Morocco) all the more unconventional.

Bird Bishop acknowledged in her work that travel both improved her physical health and appeased a sense of loneliness and dissatisfaction that she associated with what she had once referred to as her "stationary" life at home.

Whatever its physical or psychological attractions, travel seems primarily to have satisfied a desire for intellectual stimulation. Making good use of what she had learned from the wide reading of her childhood and adolescence, she transformed her travels into a form of cultural study, observing and analyzing everything from the natural habitat to the living conditions and social structures of the countries she visited. Her religious heritage and early philanthropic work may also have contributed to the efforts she made while traveling, to establish medical missions throughout the underdeveloped world. Because many of these missions were affiliated with the Church Missionary Society, biographers and critics of Bird Bishop have tended to view her work as evangelical and conservative in nature. Yet much of her writing also reflects an open-mindedness to other cultures and a corollary willingness to critique features of her own society, including what she viewed as the false sense of superiority with which many European travelers approached the broader world. Furthermore, while Bird Bishop did not use her writing as a forum to champion women's rights, her efforts to obtain admittance into male-dominated learned societies such as the Royal Geographic Society, as well as the attention paid within her travel accounts to the relative freedom that she enjoyed as a woman traveler outside her native country, both testify to an underlying interest in establishing equality between the sexes.

Bird Bishop's most well-known travel books share the hybrid nature of many nineteenth-century women's travel accounts, blending forms often associated with private writing with content more suited to a public realm. For example, several of Bird Bishop's books appeared as a collection of letters originally written to her sister, including *Six Months in the Sandwich Islands* (1875) and *A Lady's Life in the Rocky Mountains* (1879). These letters, however, extend well beyond descriptive accounts of her travels and experiences into lengthy analytical examinations of topics as varied as a country's architecture, educational system, medical facilities, and religious customs. The ethnographic interest of her work is complemented by its appeal as adventure writing, a dimension of her writing that no doubt contributed to its widespread popularity. Often emphasizing the sheer physical fortitude which her travels required, as well as the sometimes hostile physical and social conditions that she encountered, Bird Bishop implicitly challenged the ideology of fragile womanhood and quickly became one of Victorian Britain's most "celebrated" women travelers. More importantly, her works were favorably reviewed both in Great Britain and in the United States, with critics noting in particular her attention to the natural world.

Central to Bird Bishop's professional credibility and reputation was her determination to continue writing during those years in which she had returned to Great Britain, and her work at home took several forms. She wrote regularly for periodicals as varied and influential as the *Contemporary Review*, the *Monthly Review*, the *Leisure Hour*, and *St. James Gazette*. While some of these articles and reviews were based directly on her travels, others broached such topics as "Christian Individuality" (*North British Review*, November, 1862), "Religious Revivals" (*Quarterly Review*, January, 1860), and "The American Secession" (*North British Review*, May, 1861), hence indicating the extent to which Bird Bishop's travel experiences had helped to authorize her as a cultural critic. In addition, she sat on the committees of several missionary societies and gave public lectures throughout the country on an array of subjects. For example, in 1891, shortly after she had published an article titled "The Shadow of the Kurd" in *The Contemporary Review*, she was invited to speak before a committee of the House of Commons on "The Armenian Question."[1] Taken collectively, Bird Bishop's work illustrates well the ways in which Victorian women used travel experiences to garner cultural credibility and to challenge the rigidity of a separate spheres ideology that would otherwise seem to confine their writing to the domestic areas.

Although focused primarily on those years in which Bird Bishop was traveling, Pat Barr's *A Curious Life for a Lady: The Story of Isabella Bird, A Remarkable Victorian Traveller* (1970) provides good biographical coverage and supersedes the other full-length biographical study of Bird Bishop, Anna Stoddart's *The Life of Isabella Bird* (1906). Maria H. Frawley's *A Wider Range: Travel Writing by Women in Victorian England* (1994) situates Bird Bishop's narratives within the broader context of Victorian women's travel writing. The introductory chapters that preface Virago/Beacon editions of Bird Bishop's travel books provide the best critical analyses of her work available. For an effective example of Bird Bishop's critical reputation in the nineteenth century, see the chapter titled "Miss Isabella Bird" in *Celebrated Women Travellers of the Nineteenth Century* (1883) by W. H. Davenport Adams.

Maria H. Frawley,
Elizabethtown College

Notes

1.   In her article "The Shadow of the Kurd," published in the June, 1891 issue of the *Contemporary Review*, Bird Bishop condemns the Kurds for their attacks on Armenians, whom she portrays as ignorant of political grievances but loyal and industrious Christians worthy of English sympathy. She based her beliefs on a journey of two and a half months through Kurdistan which she had undertaken in the autumn of 1890. The "Armenian Question" was one of many discussions related to the conditions of Asiatic Turkey that Parliament had embarked on in the early 1890s.

19. Letter XXVI from *Six Months Among the Palm Groves, Coral Reefs, and Volcanoes of the Sandwich Islands*

Introduction

The following selection appears as Isabella Bird Bishop's "Letter XXVI" from *Six Months Among the Palm Groves, Coral Reefs, and Volcanoes of the Sandwich Islands*, which was first published in 1875, just four years before *A Lady's Life in the Rocky Mountains*. This selection has been taken from the second edition of the book, which was published by John Murray in London in 1876. The letter is representative of much of Bird Bishop's travel writing, emphasizing as it does the rugged conditions in which she traveled as well as her unusual status as a lone female traveler. Utilizing a trope common among many Victorian women travel writers, she indicates in her preface to this volume that she decided to publish an account of travels only after friends convinced her that her work was valuable. Claiming in this preface that she had "so completely lived the island life" as to have been regarded as a "kamaina," or old resident, Bird Bishop encouraged her readers to recognize the extent to which her work went beyond the historical interest of previous writing on Hawaii to explore the domestic side of native life known only to those few travelers who had immersed themselves in its culture. In "Letter XXVI," Bird Bishop reveals her familiarity with this culture by interspersing Hawaiian names and terminology throughout her narrative. Also distinguishing her work from others was her sustained attention to the natural environment of Hawaii, and it was this dimension of the work that contemporary critics praised.

Letter XXVI from *Six Months Among the Palm Groves, Coral Reefs, and Volcanoes of the Sandwich Islands*

Alone with Nature—A Light Equipment—Kahélé—A Garrulous Assemblage—A Paralysed Village—Hilo.

"MY CAMP," HAWAIIAN SLOPES, *May* 21.

This is the height of enjoyment in travelling. I have just encamped under a *lauhala* tree, with my saddle inverted for a pillow, my horse tied by a long lariat to a guava bush, my gear, saddle-bags, and rations for two days lying about, and my saddle blanket drying in the sun. Overhead the sun blazes, and casts no shadow; a few fleecy clouds hover near him, and far below, the great expanse of the Pacific gleams in a deeper blue than the sky. Far above, towers the rugged and snow-patched, but no longer mysterious dome of Mauna Kea; while everywhere, ravines, woods, waterfalls, and stretches of lawn-like grass delight the eye. All green that I have ever seen, of English lawns in June, or Alpine valleys, seems poor and colourless as compared with the dazzling green of this sixty-five miles. It is a joyous green, a glory. Whenever I look up from my writing, I ask, Was there ever such green? Was there ever such sunshine? Was there ever such an atmosphere? Was there ever such an adventure? And Nature—for I have no other companion, and wish for none—answers, "No." The novelty is that I am alone, my conveyance my own horse; no luggage to look after, for it is all in my saddle-bags; no guide to bother, hurry, or hinder me; and with knowledge enough of the country to stop when and where I please. A native guide, besides being a considerable expense, is a great nuisance; and as the trail is easy to find, and the rivers are low, I resolved for once to taste the delights of perfect independence! This is a blessed country, for a lady can travel everywhere in absolute security.

My goal is the volcano of Kilauea, with various diverging expeditions, involving a ride of about 350 miles; but my health has so wonderfully improved, that it is easier to me now to ride forty miles in a day than ten some months ago.

You have no idea of the preparations required for such a ride, and the importance which "littles" assume. Food for two days had to be taken, and all superfluous weight to be discarded, as every pound tells on a horse on a hard journey. My saddle-bags contain, besides "Sunday clothes," dress for any "gaieties" which Hilo may offer; but I circumscribed my stock of clothes as much as possible, having fallen into the rough-and-ready practice of washing them at night, and putting them on unironed in the morning. I carry besides, a canvas bag on the horn of my saddle, containing two days' provender, and a knife, horse-shoe nails, glycerine, thread, twine, leather thongs, with other little et ceteras, the lack of which might prove troublesome, a thermometer and aneroid in a leather case, and a plaid. I have discarded, owing to their weight, all the well-meant luxuries which were bestowed upon me, such as drinking cups, flasks, etnas, sandwich cases, knife cases, spoons, pocket mirrors, &c. The inside of a watchcase makes a sufficient mirror, and I make a cup from a *kalo* leaf. All cases are a mistake,—at least I think so, as I contemplate my light equipment with complacency.

Yesterday's dawn was the reddest I have seen on the mountains, and the day was all the dawn promised. A three-mile gallop down the dewy grass, and slackened speed through the bush, brought me once again to the breezy slopes of Hamakua, and the trail I travelled in February, with Deborah and Kaluna.[1] Though as green then as now, it was the rainy season, a carnival of rain and mud. Somehow the summer does make a difference, even in a land without a winter. The temperature was perfect. It was dreamily lovely. No song of birds, or busy hum of insects, accompanied the rustle of the *lauhala* leaves and the low murmur of the surf. But there is no hot sleep of noon here—the delicious trades keep the air always wakeful.

When the gentleman who guided me through the bush left me on the side of a *pali*, I discovered that Kahélé, though strong, gentle, and sure-footed, possesses the odious fault known as balking, and expressed his aversion to ascend the other side in a most unmistakable manner. He swung round, put his head down, and no amount of spurring could get him to do anything but turn round and round, till the gentleman, who had left me, returned, beat him with a stick, and threw stones at him, till he got him started again.

I have tried coaxing him, but without result, and have had prolonged fights with him in nearly every gulch, and on the worst *pali* of all he refused for some time to breast a step, scrambled round and

round in a most dangerous place, and slipped his hind legs quite over
the edge before I could get him on.

His sociability too is ridiculously annoying. Whenever he sees
natives in the distance, he neighs, points his ears, holds up his heavy
head, quickens his pace, and as soon as we meet them, swings round
and joins them, and can only be extricated after a pitched battle. On a
narrow bridge I met Kaluna on a good horse, improved in manners,
appearance, and English, and at first he must have thought that I was
singularly pleased to see him, by my turning round and joining him at
once; but presently, seeing the true state of the case, he belaboured
Kahélé with a heavy stick. The animal is very gentle and
companionable, and I dislike to spur him; besides, he seems insensible
to it; so the last time I tried Rarey's plan, and bringing his head quite
round, twisted the bridle round the horn of the saddle, so that he had to
turn round and round for my pleasure, rather than to indulge his own
temper, a process which will, I hope, conquer him mercifully.

But in consequence of these battles, and a halt which I made, as,
now, for no other purpose than to enjoy my felicitous circumstances,
the sun was sinking in a mist of gold behind Mauna Loa long before I
reached the end of my day's journey. It was extremely lovely. A heavy
dew was falling, odours of Eden rose from the earth, colours glowed in
the sky, and the dewiest and richest green was all round. There were
several gulches to cross after the sun had set, and a silence, which was
almost audible, reigned in their leafy solitudes. It was quite dark when I
reached the trail which dips over the great *pali* of Laupahoehoe, 700 feet
in height; but I found myself riding carelessly down what I hardly dared
to go up, carefully and in company, four months before. But whatever
improvement time has made in my health and nerves, it has made none
in this wretched, zoophyte village.

Leading Kahélé, I groped about till I found the house of the
widow Honolulu, with whom I had lodged before, and presently all the
natives assembled to stare at me. After rubbing my horse and feeding
him on a large bundle of *ti* leaves that I had secured on the road, I took
my own meal as a spectacle. Two old crones seized on my ankles,
murmuring *lomi, lomi*, and subjected them to the native process of
shampooing. They had unrestrained curiosity as to the beginning and
the end of my journey. I said "*Waimea, Hamakua,*" when they all
chorused, "*Maikai;*" for a ride of forty miles was not bad for a *wahine*

haole. I said *"Wai lio."* (water for the horse), when they signified that there was only some brackish stuff unfit for drinking.

In spite of the garrulous assemblage, I was asleep before eight, and never woke till I found myself in a blaze of sunshine this morning, and in perfect solitude. I got myself some breakfast, and then looked about the village for some inhabitants, but found none, except an unhappy Portuguese with one leg, and an old man who looked like a leper, to whom I said *"ko"* (cane) *"lio"* (horse), exhibiting a rial at the same time, on which he cut me a large bundle, and I sat on a stone and watched Kahélé as he munched it for an hour and a half.

It was very hot and serene down there between those *palis* 700 and 800 feet high. The huts of the village were all shut, and not a creature stirred. The palms above my head looked as if they had always been old, and there was no movement among their golden plumes. The sea itself rolled shorewards more silently and lazily than usual. An old dog slept in the sunshine, and whenever I moved, by a great effort, opened one eye. The man who cut the cane fell asleep on the grass. Kahélé ate as slowly as if he had resolved to try my patience, and be revenged on me for my conquest of him yesterday, and his heavy munching was the only vital sound. I got up and walked about to assure myself that I was awake, saddled and bridled the horse, and mounted the great southward *pali*, thankful to reach the breeze and the upper air in full possession of my faculties, after the torpor and paralysis of the valley below.

Never were waters so bright or stretches of upland lawns so joyous as to-day, or the forest entanglements so entrancing. The beautiful *Eugenia malaccensis* is now in full blossom, and its stems and branches are blazing in all the gulches, with bunches of rose-crimson stamens borne on short spikelets.

*   *   *

HILO, HAWAII, *May* 24*th.*

Once more I am in dear, beautiful Hilo. Death entered my Hawaiian "home" lately, and took "Baby Bell" away, and I miss her sweet angel-presence at every turn; but otherwise there are no changes, and I am very happy to be under the roof of these dear friends again, but indeed each tree, flower, and fern in Hilo is a friend.[2] I would not even wish the straggling Pride of India, and over-abundant lantana, away from this fairest of the island Edens. I wish I could transport you here this moment from our sour easterly skies to this endless summer and endless sunshine, and shimmer of a peaceful sea, and an atmosphere whose influences are all cheering. Though from 13 to 16 feet of rain fall here in the year the air is not damp. Wet clothes hung up in the verandah even during rain, dry rapidly, and a substance so sensitive to damp as botanical paper does not mildew.

I met Deborah on horseback near Onomea, and she told me that the Austins were expecting me, and so I spent three days very pleasantly with them on my way here.

*   *   *

The old *Kilauea* has just come in, and has brought the English mail, and a United States mail, an event which sets Hilo agog. Then for a few hours its still, drowsy life becomes galvanized, and people really persuade themselves that they have something to do, and all the foreigners write letters hastily, or add postscripts to those already written, and lose the mail, and rush down frantically to the beach to send their late letters by favour of the obliging purser. The mail to-day was an event to me, as it has brought your long-looked-for letters.

Notes

1.   Deborah and Kaluna were two of Bird Bishop's traveling companions. Deborah was a seventeen-year-old Hawaiian girl who had been raised by the Austin family, with whom Bird Bishop stayed while in Onomea, Hawaii. Kaluna also appears in "Letter X" of the volume, where he is described as "a very handsome youth of sixteen" (86). Although Bird Bishop calls him "the cousin," it is not clear whether he is the cousin of Deborah or of some other native Hawaiians whom Bird Bishop encountered.
2.   While in Hilo, Bird Bishop stayed at the home of the Severances, an American family. In "Letter III," Mr. Severance is described as Sheriff of Hawaii. In "Letter VII," his wife is described as a missionary's daughter. This is likely the "home" Bird Bishop refers to at the end of "Letter XXVI"; thus, it seems likely that "Baby Bell" was the child of servants in the Severance home.

20. Letter XV from *Unbeaten Tracks in Japan*

Introduction

The following selection appears as Isabella Bird Bishop's "Letter XV" in *Unbeaten Tracks in Japan*, first published by John Murray in 1880, and reprinted here from that edition. Although Bird Bishop had once again undertaken a journey on the advice of a doctor and represented herself in the book's preface as "a solitary health-seeker," Bird Bishop found Japan "a study rather than a rapture." Like other Victorian women travelers, she was eager to promote the novelty of her endeavors, stressing in her preface her status as a "lady travelling alone" and suggesting that she was "the first European lady who had been seen in several districts" of Japan. Letter XV is particularly representative of Bird Bishop's later travel writing. Like a professional ethnographer, she attends carefully to the documentation of village life, emphasizing—in a fashion typical of many Victorian travelers—the filthy conditions she encountered. Addressing the topics that would increasingly become central to her mission as a traveler, her letter focuses on villagers' lack of education regarding what she considered to be proper sanitation as well as on the village's need for medications. Referring in a footnote to the challenges her government faced in its efforts to "raise" a population as "deficient" as the one she described, Bird Bishop exposes the embeddedness of travel writing in the imperial discourse often associated with this particular period of British history.

Letter XV from *Unbeaten Tracks in Japan*

A Fantastic Jumble—The "Quiver" of Poverty—The Watershed—From Bad to Worse—the Rice Planter's Holiday—A Diseased Crowd—Amateur Doctoring—The Hot Bath—Want of Cleanliness—Insanitary Houses—Rapid Eating—Premature Old Age.

KURUMATOGÉ, *June* 30.

After the hard travelling of six days the rest of Sunday in a quiet place at a high elevation is truly delightful! Mountains and passes, valleys and rice swamps; poverty, industry, dirt, ruinous temples, prostrate Buddhas, strings of straw-shod pack-horses; long, grey, featureless streets, and quiet, staring crowds, are all jumbled up fantastically in my memory. Fine weather accompanied me through beautiful scenery from Ikari to Yokokawa, where I ate my lunch in the street to avoid the innumerable fleas of the tea-house, with a circle round me of nearly all the inhabitants. At first the children, both old and young, were so frightened that they ran away, but by degrees they timidly came back, clinging to the skirts of their parents (skirts in this case being a metaphorical expression), running away again as often as I looked at them. The crowd was filthy and squalid beyond description. Why should the "quiver" of poverty be so very full? one asks as one looks at the swarms of gentle, naked, old-fashioned children, born to a heritage of hard toil, to be, like their parents, devoured by vermin, and pressed hard for taxes. A horse kicked off my saddle before it was girthed, the crowd scattered right and left, and work, which had been suspended for two hours to stare at the foreigner, began again.

A long ascent took us to the top of a pass 2500 feet in height, a projecting spur not 30 feet wide, with a grand view of mountains and ravines, and a maze of involved streams, which unite in a vigorous torrent, whose course we followed for some hours, till it expanded into a quiet river, lounging lazily through a rice swamp of considerable extent. The map is blank in this region, but I judged, as I afterwards found rightly, that at that pass we had crossed the watershed, and that the streams thenceforward no longer fall into the Pacific, but into the Sea of Japan. At Itosawa the horses produced stumbled so intolerably that I walked the last stage, and reached Kayashima, a miserable village of fifty-seven houses, so exhausted, that I could not go farther, and was obliged to put up with worse accommodation even than at Fujihara, with less strength for its hardships.

The *yadoya* was simply awful. The *daidokoro* had a large wood fire burning in a trench, filling the whole place with stinging smoke, from which my room, which was merely screened off by some dilapidated *shôji*, was not exempt. The rafters were black and shiny with soot and moisture. The house-master, who knelt persistently on the floor till he was dislodged by Ito, apologised for the dirt of his house, as well he might. Stifling, dark, and smoky, as my room was, I had to close the paper windows, owing to the crowd which assembled in the street. There was neither rice nor soy, and Ito, who values his own comfort, began to speak to the house-master and servants loudly and roughly, and to throw my things about, a style of acting which I promptly terminated, for nothing could be more hurtful to a foreigner, or more unkind to the people, than for a servant to be rude and bullying; and the man was most polite, and never approached me but on bended knees. When I gave him my passport, as the custom is, he touched his forehead with it, and then touched the earth with his forehead.

I found nothing that I could eat except black beans and boiled cucumbers. The room was dark, dirty, vile, noisy, and poisoned by sewage odours, as rooms unfortunately are very apt to be. At the end of the rice planting there is a holiday for two days, when many offerings are made to Inari, the god of rice farmers; and the holiday-makers kept up their revel all night, and drums, stationary and peripatetic, were constantly beaten in such a way as to prevent sleep.

A little boy, the house-master's son, was suffering from a very bad cough, and a few drops of chlorodyne, which I gave him, allayed it so completely, that the cure was noised abroad in the earliest hours of the next morning, and by five o'clock nearly the whole population was assembled outside my room, with much whispering and shuffling of shoeless feet, and applications of eyes to the many holes in the paper windows. When I drew aside the *shôji*, I was disconcerted by the painful sight which presented itself, for the people were pressing one upon another, fathers and mothers holding naked children covered with skin-disease or with scald-head, or ringworm, daughters leading mothers nearly blind, men exhibiting painful sores, children blinking with eyes infested by flies, and nearly closed with ophthalmia, and all, sick and well, in truly "vile raiment," lamentably dirty and swarming with vermin, the sick asking for medicine, and the well either bringing the sick or gratifying an apathetic curiosity. Sadly I told them that I did not understand their manifold "diseases and torments," and that if I did, I had no stock of medicines, and that in my own country the constant washing of clothes, and the constant application of water to the skin, accompanied by friction with clean cloths, would be much relied upon by doctors for the cure and prevention of similar cutaneous diseases. To pacify them, I made some ointment of animal fat and flowers of sulphur, extracted with difficulty from some man's hoard, and told them how to apply it to some of the worst cases. The horse, being unused to a girth, became fidgety as it was being saddled, creating a *stampede* among the crowd, and the *mago* would not touch it again. They are as much afraid of their gentle mares as if they were panthers. All the children followed me for a considerable distance, and a good many of the adults made an excuse for going in the same direction.

I was entirely unprepared for the *apparent* poverty and *real* dirt and discomfort that I have seen since leaving Nikkô. With us poverty of the squalid kind is usually associated with laziness and drunkenness, but here the first is unknown, and the last is rare among the peasant proprietors. Their industry is ceaseless, they have no Sabbaths, and only take a holiday when they have nothing to do. Their spade husbandry turns the country into one beautifully kept garden, in which one might look vainly for a weed. They are economical and thrifty, and turn everything to useful account. They manure the ground heavily, understand the rotation of crops, and have little if anything to learn in the way of improved agricultural processes. I am too new a comer to venture an opinion on the subject. The appearance of poverty may be produced by apathy regarding comforts to which they have not been accustomed. The dirt is preventible, and the causes of the prevalence of cutaneous diseases among children are not far to seek. There can be no doubt of the want of cleanliness in nearly the whole district that I have passed through, and this surprises me.

The people tell me that they take a bath once a week. This sounds well, but when looked into, its merit diminishes. This bath in private houses consists of a tub four feet high, and sufficiently large to allow of an average-sized human being crouching in it in the ordinary squatting position. It is heated by charcoal in such a way that the fumes have occasionally proved fatal. The temperature ranges from 110 to

125, and fatal syncope among old people is known to occur during immersion. The water in private bath tubs is used without any change by all the inmates of a house, and in the public baths by a large number of customers. The bathing is not for purification, but for the enjoyment of a sensuous luxury. Soap is not used and friction is apologised for by a general dabbing with a soft and dirty towel. The intermediate washing consists in putting the feet into hot water when they are covered with mud, washing the hands and face, or giving them a slap with a damp towel.

These people wear no linen, and their clothes, which are seldom washed, are constantly worn, night and day, as long as they will hold together. They seal up their houses as hermetically as they can at night, and herd together in numbers in one sleeping-room, with its atmosphere vitiated to begin with by charcoal and tobacco fumes, huddled up in their dirty garments in wadded quilts, which are kept during the day in close cupboards, and are seldom washed from one year's end to another. The *tatami*, beneath a tolerably fair exterior, swarm with insect life, and are receptacles of dust, organic matters, etc. The hair, which is loaded with oil and bandoline, is dressed once a week, or less often in these districts, and it is unnecessary to enter into any details regarding the distressing results, and much besides may be left to the imagination. The persons of the people, especially of the children, are infested with vermin, and one fruitful source of skin sores is the irritation arising from the cause. The floors of houses, being concealed by mats, are laid down carelessly with gaps between the boards, and as the damp earth is only eighteen inches or two feet below, emanations of all kinds enter the mats and pass into the rooms. Where the drinking water is taken from wells situated in the midst of crowded houses, contamination may be regarded as certain, either from the direct effect of insanitary arrangements within the houses, or from percolations into the soil from gutters outside, choked with decomposing organic matter. In the farming villages, as a general rule, the sewage is kept in large tubs sunk into the earth at the house door, from whence it is removed in open buckets to the fields.

The houses in this region (and I believe everywhere) are hermetically sealed at night, both in summer and winter, the *amado*, which are made without ventilators, literally boxing them in, so that unless they are falling to pieces, which is rarely the case, none of the air vitiated by the breathing of many persons, by the emanations from their bodies and clothing, by the miasmata produced by defective domestic arrangements, and by the fumes from charcoal *hibachi*, can ever be renewed. Exercise is seldom taken from choice, and unless the women work in the fields, they hang over charcoal fumes the whole day for five months of the year, engaged in interminable processes of cooking, or in the attempt to get warm. Much of the food of the peasantry is raw or half-raw salt fish, and vegetables rendered indigestible by being coarsely pickled, all bolted with the most marvellous rapidity, as if the one object of life were to rush through a meal in the shortest possible time. The married women look as if they had never known youth, and their skin is apt to be like tanned leather. At Kayashima I asked the house-master's wife, who looked about fifty, how old she was (a polite question in Japan), and she replied twenty-two—one of many similar surprises. Her boy was five years old, and was still unweaned.

This digression disposes of one aspect of the population.[1]

Letter XV.—(*Concluded*.)

A Japanese Ferry—The *Wistaria Chinensis* —The Crops—A Chinese Drug—Etiquette in Cultivation—A Corrugated Road—The Pass of Sanno—Various Vegetation—An Ungainly Undergrowth—Preponderance of Men—The Shrines of Nature-worship—Apparent Decay of Religion.

We changed horses at Tajima, formerly a *daimiyô's* residence, and, for a Japanese town, rather picturesque. It makes and exports clogs, coarse pottery, coarse lacquer, and coarse baskets.

After travelling through rice-fields varying from thirty yards square to a quarter of an acre, with the tops of the dykes utilised by planting dwarf beans along them, we came to a large river, the Arakai, along whose affluents we had been tramping for two days, and, after passing through several filthy villages, thronged with filthy and industrious inhabitants, crossed it in a scow. High forks planted securely in the bank on either side sustained a rope formed of several strands of the wistaria knotted together. One man hauled on this hand over hand, another poled at the stern, and the rapid current did the rest. In this fashion we have crossed many rivers subsequently. Tariffs of charges are posted at all ferries, as well as at all bridges where charges are made, and a man sits in an office to receive the money.

The wistaria, which is largely used where a strength and durability exceeding that of ordinary cables is required, seems universal. As a dwarf it covers the hills and road-sides, and as an aggressive *liana* it climbs the tallest trees and occasionally kills them, cramping and compressing them mercilessly, and finally riots in its magnificent luxuriance over their dead branches. Several times I have thought that I had come upon a new species of tree of great beauty, and have found it to be an elm or cryptomeria killed and metamorphosed by this rampageous creeper. Some of its twisted stems are as thick as a man's body. In pleasure-grounds it is trellised and trained so as to form bowers of large size, a single tree often allowing 100 people to rest comfortably under its shadow.

Villages with their ceaseless industries succeeded each other rapidly, and the crops were more varied than ever; wheat, barley, millet, rice, hemp, beans (which in their many varieties rank next to rice as the staple food), pease, water melons, cucumbers trained on sticks like peas, sweet potato, egg plants, tiger lilies, a purple colea the leaves of which are eaten like spinach, lettuces, and indigo. Patches of a small yellow chrysanthemum occurred frequently. The petals are partially boiled, and are eaten with vinegar as a dainty. The most valuable crop of this region is *ninjin*, the Chinese *ginseng*, the botanical *Panax repens*. In the Chinese pharmacopeia it occupies a leading place (even apart from superstitions which are connected with it), and is used for fevers as we use quinine. It has at times been sold in the east for its weight in gold, and, though the price has fallen to 40*s*. per lb., the profit on its cultivation is considerable. The ginseng exported annually from Japan is worth, on arrival in China, £200,000, and in another two years more than double the present crop will be placed in the market. The exquisite neatness of Japanese cultivation culminates in *ninjin*.

It is sown on beds 27 feet long, 2 1/2 broad, 1 high, and 2 apart. In each bed there are 438 seed holes, and in each hole three seeds. I mention this as an instance of the minute etiquette which regulates all processes in this curiously formal country. As a protection from the sun, neatly-made straw roofs cover the beds both in winter and summer. Only the strong plants are allowed to survive the first year. In the fifth year the roots are taken up, scalded, and roasted in trays at a gentle heat from four to eight days, according to their size. The stalks and leaves are boiled down to make a black, coarse jelly, much like liquorice, but very bitter, which is used in cases of debility. *Sesamum Orientale*, from which an oil is made, which is used both for the hair and for frying fish, began to be cultivated. The use of this in frying is answerable for one of the most horrific smells in Japan. It is almost worse than *daikon*.

The country was really very beautiful. The views were wider and finer than on the previous days, taking in great sweeps of peaked mountains, wooded to their summits, and from the top of the Pass of Sanno the clustered peaks were glorified into unearthly beauty in a golden mist of evening sunshine. I slept at a house combining silk farm, post office, express office, and *daimiyô's* rooms, at the hamlet of Ouchi, prettily situated in a valley with mountainous surroundings, and leaving early on the following morning, had a very grand ride, passing in a crateriform cavity the pretty little lake of Oyakê, and then ascending the magnificent pass of Ichikawa. We turned off what, by ironical courtesy, is called the main road, upon a villainous track, consisting of a series of lateral corrugations, about a foot broad, with depressions between them more than a foot deep, formed by the invariable treading of the pack-horses in each other's footsteps. Each hold was a quagmire of tenacious mud, the ascent of 2400 feet was very steep, and the *mago* adjured the animals the whole time with *Hai! Hai! Hai!* which is supposed to suggest to them that extreme caution is requisite. Their shoes were always coming untied, and they wore out two sets in four miles. The top of the pass, like that of a great many others, is a narrow ridge, on the farther side of which the track dips abruptly into a tremendous ravine, along whose side we descended for a mile or so in company with a river whose reverberating thunder drowned all attempts at speech. A glorious view it was, looking down between the wooded precipices to a rolling wooded plain, lying in depths of indigo shadow, bounded by ranges of wooded mountains, and overtopped by heights heavily splotched with snow! The vegetation was significant of a milder climate. The magnolia and bamboo re-appeared, and tropical ferns mingled with the beautiful blue hydrangea, the yellow Japan lily, and the great blue campanula. There was an ocean of trees entangled with a beautiful trailer (*Actinidia polygama*) with a profusion of white leaves, which, at a distance, look like great clusters of white blossoms. But the rank undergrowth of the forests of this region is not attractive. Many of its component parts deserve the name of weeds, being gawky, ragged umbels, coarse docks, rank nettles, and many other things which I don't know, and never wish to see again. Near the end of this descent my mare took the bit between her teeth and carried me at an ungainly gallop into the beautifully situated, precipitous village of Ichikawa, which is absolutely saturated with moisture by the spray of a fine waterfall which tumbles through the middle of it, and its trees and roadside are green with the *Protococcus viridis*. The Transport Agent there was a woman. Women keep *yadoyas* and shops, and cultivate farms as freely as men. Boards giving the number of inhabitants, male and female, and the number of horses and bullocks, are put up in each village, and I noticed in Ichikawa, as everywhere hitherto, that men preponderate.[2]

Everywhere there are conical hills densely wooded with cryptomeria, and scarcely one is without a steep flight of handsome stone stairs with a stone or wooden *torii* at its base. From below, the top is involved in mystery, but, on ascending into what is truly a "solemn shade," one usually finds a small, wooden shrine, and some tokens of worship, such as a few flowers, a little rice, or a sprig of evergreen. These "groves" and "high places" are the shrines of the old nature and hero worship which has its symbols "on every high hill, and under every green tree." In some places there is merely a red *torii* with some wisps of straw dangling from it at the entrance of a grove; in others, a single venerable tree or group of trees is surrounded with a straw rope with straw tassels dangling from it—the sign of sacredness; in others, again, a paved path under a row of decaying grey *torii* leads to nothing. The grand flights of stone stairs up to the shrines in the groves are the great religious feature of this part of the country, and seem to point to a much more pious age than the present. The Buddhist temples have lately been few, and though they are much more pretentious than the Shintô shrines, and usually have stone lanterns and monuments of various kinds in their grounds, they are shabby and decaying, the paint is wearing off the wood, and they have an unmistakable look of "disestablishment," not supplemented by a vigorous "voluntaryism." One of the most marked features of this part of the country is the decayed look of the religious edifices and symbols. Buddhas erect but without noses, moss and lichen covered, here and there, with strips of pink cloth tied round their necks, and Buddhas prostrate among grass and weeds, are everywhere. One passes hundreds of them in a single day's journey.

In contrast to the neglect of religious symbols is the fact that the burial-grounds, even the lonely ones of the wild hill-sides, are always well kept, the head-stones are always erect, and on most graves there are offerings of fresh flowers. Near several of the villages there are cemeteries less carefully kept, with monuments of quite a different shape, where the pack-horses of the region are interred. This evening is so very fine that I will break off my letter here. It is more than long enough already.

Notes

1.   Many unpleasant details have necessarily been omitted. If the reader requires any apology for those which are given here and elsewhere, it must be found in my desire to give such a faithful picture of peasant life, as I saw it in Northern Japan, as may be a contribution to the general sum of knowledge of the country, and, at the same time, serve to illustrate some of the difficulties which the Government has to encounter in its endeavour to raise masses of people as deficient as those are in some of the first requirements of civilisation. [Bird Bishop's note]

2.   The excess of males over females in the capital is 36,000, and in the whole Empire nearly half a million. [Bird Bishop's note]

IX. Helen Taylor
(1831–1907)

Helen Taylor played a significant role in the political and educational reforms taking place in Great Britain during the mid-1800s. As one of the founding members of the National Society for Women's Suffrage, she was able to recruit a number of influential people to join the cause, including Florence Nightingale and Mary Carpenter. Taylor also wrote reviews and essays that broached diverse subjects, including religious and political toleration, women's suffrage, political economy—even the relevance of Sir Thomas More's *Utopia* to a Victorian audience. Most likely, Taylor also helped ghostwrite many of John Stuart Mill's speeches and much of his correspondence, as well as helping him draft his influential work, *The Subjection of Women* (1869). Taylor later served on the London School Board and participated in the Land Nationalization Society.

She was born on July 27, 1831, the third and last child of John Taylor, a prosperous druggist, and Harriet Hardy Taylor, a controversial feminist writer whose scandalous friendship with John Stuart Mill led to their marriage in 1851, after her husband's death. Helen Taylor was educated at home, where she studied philosophy, history, theology, literature, French, German, and Italian. Her passionate adolescent interests included music, cathedral architecture, and writing plays. In fact, Taylor so much enjoyed the stage that she decided to become an actress. In 1856, after having spent nearly a year cajoling her mother to allow her to leave home to begin an acting career, Harriet finally acquiesced—under the condition that Taylor take a stage name ("Miss Trevor") and conceal her whereabouts.

Taylor's stage career began slowly, with some long intervals between performances, but by 1858, "Miss Trevor" had become an established actress in Glasgow and Aberdeen. Just as her stage career was beginning to blossom, Taylor's mother developed another of her frequent fevers and coughs—this time when traveling with Mill to Avignon. Less than two weeks after she developed the fever, she was pronounced dead on November 3, 1858. Taylor immediately left Scotland. She travelled to Avignon to comfort her stepfather and apparently decided to abandon her acting career; she remained with Mill until his death in 1873.

Taylor's interests shifted to the women's rights movement after she and Mill returned to London. She assisted members of the Langham Place Group, including Barbara Leigh Smith Bodichon, Jessie Boucherett, Emily Davies and Bessie Rayner Parkes, in advertising the tenets of the suffragists' agenda, and she was particularly instrumental in convincing prominent periodical editors to publish women's rights essays, including her own "Women and Criticism" (*Macmillan's Magazine*, 1866) and "The Ladies' Petition" (*Westminster Review*, 1867). As a result of her shrewd negotiations with editors, she helped ensure that a large reading public was exposed to the activities of women's rights activists.

In 1876, three years after Mill's death, Taylor took the opportunity to begin her own political career. When a Southwark radical workingmen's club asked Taylor to run for the London School Board, she accepted the invitation and ultimately won a seat. Although she continued to be an active suffragist, much of her time was now consumed with her work as an education reformer. Her reputation for taking uncompromising positions, however, made her as many enemies as it gained her supporters.

Throughout her life, Taylor wrote for a variety of periodicals, ranging from the popular *Macmillan's Magazine* to the more specialized *Englishwoman's Review*. In comparison to the writing of her male peers, Taylor's work is often more impassioned, but is also tightly argued and at times humorous and sarcastic. One can tell from her prose that she was not only acutely aware of the pressing political and social issues of her time but also had talent for analyzing difficult questions, especially those involving universal suffrage and the amount of control the State should have over education and religion. By concentrating on her most important women's rights essays, we also see how adept Taylor was at combining her private, radical theories with the more conservative editorial policies of mainstream periodicals.

As with many other radical women, Taylor deliberately couched her demands for reform in a language and style that was designed to attract followers, rather than offend the sensibilities of more conservative readers.

Most of our information on Taylor's life and career comes from Michael St. John Packe's *The Life of John Stuart Mill* (1954). Packe includes excerpts from Taylor's unpublished adolescent diary, as well as a discussion of her involvement with Mill's intellectual circle and with the women's rights movement. For the most helpful primary source on Taylor's background, consult Mill's *Autobiography* (1873). For Taylor's detailed discussion of women and education, consult her article "Industrial Education for Ladies," in the *Englishwoman's Review* (January, 1874). "The Influence of Women on Temperance," also published in the *Englishwoman's Review* (February, 1877) is helpful in delineating Taylor's opinion of women's roles in temperance movements. Valuable secondary sources on Taylor include F.A. Hayek's *John Stuart Mill and Harriet Taylor: Their Friendship and Subsequent Marriage* (1951), and Josephine Kamm's *John Stuart Mill in Love*, which is primarily devoted to biographies of Mill's mother as well as of Harriet and Helen Taylor. Patricia Hollis's *Ladies Elect: Women in English Local Government* (1987), contains an insightful analysis of Taylor's career on the London School Board, and for a discussion of how Taylor's essays fit into a wider context of women's intellectual prose, consult Andrea Broomfield's "Forging A New Tradition: Helen Taylor, Eliza Lynn Linton, Millicent Garrett Fawcett, and the Victorian Woman of Letters" (Ph.D. dissertation. Temple University, 1994).

Andrea Broomfield,
Eastern New Mexico University

21. Women and Criticism

Introduction

Helen Taylor's "Women and Criticism" appeared in the May, 1866, edition of *Macmillan's Magazine* and is reprinted here from that periodical. Although the article is only signed "H.T.," editors of the *Wellesley Index to Victorian Periodicals*, Volume I, have found evidence from Taylor's correspondence to Emily Davies (dated August, 1866), that it was indeed Taylor's piece.

Writing before any overt women's suffrage articles were published in mainstream periodicals, Taylor is careful in "Women and Criticism" to refer to suffrage in only a covert fashion. Instead, she focuses attention on less controversial notions; namely, that women should be allowed the same educational opportunities as men, and that they should have a right to compete freely for jobs in a laissez-faire economy. Only when men and women are allowed equal opportunities, Taylor suggests, will we reach objective conclusions as to what women can and cannot do.

Women and Criticism

Few things are more interesting to an observer of mankind than
the endless variety and absolutely contradictory nature of the objections
raised, in society and contemporary literature, to every possible
proposal for altering anything. It seems to be in the nature of the
human mind to hold that no reason can be necessary for doing nothing;
this is so natural a thing to do, apparently, that the inducements and the
justification for it are, at all times, self-evident to all the world. But,
when any one proposes to break in upon any established order whatever,
by any plan which is actually intended to be carried into practical
operation, then there arises a multitudinous host of objections, not
from one side only but from every side, a tumult of clashing
arguments, of opposing difficulties, a crossfire which sometimes
reminds us of Falconbridge—

> From north to south
> Austria and France shoot in each other's
> mouth,

when those who fancy themselves allies unintentionally destroy one
another's position, by blows aimed at an intermediate enemy.

It is this variety and inconsistency in the objections raised to all
reforms which is one of the chief elements in the priceless value, for
human progress, of free discussion. If the truth had to do battle alone
against all its adversaries the task would be a much harder one than it is
at present, and the result, if not more uncertain, would certainly be
much longer deferred. But, where discussion is free, the *mélée* is
generally so confused that whoever will consent to fight at all can
hardly help dealing some blows at error. He who strikes at random may
fight against truth too, but, if there is one distinguishing mark of truth
as opposed to error, it is its vital power, its strength to endure, the
ineradicable energy with which it revives from apparent annihilation. A
much weaker blow will kill falsehood, and, as a general rule, the same
weakness of mind which makes people hold an opinion on insufficient
grounds makes them find very insufficient arguments strong enough to
overthrow it. Thus, while it is true that error is manifold, yet its
opponents are manifold also. A consistent reasoner will often be
surprised at the weapons with which a victory may be gained for his

own side; yet a logical intellect is not so hard and dry a thing but that some of the most humorous scenes of the comedy of human life may receive their keenest relish from the sense of incongruity between cause and effect.

But, of all the battle-fields of confused and diverse opinion, none is more strangely and chaotically intermingled than the perennial dispute, which all the world loves to join in, as to the comparative merits, duties, faults, and virtues of men and women. Feelings, passions, fancies, sentiments, resentments, hopes, dreams, fears, come pouring in, all eager to do their part in settling the matter, so that, in this particular contest, prejudice and ignorance seem calm and rational in comparison with the rest of the combatants. Nor is this abundance of personal feeling astonishing when we come to consider the subject, since every one is personally concerned in it; no one can help being a man or a woman at some time if he lives long enough. The cattle plague may be discussed among sailors, or fine art with Quakers; in which case it might be possible to secure judges who possess the qualification, so essential in the eyes of many critics, for fitness to judge—that, however little they know of the subject, they care less. But, however little a woman may know of physiology, or psychology, or history, or politics, or social science, or mental science, or difficult subjects of that sort, she is not likely to doubt that she knows woman's nature, which, after all, is only a form of that which all these sciences put together are intended to investigate. What gentle, timid, home-keeping lady will hesitate to pronounce (firm in the consciousness of her own incapacity) what nature destined for all time to be the lot of one half the human race? Is she not a woman herself, and, being so, must she not understand women? Do we not all know ourselves? And, knowing ourselves, as we all do, so well, does it not of necessity follow that we know all who resemble us in any important respect? And, knowing ourselves, is it not evident that we must know what is good for us? And, knowing these things by nature, it cannot be going out of a woman's sphere, nor need any strength of mind, to pronounce what ought to be the relative position of men, women, and children, in politics, arts, sciences, and domestic life. It is, indeed, so difficult to find a woman unprejudiced about women, that those who think least of their own capacities are more confident as to the absence of capacity in women, than those ladies (if any there are) who lay claim to strength of mind can be as to the presence of it. For the women who profess to be in some degree competent to consider the subject, generally only hazard the suggestion that women might possibly prove equal to men if they were placed in the same circumstances, and they propose only that the law shall make no distinctions, and so leave things to adjust themselves. But those who think they know woman's proper place from their own internal consciousness, want laws to keep her there. Not content to remain in that vague state of mind which only suits scientific accuracy, and requires experiment and test before considering any fact as certain; content still less with that impartiality which may do well enough for the lawgiver or statesman, but which does not become an ignorant woman; they demand a positive recognition by law and institutions of the difference between two things, of which difference these ladies are perfectly sure, because they know one of the two quite well.

When all women, strong or weak-minded, have given in their contribution to this universally-interesting subject, it is far from being exhausted. If women naturally have an opinion upon it because they are women, men have one because they are not. Even those who think the only suitable relations between the two are those of superiority and subordination cannot deny this. The question of where the lamb was entitled to drink from, was not less interesting to the wolf than to the lamb. It would be taking a very narrow view of the matter to deny that the wolf had, at least, a right to be heard, in support of claims on which so much of his comfort in life depended. The fact is, that the nearer we could come to a complete equality between men and women in the laws and institutions under which they live, the better chance would there be of getting at something like impartial opinion on the subject. The nearer it could be brought to being nobody's interest to think one way or another about it, the nearer we should be to arriving at some cool and unbiassed judgment. No observer can help seeing at present that the interests at stake are too important to permit much impartiality. People are either, consciously or unconsciously, blinded by their personal wishes and experience, or else, making a strenuous effort to be magnanimous, they endeavour to secure themselves against being selfish by an entire renunciation of all personal claims. The common opinion that women are more enthusiastic and less reasoning than men, and that men are more deliberate, and know better what they mean when they say a thing, than women, may perhaps explain why, on the whole, most women decide against, and most men in favour of, themselves.

But, if women were really entitled in justice to any rights and privileges which most of them disclaim, it may be doubted whether the fact of their renouncing such rights from pure although mistaken motives of duty, would be any evidence of unfitness for their exercise.

Yet, among the many answers commonly given when the question is asked, Why women should not have all occupations and privileges open to them, and be free to adopt or renounce masculine, as men are feminine, pursuits? none reappears more frequently than the assertion that women themselves do not wish for any such freedom. With many persons it is a received axiom that women do not like liberty. There is nothing, it would seem, that a woman more dislikes than being permitted to do what she likes. Husbands and fathers know by experience that women never wish to have their own way. One reason for this appears to be that women are endowed by nature with so strong and peculiar an idiosyncrasy that they must necessarily run counter to it if they are let alone. The laws of nature are so powerful in women that it is essential to make human laws in aid of them. The instincts of their sex so imperiously demand of women to do what is feminine, that it is necessary for men to forbid them to do anything masculine. Therefore it stands to reason that women who wish to be guided by womanly instinct must place themselves under the guidance of men. Possessed by an innate sense of feminine propriety, women feel that if the law did not protect them against themselves they would be inclined to do many unsuitable things. With men it is different; no laws are needed to define what men may or may not do, for men, with their less acute moral perceptions, are not likely to do what is unsuited to them. But legislative enactments can alone keep women from leaving their firesides to plunge into the fierce contentions and angry passions of the political world; were they free to choose for themselves it is to be feared they would desert their infants in order to command armies; their love of beauty and their physical weakness would induce them to apply themselves to the most repulsive and laborious occupations, such as no man would like to see a woman employed in, and from which they would naturally, but perhaps very unfairly, drive out their more robust masculine competitors. Then, too, being gentle, docile, and retiring, naturally fitted to obey, is it not likely that if left to their own guidance, they would show themselves quarrelsome, self-willed, and altogether unmanageable?

Leaving those who will to unravel these very curious series of
logical sequences, or perhaps leaving these contradictory propositions to
neutralize one another, it may be worth while to go on a few steps
further, and consider the question on the ground of general principles,
which cover a much larger space than the mere distinction between men
and women: for, the moment we step beyond the charmed circle which
shuts in women in most people's imagination, we find ourselves on
ground where it is comparatively usual to appeal to reason, and to
expect that reasons shall have some sort of consistency in them. On no
other subject is it commonly held that so small an amount of
experimental evidence is sufficient to build up such a wide induction as
on this. It is the commonest thing in the world to hear even educated
people, who, on other topics, pride themselves on having some
foundation for what they say, confound together in one group millions
of women, of different races and different religions, brought up in
different climates, and under different institutions, and predict, with
quiet security, how all these would act under utterly untried
conditions—such as perfect political and social freedom—of which the
history of the world has never yet furnished even a single instance
whereon to ground a sober judgment. How utterly this whole way of
treating such a subject is opposed to all the scientific tendencies of our
time, it is hardly worth while to stop to point out.

The growing habit of studying history from a philosophical
point of view, and drawing generalizations from its teaching in a
scientific spirit, will, no doubt, do much to induce men (and women
too) to consider the destinies, the duties, and the rights of women in a
serious and logical manner, and to lay aside the jokes and the
sentimental preferences which at present encumber and entangle all
discussion on the subject. It may even be presumed, that, fortified with
such studies, some women may no longer shrink from being called
"strong-minded," as from an abusive epithet, and that men may only
hesitate to apply it to them, as being more complimentary than they are
often likely to deserve.

But, when rational habits of thought, and a comparatively widely
extended acquaintance with scientific methods of observation and
experiment, have done much good work on the public mind, still we
cannot expect a thorough cure in the fanciful method of treating
women's rights, until legislation, by loosening a little the tightness of
its bonds, opens the door to observation, and permits a few, however

timid, experiments to be made. At present it is hard to complain of those who appeal to their own imagination as warrant for their highly imaginative assertions of what would happen if any changes were introduced into the condition of women, for to what else can they appeal? The truth is, as we take it, that the law is a great deal too minute in its legislation on this subject; for, if we come to consider it, we find that it is marked in the highest degree by the characteristic of early and antiquated legislation: it protects the interests of both men and women a great deal too much, and, by taking too much care of them, will not allow them to take care of themselves. It is this same meddlesome spirit which in former times produced sumptuary laws, and fixed the rate of interest and of wages; which forbade the exportation of gold and other valuable commodities from the realm, and gave rise to the whole system of commercial protection.

But the striking and brilliant success of free trade principles has happily had a powerful effect in opening the eyes of every civilized people to the mischievous effects of over-legislation. The benefit of the promulgation of such principles ought not to stop even at this result, great as it is. For the philosophical principles, and the whole train of reasoning which lead to free trade, not merely indicate that over-legislation is a check upon individual energy and enterprise, but point to the direction which all the legislation should take, viz.—to development, and not to the repression, of the faculties of those who have to obey it. That the law is made for man, not man for the law, is the spirit of modern legislation, and we recognise the working of this spirit where we see the law removing hindrances to human energy, not where we see it imposing them. The hindrances that we are willing to see imposed by the law are only those that prevent people from hindering one another, not such as are imagined to be beneficial to themselves. We are willing to see a man hindered from stealing another man's goods, but we murmur if he is not allowed to sell his own at as low a price as he pleases. The application of any such principle will show at once how very defective is our present legislation as regards women, and how antiquated is the train of reasoning by which such legislation is defended. Indeed, the only logical defence of our present legislation would be that it considers only the interests of men, and looks upon women as a subject, and even as an antagonistic class, whose hands are to be bound for the benefit of those whom the law really intends to protect. It is not impossible that some such point of

view was that which really actuated those who originated our present
system, many parts of which have come down to us from times when
men had not, even in thought, got beyond the idea that—

> Those should take who have the power,
> And those should keep who can.

But the most violent assertor of the sacred rights of sex would shrink
now from making such a notion the ground either of his own claims or
her own abnegation. Agreeing, therefore, as most disputants would
probably do, that no one wants to oppress and enslave women for other
people's benefit, we are thrown back upon the theory, that, solely for
their own good, they are excluded from all the professions, from all
political rights, from a share in the great national institutions for
education, and from every other privilege possessed only by men. The
energy and the enterprise women might show in any of all these
departments is checked by the law, only in order to protect them, just as
our traders and manufacturers used to be protected against foreign
competition. The development of their faculties is forbidden to take
place in these directions, only in order that they may be turned into
more healthy and natural channels, just as particular industries used to
be encouraged by law because it used to be thought that our island
possessed peculiar facilities for those, and just as particular methods of
manufacture used to be enjoined because it was supposed that our
people would employ wrong methods if the law did not restrict them to
right ones. Now, on the supposition (which lies as the root of the
Protective system) that our lawgivers know the true interest of every
individual of the nation better than he can know it for himself, there can
be no objection to all this as a whole, and, if we think we see reason to
object to the working of any particular portion of the system, we must
set ourselves to show what are its specially inconvenient results, and
what good might be expected to come from the relaxation of particular
restraints. Just as, under a system of commercial protection, it would be
necessary to show that some particular trade is an exceptional one in
order to get it freed from the general rule, so, on such a supposition, we
must show that some particular profession or occupation is (unlike the
majority of others) suited for women, before we can get it opened to
them.

It is precisely this necessity, arising, as we have endeavoured to
show, from ignoring the fundamental principles of modern government,

that opens the door to the flood of peculiarly contradictory and imaginative discussion which characterises every attempt at carrying out some little modification of the highly "protected" condition of women. For how can discussion on this subject be otherwise than imaginative? By the nature of the case those who are urging change are asking to be allowed to try experiments. Until experiments have been tried, we can only imagine what would be their practical results. When we are reduced to imagination one man's imagination is as good as another's, and the Irishman in the story would perhaps have said that a conservative's imagination is "better too." The reformer imagines great benefits, the conservative imagines dire disaster, to be the consequences of most change. What can decide between the two, except that invincible "logic of facts" to which protective law sternly forbids a hearing? Deprived of this impartial umpire, people disport themselves in all the wide regions of fanciful conjecture; analogy is put forward for sober argument; figurative phrases as logical proof; a single example as conclusive evidence; personal taste as the law of nature; accidental circumstances as the immutable condition of the universe. And it is the natural consequence of such discussion's being fanciful that it should also be contradictory. For no two men's imagination depicts a thing exactly in the same light. No two reformers desire, and no two conservatives dread, a change for precisely the same reasons. One man wishes a thing because it does what another man deprecates it for not doing. Thus many persons at the present moment shrink from opening the medical profession to women, because they think it might make them less delicate; others fear that such a movement, by enabling women always to consult physicians of their own sex, might foster a morbid degree of delicacy. Thus two different descriptions of imagination may figure the results of the same change as making women too delicate and not delicate enough. In this particular instance, as in many others of the same sort, it is not difficult to detect that the fancy of the objectors has seized hold of different parts of the same subject, and exaggerated a part into the whole. One class persists in regarding exclusively the probable effect upon the physicians, the other that on the patients; and both are apt to forget that, in so very extensive a portion of humanity as the whole female sex, there may easily be room for such varieties of character as would be healthily affected by both sets of influences.

From all these workings of the imagination there is no final appeal but to facts. Experiments must be tried before we can hope to arrive at trustworthy conclusions. They can be tried cautiously if we fancy, as many people do fancy, that, in dealing with women, we are dealing with very explosive materials. But, until we are willing to try them in some way, we cannot deny that those who are willing to appeal to facts are more candid, and those who desire to have recourse to experiment are more practical, than those who are content to defend the present state of things by vague predictions of possible evil, while they refuse to put their own predictions to even the most gentle test.

Just such predictions of national ruin were made arguments against free trade, and against such arguments no reply could be so effectual as the national prosperity which free trade has produced. But, until free trade had actually been tried, this argument was not available for its supporters. Having been tried, and having succeeded, free trade, however, remains an example of how human energy can find the best and easiest channels for itself when relieved from all restrictive legislation; an example likely in time to modify old opinions on many topics, and perhaps on none more than on the freedom that can safely be allowed to women.

22. The Ladies' Petition

Introduction

Helen Taylor's "The Ladies' Petition" appeared in the January, 1867, edition of the *Westminster Review* and is reprinted here from that periodical. In her article, Taylor calls attention to and defends this first major women's suffrage petition, which was presented to the House of Commons by J.S. Mill on June 7, 1866. Although the article is explicitly in favor of granting women suffrage, Taylor felt compelled to limit her support of enfranchisement to single, property-owning women—not all women, as she initially had planned. To have advocated enfranchisement for all women, irrespective of their marital and class status, was still too radical a stance for mainstream periodicals (even "highbrow" ones like the *Westminster*) to print. Taylor's decision to minimize publicly her support was, however, in line with her overarching philosophy: only by advertising the suffrage movement "as far and wide as possible," would the suffragists ever gain the support they needed to win the vote.

The Ladies' Petition

Petition presented to the House of Commons by Mr. J.
Stuart Mill, June 7th, 1866.

Among the demonstrations of opinion which the discussions on
Parliamentary Reform have drawn forth during the past session, no one
was more remarkable than the petition signed by fifteen hundred ladies,
which was presented to the House of Commons by Mr. J. Stuart Mill.
This petition is comprised in a few short sentences, and sets forth that
the possession of property in this country carries with it the right to
vote in the election of representatives in Parliament; that the exclusion
from this right of women holding property is therefore anomalous; and
that the petitioners pray that the representation of householders may be
provided for without distinction of sex.

This claim, that since women are permitted to hold property they
should also be permitted to exercise all the rights which, by our laws,
the possession of property brings with it, is put forward in this petition
on such strictly constitutional grounds, and is advanced so entirely
without reference to any abstract rights, or fundamental changes in the
institutions of English society, that it is impossible not to feel that the
ladies who make it have done so with a practical purpose in view, and
that they conceive themselves to be asking only for the recognition of
rights which flow naturally from the existing laws and institutions of
the country.

That a considerable number of ladies should think it worth while
to examine into their actual political status, and finding it to all
appearance inconsistent with the principles of the British Constitution,
should proceed to lay what they term the "anomaly" before the House of
Commons, is assuredly an important symptom of our national
condition; an evidence that the minds of English people, men and
women, are actively at work in many directions where they might have
been but little expected to penetrate. It is, at the same time, a sign of
that disposition which various causes (partly political and partly
philosophical) have tended to foster of late years, to seek the reform of
existing evils rather in the development than in the overthrow of the
present order of things.

It may appear, at first sight, as though in proportion to the millions of Englishwomen who live happily under our laws, or who groan under all the miseries of wife-beating and other social evils, without a thought of how their condition might be affected by legislation, fifteen hundred women are too small a number to be worthy of a moment's consideration. But if we reflect a little on the peculiar position of women, and their usual ways of thinking—on their habitual reticence on all subjects which they are accustomed to consider as beyond their own sphere, their timidity and dread of exposing their names to public observation, their deference even to the most unreasonable prejudices of those who have any claim on their affections, their clinging to old associations, and their regard for the opinion of all who are even remotely connected with them—we shall see reason to think that these fifteen hundred ladies, who have not hesitated to affix their names to a public document, and to pronounce a decided opinion, open to the controversy and criticism of all the world, must represent an extraordinarily important phase of thought. It is not going too far to say, that for one woman who can and will pronounce openly on such a subject, there must be at least ten whom family hindrances or habitual timidity will prevent from expressing an opinion, even if they have formed any. And the number must be still greater of those whose minds are only partially prepared for any ideas on such subjects, who are little in the habit of arriving at any definite conclusions at all on political matters, but who, as they have passed through much of the same experience, and lived in the same state of society as their more energetic or more active-minded sisters, must have been liable to the same influences, and are not at all unlikely to adopt the same way of thinking, when it is put before them in so plausible and so little startling a form as we find it in this petition. The peculiarly dependent position of women is another circumstance which must add much to our estimate of the number really represented by these fifteen hundred petitioners. There is scarcely a family in the kingdom where a mother, or a widowed or unmarried sister, or one married to a kind husband, is not the intimate friend and confident of a daughter, a mother, or a sister in a less fortunate position. Those who have been brought up together, who have learnt from one another's experience, or who have imbibed from one another the same ways of feeling, are often separated in appearance by the political or religious opinions of their fathers or husbands, or by a domestic despotism which only allows one person to express openly what many think. Moreover, when we remember that few women are able both to form and to express political opinions at all, without the assistance and encouragement of some at least among their male relations, it becomes evident that every woman who does form such, must be looked upon as the representative of a considerable body of opinion. And when the thought thus expressed is so comparatively new as to meet with little external encouragement, it must be strongly rooted in many unseen ramifications before it can have grown vigorous enough to show itself in a clear, definite, and conspicuous shape. But even independently of any of these considerations, it is impossible to glance down the list of signatures appended to this petition (a printed copy of which has been forwarded to us) without seeing that it includes a proportion large for the actual number of names, both of the intelligence and the property of Englishwomen. With all these facts before us, we think we are justified in repeating that the appearance of such a claim, supported in such a manner, is a significant indication of the direction public opinion is taking.

What we find asked for, then, in this petition, seems to be that Englishwomen shall be included in that measure of political freedom which the wisdom of Parliament sees fit to grant to Englishmen. This amount of political enfranchisement is asked for by the means by which men and women have for ages been accustomed, in this country, to make their wants known to the legislature; namely, by petition to the House of Commons. It would appear as if the election to Parliament of a member who, before his election, distinctly enunciated his opinion that women ought to have votes, has, in the judgment of the petitioners, opened for them a new prospect of getting their claims heard. That a writer of the scientific eminence and political ability of the member for Westminster holds such an opinion, and moreover that openly proclaiming it he has been returned to Parliament by a constituency influenced only by public motives, is certainly a fact that may very justly encourage these ladies to think that the political representation of women is really a question ripe for discussion; and it may fairly give them reason to hope that if they can advance any rational grounds for their claims, they will receive reasonable attention.

This being the case, we propose to examine, in some degree, not merely into the general purport of this petition, but also into the specific reasons assigned in it for the claim which it puts forward. For although it would be in itself a remarkable thing that so many Englishwomen are now prepared to ask for some sort of political representation, yet more or less increase of the liberty allowed to women has been recommended by men and asked by women, both in this country and others, for a long time past. Some relaxation of the restrictions under which the female sex has hitherto laboured is indeed a natural and inevitable consequence of the advancing freedom and civilization of the other sex, but this movement is marked by what appear to us some novel and especially national characteristics. It is interesting to observe what form this general tendency towards freedom assumes when it shows itself among a large body of Englishwomen; by what means they propose to work it out, and by what train of reasoning they seek to recommend it to their countrymen.

The petitioners ground their request on the principles of the British Constitution. They assert that certain facts in our existing system establish that women cannot be considered to be without the pale of the Constitution, for that there are precedents to show that its general principles have already been applied to women in some particular cases. They point out that in this country the franchise is dependent upon property, and that the acknowledgment of women as sovereigns among us shows that women are not considered disqualified for government. From these two principles, both of which are undoubted parts of the British Constitution as it stands at this day—the representation of property, and government by female sovereigns—the petitioners draw the evident inference, that where the female sex is no bar to the higher, it cannot reasonably be to the lower privileges of political life, when those privileges are dependent upon conditions (such as the possession of property) which women actually fulfil. And they characterize the exclusion of half the human race from any share in self-government as an "anomaly" in our representative system.

Whether this way of treating the subject arises from the petitioners themselves only looking at it from this peculiarly English point of view, or whether it is adopted as the one likely to meet with the most general support and the smallest amount of dissent, it is equally a sign of the times. If the idea of the political representation of women has now made its appearance among us in a peculiarly English dress, and one adapted to the exigencies of the reform discussions of the past session (which have turned so specially on the representation of property, and a suitable property qualification), we cannot refuse to admit that it is all the fitter to take its place among the political ideas of the day; and that it has thereby assumed a more practical character than if it had been attempted to establish it on the grounds of any more general or philosophical systems of representation. Without attempting to go at length into the subject, it will be easily seen that the representation of women might be urged with considerable force on almost any of these systems; but it is itself more in harmony with our present institutions than they are. Nothing can be more entirely foreign to our whole English system than Universal Suffrage, or than either Personal or Class Representation. All these systems, whether we hold them to be in the abstract pernicious or beneficial, are so entirely unable to coalesce with that already prevailing among us, that if they are to be tried, it would be a wise policy to introduce them *parallel*, so to speak, to our present institutions, of which they are not the development, but properly and literally a re-form.[1] But if any of these systems be admitted, either partially or entirely, either in theory or in practice, women would find a place under them equally with men. Universal Suffrage by its very name includes them; personal representation if carried out on principle has for its necessary consequence the representation of women, since the leading idea of personal representation is the effort to secure a hearing to every individual interest or opinion in the nation, however insignificant or obscure. And the totally opposite principle, of class representation, is in the highest degree favourable to the political interests of women, who, if considered as a class, are the most numerous class in the country. Indeed, no advocate of the system of class representation can for a moment refuse in consistency to recognize the claims of so important a class, and of one which is certainly bound together by a community of interests in many of the largest branches of human affairs. Those who disapprove of all attempts at class representation and believe them to be a lingering remains of an effete state of society, and those who disapprove of special legislation grounded on difference of sex and enforcing by law the exclusion of women from all masculine occupations or privileges, may consistently object to consider women as a class, or to make any claim for them as such. But this is not possible for those who group all women together, as actual or potential wives and mothers. They, on the contrary, must in consistency admit that the wives and mothers of the nation, regarded as a class, form one before whose vital importance, and overwhelming numbers, all other classes shrink into insignificance. For independently of the consideration that women are in this country more numerous absolutely than the sum of all the many classes into which men are divided by their occupations, it is evident that if women are permitted no other interest than those which they hold in common with all women by virtue of their sex, these interests must be of proportionately greater consequence to women than the equivalent interests are to men, since men have other interests in life as well.

If therefore the lady petitioners had chosen to urge their claims simply as women, and not as English women, they would, on the theory of class representation, have been able to take up very strong ground. But, apart from all consideration of the abstract truth of this theory, it seems to us that they have done well to leave it aside. For it is, as we have indicated, diametrically opposed to the English political system, and indeed more fundamentally so than personal representation. For if the English system refuses to recognise[2] the mere individual as a political unit, and if it insists that he must have palpable evidence that he requires protection for something more precious (we presume) than life or honour, before it admits him to any share in protecting himself; still more does it refuse to protect interests which do not belong to any one in particular, but which are diffused over vast numbers of men, grouped together under the merely ideal definition of a class. Property represented by an individual is the true political unit among us; and in this we recognise the influence of those mediæval habits of thought, which, putting forward living persons as the representatives of rights supposed to be inherent in particular functions or particular localities, was itself practically an advance on those Oriental ideas of caste which survive in the privileges of class, sex, or colour. This mode of thought was due partly, no doubt, to the influence of the Church, which gave and still gives examples of it in the "incumbent" and "parson" or "persona," who derives his rights neither from privilege of birth nor even from his functions as priest, but from the induction into the enjoyment of certain property for his life, of which he has the management; and of which he becomes, so to speak, the bodily expression, the "persona," responsible for the due payment of all charges. It was diffused and perpetuated by the arrangements made under the feudal system for the protection of property in times of war and against all illegal violence; and it seems to have been held, that as only those possessing property could be obliged to furnish a contingent share towards the expenses of government, they alone had any direct interest to protect against the central authority, which, in so far as it preserved peace and order in lawless times, must have stood in the position of gratuitous benefactor towards the unpropertied portion of the people. However this may be, there can be no doubt that the principle underlying our English system of government, is that men are endowed with the privilege of voting in the election of members of the Legislature, in order to enable them to protect their property against undue taxation, or other legislative enactments that might injuriously affect it. So deeply is this idea rooted in the English mind, that long after the separation of the American colonies we find American politicians arguing against conferring votes on negro slaves, upon the express ground that slaves, not being able to hold property, do not require political representation; and for authority for this point of view we find them referring to the acknowledged principles of the British system of law, which, it is well known, is considered as the foundation of the institutions of the United States, wherever not abrogated by the American Constitution, or by special legislation.

Lord Somers, in 1703, speaking in the name of the House of Lords, lays it down that "The Lords . . . conceive that giving a vote for a representative in Parliament is the essential privilege whereby every Englishman preserves his property; and that whatsoever deprives him of such vote, deprives him of his birthright." The line of thought, or train of reasoning, plainly to be traced here, is certainly very favourable to the claim of the ladies. The "birthright" of an Englishman is defined by this high authority as the privilege of preserving his property. He is refused any birthright inherent in himself, but it is laid down that by the possession of property he comes into possession of a privilege attached to property; a privilege which is a "*birthright*" apparently, because it is "essential" to the system of law under which he is born. It is observable that this way of considering a *birthright* as not of *natural* but of *legal* origin, is in conformity with modern habits of thought in regard to civilized men, the natives of civilized societies; but exactly in proportion as it is opposed to any *à priori* theories of the rights of man, it is also opposed to any attempt to give or withhold privileges for merely *natural* reasons, such as difference of sex. It is hard to see how, if the law of England endows a woman with property, it can, consistently with this legal dictum, deprive her of the "essential privilege" (which, as we understand Lord Somers, must be her "birthright" if she is born in England) whereby her property is to be preserved. Undoubtedly, Parliament may make special enactments excepting particular classes of English subjects from the rights they would otherwise enjoy in common with the rest of the community; and from this point of view the adoption of the word "male" in every Act of Parliament which confers the suffrage, must be looked upon as the adoption of an exceptional form, used (as Lord Somers would seem to say) to "deprive" Englishwomen of property of their "birthright." Now, it is assuredly in harmony with all our institutions that any class of persons, labouring under an exceptional disability as a consequence of special legislation, should petition Parliament for its removal, and should appeal against it to the general principles of the Constitution; while the burden of adducing sufficient reasons for such an exceptional disability must, in justice, lie with its supporters.

In pointing out the quite peculiar position occupied by female possessors of property, the lady petitioners have undeniably touched upon a weak point in our present political system, a kind of gap, where in political life there exists no equivalent for what we have in social and civil life. It is an "anomaly," as they assert. For who else among us, entitled by law to hold property to a certain amount, is nevertheless deprived of the vote which the British Constitution looks upon as the safeguard of property? The answer will be—Minors, idiots, lunatics, and criminals. These, and these only, are classed politically along with women. But none of these are so classed in anything but in politics. In no other respect can their standing among us be compared with that of women. We do not mean to compliment the ladies by asserting that they may not be as weak, as foolish, as mad, or as wicked as any of all these classes of the community; but we might be as enthusiastic a woman-hater as ever wrote in the *Saturday Review*, and still a moment's reflection on the legal position of these classes would show that it has nothing in common with that of women administering their own property. However incapable these latter may be, our institutions do actually permit them to administer their property for themselves. Women do actually undertake the responsibility and enjoy the privileges of property, excepting only the privilege of voting. They are liable for debts; they can enter into contracts; they can alienate or they can purchase at their own free will and pleasure; they can devise by will or gift; they can sue or be sued in courts of law in vindication of their rights or in punishment of their shortcomings; they can release others

from legal obligations towards themselves, and they can incur legal
obligations towards others in regard of the property they hold. But
minors, idiots, lunatics, and criminals can do none of all these things.
They merely hold the right to the possession of property at some future
time when they shall have become different from what they now are,
along with the right to transfer it to their heirs. Upon them the law
bestows no power of dealing with their possessions as seems good to
themselves; no power of vindicating their own doings before a legal
tribunal; no power of prosecuting those who attack their pecuniary
interests; no power, in short, of "preserving their property" before the
civil law.

Nor is this all. The legal powers of women in regard to property
are no dead letter. These powers are not an obsolete right known only to
antiquarians, hidden away among the curiosities of the Constitution,
exercising no influence upon the world around us; a mere chance
survivor of effete customs, an anachronism in the society in which we
live. So far from it, the exercise of these powers is an established part
of our social system, and every day becoming a more prominent part. It
awakens no surprise by its novelty; it shocks the prejudices of no one
among us; on the contrary, he who should propose to deprive maiden
ladies of their little independence, and put it into the hands of their
nephews, or who should recommend the law to place all widows'
property under the control of their deceased husband's brother, would be
universally looked upon as un-English, and as either a fanatical admirer
of exploded absurdities, or a would-be introducer of Oriental ideas. Not
only therefore do our laws permit women to exercise all the rights of
property, but it is customary with us for women to do so, and public
opinion regards their doing so as usual and proper. Nor is it any novelty
among us. Although we know that in the more disturbed and lawless
periods of our history it was necessary to make haste and marry rich
unmarried girls and widows (unless they were willing to retire into
convents), in order to secure protection for their riches, still we cannot
point to any precise data when this state of things came to an end, and
when advancing civilization and general respect for law relieved rich
women from the fear of outrage, and made it possible for them to
dispense with a male protector. It is very possible that the dispersion of
the monastic houses may have hastened this stage in the emancipation
of women; it is still more probable that the rise of the middle classes
had much to do with it; but from whatever cause it originated, it has

long been an established thing with us that no woman is obliged to hand over her property to any one unless she so pleases, and that if she does not so please, law and custom allow her the fullest liberty, and an absolute equality of right with men, excepting only in the single instance of political right.

Whence, then, comes this exception? Why, when they possess the necessary property, are women, alone among citizens of full age and sane mind, unconvicted of crime, disabled by a merely personal circumstance (that of sex) from exercising a right attached by our institutions to property and not to persons? What is the historical origin of this anomaly? For an historical origin there must be, and it appears to us shortsighted to attribute it to any of those general theories about the natural functions of women which it might be necessary to have recourse to in explaining a similar anomaly in a system based on universal suffrage. The explanation must, we think, be sought in our own history, and is not far to seek. It is probably the very fact to which we have referred, that, during the earlier period of our constitutional history, society was in so unsettled a state that women could not practically administer their own property, which led to women's not being included among the voters in the elections of members of Parliament. While women did not actually fulfil the other functions of owners of property, the political functions were naturally not attributed to them. Even though it might be by no fault of their own that women could not govern their own property in those times, still it was not likely that they should be admitted to a share in the political government of property which was not actually under their management. The Constitution was perfectly consistent in permitting the feminine nominal owners of the property to derive as much benefit from their civil ownership as they could manage to do, while it ignored all personal claims on their part to political influence derived from property which they were not (from whatever causes) practically competent to administer. Many centuries elapsed after our electoral system had been brought into tolerably regular operation, before the progress of law and order enabled women, as a matter of course, to exercise openly the civil rights which the law attaches to property. It is in the natural course of things that now, after one or two centuries of the practical enjoyment of their civil rights, intelligent women begin to ask why the political rights should not accompany them.

To this question, there can, we apprehend, be but one answer in the negative, at all consistent with the general principles of English law and institutions. It may be said that society is still in too uncivilized a condition to be able to protect women in the enjoyment of their political rights; for [sic] that it is still beyond the power of the Government to prevent them from being molested by riotous proceedings at polling-booths, or coerced by undue interference on the part of their male relations. It is evident that, even if this statement had a broader foundation in fact than we believe it has, this foundation would be diminished by the natural progress of every year that passes over our heads. But it can scarcely be seriously maintained that the central authority which can preserve Hyde Park, against the whole working population of London, for the recreation and health of ladies and children of the upper classes, is incompetent to preserve order in and around polling-booths on the exceptional occasion of an election. And if neither the troops, nor the police, nor any number of special constables could prevent women from being subjected to insult on these occasions, it would still be perfectly easy to afford to them the same immunities as are already accorded to non-resident members of the Universities of Oxford and Cambridge, and to permit ladies also to record their votes by means of voting papers.

The notion that the possession of a vote would expose women to improper coercion on the part of their male relations, will still less bear examination than the theory that our Government is not strong enough to protect any class of its subjects in the exercise of whatever rights it may see fit to accord them. The strength of the motives that would be likely to induce men to interfere with their female relatives in the disposal of their property, is incalculably greater than the strength of the motives that, even in times of political excitement, would urge men to try to overawe women in the exercise of the suffrage. The law has for centuries ruled that women possess sufficient strength of mind to protect their own pecuniary interests; and it has left them to seek the same redress as men, if they find themselves subjected to force or improper influence in doing so. The will of an elderly lady is not cancelled because of the possible influence her son may have used to induce her to make it in his favour, any more than the will of an old gentleman is set aside on account of the possible interference of his daughter. The law very properly refuses to consider whether men are likely to domineer over women, or whether women are likely to cajole men, and in either case it requires ample proof before proceeding to act on particular instances of either disposition. The law, which has, most properly, left women to fight their own battle (and the battle of their heirs) against private greed, cannot be required in these days to provide exceptional protection for them against the comparatively mild force of political enthusiasm. No candidate for parliamentary honours ever more ardently desired them, than a spendthrift nephew desires that his rich aunt would leave her comfortable fortune to him, rather than to her favourite minister; nevertheless we none of us dream of depriving the poor lady of all control over her property, in order to protect her against the unprincipled importunities either of the minister or of the nephew. Yet how great is the prize that either of these may hope from the weakness of only one woman, compared to the triumph of the parliamentary candidate, even if every qualified woman in his constituency could be persuaded or compelled to vote for him! To say that such danger of undue coercion as women might be exposed to by the possession of a vote, however small, is wanton, inasmuch as women seldom care for politics, is to overlook the drift of the constitutional claim made by the petitioners, and which it has been the purpose of this paper to follow out. The English representative system, such as it is, good or bad, represents not persons but property. By holding property women take on the rights and duties of property. If they are not interested in politics their property is. Poor-laws and game-laws, corn-laws and malt-tax, cattle-plague-compensation bills, the manning of the navy, and the conversion of Enfield rifles into breech-loaders—all these things will make the property held by English women more or less valuable to the country at large of this and the succeeding generations. It is on the supposition that property requires representation that a property-qualification is fixed by the law. It is not the mere personal interests of the rich man that a property franchise is supposed to protect; were it so, the injustice of giving the franchise to the rich man only would have been too grossly palpable to have endured so long, or to be capable of as good a defence as the English Constitution; for the rich man's person is no dearer to himself or to the nation than the poor man's. Nor is it granted to him because he is supposed to be, by some mysterious dispensation of providence, endowed by the possession of a 10 *l.* house with a special capacity to understand and care for the personal happiness of himself or others. The law acts upon the supposition that he who is in actual possession of property will be keener and more efficient to protect it than any other person. The abhorrence of our ancestors for allowing land to fall into *main-morte* proceeded in part from this mode of thought; a habit of considering it as at once the general interest that land should be efficiently managed and protected, and as the most effectual way of providing for its being so, to place it under the guardianship of an individual personally interested in it. It is to us almost indubitable, that the same legislators who enacted the statute of mortmain would, if as much English property had been in the hands of women as at the present day, either have deprived them of the right of holding property at all, or else have invested them with the power of protecting it in Parliament, rather than have permitted it to remain unrepresented as it now is.

The next question that will probably be asked by such of our readers as have accompanied us thus far in the consideration of the peculiar line of argument of the Ladies' Petition, is—Supposing this petition to be granted, and that Parliament were to extend the suffrage to duly qualified women, what good would it do to them or to the country in general? And, on the other hand, what harm might be expected to arise from it? And, looking at the matter from the point of view in which it is placed by the petition, these two questions are perfectly reasonable; it is indeed in our eyes one of the merits of this point of view that it brings us so directly and so logically to the consideration of these really practical questions, and enables us to leave aside all those considerations either of abstract right or of accidental custom and sense of fitness, the discussion of which is certain to be as difficult as it is usually indecisive. For if we acknowledge with the petitioners, that the exclusion of women from the right to vote in the election of members of Parliament is an anomaly, the question of right may be granted, but the question of expediency is not. We may acknowledge that their exclusion is exceptional, the result of exceptional legislation, producing an invidious distinction under which they alone labour; and yet we may think it desirable to impose such a distinction, and to establish such an exception. But then we must be prepared with reasons for doing so. What this petition appears to us to have pointed out is, that no one who accepts the principles upon which the British Constitution and English society are established, can consider the exclusion of women from political privileges as a matter of course. On the contrary, he must look upon it as the result of anomalous legislation, requiring to be justified either by its urgent necessity or by its evident advantages. Unfortunately for anything like clearness of thought, it is very seldom that we find people willing to look at the subject in so simple and practical a manner; too often, on the contrary, the very persons who would most object to importing theories of the abstract rights of man, into a discussion on the franchise, will go off into vague generalities on the nature of women, and fancy that some such universal axioms can be somehow applicable to the legal position of particular classes of Englishwomen in the nineteenth century. Now we are far from denying that general principles must underlie not only all theory, but also all practice. We readily admit that most people do in reality either accept or reject the abstract theory of the natural equality of all men, just as they do in reality talk either poetry or prose; and so, in like manner, most people have their own theory as to the special aptitudes of women. But the theory that "all women are destined for family life" is about as applicable to any practical settlement of the franchise in this country, as the somewhat equivalent one that "all men are born free and equal." We may assent to either assertion, or we may dissent from it, without being one whit further advanced in the question under discussion; for in fact they have nothing whatever to do with it, unless we propose to pull down the whole fabric of English law and society altogether, and build it up anew from its foundations. Whether or not all women are destined for family life, all Englishwomen do not live it; whether or not women are fitted by nature to be anything else than wives and mothers, many Englishwomen are something else; whether law ought or ought not to recognise women as anything else, the law of England does so recognise them. Marriage may or may not be the only good, the only ideal existence for all women, but the law of England has long ago refused to drive women into marriage, as sheep are driven into a fold, by shutting every gate against them but the one they are intended to go through. Even if all unmarried women ought to be looked upon as stray sheep, still, as we have already seen, both law and custom in this country have bestowed upon them abundance of rights and privileges; and the assertion that such people have no right even to exist, is out of place in answer to the question, whether the rights they already possess do not naturally imply one right more?

It seems to us, therefore, that no abstract ideas of woman's mission can reasonably be brought forward as proof of an urgent necessity for the exclusion of women from the franchise under our existing system; and that if the question is asked—What good would be gained by their admission? the answer is very plain—Whatever good is to be gained by the British Constitution. If that be a good, it is evident that the carrying it out must be good. The perpetuation of an omission which originated in circumstances that have long since passed away, must do as much harm to those who are omitted as would have been done to their countrymen if the British Constitution had not existed. If it be an advantage to be able to protect one's property by the power of voting for members of Parliament, the possession of this advantage must be a good for all those who live and own property under Parliamentary Government. The good that would be done to women themselves is, in fact, not open to dispute, unless we dispute the advantage of Parliamentary Government and representation of property; and in that case we must dispute the advantage of the English system of government altogether.

If continuing to confine ourselves to a strictly constitutional point of view, we ask what would be the advantage to the country in general of the political representation of female holders of property, on the same conditions as men, we think, as we have already indicated, that the reply is equally clear. If the representation in Parliament of those who are interested in property is a national good, tending to the preservation and fostering of all property interests, to the increase of our national wealth, and to the handing down to our descendants of the national property under favourable conditions, then the disfranchisement of any class of holders of property must be an evil proportioned to their numbers, and their enfranchisement an advantage in the same proportion. Whatever may be the causes, there can be no doubt that the class of independent women is a continually increasing one in this country, and their admission to the franchise is therefore continually becoming, by the natural course of events, a question of greater practical importance.

Turning now to the question, what harm could be done by their admission? we are embarrassed by the difficulty of finding any answer whatever, unless we go out of the bounds we have prescribed to ourselves, and get beyond the limits of the constitutional point of view. Revolutionary violence is out of the question from them, and their numbers are not such as to give rise to any of the apprehensions of a disturbance of the balance of power which have been excited in some minds by the claims of the working classes. There would probably be found some duly qualified female voters in every rank of society, and among them some members of almost every religious system or political party, so that the existing interests of no single class or party or religious body could have anything to fear from them. It seems difficult to imagine a case where the principles of the Constitution could be applied with more absolute freedom from the slightest shadow of danger.

Can it be said that, although there would be no danger to the State, nor to anybody within the State, yet that private interests might suffer? We confess we do not see how this is to be maintained. If we consider the private interests of men, they cannot be concerned in the political action of independent women. Their political interests may be; but we have just seen that for these there is no danger. If it be urged that the power of voting may make women more independent than it is thought they ought to be, it appears to us, once again, that English law has already decided that women may be independent, and that a woman who is absolute mistress of her own life, person, and property, will not be rendered more independent of men by the power of giving an occasional vote for a member of parliament [sic]. There are some who think that by giving to any women whatever the power politically to protect their own interests, we should diminish that generous, disinterested, and romantic character which is so charming in women, and which indeed we all like to see in others, and most of us even to encourage in ourselves, so long as it does not expose us too defenceless to the selfishness of the selfish. Yet the remarks we have already made on the legal ability of women to defend their own pecuniary interests will apply even more appositely here. For if the sole responsibility of all their own private pecuniary affairs does not unsex spinsters and widows, and make them coarse, worldly, avaricious, grasping, and selfish, the addition of a vote, giving them a very slight direct influence on public affairs, is not likely to have so extraordinary an effect upon the most gentle and amiable half of mankind; on the contrary, as we find that the names of ladies abound on all charitable and philanthropic subscription lists, showing how kindly and generous a use they are disposed to make of their property, so we might reasonably expect that such little direct influence on politics as the possession of a vote would give to women, would probably be chiefly used in the direction of what we may call philanthropic legislation; in any case, politics in themselves certainly afford more scope for exalted and generous feeling than private business affairs. Ladies accustomed to the government of households and the management of their families, will scarcely find political affairs petty, or calculated to exercise a narrowing influence on their sympathies. Whether we consider that women ought to be especially devoted to what is beautiful or to what is good, there is much work in the interests of either to be done in politics; and if the ladies were only to take schools, workhouses, public buildings, parks, gardens, and picture galleries under their special protection, and try to send to Parliament a few members who would work efficiently at such subjects, the rest of the community would have cause to be glad of their help, without their being themselves in the smallest degree vulgarized by such a task.

But, in fact, as we have already pointed out, it is too late to be afraid of letting Englishwomen share in the life of Englishmen. We cannot shut up our women in harems, and devote them to the cultivation of their beauty and of their children. We have most of us long ago acknowledged that a perfect woman is

> Not too bright and good
> For human nature's daily food.

The fear that a womanly nature could be corrupted or hardened by politics, would strike at the root of our Western and Christian civilization, which owes much of its progress to having devolved upon women a share of the common-place practical cares and duties which go to take up the sum of ordinary human life, whether domestic or political. The ingenuity, the love of luxury, the taste, and the housewifely instincts of women, have contributed much to the comforts of modern civilization; a more rapid and efficient adaptation of these same comforts to prisons, schools, barracks, and workhouses, would be a useful and probable result of the extension of women's energies to political life. It is, indeed, remarkable how large a part of the subjects which occupy most attention in modern politics are of this quasi-domestic character; and how growing a tendency there is for them to become even more so. The homes of the working-classes, education, factory acts (regulating the labor of women and children), sanitary laws, water supplies, drainage (all municipal legislation in fact), the whole administration of the poor-laws, with its various subdivisions—care of the pauper sick, pauper schools, &c.,—all these are subjects which already, by common consent, are included in the peculiarly feminine province of home and charity. If the possession of a vote should induce more women to extend their interest to the comfort and happiness of other homes besides their own, it will certainly not have exercised a deteriorating influence on their character.

Notes

1. Mr. Hare, the enlightened and philosophical proposer of Personal Representation, has suggested precisely such a parallel introduction of his system, when he recommended the formation of voluntary constituencies within the local constituencies already existing; by which means the personal weight of minorities might be brought into action, and might supplement without replacing the local majorities. Like all that emanates from this political thinker, this proposal bears the stamp of profound thought united to great practical ability. By putting his plan to some such test its real advantages would be tried, and if Personal Representation is destined to supersede our own system (in reality a representation of property interests) no better method of introducing it gradually and without violent dislocation of our institutions can well be devised. Nor would such an experiment of Personal Representation working supplementarily to the system we already have, be an absolutely novel precedent in this country; we have it already, and in combination with the use of voting papers, in the representation of the Universities of Oxford and Cambridge. [Taylor's note]

2. Throughout the essay, Taylor alternates between "recognize" and "recognise."

X. Anne Thackeray Ritchie
(1837–1919)

Although Anne Thackeray Ritchie stands (perhaps unavoidably) in the shadow of her famous father, her work as an essayist, novelist, and biographer merits examination in its own right. With her memorials to the "great" personalities who made up William Makepeace Thackeray's circle—including Tennyson, Ruskin, Dickens, the Brownings, and of course, Thackeray himself—she achieved celebrity as a biographer of the Victorian era and more pointedly, as a privileged daughter whose birth placed her in the center of an impressive literary network. However, while Ritchie did capitalize on her unique social position, her career—spanning nearly fifty productive years—extends far beyond this limited sphere. Characterized by her fascination with women's lives, Ritchie's writing focuses, more often than not, on female subjects and subjectivity. As a memorialist, she paid tribute to women writers like Mrs. Barbauld, Amelia Opie, Felicia Felix, Fanny Kemble, and numerous others who, like Ritchie now, faced obscurity. Similarly, her essays and novels dramatize the needs and anxieties of women who longed for sympathy and for a sense of shared experience. While lacking in any radical ideology, Ritchie's work does offer important insight into the concerns of nineteenth-century women writers during a time when their authority and the value of their writing was seriously under attack.

Born in London on June 9, 1837, Ritchie was named for her paternal grandmother, Anne Carmichael-Smyth, and her mother, Isabella Shawe Thackeray, both of whom would have a profound impact on her. Early tragedies, including the death of an infant sister and Isabella Thackeray's attempted suicide, left the family broken and, after Isabella was permanently institutionalized following a mental breakdown in 1840, in financial straits. Still a struggling writer, Thackeray left "Anny" and her younger sister "Minny" in his mother's care in Paris. While her childhood lacked any conventional schooling, Ritchie's liberal access to literature usually forbidden to girls fortified her independence of mind and probably helped her resist her grandmother's rigid Calvinism.

Warm-spirited as well as precocious, she became the family's primary caretaker when Thackeray finally retrieved his daughters and settled in Kensington in 1846. It is no wonder that her works so often focus on the ideal of female nurture, as she would assume a nurturing role for countless people throughout her life, including her mother (after Thackeray's early death in 1863), her governess's orphaned children, her niece (after Minny died in childbirth in 1857), Leslie Stephen (Minny's bereft husband), and Virginia Woolf, who would later argue for her aunt's recovery as a writer who captured "the spirit" of her age.

Ritchie's adolescent participation in her father's creative process as his confidante and "secretary amanuensis" stimulated her own literary ambitions. She produced several novels and a play in her adolescence, and her first essay, "The Little Scholars" (an admiring account of her visit to a London poor school) was published in *Cornhill* in 1860. As with most writers of her day, she entered the literary scene anonymously, and there is no question that her positive reception was won independently of Thackeray. Later critics would routinely look for "traces" of her famous parent, but most (including George Eliot and Margaret Oliphant) credited her with an interesting and pleasing style— a combination of precision and "diffuseness," of realism and impressionism—that was uniquely her own. Forced to live by her pen after she and Minny were left without an inheritance, she soon became a staple writer for the *Cornhill*, where she published most of her essays, journals, memorials, stories, and novels from 1860 to 1900. She also published *Chapters from Some Unwritten Memoirs* in *Macmillan's Magazine* from 1890 to 1894. Her close ties with *Cornhill* in particular kept her abreast of the changing literary milieu, and she became friend and mentor to many aspiring authors of the younger generation, including Meredith, Swinburne and James, who would remember her as "a woman of genius." In 1877 she married Richmond Ritchie, sixteen years her junior; while the age difference raised eyebrows, the union hurt neither her popularity nor her productivity, and she continued to publish almost until her death in 1919.

Although Ritchie would turn almost exclusively to memoir writing after 1873—perhaps because it offered the ideal vehicle for her generous and sympathetic perspective—her novels are arguably her most compelling works. *The Story of Elizabeth* (1860), *The Village on the Cliff* (1864), and *Old Kensington* (which went through three editions in 1873), all center on young women who endure losses, search for female role models, and finally, "ripened" by their experiences, gain a certain power that has to do with adopting caretaking roles. In her life and work, Ritchie embraced the ideal of women's sympathetic powers, and she self-consciously reached out to everyday women who defined themselves in these terms. More than this, she highlighted women's importance to one another: just as her biographical essays suggest a need, on the part of a writer intimately associated with a literary father, to recover her literary mothers, her novels recuperate "old maids" and "maiden aunts" (typically villainized in Victorian fiction) as the nurturers and advisors of her maturing heroines. In this way, Ritchie subverted oppressive notions of womanly self-sacrifice to describe female empathy and "care" as women's source of power.

This was a meaningful move during an era when female writers were being censured for their emotionalism and for the moral ambiguities of their plots. The 1860s are most often associated with the rise of sensationalism, and female writers in particular were (given the soaring subscriptions to Mudie's) the focus of anxiety. Supposedly driven by instinct and emotion, women's "virtue"—their ability to empathize and sympathize—was also their greatest weakness, and overly dramatic heroines presented a certain danger to their female readers. Along with other women writers like Eliot and Oliphant (both of whom attempted to establish standards for what was genuinely "good" women's writing), Ritchie defended women's expressive freedoms and, as in the essay which follows, acknowledged the important role that novels played in women's lives. She emphasized the sympathy between writer and reader, and while warning against too many tears, advocated heroines who, like her own Elizabeth Gilmour, reflected real women's often mixed and "tempestuous" emotions.

Eulogizing Ritchie in 1919, Howard Sturgis reiterated the praise given her time and time again by the reviewers of two generations. Her nonfiction and fiction possessed what he called a "great gift of genuine sympathy"—a "sap stirring" and "life giving" quality through which she inspired compassion and the kind of empathetic connection she herself described as a reader of women's novels. Though sometimes seen as too unstructured or diffuse, her style struck a chord with readers and with younger writers who imitated her impressionistic digressions and meditations. Though hardly subversive, her work nonetheless dealt in important and useful ways with issues revolving around gender, marriage, and authorship.

Ritchie's life is movingly documented in Winifred Gérin's 1981 biography (named for its subject), and in her own biographical introductions to her father's collected works, reprinted in 1988 by AMS Press. Thoemms Press republished in 1995 *The Story of Elizabeth* and *Old Kensington*, with an introduction by Esther Schwarz-McKenzie. Ohio State also published in 1995 a new collection of Ritchie's often amusing and poignant letters and journals.

Esther Schwarz-McKenzie,
Temple University

23. Heroines and Their Grandmothers

Introduction

Anne Thackeray Ritchie's "Heroines and Their Grandmothers," published in *Cornhill Magazine* in May, 1865, and reprinted here from that periodical, projects a way of thinking about fiction to which Ritchie would remain faithful throughout her career. An answer to the criticism being leveled at women writers and readers who had developed a preference for "the history of feeling instead of the history of events," the essay insists on the meaningfulness of novels in women's lives. Where many writers (such as George Eliot) expressed anger and impatience with women who indulged in sensation conventions, Ritchie viewed her contemporaries in a more generous light. Stressing her kinship with them, she sought to bridge the gap between modern heroines and their more "reserved" and resilient grandmothers like Jane Bennett. In this, she was responding to what she perceived as the needs of her readers, as well as to the critical concerns about the form and "influence" of literature. In short, Ritchie saw novels as a source of nourishment and strength, especially when readers recognized their own experiences and longings reflected in the pages of an absorbing book. The increase in the production of novels was no mystery to her; it was the natural result of "the necessity for expression" on the part of writers and readers for whom fiction provided bonds of common sympathy. The expressiveness of modern heroines represented a sort of liberation, but with such liberation came other risks. These included a too extreme departure from literary realism, and a profusion of negative role models who presented "strained and affected" views of life to their readers. An insightful contribution to the discussion about female writing and reading, Ritchie's essay stresses the connection of women writers and readers to their maternal literary past.

Heroines and Their Grandmothers

Why do women now-a-days write such melancholy novels? Are authoresses more miserable than they used to be a hundred years ago? Miss Austen's heroines came tripping into the room, bright-eyed, rosy-cheeked, arch, and good-humoured. Evelina and Cecilia would have thoroughly enjoyed their visits to the opera, and their expeditions to the masquerades, if it had not been for their vulgar relations. Valancourt's Emily was a little upset, to be sure, when she found herself all alone in the ghostly and mouldy castle in the south of France, but she, too, was naturally a lively girl, and on the whole showed a great deal of courage and presence of mind. Miss Edgeworth's heroines were pleasant and easily pleased, and to these may be added a blooming rose-garden of wild Irish girls, of good-humoured and cheerful young ladies, who consented to make the devoted young hero happy at the end of the third volume, without any very intricate self-examinations, and who certainly were much more appreciated by the heroes of those days, than our modern heroines with all their workings and deep feelings and unrequited affections are now, by the noblemen and gentlemen to whom they happen to be attached.[1]

If one could imagine the ladies of whom we have been speaking coming to life again, and witnessing all the vagaries and agonizing experiences and deadly calm and irrepressible emotion of their granddaughters, the heroines of the present day, what a bewildering scene it would be! Evelina and Cecilia ought to faint with horror! Madame Duval's most shocking expressions were never so alarming as the remarks they might now hear on all sides. Elizabeth Bennett would certainly burst out laughing, Emma might lose her temper, and Fanny Price would turn scarlet and stop her little ears.[2] Perhaps Emily of Udolpho, more accustomed than the others to the horrors of sensation, and having once faced those long and terrible passages, might be able to hold her own against such a great-granddaughter as Aurora Floyd or Lady Audley. But how would she deal with the soul-workings and heart troubles of Miss Kavanagh's Adèle, or our old favourite Ethel May in the *Daisy Chain*, or Cousin Phillis, or Margaret Hale, or Jane Eyre, or Lucy Snowe, or Dinah or Maggie Tulliver's distractions, or poor noble Romola's perplexities?[3] Emily would probably prefer any amount of tortuous mysteries, winding staircases and passages, or groans and groans, and yards and yards of faded curtains, to the task of mastering these modern intricacies of feeling and doubting and sentiment.

Are the former heroines women as they were, or as they were supposed to be in those days? Are the women of whom women write now, women as they are, or women as they are supposed to be? Does the modern taste demand a certain sensation feeling, sensation sentiment, only because it is actually experienced?

This is a question to be answered on some other occasion, but, in the meantime, it would seem as if all the good humours and good spirits of former generations had certainly deserted our own heart-broken ladies. Instead of cheerful endurance, the very worst is made of every passing discomfort. Their laughter is forced, even their happiness is only calm content, for they cannot so readily recover from the two first volumes. They no longer smile and trip through country-dances hand-in-hand with their adorers, but waltz with heavy hearts and dizzy brains, while the hero who scorns them looks on. Open the second volume, you will see that, instead of sitting in the drawing-room or plucking roses in the bower, or looking pretty and pleasant, they are lying on their beds with agonizing headaches, walking desperately along the streets they know not whither, or staring out of window in blank despair. It would be curious to ascertain in how great a degree language measures feeling. People now-a-days, with the help of the penny-post and the telegraph, and the endless means of communication and of coming and going, are certainly able to care for a greater number of persons than they could have done a hundred years ago; perhaps they are also able to care more for, and to be more devotedly attached to, those whom they already love; they certainly say more about it, and, perhaps, with its greater abundance and opportunity, expression may have depreciated in value. And this may possibly account for some of the difference between the reserved and measured language of a Jane Bennett and the tempestuous confidences of an Elizabeth Gilmour. Much that is written now is written with a certain exaggeration and an earnestness which was undreamt of in the placid days when, according to Miss Austen, a few assembly balls and morning visits, a due amount of vexation reasonably surmounted, or at most "smiles reined in, and spirits dancing in private rapture," a journey to Bath, an attempt at private theatricals or a thick packet of explanations hurriedly signed with the hero's initials, were the events, the emotions, the aspirations of a life-time. They had their faults and their accomplishments: witness

Emma's very mild performances in the way of portrait taking; but as for tracking murderers, agonies of mystery, and disappointed affections, flinging themselves at gentlemen's heads, marrying two husbands at once, flashing with irrepressible emotion, or only betraying the deadly conflict going on within by a slight quiver of the pale lip—such ideas never entered their pretty little heads. They fainted a good deal, we must confess, and wrote long and tedious letters to aged clergymen residing in the country. They exclaimed "La!" when anything surprised them, and were, we believe, dreadfully afraid of cows, notwithstanding their country connection. But they were certainly a more amiable race than their successors. It is a fact that people do not usually feel the same affection for phenomenons, however curious, that they do for perfectly commonplace human creatures. And yet at the same time we confess that it does seem somewhat ungrateful to complain of these living and adventurous heroines to whom, with all their vagaries, one has owed such long and happy hours of amusement and entertainment and comfort, and who have gone through so much for our edification.

Still one cannot but wonder how Miss Austen would have written if she had lived to-day instead of yesterday. It has been often said that novels might be divided into two great divisions—the objective and the subjective: almost all men's novels belong to the former; almost all women's, now-a-days, to the latter definition. Analysis of emotion instead of analysis of character, the history of feeling instead of the history of events, seems to be the method of the majority of penwomen. The novels that we have in hand to review now are examples of this mode of treatment, and the truth is, that except in the case of the highest art and most consummate skill, there is no comparison between the interest excited by facts and general characteristics, as compared with the interest of feeling and emotion told with only the same amount of perception and ability.

Few people, for instance, could read the story of the poor lady who lived too much alone without being touched by the simple earnestness with which her sorrows are written of, although in the bare details of her life there might not be much worth recording. But this is the history of poor Mrs. Storn's[4] feelings more than that of her life—of feelings very sad and earnest and passionate, full of struggle for right, with truth to help and untruth to bewilder her; with power and depth and reality in her struggles, which end at last in a sad sort of twilight that seems to haunt one as one shuts up the book. In *George Geith*, of which we will speak more presently, there is the same sadness and minor key ringing all through the composition. Indeed, all this author's tunes are very melancholy—so melancholy, that it would seem almost like a defect if they were not at the same time very sweet as well as very sad. Too Much Alone is a young woman who marries a very silent, upright, and industrious chemical experimentalist. He has well-cut features, honourable feelings, a genius for discovering cheap ways of producing acids and chemicals, as well as ideas about cyanosium, which, combined with his perfect trust in and neglect of his wife, very nearly bring about the destruction of all their domestic happiness. She is a pale, sentimental young woman, with raven-black hair, clever, and longing for sympathy—a *femme incomprise*, it must be confessed, but certainly much more charming and pleasant and pathetic than such people usually are. Days go by, lonely alike for her, without occupation or friendship or interest; she cannot consort with the dull and vulgar people about her; she has her little son, but he is not a companion. Her husband is absorbed in his work. She has no one to talk to, nothing to do or think of. She lives all alone in the great noisy life-full city, sad and pining and wistful and weary. Here is a little sketch of her:—

> Lina was sitting, thinking about the fact that she had been married many months more than three years, and that on the especial Sunday morning in question she was just of age. It was still early, for Mr. Storn, according to the fashion of most London folks, borrowed hours from both ends of the day, and his wife was sitting there until it should be time for her to get ready and to go to church alone. Her chair was placed by the open window, and though the city was London, and the locality either the ward of Eastcheap or that of Allhallows, Barking (I am not quite sure which), fragrant odours came wafted to her senses through the casement, for in this as in all other things save one, Maurice had considered her nurture and her tastes, and covered the roof of the counting-house with flowers. But for the distant roll of the carriages, she might just as well have been miles away from London. . . . She was dressed in a pink morning dress, with her dark hair plainly braided upon her pale fair cheek, and she had a staid sober look upon her face, that somehow made her appear handsomer than in the days of old before she married . . .

This very Sunday Lina meets a dangerous fascinating man of the world, who is a friendly well-meaning creature withal, and who can understand and sympathize with her sadness and solitude only too well for her peace of mind, and for his own: again and again she appeals to her husband: "I will find pleasure in the driest employment if you will only let me be with you, and not leave me alone." She only asks for justice, for confidence—not the confidence of utter desertion and trust and neglect, but the daily confidence and communion, which is a necessity to some women, the permission to share in the common interests and efforts of her husband's life; to be allowed to sympathize, and to live, and to understand, instead of being left to pine away lonely, unhappy, half asleep, and utterly weary and disappointed. Unfortunately Mr. Storn thinks it is all childish nonsense, and repulses her in the most affectionate manner; poor unhappy Lina behaves as well as ever she can, and devotes herself to her little boy, only her hair grows blacker, and her face turns paler and paler, day by day; she is very good and struggles to be contented, and will not allow herself to think too much of Herbert, and so things go on in the old way for a long, long time. At last a crisis comes—troubles thicken—Maurice Storn is always away when he is most wanted, little Geordie, the son, gets hold of some of his father's chemicals, which have cost Lina already so much happiness and confidence, and the poor little boy poisons himself with something sweet out of a little bottle. All the description which follows is very powerfully and pathetically told—Maurice Storn's silence and misery, Lina's desperation and sudden change of feeling. After all her long struggles and efforts she suddenly breaks down, all her courage leaves her, and her desperate longings for right and clinging to truth.

> She said in her soul, 'I have lost the power either to bear or to resist. I have tried to face my misfortune, and I feel I am incapable of doing it . . . why should I struggle or fear any more? I know the worst that life can bring me, I have buried my heart and my hopes with my boy. Why should I strive or struggle any more?' And Lina had got to such a pass that she forgot to answer to herself, Because it is right— Right and wrong, she had lost sight of them both.

And so poor Mrs. Storn almost makes up her mind to leave her home, unconscious that already people are beginning to talk of her, first one and then another. Nobody seems very bad. Everybody is going wrong. Maurice abstracted over his work, Lina in a frenzy of wretchedness; home-fires are extinct, outside the cold winds blow, and the snow lies half melted on the ground. The man of the world is waiting in the cold, very miserable too; their best impulses and chances seem failing them, all about there seems to be only pain, and night, and trouble, and sorrow for every one. But at last the morning dawns, and Lina is saved.

Everything is then satisfactorily arranged, and Maurice is ruined, and Lina's old affection for him returns. The man of the world is also ruined, and determines to emigrate to some distant colony. Mr. and Mrs. Storn retire to an old-fashioned gabled house at Enfield, where they have no secrets from each other, and it is here that Maurice one day tells Lina that he has brought an old friend to say good-by to her, and then poor Herbert Clyne, the late man of the world, comes across the lawn, and says farewell for ever to both his friends in a very pathetic and touching scene.

Lina Storn is finally disposed of in *Too Much Alone*, but Maurice Storn reappears in disguise, and under various assumed names in almost all the author's subsequent novels. Although we have never yet been able to realize this stern-cut personage as satisfactorily as we should have liked to do, yet we must confess to a partiality for him, and a respect for his astounding powers of application, and we are not sorry to meet him over and over again. Whether he turns his attention to chemistry, to engineering, to figures, to theology, the amount of business he gets through is almost bewildering, at the same time something invariably goes wrong, over which he has no control, notwithstanding all his industry and ability, and he has to acknowledge the weakness of humanity, and the insufficiency of the sternest determination, and to order and arrange the events of life to its own will and fancy. To the woman or women depending upon him he is invariably kind, provokingly reserved, and faithfully devoted. He is of good family and extremely proud, and he is obliged for various reasons to live in the city. All through the stories one seems to hear a suggestive accompanying roll of cart-wheels and carriages. Poor Lina's loneliness seems all the more lonely for the contrast of the busy movement all round about her own silent, sad life. "At first it seemed to give a sort of stimulus to her own existence, hearing the carts roll by, the cabs rattle past, the shout and hum of human voices break on her ear almost before she was awake of a morning. . . . But wear takes the gloss off all things, even off the sensation of being perplexed and amused by the whirl of life."

In *City and Suburb*, this din of London life, and the way in which city people live and strive, is capitally described; the heroine is no less a person than a Lady Mayoress, a certain Ruby Ruthven, a beauty, capricious, and wayward, and impetuous, and she is perhaps one of the best of Mrs. Trafford's creation. For old friendship's sake, we cannot help giving the preference to *Too Much Alone*; but *City and Suburb* is in many respects an advance upon it, and *George Geith* is in its way better than either. *The Moors and the Fens* did not seem to us equal in power to either of the preceding works.

It seems strange as one thinks of it that before these books came out no one had ever thought of writing about city life: there is certainly an interest and a charm about old London, its crowded busy streets, its ancient churches and buildings, and narrow lanes and passages with quaint names, of which dwellers in the stucco suburbs have no conception. There is the river with its wondrous freight, and the busy docks, where stores of strange goods are lying, that bewilder one as one gazes. Vast horizons of barrels waiting to be carted, forests of cinnamon-trees and spices, of canes, of ivory, thousands and thousands of great elephant tusks, sorted and stored away, workmen, sailors of every country, a great unknown strange life and bustle. Or if you come away, you find silence, old courts, iron gateways, ancient squares where the sunshine falls quietly, a glint of the past, as it were, a feeling of what has been, and what still lingers among the old worn stones and bricks, and traditions of the city. Even the Mansion House, with its kindly old customs and welcome and hospitality, has a charm and romance of its own, from the golden postilion to the mutton-pies, which are the same as they were hundreds and hundreds of years ago. All this queer sentiment belonging to old London, the author feels and describes with great cleverness and appreciation.

George Geith is the latest and the most popular of Mrs. Trafford's novels, and it deserves its popularity, for although *Too Much Alone* is more successfully constructed as a story, this is far better and more powerfully written than any of her former stories. It is the history of the man whose name it bears—a man "to work so long as he has a breath left to draw, who would die in his harness rather than give up, who would fight against opposing circumstances whilst he had a drop of blood in his veins, whose greatest virtues are untiring industry and indomitable courage, and who is worth half-a-dozen ordinary men, if only because of his iron frame and unconquerable spirit." Here is a description of the place in which he lived, on the second floor of the house which stands next but one to the old gateway on the Fenchurch Street side:—

> If quietness was what he wanted, he had it; except in the summer evenings when the children of the Fenchurch Street housekeepers brought their marbles through the passage, and fought over them on the pavement in front of the office-door, there was little noise of life in the old churchyard. The sparrows in the trees or the footfall of some one entering or quitting the court alone disturbed the silence. The roar of Fenchurch Street on the one side, and of Leadenhall Street on the other, sounded in Fen Court but as a distant murmur, and to a man whose life was spent among figures, and who wanted to devote his undivided attention to his work, this silence was a blessing not to be properly estimated save by those who have passed through that maddening ordeal which precedes being able to abstract the mind from external influence. . . . For the historical recollections associated with the locality he had chosen, George Geith did not care a rush.

George Geith lives with his figures, "climbing Alps on Alps of them with silent patience, great mountains of arithmetic with gold lying on their summits for him to grasp;" he works for eighteen hours a day. People come up his stairs to ask for his help—

> Bankrupts, men who were good enough, men who were doubtful, and men who were (speaking commercially) bad, had all alike occasion to seek the accountant's advice and assistance; retailers, who kept clerks for their sold books, but not for their bought; wholesale dealers who did not want to let their clerks see their books at all; shrewd men of business who yet could not balance a ledger; ill-educated traders, who, though they could make money, would have been ashamed to show their ill-written and worse spelled journals to a stranger; unhappy wretches, shivering on the brink of insolvency;

creditors who did not think much of the cooking of some dishonest debtors' accounts;—all these came and sat in George Geith's office, and waited their turn to see him.

And among these comes a country gentleman, a M. Molozane, who is on the brink of ruin, and who has three daughters at home at the Dower House, near Wattisbridge.

There is a secret in George Geith's life and a reason for which he toils; and although early in the story he makes a discovery which relieves him from part of his anxiety and need for money, he still works on from habit, and one day he receives a letter from this M. Molozane, begging him to come to his assistance, and stating that he is ill and cannot come to town. George thinks he would like a breath of country air and determines to go. The description of Wattisbridge and the road thither is delightful; lambs, cool grass, shaded ponds and cattle, trailing branches, brambles, roses, here a house, there a farmyard, gently sloping hills crowned with clumps of trees, distant purple haze, a calm blue sky and fleecy clouds, and close at hand a grassy glade with cathedral branches, a young lady, a black retriever and a white poodle, all of which George Geith notices as he walks along the path, "through the glade, under the shadow of the arching trees, straight as he can go to meet his destiny."

Beryl Molozane, with the dear sweet kindly brown eyes, that seemed to be always laughing and loving, is as charming a destiny as any hero could wish to meet upon a summer's day, as she stands with the sunshine streaming on her nut-brown, red golden hair. She should indeed be capable of converting the most rabid of reviewers to the modern ideal of what a heroine should be, with her April moods and her tenderness and laughter, her frankness, her cleverness, her gay innocent chatter, her outspoken youth and brightness. It is she who manages for the whole household, who works for her father, who protects her younger sister, who schemes and plans, and thinks, and loves for all. No wonder that George loses his heart to her; even in the very beginning we are told when he first sees her, that he would have

> Taken the sunshine out of his own life to save the clouds from darkening down on hers. He would have left her dear face to smile on still, the guileless heart to throb calmly. He would have left his day without a noon to prevent night from closing over hers. He would have known that it was

possible for him to love so well that he should become
unselfish. . . .

One cannot help wondering that the author could have had the
heart to treat poor pretty Beryl so harshly, when her very creation, the
stern and selfish George himself, would have suffered any pain to spare
her if it were possible. It is not our object here to tell a story at length,
which is interesting enough to be read for itself, and touching enough
to be remembered long after the last of the three volumes is closed. To
be remembered, but so sadly, that one cannot but ask oneself for what
reason are such stories written. Is it to make one sad with sorrows
which never happened, but which are told with so much truth and
pathos that they almost seem for a minute as if they were one's own? Is
it to fill one's eyes with tears for griefs which might be but which have
not been, and for troubles that are not, except in a fancy, for the sad sad
fate of a sweet and tender woman, who might have been made happy to
gladden all who were interested in her story; or are they written to cheer
one in dull hours, to sooth, to interest, and to distract from weary
thoughts, from which it is at times a blessing to escape?

A lady putting down this book the other day, suddenly burst into
tears, and said, "Why did they give me this to read?" Why, indeed! Beryl
might have been more happy, and no one need have been the worse.
She and her George might have been made comfortable together for a
little while, and we might have learnt to know her all the same. Does
sorrow come like this, in wave upon wave, through long sad years,
without one gleam of light to play upon the waters? Sunshine *is*
sunshine, and warms and vivifies, and brightens, though the clouds are
coming too, sooner or later, and in nature no warning voices spoil the
happiest hours of our lives by useless threats and terrifying hints of
what the future may bring forth. Happiness remembered, is happiness
always; but where would past happiness be if there was some one
always standing by, as in this book, to point with a sigh to future
troubles long before they come, and to sadden and spoil all the pleasant
springtime, and all the sport and youth by dreary forebodings of old age,
of autumn, and winter snow, and bitter winds that have not yet begun
to blow. "So smile the heavens upon that holy act," says the Friar,
"that after sorrow chide us not." "Amen, amen," says Romeo; "but
come what sorrow can, it cannot countervail the exchange of joy that
one short minute gives me in her sight." And we wish that George
Geith had been more of Romeo's way of thinking.

A sad ending is very touching at the time, and moves many a sympathy, but in prose—for poetry is to be criticised from a different standard—who ever reads a melancholy story over and over and over as some stories are read? The more touchingly and earnestly the tale is told, the less disposed one is to revert to it, and the more deeply one feels for the fictitious friends whom one cannot help loving at times, almost as if they were real ones, the less heart one has to listen to the history of their pains, and fears, and sufferings—knowing, as one does, that there is only sorrow in store for them, no relief coming, no help anywhere, no salvation at hand. Mr. Thackeray used to say that a bad ending to a book was a great mistake, that he never would make one of his own finish badly. What was the use of it? Nobody ever cared to read a book a second time when it ended unhappily.

There is a great excuse in the case of the writer of *George Geith*, who possesses in no common degree sad powers of pathos. Take for instance the parting between George and Beryl. She says that it is no use talking about what is past and gone; that they must part, and he knows it.

> Then for a moment George misunderstood her. The agony of her own heart, the intense bitterness of the draught she was called upon to drink, the awful hopelessness of her case, and the terrible longing she felt to be permitted to live and love once more, sharpened her voice and gave it a tone she never intended.
>
> 'Have you grown to doubt me?' he asked. 'Do you not know I would marry you to-morrow if I could? Do you think that throughout all the years to come, be they many or be they few, I could change to you? Oh, Beryl, do you not believe that through time and through eternity I shall love you and none other?'
>
> 'I do not doubt; I believe,' and her tears fell faster and her sobs became more uncontrollable. . . .
>
> What was she to him at that moment? More than wife; more than all the earth; more than heaven; more than life. She was something more, far more, than any poor words we know can express. What he felt for her was beyond love; the future he saw stretching away for himself without her, without a hope of her, was in its blank weariness so terrible as to be beyond despair. Had the soul been taken out of his body, life

could not have been more valueless. Take away the belief of
immortality, and what has mortality left to live for?

At the moment George Geith knew, in a stupid, dull
kind of way, that to him Beryl had been an earthly
immortality; that to have her again for his own, had been the
one hope of his weary life, which had made the days and the
hours endurable unto him.

Oh! woe for the great waste of love which there is in
this world below; to think how it is filling some hearts to
bursting, whilst others are starving for the lack thereof; to
think how those who may never be man and wife, those who
are about to be parted by death, those whose love can never be
anything but a sorrow and trial, merge their own identity in
that of one another, whilst the lawful hands of respectable
households wrangle and quarrel, and honest widows order their
mourning with decorous resignation, and disconsolate
husbands look out for second wives.

Why is it that the ewe-lamb is always that selected for
sacrifice? Why is it that the creature upon which man sets his
heart shall be the one snatched from him? Why is it that the
thing we prize perishes? That as the flower fades and the grass
withereth, so the object of man's love, the delight of his eyes
and the desire of his soul, passeth away to leave him desolate?

On George Geith the blow fell with such force that he
groped darkly about, trying to grasp his trouble; trying to
meet some tangible foe with whom to grapple. Life without
Beryl; days without sun; winter without a hope of summer;
nights that could never know a dawn. My reader, have
patience, have patience with the despairing grief of this
strong man, who had at length met with a sorrow that crushed
him.

Have patience whilst I try to tell of the end that came
to his business and to his pleasure; to the years he had spent
in toil; to the hours in which he had tasted enjoyment! To the
struggles there had come success; to the hopes fruition; but
with success and with fruition there had come likewise death.

Everything for him was ended in existence. Living, he
was one as dead. Wealth could not console him; success could
not comfort him; for him, for this hard, fierce worker, for the
man who had so longed for rest, for physical repose, for
domestic pleasures, the flowers were to have no more
perfume, home no more happiness; the earth no more
loveliness. The first spring blossoms, the summer glory on

the trees and fields, the fruits and flowers, and thousand tinted leaves of autumn, and the snows and frosts of winter, were never to touch his heart, nor stir his senses in the future.

Never the home he pictured might be his, never, ah, never! He had built his dream-house on the sands, and, behold, the winds blew and the waves beat, and he saw it all disappear, leaving nought but dust and ashes, but death and despair! Madly he fought with his sorrow, as though it were a living thing that he could grasp and conquer; he turned on it constantly, and strove to trample it down.

No comment is needed to point out the power and pathos of this long extract. The early story of George Geith is in many respects the same as the story of Warrington in *Pendennis*,[5] but the end is far more sad and disastrous, and as it has been shown, pretty bright Beryl dies of her cruel tortures, and it is, in truth, difficult to forgive the author for putting her through so much unnecessary pain and misery.

One peculiarity which strikes one in all these books is, that the feelings are stronger and more vividly alive than the people who are made to experience them. Even Beryl herself is more like a sweet and tender idea of a woman than a living woman with substance and stuff, and bone and flesh, though her passion and devotion are all before us as we read, and seem so alive and so true, that they touch us and master us by their intensity and vividness.

The sympathy between the writer and the reader of a book is a very subtle and strange one, and there is something curious in the necessity for expression on both sides: the writer pouring out the experience and feelings of years, and the reader, relieved and strengthened in certain moods to find that others have experienced and can speak of certain feelings, have passed through phases with which he himself is acquainted. The imaginary Public is a most sympathizing friend; he will listen to the author's sad story; he does not interrupt or rebuff him, or weary with impatient platitudes, until he has had his say and uttered all that was within him. The author perhaps writes on all the sad experience of years, good and ill, successes, hopes, disappointments, or happier memories, of unexpected reprieves, of unhoped-for good fortunes, of old friendships, long-tried love, faithful sympathies enduring to the end. All this, not in the words and descriptions of the events which really happened, but in a language of which he or she alone holds the key, or of which, perhaps, the full significance is scarcely known even to the writer. Only in the great unknown world which he addresses there surely is the kindred spirit somewhere, the kind heart, the friend of friends who will understand him. Novel-writing must be like tears to some women, the vent and the relief of many a chafing spirit. People say why are so many novels written? and the answer is, because there are so many people feeling, thinking, and enduring, and longing to give voice and expression to the silence of the life in the midst of which they are struggling. The necessity for expression is a great law of nature, one for which there is surely some good and wise reason, as there must be for that natural desire for sympathy which is common to so many. There seems to be something wrong and incomplete in those natures which do not need it, something inhuman in those who are incapable of understanding the great and tender bond by which all humanity is joined and bound together. A bond of common pain and pleasure, of common fear and hope, and love, and weakness.

Poets tell us that not only human creatures, but the whole universe, is thrilling with sympathy and expression, speaking, entreating, uttering, in plaints or praise, or in a wonder of love and admiration. What do the sounds of a bright spring day mean? Cocks crow in the farmyards and valleys below; high up in the clear heavens the lark is pouring out its sweet passionate thrills; shriller and sweeter, and more complete as the tiny speck soars higher and higher still, "flow the profuse strains of unpremeditated art." The sheep baa and browse, and shake their meek heads; children shout for the very pleasure of making a sound in the sunshine. Nature is bursting with new green, brightening, changing into a thousand lovely shades. Seas washing and sparkling against the shores, streaks of faint light in distant horizons, soft winds blowing about the landscape; what is all this but an appeal for sympathy, a great natural expression of happiness and emotion?

And perhaps, after all, the real secret of our complaint against modern heroines is not so much that they are natural and speak out what is in them, and tell us of deeper and more passionate feeling than ever stirred the even tenour of their grandmothers' narratives, but that they are morbid, constantly occupied with themselves, one-sided, and ungrateful to the wonders and blessings of a world which is not less beautiful now than it was a hundred years ago, where perhaps there is a less amount of sorrows, and a less amount of pain most certainly than at the time when Miss Austen and Miss Ferrier[6] said their say. Jane

Austen's own story was more sad and more pathetic than that of many and many of the heroines whom we have been passing in review and complaining of, and who complain to us so loudly; but in her, knowledge of good and evil, and of sorrow and anxiety and disappointment, evinced itself, not in impotent railings against the world and impatient paragraphs and monotonous complaints, but in a delicate sympathy with the smallest events of life, a charming appreciation of its common aspects, a playful wisdom and kindly humour, which charm us to this day.

Many of the heroines of to-day are dear and tried old friends, and would be sorely missed out of our lives, and leave irreparable blanks on our bookshelves; numbers of them are married and happily settled down in various country-houses and parsonages in England and Wales; but for the sake of their children who are growing up round about them, and who will be the heroes and heroines of the next generation or two, we would appeal to their own sense of what is right and judicious, and ask them if they would not desire to see their daughters brought up in a simpler, less spasmodic, less introspective and morbid way than they themselves have been? Are they not sometimes haunted by the consciousness that their own experiences may have suggested a strained and affected view of life to some of their younger readers, instead of encouraging them to cheerfulness, to content, to a moderate estimate of their own infallibility, a charity for others, and a not too absorbing contemplation of themselves, their own virtues and shortcomings? "Avant tout, le temps est poseur," says George Sand, "et toi qui fais avec d'esprit la guerre à ce travers, tu en es pénétré de la téte aux pieds."[7]

Notes

1. *Evelina, or The History of a Young Lady's Entrance into the World* (1778), and *Cecilia, or Memoirs of an Heiress* (1782) are novels by Fanny Burney. Emily is the protagonist of Ann Radcliffe's *Mysteries of Udolpho* (1794). Maria Edgeworth (1767–1849) was an Irish novelist.

2. Elizabeth Bennett, Emma, and Fanny Price are heroines from Jane Austen's novels.

3. *Aurora Floyd* (1863) and *Lady Audley's Secret* (1862) are novels by Mary Elizabeth Braddon. Adèle is the protagonist in a Julia Kavanagh novel; Ethel May is the protagonist in Charlotte Yonge's *The Daisy Chain* (1856); Margaret Hale is the protagonist in Elizabeth Gaskell's *North and South* (1855); Jane Eyre and Lucy Snowe are the protagonists in Charlotte Brontë's novels; Dinah, Maggie Tulliver, and Romola are protagonists in George Eliot's novels.

4. Mrs. Storn is the protagonist in Mrs. J.H. Riddell's novel *Too Much Alone* (1860), which Ritchie proceeds to critique. Ritchie will later discuss several of Riddell's other novels: *George Geith of Fen Court* (1864), *City and Suburb* (1861), and *The Moors and the Fens* (1858). Riddell often wrote under the pen name F.G. Trafford.

5. *The History of Pendennis* (1849–50), by W.M. Thackeray.

6. Susan Edmonstone Ferrier (1782–54). Novelist known for *Marriage* (1818), *The Inheritance* (1824), and *Destiny* (1831).

7. French for: "Above all else, time is a poseur," says George Sand, "and you who lead a spirited struggle against these odds are imbued with it from head to toe."

XI. Alice Brooke Bodington

(1840–1897)

Alice Bodington, née Brooke, would have been known to her contemporaries as a popularizer of scientific theories, especially those focusing on evolution. Writing primarily for the "Independent Section" of the *Westminster Review* (which contained articles differing from the periodical's editorial stance), Bodington covered a variety of topics, including brain development in humans and other mammals, the question of marriage from a scientific viewpoint, women's rights, the tension between science and religion, and—most notoriously—an article on evolution and the inferiority of Africans. Bodington also wrote *Studies in Evolution and Biology* (1890), which summarizes various evolutionary and physical science theories; more importantly, the book offers insight into this virtually unknown woman's perception of herself as an author. In her preface, she states, "I am at a loss to imagine why it is considered almost wrong to write about physical science without having made original experiments. A historian is not required to have fought in the battles he describes, nor a geographer to have personally traversed the wilds of Africa." In a short review of Bodington's book, an anonymous *Westminster Review*er curtly responded, "[the] advantage of having made original experiments leads a writer to greater exactness, and, above all, to appreciate the relative value of statements and facts." In spite of this reviewer's dislike of Bodington's methodology, she most likely gained admirers due to her ability to simplify theories and articulate ideas that were currently in vogue.

Harriet Martineau, who was also often remembered by readers as a popularizer of others' ideas, has experienced a steady comeback in literary studies, whereas Alice Bodington has not. And there is good

505

reason for this. Martineau did more than popularize; indeed, her advanced thinking on race, gender, education, class, and government not only influenced many of her followers in the 1830s and 40s, but it continues to draw scholars to her work precisely because her ideas remain valuable. Bodington's writing on race, however, most closely resembles Thomas Carlyle's work on this subject. But unlike Carlyle, Bodington wrote on little else to redeem her reputation among modern-day readers. Instead, she focused on disseminating theories that have since, especially due to the Jewish Holocaust and other heinous, racially motivated crimes, made her thinking anathema to most persons.

Bodington's writing, in particular "The Importance of Race and Its Bearing on the 'Negro Question'," was nevertheless representative of attitudes and beliefs that many of her Anglo-British contemporaries espoused during the latter part of the nineteenth century. When her work is studied in conjunction with eugenists and some social Darwinists, readers gain a realistic perspective on how the British utilized a mishmash of evolutionary theory and racial politics to construct, as well as justify, an Imperialist agenda that took British rule to all parts of the globe, including huge segments of Africa.

By no means an "enlightened" thinker, let alone an original one, Bodington nevertheless deserves attention because her work exemplifies the sort of writing produced by hundreds of Victorian men and women specifically for periodicals. These long-forgotten Victorian writers, including Bodington, resemble in many respects present-day pundits and "expert" commentators to whom mass audiences turn for guidance in deciding how to think and act.

Walter Hajduk,
Temple University,
and Andrea Broomfield,
Eastern New Mexico University

24. The Importance of Race and Its Bearing on the "Negro Question"

Introduction

Alice Bodington's "The Importance of Race and Its Bearing on the 'Negro Question'," published in October, 1890, in the *Westminster Review*, and reprinted here from that periodical, is a blatant example of Bodington's tendency towards generalization and supposition, and an illustration of her constant effort to disguise opinion as fact. The intent of her article is to justify British imperialism, as well as to argue against allowing Black Americans full United States citizenship.

Bodington attempts to provide a historical basis for British and United States ascendency over other countries by tying the Anglo-Saxons to their Rome-conquering Teutonic forbears, and eventually to the pseudo-mythical Aryan race of antiquity. She creates a paradigm wherein the rising and falling of the different "branches" of the Aryan race constitutes a never-ending progression, an ultimately successful campaign for supremacy, predicated upon the Teutonic people's superior moral fiber, adaptive skills, intellect, and political organization. She portrays the British and the European-Americans as benevolent fathers leading the less-endowed races, caring for their shortcomings, and protecting them from their inherent deficiencies.

The Importance of Race and Its Bearing on the "Negro Question"

It has been only within the memory of those now living that the master key to the problems of history has been found. Even the genius of Gibbon could only place before the mind's eye a long succession of events, leading no whither, showing no moral, and giving no clue to the philosophy of history. Throughout the *Decline and Fall of the Roman Empire* there is not the slightest premonition of the stupendous upheaval which was on the verge of taking place in Europe.[1]

He recounts the conquest of the decaying Empire of Rome by successive tribes of Teutons, but no appreciation is expressed by him of the subtle new leaven which immediately began to work, when the highest branch of the Aryan race was brought into contact with the civilisation and the religion of Rome. The Celtic peoples of Europe had for some centuries enjoyed the benefit of Roman civilisation, and had during a considerable period been converts to Christianity, but these influences did not act on them as a ferment. They assimilated what they found, and went no further. The strange unrest, the new institutions, the constant changes, the ceaseless progress of Western Europe began only with the Teutonic conquest, and the adoption by the conquerors, not only of the civilisation, but of the religion of Rome. The possession of one common faith, held with a primitive intensity of belief, made of Western Europe one living whole. No pulse could throb in one part of this organism, whose members were nations, without a responsive throb in the most distant arteries. No bond stronger than that of a common faith held with primitive belief could have existed in that stormy birth hour of modern Europe. Whilst its influence was still at the strongest, the twin institutions of the Feudal system and of Chivalry arose to unite the Western nations still more closely. As the time approached when the old primitive faith began to lose its power, and a violent schism rent the Church in two, other influences, not less powerful, had begun to work. Contemporaneously came the Reformation, obliging men to use their own reason as to what they would believe; the Renaissance which poured forth a thousand fertilising streams from the well-springs of Greek and Roman literature and art; and the discovery of America and first circumnavigation of the globe which opened out new worlds, not only to commerce, but to imagination.[2]

Still later, as these forces lost their first strongly impulsive power, other forces not less strong arose, which are exercising their utmost activity at present. More correctly, I should say, one force arose, of which all others are the manifestations; namely, that untrammeled use of the human reason in the observation of facts, and the fearless deductions from those facts, which we call science. I have purposely used the metaphor of a ferment to express the rise of modern civilisation through Teutonic contact with the civilisation and religion of Rome. The conquerors, except in the original Teutonic countries, and in England, after the Saxon invasion, were generally far inferior numerically, to the conquered, yet they impressed their own restless progress upon all. A similar phenomenon may be seen in the United States, where the heterogeneous assembly of European immigrants is assimilated by the ruling race in the course of one or two generations. This process may go on safely, and even advantageously, where the mixture is of one branch of the Aryan race with another; except when the superior vitality of the Celtic stock (a well-known physiological fact) threatens to *live down* the Saxon, through its power of multiplication, and of successful endurance of adverse conditions. This is no imaginary evil, but an active danger in more countries than one. On the assumption followed throughout this article, that the Teutonic is the highest branch of the Aryan race, and that degeneration will take place where its influence declines, I deliberately use the term evil. History shows the Celtic race as specially conservative of old ideas and institutions; slowly and unwillingly imitative; and relapsing into its original habits, when the stimulus given by other branches of the Aryan race is withdrawn. On the other hand, the due intermixture between Saxon and Celt has produced a type to which the British Empire has owed some of its most brilliant sons. The names of Goldsmith, Burke, Grattan, Sheridan, the Wellesleys, and of one happily still living to serve his country—the Earl of Dufferin, arise instantly to the mind.

The Frankish ruling element was almost destroyed, in any case was greatly weakened in France, during the first Revolution, and French writers of the present day bewail in every way "la décadence" of their nation. In Spain the Visigoth "blue blood" degenerated through close and continuous intermarriages. At the end of the last century, a lady wrote from Madrid: "When I hear of a grandee of Spain, I expect to see a creature like a monkey." The peasantry of Spain is one of the finest in the world, but the vital ferment which *creates* fresh developments is there no longer. What Spain was before her decadence is written on the most brilliant pages of mediæval history.

The possibility of a scientific study of history we owe to philology. Science, when wooed only for herself, has rich unlooked-for gifts to bestow, in the direction perhaps least dreamed of by her votaries. When the first researches were made in the grammar and construction of Sanskrit, no one dreamed that it would afford a key to history, much less that Hindu and Persian, Celt and Sclav, Greek and German are of the same race; a race which, though rising and falling in its various constituent members, *has, as a whole, perpetually advanced and improved.* Viewed in this light modern history is the story of the struggle of this race with its various opponents; of the sore straits to which it has often been reduced, as in the periods of Arab and Tartar temporary success; of the victory, often long deferred, but inevitable, over every foe; and in our own day, of its headlong rush towards new discoveries, new conquests, its search for more satisfactory bases of sociology, and, in this its moment of supreme power, perhaps of most importance to the world, its recognition of duties towards the weak and helpless. Nature knows nothing of duties to the weak and helpless, except where the preservation of the species is concerned. As a moral sense this recognition of duties towards the weak is of all others the most distinctly human, and in its most important developments the most distinctly modern.

Until the essential unity of the Aryan race was revealed, the study of history was saddening and disappointing. As Shakespeare says of life, history was as

A tale
Told by an idiot, full of sound and fury,
Signifying nothing.

Nations rise and fall, empires wax and wane; whatever their virtues and their heroism, how wide soever their conquests in arts or arms, the result is the same—decline and decay. The Chaldean, the Egyptian, the Greek, the Roman, succeed one another as the supreme ruling power of their time. They attain to a high degree of civilisation, and when the topmost peak of ambition is reached, the inevitable decline sets in. Their mental progress stops, their moral and political status degenerates. Then the end comes, often by violent means, or the effete nations live on, like the Struldbrugs of Swift's terrible satire, objects of contempt to all around them.[3]

From the standpoint of race, we behold history in a very different light. Where all seemed chaos, we recognise orderly sequence; where formerly we beheld progress, followed by inevitable degeneration and decay, we can now recognise a constant advance from the lower planes of civilisation to the highest point yet attained by men. History, if we look upon Herodotus as its "father" is the story of world conquest by the Aryan race, a world conquest which even our children may see completed. The struggle for the possession of Africa is the last act of the drama, the greatest, assuredly, ever played upon this earthly stage.

Going back into that record of the ages contained in the sacred books of the Jews and Hindus, we see the first race-victories of the Indo-Persian division of Aryans; the conquests of the aboriginal tribes of India, and the great Egyptian and Chaldean monarchies. In the Hebrew Scriptures, the earliest struggles for mastery are going on between the Hamitic and Chaldean races, and later between the Chaldeans and the Semites. The Persians appear, and all other combatants go down before them; Babylon, Egypt, and Palestine are conquered. In their turn, the Persians succumb to Alexander the Great, and the Western Aryans are seen in the position of pre-eminence, which they never afterwards lose. The Greek empire over the mind can never lose its sway, but she held only for a brief space the material sway over civilised men. The Romans, the most closely allied branch of the race to the Greeks, succeeded next to supreme power, and in their turn succumbed to the Germans, after impressing their civilisation and their religion upon their conquerors. But from the first appearance of the Persians on the scene we are beholding *the development of one race.* That which happened when Greece became a Roman province, occurred also when Rome herself fell before the Teutons, who, after a period of terrible convulsion, in which the very foundations of society seemed broken up, emerged masters of Europe from the wreck of the Roman Empire. The conquered in the field of physical force were masters of their victors in the empire of mind. The victorious Teutons eagerly sought lessons in mental and moral philosophy, in the arts and sciences, from their learned slaves. The classical languages and literature, the great code of Roman law, studied eagerly at the

Universities of the Middle Ages, the humanising religion which made
an abiding link between the abiding nations of Christendom; all these
contributed to the marvellous development of the hitherto barbarian
Teutons, and all were derived from the conquered Romans. The first
steps were hewn out of the rock of knowledge ready for our feet, and in
every advance in human society the proverb, "ce n'est que le premier
pas qui coûte,"[4] is strikingly true. We see the keenest intellects of a
given age approach so near to some new truth, or some important
discovery, that we think they must become aware of it, but the first
step in the new departure is never taken. The Romans showed a
political instinct keener than that of any other people, except those of
the Anglo-Saxon race. The stroke in policy which made the inhabitants
of the Italian cities free citizens of Rome was a masterly one. It
converted implacable enemies into men with the feelings of a common
nationality. Yet the Romans, with all their political genius, could never
go a step further, and imagine the principle of representative
government; the only possible machinery by which a great nation can
govern itself. As the empire of Rome extended, fresh nations gained the
privilege of citizenship. No machinery existed by means of which these
immense numbers could record their wishes and their votes, and an
autocratic government was the necessary result. So, too, the most acute
intellects of Greece and Rome could never devise any system of
notation less clumsy and unworkable than the one they possessed, and
we are indebted to the Semitic race for our numerals, as well as our
alphabet.

    If we except the terrible episodes of the two great Tartar
invasions, exhibitions of brute force directed against a divided Europe;
the only serious rivals of the Aryans, mentally, morally, and
physically, have been the Semites. It is hardly too much to say that the
present unquestioned superiority of the former race has not been owing
to any striking mental, or moral, or physical advantages beyond those
of their rivals, with the exception of one point only. But this one
point, in so hotly contested a game, has been the winning one. The
Aryan race has proved itself immensely superior to the Semitic in its
capacity for political organisation. The downfall of the great Arab
Empire of the Caliphs is distinctly traceable to lack of political instinct
and organisation. The Arabs could be held together under the strong
hand of a conquering prophet or Caliph, but they were utterly unable to
construct anything possessing the adhesive powers of our Feudal

system, much less of passing on to systems of self-government and federation. The mental discipline which self-government gives to the great mass of the people is a priceless boon. It has been said that a benevolent despotism would be the best form of government if the despot could be immortal. One might as well say that a nurse and leading strings would be the best form of government for a growing boy! Better all the tumbles, and the bruises, and the manifold blunders of the growing boy, and of a liberty loving people, than the best despotic government that was ever devised. But this is not saying that self-government is the best for all peoples. On the contrary, it is the very highest and most difficult of all forms of rule; it has been slowly evolved by the highest race of man, has grown with its growth, and is still far from the purity of spirit and perfection of form it may attain at some future day. Yet with all its faults, it is incomparably the best form of government for *us*, and the only one under which we can grow to our full mental and moral stature. But if the question is asked whether it is the best form of government for all people, I, for one, would unhesitatingly answer in the negative. The members of the Semitic race who are dwellers with us, are perfectly capable of adopting all advances we ourselves make, and therefore of using our political system to advantage. Whether they could do if they again became possessed of a country of their own, remains to be proved; all that they have hitherto done has been imitative. Putting aside the Jews, as practically our equals, whilst too few in numbers to be our rivals, we will consider the case of the inferior races. Rousseau's maxim "all men are born free and equal" can be interpreted as Professor Huxley[5] says, only as a permission from Nature for man, in common with other animals, to be just as free and as equal as they can contrive to be. These natural rights, include the rights of the tigress to find a meal for herself and her hungry little ones wherever she can, whether the meal appear in the shape of a cow, or an Indian villager, and the right of the villager to kill the tigress—if he can. Nature allowed the red man and the buffalo to roam at liberty over the continent of North America; she allowed the red man to scalp the newly arrived pale-faces whenever he could; and she allowed the pale-faces to do their very best to exterminate the noble savage in return. In fact, natural rights mean in practice unceasing warfare; the rights of the strong to anything and everything they can get by any means they choose to employ. The weak of course have no rights, and can survive only by elaborating means of hiding or escape, as we see in the rabbit and the deer respectively; or by abject submission and usefulness as slaves. In the history of ethics, the first dawn of a moral sense is shown in injunctions to be merciful to the poor and helpless members of the lawgiver's own nation, admirably shown in the provisions of the Mosaic law. But a savage cruelty to enemies, both to non-combatants and to the vanquished in battle, persisted for many centuries later, showing how deeply ingrained are the instincts of man as an animal, in this respect. It appears in all its atrocity in the Homeric Greeks; nor do their descendants appear to have improved much in this respect, as in the notable example of the awful sufferings of the Athenian captives in the fatal quarries of Syracuse. Gradually a conqueror was found here and there, who showed mercy to his vanquished enemies, and respected the honour of his female captives. There is an instinct which recognises the good, and men loudly applauded this new and strange departure. The very praises which were bestowed on Alexander, Scipio and Bayard,[6] show what a new departure their virtues secured to the men of their age. I have seen the question seriously discussed whether it is preferable that a given virtue should be the result of conscious effort, or should be practised as a matter of course. I do not think prisoners of war, or captive women would hesitate much in coming to a decision on that point. It is a great deal better that the soldiers of a modern army should be merciful to prisoners, and scrupulously respectful to women, as a common everyday matter for which no one thinks of praising them, than that the unrestrained horrors of brute passions should be lighted up occasionally by the rare virtues of a Scipio or a Bayard. It means that the race has advanced as a whole to the stature of those who were once regarded, and justly regarded, as moral giants.

Another great advance in ethics is shown in the utter detestation in which the institution of slavery is now held. Till within the last two hundred years, slavery pure and simple, or slavery in its modified form of serfdom, was looked upon as a part of the natural order of things. The theory that slavery is necessarily as deteriorating in its effects upon the master as upon the slave expresses our feelings and not real facts. The Athenians and the Spartans of the age of Pericles and Lycurgus, the victors at Marathon and Salamis would have been astonished to hear that they were in a condition of deterioration because they were owners of slaves. The Romans of the age of the Gracchi, or of the Scipios, or of Julius Cæsar would also have been astonished to hear that they were in a condition of deterioration.

Many centuries later, when our excellent Alfred the Great left sundry villages of serfs for the possession of the Church, he would have been astonished indeed had he been accused of committing an immoral act. Our present horror of slavery is the outcome of our own advance in ethics, and the instinct which makes *us* feel that slavery has a deteriorating effect is a perfectly sound one. Every step that takes us further away from the exercise of those odious "natural rights" which sanction oppression of the weak by the strong, is a step in the development of our highest selves; a step further away from the brute and the savage. On every side we see that the endeavour is to treat subject peoples with justice and kindness, and to make the Aryan rule a benefit to them. England may point with pride to her Indian Empire, where, with whatever drawbacks and imperfections, the welfare of the native races is the great object of the ruling class. The conquest of Ireland, when the English were at a lower ethical stage, presents the spectacle of as many ghastly and irretrievable blunders as the conquest of India has displayed brilliant successes. The English of Queen Elizabeth's and of Cromwell's time were by no means without good intentions towards those "mere Irish," whom they had left alive. But their goodwill was as misplaced as that of the benevolent female elephant who had inadvertently crushed a hen partridge on her nest— "Poor little things," said the elephant as she compassionately beheld the motherless little ones; "I will be a mother to them," and without further ado she sat down on the nest. The English had no idea of benefitting the Irish except by forcing all their own institutions upon them, from their Church to their land laws. We now recognise the elementary fact that the laws, customs, and institutions of a people are natural growths, and can no more be suddenly altered or replaced than our own heads could be fixed upon other people's shoulders. An imitative people will adopt our ways, at least superficially, with rapidity, but cannot be suddenly forced into them. A Red Indian will not be made into an agriculturist by presenting him with a piece of land, some corn, and a plough; he will sell his land and his plough, eat his corn, and starve with dignity. A South Sea Islander does not attain our moral standpoint by the possession of a Bible and a pair of trousers. And the American negro, the offspring of many generation of slaves, and a member of the lowest ethnological race in the world, is not made the equal of the white man by the possession of his personal freedom and a vote. It is a favourite assertion that the only difference between the white man and the negro is, the latter has a "black skin." It is unnecessary to say that, from a scientific point of view, the colour of a man's skin, whether it be red, black, brown, or variegated, is a matter of utter indifference. It is the general conformation of the negro, and above all his brain, that we have to consider. Ethnologically he is the lowest, as the Aryan is the highest, of all races of men. The various peculiarities by which he approximates more closely to the anthropomorphic apes than do other members of the genus "homo," may from sheer want of space, be left out of account. But the difference in brain weight between the negro and the white races, and the fact that the cranial sutures in the negro close at sixteen, instead of at twenty or twenty-two years of age as in the white man, are essential points. The negro has a brain not only relatively much smaller than that of the white man, but the early closing of the sutures forbids any possibility of equal development. And it is superiority of brain, and nothing else, that has given man his present ascendency over all other animals, and to Aryan man his ascendency over all other men. *The negro can never be our equal.*

Now the voting capacity must rest upon the "force majeure" as a last resort. A vote conflicting with the general sense of those who alone have the power to enforce its execution would be null and void. Women may vote, and may become members of legislative assemblies; but if the feminine vote should carry any measure repugnant to the general sense of the male population, that measure could not be enforced. The individual capacity of woman is in many cases very great, and the sex which has produced a Zenobia of Palmyra[7] and an Elizabeth of England, cannot be said to be wanting in capacity for government. But even when judged as individuals, women are far inferior to men; Zenobia could not "hold a candle" to Napoleon, nor Queen Elizabeth to Charlemagne. And in many directions of thought, science, and art women may be left out of our calculations; a female Beethoven, Shakespeare, or Newton, would be a wonder indeed. Whatever then may be their individual capacity, women can never, *as a body*, possess the "force majeure," and their real strength must be in influence. It is a truism to say that influence will be good or bad in its effects in exact proportion to the mental and moral qualities of the persons exercising it. It may be the influence of a Torquemada, or of a Wilberforce, or of a Catherine of Siena, or of a Pompadour.[8] The influence of the best and most cultivated (I do not use these terms synonymously) women of the Anglo-Saxon race, may, on the whole, be safely relied upon as likely to be beneficial, and conducive to the ethical advance of humanity. It is removed, as widely as the poles apart, from that wily cajoling of harlots and slaves, which has strewed the pages of history with the annals of private shame, and of national ruin. Within the last thirty years incredible victories have been won by brave and highly cultivated women, and won by influence alone. There may still be victories to win, but in my personal opinion, man has granted already as much as woman can safely demand; and if she still has grievances, she must find fault with Nature herself. It is some comfort to think that Nature has revenged, in another line of animals, the humiliations of the female sex amongst the Mammalia, and an injured lady of the Buddhist persuasion might cruelly rejoice, as she beheld a poor gentleman spider expiring in the capacious jaws of his enormous and ferocious bride.

The same line of reasoning, which leads those who adopt it to the conclusion that the vote of women would be practically null and void, applies with incomparably greater force to the negro. To take a metaphor from the animal world, we have hitherto been comparing the lion with the lioness; we have now to compare the lion with "Brer Rabbit." The vote of the women of the Anglo-Saxon race would at least carry with it great moral force, or in the view of those who consider women morally superior to men, a preponderating moral force. Personally, I think women are no more the equal of men from this point of view than from any other, unless morality is understood in the narrowest possible physical sense. The names of the great leaders in morality and ethics, will be found as surely to be names of men, as those of the great leaders in any other line of human advance. Moses, Buddha, Saint Paul, Socrates, Luther, Howard, and Wilberforce, will occur to the thought, before that of any woman presents itself.

The vote of the negro can have no force at all, mental, moral, or physical. If he voted in the majority on any question in which that white minority disagreed with him, the measure passed by such a vote would never be carried out. If he attempted to resort to physical force, so much the worse for our poor "black brother." The story of the Indian Mutiny shows of how little value is numerical superiority, in a contest where every other kind of superiority is on the side of a very small minority. Voltaire gave us an exquisite epigram when he said, "Providence is on the side of the big battalions;" but he said something very nearly the reverse of the truth. Ultimate victory is never on the side of mere physical force. One other favourite argument must be alluded to before passing on to the true "rights" of inferior races. It is asserted that the black man should have equal privileges with the white, because "all souls are equal before God." This is a question for the theologian, and if true may have great value in another world. But on this earth it can hardly be considered a question of practical politics, because it applies equally to the negro, the Red Indian, the Chinese, and the Jackoon[9] of Borneo. Whatever may be the facts as to the souls of these various races, their bodies and minds are very far from being equal, either as compared with one another, or with the white man. Red Indians and Chinese are not admitted to equal rights with the citizens of the United States, on the ground that they have souls, it is always the negro, especially, who has a soul conferring political privileges.

Have we, then, no duty to the negro; has he no rights? He has the rights conferred upon him, and upon all inferior races, in our own day, not by nature, but by the high ethical development of the white race amongst whom he dwells. This high ethical development *concedes* rights to all the weak and helpless, rights to protection and kind treatment, and (where possible) to education and careful guiding to a higher plane. In a word, for the weaker races paternal government is the best and kindest form of rule, as self-government is the best form for the white race which has arrived at political manhood. To expose the negro to all the cruel experiences which must attend the concession of his "natural rights"—that is, of his right to do as he pleases, and of the white race to do to him as *it* pleases in return—to expose him to this fate would be the refinement of cruelty. It can only result in his being crushed and oppressed; and as the press of the white population south becomes greater, to his extermination by direct or indirect means. On the other hand, the recognition of the right of the negro to care and protection from the citizens of the United States, under penalty of certain moral deterioration to the white race if they deny him this right, affords him safe and solid ground to stand on. History has fearful examples to show of the Nemesis which attends a systematic denial of these *human* rights to the weak. The high-spirited and courageous nobles of Poland saw their country obliterated from the map of Europe, because the wretched serfs had neither heart nor will to fight for the independence of cruel masters. The oppressed and starving peasantry of France washed out the wrongs of centuries in rivers of blood. The

Russians present the picture of an educated class exhausting itself in agonising struggles for liberty and self-government—of a head which has come to life, united to a hopeless, inert mass, sunk in the most abject superstition and ignorance, incapable of being roused to life, and thus taking a horrible revenge for centuries of serfdom.

Instead of a freedom and equality which can never exist except on paper, why should not the real truth be honestly faced? The sudden emancipation of the slave, and his theoretical admission to all the rights and privileges of an American citizen arose from a supposed political necessity, and rested on an immense accumulation of religious and sentimental ideas, all equally untenable from a scientific point of view. If it were possible, which fortunately is not the case, that this theoretical equality could be made a reality, the consequences would be appalling. A mingling of the white race with the negro in marriage; the admission of negro theories as to the laws of *meum* and *tuum*, and of his ideas as to morality generally—what need to complete the picture where all would be hopeless degeneration! I venture to think that if the illusory right to vote as an American citizen were withdrawn from the negro, and on the other hand, if his real welfare and protection were made the whole business of a special bureau, he would be in a far better position than he is now. Nor need the negro race be deprived of the chance of a gradual education in self-government.

There could be no possible objection to the free election by coloured people, of representatives who might discuss all matters of special interest to the coloured portion of the community. These representatives might, in their turn, elect a limited number of delegates to appear for them in Congress. The delegates would be persons in whom the negroes placed special confidence, and might be black or white. But the choice must be absolutely free, and no canvassing of any kind must be allowed on the part of the candidate for this vitally important office.

The ordinary affairs of the community would be dealt with by the whole body of coloured representatives, *subject in all cases to the inspection, the revision, and, if necessary, the veto of a special department at Washington*. Matters of grave interest and importance; grievances real or imaginary; should be laid directly before Congress by the small, specially selected, number of delegates, and thus brought to the bar of American public opinion. The points of real importance are that the welfare of the negro, and the best measures for its attainment should be studied by men who should make these questions their special business; that the "red tapeism" apt to arise in the best official department should have some check from public opinion in important matters; that the guidance of the white man should always be retained; and that no risk should be run of deterioration of the white race by admixture with an ethnologically inferior stock. I may be asked if I propose excluding all persons of mixed blood from the privileges of American citizens. I think no risk would be run if octoroons were admitted to these privileges, provided they entered into marriage relations only with octoroons or pure whites. Marriage with a negro or a mulatto should involve the forfeiture of these rights, and limit the octoroon to the political status of the coloured population.

There is in social affairs what has been often called the "swing of the pendulum." Public opinion long fixed in one direction is apt to rebound as far in the opposite direction, and many oscillations are required before the mean point is attained. It is an axiom with classical scholars that Horace has said all the good things that can be said, and he expresses the idea contained in the metaphor with his accustomed epigrammatic force:

> Dum vitant stulti vitia in contraria,
> Currunt. . . . . Nil medium est.

We have only to recall the changes in public opinion with regard to corporal and capital punishment respectively. There was the same rebound of the pendulum in public opinion about slavery. From regarding slavery as a divine institution, and as a necessary part of the machinery of society, men rushed to the opposite extreme, and could see no salvation except in granting to the black man exactly the same rights as the white. That the negro can fairly be called upon to render some return for the protection he now receives in civilised States, seems not to have occurred to any one. The more we hear and know about the negro in his own country, the more utterly wretched does his position appear, a martyr to the most horrible and degrading superstitions, the helpless prey of the Arab slave-trader, the trembling victim of a fellow savage decked with the title of king. Amongst the negroes, some tribes are of course superior to others, but their independence is preserved only by unceasing warfare, and they exert their "natural rights" to the full over-weaker [sic] neighbours. Of these warlike and independent tribes, such as the Masai and the Zulus, the

American negro is not a descendant. His lot was cast amongst the weaker brethren in that paradise of natural rights, Africa. He is now allowed to live in a land which he could by no possible means conquer or keep for himself; he can till his fields, or sprawl in his melon patch at his own sweet will, protected by the *pax Americana*. If he is oppressed, it is most assuredly against the will of the vast majority of the American people, who would have hailed him as their equal, if Nature had made this possible. In return for peace and protection I believe that the State, representing the whole body of citizens, has a right to demand certain duties from the negro, and to enforce the carrying out of any rules it may choose to make, remembering only that those duties and rules should be enforced in a spirit of kindness and justice. If the State considers that the negroes should be removed into certain portions of the country specially reserved for them, if it decrees that negroes residing in the United States should do a certain amount of labour in return for the protection accorded to them, I believe the State will be within its "rights," in the sense in which we now regard this word. If when the white population presses on the means of subsistence, the State decrees that the coloured people should be settled in Africa or the West Indies, it would again be within its right, because altruism cannot be exercised by a State beyond the limits required by self-preservation; but a foul wrong would be done, if a child-like people were expatriated, without receiving in their new country some enlightened guidance, and the same humane care which can alone give the State the moral right to decide for them. If England can rule millions of Hindus with an anxious care for the welfare of those, who by a polite fiction are called our "fellow-subjects," the United States could equally care as guardian for the welfare of their coloured wards beyond the seas.

Notes

1.   The last volumes of the *Decline and Fall of the Roman Empire* were published in 1788; the convocation of the States General, the first scene in the drama of the French Revolution, occurred in May 1789. [Bodington's note]

2. If we date the commencement of the Renaissance from the dispersion of Greek men of learning after the taking of Constantinople in 1453; the commencement of the Reformation from the ban of the Pope pronounced against John Huss and the "Wickliffite heresies" in 1409; and the era of great maritime discoveries, from the circumnavigation of the globe accomplished by Vasco di [sic] Gama in 1497, and the discovery of the mainland of America by Columbus in 1498, these three great motive forces took their rise within the same century, and displayed their strongest activities during the ensuing century, the sixteenth. [Bodington's note]

3. Struldbruggs, or Immortals, were born with a red circular dot over the left eyebrow, thus marking them as persons who would live forever. From Jonathan Swift's *Gulliver's Travels*, Part. 3, Chapter 10.

4. A French proverb, roughly translated as: the first step is what really counts.

5. Thomas Henry Huxley (1825–95).

6. Alexander "the Great" (356–323 B.C.). King of Macedon 336–323 B.C., who, on his succession, immediately began the invasion of the Persian empire. He also liberated the Greek cities in Asia Minor, and defeated the Persians in Egypt, Syria, and Mesopotamia. Scipio (185/4–129 B.C.). A Roman general who achieved distinction in the third Punic War; he blockaded and destroyed Carthage in 146 B.C. Pierre du Terrail, Seigneur de Bayard (1473–1524). A French soldier known for his great valor and chivalry. Also known as the knight "fearless and above reproach" ("sans peur et sans reproche").

7. Zenobia (3rd c.). Queen of Palmyra who succeeded her murdered husband as ruler. Ultimately she conquered Egypt and much of Asia Minor.

8. Torquemada, Tomás de (1420–98). Spanish cleric and Dominican monk who became the Inquisitor-General of Spain. He transformed the Inquisition into an instrument of the state, and gained a reputation for ruthlessness and cruelty. He also expelled the Jews from Spain from 1492 onwards. William Wilberforce (1759–1833). A prominent Evangelical who, as an MP, was instrumental in ending British participation in the slave trade by 1807. Catherine of Siena (1347–80). Saint of the Roman Catholic Church who was born in Siena, Italy. At age sixteen she joined the Dominican Tertiaries, and held a unique position as an advisor to civil and religious leaders.

9. A race of peculiarly simian appearance and habits, living on platforms in the trees of the forests of Borneo. [Bodington's note]

XII. Edith Jemima Simcox
(1844–1901)

Edith Jemima Simcox was a woman of manifold talents and interests. As a literary critic, she championed realism and moral aesthetics in the fiction she reviewed. As a feminist, she urged the public to take heed of women's intellectual and social accomplishments, and she took to task those nineteenth-century philosophers who advocated fallacious stereotypes of women. As a trade-union activist, Simcox improved the working conditions of exploited textile workers, especially women. Finally, as an essayist, Simcox wrote about the experiences of women oppressed by poverty that she saw brought on by patriarchal tyranny.

Simcox was born on August 2, 1844, the only daughter of Jemima Haslope and F. George Price Simcox, a middle-class merchant. Little is known of her education. She learned French and German in school, quoted Latin easily, and knew enough Greek to read Plato's *Symposium* and the works of Herodotus. While working as a trade unionist, she also learned the rudiments of Italian and Flemish. Furthermore, her writing indicates that she must have been a voracious reader and well acquainted with the works of major intellectual and social thinkers. Although she characterizes her studies as desultory in her unpublished "Autobiography of a Shirt Maker," her older brothers, George Augustus and William Henry (both of whom were Oxford Fellows), probably gave her educational guidance. George Eliot had an especially profound effect on Simcox, ultimately influencing many of this younger woman's theories regarding literature and philosophy.

According to her biographer K.A. McKenzie, Simcox's "main social interest was in improving the lot of the toiling masses of mankind in general." She used her own earnings as a writer to support many reform initiatives. On the educational front, Simcox lectured at the numerous workingmen's clubs which provided members with instruction; she also served on the London School Board from 1879 to 1882, working tirelessly to make secular education compulsory for all children. However, Simcox's major social contributions came from her work as a trade unionist. As the result of a cooperative shirt making venture with reformer Mary Hamilton, Simcox helped organize the Shirt and Collar Makers Union in 1875. She also became involved with the Women's Protective and Provident League. Emma Paterson and Edith Simcox then became the first women delegates to the Trades Union Congress, held in Glasgow in 1875. Always anxious to disseminate information on such labor activity as widely as possible, Simcox translated into French the delegates' resolution from the Workman's International Conference held in October, 1883. Simcox contended that real improvement for workers could best be realized through international trade unionism—a theory contested by most British trade union leaders of her time.

When not working at educational or trade union reform, Simcox wrote on a wide range of topics, including literary reviews and essays on art, literature, philosophy, trade-union and labor theory, politics, and other social issues. Assuming the pseudonym H. Lawrenny, Simcox began her writing career in 1869 as a reviewer for the *Academy*, sharing with her university-educated male colleagues the task—or privilege—of educating the reading public about culture. Besides reviewing for the *Academy*, Simcox also contributed essays and reviews to *Longman's*, *North British Review*, the *Fortnightly Review*, *Nineteenth Century*, *Contemporary Review*, *Macmillan's Magazine*, and *Fraser's*. Although mainly known for her periodical contributions, Simcox also published three significant full-length studies: *Natural Law: An Essay in Ethics* (1877), *Episodes in the Lives of Men, Women, and Lovers* (1882), and *Primitive Civilizations* (1894). Of the three, *Episodes* is best known to modern readers, due to Simcox's admiring discussion of George Eliot. Although *Episodes* has been long out of print, five chapters were published in *Fraser's Magazine* in 1881, and thus are still accessible.

Although Simcox's connection with George Eliot has saved her from permanent obscurity, her stature as a Victorian writer and reformer has suffered thereby. Undoubtedly, when the manuscript of Simcox's "Autobiography" became available to the Bodleian Library in 1958, it allowed biographers such as Gordon Haight to formulate a more complete picture of Eliot's life; however, the portrait of Simcox which resulted has been that of an emotional spinster forever pining away for a kind word from her Madonna. McKenzie's biography—the only lengthy study of Simcox's life and work—does not stray far beyond what Simcox had to say about Eliot in the "Autobiography." Except for a discussion of Simcox's *Episodes*, McKenzie does little to further Simcox's reputation as a writer.

A re-evaluation of Simcox's writing would ideally be situated within the context of her work as a social reformer. Rather than assuming that Simcox simply left scholars essential information regarding George Eliot's life and thoughts, we should begin assessing how her work compelled a vast reading audience to consider the ill effects of a free market economy on untrained factory girls. Much of Simcox's writing, including her literary criticism, reflects her concern about worker exploitation. Even in "Autobiographies" (*North British Review*, 1870), Simcox draws attention to the goldsmith Benvenuto Cellini's heroic "championship of men of genius against their employers."

Recent critical evaluations of Simcox's work are very limited. Lynn Reese Register Atkins's "Expanding the Limits of Domesticity: Nineteenth Century Nonfiction by Women" (Ph.D. diss., Wayne State, 1984), and Kathy Wingerd's "New Voices in Victorian Criticism: Five Unrecognized Contributors to Victorian Periodicals" (Ph.D. diss., Kent State, 1987) both examine Simcox's writing on the woman question, as well as her literary criticism. Aside from these dissertations, the most important sources available on Simcox remain K.A. McKenzie's *Edith Simcox and George Eliot* (1961; rpt.1978) and Simcox's own books and articles. Gordon Haight's collection, *The George Eliot Letters* (1954–6; 1978–9) also contains extracts from Simcox's work.

Laurie Zierer,
The Pennsylvania State
University

25. Autobiographies

Introduction

Published in the *North British Review* in January, 1870, and reprinted here from that periodical, Edith Simcox's "Autobiographies" is a critical analysis of published autobiographies ranging from Darius, King of Persia (reigned 521–486 B.C.) to John Henry Newman (1801–90). Using Auguste Comte's "three historical periods" as a framework for her discussion, Simcox argues that the autobiography has evolved in three stages: the Elementary, the Positive, and the Analytical.

Although the article was written before most of the major Victorian autobiographies (including those by Mill, Martineau, Carlyle, and Oliphant) were published, Simcox does include John Henry Newman's 1864 spiritual autobiography, *Apologia pro Vita Sua*; her comments on this and other classic autobiographies established her as one of the first scholars to construct a theory of the genre. In "Autobiographies," as in her other analyses of literary works, Simcox saves her praise for those authors who paint a faithful picture of reality and enlarge the moral and intellectual sympathy of their readers.

Autobiographies

There is nearly as much difference between the motives which
men have alleged for writing histories of their own lives as there is
between the tenor and literary merit of the works themselves. The
undertaking is at one time vindicated as a concession to the affectionate
curiosity of friends or descendants; at another by a reference to the
importance of the events concerned. Sometimes the writer boldly
announces a claim to public admiration, or apologizes for listening to
the dictates of private partiality, or professes a wish to elucidate his
published works, or to recommend his principles by his example. More
rarely he proposes to rebut current calumnies; most often, perhaps, to
satisfy an ambition which has found no other direction for its hopes.
The action of this last motive, the influence of which may be suspected
in every classical autobiography, is best analysed by Cardan in language
which seems prophetic of Comte.[1] Men, he says, have a twofold
existence, a single private personality, and a share in the common life
of the world or humanity. The appetite for immortality (subjective
immortality that is, though he does not formulate the distinction) is
irrational, irreducible, inexplicable, and indestructible, but admitting
two kinds of satisfaction. The founder, the conqueror, the destroyer of
empires and cities—a Cæsar, Alexander, or Eratostratus,—has placed
his immortality beyond the reach of vain report; and the history of his
deeds adds nothing to his greatness. The world is the monument of such
men, whether their names are inscribed on it or no. But the ambition of
Cæsar is folly; for the lapse of years left the Roman empire but a
ridiculous and unheard-of shade in Germany. If the mind is eternal,
renown profits it nothing; if it is mortal, the noisiest fame is empty.
And yet men whom a thousand obstacles shut out from failing with
Cæsar seek fresh ways of fixing upon the world's memory the fact that
they have been. This too is vanity, and stupidity even more extreme
than the former. For what these men write will not be read; or if it is
read, they can count the years after which it will be forgotten,
contemned, and neglected. Let go the shadow and seize the reality, carpe
diem, live while you live, follows as the substance and the sum of
practical philosophy. But if the reality is not to be attained—if, after
all, the present is unsatisfying or worse—then any future that can be
looked forward to is a gain; and it is well to despise actual evils in view

of an immortality that shall be free from them. A man's qualities are himself in a closer sense than his actions; and to build a monument in the memories of men to come, without laying its foundation in the physical fortunes of their ancestors,—to interest ages in a story of wishes, failures, feelings, and tendencies that stop short of action,—is a hope which may tempt even a more exacting egotism than the hollow glory of unbounded power.

The man who has courage and patience to write a history of his life does not go unrewarded. As a hero, he need not fear detraction; as an author, there is no risk of his materials failing; his own theme and his own critic, he can suppress in the second character whatever seems unworthy of himself in the first. On the other hand, to go over again the whole of a life which has already begun to decline, to dissect the still palpitating corpse of decaying consciousness, is a laborious, and, as it proceeds, increasingly thankless task. It can only be undertaken, not to say completed, under the pressure either of a strong conviction on the part of the writer's friends that his life is full of interest to his contemporaries, or else of a still firmer persuasion on his own part that the revelations he has to make are such as will tend to gratify the unappeasable curiosity of the human race touching all that bears upon the standing difficulties of the anatomy of the human mind. In the former case the work is likely to be disappointing in itself, however indispensable the light may be which it throws upon the private history of the author. In the latter case, a sort of instinct seems to guide and correct the motions of simple self-love; and unconscious tact saves from an attempt, which must have failed, the vast majority of those whose outward circumstances have been commonplace, who have no mental history to speak of, or whose consciousness of what takes place in and around them is too confused and fugitive to be revived after the laps of years in a literary framework.

The temptation to attain what, at first sight, seems so easy an immortality, is of universal application; and if the class which succumbs to it is small, it is natural to suppose some common qualities in its members, underlying their obvious differences. The point of union, even if it could be determined, would not, it is true, offer much basis for generalizations; and a division of mankind into those who have and those who have not written autobiographies might be unfruitful as well as arbitrary. But since, apart from questions of style, every autobiography depends for its value and interest upon the

measure of common human passion and experience concentrated in its
pages, or on the degree of vividness with which they depict common
human situations and sentiments, every autobiographer is a
representative man, and one not of a representative class, but of a class
of representative men. In point of fact, existing autobiographies may be
arranged in three principal groups, corresponding roughly to Comte's
three historic periods, though the chronological order is different, and
subject to individual aberrations.[2] These groups may be distinguished
critically as the Monumental or Elementary, the Positive, and the
Analytic, or, to keep up the analogy, the Metaphysical. The first of
these schools is epic in style and heroic in substance; each of its works
is that of an imaginative autocrat—a story of action told with primitive
energy, unmixed self-approval, and spontaneous art. The second school
contains artists of a sort, but no heroes. It is literal, realistic, and in
form dramatic. The writers depict themselves only as a means or
accessory to the representation of the age in and for which they live.
They write with unsurpassed depth of conviction what every one knows
and believes; they give expression to a sublimated common sense; and,
as their observations are authentic and their judgements unimpeachable,
the universal reason of mankind admires and applauds. The last variety
of autobiographical writing is more complicated. To the
autobiographer, at any rate, humanity consists of the ego and the non
ego. It is possible to him to view the world as subordinate to himself,
or to treat himself in subordination to the world; but a third alternative
is not easy to find. Decaying originality may take refuge in a sort of
criticism: but criticism of the outer world does not naturally take the
form of autobiography, criticism of the writer's self paralyses the
course of a narrative, and criticisms of the relations between the two are
not naturally suggested by the events of an ordinary life. The only
remaining possibility is to chronicle thought instead of action, changes
of opinion instead of succeeding experience, or else to represent the
influence of imaginary circumstances upon a real mind. To surround a
fictitious hero with incidents founded upon fact can scarcely be said to
constitute autobiography at all.

One of the earliest, and, in some ways, the most admirable of
autobiographies, that of Darius Hystaspes,[3] whether composed by
himself or a confidential secretary or clerk of the works, speaks a moral
unity, a command of memory, and a confidence in the facts to be stated,
which is scarcely approached even by Benvenuto Cellini, and looks for

its response to a reverential and uncritical nation. The simple loquacity of the best memoir-writers disappears in busy, learned, or earnestly controversial ages that might question its purpose and its use. Confessions, real or fictitious, designed to express a romantic opposition to the existing order of creation, or a speculative disapproval of any possible order, indicate a transitional period of moral exhaustion and intellectual despondency, trained to tolerate a want of faith and courage, if not of candour, in its representatives. But whether the work be in the form of an autobiography, a journal, or a philosophical romance, literary success depends upon the distinctness of the outline, the freshness of the colours in which the hero's person appears before us, the completeness of our sympathy with him, and the frankness with which he seems to rely on it. What we really value most in the author who admits us behind the scenes of his career, is the revelation of something—however commonplace, however obviously probable— which we could not have known as certain and actual without his assistance. The virtues and achievements of an eminent man do not come into this category; and hence the impatience with which we hear from themselves how Cicero saved Rome, or how Napoleon wished to save Europe. Information which newspapers might give, gains little in purely literary interest by coming at first hand; and direct statements of fact by historical characters may easily have less authority than incidental, so to speak, inanimate evidence. To the critic, the fact that a thing has been said is very far indeed from being a sufficient reason for believing it; and when the publication of a volume of memoirs is only one act, if perhaps the last, of a complex political activity, it has often little more than the weight of a diplomatic note addressed to posterity.

The memoirs of men who have taken a prominent part in public affairs are not, of course, without value, but their price to the historian or the antiquarian is not in direct proportion to their psychological interest. The Commentaries of Cæsar, for instance, reappear in every History of Rome, and have inspired libraries full of archæological lore; but when the object is to advance further into the penetralia of Cæsar's mind than into the thoughts of Alexander or Charlemagne, we are balked of the expected revelations, and can only draw inferences from our disappointment. A character where energy leaves no space for reflection, a will that leaves itself no leisure for self-questioning, a personality squandered upon the subjects of its influence—if this is all that one of the three or four accepted giants of history can show us of himself over and above his actions and motives, there is compensation for men of smaller stature, Cæsars of private life, who contrive to pose as heroes to themselves, and have the art of concentrating on their persons the attention which their achievements could scarcely command. The attraction in this case is not exclusively either in narrative or narrator; but when a person of marked or singular character has met with or sought out adventures equally uncommon, his own account of the sensations he experienced meanwhile has a twofold, irresistible interest. Works that completely satisfy this condition are few: and if we attempt to include in the first rank of autobiography the Lives of Benvenuto Cellini and Alfieri, the Confession of St. Augustine, Dr. Newman's *Apologia*, the acts of Giraldus Cambrensis and the Chevalier de Grammont, and the early part of Stilling's *Lebensgeschichte*, it is difficult to give a satisfactory reason for consigning Goldoni, Marmontel, Hume, Gibbon, Lilly, or the prince of journalists, Pepys, to a lower literary level.[4] The difference—if, as may be suspected, there is a difference—is in the more powerful imagination possessed by the first class; not that in any sense unfavourable to their accuracy or sincerity they embellish their characters and magnify their exploits, but that their recollections have a clearness resembling that of direct poetic intuition, so that at the moment of writing, the picture of their past lives appears to themselves as a complete artistic whole, with what faults or beauties the spectator may judge, but at least an unbroken block of nature, chiselled by the force of a single human will into the form we see. In the best writers of diaries, it is perception rather than memory that rises to the dignity of inspiration. The creative finger of poetry fixes the surrounding circumstances and occurrences of the life; but the author is only one figure in the scene which he observes intensely and acutely, whilst, apart from the act of attention, his own mind is either passive or bent on minor affairs of practical interest. And this, which is true of Pepys, is still more true of politicians and men of letters, who write when the original vividness of sensation has worn off, instead of seizing the humour or experience of the moment.

Historical memoirs by men who had witnessed or taken part in the events they commemorated, were as common in ancient as they are in modern literature. But the introduction of a personal element was a later step; and before the habit had been formed, the decay of national and private energy had left nothing to tempt the skill of qualified pens.

The dissolution of the old world might, it is true, have bequeathed to us the corrupt protests, the unavailing complaints, of a provincial Rousseau or Werther;[5] but such fragments may not have been written, and they were certain not to be preserved. The last remonstrances of Paganism looked outwards in appeal to an objective past rather than to a new inward standard; and the confidences of M. Aurelius or the Emperor Julian are neither circumstantial nor sentimental enough to supply the want.[6] S. Augustine's *Confessions*, indeed, are connected by one side with the analytic or subjective school of autobiography, which will have to be treated later on as a note of moral and literary decadence; but by another they belong to the primitive, epic, or heroic class, and may as easily be reckoned first of the modern, as last of the ancient order of thought.

The earliest formal autobiography of any importance is that of Giraldus Cambrensis in the twelfth century. It is the first that begins at the beginning with the parentage, birthplace, favourite games, and earliest school triumphs of the hero; and it is one of the chosen few in which the hero's character is neither obscured by the history of his deeds, nor made the subject of minute and tedious description. Unfortunately, out of the two hundred and seventy-three chapters of the original work, *De rebus a se gestis*, only the first fifty-three have been preserved to posterity; but these bring the author down to the age of fifty or thereabouts (for the chronology of his life is not absolutely certain); and the loss of the remainder is compensated by the abundant details of his career afforded in the *Invectionum Libellus*, or his later work, *De jure et statu Menevensis Ecclesiæ*. Of course these details owe great part of their value to their early date and the light they throw upon contemporary history; but on his own merits, the Welshman takes a creditable place between literary autobiographists and authors of political memoirs; and he is particularly happy in avoiding the standing difficulty of egotists of his class,—the danger lest the interest should flag and the story lose its freshness as age overtakes the narrator.

The main features of the history of Giraldus are well known:— how he defended the rights and dignity of S. David's see against his Welsh neighbours, against the metropolitan Canterbury, against kings and nobles, and before the Pope; how he laboured to restore ecclesiastical discipline amongst his barbarous countrymen; how he traversed Ireland, chronicled its conquest, and described its people; how Paris hung upon his expositions of the canon-law; how he refused

English, Irish, and even Welsh bishoprics; how his Latinity was praised
by the Pope; how he outwitted his perjured adversaries; how his courage
never failed in the direst extremities; and how, when the hopelessness of
his efforts was apparent, he scorned to harass his opponent with merely
captious resistance, and startled friends and enemies alike by resigning
the contest with a good grace. All this is set forth in his published
works, with a minute candour that takes the place of humility. When
we are told so much about a man, we are likely to be told more than he
knows himself; and we can see that the vivacious archdeacon was
marked out for failure in his cherished ambition by other causes than
his affinity to the royal family of Wales. An ecclesiastical "enfant
terrible," his first victory would have given him an importance which,
as the controversy between Church and State then stood, could only
have been embarrassing to himself. The king and the archbishop knew
better than to provide themselves with a third in the dispute, as
inflexible as either, and with interests separate from both. The would-be
Metropolitan of Wales was too great a patriot for Hubert, too good a
churchman for John, too conscientious or too thoughtless to play them
off against each other.[7] His nationality was his real misfortune, in a
wider sense than he suspected. As an Englishman or Italian, he would
have represented a popular and important principle; even as a Scot, he
might have deserved well of his country; but as a Welshman, he could
only act as a drag upon the wheels of imperial progress. His principal
distinction is to have fought a losing battle with singular grace and
dignity; and his example certainly tends to verify Cardan's theory of the
alternatives of ambition.

If Giraldus's public life had been more fortunate, if a more
propitious set of circumstances had provided him with material scope
for his activity, if he had exercised a perceptible influence on the fate of
Wales or her church, the constantly vanishing traces of his work would
have been his memorial; he would have had no leisure to struggle with
impending oblivion; and he would not have felt the need to register his
protest against the injustice of fate. His best efforts must have failed—
they were scarcely even directed—to attain material immortality; but
any ordinary vanity might be satisfied with the fame he has secured to
his person, and his adventures. In himself, Giraldus rather recalls the
temperament of another itinerant philosopher of later date, with the
same knack of fluent invective, the same talent of falling out of one
quarrel into another, the same good-humoured arrogance, and the same

apparent unsuccess. But Giordano Bruno's extravagances are covered by his tragical end.[8] He was a missionary of the rising astronomical system; his tenets are of the sort that admit of perennial rediscovery; the autobiographical notices in his works are lively; and his uncomplimentary account of the Oxford of Queen Elizabeth yields to none of the descriptions of Giraldus Cambrensis in piquancy. But the Italian relied upon the intrinsic value of his theories, their absolute truth, and their unchanging importance; he claimed respect for himself, because he believed the earth to go round the sun, not for his imaginative pantheism, because it was preached by a versatile and witty traveller. A divided allegiance weakened his chance of reward; he thought too much of himself to be identified and immortalized with his cause, too much of his beliefs to treat them as mere accessories to his history. Copernicus and Cellini have a stronger hold upon posterity.

It is possible to define genius as the exaggeration of a few ordinary faculties; but the intensification of any common taste or tendency is enough to make the subject of a good autobiography. The essential point is to present the maximum of life and motion compatible with the calm of self-analysis and the composure of unalterable self-respect; the rest is only an affair of skill in style or composition. The subtle genius which delineates character is midway between the art of the portrait-painter and the historian; but the illusion produced by representations of this class must be perfect. We must see the individual with all the indescribable shades and mixtures of his temperament, not merely infer his qualities from his conduct, still less accept uncritically his own description of them. We require a confidence so special that it will enable us to predict what the hero would do under any given circumstances, so minute that at any fresh trait we may spontaneously recognise to whom it belongs. We wish to see his impulses in his actions, his principles in his account of them; and we expect both to be original, neither eccentric. An Admirable Crichton,[9] a model author, artist, or ecclesiastic, would have to be described with too many and too congruous superlatives, in terms too suggestive of an epitaph, for the picture of his life to stimulate curiosity. The tints of language are not fine enough to distinguish one such phœnix from another. There might be fifty Evelyns,[10] but there is only one Pepys. In existing specimens of autobiography, the difficulty is to obtain the necessary variety of form without introducing too many and too black shadows. Men who have the courage to show us their worst side are seldom afraid of allowing that side to be sufficiently bad. Characters of concentrated willfulness are tempted to obey their least laudable impulses by the very ease with which they can override opposition; but men of this type do not care enough about the warrant of laws, human or divine, to tamper with those that condemn them, or to seek to modify them in their own interests. They only endanger the cause of morality by the reproach they bring on originality, and by confounding for a moment the attempt to try them by the standard of common right and wrong.

In everything except date Benvenuto Cellini's life belongs to a ruder and more primitive age than that of Giraldus; his moral ideal differs more from that of the present time, and his intellectual culture is more individual, less coloured by the traditions of a still remembered antiquity. At bottom a healthy and intelligent savage, he had learned drawing from Leonardo and Michel Angelo, letters from Boccaccio and Petrarch; and this appearance of irrepressible barbarism, adorned with all the splendours of the Renaissance, produces the most paradoxical results. No other autobiography shows so plainly how far it is possible to diverge from common types without overstepping the recognised limits of nature. A talented artist, a truculent soldier, a diligent tradesman, a courteous gentleman, an unprincipled bravo—one character is no more proper to him than another. He is, first of all, himself; next, the sixteenth century in person, only without the scepticism that might have disarranged his life or disturbed his narrative. The union of precocious maturity with indestructible youthfulness is indispensable to the writers of memoirs; for the thought of follies, pronounced irrational on reflection, would be fatal to retrospective self-respect, whilst any concessions to the lassitude of old age would interfere with the labour of composition. At sixteen, Cellini was already master of a trade which would make him welcome in any town in Italy. He could get his own living, assist his father, dress handsomely, wear a sword, draw it at every provocation, and all the while labour devotedly to improve in the higher branches of his art. Perhaps the only feature in his career on which it is possible to dwell with unalloyed satisfaction is his championship of men of genius against their employers. It may be that his trade helped to make him (like Blake) more independent in his art; he is, perhaps, the only artist to whom discouragement and disappointment were unknown. Even in that munificent age, patrons were often found more ready to promise than to perform, to praise than to recompense; and painters and sculptors suffered without remedy. But not so Cellini. King, pope, and emperor, prince, cardinal, and duke, whoever had the misfortune to offend the irascible goldsmith, might get their medals struck, or their jewels mounted as they could: he would only work on his own terms; and they were lucky to get him on those. Now Michel Angelo was old, not another man living could have cast his Perseus. It was—strictly speaking—priceless; but if he condescended to take ten thousand crowns for it, what mad blindness to chaffer with him! Change the circumstances; throw him into prison with a broken leg, and he will write verses, see visions, and almost repent of his many murders. But in every situation he remains master of himself; and it is impossible to doubt his substantial good faith. At the same time, it must be admitted that his reasonable estimate of the dignity of art is apt to take the form of personal insolence, and that the truth of his narrative is occasionally what has been called regulative rather than absolute. A little imagination in recounting his exploits was necessary to give a complete idea of the boundlessness of his aspirations. The explanation, for instance, of his most flagrant myth— his defence of Rome, and single-handed slaughter of the Constable de Bourbon—is really this: The Constable was slain by an arquebus;[11] who so likely to have fired it as the man who felt within himself power and inclination to shoot not only one but a dozen Constables, as occasion might serve?

As we advance into more sophisticated ages it becomes less easy to draw the line between harmless and communicative self-deception and interested misrepresentation. No autobiographies are intentional impostures throughout, if for no other reason, from the impossibility of making a forgery consistent; but there are varieties of falsehood and degrees of truth. Facts and intentions admit equally of mis-statement; real actions may be explained erroneously, and imaginary conduct accounted for by real motives. Such writers, for instance, as William Lilly, "student in astrology," and Jung Stilling, do not, like Rousseau, make an art of insincerity, or we should be less indulgent to the solemn quackery of the one, and the lucrative unworldliness of the other; but what they say, and still more what they leave unsaid, makes it plain that they had to choose, in the last resort, between deceiving themselves and deceiving the public. The compromise by which we are enabled to trace the mental processes of pseudo-scientific imposture, and to estimate the degree of unconsciousness compatible with religious hypocrisy, disarms the severity with which we might otherwise visit the self-betrayal of our authorities. In the case of Lilly, it is difficult, primâ facie, to believe that a respected professor of a still esteemed art should *consciously* divide mankind into the two sections of accomplices and dupes; and this difficulty is increased by the sincere contempt which he evidently feels for the small practitioners who decide cases of loss, restore stolen goods, and cast flattering horoscopes for money. Lilly was a power in the State; and it is in checking his political prophecies that we can best estimate the qualified faith with which they inspired their author. The civil war simplified his task amazingly; for the weal or woe vaguely announced to befall the country was certain to overtake one side or the other; and at the critical moment the prophet could verify his own prediction by identifying himself with the winners. Cardan is said to have starved himself at the age of seventy-five in obedience to his horoscope, after several times surviving the fated day of his calculations. But when in June, 1645, Lilly had proclaimed, "If now we fight, a victory stealeth upon us," and fortune declared for the Parliament at Naseby, he had only to begin to write himself Roundhead instead of Cavalier, and the credit of his prognostications was saved. Astrology in its palmy days was not a mere system of arbitrary imposture: it had fixed principles and methods; and of course the greatest master of these was able to make the most numerous and the most various predictions. The quackery was in the ambiguous expression of the oracles, and in their interpretation après coup. Lilly's prophetic style is a mixture of Emerson, Mr. Home,[12] and the pamphlets of his time. It was enough for many to find current events or their own projects alluded to by name in the inspired hieroglyphics; and there was a general understanding that the exact meaning and application might wait till fate revealed it to all the world at once. If the stars spoke too plainly—and in a certain conventional language they did speak—their interpreter could generalize and confound their utterances, so that it was scarcely possible for them to be ever wrong, and certain by the law of chances that they would sometimes be right. Thus Lilly's *Monarchy or no Monarchy*, published in 1651, contained representations of a great fire and a great mortality; but fifteen years was long enough for the non-fulfillment of any prediction to be forgotten, as well as for the strangeness of its accomplishment to be abated. And that this was felt by Lilly's friends and enemies, is proved by the little molestation he suffered in the popular excitement of 1666.

Heinrich Jung belongs in every way to a later period than Lilly; and it is a relief to turn from the embarrassing questions of mental casnistry [sic] which they raise to the thoroughly safe triviality of Michel de Marolles. His only distinction is that of having written, in cumbrous French, an uninteresting account of an uninteresting life, which, nevertheless, such is the charm of autobiography, was held by his contemporaries to atone for other still duller works. Born just a century after Cellini, he transports us at once from a state of nature to one of convention, from an age of action to one of reflection. He is the first, as well as the most obscure, representative of the positive school of autobiography—a school which, in a sense, includes all genuine memoirs, diaries, or journals, all merely descriptive narratives of a life that anybody might have lived, that is only interesting because some one did live it. Their value is not in clear representations of the author's character, for he need not have much, and what he has we are content to infer from the part he plays in the scenes it is his pretension to recall. But he must have lived in a time of which we know enough to wish to know more, he must not have forgotten himself in his career; and his personal life must have had at least variety enough to supply a thread of connection to the narrative. If, in addition to this, he observes acutely, judges impartially, and writes without regard to either present or future, there is some hope of his name outlasting that of greater men. Marolles's share of these qualities is sufficiently modest; yet even his volumes are not quite without interest. The son of a country gentleman of moderate means, his earliest recollections of hay-time and harvest, of genuine rustic merry-makings, and of a contentment common to the village and the château, are valuable illustrations of the "good old times" of Henry the Fourth, and help us to believe in a real, though brief, interval between the wars of the League and the Fronde, in which the provinces were preparing an advance in civilisation and prosperity which would have saved France from most of her troubles. Of Paris and the Court our notions are not so scanty as to make Marolles an important authority; but his extravagant admiration for the courage and spirit of his pupil, the Duke de Rethelois, in daring to jest superciliously with the favourite, Luynes, is significant in its way. He was present when Louis XIV. repeated inaudibly the lesson which was to make his mother sole regent; he was intimate with the most eminent of his contemporaries; and when he retires from the scene with the dignity of Abbé of Villeloin, in acknowledgment of his father's services, it is pleasant to find the office not yet a sinecure, and its holder as much devoted to decorating his church and looking after his monks, as to collecting prints or presentation copies.

As memoirs multiply, we find ourselves embarrassed with an increasing supply of works of this sort, whose interest is in no sense personal, though their contributions to social, literary, or political history cannot be ignored. French literature is inundated with such; and from Saint Simon and Saint Evremond[13] the descent is so gradual to the commonplace compilations of any minister's secretary, that it is difficult to say where autobiography ends and book-making begins. In the Chevalier de Grammont we get glimpses of the higher art; and perhaps nothing in literature exhibits better than the classic episode of the waistcoat, that placid faith in himself and his star, which is the peculiar property of the hero. Every one knows how the Count was to appear at a fancy ball in a suit brought express from Paris, and how the night arrived, and the valet, but not the costume. The Count presented himself well dressed as usual, but not in the anticipated splendour; but when he begins to relate, before all the Court, the one grave man there, how, Heaven be praised! Termes had arrived, though the valise was lost in the depths of a quicksand at Calais, of which quicksand he came, as in duty bound, to give the earliest intelligence to the King, there is an end of everything except amusement, and we do not even care to hear the rest of the veracious history.

It is easier to see why so many lives of mediocre interest are written, than why so few men of the duly qualified heroic class, who have done or felt, as well as witnessed, what we are eager to hear about, care to transmit direct and circumstantial confidences to posterity. The motives for the effort are stronger, but less various than those against it; and the inclination must be very strong to override the certain difficulties of execution. Men whose whole lives have been public property, who have had their actions criticised, their motives canvassed, and their tastes discussed without ceasing, may be excused if they themselves are bewildered by the murmur of opinions, and do not set their own hesitating self-judgments against the confident affirmations of partisan biographers. The primitive merits of Cellini's work demand an untried, an unhackneyed subject; in Garibaldi's life, arranged by Dumas, they are conspicuous by their absence. Besides those autobiographies which we lose through the impatience of contemporaries who take the words out of the mouth of the proper orator, we are disappointed of others by the scepticism, and of many by the enthusiasm, of the heroes. Some are too critical, too cynically uncertain of the value of their life's work, to confront their real self, and ask for a judgment upon its absolute merit; others are too disinterested, or perhaps too narrow-minded, to find room at the same time for devotion to a cause and the most legitimate self-assertion. But these difficulties apply principally to men of action. Enthusiasm in men of letters will lead them to wish to record and preserve their contributions to knowledge, or the feats of their imagination; nor is it distrust of themselves or their methods that deters the greatest thinkers from minute self-examination, and causes the greatest poets to dwell on anything rather than the details of their personality. Every grace of style, and almost every mental attribute of value, may find a place in memoirs, with one exception, one deficiency, not to be supplied, disguised, nor easily forgotten, and which of itself explains why we should be aghast at an autobiography of Shakespeare. The ideas of autobiography and humour exclude each other.

Humour is not much easier to define than genius; but if we call it an intuitive sense of proportion, an instinctive appreciation of the fit and the incongruous, bringing with it an incurable sensibility to bathos, it will at once be seen that a humourist can indeed show us traits of his character, or introduce us to episodes or aspects of his life, but never adventure on the task of reconciling dignity and candour through a complete set of confessions. The autobiographer lives in a glass house; and it is the humourist's profession to throw stones at every transparent fabric, and to see through apparently solid ones. Swift and Sterne and Richter[14] and Lamb, knew better than to make themselves the first victims of their skill; but Voltaire was not willing to be less brilliant than Swift, and wrote too much to be able always to avoid writing of himself. In the fragmentary memoirs, which contain an account of his intercourse with the King of Prussia, we see the pressure of a devouring fear lest something in his past conduct, or in his present estimate of his past conduct, should, somehow or other, give a handle to the satirists. He is equally afraid of apologetic gravity and naïve self-surrender; but in his endeavour to forestall the laughters by laughing at himself, he descends not less surely from the pinnacle of heroic dignity accessible to those with whom truth is a primary motive, and the equal importance of all self-regarding truths a fundamental axiom. The spell of reality, by which Pepys and his fellows fix our sympathy, even when our curiosity flags, would be broken by a touch of irony. Here and there, of course, they allow us a hearty laugh at a situation, a comfortable smile at a neighbour; but the writer is in too business-like earnest often to give us the opportunity of laughing with him, and if we do not like him too well to wish to laugh at him how can he expect us to care about what he has for dinner? If a man is absurd, why write his life? but a life in which the humourist can see no absurdities must be a series of negatives, impossible to write. The incongruities are there, an essential part of humanity; and we resign ourselves as we can to the author's unconsciousness of them. When Pepys has just raised a laugh by answering the King that he is on his way to "our masters at Westminster," it is irritating to find him recording a solemn resolution never to do so again, though we do not mind his being "sorely troubled for fear some Parliament-man should have been there." But if he had been of the number of those whose gravity is always exactly proportioned to the occasion, he might have had the humourist's dread of a truism. As it is, he is not afraid to comment naturally on the short-lived grief of a jointured widow; and he can moralize on the cost of an evening party without interspersing general reflections on the vanity and misery of life. All his observations have a particular occasion; and that is why so many of them appear always new. His widow is received in the reader's mind as the immortal type of consolable widowhood. It is a division of labour. The humourist sees the world motley on a black ground; the autobiographer sees one figure in relief, lighted up with a searching, inextinguishable consciousness. We instinctively put ourselves in the writer's attitudes; and we are confronted with a moral looking-glass. The diary is a mouse-trap, like Hamlet's play, to catch consciences.

If truth of character, precocious maturity, and realistic vividness, give Pepys's nine years' journal a right to rank with complete autobiographies, Montaigne's Essays ought not to be excluded by the disconnected form of his confidences. But though the minds of the two men have much, their writings have little, in common. Montaigne himself explains that he was unobservant to stupidity of what took place around him; and this is the more credible, since, with all his descriptions of his house, his habits, and his circumstances, we have at the end a clear idea of nothing but his tastes and his principles of morality. He and Pepys would have formed the same opinions from the same materials; but Montaigne would not have observed the facts, nor Pepys formulated the judgment. Montaigne's imagination is too sluggish for his century: he describes his intellect instead of dramatizing his character; and he tells us either too little or too much. There is more egotism in partial than in complete confidences. It would be rash to maintain against a consensus of critics that Pepys was neither vain nor an egotist; but there is a confusion in the notion of egotism which may be cleared up to his profit. To keep a diary may be a proof of regard and respect for the personality to which such a monument is erected; but that is nothing to the point so long as partiality is avoided. Ambition is not vanity; and whatever Pepys's failing may be, his defence is that he makes none. Of all autobiographers he would be the least capable of a vaunt like Rousseau's, though he is the only voluminous one in whose mouth it would have any plausibility. Egotism, in the unfavourable sense of unfounded self-admiration, only begins to disfigure autobiography as the lives written become emptier, the characters less pronounced, and the social machinery so intricate that mere perception requires as much native energy as might once have sufficed for original creation. To revive an old distinction, the autobiographer is essentially and radically *glorious*; he is satisfied with himself and his actions as a whole; to misrepresent them in any particular would be an act of high treason against his conscience and his self-esteem, which are nearly related to each other. We call the man who is afraid of unembellished truth, and proud of forged credentials, *vainglorious*. But the vanity which tampers with *fact*, and embroiders states of mind, implies a doubt whether the absolute and unadorned truth is the most creditable possible to the narrator; and that which can co-exist with candour is scarcely a vice in an autobiographer.

The popularity of works like Pepys's Diary proves that their individualism is not excessive; but this individualism itself depends for appreciation upon some tendencies, and for expression upon some development of the social instincts. Without this, autobiographies could have no representative value; they would throw no light upon questions of moral progress, and could only serve to amuse a gossiping curiosity. In virtue of this they enable us to follow the history of the last three centuries in a sort of miniature reflector of the outer world, in a parallel current of action, thought, and criticism, leading—it is true with interruptions and irregularities, but in the main continuously,— from the age of Cellini, Luther, and Macchiavelli, past Madame de Sévigné,[15] Voltaire, and Gibbon, to Faust, and the many recent illustrations of the phases of waning and waxing faith.

The memoirs of the seventeenth century interest, as we have said, the matter of fact element in man; and no popularity is wider, less ephemeral, or more just. For the worst that can be said of this kind of social positivism is that it formulates the commonplaces of commonplace minds, and reveals the ubiquity of their influence. Since Louis XIV. and the Stuarts, there have been no changes in the moral habits of Europe radical enough to make a stranger of Pepys; and it is human nature, both that more people should take an exclusive, and that more should take a passing interest in the doings of courtiers and actresses, than in literature or the history of letters.

The eighteenth century was pre-eminently the age of authors. A single writer might give an impetus to popular thought, gather a party round his name, and create a demand for information as to the history of his opinions, the occasion of his principal works, the character of his conversation, of his private relations, his personal habits, and, generally speaking, the connection between his inner and his outer man. Of course this curiosity is in part frivolous—too much so for the greatest men to stoop to gratify it; and where it is most serious—relating to the secret history of important works—its gratification implies least literary merit. The lives of Marmontel and Goldoni are more amusing than those of Gibbon and Hume, though the studied simplicity of the last is a model in its kind. Indeed, if the absence of tragic interest allowed us to call it heroic, its candid brevity might almost entitle it to rank with the epic variety of narrative. When the writer has told us that all his books began by failing, and he did not mind it; that they ended by succeeding, and he did not mind that either; that he was poor and contented when he was young, and rich and not less contented when he was old; and that it was his intention to die in perfect and philosophic charity, with a world which had never done him any harm, we know all that can be said about a happy temperament exactly suited to its circumstances. But Hume's account of his life is not circumstantial enough to command the popularity proper to autobiographies; and it is possible to suspect both him and Gibbon of being influenced by an ostentation akin to Addison's. In their compositions, and in their friends' anxiety to give an account of their last moments, the motive is a little too plainly to call on the orthodox world to observe and admire how deists can live and die. Gibbon's style is too cumbrous to enliven the account of an uneventful career; he seems to know no more about his character, and to tell no more about his life, than any qualified biographer might do. An independent man of letters, his life is the life of a class; that is to say, he existed, and he wrote books, and before writing a book he meditated on the Roman Empire and the Swiss Republics. The author is lost, his personality sunk, not in his thoughts, which are a part of himself, as we may take to be the case with Bruno or Campanella, but in his writings, of which the interest is altogether external, like a measure of Richelieu's or Sully's.[16] The extreme of civilisation begins already to meet the extreme of rudeness. Mere intellect is as little capable of dramatic self-consciousness as mere animalism; and by the time the mind has become aware of this, we shall probably find ourselves in a period of romantic or pietistic revival, full of zeal and enthusiasm, but without the confident simplicity of a first literary dawn.

Goldoni's Memoirs are transitional. The indispensable conditions of variety and originality are supplied partly by his adventures, which in the earlier half of his life succeed each other with Gil-Blas-like[17] rapidity, and partly by the observant nonchalance proper to him as a dramatist. The professional element in him is as strongly marked and prominent as that in Gibbon; but it is narrowed so as to produce more of the effect of individuality. He is the typical comedian, not only in his literary tastes and aptitudes, but in the education which seemed forced on him by a kind of fatality; and, so long as the scene of his career is laid amongst the towns and provinces of Italy, the abundance of material for his sketches conceals the essentially passive character of his attitude and disposition. As in the case of Goethe, a grandfather and a puppet-show are amongst his earliest reminiscences. He wrote a play when he was eight years old, on the strength of which he was sent to school, where he distinguished himself by a scrambling precocity in composition. While still a boy he was placed with a family at Rimini, to study philosophy, with a view to embracing his father's profession, that of medicine. From thence he eloped, on the invitation of a troop of comedians, with no motive but that of visiting his mother, and making a short voyage in the company of his dramatic friends. His escapade was forgiven; and, as he found the introductory study of scholastic philosophy unattractive, his father undertook to introduce him at once into the mysteries of medical practice. The boy of fifteen soon became restless again, and was sent to Venice to read law. Then the offer of a sort of scholarship at the University brought him to Pavia, where he received the tonsure; and, since the conditions of the foundation required him to be in his nineteenth year, he found himself next morning more discreet by two years than when he went to bed. In the vacation he again visited Chioggia, this time more in the style of the Decameron than of Wilhelm Meister's vagabondage: youths and ladies sailed down the Po, stopping by night to dance and enjoy the entertainments everywhere offered them, by day bringing all the country people down to the river's brink by their songs and music. Goldoni was the laureate of the party, and on his return home won golden opinions by composing edifying orations for a convent of nuns patronized by his mother. But this new facility had its dangers, as the author found when he began to try his hand at satire. Feuds between town and gown had long raged at Pavia; and the wives and daughters of the citizens were accused of unbecoming partiality to the stranger youths. At last the marriageable townsmen bound themselves by a covenant not to solicit the hand of the daughters of any house in which students were received. Goldoni, after paying a series of afternoon calls, and finding every door closed to him, was urged by his friends to revenge, and the result was an Atellan comedy, describing the construction of a colossal statue of Beauty; to this statue each of the eligible young ladies of Pavia was supposed to contribute a feature, which immediately became the subject of criticism by artists and dilettanti. The ingenious author was promptly expelled the University. But his parents received the prodigal with indulgence; and the problem of his destiny in life was as far from solution as ever.

It was not till 1746, when he was thirty-nine, that he began to write for the stage as a profession, and conceived the reform of Italian comedy as the object of his life. The interval is filled up with many changes of place and occupation, secretaryships, doctor's degrees, practice in civil and criminal law, marriage, amateur authorship, and the vicissitudes of an adventurer's life; but in all the accidents which befall him, each misfortune is tempered by a shade of the ridiculous, and never quite reaches tragic proportions. His rôle is that of an easy-tempered victim, amused by his wrongs, and consoled by the jests he passes on their perpetrators. He wooes the waiting-maid by mistake for the mistress, wins the affections of the aunt instead of the niece, is despoiled by card-sharpers, deceived by swindlers, and has his first opera refused by a committee of actors. At this last blow indeed he began to despair. He returned to his hotel, ordered a fire instead of a meal, and grimly committed the history of *Amalasunta* to the flames. But this was the turning point in his fortunes. The comedian element in him re-asserted itself. He reflected that neither in love nor war had he ever lost his appetite before: he ordered supper, "ate well, drank better, and slept profoundly and with relish." After this he met with only ordinary troubles at the hands of actors and critics, for which he used to take a harmless revenge. The actors were punished by having to represent their own delinquencies on the stage; and the critics either had the worst of it in a humorous prologue, or were silenced and crushed by the success of sixteen new comedies a season. But the analysis of these sixteen comedies is less amusing than the account of the varied experience of Italian life and character which went to supply plots for them. Goldoni's Memoirs, as they proceed, take increasingly the form of mere materials for a history of the Italian stage. This might perhaps have been no disadvantage, if he had really heralded a new era in Italian comedy; but he was not more successful than Alfieri in founding a school; and his own importance as a dramatist was not such as to give lasting value to the detail in which he describes his compositions and their reception. It throws some light on the society for which he wrote, to find that he might rally the institution of Cicisbeatura, but on no account attack it, that the native Harlequin and Pantaloon still had energetic defenders against his Gallicizing reforms, and that he was obliged to transform his *Pamela* into the unknown heiress of a Jacobite noble before his audience would consent to the reward of her lowly virtues by the hand of a Milordo. But this is not autobiography; or, if so, it is a confession that the autobiographer has outlived his moral energy, and has become either the subject of his circumstances instead of their ruler, or else an original and independent rebel—the only characters in which he has a right to disregard grace of style and the comparative unimportance of his personal history.

Marmontel's Life stands to the history of the Republic of Letters in France, in the same relation as the political memoirs of the preceding age to the history of the French monarchy. The brilliant assemblage of literary celebrities gathered together in Paris in the middle of the eighteenth century deserved to find a Boswell; and Marmontel's share of cultivation and common sense exactly fitted him for the task of portraying the society to which he belonged. The cynical self-distrust which disfigures Voltaire's amusing Memoirs takes the form in a less eminent man of gentle irony, which is no more than sufficient to guard his evidence against the distrust excited in literary matters by too simple second-hand enthusiasm. Marmontel mixed letters and philosophy so as to be on good terms with both, and the devotee of neither. But the age and the country were too frivolous, too critical, too doctrinaire for a great autobiography to be produced, except by rare accident; and Marmontel's *mémoires pour servir* the history of society and contemporary thought only give a sketchy and unsatisfactory picture of their author. The work is homogeneous, though it is difficult to see how the ostensible purpose of edifying and instructing the writer's young family should be served by the account of his relations with Mlle. Clairon, and the more or less celebrated ladies in whose affections he succeeded or supplanted Marshal Saxe. The Life, which ends with serious reflections on the course of the French Revolution, begins with a scene of school life in Auvergne; and it is a curious coincidence that the author, whom time was to turn into a reluctant conservative, expends eloquence enough to overturn a monarchy in exhorting his companions to resist the tyranny of the head-master, who, for some supposed offence, had dared to threaten a member of the rhetoric class with the barbarous and humiliating rod. Fifty years before Camille Desmoulins,[18] Greeks and Romans were invoked pell-mell to attest the wrongs of enslaved humanity; a solemn oath of fraternity and solidarity was sworn upon an altar which was at hand; and—not least bewildering to the preceptors—a noisy *Te Deum* was chanted in honour of the successful revolt. The passion for reform might have found milder expression in the Gironde and the Mountain, if the leaders of those parties had been inoculated, so to speak, with the principles of revolution in this harmless manner in their youth. Marmontel's combination of peasant breeding, literary culture, and aristocratic connections, gave him a moderation which the separation of classes had made dangerously rare. His *Contes Moraux* bridge the distance from *Paul et Virginie* to *Harry and Lucy*. His master prophesied that he would grow up a dangerous and turbulent character, which might very possibly have been the case if political significance had been attributed to his unruly vivacity at Mauriac; but the provinces were more philosophical than Paris. Already in Marolles we find the neutralization of school-boys as far from acceptance under Richelieu as under the Republic; and the neglect of one educational axiom brings others with it.

Of Marmontel's other works, *Bélisaire* has shared the common fate of books which owe their popularity to a censorship; his *Incas* scarcely continues to furnish reading-books with extracts; and his *Contes*, though not perceptibly duller than their modern counterparts, naturally find little favour in a society which is not content with plots that end in happy marriages, domestic reconciliations, and the conversion of giddy matrons or undutiful children. But his Memoirs are not only still amusing in themselves; they form a link in the chain of social and personal history, which the devotees of autobiographical art would wish to see unbroken in its parallel illustrations of the known course of public events. Not the least interesting part of the *Histoire de ma vie* of George Sand is that which is devoted more particularly to the history of her grandmother, the Aurore de Saxe for whom Marmontel procured a Parliamentary decree confirming her claim to an illegitimate descent from Marshal Saxe. Except in this curious proceeding, Aurore appears to great advantage in her granddaughter's pages, and the letters preserved in them. One of the few ladies of the old Court whose reputation had never been approached by scandal, she devoted herself on the death of her second husband, M. Dopin de Francueil, frequently mentioned by Marmontel and Rousseau, to the education of her son, Maurice, the father of the novelist. Mme. Dupin remained all her life a consistent Voltairian, forgave the Revolution its inroads on her property, distrusted the Empire, and held aloof at the Restoration from the faubourg Saint Germain. The admirable practice of preserving family papers, observed in France, enables us to follow her sentiments as a liberal aristocrat in the prisons of the Terror, to watch the conflict of prejudice and principle when her son enlisted in the armies of the Republic, and to trace the growing discontent with which representatives of the old school of enlightenment submitted to the parvenu airs of the Napoleonic dynasty.

The period in which these reminiscences are supplemented by Marmontel's narrative is the date—so far as the rise of a tendency can be dated—of the third and latest development of autobiography. Rousseau is the herald of this development, though not its representative. His works are the product of an unhealthy social and political atmosphere: but his genius was anomalous; and it would be unjust to any age to hold it responsible for the diseased working of his imagination. Merely vicious sophisms, like those by which the author of *Emile* professed to convince himself that it was for the good of his children to be brought up at a Foundling hospital, could not make disciples; the *Contrat social* and *Julie* might attract those who were tired of scepticism, or who wished for new passions to enliven a new organization of the State; but even the inspiration of Oliver Goldsmith, "who wrote like an angel, and talked like poor Poll," was equable and consistent compared with Rousseau's, who did not talk at all, and invented a complete system of social ethics to dispense himself from the necessity of making a bow or accepting an invitation to dinner. None of the merits of the writer extended to the man; and except in the *Confessions*, the defects of the two were kept equally distinct. Rousseau was not mad enough to be treated as an interesting case; and he was too powerful to be ignored as a vicious nuisance. But though a madman's diagnosis of his symptoms would have one value, as Cellini's barefaced avowals of crime have another, the accident, so to speak, of identity between an imaginative philosopher and a vain, querulous, and unprincipled musician does not lend importance to the life of the latter.

It is however true, that with Rousseau sincerity ceases to be a matter of course in the composer of his own Life or Memoirs. The stereotyped preface to such works, to the effect that the narrator has no ambition or desire but to be known as he really is, either ceases to have any meaning, or becomes far more individually significant than before. The earliest autobiographers believed simply and firmly that posterity would be glad to inherit an authentic likeness of the man who had done such and such deeds amidst such and such surroundings. His first business was to live; and this he did so completely to his own satisfaction, that he had no doubt of imparting the feeling to his readers. But this was at most secondary object. We see signs of the coming change in Goldoni, who was thankful for having lived so as to have no need for concealment, as if there was a recognised standard, divergence from which had to be concealed. Even Alfieri seems to think that his own veracity needs accounting for, and suggests that it may be due to the horrible torments which he suffered when a child, from being taken to church in his nightcap as a punishment for story-telling. The cause seems inadequate to so admirable an effect; but Italian character, versatile and exuberant, long after other countries had contentedly sacrificed individuality to systems, was not to be swamped in the level current of modern progress without a last remonstrance. The interval between Alfieri and Goethe may, at first sight, seem less wide than that which separates Rousseau from Goldoni; but it is profounder and more final. The hereditary self-confidence which lingers longest in the castles of a rustic nobility carried the young aristocrat, without loss of dignity, through the crass ignorance of his boyhood and the romantic extravagance of his youth, harmonizes with the writings of his maturity, and emboldens him, at the age of forty-eight, to encounter the difficulties of the Greek grammar and alphabet. Where Goethe breaks hearts with idyllic tearfulness, Alfieri crosses swords, a pure hero of melodrama. Whilst the German accepts gratefully the favour and honours of a petty Court, the Italian reconciles his habits and the rights of man by allowing his servants to return his cuffs, and by making it a principle not to cane them as a superior, but only to throw chairs and boots at their heads as an angry fellow-mortal. The story of Count Mirabeau and his lacquey shows that such a piece of self-conquest is not to be despised; but the fact is nothing to the manner in which it is related. Alfieri is not a poet of the first rank; and the interest of his adventures may be matched by many; but in the confidence with which he tells his story, his indifference whether his narration may invite amusement or condemnation, above all, his assumption that whatever he has done needs no explanation, and scarcely any justification beyond the fact that he did it—in all this there is a degenerate heroism, a rudimentary positivism, which, whatever the defects of both material and style, are removed toto cœlo from the depressing irresolution of the metaphysical period in the history of egotism.

The *Lebensgeschichte* of Heinrich Jung is a connecting link between the religious memoir, which is always the same, and the sentimental autobiography of which Werther was soon to set the fashion. Written by Goethe's advice, the story of his woes and religious faith had a brilliant success; but it takes all the power of Goethe's name to make us believe in the sincerity of the tailor-schoolmaster turned oculist, who wept tears of pity when young ladies went out of their minds in compliment to his mind and person, who with tears of gratitude invoked everlasting happiness to reward his employer's gift of a Sunday suit, and half-a-dozen pairs of beautiful stockings, and who drew cheques upon Providence and the religious world which were sometimes rather too near being dishonoured. Perhaps the key to his character lies in a trait of his youth, when he used to tell lies to avoid the correction of a severe father, and then pray that they might not be found out. In later life he ran into debt, and prayed for money to discharge his liabilities; and in each case his prayers were so often heard that he forgot to repent of the preceding offence against secular canons

of morality. but without this peculiarity his Autobiography might have
been tedious, as indeed it becomes as his years and income increase. In
the early and more poetical chapters, the mild and apparently modest
youth has really more in common with the placid arrogance of the
Chevalier de Grammont than with the slightly fatiguing good faith of
ordinary religious diaries.

Autobiographies written for the sake of edification differ amongst
each other less in substance and tenor than in the success with which
the writer expresses real and genuine feelings as if they were original as
well as real. Baxter[19] gives us a reason for reticence touching the "heart
occurrences" of his later years, that "God's dealings with his servants
are the same in the main," and thinks it "unsavory" to dwell too much
on intimately personal matters; and his instinct is justified by the
monotony of those religious memoirs which neither stop short with the
crisis of the writer's spiritual history, nor yet have anything important
to relate of his subsequent influence in the religious world. From the
"Friends of God," in the fourteenth century, the Germans have always
been fond of this class of autobiography. The difficulty of keeping up
an active, conscious, religious life, without mysticism and without
practical fields of labour, led that famous confraternity into dangerous
reliance upon mysterious machinery and secret agencies for political or
other proselytism; and with Francke and the later pietists its effect is
simply to lower the standard of spiritual exaltation. The Covenanters of
the seventeenth century have far more to say about their armed risings
and the sins of their rulers than about their personal trials and
temptations; and Veitch, Brysson, and Blackader throw more light on
the history of their times than on their own characters, and less on
either than a thoroughly original writer and politician like Knox.[20] But
Knox had never leisure, nor perhaps repose of mind enough, to add an
autobiography to his history; and the age of Pepys is not represented
amiss in the field of religious autobiography by Richard Baxter and
George Fox.[21] They are the two extremes of the movement which finds
a faint and degenerate echo in the missionary journals of the first
Methodists. Fox's Journal is perhaps the more able, certainly the more
imaginative, of the two; and the touch of fanatic extravagance, which
might be a drawback anywhere else, only serves here to give an air of
genuineness to the story of the writer's conversion and persecutions. It
was a saying of his school-fellows, "If George says 'Verily,' there is no
moving him;" and in the most important qualification of self-confidence

he yields neither to Stilling nor Cellini. It is imagination vivid to the point of disease that led him to see a material resemblance between the congregation of the "steeple-house" at Nottingham and a "field of fallow-ground," with the priest "like a great lump of earth" standing in his pulpit above. The forms taken by his horror of steeple-houses were sometimes quaint in the extreme, the spires of Lichfield, in particular, moving him to a bona fide cross-country chase, which he describes with great gusto: but it cannot be denied that episodes of this sort do a good deal to enliven the spread of Quakerism. Baxter is more dignified, and, for the reason above quoted, restricts himself to the history of his labours and their success and hindrances, only resuming at intervals the changes which he traces in his character. Of these the most notable was a steady increase in tolerance, or, as his enemies said, indifferentism—a slowness to proselytize, arising partly from a respect for his neighbour's personality and conscience, and partly from a belief in the impossibility of assisting a soul in distress, except indirectly and at the appointed time.

To class together Byron, Shelley, and Sénancour,[22] Goethe, Newman, George Sand and the Guérins, may seem the reductio ad absurdum of the chronological theory which connects them. But the step from Macchiavelli to Montesquieu[23] is exactly that from practice to theory, as the step from Alfieri to Gibbon is that from action to thought; and if we have already outlived the men who record dispassionately the arbitrary course of their lives, and those who represent with truth and complacency the life of a period or a class, nothing remains but to misrepresent one or the other, or the represent a relation or compromise between the two. A similar intensity of character, or an identical method and habit of mind, connect S. Augustine and Cellini, Marmontel and Pepys: and the heterogeneous list, which should include all authors of the present century whose works contain autobiographical details, avowed or easily recognisable, is held together by a common absorption in certain problems, by the use of similar methods for their solution, and by the arrival at kindred conclusions, or at least by two out of the three possible points of contact. The egotism of introspective autobiography takes several forms, but rarely one which can be satisfied with the undiscriminating historical candour of professed memoirs. For a man to describe his own character is to confess a doubt whether his actions and his declared opinions represent it fully and worthily; but to disclaim the description is in addition to admit a doubt, not merely whether the author's real character, but whether his favourite idealized rendering of it, has the artistic propriety without which it should not have been made the subject of disquisitions in prose or verse. Shelley's *Alastor* and *Laon* are a mixture of Shelley's notion of himself and his notion of perfection;[24] and if the presence of the Shelleyan element is objected to as marring the abstract truth of the poems, the poet is compelled to answer that the choice of an ideal implies a tendency to approximate to it. But Shelley's imagination would have outlived his theories; and even before his intellect had rejected these, his taste warned him off from the morbid portraiture of a mere exaggerated second self in *Prince Athanase*. Byron, on the other hand, is a complete example of that curious development of vanity which allows its victims to wish to be admired not for what they are but for what they are not. The uniform character of his heroes, and the taste for magnanimous mysterious misery which is common to him and them, make it impossible to take his word for their being altogether independent creations. When the poet, therefore, speaks in terms of condemnation of his favourite characters, the artifice is as transparent as when he appeals to the mere difference of scenery as distinguishing himself from the corsair or the Giaour.[25] But this tergiversation is the least part of his sins as an autobiographer. When Rousseau wished to pass for an example of antique virtue and primitive simplicity, he bought a scratch-wig, sold his watch, and wore coloured stockings, that he might be the more readily mistaken for a high-minded philosopher; Schiller's Karl Moor[26] really made converts to highway robbery; and Werther provoked and prevented an appreciable number of suicides. But Byron's ideal was not definite enough for even its author to think seriously of approaching it in practice. Without being inconsistent, it was incomplete. It asked too much from the imagination, whilst withholding all tangible food from that much-enduring faculty; and with the best intentions, his imitators could not find out exactly what it was they had had to do to their wives, their friends, or the laws of the land, before they would be entitled to look down with Manfred, Lara, and Childe Harold, upon the duties, pleasures, and concrete misfortunes of humanity. The only object held in view by the school was to reach a non-natural frame of mind, unmotived, objectless, and morally unfruitful. Werther, Réné,[27] and Obermann are true by comparison. When Byron wrote, the days of piracy and lordly debauch were over. They had been weighed in the balance, and had been found wanting in beauty, use, and intrinsic propriety; to rehabilitate them as subjects of high art was an anachronism of which a poet with deeper imaginative insight would not have been guilty. Obermann, on the other hand still—still more Réné,—were, at the time of their appearance, new and genuine, even where weak and fantastical. With them ennui was more than a personal, half-formed sentiment of discontent; it was a positive and resentful protest against the action and the thought, the failures and the successes, of preceding generations. These young apostles of incurable melancholy passed in review nations, empires, and religions, life, death, and the unalterable conditions of existence; and in their summary condemnation of all and everything they were guided, not by principles which might be controverted, nor by experience which might be enlarged, but by a moral taste above discussion and above reason, as well as above sublunary satisfaction. The first step was taken when the private griefs of a Werther were set forth to be shared or compassionated by thousands of readers. But it was the sentiment, not its provocation, that enlisted sympathizers; and when Réné and Obermann ultimately failed to find relief, even in the indulgence of their melancholy, those who were conscious of having no specific to suggest for an abstract infinitude of unprovoked suffering accepted cynically all that could be urged against the natural order which includes diseases without remedy.

The new and peculiar feature of these sentimental pseudo-autobiographies is that the supposed author not merely despairs of finding consolation himself, but denies *à priori* the possibility of its being found by any one. He has no conviction, no ambition, and no desire but that for personal contentment; but, as the causes of his discontent are internal, the new philosopher's stone, the idea of happiness, has to be developed out of the subjective moral consciousness of the seeker; and the most serious and lachrymose of pessimists hardly differs from Sir Walter Scott in estimating the success of the search. But this failure does not, like a mere political or controversial defeat, leave its subject disposed to claim his revenge at the bar of posterity. Neither personal nor literary amour propre is satisfied by proving a problem to be unanswerable, of which the first comer may dispute the premises. The real Werthers have not energy to commit their sorrows to paper; and the few whom constitutional despondency really sends to a premature grave leave little mark upon their age, and at most have their memory preserved by a friendly and more favoured contemporary. If, like Chateaubriand[28] and Goethe, the author outgrows the tendencies of his youthful representative, and writes an autobiography in form, there will still be reasons why it should not come up with the highest examples of the past. It is only another form of the fundamental scepticism of the youth which makes the man content to throw one section of his life after another behind him, not in search of a final resting-place, but because moral progress is the highest end he can discern. The choice is substantially that of Lessing;[29] only Lessing's resignation to the infinite duration of the pursuit of infinite and absolute truth was natural and spontaneous, and left his life as full as ever of objects and interests. But if the progress is the end, and the only object of art and philosophy is to enable the student to interpolate as many stages as possible between his natural self and an indifferent goal, then material events are only important in so far as they further or retard this endeavour, and historical accuracy of narration becomes a secondary matter. But the internal and external lives of individuals do not run in parallel lines, nor advance at an equal pace; and the attempt to make their crises synchronize only distorts the real succession of events and opinions. The immortality of Lotte and Frederika is perfectly legitimate, and consoles us for the easy passage from *Werther* to the *Wahlverwandschaften* [sic], and thence to such *Confessions* as Alfred de Musset's. But the ready abuse of which this sentimental style admits makes it doubtful whether any loss results from its necessarily fragmentary character.

In the parallel variety of analytic autobiography, Goethe does not, like Byron or Shelley, Lamartine,[30] Rousseau, or Sénancour, attempt to connect his solution of the difficulties of modern life with his individual character and temperament. In *Faust* it is the history of the intellectual, in *Wilhelm Meister* the consciousness of the emotional and materialistic sides of human nature that he generalizes and abstracts: but he far more often disguises his own adventures to bring them into harmony with his ideal existence than modifies the latter to adapt it to his own preferences. The doctrine of the new Ecclesiastes is less complicated in its substance than in the preparatory steps of initiation. Enjoy, renounce, and—if you can—understand, is the formula which resumes the conviction that to enjoy is a necessary, commendable, and unsatisfying weakness, that to renounce is a necessary, attractive, and unfruitful discipline, and that, for what concerns comprehension, it is a happy thing that there are some wise enough not to wish to fathom the depths of their own wisdom. As Goethe's apprentice draws near his emancipation, mentor after mentor brings out the moral—"Words are good, but they are not the best; and the best cannot be explained by words"—to the exaltation of the "magnificent moment" in which the commonness and stupidity of the comprehensible is first revealed. The state of mind of a wise man, which is too good to be expressed by words, may be better than an act or a thought, worthy and capable of distinct remembrance; but, ex hypothesi, volumes of written words can throw no light upon its nature; and this is exactly the point of uncertainty and credulous doubt at which voluntary ignorance has the advantage of unsuccessful science. A generation predisposed to condemn in the mass what it is not qualified to judge in detail, to resent the limitations of the knowable without having attained the limits of the known, to reject all possible enjoyments because there are, or rather are not, impossible ones—such a generation will be glad of an elaborately obscure excuse for reverting, by a circuitous route, to what is after all only a new name for the old practical wisdom of making the best of things. The first part of *Faust* is complete as a poem; and, if art had been all with Goethe, he would have been content to leave it so. But we have seen that his capital principle, the finality of progress, is adverse to the repose of classical art, as well as to the confidence of positive science; and, this being so, it seems almost in spite of the author that the second part of *Meister* and the second part of *Faust* meet in the same final and inevitable result. This result is of course disappointing to those who have not followed the poet through the preliminary steps in his pursuit of an object to pursue. That Wilhelm Meister, at the close of his *Wanderjahre*, should take to surgery, his son to horse-breaking, Jarno to mining, and Philina to dressmaking on enlarged principles, may seem a lame and impotent conclusion to the most elaborate Pilgrim's Progress devised by the natural reason; but at any rate the inventor of such a climax is not disqualified for autobiographical success by an unduly keen sense of humour, and if Goethe was serious about anything it was probably in this very quaint provision for the mature age of his renuntiants. It is not quite a platitude to recommend, as conducing to peace of mind in the individual, what is not, in itself, an adequate end for his desires; and the rehabilitation of primitive tastes and motives is completed in *Faust*. The moral—in any case rather trite—that magic is apt to turn out badly for the wizard, may be read against the wish for

superhuman faculties, as well as against their unlawful possession; but
the elaborate machinery for satiating Faust with power, love, and
wealth, is really subordinated to the crowning moment, in which he
rejects their most perfect appearances for the mere thought of some
philanthropic improvements to be carried out on his estate. On their
completion—

> Zum Augenblicke dürft' ich sagen:
> Verweile doch! du bist so schön!
> *Es kann die Spur von meinen Erdentagen*
> *Nicht in Aeonen untergehn* —[31]

an undisguised return to the most simple, and, so to speak, disinterested
phase of positive ambition. The same incompleteness marks all
successive writings of the school of introspective sentiment.
Obermann, after a vain search for the complement of his being,
subsides into a surly quietism, which at any time might make way for
the ordinary machinery of unideal life; and more original writers only
find a fresh poison for every antidote suggested in their velleities of
hopefulness. The complement of *Meister* is an age of imaginative
industrialism; the complement of *Lelia* [sic] is an age of imaginative
immorality; but since neither immorality nor industrialism was ever
less imaginative than in the nineteenth century, the conclusion is
inevitable, either that Goethe and George Sand have misunderstood their
age, or that their age has an aversion to being understood, which is
peculiarly trying to those who take their humanitarianism from Goethe
instead of Cardan, and value the individual life in proportion to its
harmony with the general mass.

The tendency of contemporary autobiography is to become a
record either of sentiments or opinions; but in either case, Scylla and
Charybdis, the extravagant and the commonplace, are separated by an
ominously narrow passage. The popularity of Silvio Pellico[32] and
Mademoiselle de Guérin shows that it is possible to escape, however
narrowly, the two dangers in journals of sentiment; but in a history of
thought there is less license allowed. Philosophic or theological
Retractations may take one of two roads to significance. They may trace
the original course of an individual mind, or they may resume the
inevitable results of certain tendencies in kindred minds. In the one case
they exhibit a chain of opinions which depend from each other
naturally, if not necessarily: in the other, a series of thoughts which

follow necessarily, if not by a plainly natural process, from the mental organization of the thinker. In the first case, our sympathy is claimed for a man: in the other, for a group of propositions. In *Phases of Faith*, a fair example of the later class of narrative, the views of which the author gives an account, are always such as might be held by a party. The connection and interdependence of his arguments is objective; and it did not require much penetration on the part of his evangelical friends to predict in advance the steps by which he would abandon their fellowship. Where the controversial element so far outweighs the historical, the work is always in danger of ceasing to be individual, without becoming really representative. Such narratives may command the active assent of a small body of sympathizers; but, here as elsewhere, material success, the triumph of the favourite doctrine, demands some moral self-abnegation in the advocate whose personality is merged more and more in the narrow or extreme symbol of a sect. Every believer in a peculiar doctrine feels as if he had discovered or invented it himself, and pays less respect to the spokesman of his party than even the member of a dominant majority, who sees in *his* organ simply a mouthpiece of the universal reason. But a mere Pepys of rationalism would find his materials too scanty. The axioms of sense and the fallacies of common sense are soon exhausted or detected; and the history of their acceptance or rejection is concluded in the moment in which their drift is apprehended. Less originality is displayed in thinking everybody's thoughts than in living everybody's life; for people who have intellectual convictions think it a duty to formulate them for themselves, whilst to retain a clear and vivid conception of the experiences of social life is plainly optional. At any rate, it is impossible to treat the first process historically.

The opposite extreme of individuality offers one of the knottiest problems of autobiography—that of reconciling common and received principles of thought with new original methods of development and inference. The writer has to tell both what he believes and how he came to believe it, with a clearness and imaginative cogency which shall seem to prove that what was must have been, and convince those who finally differ from him most that it was in their common human nature to have agreed. The task has not perhaps been accomplished more than once; certainly it has never been accomplished with the same brilliant success as by the author of *Apologia pro vita sua*; but that instance would alone be sufficient to cast doubt on a desponding conclusion that autobiography was one of the arts lost by over-civilisation. The mindful accuracy which we miss in Goethe—that leaves every period its real temper, the precision of feeling for want of which *Obermann* and *Lélia* are unreal and inconclusive, a recognition that doctrines are made for man, not man for the truest opinion,—the simple eloquence of S. Augustine, the candour of Pepys, the self-respect of Benvenuto Cellini, combined in an unhackneyed style, make Dr. Newman's history of his religious opinions a literary masterpiece. It is the true history of a real mind; and so far it is truly representative of an age in which men of original character are thrown back upon solitary thought, or comparatively selfish sentiment. But the form of which the *Apologia* is an ideally perfect specimen is less permanent and universal in interest than some others. The tendency to distinguish between action and thought as alternative fields of energy leaves the former contentedly monotonous, mechanical, and unfruitful, and causes the latter, properly a method or instrument, to be mistaken for an end in itself—the chart, that is, for the voyage, the compass for the desired land. When the particular circumstances are forgotten which gave occasion to trains of reasoning only connected together by their affinity to the same mind, it is hardly possible to revive a sense of their significance; and Pepys may be read with unflagging amusement when Dr. Newman's equally lifelike narrative will only serve as a contribution to history, and to delight at long intervals a curious and sympathetic reader.

But nothing bears its date so plainly and so fatally as works of fiction. When passages of mental autobiography are thrown into the form of a story, such as *Yeast, The Nemesis of Faith*,[33] or the French romances so often alluded to, the authors are even more at the mercy of changes of literary fashion than they would be in narrating commonplace or too exceptional experiences. A truth is at worst trivial: a trivial invention is absurd and impertinent. Autobiography has duties as well as rights; and the authors who have neither the courage of their opinions, nor what may be called the courage of their characters, are not entitled to entertain society with a garbled version of their mental history. A novelist cannot, of course, be charged with a lack of moral courage for drawing upon his own experience to the extent found in *Pendennis* or *The Professor*,[34] and no further. But a master of realistic fiction like Thackeray has as little temptation as a poet to identify himself exclusively with any one of the characters he creates; and though Charlotte Brontë's heroines are all of one type, it by no means follows from this that all or any of them were successful representations of herself. Yet perhaps even these writers are as near to genuine autobiography as the Journals or Recollections published from time to time by statesmen, travellers, detectives, missionaries, and self-made men, or the crowd of inferior littérateurs who, wishing to write a book, take the first worthless subject that comes to hand.

Notes

1. Jerome Cardan (1501–76), mathematician, naturalist, physicist, and philosopher, who finished his candid autobiography *De Propira Vita* a few weeks before he died.
2. Simcox arranges autobiographies into three groups corresponding with Auguste Comte's Law of Three Stages as outlined in *Cours de philosophie positive* (1830–42), and *Système de politique positive* (1851–54).
3. Darius I (550?-486 B.C.). "Darius the Great." A Persian king from 521 B.C. until his death.
4. Giraldus Cambrensis (1147–1223), whose literary name was Girald de Barri, was a Norman-Welsh historian and ecclesiastic. Comte Philibert de Grammont (1621–1707). French courtier whose *Mémoires*, first printed in 1713, focused on the intrigues of Charles's court. Johann Heinrich Jung (1740–1817), known as Heinrich Jung-Stilling, was a German writer whose autobiography, *Heinrich Stillings Jugend*, was edited by Goethe. Carlo Goldoni (1707–93). Venetian dramatist whose *Memoirs* were published in 1787. Jean-François Marmontel (1723–99). French author of tragedies and operas whose *Mémoires* was published posthumously in 1804. David Hume (1711–76). Scottish philosopher of the Enlightenment. Edward Gibbon (1737–94). British historian who wrote *Decline and Fall of the Roman Empire* (1776–88). William Lilly (1602–81), British astrologer whose *History of His Life and Times* was published in 1715. Samuel Pepys (1633–1703). British author whose diary includes descriptions of the Great Fire of London (1665) and London plague (1666).
5. Werther is a character in Goethe's *Die Leiden des jungen Werthers* (1774).
6. Marcus Aurelius Antoninus (A.D.121–180). Roman emperor famous for his Stoic philosophy and *Meditations*. Julian (A.D. 331?-363), Roman emperor from 361–363, who attempted to restore the dominance of paganism.

7.   St. Hubert, or in German, Hubertus (d. 727). Patron Saint of Hunting, Bishop of Lüttich. John (1167–1216). King of England during Cambrensis's lifetime.

8.   Giordano Bruno (1548?-1600). Italian philosopher who developed a cosmic theory of an infinite universe.

9.   James Crichton (1560–82), the "Admirable." Renowned Scottish adventurer and intellectual prodigy who died at the age of 22 in a brawl in Italy.

10.   John Evelyn (1620–1706). English diarist.

11.   arquebus or harquebus, a heavy portable matchlock gun invented during the 15th century.

12.   Daniel D. Home (1833–86). British Spiritualist who won fame as a medium and popularizer of tableturning and levitation in the United States in 1850 and in London in 1855. He is the author of *Incidents of My Life* (1863–72).

13.   Louis de Rouvroy, Duc de Saint-Simon (1675–1755), prepared his *Mémoirs* on court life before his death, but the first edition was not published until 1830. Charles Marguetell de Saint Denis, Seigneur de Saint-Evremond (1610–1703), was a French writer and wit, whose *Life* was published in 1705.

14.   Johann Paul Friedrich Richter (1763–1825). German poet whose unfinished *Autobiography* was published in 1826.

15.   Madame de Sévigné, née Marie de Rabutin-Chantal (1626–96). French author whose twenty-five years of letter writing reveals the history of her times.

16.   Tommasco Campanella (1568–1639). Italian philosopher who was confined in a dungeon for twenty-seven years as a theological and political heretic. Armand Jean du Plessis, Duc de Richelieu (1585–1642). French prelate and politician who wrote *Mémoires*. Maximilien de Béthune, Duc de Sully (1560–1641), French politician and chief minister to Henry IV. His *Mémoires* (1634) detail the events of Henry IV's reign.

17.   *Gil Blas de Santillance* (1715). A picaresque novel by Le Sage.

18.   Camille Desmoulins (1760–94). Journalist who was executed during the French Reign of Terror.

19.   Richard Baxter (1615–91). English Putitan whose autobiographical *Reliquiae Baxterianae* was published posthumously in 1696.

20.   John Veitch (1829–94). Scottish author who wrote on Scottish history and poetry. Brysson. It is unclear as to which Brysson Simcox is referring to here. John Blackader (1615–86). Scottish minister whose *Memoirs* were published in 1823. John Knox (1514?-72). Scottish religious reformer who founded Scottish Presbyterianism; he is author of *History of the Reformation in Scotland*.

21.   George Fox (1624–91). Founder of the Society of Friends, or Quakers, who is known for his *Journal*.

22. Étienne Pivert de Sénancour (1770–1846). French author of *Rêveries* (1799) and *Obermann* (1804) who was greatly influenced by Goethe's *Werther*.

23. Charles de Secondat, Baron de la Brède et de Montesquieu (1689–1755). French philosopher and jurist whose *Lettres persanes* (1721) was a satire on French society.

24. Percy Bysshe Shelley's *Alastor* was published in 1816; *Laon and Cythna*, first written in 1817, was published in 1818 under the new title, *The Revolt of Islam*.

25. *Giaour* (1813). One of a series of Turkish Tales by Byron.

26. Karl Moor, the noble revolutionary hero of Schiller's first play, *Die Räuber* (1781).

27. Réné is a fictional character created by the French author, François René Vicomte de Chateaubriand (1768–1848).

28. Chateaubriand's autobiography, *Mémoires d'outre-tombe* (*Memoirs from Beyond the Grave*), appeared before his death.

29. Gotthold Ephraim Lessing (1729–81). German philosopher and dramatist.

30. Alphonse Marie Louis de Lamartine (1790–1869). French poet, statesman, and historian known for his autobiographical *Confidences* and *Raphaël*.

31. Roughly translated: At this moment, I feel I should say: / Stay awhile! You are so beautiful! /*The traces of my earthly existence / Cannot descend into eternity with me —.*

32. Silvio Pellico (1788–1854). Italian writer who wrote an account of his fifteen-year imprisonment entitled *Le mie prigioni* (1833).

33. *Yeast, A Problem* (1851) by Charles Kingsley. *Nemesis of Faith* (1849) by J. A. Froude.

34. *Pendennis* (1850) by W.M. Thackeray. *The Professor* (1857) by Charlotte Brontë.

26. Women's Work and Women's Wages

Introduction

Edith Simcox's article, published in *Longman's Magazine* in July, 1887, and reprinted here from that periodical, is intended to educate the public about how trade unionists grapple with the problems of the poor. Simcox relates the history of trade unionism by discussing the careers of three activists: Emma Paterson, Mrs. Mason, and Jeannette Wilkinson. By examining the lives of these women, Simcox is able to publicize their efforts as well as praise their accomplishments. In a rallying cry, Simcox calls on women of all classes to reform an unjust economic system by supporting those who work and by educating those who buy. At the same time, Simcox merges literary and social critique; she reiterates her stand on the moral responsibility of authors to provide some sort of guide to life. As with her articles "Ideals of Feminine Usefulness" (*Fortnightly Review*, 1880) and "The Capacity of Women" (*Nineteenth Century*, 1887), Simcox draws on women's common experiences. She shows the public how women are frustrated early in their careers and how the St. Theresas of her age are victimized.

Women's Work and Women's Wages

When the incredible has happened once it becomes almost reasonable to expect that it may happen again. It has happened once for an imaginative writer to trace, regardless of expense, the outlines of an altogether ideal scheme for making life less uniformly dismal for two or three millions of his fellow-mortals. Fortune aiding the seductiveness of Mr. Besant's pen,[1] East London will shortly be in possession of as fair an imitation of a "Palace of Delight" as can well be set up in bricks and mortar. The critics who denounce all "novels with a purpose"[2] would perhaps have forgiven the author of that "impossible story" concerning "all sorts and conditions of men" had he been content to plead immunity for a first offence and agreed not to trespass again. But, as the readers of LONGMAN best know, Mr. Besant's imagination was still happily unexhausted, and after seeing visions and dreaming dreams about the holiday hours of Whitechapel, he has gone on to take the same liberty with the working-days of Hoxton. The newspapers and the novel-readers don't half like it. People do *not* like being made uncomfortable, and when a favourite author turns upon them, and actually produces a dim feeling of *malaise* in the recesses of well-bred easy-going consciences, they nourish a certain sense of injury. They can't say that Mr. Besant is dull, or his characters unreal, or his plot more impossible than he intends. But they grumble at the novelist with a purpose, and protest against being made uncomfortable for nothing; they complain of the mixture of powder and jam, and pretend that they would rather take their morals and economics unsweetened in church or lecture-rooms. Of course we know better. No one sits under preachers or professors who really succeed in making them uncomfortable, and the novelist who gets read in spite of that achievement has really won so great a victory, that he may, Napoleon-like, blot the word "impossible" out of his dictionary.

In plain fact, anything is possible, however large, difficult, or distant, if the object is clearly defined and resolutely pursued. At one time it would have been thought wildly impossible to teach every child in England to read; but as soon as the State determined that schools enough for the purpose should be built, the impossible ceased to be even difficult. It would be just as easy to provide free amusements, after the Beaumont Palace fashion, for the whole population as to provide

elementary schooling. But free amusements are of no use to those v
work sixteen hours out of the twenty-four for wages that only buy brea
and tea, and it takes a robust imagination like Mr. Besant's to conceive
so radical a reconstruction of the social order as would be involved in
halving the work and doubling the wages of Melenda and her tribe. Yet
such a reconstruction is in the nature of things quite possible, and not
more difficult than the complete revolution in our industrial economy
effected [sic] by the introduction of the factory system. It only requires
such a *consensus* of opinion as that which passed the Education Act of
1870,[3] such a *consensus* of goodwill as that which has founded the
People's Palace, in fact, such concerted action upon the labour market
as can be brought to bear when ten thousand Valentines and a hundred
thousand Melendas have agreed upon a plan of campaign.

Now that the Beaumont Palace is a fact, there are plenty of good
people who say, quite truly, that they wished and asked for something
of the kind long before Mr. Besant's book was published; and of course
his book would not have produced its effect if people's minds had not
been already predisposed to accept such a scheme as soon as it was set
forth in sufficiently lively and attractive colours. Similarly, we should
have no hope of any corresponding outcome from "The Children of
Gibeon" if there were not already amongst men and women of all
classes a strong and growing feeling that something must be done to
alter and amend the conditions of women's work.

The object of these pages is to describe one attempt in particular
which has been made to grapple with this problem, and to suggest the
possibility of a wider organisation to concentrate and direct all the
unemployed and misguided sympathy with the hardships of the working
poor which is really floating about in the social atmosphere,
notwithstanding "that strange hardness of woman's heart towards
women" which Mr. Besant justly denounces as "a wonderful and
monstrous thing."

If women work for wages like men, and are liable to have their
wages reduced through the competition of employers for custom and the
competition of workers for employment, they must at least endeavour
to protect themselves, as men do, by union and combination, against
the forces which singly they are unable to resist. Men, it is said, by the
help of trade unions, have shortened their hours of work and raised, or
prevented the reduction of, the general rate of wages: women in the
same position, to obtain the same results, must use the same means.

women of all classes are a shade more sensitive to the breath of ...lic opinion than men are, and working women are not likely to seek ...ch help as trade unionism can give them until they are well assured that the last remains of ancient prejudice against trade unionism have been dispelled. Everyone agrees now that trade unions are lawful, but many good people still entertain a lingering doubt as to the expediency or utility of their action, and this doubt must be removed before even the women who most need protection can be induced to seek it through combination.

The trade unions of men have always had two chief objects in view—to shorten the hours of work (practically whenever possible to a "nine hours day"), and to fix a *minimum* rate of wages to be received by all ordinary workers, such as is considered sufficient for the maintenance of the worker and his family.[4] Starting from the sound principle that work is a good thing, the early unionists were blamed for making rules which prevented their members from working as a rule more than certain specified hours; ladies and gentlemen of leisure asked quite sincerely, Is it not a shocking thing, if an industrious man wants to work extra hours for extra money for the sake of his family, that he should be forbidden to do so by a tyrannical society? Even now it may seem rather paradoxical to maintain that it is the idle and drunken, not the industrious and thrifty workers, who as a rule like working overtime. And yet the fact is so. After a nine hours day, the walk home, the evening wash, and the family supper, how much time is there left for the ideal British workman to rest by the domestic hearth and enjoy the company of his wife and children? A bare hour or two at most before bed-time; and if a man's regular wages will not allow him to indulge in this one cheap and innocent and wholesome pleasure, they are obviously too low, and very low wages are fatal not only to domestic happiness but to industry and thrift. For suppose the day's work extends over twelve or fourteen hours instead of nine, the man leaves his workshop tired out, physically faint and nervously irritable, and must stop for "a glass" before he feels equal to the tramp home; he gets in late, too tired to eat; and the wife, who never knows when to expect him, has, of course, got supper too early or too late, and is herself worried with waiting—with the daily result of probable quarrels and certain drink. Habitual long hours and habitual drinking always go together. The clever, idle, thriftless worker, who does not dislike working overtime, does not, and never did, spend his extra earnings on his family. He either drinks the surplus as he earns it, or he saves up a few pounds from high wages to spend "upon the spree," only returning to work when all the family property has been pawned, and he again begins to work double tides to keep himself going with drink while he is redeeming it.

At a time when philanthropists could only shake their heads at the improvidence and intemperance of the poor, and lament that they were none the better for high wages when they got them, the early unionists set themselves to remove the chief cause of these evils in excessive and irregular hours of labour. *They* knew that overwork was neither a cause nor an effect of industry, and they were moved almost exclusively by motives which every philanthropist must approve, when he understands them, in their struggles against habitual overtime. When engineers worked as long hours as tailors they used to drink as much or more; now the engineers have shortened their hours and their drink-bill, and the tailors have not. Human nature is responsible for the result, which is not even peculiar to masculine depravity. Women are demoralised just as men are both by chronic long hours and by the extra wages earned at the expense of chronic overtime; and there are still clever shirtmakers and tailoresses who alternate between weeks of intemperate work and intemperate play.

Evidently, then, benevolent public opinion must go heartily with trade unions in their efforts to secure a moderate and uniform length for the day's work.

The case for a *minimum* rate of wages is even simpler. Trade unions have never wished to have all workers, good or bad, paid at the same rate; all they ask is that the average worker, the man who is thought good enough to be employed, shall be paid at some certain rate which has been accepted in the trade as just sufficient for a decent maintenance. Extra skill and extra speed may be paid for extra, as much as the employer pleases; what trade unionists object to is paying ordinary wages to the extra good hands, and something less than that to the ordinary ones. Ordinary folk are the rule, and if all ordinary workers were to go on half rations it would be a bad look-out for most of us.

Thirteen years ago, a young woman of great energy and ability,[5] who had had singular facilities for approaching the labour question from the worker's side, began for the first time seriously to advocate trade unionism as a remedy for the notorious evils affecting the industrial position of women. She was the daughter of a highly-educated elementary schoolmaster; and on her father's death,[6] when quite a young girl, she was engaged as secretary, or assistant, by an elderly lady, who herself acted as clerk to the secretary of the Workmen's Club and Institute Union.[7] She made herself so useful in this capacity that she was soon afterwards appointed secretary to the Union itself. Nearly all the workmen's clubs in London are affiliated to this Institute, and the ordinary course of its business brought Miss Smith into constant and friendly intercourse both with the leading working-men and with persons of every class interested in social and industrial problems. After some years of this work she married one of the ablest and most disinterested of the men associated with the Club Union, Mr. Thomas Paterson, formerly a cabinetmaker, a speculative metaphysician of considerable originality, and a man of singular uprightness and generosity of character.

Immediately after her marriage Mrs. Paterson began to organise the movement which must be permanently connected with her name, in favour of trade unionism among women.[8] She saw that in women's trades, at their best, there was the same need for mutual help and protection as in the trades of men, while every form of charitable help had been tried and found ineffective to deal with the chronic starvation prevailing in women's trades at their worst. She knew that working-women, as a class, are too poor, too busy, and too timid to start any even mildly militant organisation for themselves; and at the same time she believed that there were men and women of leisure, dissatisfied with the machinery of so-called charity, who would be ready and willing to help and encourage the workers to combine to help themselves.

A society upon these lines was formed in the summer of 1874,[9] with the good wishes of all well-known friends of the working classes as such, together with the friends of women as such. Some conservative ladies, who still had their doubts about trade unionism in general, trusted to the discretion of their sex to revise its platform so as to eliminate all doubtful elements, and working-men, who objected in theory to all female labour, admitted that it was really the competition of disorganised female labour that they objected to, not the employment of women who had learnt to ask a fair day's wages for a fair day's work. Public opinion was thus, within a certain area, prepared to look with favour upon a *bonâ fide* trade society of working-women, if the women of any trade should be pleased to form one; and the women employed in book-folding and book-sewing were happily ready to rise to the occasion.[10] With the co-operation of the men in the trade a public meeting was called, at which about three hundred women were present, and the first women's trade union was forthwith established. About three hundred members were enrolled in the first year, and rules were adopted which have been the model for most of the women's unions subsequently formed. A shilling entrance fee, and a weekly subscription of twopence, entitle members to receive, after a year's probation, 5s. a week as sick or out-of-work pay for not more than eight weeks in a year. No exact actuarial calculations can be made as to the payments necessary to cover trade benefits, but the experience of the women bookbinders shows that the scale of pay and benefits first suggested by Mrs. Paterson is such as can fairly be maintained. The Society since its formation has paid over 200*l.* as sick and over 100*l.* as out-of-work allowance, and has a balance in the bank of over 300*l.* to meet any strain upon the funds. The average earnings of the women in this trade, *when fully employed*, are about 10s. to 12s. a week; but we must not conclude from this that their average yearly income amounts to 26*l.* or 31*l.* There are many weeks in the year when the publishing trade is slack, and the women, though not literally "out of work," and so entitled to the Society allowance, are only working half-time or less, and perhaps not earning even so much as 5s. In fact, if we are to form any conception of the marvellous exercise of thrift and self-denial habitual amongst working-women, we must in all cases make a deduction of about 25 per cent. from the so-called "average earnings."[11]

The Upholsteresses' Society,[12] which was formed next, has fewer members, but, owing to the depression of trade, especially in the last two years, it has paid nearly as much in benefits, and more than twice as much in out-of-work allowance, as in sick-pay. Hence its funds are at a low ebb. In this trade the "average wages" would be probably described as reaching 15s. a week; but the uncertainty of employment, as already seen, is greater, and the trade as a whole is suffering from the action of a few shops (much esteemed, alas! by the middle-class lovers of cheapness), which extend their trade first by cutting wages and prices down to the lowest possible point, and then again by reinvesting the profits so acquired in the shares of companies, hotel or other, which have orders for showy furniture to bestow. Respectable and liberal employers who do not engage in this class of speculation are being increasingly driven out of the trade by the competition of such firms.

Shirtmakers, tailoresses, and dressmakers in London have formed similar societies, the largest branch of the Tailoresses' Union consisting of women employed in the Government Army Clothing Factory, where energetic officials are always ready to justify their own receipt of a handsome salary by pointing to economies effected in the wages of their subordinates.[13] In 1875 the first women's unions were represented at the Glasgow Trades Congress by Mrs. Paterson and the present writer, not a single objection being raised by the other delegates to the representation of *bonâ fide* trade societies of women. Indeed, then, and on all future occasions, leading members of the Congress were ready and glad to assist in organising new local societies, and in recommending the principles of unionism to women. Any doubts or suspicion that might otherwise have been felt were tranquillised by the confidence felt by the many working-men to whom she was known in Mrs. Paterson's judgment and clear-headed devotion to the interests of labour.

Her work in connection with the Unionist Propaganda falls naturally into three divisions. The London trade societies were, of course, in constant communication with her, each secretary of a union being *ex officio* a member of the committee of the central parent society, called the Women's Protective and Provident League.[14] A library, a swimming-club, a monthly journal, winter evening entertainments, lectures, and conferences on subjects of interest, such as factory inspection, co-operation, &c., were provided or organised by the League for the benefit of the societies, and the cost of public meetings, printing, and other preliminary expenses connected with the formation of new societies were met in the same way; but the unions, once formed, have been from the first entirely self-governed and self-supporting. In the provinces, on the other hand, the League has sometimes started, and sometimes only been called upon to encourage, independent local efforts. In the former case, except in Oxford, little permanent success can be recorded, apparently for want of just such help and encouragement to the young and struggling societies as has been given continuously to those in London by the League. On the other hand, in two cases at least, important trade movements have been successfully conducted by women, who were pleased to be invited to give an account of their exploits at the Annual Meeting in London.

The first case was that of the Seamers and Stitchers' Union in Leicester. The women employed in finishing hosiery had always been paid at a very low rate, and organisation was particularly difficult, as the workers were scattered in about forty villages round. In 1874 some of the more courageous applied to the manufacturers for an advance, and many expressed their willingness to grant it if a "list price" was prepared and accepted by the workers. This was done by the townspeople, and thereupon the employers who refused the advance sent their orders to the villages. Then the women went out into the villages, tramping through deep snow, canvassing and collecting from house to house, till twenty-seven out of thirty-seven villages had joined the union, and it had 300*l.* available for "strike pay." All this was described by one of the actors in broad, picturesque dialect, with the most graphic details, concluding with the statement that "the advance gained by the list was for some of the women as much as 2*s.* per week on earnings of from 5*s.* to 7*s.* per week."

The story of the Dewsbury Woollen Weavers' Union told in 1880 was substantially similar. About 700 members were enrolled, and in 1879 the Society spent "in resisting reductions" 66*l.* 7*s.* 6*d.*, while its income was 155*l.* 8*s.* 11*d.* This Union was formed in consequence of an association of the masters, formed to equalise the prices paid for the same class of work throughout the district. The masters naturally proposed to level down, while the workpeople reasonably advocated the opposite course; with the result of securing an advance of 2*s.* 4*d.* for eight days' work in one case, and in general raising the rate of wages in bad firms instead of lowering it in good ones. With larger funds and a larger number of active members the League would be able to render great service to country unions by keeping them in communication with each other, and promoting the establishment of permanent benefit branches, which prevent members from falling off after the satisfactory arrangement of trade disputes.

Of course, taking the country as a whole, women's unionism is still in much too rudimentary a state to exercise any general influence upon the rate of wages or the hours of work. The few who do belong to a society obtain certain definite advantages, which are worth having in themselves; and they are also firmly convinced that they are treated with more respect and consideration in their workshops when it is known that they are no longer collectively penniless or unbefriended. The societies in London are fully recognised by the employers, who send to the office when in want of workers, and besides the unbounded gratitude and affection felt for Mrs. Paterson herself by the members of the

Women's Unions, they also certainly count among the advantages they have gained by association, the discovery that there are persons in other ranks of life capable of valuing their friendship, able to understand their wants, and honestly anxious to enable them to improve their position to an extent which they would hardly venture to hope for if quite all the world were to be against them always.

What has been learnt in the last dozen years by the outside friends of the unionists would take longer to describe, and not all the knowledge so acquired is of a pleasurable nature. We see that besides the thriftless, helpless, more or less incompetent or undeserving poor, who are the chronic objects of fitful and ineffective charity, besides the ignorant and sickly residuum whose work is at best worth little more than the mere nothing which it fetches—besides all these, whose number is more than enough to baffle us by itself, we find that there are perhaps a million of respectable, self-supporting, self-respecting, fairly skilled female operatives, often the sole maintenance of a family, whose clear average weekly earnings, with a long day's labour, are more often under than over ten shillings a week. We believe that there are still well-to-do people who say and think that ten shillings a week are very good wages for a singe woman; but that opinion is seldom supported by a detailed budget. Let us see for ourselves how much spending there is in such a sum. The rations allowed to the old people in Whitechapel Workhouse cost, according to Mrs. Barnett, 3s. 11d. a head per week. In quantity they are scarcely equal to the amount physiologists consider necessary for the healthy maintenance of an able-bodied adult, and a lone woman can hardly buy as cheaply as contractors. Still, we will suppose our working-woman to be content with the same diet as the aged paupers, and to spend only 4s. a week in food; 3s. is an ordinary rent to pay in London for such a small back room as she will occupy; lights, firing, and washing can hardly cost her less than another shilling, and if she belongs, as we will hope, to a trade union, her necessary weekly expenses are brought up to 8s. 2d. without any provision for clothes, holidays, amusements, or saving; for all these and other purposes she has a balance available varying, let us say, from 4d. to 1s. 10d. a week, or from 17s. 4d. to 4l. 15s. 9d. a year![15]

And yet there are ladies, whose cheapest dress costs as much as the whole year's pocket-money of an industrious bookfolder, who have the audacity to talk about thrift to these passed mistresses in the art of "going without!"

Such hard habitual penury is not, we submit, good even for a single woman, and probably few people who take the trouble to realise for themselves the sort of existence implied by the nominal wages of 10*s.* a week will fail to join in the wish that women's trade unions might become strong enough to establish as their *minimum* rate something like half-a-crown a day, or 15*s.* a week, instead of 10*s.* or less, for workers of ordinary ability. But if, in one way, it is painful to discover how hard a life is led even by the more skilled and fortunate of our women workers, the unions provide us with new grounds of hope for the future.

Whatever differences there may be between men and women as such, it is an old observation that common experiences give to men and women of the same class some common characteristics overriding the usual differences of sex. The male slave becomes servile and the woman aristocrat imperious, while similarity of position and education will efface the distinctions of class as well as sex, so that in the mediæval hierarchy the sons of noble and peasant have more in common with each other and with St. Catherine or St. Theresa than with their lay contemporaries. Again, we find that all education, if good of its kind, develops the same sort of valuable qualities: the workshop is a good substitute for the school, and the mechanic who is accustomed to administer the affairs of his trade society is receiving the best training for practical politics. We owe to Mrs. Paterson the discovery that the education of the workshop is just as effective in producing a class of intelligent working-women as in developing the intelligent working-man of whom we have heard so often and so long. Girls who only work at a trade for a few years of course do not receive the full benefits of this sort of technical education; but in every trade there are large numbers of women who from one cause or another have worked almost or quite continuously. Single women; wives with sick, or idle, or unlucky husbands; widows with children, and girls of unusual character or education—all these classes take their trade seriously, welcome the idea of trade combination, and are proved by experience to possess all the qualities necessary for organising and administering a trade society. These women are certainly, as a class, more intelligent, enterprising, and resourceful than the average workman's wife or the "poor women" known to district visitors. They have, as a rule, the same domestic experience as other women, with that of the workshop in addition. They cannot help knowing a great deal at first hand about the conditions of work in their own trade, and their own experience serves to interpret the secondhand knowledge of other trades which they pick up, equally without effort. These women know the needs and the failings of their own class infinitely better than their well-to-do would-be benefactors; and until they are taken into council there is little hope of doing anything permanent for the lower class of workers. But the more reason we find to esteem and value the most intelligent of the women operatives, the more grievous it is to realise that even these women are living permanently on the borderland of poverty and want.

We have mentioned the achievements of the Leicester Seamers and Stitchers' Union. Mrs. Mason, one of the members of the original committee, who engaged in the missionary tramp through the snow, was a fair representative of the best type of unionist. Eloquent, humorous, and thoroughly capable, she and her husband, who worked at the same trade, would have been counted among the *élite* of the working-class. Their joint earnings maintained a comfortable home; they were zealous gardeners, thanks to the plots available round the town of Leicester; active co-operators, and ready at any time to sacrifice a few days' wages to promote the cause of unionism in other parts. It gives a painful reality to the statistics which tell of the different duration of life in different social classes when we read the obituary notices in trade organs and see how young the elder unionists are when they die. Mr. Mason died, suddenly, of heart disease; his wife ten months later, at the age of forty-nine, leaving three children, the youngest eleven, and so, it was said, all able to help themselves; but we can understand that when the struggle for existence begins so early it must end early too.

The first secretary of the Upholsteresses' Society, Miss Wilkinson,[16] was also lost prematurely to the cause of Unionism by her early death last autumn; and no one who had heard her describe, evidently from personal experience, the hardships of the search for work, with failing shoe-leather, before the existence of the Society, with its free registry and out-of-work pay, could doubt that it is by the ordinary everyday hardships and vicissitudes of industrial existence that such lives are cut short. Miss Wilkinson herself was not latterly engaged in the trade, but employed as a lecturer by the Women's Suffrage Society, the Birkbeck Institute having furnished her with the means of self-education. She was one of the first to welcome Mrs.

Paterson's suggestions as to the need for trade organisation, and never ceased to take an active part in the propaganda of the Women's League. Thus we find, on the one hand, with satisfaction, among the workers themselves women of character, intelligence, and education, able and willing to devote themselves to the interests of their own class; and on the other hand, we find, with a sort of horror, that these most valuable members of society have on the whole, let us say, an average "expectation of life" less by twenty years than the women who spend their time in comfortable idleness, or industry tempered with the ease and comforts of middle-class life. Death had not yet done its work, and in December 1886 Mrs. Paterson also died, at the early age of thirty-nine, from a constitutional malady, aggravated, there can be little doubt, by overwork and the anxiety which she underwent after her husband's death when endeavouring to continue all the honorary work she had undertaken for the benefit of others, while at the same time compelled to seek remunerative employment for her own support.[17]

There are many well-known "movements" under benevolent patronage, taking up a much larger space in the mind of the general public than the one founded by Mrs. Paterson, which have failed to elicit anything like the same amount of gratitude and recognition on the part of the class intended to be benefited. Many of our readers, no doubt, may here meet with her name for the first time; but working-men throughout the country, and working-women in London and those parts where she was personally known, would name her rather than any of our middle-class philanthropists, if asked what woman had laboured most, and most wisely, to improve the industrial position of women.

In the last report of the society to which she was honorary secretary, prepared only a fortnight before her death, Mrs. Paterson quoted from Mr. Besant's story the saying, "the impossible way [of helping working-women] is that the ladies of the country shall unite to form a protection league for their working sisters," and appealed to educated women of leisure to prove the reproach unfounded by taking part in the attempt already begun to enrol both classes in such a league for the protection of the weak. Will any help come from this quarter, or is the novelist's indictment true? "Ladies deliberately shut their eyes; they won't take trouble; they won't think; they like things about them to look smooth and comfortable; they will get things cheap if they can. *What do they care if the cheapness is got by starving women?* What is killing this girl here? Bad food and hard work. Cheapness! What do the ladies care how many working girls are killed?"

"What the eye doesn't see the heart doesn't grieve for," and, honestly, I am afraid that ladies *don't* care how many working-girls are killed so long as they know nothing about it. They will even go so far as to say, What is the use of knowing or caring if it can't be helped? To which the answer is, It *can* be helped if only enough people will begin to know and care. Unionism by itself will do a good deal for women, as it has for men; but there are special difficulties in the way of their organisation, and the first thing their friends can do for them is to help to remove these difficulties. Trade-unionism, however, is not, any more than co-operation, a panacea for all the evils and dangers of our industrial system: it deals only with two out of the three great factors of the problem; as if the capitalist and the labourer could decide their quarrels without the intervention of that virtual employer of both—the consumer. The only real and effective protection that can be extended to the starving workgirl must come from a universal conspiracy of consumers not to buy the produce of stolen or half-paid-for labour, spending, of course, the money so economised in employing at first hand a corresponding number of women at trade-society wages. No doubt if we all were to buy only what we could afford to pay for honestly, some of us would get, as the lovers of cheapness say, less for our money; but a clear conscience would be thrown in as compensation, and the industrial interests of the community would not suffer, since as large a proportion of the national income would still be spent on the products of agriculture and manufactures, though a larger proportion would be spent and consumed by the producers themselves.

To bring about this conspiracy or alliance between women of all classes, two things are needed first—namely, to give courage to the women who work, and knowledge to the women who buy; or rather, since they can so easily give each other encouragement and information, the one thing needed first is to bring the two classes into contact with each other. We have shown how this has been done upon a small scale through the initiative of Mrs. Paterson, whose life and labours it is proposed to commemorate by the foundation of a Central Trades Hall and Working Women's Club, to be used and administered by the women unionists of London, present and to come. The society founded by Mrs. Paterson will, no doubt, have its headquarters in the same premises, and working-men unionists of wide experience agree with the women in believing that the mere possession of such a central house of call will give a great impetus to the cause of unionism. At present whenever a public meeting has to be held preliminary to the organisation of a new trade, premises, often expensive or inconvenient, have to be hired, and many who would come to a place they know and feel at home in are deterred by having to hunt up some unknown address in a strange quarter. As Miss Wilkinson used to say, the working-woman has always two days' work to do in the twenty-four hours—half-a-day's housekeeping, namely, before and after the day in factory or workshop. Her time available for public interests is therefore shorter than a man's, and the public house, still used perforce, even though reluctantly, as an office by the men's unions is fortunately not considered available for women. The established unions can, and do, pay a reasonable sum as office rent for the use of premises provided by the League; but larger and better premises would attract and accommodate more members and more societies, all of which would become self-supporting as soon as formed.

Of course the world cannot be reformed by subscriptions to any society or any institution, however useful or well-intentioned; but there is a clear generic difference between unproductive charity—money given, that is, to meet some particular want, which is spent and done with, leaving just the same want to present itself again next day—and money invested in furthering a movement which gathers impetus as it proceeds, and looks forward to uprooting the very seeds and germs of social distress. On this ground alone, all those whose consciences are troubled by their share of responsibility for the sufferings of those who hew wood and draw water in our service should be glad to enrol themselves in the Holy Alliance or protective league preached by Mr. Besant, and founded in embryo by Mrs. Paterson.

But this is not all. The responsibility for the existing evils of our social order is distributed over all classes of society. Neither the labourer, nor the capitalist, nor the much-abused middleman, can bear the whole burden. From the ducal agent running up rents to the frugal housewife running down prices, we all contribute something to the influences which starve Melenda, body and soul. For the most part we act in ignorance; we do not mean to be cruel; we wish to buy that suit for little Harry cheap; we don't *wish* the tailoress who makes it to starve; and we don't know that 3*d.* has to come off her price, and a shilling or two off her 8*s.* 6*d.* of weekly wages in order that we may be tempted by 9*s*. 11*d*. instead of 10*s*. 6*d*. upon the ticketed price of an enterprising tradesman. Hitherto, all our attempts at reform have started on the hypothesis that the rich know what is wrong and can teach the lower orders, who do it, how to amend their ways. And yet society is very much where it was when philanthropists began to tinker at it. Judging from results, they have somehow failed to go the right way to work; they must have either preached the wrong remedy, or preached the right remedy to the wrong people. They have preached thrift to the poor: is it possible that they ought to have preached it to the rich instead? They have preached industry to the workers: would it perhaps be better were they to practise it themselves?

These and other such-like revolutionary doubts suggest themselves when we begin to compare what the women unionists have to teach with what they, like the rest of us, have still to learn; and we have no hesitation in maintaining that the projected Paterson Hall will be just as useful as an institution for the economic instruction of our ladies of leisure as it will be as headquarters for trade-unionist propaganda. Even now, consumers may learn from members of the existing unions which of two firms, with perhaps equal prices, equal civility, and an equal display of plate glass, has the repute of a "fair shop" among the workers, and which is shunned as a "stoneyard" or refuge for the destitute in funds or character. Let us suppose the existing organisation strengthened and extended, and there is surely nothing impossible in the idea that the valued customers of a fashionable shop should allow themselves to remonstrate with its courteous proprietor when they hear of fines or reductions, insanitary workrooms, or other subterranean grievances of the operatives. Let it become the fashion for ladies to ask, not merely what is done for the resident shop-assistants, but how the workroom and the out-of-door "hands" are treated. It will then become the fashion among respectable firms to patronise the unions and boast of paying "list prices" only; it will become the fashion among the workers to join their trade society; and a coalition of workers, customers, and employers with a character to lose would easily suppress any tendency among needy or unscrupulous masters to rebel against the necessity of paying decent subsistence wages even to the women they employ. Of course there will be grumbling: shopkeepers will lay the blame of every fancy price upon the workers' claims, and the ruin of England will be prophesied as confidently as when its prosperity was held to turn upon setting babies of five to work in factories, or harnessing naked women to draw wagons in coal-mines. There is no cheaper beast of burden than a woman, but somehow the national income has proved equal to the strain of providing more costly quadrupeds for the latter work. And, supposing the same income to be further drawn upon to the extent of providing food, clothes, and a little leisure for our whole working population, there will still stand between us and bankruptcy, not merely the produce of conscientious "thrift" amongst the wealthy and comfortable classes, but also all the expenditure now thrown upon the community by chronic poverty, disease, and the demoralisation that results from hopeless misery.

It is a commonplace of the old political economy that it is cheaper to pay a labourer wages that he can live upon, and let him keep himself, than to buy his labour cheaper and eke out his wages by state or charitable doles. The organisation of women's industry will help the community to understand that every sound economic principle applies to women as well as to men, and it is therefore hardly Utopian to believe that a good day may come, and even quickly, when we shall all see that the labour of starving workgirls is not really even "cheap" while the conditions under which it is bought and sold are quite intolerably "nasty," and such as must be relentlessly proscribed by any duly enlightened public opinion.

Notes

1.   Simcox refers to two of Sir Walter Besant's popular novels that generated sympathy from the wealthy for the East End poor and stimulated the social regeneration of the area. In one part of *All Sorts and Conditions of Men* (1882), Harry Goslet tells Angela Messenger, a wealthy reformer who sets up a dressmaker's cooperative, of his dream of a Ruskinian People's Palace of Delight for Eastenders. Besant helped to give this fancy reality. With the help of a wealthy donor and publicity from *Longman's*, it was built, and the People's Palace was opened by Queen Victoria on May 14, 1887. The Palace eventually developed into East London College, which was recognized as a branch of London University in 1908. During this time while *Longman's* popularized Besant's cause, the magazine published *Children of Gibeon* from January through December of 1886, another novel of working-class East End life.

2. During Victorian times, according to Kenneth Graham in *English Criticism of the Novel: 1865–1900* (1965), readers and critics demanded that novels should be pleasing before they are realistic, and that they should have a moral purpose without becoming didactic.

3. In 1870, Forster's Education Act made elementary education available to all children in England and Wales.

4. Compare Simcox's arguments to Clementina Black's in "The Coercion of Trade Unions," published in Oct., 1892 in the *Contemporary Review*.

5. Emma Smith Paterson (1848–86).

6. When her father, who only earned £60 a year, died of typhoid fever, Emma Paterson and the rest of her family were in financial straits.

7. In 1867, Paterson became assistant secretary of the Working Men's Club and Institute Union. Founded in 1861, the organization worked to reconcile conflicts between employers and workers.

8. While honeymooning in America, the Patersons were inspired by the success of New York trade unions, the Women's Typographical Society and the Female Umbrella Makers Union.

9. On July 8, 1874, the Women's Protective and Provident League was formed.

10. At a WPPL meeting held on September 12, 1874, the Society of Women Employed in Bookbinding was formed with 300 members.

11. In a factory, employing 2,000 women, it was said quite sincerely, in answer to a question about the rate of wages: "Oh, they earn 10*s.* or 11*s.*"; but the average weekly wage bill, when divided by 2,000, gave only a real weekly average of 8*s.* 6*d.* a head, and the experience of large men's unions frequently gives a similar result. [Simcox's note]

12. The Society of Upholsteresses was formed in 1875.

13. In 1879, 1500 Royal Army clothing workers in Pimlico were discharged. The government offered to hire them back with a 15% reduction for piece work and without the option of working at home. The WPPL stepped in and the Pimlico Branch of the London Tailoresses' Union was formed with a membership of 140 women. It took the union two years to secure their aims.

14. Further information respecting this Society can be obtained from the Secretary, Miss Black, at its office, Industrial Hall, Clark's Buildings, Broadstreet, Bloomsbury, W.C. [Simcox's note]

15. Compare Simcox here to Clementina Black in "What Is a Fair Wage," published in the *New Review* in May, 1893.

16. Jeannette Gaury Wilkinson (1844–86).

17. Paterson suffered from diabetes.

27. The Capacity of Women

Introduction

Edith Simcox's "The Capacity of Women" appeared in September, 1887, in *Nineteenth Century*, and is reprinted here from that periodical. In this essay, Simcox argues that George Romanes's evolutionist polemics in "Mental Differences Between Men and Women" (*Nineteenth Century*, May, 1887) is misguided. Romanes argued that women are inferior intellectually because they have been poorly educated, and that, according to him, their "inferiority displays itself most conspicuously in a comparative absence of originality." In response, Simcox argues that Romanes's claims are based more on stereotypes than on a critical examination of women's accomplishments. Simcox centers the issue of women's advances in an analysis of class, arguing that "the ruling minds of the ages have always been a *minority of a minority*." Simcox further argues that women have the right to pursue a career outside the home. For Simcox, thwarting women's attempts to pursue work of their choice is ultimately a crime against not only women, but also against intellectual and social progress.

The Capacity of Women

Mr. Romanes's article, published in the May number of this Review, is so excellent an example of the manner in which this subject should be treated, that it invites a few supplementary remarks and qualifications, which scarcely amount to criticism, as they in no way invalidate the general practical conclusions which he advocates.[1]

Mr. Romanes is of opinion, for assignable and intelligible reasons, that "in the animal kingdom as a whole the males admit of being classified, as it were, in one psychological species and the females in another." And he is also persuaded that, among human beings, the course of history has resulted in bringing the minds of men and the morals of women respectively to a higher degree of development. The first of these propositions is no doubt true in the main; but so long as vague metaphysical notions about an *Ewigweibliche*[2] continue to becloud the atmosphere, it is important and interesting to note that the psychological and other distinctions of sex are among the after-thoughts of the primæval mother nature.

Who would have ventured to predict, after comparing a rudimentary vertebrate in the undated past, say, with the common ancestor of ants and bees, that the future did not belong to the insects? There is a vast region of animal life in which existence seems renewed by transmigration rather than birth, where parentage is virtually unknown, and where the community is differentiated into castes rather than sexes. By an easy flight of the imagination, we can suppose ants and bees or butterflies to have developed on their own lines to a point as far removed in organisation, morals, and intelligence from the typical rudimentary insect as man is from the rudimentary vertebrate. The psychological distinctions of sex, noted by Mr. Romanes, would have no place in such a world. Even among the vertebrates, it was not a foregone conclusion from the first that the mother bird or fish should hatch and protect the young: this function is shared or monopolised by the male so often that we can not be certain, if the rulers of the world had been developed from the races that swim or creep or fly, that intellectual birds or moralised reptiles would have noticed the same psychological sex distinctions as ourselves.

Of course it will be said that the existing distinction has emerged and survived because of its natural fitness; that is, that it has proved favourable to the life and development of the higher vertebrates; but there is a difference between things practically useful under given material conditions and things belonging to the eternal and immutable "nature of things." Science teaches that nature is eminently mutable, and that all elaborate qualities are the products of lengthy and complex processes of manufacture. Supposing the kind and degree of sex differentiation which was advantageous to mammoths to prove inconvenient to man, we shall find Nature as much open to the reasoning of facts now as in the days when she decided against the sociological experiments of insects and fishes. If the social life of men and women is not modelled upon that of seals or stags, any human propensities which are a mere survival from earlier stages of mammalian development will die out after a few ages of inappropriateness. This is in fact the conclusion at which Mr. Romanes's argument arrives, and we can only hope that it will not lose any of its force from being allowed to begin a stage further back.

With regard to the mental inferiority and moral elevation of women, there are one or two grounds for doubting whether either is quite as considerable as even Mr. Romanes is disposed to maintain. It may seem ungracious to disturb a complimentary consensus of opinion to the effect, as Mr. Romanes expresses it, that "purity and religion are, as it were, the natural heritage of women in all but the lowest grades of culture." But if the statement is not quite unassailable historically, its correction had best take the form of a modest disclaimer on the part of women themselves before some brutal misogynist demolishes the flattering illusion, and with it our last poor claim to some impartiality of judgement.

The exceptive clause, that women are devout and virtuous "in all but the lowest grades of culture," is not wide enough. The primitive saint, the primitive sage, and the primitive humourist agree, it must be admitted, in taking a low view of feminine morality. The typical view of the typical woman is as a daughter of Eve, on intimate terms with the old serpent and given to the beguiling of men. The picture may have been—and to a certain extent was—unjust, but it was the one sketched by man while he monopolised the arts of portraiture. Indian rishis and mediæval monks took this view. Their ideal being ascetic, if a woman appeared on the horizon at all, it could only be as an ally of the lower nature they were endeavouring to subdue, and so, not unnaturally, from their point of view, they concluded every woman to be all "lower nature." This was unjust because the mass of men who were not ascetics had just as much "lower nature" as the women, and it was not the fault of the latter that imperfect ascetics found their existence a trial or temptation.

Primitive philosophers have as a rule less to say about women than ascetics, and in place of moral disapprobation feel only a little mild contempt for their intelligence and want of moral elevation; but even in this there is a measure of injustice. The sage despises all women because they are ignorant of philosophy, but he does not despise all men, who are equally ignorant, because some men, he himself at least, have obtained knowledge. Later on, no doubt, cross divisions are established, and a "religious" woman may be ranked as higher than a lay or lewd man; but from the earliest times even until now, I think, our comparative estimate of the virtue and intelligence of the average man and of the average woman is influenced by the fact that when we talk of men in general we mean all men, the great known to history and the small known to us in the flesh, and that when we speak of women in general we think of the ordinary known sort only.

The first thinkers of the first ages were taken from the class of gentlemen of leisure, rulers of men, possessed of whatever experience life then could teach; their leisure was secured by the industry of wives and slaves, and any latent aptitude their sisters might have had for religion or philosophy was sacrificed to the necessity for grinding corn or looking after the maids. The educational privileges, as one may call them, enjoyed by the favoured few, as a class, were utilised by the tiny cluster of individuals whose natural faculties allowed them to seize the happy moment. But from the prehistoric days when unknown sages translated the experience of primitive *Weltweisheit*[3] into the language of an ancient saw, from those days down to the last moment of our own degeneracy, it has been and remains true that the ruling minds of the ages have always been a *minority of a minority*, the units selected from a select few, the cream of the cream of the intelligence of their time.

The immortals whose names stand upon the brief list agreed upon by the whole civilised world were men who towered above the heads of a generation of great contemporaries, who as a rule had the way opened before them by an age of great precursors. In art, in literature, in philosophy, this is almost uniformly the case. Suggestive teaching, training that inspirits or provokes to growth, combine with the happy moments of historic and ethnic destiny to produce the cluster of eminent talent which all becomes articulate and effective at the same time. The great men of the great generations educate each other, and the greatest generations produce an immortal or two apiece. The thesis is almost too obvious to need illustration. Plato and Aristotle follow Socrates and the Sophists, as Raphael and Michelangelo succeed Giotto; Shakespeare, Chaucer; and Goethe, Klopstock *plus* Winckelmann, Lessing, and the vernacular *Reineke Fuchs*.[4] So much will be conceded readily, but it is not so easy to understand what the immortals, whose features alone show clearly through the haze of time, may have owed to their long since forgotten contemporaries. Probably, since a heightened sensitiveness to all immaterial influences is a part of genius, the immortal owes even more than lesser men to all that is fortunate in his surroundings, and we can more easily imagine the wits of the "Mermaid" without Shakespeare than a Shakespeare stranded on a realm of Hayleys.[5] To drop into the familiar regions of modern literary biography, we know what Goethe owed to Schiller, and Coleridge and Wordsworth to each other, as well as to the lesser lights of their society; conscious and unconscious feelings of emulation drove Byron and Shelley to do their best work for each other, just as Thackeray was stirred by his admiration for *David Copperfield* to accomplish *Esmond* and prepare for Colonel Newcome.

If the fashion of the day causes all available talent or genius to be applied to some special branch of study, astronomy, theology, metaphysics, or whatever it may be, the result is of course still more obvious, and all Europe produces schoolmen as France of the Restoration produces romantic fiction in prose and verse. Héloïse and George Sand yield to the spirit of the age like Abelard or Victor Hugo—if they have learnt to read, and the chapter of accidents brings them into the current of intellectual life. But before we can form any opinion as to the fitness of their sex to produce half a dozen immortals in a millennium, we must first ask if historic and social influences have produced a generation of womanly precursors, and a group of women of talent, out of which the missing immortal might have emerged. It does not quite settle the question to say, what is no doubt true, that if women had had stronger brains they might have produced both. The brains both of men and women exercise themselves habitually upon such stuff as the customs of their age and race set before them. An enormous part of the brain power of mankind has been spent, or wasted, in smiting the Philistines hip and thigh: an enormous part of the brain power of womankind has been spent, or wasted, in cajoling Samson.[6] But the victories of Samson pave the way for the victories of Saul, and the victories of Saul lay the foundations of the throne of Solomon. The daughters of Delilah found no dynasty, though they help to upset a good many. In other words, by following the fashion which required men to fight, the men on the winning side may drift into social and political relations favourable to the growth of civilisation; while the primitive division of labour, which confined women to the tent or homestead, cut them off, as a class, from the educational influences of power and free association with powerful equals. Here and there a woman of exceptional capacity and position might appear by chance among the rulers of men, but the opportunity would be owning to her connection by birth or marriage with the privileged class, and would make no opening for others of her sex.

Once the gulf was formed between the occupations and interests of men and women, it tended naturally to widen and perpetuate itself, until civilisation had made such progress that uncivilised wives went out of fashion, and women began to learn to read. If the workings of intelligence were quite unconditioned, we might ask why, when this first step was taken, women with some masterpieces of literature behind to help them did not develop intellectually, say, like men in and after the Homeric age. But the omission is perfectly intelligible if we are right in supposing that all intellectual movements, and especially such as culminate in the production of a world-famed genius, originate when a whole class of persons are engaged together in occupations which suggest and stimulate fresh thought and action, under circumstances which allow the individual and the group to act and react upon each other, striking out fresh combinations, and multiplying suggestions and possibilities for those who come after.

Until the present day, even in the most civilised communities, it cannot be said that this social life of the intellect, as one may call it, has been open to women in appreciable numbers. The two above named reached their fame by chance; happily married or happily cloistered—and both had by nature as good a chance as other women of such a fate—both would have remained unknown to letters. Thrown by chance into the current of contemporary thought, their brains began to work to the same tune as their neighbours', and we find them to be made of the same intellectual paste as those able men of a period who, once in a way, find a genius to out-top them. While it is the exception for a woman to find herself in a position to produce anything, it is virtually inconceivable that she should produce immortal work. Nor is it altogether unscientific to hold our judgment in suspense as to what feminine brains may do, should circumstances ever become propitious to their productiveness; for we observe in the past that on the rare occasions when similar demands have been made upon the minds of men and women, chosen in the same way, the nature of the response has been surprisingly similar. Curiously enough, the demands thus made and met are such as the most ancient *à priori* theories of feminine frailty would have thought most inappropriate. Our primitive sage would certainly have been as ready to believe that women could write immortal poems as that they could discharge the higher functions of government or enter into the higher emotions of the religious life. We may not perhaps think very highly of the wisdom of crowned heads, or altogether endorse the mediæval ideal of saintliness, but we note that when public opinion has called upon women of high birth to rule, they have done so readily and with an amount of intelligence and good-will fully equal to that displayed on the average by masculine potentates.[7] Again, when opinion called men and women equally to embrace a life of religious devotion and asceticism, women were found as able and willing as men both to follow and to lead, to organise and administer in the interests of the church on the one hand, and on the other to control the hostile forces of the world itself by purely spiritual influences. Here for the first time we find clever women, as a class, provided with a career, in the religious life, and much ability was shown by divers saints, abbesses, and founders or reformers of religious orders for women. Many of them were certainly quite clever enough to have addled their brains over the subtleties of the scholastic philosophy, but public opinion called on them to become saints and did not call on them to become theologians or metaphysicians, and then, as always, popular expectation fulfilled itself.

But, it will be said, men of genius or eminent talent have manifested themselves in social strata where intellectual eminence was neither looked for nor desired. The Ipswich butcher's son is called by his circumstances to be a butcher, not a cardinal, and the long list of "self-made men" is quoted as a reproach to the other sex, as if women rich and poor had at least had no worse chances than the men who have triumphed over the difficulties of poverty alone. We may observe in passing that the inner circle of immortals is not recruited from the otherwise most justly honoured ranks of the self-taught. The non-existence of a phenomenon must not be mistaken for its impossibility; but we note that men who have had to fight for the rudiments of humane learning have not as a matter of fact ever subsequently reached the very topmost summits of human achievement. But there is a standing difference between the position of the boy or man who has to contend with adverse circumstances before his natural talents find fair play, and the position of girls or women even belonging to the leisured class. The difference is that the boy, if he escapes from the thrall of poverty at all, escapes into the surroundings to which he belongs by nature. The carpenter's boy with a turn for mathematics makes his way to Cambridge; the barber's lad with a taste for cuneiforms gets into the British Museum, and for all purposes of self-development and production the difficulties of birth and origin are left behind. Natural genius and cultivated talent meet on equal terms, and the education of comradeship and emulation is not less available to the poor man's son than to those with whom a kind of learned mediocrity is hereditary, or to those who inherit the means of cultivating all their natural aptitudes to the utmost. Every age and every branch of thought has its first and second rate men, who rise above a crowd of fellow-workers as the rare immortal rises above a great generation. But first-rate achievement never crowns a lifetime of continuously solitary work, and in many, if not most cases, first-rate ability does not declare itself until promising natural faculties have been matured by exercise and polished by intercourse with other minds in the prime of their activity. Any intellectual coterie may serve to this extent the purpose of a university, and the debates and readings of Mill and the other young utilitarians in London were just as academic as the society in which Arthur Hallam was the leading figure.[8]

It is needless to say that the most studiously disposed or gifted of young women in past generations have been cut off by custom as absolutely from the stimulus of such common intellectual life as from the advantages of university teaching in its stricter form. Middling abilities suffice to enable us to learn what we are taught, and we may agree that no youth is to be called exceptionally clever who cannot pick up, let us say, Greek or algebra without a teacher. But what clever man, who looks back upon the modicum of such learning acquired in or out of school, can imagine the cleverest youth proceeding to do any good with such acquirements amid the trivial occupations and mental solitude of the ordinary middle-class maiden? Youth insists on being amused, and clever youths find intellectual amusements the most fascinating of any; but, as children say, it is dull to play by oneself, and if the game is spoilt for want of schoolfellows, the delightful play of young minds, instead of leading up to still more delightful work, gradually loses its charm, and one more of the clever girls, who might have grown into an able woman, drops out of the field altogether, and spends or wastes her brain power in some quite different direction.

Ruling minds, we began by saying, are a minority of a minority, but in fact we arrive at them by a process of winnowing indefinitely repeated and renewed. We have a senior wrangler at least every year; every university generation has its cluster of best men, but the best men of bad years soon drop out of sight, and even the best men of brilliant generations often fail to survive the rigorous tests of after life, and disappoint the hopes which centred on their future. The ability believed in may have been real, but besides the accidents which may cause a man to obtain less success or reputation than his deeds or powers deserve, there are a thousand circumstances which may prevent powers from turning into achievement, may cause good work to produce less than its fair proportion of result, may make good qualities neutralise instead of reinforcing each other, and, as a result of these or countless other discouragements, may prevent the promises of youth from being fulfilled and leave the man of exceptional ability, who had every chance at starting, after all as unproductive of great works as any woman. Then, again, the man in whom his contemporaries have seen the promise of immortality may, through some fault or merit in his character, become, womanlike, content to do something else with his mind. So Charles Austin, held to be the most brilliant man of a brilliant set, was content to spend his life in making a fortune at the Parliamentary bar.[9] Brain force can spend itself on such work, and Charles Austin's cleverness still made itself felt in the narrow sphere he had chosen. But if men, who begin by dreaming of immortality and counting upon celebrity, are constantly found ready to subside into ordinary professional existence, can we wonder that women, who have never had so near a view of the tempting prizes of ambition, should be content to occupy their minds, even when these are really "strong," with the ordinary incidents of social and domestic life? Even supposing that there were at a given moment as many girls as boys naturally capable of attaining some degree of intellectual eminence, it would be natural, under all past conditions, for the girls to be choked off into contented obscurity in each case at an earlier stage of their intellectual development than would be the case with a boy of corresponding character, while of those who were not so finally choked off an overwhelmingly larger proportion would swell the ranks of comparative unsuccess, of those who apparently "might have been" but are not exactly great.

It may even rest with circumstances to decide whether the flower of genius shall show itself or not upon the stock of natural talent. The extraordinary mathematical power of Mrs. Somerville is sometimes quoted as a proof that women at their best are without originality, since Mrs. Somerville at last had as much knowledge as men who do original work, and yet did none herself.[10] But what are the facts? With ordinary teaching, it will no doubt be admitted that such a born mathematician would have been senior wrangler at Cambridge at the usual age, but poor Miss Fairfax was eighteen before she could get hold of a Euclid, could then only read it in bed at night, and was deprived even of that resource by the confiscation of her candles. She was clever all round at the learning of schools, having taught herself some Greek and Latin as well as algebra, yet, human-like, she was led to go in the groove society prescribed, and submitted to marry, uncongenially, at twenty-four, and to spend her brain power in keeping house and minding babies on a small income. She was over thirty before she obtained possession of such a mathematical library as an undergraduate begins his college course with. When she was over forty she taught herself to stop in the middle of a calculation to receive morning callers, and to take it up where she had left off when they were gone. Can we wonder that no original work was done in a vocation thus cavalierly treated? The young mathematician of genius talks and thinks and dreams of formulæ; his very jokes are in their jargon; facility of manipulation reaches its highest point by constant exercise, and the constant familiarity with certain conceptions not only makes apprehension easier, but also keeps the whole field of mathematical thought so constantly present to the mind that discoveries, as it were, make themselves, in the recognition of new relations, on the suggestion of the known relations embraced in a single glance.

In such a science one sees clearly that genius is only talent carried to a higher power. In all cases, it is by the constant application of the mind to operations of the same character that intellectual work, of whatsoever nature, is made easy to those who are by nature able to perform it; and real mastery of this kind is seldom unrelieved by flashes of more or less brilliant inspiration, unless it is attained too late, after the first vigour of intellectual maturity is exhausted and worn out. But there is a further element of good fortune even in the productiveness of solid work. Circumstances determine whether there is room in this or that field for an epoch-making inspiration, and we cannot tell whether women will furnish their due proportion of original discoveries till we have a due proportion of them engaged in lifelong diligent day labour in the service of thought and knowledge. Probably most of us know venerable "double-firsts"[11] who have by no means set the Thames on fire, and we must no more expect certain, prompt, and conspicuous eminence from every girl who takes a good degree than we do from men with the same record.

After all, the practical interest of the question is of the smallest. If women are to do any kind of literary or other intellectual work, however humble, it is for the interest of the community that they shall be taught and required to do it as well as their natural faculties will allow. This is the practical conclusion to which Mr. Romanes' argument points, and it is quite unnecessary for us to waste time and energy in guessing how good their best may prove in the ages which are to come. Reading women are no doubt interested in increasing the amount of good work of all sorts, and in the apparition of immortal works as often as niggard fate allows; but there is no room in the great republic of letters for the small jealousies of sex or nationality. If England has no immortal to produce, we shall be thankful to welcome one from France, and we should be sorry for the world to refrain from producing, if it could, an immortal man in the next decade, in order that an immortal woman—should the twentieth century give birth to such— might reign in more unrivalled eminence. The world and even its immortals exist after all for the many, not the few, and in the case of both men and women alike the main business of education must be to teach the many to understand and enjoy, while the very, very few who can originate or impart will educate each other, if we leave them free to do it and guard against having the light of any promising capacity snuffed out by discouragement in the tender years of youth with their irrecoverable treasures of vitality.

The intellectual capacity of women, then, is a problem—and not a very pressing one—for the future to decide, while their present moral apacity is a matter of observation. Granted that popular opinion may have somewhat underrated the powers which have as yet been imperfectly tested, there is no very apparent reason why it should have overrated the merits which could be proved and numbered, unless indeed there is somewhere hidden in the recesses of the public mind a conviction that after all men and women are "pretty much of a muchness," and that therefore, if for any reason we credit one or other of them with any special merit, we must in fairness discover or invent some counterbalancing merit or defect that will make the scales as even as our widest involuntary generalisations declare them to be. We know of men incomparably wise, we know of women incomparably good, and so it seems natural when we want to generalise about the good qualities of the sexes to speak of men as naturally clever and women as naturally good. But are not the best of men really as good as the best of women? Have there not been in the world's history as many men as eminent for goodness? We have endeavoured to show why the natural cleverness of women—assuming it to exist—has remained comparatively undeveloped and unproductive; but as regards both cleverness and goodness, is not any kind of eminence in either sex so far the exception as to make us hesitate in claiming either as a psychological sex characteristic?

The earliest comparative estimate of the sexes regards women as both morally and intellectually inferior to men.[12] Subsequently, public opinion has demanded some domestic virtues from women, and, with really commendable consistency, has to a certain extent supplied them with the means of cultivating the same. Accordingly the one virtue of which popular tradition formerly held women to be incapable is now ascribed to them as "a natural heritage." Is it not, however, historically certain that the superior chastity of civilised women is the product of sustained, deliberate pressure, legal, social, and religious, and in itself, so far as it exists, a proof of the extent to which the human race has power to realise its own ideals?

It is difficult to assign a date for the beginning of such pressure. Every community as it emerges from barbarism tries its own experiments, and if these are so far unsuccessful that culture and morals in the end break up together, the work has to begin again not very far from the beginning. The ideal of spiritual purity in mediæval Europe is embodied in the conception of a perfect knight, a Percival or Galahad, to whom we find no feminine counterpart or equivalent; the untamed maidenhood of Brunehild of course belonging to a quite different and more archaic legendary cycle, without any moral significance. In the time of Boccaccio, it seems that ladies were required to disguise their amusement when very scandalously loose stories were told in their presence; but as they also tell such stories themselves, their protests are evidently more a matter of manners than morals, and in the days of the *Decameron* the sex had evidently not yet entered upon the enjoyment of its heritage.

It is a long way from Boccaccio to the ladies' novelist of five centuries later, but our fastidiousness evidently grows at an accelerated rate, for Richardson himself appears to our present taste to pitch the standard of feminine virtue rather insolently low; at least he would be open to such a charge if we did not make allowance for the tone of feeling of the age, which was still a shade more barbaric than his own.[13] As regards the particular virtue which poor Pamela was supposed to illustrate, our ideal has certainly been so far raised that she at least no longer satisfies it. But the whole duty of woman cannot be reduced to the single chapter, whether to marry—or not to marry—a rake. And it is an ethical blunder, nearly as offensive as any of Richardson's, to praise the virtuousness of women as a class merely on the assumption that they are all that Pamela was meant to be. Perhaps the assumption now current would add that they sometimes nurse in hospitals and are concerned for the happiness of dogs and cats; which is also in itself a good thing, and a sign of moral progress, since the natural woman is as prone as the natural man to enjoy bull fights and even gladiatorial shows. But civilised man is overtaking civilised woman in the distaste for bull fights, and even this acquired extension of the sympathetic sensibilities is not the whole of human duty.

If it is a damaging illusion to believe that all men are intelligent and well-informed because they are on an average better taught than women, it is not less damaging to assume that all women are fine moral agents because they are more chaste, and dislike the sight of pain more than men. As was argued long ago by an immortal moralist, wisdom and virtue, ignorance and vice, are inseparable, and it is a fact that our women would have been wiser, would have sought and seized knowledge and the means of obtaining it more resolutely for themselves, if their moral fibre had been of a finer and stronger cast than it could be while knowledge was still wanting. A secondary proof, if one is needed, that the intellectual superiority of mankind cannot be so marked as has been supposed, is supplied by the very fact that we do not find in men the marked moral superiority which should go with superior wisdom. But to suppose that superior virtue all round can co-exist with inferior wisdom, is to suppose walls and towers to be raised without scaffolding and sustained without foundations. In fact, where the knowledge and practical experience of women are defective, so also is their sense of moral obligation. The intellect of women, as a class, has been concentrated and expended upon the incidents of private life and the domestic relations, and within these limits, as a natural consequence, their sense of moral obligation has been developed. Their participation in the public life of the community has been restricted, and hence their knowledge of the needs and duties arising from social and political relations is still very incomplete, while it is impossible alike with men and women for the conscience to speak concerning matters of which the mind has no consciousness at all.

If we are disposed to take a cheerful view of the moral future of the race—and all evolutionists are optimists at heart—we must look forward, not to a continued difference between the functions and ideals of the sexes, but to the evolution of an ideal of human character and duty combining the best elements in the two detached and incomplete ideals. Great men, we have seen, educate each other, and we shall never have both men and women at their best and greatest until we have the cream of the cream of both sexes educating each other towards the highest standard of all imaginable human excellence.

Notes

1.   Simcox's article was in response to Romanes's thesis of feminine intellectual inferiority published in the May number of the *Nineteenth Century*. George John Romanes (1848–93) was a researcher in physiology and mental evolution. He claimed that secondary sexual characteristics of a "mental kind" differentiated men and women: "Seeing that the average brain-weight of women is about five ounces less than that of men, on merely anatomical grounds we should be prepared to expect a marked inferiority of intellectual power in the former."
2.   German for "eternal in woman."
3.   German for "philosophy or world wisdom."

4. Friedrich Gottlieb Klopstock (1724–1803) was a German poet; Johann Joachim Winckelmann (1717–68) was a German archaeologist and antiquarian; Gotthold Ephraim Lessing (1729–81) was a German critic and dramatist; *Reineke Fuchs* (1794) was an epic poem by Goethe.

5. Simcox most likely is referring to the Mermaid Tavern. Sir Walter Raleigh supposedly founded a writing club which met there every Friday night. [cited by Jesse Swan]

Although spelled "Hayley" by Simcox, she is referring to Halley's Comet, named after the English astronomer Edmund Halley (1658–1742).

6. Samson, from the Old Testament, was an Israelite servant of God. He used his amazing strength to fight the Philistines on numerous occasions. Eventually his lover, Delilah, tricked him into believing that his strength lay in his uncut hair. While he slept, Delilah cut his hair, called to the Philistines, and they captured Samson and blinded him. When his hair grew back, Samson pulled the Philistine banquet hall down on top of them.

7. At one time in China a succession of able empress-mothers succeeded in establishing something like an irregular feminine dynasty. [Simcox's note]

8. Arthur Hallam (1811–33). An English essayist whose early death was commemorated by Alfred Tennyson in *In Memoriam*. Hallam was a member of the Cambridge Apostles, a society which brought together an intellectual and literary elite among Cambridge university undergraduates.

9. John Stuart Mill describes the influence Charles Austin (1799–1874) had over his peers at Cambridge in Chapter Three of his *Autobiography*. In 1847, during the railway boom, rumor circulated that Austin had earned as much as 100,000 pounds.

10. Simcox also discusses the life of Mary Somerville (1780–1872) in a review of *Personal Recollections of Mary Somerville* for the *Fortnightly Review* in 1874.

11. A double-first is the highest rating for a university exam.

12. "A Mediæval Latin Poem," reproduced in the *English Historical Review*, July 1887, may be referred to as a specimen of a copious kind of literature. [Simcox's note]

13. Samuel Richardson (1689–1761). English novelist whose work *Pamela* (1740–41) dealt with questions of a maid's virtue.

XIII. Clementina Black
(1853–1922)

Both the life and work of Clementina Black, author, labor reformer, and suffragist, are characterized by unshakeable pragmatism and persistence. While she is the author of numerous novels, histories, translations, and collections of short fiction, it is her work in the labor and suffrage movements that designates her place in Victorian history. She was instrumental in the development of British trade unionism, in particular its inclusion of working women, and she brought to the middle-class reading public the voices and experiences of British workers.

Clementina Black was born in Brighton, the eldest daughter of Clara Patten Black, who was daughter of prominent portrait painter George Patten. Her father, David Black, was a coroner and town clerk. The family's travels in Europe and their acquaintance with artistic and intellectual figures of the day must have influenced young Clementina's education, for which her mother was principally responsible. The male children of the family assisted in the mathematical training of their sisters, and Clementina herself was educated primarily at home. It is also of note that all the Black children were raised as atheists. After her mother's death in 1875, Black moved to London, where she studied privately at the British Museum and was aided by Richard Garnett, her sister's husband. Garnett exerted profound influence over Black; through him and through her sister Constance's involvement with the Fabian Society, Black met many of the people who were to influence her career, including Eleanor Marx, Emilia Dilke, the poet Amy Levy, and John Burns.

Following the Trafalgar Square riots in 1886, Black became involved with the Women's Protective and Provident League, thus beginning a career in the trade union movement which would prove distinguished and productive. After serving as secretary of the League, Black helped form the militant Women's Trade Union Association. Her greatest contributions to the movement sprang from her concern that working women were inadequately represented in both unions and union rhetoric. This conviction resulted in her forming, with Burns, the Women's Industrial Council in 1894, an organization dedicated to legislative lobbying and to garnering the involvement of both sexes and all classes in the labor struggle. Black's activities in the women's suffrage movement were also predicated on her concern for British working women, and her emphasis on their right to play a part in their own political fate is notable. Black continued to work in the labor and suffrage movements until her death from cardiac arrest in 1922, holding office not only in the WPPL and the WIC, but also in the London Society for Women's Suffrage, the National Union of Women's Suffrage Societies, and the National Anti-Sweating League. Throughout her life, Black's social work had been volunteer; she supported herself and her orphaned niece for two and a half decades on a £1000 inheritance. Her will left the remaining £39 to that niece.

Black's nonfiction prose is grounded in the same pragmatism that must have been the basis for her frugality. Unlike many canonical Victorian prose writers, Black is fundamentally uninterested in philosophical abstraction. Her seventy-odd essays, published between 1887 and 1919, appear in a wide range of periodicals, from the mainstream *Longman's Magazine*, *Contemporary Review*, and *Fortnightly Review*, to the highly specialized *Common Cause*, *Women's Industrial News*, and the *Englishwoman*. Most of her essays address specifically the major labor and women's issues of the day. Clarity and debate-like rhetoric are the hallmark of such significant essays as "Caveat Emptor" (*Longman's*, 1887), "The Coercion of Trade Unions" (*Contemporary Review*, 1892), and "What Is a Fair Wage?" (*New Review*, 1893). She was equally concerned with the education of the working classes themselves: in 1900 she published *The Rhyme of the Factory Act*, a catalog in rhyming tetrameter of worker's rights and responsibilities under the current legislation, and in a later series of articles which became *A New Way of Housekeeping* (1918), she outlined a proposal for the organization of domestic service. It is perhaps this pedagogical style, in an age characterized by flamboyant rhetoric and exalted subject matter, which has caused Black to fade from literary attention. However, this explanation alone is inadequate to account for the disappearance from social history of a woman who, along with Emma Paterson and Edith Simcox, was a primary force of the British women's labor movement. In light of her considerable influence on British attitudes regarding labor, her career—especially her writing—deserves a second look.

The critical biography of Black has yet to be undertaken. Liselotte Glage's *Clementina Black: A Study in Social History and Literature* (1981) does contain the biographical footwork, but is thin, and principally concerned with Black's fiction. For accounts of how Black's activism fit into the larger picture of Victorian social work, consult Carl Chinn's *They Worked All Their Lives: Women of the Urban Poor, 1880–1939* (1988) and Ellen F. Mappen's "Strategists for Change: Social Feminist Approaches to the Problems of Women's Work" in *Unequal Opportunities: Women's Employment in England, 1800–1918* (1986), edited by Angela V. John. A substantial obituary appeared in the *Times* on December 20, 1922.

Alison Valtin,
Temple University

28. The Coercion of Trade Unions

Introduction

Clementina Black's "The Coercion of Trade Unions," reprinted here from the October, 1892, *Contemporary Review*, appeared during the most active years of the early British trade union movement. Black had recently resigned from the Women's Protective and Provident League and was deep in the process of organizing what would become the Women's Industrial Council, one of the most influential labor lobbying groups of the day.

As a concise pedagogical introduction to the operation and function of organized labor, this essay can scarcely be equalled. Presupposing an antagonistic reading audience, Black structures the article as a debate, anticipating virtually all conceivable counterarguments and dispensing with each of them in their turn. Her tone is never strident or argumentative; it does occasionally, however, indulge in a gentle ridicule of upper-class ignorance of working life.

The Coercion of Trade Unions

Yes, Trade Unions do exercise coercion. To deny or to blink the fact is to misunderstand the reason of their existence. They do, undeniably, compel their members to accept or refuse certain conditions of employment, according, not to individual contracts, but to rules made by the Union. Furthermore they do, to the utmost of their power, prevent persons who refuse the Union conditions from getting work at all.

That they do these things is the burden of the complaints and accusations brought against them by persons who know the facts. Other complaints and accusations are indeed often made, but only by persons who do not know the facts. Nothing, for instance, is commoner than to hear a middle-class speaker arise in a meeting and declare that the one thing which he cannot pardon in Trade Unions is their unfair plan of insisting that all men shall be paid alike, and that a man who does better work than another shall not receive better pay. The fact is that no such rule exists in any Trade Union of which I ever heard; and I do not believe that even the least enlightened of Trade Unionists would dream of advocating such a plan. What a Union does enact is, not that there shall be a universal rate, but that there shall be a *minimum* rate, below which no man's pay shall fall. If any man can, by private arrangement or personal ability, secure a higher rate, he is at perfect liberty to do so. That so few, even with the Union rate as a platform, do succeed in rising much above it, only shows how well the Unions have mostly succeeded in pushing up the general rate.

There are, indeed, some cases in which the extra wage of one worker would tend to drive downward the general rate; and in these cases Unions do interfere to prevent the acceptance of that extra wage.

Here is a typical example—one of a dozen within my own observation. Some years ago, a few women in a tailoring factory received coats of a new pattern to make, and were paid for them at a slightly better rate than usual. One woman, by great exertions, by working in her meal hours, by leaving late and coming early, succeeded more than once, in making three coats in the time hitherto employed in making two. Her companions warned her. They said: "You'll make it hard for all of us. The prices will be put down, and we shall have to slave our hardest to make three coats in the time of two." She, poor woman, was in great need of the few additional shillings, and she gave no heed. In a few weeks the prophesied reduction came, and she and her companions were alike compelled to work at increased pressure in order to earn their previous wage.

Now, if there had existed in this case a Trade Union of any validity, this too strenuous worker would undoubtedly have been subjected to coercion. She would not have been allowed to overwork herself and gain better pay for a few weeks, at the price of having to overwork ever afterwards without getting better pay. This woman was not thus coerced by a Trade Union. But I think it will be pretty obvious to any fair-minded person that, though it was not the Trade Union which coerced them, yet she and her companions were to all effects and purposes subjected to a very real coercion. Because one of them had not been compelled by the organised will of her fellow-workers to refrain from overwork, therefore all were compelled, by the pressure of unorganised competition, to submit to overwork.

The truth is that there is no such thing as "free" labour for the wage earner who stands alone without a Union. The single worker, unless his skill is such as to give him a practical monopoly, or unless no other man is asking for the same work, cannot at present make a free contract with his employer. That, I am well aware, will seem to many readers a preposterous statement. But what are the facts? He must have work or starve, and he cannot hold out for better terms, because some other man needing work equally, and equally pressed by starvation, will come in and take his place. Nay more, in nine cases out of ten, the employer cannot make a free contract either; he cannot, if he would, offer higher payment, because some other employer will take that other worker at a lower wage, and will be able, by that means, to sell lower in the market, and so draw away his custom.

I am anxious to put clearly the tyranny to which both employers and workers are subject in a state of unrestricted competition, because many persons see in Trade Unions only the objectionable feature that they interfere with freedom of action. It is quite true that they do interfere with freedom of action, but it is also true that freedom of action ceases to exist where there are no Trade Unions. That is what middle-class and upper-class critics for the most part entirely fail to comprehend. Mr. Gladstone, for instance, perceives that there would be an excessive interference with personal liberty "in prohibiting a seamstress from working unlimited hours in her own home," but he appears quite blind to the infringement of liberty betokened by the mere fact of her so working. Yet it is pretty obvious that no woman would work fourteen or sixteen hours a day for a pittance of a few shillings weekly, if she had any liberty of choice in the matter.

To be under the compulsion of the law of unlimited competition, which may force him to work at a lower rate, whether he will or no; or to be under the compulsion of the Union rules, which may restrict him from working at a lower rate, whether he will or no; these are, in plain truth, the alternatives offered to the worker. Beyond these, there remains to him only the liberty of dying—a liberty, it may fairly be remarked, shared by every slave since the world began.

Now there are material differences between these two forms of compulsion.

First.—The one is an intentional guiding of effects by a reasoned adjustment of causes; the other is the resultant of unguided, disconnected actions, pressing in an unintended and undesired direction.

Second.—The one compulsion forces men positively to do something; the other only forces them to abstain from doing something; and to be compelled against one's will to do, is more unpleasant than to be compelled against one's will to abstain.

Third.—The one compulsion enforces something naturally displeasing to most men—*i.e.*, lower pay and longer hours of work; the other enforces something naturally pleasing to most men—*i.e.*, higher pay and shorter hours of work.

When we have fully grasped these differences, and when we have made quite clear to ourselves that compulsion is just as much compulsion when it is exerted by the blind forces which result from no man's will but from all men's unregulated action as when it is exerted by any organised body of men or by an Act of Parliament, we begin to understand the real nature of the struggle between the Unionist and the non-Unionist. It is, in the long run, a struggle to decide whether all men and women shall be prevented from working under bad conditions or whether all men and women shall be driven to do so. For, speaking largely and disregarding exceptions, it must be all one way or all the other. Let me quote, on this point, an impartial man, who understood these things, and was not afraid to utter his knowledge more than twenty years ago—the late Professor Fleeming Jenkin:

> If any individual who pleased could work overtime without entailing equal work on all his fellows, there would

be little or no objection to overtime, but if overtime is made
at all, it must be made by the large proportion of men
employed in a shop. The engine must be at work, the gas
burning, the timekeeper at the gate, the foreman present; and
does any one suppose that this can be done for an odd man
here and there who wishes to get on, or earn extra pay? No;
the rule in a shop is that all or none work overtime. . . . It
may be inconvenient to a few of their number not to have the
opportunity of making more, but it would be intolerable that
a mass of workmen should night after night, and year after
year, have all of them to work till 10 o'clock, in order that 1
per cent. of their number should rise to be a master, or even
that 5 per cent. with extra large families should be more at
their ease.

It is thus strictly true that the Unionist is always fighting for
better conditions for the non-Unionist as well as for himself, while the
action of the non-Unionist is always tending to lower the working
conditions of the Unionist. And the Unionist is conscious of the fact,
while the non-Unionist is only conscious that the Unionist casts
opprobrious epithets at him for taking work where and how he can get
it, and for refusing obedience and contributions.

The Unionist, in short, is in the position of a citizen, who, in
the absence of any paving and lighting rate, should join a voluntary
association for paving and lighting his district. I[t] would not be
possible to exclude from a share in the use of these improvements any
non-contributors whose houses abutted on the paved and lighted
highways; and such inhabitants would enjoy these advantages at the
expense of their neighbours. It may be quite true that it may be worth
the contributors' while to pay the extra shares rather than do without
the improvements, but it is also true that each has to pay more for
them than if all who enjoyed them paid a share; and it is natural—it is
even just—that those who pay should resent the non-payment of other
participators. This resentment must not, in any moderately civilised
community, be permitted to go the length of flinging the disputed
paving-stones at the non-subscribers' heads, or applying to their houses
a light from the disputed lamps; but it might, and probably would, go
the length of "cutting" these offenders. People who paid the voluntary
toll would, by preference, give their custom to tradesmen who paid it; if
they had houses to let, they would prefer tenants who would pay it;
they might even go so far as refusing to take a house from any landlord

who let other houses to non-contributors, and thereby increased their own proportional payments.

In the end, however, the toll-paying majority would probably insist upon placing the whole matter of paving and lighting in the hands of a representative, publicly organised body, which would thenceforward collect rates from all residents alike, whether they individually desired lamps and sidewalks, or whether they preferred a continuance of mud and darkness. A distinct inclination is shown by the younger Trade Unionists to follow a similar course, and to secure for each new advance which they may gain, the permanence of parliamentary enactment. Personally, I believe this course to be a logical development, and likely to lead, on the whole, to beneficial results. To expound this view, however, or to forecast these results, would be beyond the scope of the present paper.

Meanwhile, the Trade Unions, as voluntary combinations for objects believed to be desirable on behalf of all workers alike, are doing their best, in the channels allowed them by law, to secure their main aim of better pay and better conditions.

Let us consider briefly—first, whether they have attained these ends; secondly, what have been their methods; thirdly, whether in trying to attain or in attaining these advantages they have brought about other disadvantages, and, if so, whether these disadvantages do or do not outweigh the gains.

The object of many of the older Unions is defined in substance as "the securing of fair pay and good conditions of work for all its members." Some Unions, however, include "all workers in the trade," and many "new" Unionists declare "the abolition of poverty" to be the aim and end of Trade Unionism.

That Trade Unions have improved the industrial position of their own members is, I think, indisputable. The workers in well-organised trades are appreciably better paid than those in less organised kindred trades, or than their own predecessors in the days before the Union. This is true of unskilled trades no less than of skilled ones. The shortening of working hours, in almost all cases where it has been attained, has been the result of Trade Union action. Moreover, Trade Unions have, in a considerable measure, taken on themselves burdens which must otherwise have fallen on the rates. Many of them grant allowances in sickness, lack of work, and old age; and many men whose cases are not provided for under the Union rules are prevented from coming upon the rates by the voluntary assistance of their fellow members, to whom the circumstances are known. In another way Trade Unions indirectly diminish poverty by helping to prevent the fall of wages to that point at which apprenticeship is made impossible by the fact that the parents cannot afford to let the child's time go unpaid for. The children of very ill-paid parents cannot afford the training of the skilled worker; they press in to the over-full unskilled market and help to intensify the poverty already existing.

Unions then have in some measure mitigated the evils of low wages as far as their own members are concerned.

We are next to consider what are the methods in which Trade Unions deal with (*a*) their own members; (*b*) the non-Union workers; (*c*) the employers. The methods by which a Union tries to enforce its decrees upon workers may be briefly and fairly described as voluntary association supplemented by moral pressure and the boycott.

(*a*) Of its own members it requires regular contributions, and the sacrifice of their personal desire whenever they desire to work under conditions of which the universal enforcement would be an injury to workers at large. In return, the Union guarantees that each shall himself in like manner be protected from the risk of competition on the part of any other member.

(*b*) As to non-Unionists, the true aim of a Trade Union is to bring them in; and failing that, to make it unpleasant for them to remain outside. A few Unions have, at times, been so stupid as not to perceive this primary need of inclusion, and have made it difficult for non-Unionists to obtain membership—a most mistaken policy. Beyond persuasion and argument, the legitimate weapon brought to bear on the non-Unionist is a refusal to work beside him. I say the "legitimate" weapon, because the right to refuse to work for any particular master is one which can be denied to no man without reducing him to the level of a slave. So long as the Union says "We will not work," it is within its lawful limits; so soon as it begins to say, "You shall not work," or, "You shall not employ," it transcends them—a difference which has not always been clearly apprehended by legal gentlemen sitting in the seat of judgment. The refusal to work with the non-Unionist is defended on the ground that either the action of the non-Unionist imperils the Unionist's position by making easier a general reduction of wages, or else the non-Unionist is getting the advantages of the Union conditions without paying for them. Intimidation—that is, threats and violence—

are supposed by some ignorant persons to be habitual weapons of a Trade Union. This is emphatically not the case. I do not say that the conduct of the too zealous Unionist who, in the heat of conflict, breaks the head of the blackleg, has always been treated by his executive with the reprobation which it undoubtedly deserves, but I do say that an executive, as such, seldom or never promotes intimidation; and further, that, if it did, it would lose its authority with the majority of its members.

(c) As regards the employer the methods of the Union are two: discussion, through official representatives, and a combined refusal to work. The weapon of the Union is, in short, the power of striking. Yet, paradoxical as it may appear, the existence of a strong Union diminishes the number of strikes. The strike is the first resource of the disorganised; it is the last resource of the Union. The inordinate number of petty strikes which take place among non-Union workers in scattered factories is a thing of which I had no suspicion until I came into close relation with the poorer class of London factory workers. The leaders of such strikes have no influence with newspapers, and the public never hears of them; whereas publicity is immediately sought by a Union whose members are on strike. It is true that Union strikes, though fewer—much fewer—in number, are more severe and prolonged than strikes of the unorganised or ill-organised. They are, in short, not guerilla skirmishes, but decisive battles. As such, they are prefaced by diplomatic dealings—representations, discussions, conferences; and these give to both sides time for reflection and an opportunity of coming to a better understanding. In nine cases out of ten, an actual strike is averted by these preliminaries. On the whole, Union strikes are undertaken after the cost has been counted, reasons weighed, and preparations made. No doubt, in spite of all this, there have been injudicious Union strikes but to say that, is only to say that Trade Unions, like other human institutions from the House of Lords downwards, are not infallible.

The question remains whether, in trying to attain their ends, the Trade Unions have brought about other disadvantages, and if so, whether these new evils are less or greater than the old.

As regards the Trade Unionist, what harm does the Trade Union do him? It sometimes, no doubt, keeps him out of work, when he might have work on non-Union conditions. In return, however, it gives him an allowance in lieu of that lower wage, and his chance of sharing the advantage of a higher wage all round. There are undeniably cases in which the total defeat of a Union has meant ruin to many of its members. I will not quote instances; they are not many, but they are still too bitterly remembered to be good to think or speak of. In comparison with the general improvement in the condition of Trade Union workers, however, the losses are proportionately very small.

As regards the workers outside the Union, what injury, if any, do Trade Unions do? They do, I have no doubt at all, make the battle of life harder for the incompetent and the shiftless. They tend to make a clear boundary line, on the one side of which is the well paid man in work, and on the other side, the absolutely unpaid man out of work. That is, undoubtedly, a hardship for the one incompetent and feckless individual, but is it an injury to the community? Is it not very much to be desired that the problem of the unemployed—a real problem, though a problem involving, I believe, a far smaller number of persons than it now appears to involve—should be left uncomplicated by the presence of the vast class of half-employed and half-paid persons who, in effect, subsist partly on the labour of some one else, and help to drag that some one else down to their own level? It cannot, I fear, be doubted, that there exists among us a class of persons who cannot, in our present commercial system, be employed with profit to themselves and others. For these the Trade Union has no help. Their own work will not keep them; our civilisation forbids us to leave them avowedly to starve. In the long run the nation has to keep them; and the sooner the nation faces the problem and sets to work to keep them systematically, humanely, and cheaply the better for us all.

Finally, as to the great indictment of all; have Trade Unions done harm to the country by driving away trade? The question is difficult to answer, because every particular instance has different factors and requires to be examined separately, and to do this exhaustively would demand a volume. That the action of Trade Unions shortens the agony of any inevitably declining trade, I cannot doubt; and I think it more than likely that there are certain trades in which more work would be done in England if there were no Trade Unions. But then such work would be done at a lower wage-rate; and low wages, no less than diminished employment, mean low purchasing power on the part of workpeople, who form the largest class of purchasers; and low purchasing power means diminution of trade in one direction or another.

What amount of national wealth this country might have secured if Trade Unions had never existed it is impossible to say; but we do know that, with things as they are, the average national income—the amount per head—goes on increasing. We know that on the whole our Trade Unions have got for their members shorter hours and better pay than belong to any other working-class in Europe; we also know that this country, in which the Unions are strongest, is the most prosperous in Europe. These facts prove that the action of Trade Unions does not prevent a high and increasing degree of national wealth; they do not, of course, prove that the Unions have been the cause of this prosperity, but they go far to suggest that their existence has at least been one of its factors.

29. What Is a Fair Wage?

Introduction

Clementina Black's "What Is A Fair Wage?," published in the *New Review* in May, 1893, and reprinted here from that periodical, was written during Black's most active years in the labor movement. Aimed at the magazine's middle- and upper-class readership, it is a response to the prevailing argument that wages could be determined by their market value without regard for the worker's ability to subsist on them. In this article, Black counters that assertion with a concise point-by-point, working-class perspective on the market-based wage system.

"What Is A Fair Wage?" exemplifies Black's two principal rhetorical goals. First, it introduces into the labor debate the voice of working-class experience—an experience which only infrequently appears in middle-class periodicals. Second, it vividly evinces Black's clarity and conviction in her argument for a new wage system.

What Is a Fair Wage?

There are few phrases more current at the present day than those which include the expression "a fair wage." All workers demand it, and I never met an employer who did not maintain that he paid it, though I have known some who frankly admitted that their "fair wage" was one on which the worker who received it could not live. To any timid inquirer venturing to point out this peculiarity the reply is given: "But the work is not worth more," and the reply generally silences the inquirer for a moment—whereby the employer comes to believe it unanswerable.

In the inquirer's mind arise eventually two questions: "Can a wage be fair on which the wage earner cannot live?" and "Has labour a worth measurable otherwise than by the market price?"

The present paper is an attempt to set forth the answers which have gradually shaped themselves in the mind of one inquirer since the day—five years and a-half ago—when she first heard a wealthy employer say cheerfully, and without shame: "Oh no, they can't live upon it; but they live at home with their parents." These notes do not pretend to offer a detailed "log" or scale of fair payments; their utmost aim is to set forth a general principle.

When we begin revolving that statement that "the work is not worth more," it presently occurs to us that the "worth" of work has two aspects: that its price to the buyer and its cost to the worker are not the same. The price to the buyer, which is its "worth" in the phrase quoted, is neither more nor less than its market price, or, in other words, the price brought about by the balance of the competition between those who want to buy work and the competition of those who want to sell it. This price is regulated solely by the numbers competing on either hand, and by their greater or less degree of combined action. But the cost of work to the worker is the expenditure of energy which he has made upon it. Labour, like every other commodity, has a certain cost of production. Every hour's work takes out of the worker a proportion of health, strength, and tissue—of vital energy, in short; and this expenditure can only be made good by a corresponding amount of nourishment, rest and warmth. When we extract from the worker a greater expenditure than he can restore out of the amount we pay him, he is, in the truest possible sense, a loser by the transaction, and the wage we have paid him must, if the word "fair" is to retain any significance at all, be called an unfair one. When, for example, a railway servant is kept on duty for sixteen hours a day, he wastes more force in those sixteen hours than can be made up in the remaining eight, and no conceivable wage can be adequate repayment, because no money can enable him to put ten hours' repose into eight. He has, in very truth, *payé de sa personne*.

Here, then, we appear to approach something like an equitable measure of a fair wage for labour. A remunerative price for any commodity is one which repays the cost of production and leaves a margin—that margin being the seller's profit. The cost of production of labour is the cost of keeping in efficient condition, physically and mentally, the human being who produces it, and we must reckon among the items of this efficiency the cost of supporting old age and childhood. Thus, a man whose merchandise is his own labour may reasonably consider that, unless he can make up all that he has expended in the way of bodily substance, he has not been repaid his cost of production, and that until he has received something in addition he has made no profit on the sale of his labour.

When, therefore, we pay for an hour's work at such a rate that the worker could not, in a moderate day's work at that rate, receive enough to cover the expenses of keeping himself in health and strength, we are taking from him more than we give him back; in other words, not only are we not paying him anything for his work, but we are not even repaying him what his work actually costs him; and the lowest wage that can possibly be a fair one is a wage which, applied to a reasonable number of hours of work, would form a comfortable, healthy living for the worker and enable him to provide for the incapable years of his own age and his children's youth.

It may be worth while to consider the results which follow from the payment of unfair wages at the present time.

Unfortunately there is a good deal of labour which is performed thus at a loss to the worker. On each transaction he pays out a little more than he receives back. He becomes, at each step, a little poorer in bodily resources. He is never quite sufficiently clothed, quite sufficiently fed, or healthily housed; and he never has that reasonable certainty of the morrow's provision which goes so far to give peace of mind and health of body. Finally, he becomes bankrupt; that is to say, he either dies—several years earlier than the average of men who are better paid—or he sinks into the invalid condition of the pauper.

Yes, some reader will say, it is bad that these persons should be so inadequately paid, but it is better than if they had no work, and therefore no pay, at all. "Half a loaf is better than no bread." No doubt—if that were the choice, and if each individual stood solitary. But we are so locked together that the acceptance by a few workers of half a loaf instead of a whole one means half loaves for the workers all round. And that any whole class of workers should be unable to earn a living wage by working is a far worse state of things than that some members of that class should be unable to get work. To underpay a person who would else have nothing tends, like alms-giving, to aggravate on a large scale the woes which it relieves on a small, and for the same reason, namely, because it tends to lower the average rate of wages. Every person who in any department of labour is receiving less than a subsistence wage is helping to make a non-subsistence wage the rule in that department, and thereby rendering it impossible for any man or woman to live by that sort of labour—a point which cannot be too often repeated to women, who desire, as they say, "to make a little," and who forget that they are making it impossible for other women to earn a livelihood. Moreover, it may fairly be pointed out that every person who is not living solely upon the payment for his own work is living partly upon the payment for somebody else's, and thereby reducing that somebody's income.

Yes, the unsatisfied reader will say once more, it is no doubt very desirable that every person should receive what you would call a fair wage, but it is not commercially possible. The attempt would so diminish trade as to throw out of work an additional number of people, whose added competition would inevitably reduce the average wage to a lower level than at present. It may be remarked that this view involves the admission that we live under commercial conditions which render dishonesty not only the best but actually the only possible policy. Such a belief would appear to furnish an unanswerable argument in favour of the destruction of such commercial conditions, and it seems difficult to understand how any humane man can hold it and not become a convinced revolutionary; yet, strange to say, it is not in the mouth of the revolutionary but in the mouth of the upholder of things existing that it is heard most frequently. Is the belief true? Is it the fact that the payment of fair wages—as here defined—would mean diminished employment?

Let us examine a little what might be expected to happen in various trades, if it were no longer possible to get work at a price which would not support the worker. The various trades would fall into four classes.

1. Those in which wages are already at the "fair" level, which would undergo no change.

2. Those in which there is a margin rendering possible a rise of wages without a corresponding rise of selling price.

In these there might be a certain drawing-away of capital, consequent on the diminution of profits, and, if so, there would be a proportionate diminution, for a time at least, in the numbers employed.

3. Those in which it would become worthwhile to introduce improved methods, such as speedier machinery.

These improvements would often lead to actual reductions of selling price, and these reductions would in their turn so stimulate demand as to lead to the employment, sooner or later, of at least as many workers as were at first displaced. This class of trades would, I believe, be far the largest. The association of higher wages and improved methods of production is almost proverbial.

4. Those trades in which wages could not be raised at the present selling price without the total disappearance of profits, and in which, therefore, a rise of wages must mean also a rise of selling price.

Such trades appear to be few. We will consider in more detail one—the cheapest branch of the ready-made shirt trade—which seems, on inquiry, to be among them.

But, before passing to this, let me point out that every previously underpaid man and woman will now, according to our hypothesis, have additional money to spend, and that this additional money will be spent in putting men and women to work in some branch or another. Should the trades in Class 2 and Class 3 prove very numerous, the additional money spent by workers in those trades may suffice to employ all the persons who previously worked in the small Class 4, even if every trade in that class should become extinct.

To return to Class 4 and the cheap ready-made shirts. I have convinced myself: 1st, that the wages paid to women in this branch are not in any broad and humane sense subsistence wages; 2nd, that any employer who substantially raised those wages would, at the present selling prices, lose on the sale of his goods. This is merely another way of saying that the cheapest branch of the ready-made shirt trade is, in truth, being carried on at a loss to some of the persons concerned in it—namely, to the women employed in sewing the shirts, who, unless they are subsidised, end, like other losing traders, in the workhouse. Now, if these shirts were no longer sold at a loss, if, for instance, the shirts that can now be bought retail at 11 3/4 *d*. (I am not inventing this price; I have noted it myself more than once) could no longer be bought for less than, say, 1*s*. 2*d*., what would happen?

Clearly, the shirts would either cease to be bought, or they would continue to be bought at a higher price. If they continued to be bought, there would, on every purchase, be a diversion of twopence-farthing from some other channel of trade; and this twopence-farthing, instead of being spent in some other direction by the shirt-buyer, would now be spent (supposing, that is, that it ever percolated through her employer to her) by the shirtmaker. And since, while she goes short of that twopence-farthing, she pays the difference literally out of her flesh and blood, equity would seem to demand that she should receive it. If the shirt costs, in material, in supervision, in distribution, and in the actual substance of the women who make it, 1s. 2*d*., then to sell it or to buy it is (to speak plainly) to take part in a robbery of those women—a robbery to which they submit because it is worse to be starved than to be robbed, and because they lack the combination which would enable them to resist both robbery and starvation. It is also to do an injury to the community, which, in the long run, has to supplement the wages of these women, either by personal charity, by hospitals, workhouses, or burial expenses, in order that certain men may be enabled to buy certain shirts at a lower price than that for which they can profitably be made.

If, on the other hand, the shirts would cease to be bought at a higher price than 11 3/4 *d*., then the fact is that the demand for them is not equal to the cost of producing them: the trade is, in truth, a factitious one, and it would be better that the money and enterprise engaged in it should be turned to producing goods that are more wanted.

That individual workers, and, indeed, whole classes of workers, must suffer displacement by the cessation of this, or any other unprofitable trade, is true; but it is nevertheless better that such trades should cease: better for the whole working class, and for the whole nation. That anything is good for trade which increases the purchasing power of the largest purchasing class, *i.e.*—the workers—will hardly at this time of day be questioned; and the payment of a "fair" wage (in the sense here used) to all workers would undoubtedly increase the purchasing power of those many hundreds whose wage is to-day below the standard.

It appears, then, that the dangers apprehended by the pessimist would not follow upon the universal payment of fair wages; and that in economics, as in morals, it is true, for the race if not always for the individual, that honesty is the best policy.

30. The Dislike to Domestic Service

Introduction

Clementina Black's "The Dislike to Domestic Service" appeared in the *Nineteenth Century* in March, 1893, and is reprinted here from that periodical. The article represents Black's most overt attempt to compel her readers to consider the working class's point of view on the labor question. It was published in response to two earlier articles on the subject of domestic service, the first by Elizabeth Alicia M. Lewis and the second by George Somes Layard. Both of these earlier articles were patronizing and dismissive in their discussion of domestic service. Lewis argued that British households, because they no longer grow and prepare the bulk of their own foodstuffs, should phase out the practice of hiring a large live-in staff: domestic servants, she claimed, require too much food, too much time off, and are generally obtrusive and untrustworthy. Layard expanded on Lewis's argument by devising an elaborate scheme for replacing the "empty-headed" domestic cook with a centralized, Victorian version of the modern-day carry-out. Both articles advocated the abandonment of live-in service as a boon to the employer. Appearing after these articles, Black's support of the domestic servant from the perspective of organized labor must have been read with some incredulity.

The impact of this essay is twofold. First, it gives the object of debate—the domestic servant—a voice. More significant, however, is Black's rhetorical style. No doubt conscious that the perception of both the labor and suffrage movements as radical, violent, and irrational obstructed communication with a wide audience, Black adopts a gently remonstrative tone, just shy of condescension. In this debate, it is the conservative upper class which appears to shriek.

The Dislike to Domestic Service

Two articles have lately appeared in this Review, advising a certain rearrangement of the present conditions of domestic service. Both dealt with the matter almost entirely from the point of view of the employing householder. The following brief paper (which was in great part written before the appearance of the earlier article) approaches the same question from the point of view of the servant.

That most young women of the working class dislike domestic service is generally admitted; and there is a certain inclination on the part of persons who find this dislike inconvenient, to preach against it as a sort of depravity. The truth, however, is that these young women—like other classes of working people—understand their own needs and their own discomforts a great deal better than these are understood by their middle-class critics.

The conditions of domestic service are still those of an earlier industrial and social system, and this earlier form does not harmonise with the sentiments of to-day. In other employments, the person employed sells a certain number of hours of labour, and, when those hours are over, all relation ceases between employed and employer. The worker has, in short, a life of her own, absolutely apart from her industrial life. The servant has no such life of her own. Her existence may, perhaps, best be realised by a perusal of those chapters of Madame d'Arblay's Diary in which are recorded her experiences as an attendant on Queen Charlotte. In this instance, the waiting-maid—for a waiting-maid in truth she was—regarded her position as one of distinction, and professed an almost religious regard for her mistress. Yet is there any reader of her vivid narrative to whom the position does not seem intolerable? She is at beck and call from morning till night: her companions and her immediate superior are not of her own choosing, and are not sympathetic. She is exiled from her family and from her personal friends. Smiles and civility are expected from her, whatever her mood or state of health, and whatever the conduct towards her of the persons with whom she is brought into contact, even when one of these is a son of the household in a state of intoxication.

The domestic servant, in short, still lives under a system of total personal subservience. Now, a feeling has gradually grown up that total personal subservience is intolerable and degrading; and it is this feeling which causes domestic service to be held in low social esteem by women who are often harder worked and less materially prosperous than most servants. The servant is despised, not because she cooks, or scrubs, or nurses a baby, still less because she has to yield obedience to orders—every factory worker has to do that in working hours—but because she consents to put herself permanently at some other person's beck and call.

One consequence of this position is that the servant is practically removed from her own circle and placed in another. I am afraid that a good many of the well-to-do are apt, in the ignorance of their Pharisaism, to regard such transplantation as an unmitigated advantage to the working man's daughter. Yet it is surely obvious that, whatever may be a young girl's social station, there are dangers in withdrawing her from the family influences in which she has grown up, and from free intercourse with her social equals. These dangers are increased if her education has left her comparatively unable to keep up an intimate correspondence by letter, or to fill up her solitude by any study. Yet more are these dangers intensified if young women thus withdrawn from their natural surroundings are at the same time required to obey a fixed and conventional code of manners. A servant on duty behaves according to rules of strict etiquette—that is to say, she exercises a prolonged self-restraint. Older people—especially older people of a different social grade—are apt to consider such self-restraint very salutary, and to desire that she should remain perpetually within that barrier of etiquette. Nature, however, is of a different mind, and has made young people of all grades averse to a life thus regulated; she has given them an eager hunger for equal companionship, for change, and especially for freedom. If the longing for these things does not find gratification in safe and permitted ways, it is likely to make for itself ways that are dangerous and prohibited. This isolation, in which many servants live, remote from the restraining public opinion of their relations and their own social class, removes more than one safeguard, and leaves them exposed to dangers little realised by benevolent persons who, judging other households by their own, regard domestic service as the safest of all callings. Unfortunately, there are too many households in which an unprotected girl is liable to temptations and insults from which she would be safe in most factories and workshops. I do not wish to dwell upon this aspect of the question. It has been brought before me by instances in the experience of more than one young woman personally known to me, and it is unquestionable that the very large majority of girls who pass into Homes and Refuges have been servants. Allowance must of course be made for the fact that any known lapse from good character is a more serious obstacle to employment in the case of a servant than in that, for instance, of a factory worker; but even the most liberal deduction seems to leave the proportion excessive. No; domestic service is by no means invariably a safe haven, and to send a girl into a household of unknown character is not altogether the philanthropic action which many well-meaning persons suppose.

I must confess that, if I were a mother of girls who had to choose between factory work and service, I should give my voice unhesitatingly for the factory. The work would be probably harder, the material comforts less, and the manners rougher, but the girls would be working among their own class and living in their own home; and their health, their happiness, their companionships, would be under their mother's eye. Nor can I think that an unwillingness on the part of girls to cut themselves off from all the natural ties of kindred and surroundings, to dwell among strangers in an unknown house, and to merge their lives completely in that of an alien household, is by any means a sign of perverse folly.

The unwillingness, being thus natural, reasonable, and well-founded, is likely to be removed only by the removal of the special conditions which differentiate service from other employments. That is to say, servants must cease to be domiciled under their employer's roof, and must, instead, come to work for a specified number of hours, as dressmakers and charwomen already do. I venture to say that under these conditions domestic service would speedily become a popular department of labour. It is interesting to observe that the writers of both the articles dealing with service are advocating this same change in the interests of the employer of servants.

Of course, this change of system would require certain other alterations. It would, for instance, be quite necessary that an improved variety of registry-office should be established, which would undertake to supply competent and honest servants, each properly trained in her special branch. Already there are hundreds of small households to which such a registry would be most useful. There is, I am convinced, a profitable career awaiting the capable woman who shall be the first to organise a brigade of really good outdoor servants.

XIV. Mona Alison Caird
(1854–1932)

Mona Caird is most remembered for her polemical essays on the inequities of marriage, the corpus of which were published in the late 1880s and through the 1890s. She was also a novelist, and her best known work is the New Woman novel *The Daughters of Danaus*, which was also written in this period (1894). Like her kindred spirit and contemporary Sarah Grand, Caird's strong and unequivocal voice could not be ignored by the reading public. In fact, one of Caird's first essays, "Marriage," provoked 27,000 responses to the *Daily Telegraph*'s letters column after the essay's 1888 appearance in the *Westminster Review*.

Alice Mona Alison was born in Ryde on the Isle of Wight on May 24, 1854, and grew up in Kensington. Her mother, Matilde Ann Jane Hector, was from a well-to-do family in Schleswig-Holstein. Her father, John Alison, was an engineer and landed proprietor. At age twenty-three she married a Scot named James Alexander Henryson-Caird, a wealthy farmer, and they had a son, Alister. Little is known about their marriage or Caird's personal life in general, but from anecdotal evidence it seems that they were happily married, despite Caird's uncompromising rhetoric on the institution's injustices. She spent much time at her husband's ancestral home, Cassencary, on the southwest coast of Scotland; the wildness of the mountain country and the romance and history of the mansion fired her imagination. The novels *Daughters of Danaus* and *The Stones of Sacrifice* both take place in such a setting. When the family was not in Scotland, they spent most of their time in or near London. Caird died in St. John's Wood, eleven years after her husband.

Although Caird did not receive a university education, she was a voracious reader in sociology, history, ethnology, economics, philosophy, feminist thought and, later, some science. She also surrounded herself with intellectuals and artists, and the Cairds' friends Elizabeth and William Sharp introduced them to Walter Pater, Dante Gabriel Rossetti, J.A. Symonds, and Dr. Garnett. As her own writing became widely read, Caird became acquainted with people such as H.D. Traill, Sydney Hall, and Emily Hickey. She also knew other progressive women writers such as Mathilde Blind, Dinah Maria Mulock Craik, and Augusta Davies Webster.

Caird's obituary in the *Times* claims that she herself was not a militant suffragist, and that ultimately she sought reform, equity, and freedom in the marriage laws—not a radical alternative to the institution. She was a member, however, of the most egalitarian feminist club in London, the Pioneers. As with many intellectuals of the day, Caird was also an ardent antivivisectionist. She wrote two significant works on the issue, *A Sentimental View of Vivisection* (1893), and *Some Truths About Vivisection* (1894). She also served briefly as President of the Independent Anti-Vivisection League at a time when George Bernard Shaw and Annie Besant were members too.

After the First World War, Caird became a pacifist, and she also developed a wariness of socialism, connecting it somehow with the eugenics movement; she warned of a future in which "degenerates" and "criminals" would be killed. Was this prediction prescient or merely odd? Her interest in futurism continued until her death. In her novel *The Great Wave*, she warned of possible wartime uses for a particle containing infinite energy.

Caird's prose style, especially in the 1890s when she wrote about a subject that was in the forefront of public debate, was impassioned, florid, and highly imaginative, if frequently overwrought. This kind of inflated rhetoric was not unusual on such hotly debated topics as the Woman Question. Caird's essays on the subject include "Marriage," "Ideal Marriage," "The Morality of Marriage," and "Does Marriage Hinder a Woman's Self-Development?". Most of these essays were published in a volume entitled *The Morality of Marriage and Other Essays on the Status and Destiny of Women* (1897). In these pieces, Caird not infrequently compares the traditional concept of marriage to slavery or prison, tenaciously sustaining the metaphors. *The Daughters of Danaus*, reviled by several of the major dailies for the same uncompromising intensity, did however receive unqualified praise in a three-part review in the April, May, and June 1895 issues of *Shaft*, a progressive journal. Although Caird's work was characterized by this highly polemical style during the late 1880s and the 1890s, with more progress in women's rights, her tone became less urgent, almost complacent. In an earlier novel, *The Wing of Azrael* (1889), she had suggested a fatalistic vision of marriage, but the marriages in her later novels, *The Pathway of the Gods* (1898), *The Stones of Sacrifice* (1915), and *The Great Wave* (1931), are more egalitarian. In addition to her novels and political essays, Caird also wrote lighter works, including a collection of stories entitled *A Romance of the Moors* (1891) and a travel book, *The Romantic Cities of Provence* (1900, 1910).

Nevertheless, Caird's sharpest writing was that for which she had her most attentive, if sometimes reactionary, audience. As a critic of the institution of marriage, her role was that of thorn in the side of patriarchal tradition, and it was one that she fulfilled with a torrent of words. Informed by a keen sense of societal transition, and yet wary of the juggernauts of habit and inertia, her double-edged sensibility gave urgency to her prose, which rarely failed to hit its mark. Caird's essays and novels of that period, together with their readers' impassioned responses, constitute a rich vein in the late-nineteenth century's discourse on the Marriage Question.

Margaret Morganroth Gullette has written recently on Caird, in an afterword to her republication of *The Daughters of Danaus* (Feminist Press, 1989).[1] This highly sympathetic essay is both a celebration and a scrupulously researched discovery of a writer about whom information is difficult to unearth. Although the only published scholarship devoted exclusively to Caird, Morganroth Gullette's research is augmented by a discussion of *Daughters of Danaus* in Gail Cunningham's 1978 study, *The New Woman in the Victorian Novel.* Cunningham's book is especially useful for seeing Caird in the context of other late Victorian feminist fiction writers. Caird's nonfiction, however, has yet to receive serious study.

Lauren D. McKinney,
Eastern Mennonite University

Notes

1.   Morganroth Gullette also reprints Caird's "Does Marriage
Hinder a Woman's Self-Development" in her Appendix.

31. The Morality of Marriage

Introduction

Mona Caird's "The Morality of Marriage" first appeared in the *Fortnightly Review* in 1890, and is reprinted here from that periodical. It was later published again with several of Caird's other essays in *The Morality of Marriage and Other Essays on the Status and Destiny of Women* (1897). In this essay, Caird attacks sentimental notions of marriage and motherhood by endeavoring to expose the oppression that such notions mask. Traditional paradigms of marriage, Caird argues, are hypocritical and shallow. With a sophisticated sense of psychology and power relations, she continues by insisting that a compulsory "stolid peace" is inferior to a freely chosen "living harmony." Ultimately, the solutions she offers include contract marriages that ensure women's economic independence, wide acceptance of birth control, and less rigid divorce laws.

This essay could be considered an answer to the conservative polemics of Eliza Lynn Linton, a vocal critic of "New Women" and suffragists. "The Morality of Marriage" can also be contextualized in terms of other debates of the day, such as the concern about "degeneracy," which Caird links to an overemphasis on childbearing, or the commonly expressed desire to return to a more primitive and less artificial mode of living. Caird believes, mistakenly, that women in less "civilized" societies have fewer children and therefore more peace of mind. It is also evident in the essay that she is naive about the traumatic effects of divorce on children, which is understandable since divorce was uncommon in that day. Cultural blind spots notwithstanding, "The Morality of Marriage" is a fervent exposé of commonly held, but frequently unexamined, beliefs about marriage.

The Morality of Marriage

"If it were not for the children, I would take a dose of chloroform to-morrow!"

These are the words of the wife of a well-to-do tradesman, who, after twelve years of marriage, finds life a burden too heavy to be borne. After much theory, a little fact, hot from the lips of a simple-minded woman, without theories, but with plenty of experience, comes with a force that is somewhat startling.

This woman recognised gratefully her worldly prosperity; there was nothing fretful about her complaints. One pitied her most when she made some unconscious admission, let fall some pathetic, patient little word, which revealed how little she asked and how much she was ready to endure. Her husband is a "good fellow" with an uncertain temper. He is capricious and imprudent, and the success of the business depends on his wife, who works at it unremittingly, sending her husband and children away for a holiday now and then, while she remains to look after the customers. The wife's industry has made the business flourish, though her husband frequently develops an inclination to sell it, in spite of her remonstrance, and in this contest he has finally prevailed, having control of the purse-strings.

The work and the anxiety during the years when the business had to be made were very severe, and during that time this woman bore six children. If it were not for them, she would "take a dose of chloroform to-morrow!" Pain, weariness, broken rest, hard work, anxiety, these have been her unceasing portion. She declares that she would infinitely prefer death to having more children; she is a maimed and wounded creature with a spoiled and shortened youth, broken nerves, weary, and at the end of her strength.

Whatever may be her feelings, she has to appear cheerful, for her husband hates to see her ailing, and she always does her utmost to please him. At her worst miseries he laughs. What is so common cannot be so very severe! She feels—and this last touch seems to make the situation, when realized, absolutely ghastly—she feels that she is wholly dependent on this man, that though she works hard for her living, she is without a penny in the world that she can call her own. With or without cause, she lives in a state of incessant dread that he may get tired of her, as he did of his business, and go away and leave her and the children penniless. Probably her fears are groundless, but that they are even possible, marks the state of dependence in which she lives. Her anxiety makes her over-watchful and suspicious; she is miserable if he stays out an hour later than usual; she is jealous and in perpetual fear of his being led away by other women. Thus her fears help to bring about their own fulfilment, for this conduct is naturally very irritating to the husband.

A union, really true to the ideas of marriage, never works smoothly, unless one or both of the yoke-fellows surrender what is strong and individual in the character. Indeed, to be quite frank, a thoroughly prosperous marriage (always granted that it be not achieved by conspiracy in rebellion) brings about—or rather is brought about by—a gradual process of brain-softening, which does much to deteriorate the raw material of society.

Perhaps in the case which we are considering there would be less unhappiness if the woman ceased to feel the injustice of her lot; but if she did so, she would sink in the scale of humanity; she would lose her self-respect. At present she feels it keenly. Is it fair, she asks, that she should be claimed body and soul for a life-time, that she should work hard and suffer much, without earning a bare subsistence? Were she not the man's wife, he would pay her a salary for far less toil, and she would be a free agent into the bargain. She seems vaguely to hanker after the cook's place in her own establishment! To work without pay—what is it but to be a slave? Whence has arisen among good men and true the state of conscience which allows them to throw upon their help-mates the severest strain of the household (even supposing that they take no part in the business), while keeping them dependent to their lives' end? Many social and economic changes must take place before *all* women can, without injury to themselves and the race, earn their own living (in the accepted sense of the term), but what is there to prevent a woman having a legal claim to a salary, when she works in her husband's business? There is an ungenerous dislike on the part of many men to the idea of a wife being her own mistress. They do not realise[1] that they are demanding what they have no moral right to demand from any human being when they endow a woman with their name and their "worldly goods." Were it possible for a wife to leave her husband without penalty if the worst came to the worst, that worst, in nine cases out of ten, would never come. One seldom hears of very bad cases of ill-treatment when a woman has private means under her own control. Wives who have begun their married life without such means, and acquired them afterwards, notice that a marked difference is discernible in the husband's attitude towards them. It is the unconscious recognition of the new status.[2]

Dependence, in short, is the curse of our marriages, of our homes and of our children, who are born of women who are not free—not free even to refuse to bear them. What is the proportion of children whose mothers were perfectly willing and able to bring them into the world, willing, in a strict sense, apart from all considerations of duty, or fear of unsanctioned sentiment? A true answer to this question would shake down many brave edifices of ignorance and cant which are now flying holiday flags from their battlements.

Nervous exhaustion and many painful forms of ill-health among women are appallingly common, and people try to find round-about explanations for the fact. Do we need explanations? The gardener takes care that his very peach-trees and rose-bushes shall not be weakened by over-production (though to produce is their sole mission); valuable animals are spared in the same way and for the same reason. It is only women for whom there is no mercy. In them the faculties are discouraged and destroyed which lead away from the domestic "sphere" and "duties," the whole nature is subjected to hot-house cultivation in such a manner as to drive all the forces into a single channel. Such treatment means over-wrought nerves, over-stimulated instincts, weakened constitution, a low intellectual development, or if otherwise a development at the cost of further physical suffering.

This misdirection of nervous energy creates innumerable miseries, and some of them seem to have become chronic, or hereditary, and from being so common have lost the very name of disease. Yet with these facts before them, people still dare to argue from the present condition and instincts of average women to the eternal mandates of nature regarding them; they still fail to see that to found a theory of society upon special adaptations of structure and impulse which they now find in a long enslaved and abused race, is to found a theory of nature upon artificial and diseased development.

The nervous strain which the civilised woman endures is truly appalling. The savage, to whom the infinite little cares and troubles, responsibilities and anxieties of modern life are unknown, has also the advantage of a far less severe tax on her strength as regards her maternal functions. Nature appears to be kind to her primitive children; their families rarely exceed two or three in number, and the task of bearing and rearing cannot be compared for severity to that of the civilised mother. It is one of the many instances of "cussedness" in nature, that a more protected, well-fed, complex life causes the race to become more prolific, thus increasing the demands upon the nervous energy from every side. People are beginning to feel the danger to the race in all this; but how do they propose to meet it? By trying to hold women back from the full possession of life, by bidding them, for Heaven's sake, keep to their appointed maternal functions! One-half of the race is to be rescued at the expense of the other! A highly moral and scientific solution of the difficulty. Highly moral and scientific men have advocated this singular method of averting the danger of race degeneration, so we must conclude that the proposal shares the qualities of its authors. Women, who already are crippled in body and mind by excessive performance of the functions of maternity, are to plunge yet further in the same disastrous direction—to cut off all chance of respite and relief, all hope of the over-taxed system righting itself by more general distribution of energy. The longing and the effort—so striking among the present generation—for a less one-sided, more healthily-balanced life, must be sternly checked. Do we not see that the mother of half-a-dozen children, who struggles to cultivate her faculties, to be an intelligent human being, nearly always breaks down under the burden, or shows very marked intellectual limitations? This naturally scares the scientific imagination, and the decree goes forth: "Cease this unwomanly effort to be intelligent; confine yourself to the useful office which Nature ordains for you. Consider the welfare of the race." At this, however, there are murmurs; a rebellion is brewing.

It is too late to press "Nature" into the service. Women are beginning to aspire to try their own experiments with Nature, ignoring the old worm-eaten sign-posts of their guides, philosophers, and friends. It is idle to attempt to lure them back into their cage, the temper of the age is against it; and although much suffering is caused by the present effort to do the old duties more perfectly than before, while adding to them a vast number of fresh duties, intellectual and social, yet the result in the long run promises to be the creation of a new balance of power, of many varieties of feminine character and aptitude, and, through the consequent influx of new ideals and activities, a social revolution, reaching in its results almost beyond the regions of prophecy. The mad attempt to move backwards against the current would, if successful, be the beginning of a retrogressive evolution, which, one must not forget, is always possible at any stage of history.[3] It is remarkable that even the one function to which a whole sex is asked to devote itself is, under the old order, very badly performed. Among men we have had division of labour; among women such a thing has scarcely existed. We give the heads of our pins into the hands of specialists; the future race may be looked after by unqualified amateurs. This is a subject which is usually slurred over; therefore it is well to look it steadily in the face. First, from the least unpopular side, the injustice to the children. I do not hesitate to say that every fifth or sixth child is a deeply injured being. Indeed in most instances the case might be put more strongly. We are so accustomed to a low standard of physical and mental power, that few of us recognise the mischief, unless the child has fits or rickets, and then there is a lurking consolatory suspicion that he has them by the grace of God. Nobody counts the miseries caused by a low vitality, by an untoward start on the race of life, by a lack of that intelligent care which the most devoted mother in the world cannot give, if she has half-a-dozen other claimants to give it to, and no time or strength or heart to acquire the knowledge that must precede it. When shall we shake off the old notion, that maternal love makes up for the lack of common sense?

Now, from the unpopular standpoint, to face the question, the mother's sufferings. These have been already dwelt upon in the earlier part of this paper, and one of the sufferers spoke out of the fulness of her heart, in support of no theory, but in the desperation of a life drained of its vital force, of its very sap and savour.[4] But this woman felt only her *positive* miseries; she did not make the claim that she justly might have made, to enjoy the other faculties that were hers, to spend her allotted time not always in one fashion.

It is a hideous ideal that we have set up for our women, and the world is wretched and diseased, because they have followed it too faithfully. An interval now of furious licence, if it must be, on the way to freedom, would be a kinder potion for this sick world than another century of "womanly" duty and virtue, as these have been provided hitherto. Happily there is no necessity to pass through such a terrible ordeal, socially or politically. The Anglo-Saxon race is not naturally addicted to "ideas," but it prefers them, if the worst comes to the worst, to revolutionary changes. A new order of life and thought first creeps in, and then floods all the heavens as the sun rises in the morning.

We have now considered two of the essential attributes of marriage as it stands—the wife's dependence, economic and social, and the supposed duty to produce as many children as Fate may decide. Take away from it these two solid props, and what but a scraggy skeleton remains of this plump and prosperous institution, appearing, if anything, a trifle over-fed, with one eye on the flesh pots, the other (when anyone is looking) on the stars? It is not yet recognised that what makes the "holy estate" so firm and inflexible are its atrocious injustices—to use no harsher word—and that if one firmly uses the surgeon's knife to these he destroys nearly all that holds the thing together. Suppose an opponent to grant this for the sake of argument; would he leave standing the institution, clamped and grappled by these injustices, rather than sacrifice its essentials? or would he say, "If this be so it cannot be a fair and sacred edifice, not having power to stand without such things!"

This brings us to the crux of the question: Is it safe for society to permit men and women to have fair play in their mutual relations? is it safe to found our State upon Liberty and Justice? Dare we substitute a broad and free ideal of the womanly character for a cramped and petty one? dare we take from marriage its barbaric elements, so that a married woman may be able to look her position frankly in the face, without resort to cant and subterfuge in order to preserve her self-respect? I go so far as to assert that no clear-headed woman can do that now without vitiating her judgment by one of the myriad methods of self-beguilement which are amply provided by thoughtful teachers for the multitudes who need them. If any adventurous wife thinks that she *can* look her position approvingly in the face, let her try to answer the arguments of Guido Franceschini, in *The Ring and the Book*, when he is pleading before the court; urging that he had acted strictly within his marriage rights in matters wherein he had been blamed by public sentiment—nay, by the august judges themselves—and that the court which upheld in all severity the gist and meaning of marriage had no right whatever to call him to account.[5] Nor had it. To do so was like giving permissions to a child, and then scolding him because he availed himself of them. Listen to him, how he cuts through the sugar-crust of pretty sentiments, and lets his knife grate harsh and straight on the skeleton fact. He has been remonstrated with for the manner of his marriage: "Are flesh and blood a ware? Are heart and soul a chattel?" cry

the public, who have some sentiment. To which Guido Franceschini
replies:—

> 'Softly, sirs!
> Will the Court of its charity teach poor me,
> Anxious to learn, of any way i' the world,
> Allowed by custom and convenience, save
> This same which, taught from my youth up, I trod?
> Take me along with you; where was the wrong step?
> If what I gave in barter, style and state,
> And all that hangs to Franceschinihood,
> Were worthless—why, society goes to ground,
> Its rules are idiots' rambling. Honour of birth—
> If the thing has no value, cannot buy
> Something of value of another sort,
> You've no reward or punishment to give
> I' the giving or the taking honour; straight
> Your social fabric, pinnacle to base,
> Comes down a-clatter like a house of cards.'
>
> .   .   .   .
>   'I thought
> To deal o' the square: others find fault it seems:'

"But," urge the critics—

> 'Purchase and sale being thus so plain a point,
> How of a certain soul bound up, may be,
> I' the barter with the body and money-bags?
> From the bride's soul what is it you expect?'

To which Guido returns:—

> 'Why, loyalty and obedience—wish and will
> To settle and suit her fresh and plastic mind
> To the loyal, not disadvantageous mould!'

Here we see Guido claiming as his right that which the reiterated
immemorial custom of wives has accorded and caused to become the
expected perquisite of husbands. The law gives no definite claim here in
black and white, but usage grants a right at least as strong.
Guido goes on:—

'With a wife I look to find all wifeliness,
As when I buy, timber and twig, a tree—
I buy the song of the nightingale inside.
Such was the pact:—Pompilia from the first
Broke it.   .   .   .   .   '

Someone has suggested that perhaps Pompilia on her side
expected love from her husband. There is a right of usage here also. To
which he replies that they are talking of marriage, not of love:—

'The everyday conditions and no more:
Where do these bind me to bestow one drop
Of blood shall dye my wife's true-love-knot pink?
Pompilia was no pigeon   .   .   .   .
.   .   .   .
.   .   .   .   . ; but a hawk
I bought at a hawk's price, and carried home
To do hawk's service—at the Rotunda say,
Where, six o' the callow nestlings in a row,
You pick and choose and pay the price for such.
I have paid my pound, await my penny's worth,
So hoodwink, starve, and properly train my bird,
And should she prove a laggard—twist her neck!
Did I not pay my name and style, my hope
And trust, my all? Through spending these amiss
I am here! 'Tis scarce the gravity of the court
Will blame me that I never piped a tune,
Treated my falcon-gentle like my finch.
The obligation I incurred was just
To practise mastery, prove my mastership:—
Pompilia's duty was—submit herself,
Afford me pleasure, perhaps cure my bile.
And I to teach my lords what marriage means,
What God ordains thereby, and man fulfils
Who, docile to the dictate, treads the house?'

Guido has the right on his side; no one can gainsay him who
stands to the canon. Marriage, with its buttresses of law, religion,
usage, grants him all he asks. Not one jot nor one tittle dare we deny
him, and remain of the faithful. He may be urged to forego his
privilege, to be merciful—even that is a dangerous admission of
fallibility—but the claim is undeniable. By the law of the land, by the

service of the Church, by all that we cling to and uphold in the existing order of society, Guido Franceschini is supported in his demands. Few people will face that truth; few have the courage to stick to their colours—they are so very ugly in the full sunlight. It is preferable to drape one's idol in sentiments, vague but very lofty, the loftier the better, for they may console Pompilia, who lies bleeding beneath the wheels of the social order. It may soothe her immensely to know that those who support it, and all that appertains thereto—for sundry things one does not like to speak about, having refined feelings—incidentally accompany the triumphal procession which, alas! crushes a victim here and there, a painful sight to be avoided by delicate nerves—it may, I say, console Pompilia very much to know that those who organize the triumph have sentiments that would in sooth do honour to a brood of callow angels!

This is not a mere form of speech. It is a simple truth that the ugly skeleton of fact in the edifice that we call Society, above all in the institution which is said to hold it together, is kept out of sight by a mouldy growth of irresponsible sentiment; and we are so taken up in admiring the pleasing details of this ornamental vegetation that we do not consider the rotten rafters on which it grows. That few people *do* know what they are supporting is evident from their criticism of husbands as logical as Guido Franceschini. The mould confuses them!

What business have they to criticise the man who simply claims what his indulgent country offers? The marriage cultus would have a short life without its unconscious heretics! It is they who keep it standing, they who bring to it undeserved glory and honour, they who rescue it from sheer impossibility. An outbreak of Guido Franceschinis would strain its timbers ruthlessly.

Apart from the drapery of sentiment, it is undeniable that the normal conditions of sex-relationship are growing out of date. One great fact must be faced: the woman is claiming to be released from perpetual tutelage, not only in her own name, but in the name of humanity itself: she must cease to be swallowed in the family; she demands a life of her own, the right to test things for herself, not, indeed, because she wishes to be less the companion and friend of man, but (among other things) because she desires to be infinitely more so. And every one who thinks at all knows that a real union is between two individuals, not between an individual and a set of commendable qualities made to order.

If the woman's claim were granted, if she could secure a liberty as great as that of man, in all the relations of life, *marriage, as we now understand it, would cease to exist;* its groundwork would be undermined.

The change will not and ought not to come through sudden and impulsive legislation (though some legislation is needed), but by weeding out those elements of the institution which work the evil, and are out of touch with the spirit of the age.

Having thus realised the enormous difference which real sex-equality would make in the conditions of this relationship, let us face the questions that spring up to confront us as to the consequences of such a change, and of the further changes which would inevitably follow: for after all, that change would not end the movement. Freedom is a life-inspiring thing, and would foster fresh aspirations. There would be no pause till absolute liberty had been achieved.

Can we face this prospect? or must we take our conscious stand upon injustice? Injustice that has not realised itself is one thing; injustice that is wide-awake, cool, and deliberate is quite another. Under the first we can painfully struggle on, but the last, nationally speaking, is suicidal.

We are reminded again and again of the sea of licentiousness which underlies all society, and of the absolute necessity for severe restraint, in order to avoid being altogether submerged.

It was once thought impossible to bring up children without perpetual chastisement. This idea has been found to be false and barbarous. Not only does it fail to restrain, but it excites every evil impulse, and an inclination to repeat the transgression, if possible without being found out. Adult natures are no doubt more complex than children's, but experience tends to show that coercion acts upon them very much in the same manner as it does upon children.

And in this argument about licentiousness one thing is always forgotten: that if marriage moves towards freedom by gradual steps—by raising women to the position of independent human beings, by releasing them from the curse of unwilling motherhood, and from that of overwrought maternal instinct (a far cry still, I admit); if there is co-education of the sexes and the radical alteration of life and feeling which all these movements imply, we shall have a totally different kind of people to deal with from the men and women of to-day. The elements of human nature will remain, but their *proportions* and *relations* will be altered. New impetus creates new direction; new ideals new tendencies. Granted that an ideal is Utopian; still it is a soul that moulds to itself a body. The old body cannot long remain when a new soul is within it. Motives once all-powerful, now cease to influence; others have taken their place; time, circumstance, the growth of opinion: these are the forces of the world, and these are in a state of perpetual change and progression. Ideas about life and duty are rapidly altering, old notions disappearing. The future creed that no man or woman has a moral right to possess another, to coerce, cramp, and restrain, is in itself an education in just and liberal living, since it emphasises the rights of those in close relationship, those unlucky persons who, of all others, are most interfered with and trampled upon. A little girl, of evidently advanced views, was once heard to enquire with bitterness: "What is the use of being a citizen of a free country if one has to be tyrannized over by one's nurse?" Her elders were all immensely delighted and amused by the remark. Yet each of them might with propriety have expressed a similar sentiment: What is the use of being a citizen of a free country if one has to be tyrannized over by one's family?[6]

There is, perhaps, no more difficult relation in the world than that of husband and wife. Peace is not so very hard to achieve, nor an apparent smoothness which passes for harmony. The really rare thing is a unity which is not purchased at the expense of one or other of the partners. The old notion that the man ought to be the commander, because one must have a head in every commonwealth, is an amusingly crude solution of the difficulty, to say nothing of its calm and complete injustice.[7] Between two nations, it is easy to keep peace by disabling one of the combatants. That sort of peace, however, is of a somewhat "cheap and nasty" order, and can scarcely be described as international harmony. Between husband and wife it is absolutely degrading, not only to the disabled, but to him who disables. It is the fatal sense of power and possession in marriage which ruins so many unions and acts as a sort of disenchantment to the romance of pre-marital days. Through it the woman loses half her attraction, and it is this loss of attraction, observed *apart from its cause*, which creates so much fear of the effects of greater marital freedom. Ardent upholders of the present status point out that men would leave their wives without hesitation if they could, a curious admission that most marriages hold together by law rather than by affection.

What could possibly be more fatal to the wife's continued influence over her husband than the fact that she is *his* absolutely and for ever; that her beauty, her talents, her devotion are in duty bound dedicated to him for the rest of her life? He marries expecting exorbitantly. If the wife does not give him all he expects, he is disappointed and angry; if she does give it—well, it is only her duty, and he ceases to value it. It becomes a matter of course, and the romance and interest die out. The same thing in a lesser degree happens to the wife. She, too, may make vast claims upon her husband, curtail his liberty of action and even of thought; she may drag him about with her, on the absurd assumption that it is not "united" in husbands and wives to have independent tastes and pursuits, as other people have; she may even ruin a great talent, and fritter away an otherwise useful life, through her exactions.

Often indeed the claims on both sides are willingly recognised, but that saves neither of the pair from the narrowing influences of such a walled-in existence. Marriages of this kind are making life, as a whole, breathless and lacking in vitality; social intercourse is checked, the flow of thought is retarded; and these unions also have the very evil effect of cutting off, in a great measure, both the husband and wife from intimate relations with others. The complaint among friends is universal: when a man or woman marries a great curtain seems to fall; as human beings they have both lost their position; they are more or less shut away in their little circle and all the rest of the world is emphatically outside. As society is made up, to a large extent, of married couples—all tending to this self-satisfied isolation amidst the dust of undisturbed prejudices—it suffers from a sort of mental coagulation, whose effects we are all feeling in a thousand unsuspected ways. Life is tied up into myriads of tight little knots, and the blood cannot flow through the body politic. Ordinary social intercourse does little or nothing to loosen this stricture. The marital relationship of claims and restraints is, perhaps, in its vaunted "success" more melancholy to witness than in its failure.

In a marriage true to the modern spirit, which has scarcely yet begun to breathe upon this institution, husband and wife regard one another as absolutely free beings; they no more think of demanding subordination on one side or the other than a couple of friends who had elected to live together would mutually demand it. That, after all, is the true test. In love there ought to be *at least* as much respect for individuality and freedom as in friendship. Love may add to this essential foundation what it pleases, but to attempt to raise further structures without this as a basis, is to build for oneself a "castle in Spain." It cannot last and it does not deserve to last. The more intensely humanity begins to feel its unity, its coherence, the more deep must be the reverence for each individuality.

Stolid peace, but not living harmony, is possible without it. Under the present set of ideas, there is something terribly disappointing in marriage even to those who start with the highest hopes and resolutions. Human nature is too severely tried. It finds itself in possession of almost irresponsible power, its claims (by supposition just) are innumerable; there is scarcely a moment in the life of husband or wife which cannot be brought to judgment and criticised. How is it possible for two people to satisfy one another in every word and look and deed? How can one invariably fit every detail of conduct to the preconceptions of the other, affected as each must always be by moods, health, chance influences, and hereditary feelings? It is simply insane, as well as a piece of intolerable impertinence to expect it. We do not ask our friends to shape their conduct always according to our opinion; neither ought those who are married and (presumably) anxious to be mutually helpful to lay this terrible burden on one another. How often is the courtesy and respect which is instinctively given to a mere acquaintance withheld from the husband or the wife! Roughness, lack of refinement in thought and word, which often disfigure this relationship, have much to do with the passing away of the first love and enthusiasm, the first so-called illusion, which was no illusion but the beautiful flower of life's poetry, deliberately crushed under foot. The marriage relationship can never exist in its finest form until the wife can say to the husband what the heroine of Tchernuiskevsky's novel says to the man who has given her real freedom in marrying her: "Sasha, how greatly your love supports me! Through it, I am becoming independent: I am getting independent even of you!"[8] Such an ideal may be held by the few, spreading gradually to the many, long before legal freedom is attained or even attempted, and this ideal makes that freedom at once necessary and safe.

It would be madness indeed to ignore the licentious tendencies of mankind, but can we acquit the present restrictive dual-morality system of its share in increasing those tendencies? Can we forget how much the allotted scapegoats of society have to endure in the interests of purity among the elect?

Is this licentious element in human nature to be a perpetual stumbling-block, causing life to crystallize into hard patterns, separating people into inexorable groups, each with its evils, sorrows, limitations, despairs? This is what happens in consequence of our precautions against disorder. Does licentiousness indicate a state of physical and mental health or of disease? If a state of disease, is it incurable? What serious attempt have we ever made (except through asceticism, which is worse than useless) to cope with this dangerous force? We destroy a thousand possible joys, crib, cabin, and confine the lives of harmless people, set apart a great body of women for a purpose which we account disgraceful—and strange to say we make them no apology for our conduct, we only heap insults upon them—but what do we do to conquer this tyrant who destroys so much happiness, usurps so large a proportion of energy, runs amuck through all society? Our one idea is restraint, punishment, strict laws, suspicious, petty, watchful social usages.

All this emphasizes the idea it pretends to repudiate, and creates lip-service, while it gives sheltered hiding-places to the enemy. The atmosphere is growing daily more unwholesome; the finger of "Propriety" is leaving everywhere its stain. More liberty would mean less licence. In this matter women will have much to say and to do. Education—in its widest sense—must grapple with the problem; the tendencies, pleasures, interests of mankind must be raised to a higher level; the curtain that hides from vast multitudes of average men and women the marvels of nature, the dramatic splendours of life, must be lifted, and the art of living made familiar to all.

But practically, what is to be done? How would a free system work? We must face the unpalatable fact that a cut-and-dried scheme which will now seem plausible is just as impossible as our present state of society would have appeared to the "practical man" of the Middle Ages. Social changes are too gradual and subtle for such draughtsman-like forecasts to be of any use or meaning. All that can be done, at any given time in the world's history, is to indicate the next direction of development, initiate or emphasize the tendency of human thought, sentiment and institutions, for some new conception. Far more stupendous changes come to pass in average human action than any one would dare to predict, and even now a great movement affecting

in the profoundest manner human ideals and standards is taking place. It
is futile to say that human nature is incapable of this or that, since
human nature is precisely the author and creator of the new heavens and
the new earths.

I have suggested that the licentious element in mankind may be
reduced to more manageable proportions; and this is surely not an
entirely vain hope, unless it is also vain to hope to bring men and
women into better conditions of mind and body; unless it is vain to
hope that thought and will count for something in human destiny. The
conditions of life, sentiment, fashion, which induced our ancestors to
get drunk every night have passed away, and human nature on the whole
finds that, without any conscious effort or restraint, the impulse to
excessive drinking is no longer so imperious, and it will probably
become progressively less so. The freer, richer, healthier, more full of
interest a life becomes, the less need will there be to drown misery or
chase away dulness by merely sensual pleasures. And for this rich and
full life men need the society and influence of women, and women that
of men, without let or hindrance. On matters of sex too much stress is
laid by our network of laws and restraints. The Puritan spirit is greatly
to blame for this; it casts an ugly, self-conscious light upon all things
wherein men and women are concerned, creating evil where none need
be; it fosters a heated, unnatural atmosphere, and makes artificial sins
which are the parents of a swarm of unnecessary sorrows. The new ideas
of education—the training of the mind in accordance with its own
natural impetus, the awakening of vivid interests, the bringing forth of
latent talent, and the powers of acquirement and concentration—all this,
after a few generations, must have a profound influence upon the
leading impulses and motives of mankind. Then we must remember
that licentiousness is—in general—the preying of one sex upon the
other; women, respectable and outcast alike, are dependent on men for
their bread and butter. They have no voice in determining the relations
they will bear to them. They are supported on the one condition:
subjection of body and of soul. Were this dependence no longer
existing, is it conceivable that women would continue to allow
themselves to be doomed to so ghastly a fate? There are no doubt many
prostitutes who crave for the excitement that their life affords, but is
not this largely because Respectability carefully provides that the
reputable life shall be so deadly dull? It is surely undeniable that if
women were as free as men to say "Yes," and "No," the condition of

society as regards these matters would be entirely transformed. It would not necessarily change in a direction to please Mrs. Grundy; in fact it would probably cause a serious shock to her nervous system; but it is almost inconceivable that the most ghastly evils would not disappear, for these are of a kind that implies a victim and an oppressor.

Does not, in fact, licentiousness have for a condition the subjection of women?

If this be admitted, there is comparatively little left to admit. If the independence of women had the effect of destroying or greatly lessening prostitution and mercenary marriage, what object would there be in binding people together by adamantine chains and subjecting them to vexatious rules and restrictions? Neither man nor woman would then submit to it.[9]

Once more I must repeat that to demand what would appear to be an *immediately* workable system of free marriage is as unreasonable as it would be to ask a cattle-lifting clan of the Middle Ages to turn over a new leaf and earn their living on the Stock Exchange. The motives that are all potent to the Stockbroker are non-existent for the Highlander. Both conceptions of existence are, however, possible and workable, and both are the outcome of that most plastic material—human nature.

It would indeed be easy enough to suggest general outlines of a social system in which marriage should be free, but its workability entirely depends upon whether humanity is going to educate itself in that direction, whether it will take less jealous and possessive views of sex-relationship, and whether the conception of true liberty will penetrate from public into domestic life, where at present it is practically unknown. Love now comes with a vast bundle of claims in her hand, and she even passes on these claims to mere kinship, which presses them with the persistency of a Shylock. Free marriage is not for those who understand freedom no better than this. All such ideas of restriction and interference, on any plea whatsoever, must be swept away. If we cannot grant or claim liberty in one relation of life, we are incapable of it in another. This is a great lesson that has yet to be learnt. In learning it humanity will be fitting itself for the next development. But there is no reason why those who *do* understand the idea should not carry it into practice wherever individual circumstances permit.

When freedom is no longer merely political and civic, when it becomes as the breath of our nostrils in the most intimate relations of life, our notions of morality must undergo a very serious modification. A glimpse of the end of the twentieth century might puzzle even those who are most prepared for change.[10]

It is impossible to be "practical" on this subject, if we consider its entire scope, for we are dealing with social movements affecting the beliefs, feelings, the very temperament of the whole people; we are not dealing with mere outward adjustments of the machinery. Critics generally assume that a change of machinery is chiefly demanded, and if it can be shown that, at the present moment, this would result in disorder, the whole doctrine is supposed to be crushed. This is simply to misunderstand the doctrine. It implies a complete revolution in our present conceptions of sex and family relationship, and therefore it is evident that no new law suddenly launched upon a people still under the spell of the old ideas could have any triumphant effect. The fears entertained of the working of a freer law are, I believe, wildly exaggerated, but it is certain that legal relaxation can never take the place of moral evolution. Still the law must not lag too far behind the change of thought, and there seems no reason why it should not at once become more flexible to individual needs in the marriage relation. This could be done without relinquishing the supervision and restraint which is still thought necessary on the part of the State.[11] Less rigid divorce laws, equal for the two sexes; the right of the mother to the control of her children; these are the next practical steps which civilization demands. As soon as the principle of equality between the sexes is sincerely accepted, there remains no valid reason against the immediate adoption of contract-marriage under certain limitations. The idea of equality would at once sweep away the one-sided divorce laws, enabling man and woman to obtain divorce on the same grounds. Contract-marriage would permit them to agree upon these grounds, subject to certain restrictions which would guard against the selection of absurd or frivolous reasons.

A couple would draw up their agreement, or depute the task to their friends, as is now generally done as regards marriage-settlements. They agree to live together on such and such terms, making certain stipulations within the limits of the code. The breaking of any of these promises may or may not constitute a plea for separation or divorce—again according to agreement. The husband might bestow on the wife a certain sum as her exclusive property, this being her reward for her share in sustaining the household, and as the security for her independence.[12] In case of the union proving unsuitable, a certain time shall be specified which shall elapse before application is made for divorce or separation, and the State would then demand a minimum interval between the notice and the divorce itself, if still desired after that interval is over.

A more morally developed people would demand greater freedom than could now be safely accorded; the limitations under which the contracts would be drawn up would provide a sure check upon the unscrupulous and capricious, while the contract system would give relief in most cases where the union ought to be dissolved.[13]

The doubt and anxiety which people feel with regard to the children under a freer condition of society, ought to be transferred to their condition under our existing regime. If only for their sakes, the present marriage system stands condemned.

The very existence of a large proportion of our children is a wrong to them and to their mothers; the continued union of their parents is another wrong, and the popular mode of training and education dependent on existing marriage ideals, is yet a third. This is initial, fundamental; nothing can atone for it completely. The wrongs of children are in their way, as great as those of men and women. Under a freer system—each child having been willingly brought into being—the responsibility of parents would be more deeply felt than it can be now, when a human creature is turned loose upon the world, as one might turn out a horse to grass. Freedom, more than anything else, fosters the sense of responsibility. The very housemaid ceases to feel responsible, if her mistress watches her every minute of the day. The onus rests then with the mistress. The maid simply acts under compulsion. Responsibility vanishes. The State must when necessary protect its helpless members against neglect and ill-treatment; it must demand of the parents that they shall support and educate their children at all hazards; but surely, in order to provide for the exceptional cases in which neglect might happen, it is not necessary to hold an entire people in bondage, ruin innumerable lives, and create all the subtle, deep-reaching evils which a relationship that is enforced brings in its train. This method reminds one of the policy of people who keep their whole family in unventilated rooms, because now and then somebody in a weak state of health might take cold from an open window. The ordinary, everyday, necessary good is sacrificed to the possibility of an exceptional evil. It is surely childish to suppose that people in a free society who had full opportunity of forming suitable unions, who had willingly incurred the responsibility of children, would be perpetually breaking these ties, snapping all associations and affections, and flying off to other partners. There would be a public opinion then as now, that would discourage such tendencies, and society also has a way of adjusting its habits, after certain fashions, according to comfort and convenience, not to mention the influence of ideals of character and conduct which never cease to exist.

Granted, however, for the sake of argument, that a larger number of couples separated than is now the case. Remembering the altered conditions and motives that are implied by the freedom to separate, what serious evil would result? The parents being unhappy together, or for some reason unsuitably matched, it is better for the children not to live in the home-atmosphere inevitable in such circumstances. They need not necessarily be entirely separated from either parent (under present conditions, school-life separates them during the greater part of the year from *both*), nor need they suffer more than is unavoidable in every case when parents are not completely at one. The difficulties are almost entirely imaginary, and they take their very shaky stand on the unformulated assumption that the father and mother both have a large and constant part in their children's education and training, that the parents continually live as central ornaments to a group of clustering offspring from whom they are unwillingly torn each evening when the unwelcome nursemaid comes to distribute them among their respective cots.

I have elsewhere stated at length why it seems to me that the mother has a moral right to final authority over her children, and not the father, so I will not touch upon this unpopular point here again, but that idea is essential to what appears to me a just arrangement in case of the separation of parents. The mother should be able to claim her children if she desires to exercise her rights to the full, and under new economic conditions, she would have no difficulty in supporting the one or two that she would be likely to have. More often, however, some compromise would be made, and there is no reason to suppose a greater separation from the parents than is now *invariably* necessary, through the practice of depriving children of home-influence during the most susceptible time of their lives, by sending them to public schools. Anything more astonishingly trustful than such conduct on the part of parents is difficult to conceive! Boys are plunged suddenly into a new and not exactly beautiful or moral world without guide or compass, without preparation, and Providence must decree what influences shall prevail upon the unformed spirit. Providence must have its hands full! Yet nobody objects, nobody says, "How sad for those boys to be deprived of the joint-guardianship of father and mother! How sad that the parents are not able to watch over their welfare!" If parental care from both sides is so essential, why is this system of exile from the home not condemned; if it is *not* essential, why is there so much horror at the partial separation from one of the parents? Were home-life less restrictive and dull—were its influence extended much later in life than it now is, a child would undeniably have a better chance of developing mentally and morally, than he now enjoys. If, in such a case, the father and mother were separated, still the child would have a home where he spent much of his time, during the years of education and development. The enormous importance that is given to the possession of two parents under the same roof, whether or not they live harmoniously and willingly, seems to savour very strongly of superstition.

This problem of the children, however, touches on so many burning questions, offends so many rooted ideas, that every available argument runs straight against an objection, old and stiff, and for the moment immovable. The kindred topic of educational methods affects the question also, but cannot be entered upon here.

The chief, the essential point to consider in this question is the altered conception of life and morality which its development implies. That which has been held fair and beautiful is becoming unlovely; that which was formerly a right will transform itself into an aggression; where there were claims there will be unrestraint; while liberty and love will no longer be for either sex, the stern alternatives. A new endeavour takes the place of the old, and as the altered feeling tends to shape the thoughts and actions, even of those who are making no effort, but are merely breathing the mental atmosphere of their day, the conditions of life shift slowly but surely till a fresh horizon opens, and the race gathers strength in an interval of rest for the next discovery and conquest.

It must not be forgotten, in considering this most complex of questions, that while there has been much evil from licentious excess on the one hand, there has been also suffering among those who have led a strictly single life on the other. The excess, carried on from generation to generation, probably partly explains the suffering of the self-controlled.

Society demands this endurance from women but not from men: men hand on to the race exaggerated instincts to devastate other lives, and the brunt of those unsatisfied instincts must be allowed to destroy the health and sometimes the reason, because the sufferer belongs to the sex that has no choice in these matters. Duty or sin: stern, strict, savage, intolerable duty, or black, polluting, unforgivable sin! These are the woman's alternatives! It is not true that we women reap what we sow: we reap what other people have sown for us!

As if to aggravate this evil, so subtle and so difficult to deal with, there is the terrible monotony and greyness which Heine felt so oppressive in English life. At midnight, he says, as he "passed the fatal window of Whitehall, I felt the humid, chilly prose of England's modern life freezing my veins."

The emotional nature is starved, or stimulated in one sole direction; the heart is half empty, ready to go forth at the first hope of something to fill the void. The interest and attraction which men feel for women and women for men have no complete and healthy opportunity. The satisfaction of the emotional nature must be purchased at the cost of a bondage that lasts for life, with all its responsibilities and risks. The most orthodox usually admit that it is bad to assume these responsibilities too young, but they do not admit that it is bad also to forego the society and the interests for which there is so strong a desire.

If there are dangers in freedom, they are nothing more than the price that must be paid for everything that is worth having. We do not prevent people from falling in love by our restrictions; we only prevent them from falling in love suitably. Fulness of life, mental and emotional, is calming and steadying to the judgment; its dangers are greatest when it is enjoyed as a solitary privilege.

There are worse things for society than the play of passion. We have those worse things now in the play of lust, cruel and cold, in sapless lives and pinched souls, in organisms that seem a sort of cross between a corpse and a lay figure.

Experience tends to prove that freedom is the right and beneficent condition for all things human: there may be necessity for restraint, or for guidance which has power to become restraint, at times and seasons of development; but freedom invigorates, purifies, suggests, inspires; it promotes growth and makes room for it. Of it must be the atmosphere of Heaven.

There are already individual souls in whom the spirit of a new freedom in social life is powerfully working. It has come to them as an inspiration, re-moulding their lives and characters down to the minutest fibres. This enthusiasm is infectious, for it belongs to the spirit of the age and harmonizes with all its vital movements. Through these scattered individuals the impossible becomes fact.

We shall sooner or later have to consider whether our ideas of what we are pleased to call "high" and "pure" are precisely square with facts; whether those men and women who keep most closely to the current models of the commendable are really the most joy-inspiring and beneficent people. If we accept the scientific view of morality—the school of Bentham, Mill, Herbert Spencer, Clifford—that is the test which must be applied.

What, after all, is "purity"?

Does it not come very close to charity which "vaunteth not itself, is not puffed up, seeketh not her own, thinketh no evil"? The "purity" that sits up aloft under the presidency of Mrs. Grundy vaunteth itself exceedingly, is puffed up very much indeed, seeketh her own, to the entire forgetfulness of the manner in which she acquires it, and occupies all her leisure in thinking evil. This kind of purity has a beautiful sister, who unquestioningly adopts the elder's rules, but obeys them in a devotional spirit, believing them to come straight from heaven, with the light of holiness still upon them. And for these she is ready to suffer—and often has to suffer—martyrdom. Both these forms of purity, noble and ignoble, begin to grate against fact. There is yet another kind.

This purity came into being with the love of nature, the vivid modern sense of the splendour of life, the "beauty of the world." She is fostered by that passionate love of liberty, of health, sunlight, freshness, which is becoming one of the regenerative and moving forces of the century. She is fresh as a sea-breeze, full of the breath of life, open-eyed, straight of glance and utterly without fear. This is the purity (the name with its pale, cramped associations seems to mock her!) of an age of science and the poetry of science, of an age which permits no roofs and domes to stand between itself and the light of truth, which finds its hope and its inspiration in the service of man.

Notes

1. Caird alternates between "realize" and "realise."

2. In one singular case of this kind, the relations between the couple had been happy and friendly from the beginning, and the wife thought she was far from having anything to complain of. Yet even she noticed a startling change of attitude after she became the possessor of a small income, which gave her a position of independence. [Caird's note]

3. ". . . toutes les fois qu'un peuple placé en tête de l'humanité est devenu stationnaire, les germes du progrès qui se trouvaient dans son sein, ont été aussitôt transportés ailleurs, sur un sol où ils pouvaient se développer; et l'on a vu constamment dans ce cas, le peuple, rebelle à la loi humaine, s'abîmer et s'anéantir comme écrasé sous le poids d'un anathème."—Bazard et Enfantin, followers of St. Simon. [Caird's note] French for: ". . . no sooner are a people set at the fore of humanity than they become stationary, and the seeds of progress that were found in their midst are transferred elsewhere, onto a soil where they might expand; and it is always observed in such cases that the people, impervious to human law, fall into ruin and are abased as if crushed under the weight of a curse."

4. The common contention that the woman is abnormally weak who suffers in this way is not borne out in this case. She began life in perfect health and buoyant spirits. The marvel is that any creature born of woman *can* so begin it! [Caird's note]

5. Caird is referring to Robert Browning's *The Ring and the Book* (1868–69), which is based on the actual murder of Pompilia and her family. Pompilia's tyrannical husband, Count Guido Franceschini, was charged for murder in 1698, and in spite of arguing that he had a right to kill a wife who had—as he claimed—committed adultery, the court ordered his execution.

6. "The patriarchal power [among the Aryan family groups] extends over the life and liberty of the members of the family. The wife and children are absolutely in the power of the head of the family, and he has not to give account for any of his actions. We saw that the Brazilian community was constructed on these lines, which afford the typical form of brute force."—*The Primitive Family* (Starcke). It is this "typical form of brute force" which survives in our own idea of the necessity for a "head" in every family. [Caird's note]

7. "Elle [la loi civile] déclare la femme mineure pour toujours et prononce sur elle une éternelle interdiction. L'homme est constitué son tuteur, mais s'il s'agit des fautes qu'elle peut commettre, des peines qu'elle peut subir, elle est traitée comme majeure, tout à fait responsable, et très-sévèrement. C'est du reste la contradiction de toutes les lois barbares. Elle est livrée comme une chose, punie comme une personne."—*L'Amour* (Michelet [sic]). [Caird's note] French for: "It [civil law] declares the woman to be a minor for all time and pronounces upon her an eternal prohibition. The man is appointed as her guardian, but where mistakes that she might commit or penalties that she might suffer are concerned, she is treated—very severely—as an adult who is

completely responsible. Yet such is the contradiction of all these barbarous laws. She is handed over like a thing, but punished like a person."

8. *A Vital Question; or, What is to be done?* By N.G. Tchernuiskevsky. [Caird's note]

9. I do not here attempt to deal with the economic question upon which the pecuniary independence of women partly hangs. That is a gigantic question, affecting the whole of society, and to touch upon it now would be to confuse the issues that we are considering. [Caird's note]

10. "The sense of duty is not the highest moral principle, and not only does it seem that it will undergo purification or such modification as will replace it by a higher conception, but the process has already begun. The ground of the defect of duty lies in what has been already noticed, that it conceals the spontaneity of morality. It leaves out of sight that morality in the direction in which the individual naturally moves; what is the natural direction having been determined by eliminating all other [i]deas."—*Moral Order and Progress* (Alexander). [Caird's note]

11. "So long as the legislature determines to consider adultery the only ground for divorce, and attempts to place 'by law' a stigma on certain conduct and certain acts, so long our marriage laws will continue in a vicious circle."—"Marriage and Divorce," *Fortnightly Review*, George H. Lewes, May, 1885. "Yet our divorce court to-day is as savage and barbarous an institution ethically as the fixing up on spikes of the heads of criminals was in old days on London Bridge." [Caird's note]

12. This would be like the old *Morgengabe* or the *Gerade*, the first being the gift of the husband, consisting of flocks and herds and other valuable property, the latter being generally provided by the woman's family, to be thereafter inherited by the women of the tribe, while the men have their Heergewäte—armour and weapons—handed down in the same way. [Caird's note]

13. In Germany divorce is allowed for incompatibility of temper, yet there are rather fewer divorces in that country than with us. In Ibsen's *Lady from the Sea*, he depicts the morbid desires and uneasy longings created by a state of bondage, however good and amiable may be the person who holds the power. At the close of the play we see the wholesome, steadying effect of freedom. [Caird's note]

XV. Sarah Grand
(Frances Elizabeth Clarke McFall)

(1854–1943)

A feminist whose essays and novels exposed the most sensitive issues of Victorian sexuality to direct sunlight, Sarah Grand was well known for her radical ideas, daring style, and aggressive wit. Credited with coining the term "New Woman," she was a prominent figure in the 1890s debates about what women were, should be, or could be. In her fiction and in essays appearing in *Lady's Realm* and *Living Age*, Grand argued tirelessly in support of women's education and against the sexual double standards that endangered and degraded women. Confident that hers was an era of transition and progress, Grand hailed the emergence of the New Woman as inevitable, and believed that women's efforts on behalf of social reform would advance both sexes. To this end, she called on women to recognize their value to each other and to the human race. In the exacting manner of a physician, Grand analyzed the reigning attitudes towards womanhood, marriage, and female child rearing; and, while revealing the hypocrisy of these attitudes, she demanded that women enact a "remedy." This meant setting new standards in marriage, and particularly in the parenting of young women whose ignorance about sex, venereal disease and wife abuse ensured their oppression by men. Turning the rhetoric that defended traditional gender ideals on its head, Grand challenged the very manliness of men who bawled in opposition to women's political and expressive freedoms; equally important, she reminded women of their duties not to men, but to the sisters and daughters who could benefit from their experience.

Despite the activism that won Grand celebrity status by 1893, surprisingly little is known about her early life and the influences that shaped her consciousness. Born Frances Elizabeth Clarke, she was the fourth child of Margaret Bell Sherwood and Edward John Bellenden Clarke. After the death of her naval-officer father in 1861, her mother moved the family from Ireland to her native Yorkshire, where Grand lived until enrolled at a naval boarding school in Twickenham in 1868. Dismissed within a year—apparently because of already pronounced radical attitudes and religious skepticism—she briefly attended finishing school at Holland Road, Kensington. At sixteen (young even by Victorian standards), she married David Chambers McFall, a military officer and royal surgeon who, at thirty-nine, was more than twice her age. With McFall, his two sons by a previous marriage, and her own infant, Grand traveled to Singapore, Ceylon, China, and Japan until 1879, when the family settled in England. At this point, Grand had already published several short stories in children's magazines, but it was with the return home that her ambitions as a writer became serious. Her first overtly feminist novel *Ideala*, was completed in 1881 and published in 1888. Though the novel and its author met with rejection by family, friends and publishers, Grand was nonetheless destined to become one of the most popular writers of her day. *The Heavenly Twins* (1892), which deals explicitly with "taboo" subject matter, especially venereal disease, sold over 20,000 copies immediately after its publication by William Heinemann. It established Grand overnight as a major player in the suffrage movement.

Between 1893 and 1898, New Woman fiction—thematically focused on women's rebellions against arbitrary authority and even on an open recognition of female sexuality—was a significant cultural influence. A site of controversy in the journals of the period, these novels evoked powerful emotions in readers and reviewers, and Grand's popularity made her a primary focus of celebration or censure. For women writers, mention of Grand's name signaled feminist awareness along with ideas such as studying at Girton or owning a latchkey. For critics, however, Grand's work was a source of despair and outrage. Focusing more on her "snarling" personality and broken marriage (she left McFall in 1890) than on her literary talent, writers like G. Noyes Miller and Frank Harris called her "aboriginal" rather than "original," and insisted that she was "unfit to be received by decent people." As the following essays will demonstrate, Grand was up for the challenge. Dissecting the myths and arguments of the "Bawling Brotherhood," she asserted, in regal style, that women would no longer listen to such men about what to think. If anything, the critics' denouncements seemed to fuel Grand's determination, energy, and creativity. By the turn of the century she had produced several novels, short stories, and essays, including *Singularly Deluded* (1892), *The Beth Book* (1897), *The Modern Man and the Maid* (1898), and *Our Manifold Nature* (1893?). Many of Grand's essays are among the most interesting and astute contributions to the New Woman debate.

Although Grand has, until recently, been primarily remembered for her critique of patriarchy, the topic of women—their responsibility to each other, their potential for intellectual growth, power, sympathy, even joy—was her primary concern. She believed that literature had the capacity to change people's lives and she saw herself as an educator and role model whose hand was extended to the Modern Girl. Like many of her New Woman contemporaries—including George Egerton, Iota, and Emma Frances Brooke—Grand deserves renewed attention not only for her ideas, but for her innovative play with literary form and novel structure. *The Heavenly Twins* in particular stands out as a critique of linear narrative, the marriage plot, and the conventions of chivalry and romance—all of which informed contemporary thinking about gender. Savvy and articulate, her essays convey keen psychological insight into the politics of human relationships that will continue to have relevance so long as we grapple with issues of gender, education, and equality.

By 1900, the fervor over the New Woman had died down, perhaps because writers like Grand had so thoroughly disseminated ideas that had consequently become less shocking and dangerous. With the National Union of Women's Suffrage Societies (the NUWSS) intensifying its campaign for the vote in 1898, Grand turned her energies to lecturing and to participation in various women's organizations, including the Women Writers' Suffrage League. She also became President of a branch of the NUWSS. Whether she finally became tired of attacks on her character or simply felt that, by the close of the decade, her objectives could best be met in other ways, Grand stopped publishing between 1898 and 1908. Her last two novels, *Adnam's Orchard* (1912) and *The Winged Victory* (1916), are noticeably toned down and do not appear to have received much attention. From 1922 to 1929 she served under widower Cedric Cheevers as the "mayoress" of Bath, during which time a younger woman admirer, Gladys Singers-Bigger, documented her later life in personal diaries. Gillian Kersley's *Darling Madame: Sarah Grand and*

Devoted Friend (1983), which tends to identify Grand with her fictional characters, is the only full-length biography to date. For reviews, obituaries, etc., see Joan Huddleston's *Sarah Grand (Mrs. Frances Elizabeth McFall, née Clarke), 1854–1943: A Bibliography* (1979). For background on New Woman writers, see Ann Ardis's *New Women, New Novels: Feminism and Early Modernism* (1990). Thanks to the University of Michigan Press and Thoemms Press, *The Heavenly Twins*, with an introduction by Carol Senf, and *The Beth Book*, with an introduction by Sally Mitchell, have recently become available for new generations of readers and students.

Esther Schwarz-McKenzie,
Temple University

32. The New Aspect of the Woman Question

Introduction

Sarah Grand's "The New Aspect of the Woman Question" appeared in *North American Review* in 1894, and is reprinted here from that periodical. Emerging from a long period of dormancy and "apathy" (almost like butterflies from cocoons), women are—in Grand's vision here—ready to take responsibility for themselves and exercise moral and political power. Contradicting the ideas of biological determinism, Grand boldly rewrites history as a matter of choices; in short, women have long been too trusting of men, and therefore deserve "blame" for their intolerable situation. But Grand then asserts that women now have the ability to promote advances that will benefit both sexes. Subverting the terminology used to justify the oppression of women, Grand attacks men for lacking in "manliness," which here means an ability to live with women honestly and as equals. Scrutinizing the hypocrisy with which the "Bawling Brotherhood" defends its superiority, she concludes that women do want marriage, but that they want husbands whom they can respect. Creating new standards for marriageable men would be a first step toward putting "the human house in order." Using familiar language, Grand impressed upon women their responsibility to clean out the "dark corners"—the marriage market and prostitution—that enabled the status quo. By changing their expectations of men, women could protect one another and use their mutual compassion as a revolutionary force.

The New Aspect of the Woman Question

It is amusing as well as interesting to note the pause which the
new aspect of the woman question has given to the Bawling Brothers
who have hitherto tried to howl down every attempt on the part of our
sex to make the world a pleasanter place to live in. That woman should
ape man and desire to change places with him was conceivable to him
as he stood on the hearth-rug in his lord-and-master-monarch-of-all-I-
survey attitude, well inflated with his own conceit; but that she should
be content to develop the good material which she finds in herself and
be only dissatisfied with the poor quality of that which is being offered
to her in man, her mate, must appear to him to be a thing as monstrous
as it is unaccountable. "If women don't want to be men, what do they
want?" asked the Bawling Brotherhood when the first misgiving of the
truth flashed upon them; and then, to reassure themselves, they pointed
to a certain sort of woman in proof of the contention that we were all
unsexing ourselves.

It would be as rational for us now to declare that men generally
are Bawling Brothers or to adopt the hasty conclusion which makes all
men out to be fiends on the one hand and all women fools on the other.
We have our Shrieking Sisterhood, as the counterpart of the Bawling
Brotherhood. The latter consists of two sorts of men. First of all is he
who is satisfied with the cow-kind of woman as being most convenient;
it is the threat of any strike among his domestic cattle for more
consideration that irritates him into loud and angry protests. The other
sort of Bawling Brother is he who is under the influence of the scum of
our sex, who knows nothing better than women of that class in and out
of society, preys upon them or ruins himself for them, takes his whole
tone from them, and judges us all by them. Both the cow-woman and
the scum-woman are well within range of the comprehension of the
Bawling Brotherhood, but the new woman is a little above him, and he
never even thought of looking up to where she has been sitting apart in
silent contemplation all these years, thinking and thinking, until at last
she solved the problem and proclaimed for herself what was wrong with
Home-is-the-Woman's-Sphere, and prescribed the remedy.

What she perceived at the outset was the sudden and violent
upheaval of the suffering sex in all parts of the world. Woman were
awaking from their long apathy, and, as they awoke, like healthy

hungry children unable to articulate, they began to whimper for they knew not what. They might have been easily satisfied at that time had not society, like an ill-conditioned and ignorant nurse, instead of finding out what they lacked, shaken them and beaten them and stormed at them until what was once a little wail became convulsive shrieks and roused up the whole human household. Then man, disturbed by the uproar, came upstairs all anger and irritation, and, without waiting to learn what was the matter, added his own old theories to the din, but, finding they did not act rapidly, formed new ones, and made an intolerable nuisance of himself with his opinions and advice. He was in the state of one who cannot comprehend because he has no faculty to perceive the thing in question, and that is why he was so positive. The dimmest perception that you may be mistaken will save you from making an ass of yourself.

We must look upon man's mistakes, however, with some leniency, because we are not blameless in the matter ourselves. We have allowed him to arrange the whole social system and manage or mismanage it all these ages without ever seriously examining his work with a view to considering whether his abilities and his motives were sufficiently good to qualify him for the task. We have listened without a smile to his preachments, about our place in life and all we are good for, on the text that "there is no understanding a woman." We have endured most poignant misery for his sins, and screened him when we should have exposed him and had him punished. We have allowed him to exact all things of us, and have been content to accept the little he grudgingly gave us in return. We have meekly bowed our heads when he called us bad names instead of demanding proofs of the superiority which alone would give him a right to do so. We have listened much edified to man's sermons on the subject of virtue, and have acquiesced uncomplainingly in the convenient arrangement by which this quality has come to be altogether practised for him by us vicariously. We have seen him set up Christ as an example for all men to follow which argues his belief in the possibility of doing so, and have not only allowed his weakness and hypocrisy in the matter to pass without comment, but, until lately, have not even seen the humor of his pretensions when contrasted with his practices nor held him up to that wholesome ridicule which is a stimulating corrective. Man deprived us of all proper education, and then jeered at us because we had no knowledge. He narrowed our outlook on life so that our view of it should be all distorted, and then declared that our mistaken impression of it proved us to be senseless creatures. He cramped our minds so that there was no room for reason in them, and then made merry at our want of logic. Our divine intuition was not to be controlled by him, but he did his best to damage it by sneering at it as an inferior feminine method of arriving at conclusions; and finally, after having had his own way until he lost his head completely, he set himself up as a sort of a god and required us to worship him and, to our eternal shame be it said, we did so. The truth has all along been in us, but we have cared more for man than for truth, and so the whole human race has suffered. We have failed of our effect by neglecting our duty here, and have deserved much of the obloquy that was cast upon us. All that is over now, however, and while on the one hand man has shrunk to his true proportions in our estimation, we, on the other hand, have been expanding to our own; and now we come confidently forward to maintain, not that this or that was "intended," but that there are in ourselves, in both sexes, possibilities hitherto suppressed or abused, which, when properly developed, will supply to either what is lacking in the other.

The man of the future will be better, while the woman will be stronger and wiser. To bring this about is the whole aim and object of the present struggle, and with the discovery of the means lies the solution of the Woman Question. Man, having no conception of himself as imperfect from the woman's point of view, will find this difficult to understand, but we know his weakness, and will be patient with him, and help him with his lesson. It is the woman's place and pride and pleasure to teach the child, and man morally is in his infancy. There have been times when there was a doubt as to whether he was to be raised or woman was to be lowered, but we have turned that corner at last; and now woman holds out a strong hand to the child-man, and insists, but with infinite tenderness and pity, upon helping him up.

He must be taught consistency. There are ideals for him which it is to be presumed that he tacitly agrees to accept when he keeps up an expensive establishment to teach them: let him live up to them. Man's faculty for shirking his own responsibility has been carried to such an extent in the past that, rather than be blamed himself when it did not answer to accuse woman, he imputed the whole consequence of his own misery-making peculiarities to God.

But with all his assumption man does not make the most of himself. He has had every advantage of training to increase his insight, for instance, but yet we find him, even at this time of day, unable to perceive that woman has a certain amount of self-respect and practical good sense—enough at all events to enable her to use the proverb about the bird in the hand to her own advantage. She does not in the least intend to sacrifice the privileges she enjoys on the chance of obtaining others, especially of the kind which man seems to think she must aspire to as so much more desirable. Woman may be foolish, but her folly has never been greater than man's conceit, and the one is not more disastrous to the understanding than the other. When a man talks about knowing the world and having lived and that sort of thing, he means something objectionable; in seeing life he generally includes doing wrong; and it is in these respects he is apt to accuse us of wishing to ape him. Of old if a woman ventured to be at all unconventional, man was allowed to slander her with the imputation that she must be abandoned, and he really believed us of trying to emulate him in any noble, manly quality, because the cultivation of noble qualities has not hitherto been a favorite pursuit of his, not to the extent at least of entering into his calculations and making any perceptible impression on public opinion; and he never, therefore, thought of considering whether it might have attraction for us. The cultivation of noble qualities has been individual rather than general, and the person who practised it is held to be one apart, if not actually eccentric. Man acknowledges that the business of life carried on according to his methods corrodes, and the state of corrosion is a state of decay; and yet he is fatuous enough to imagine that our ambition must be to lie like him for our own benefit in every public capacity. Heaven help the child to perceive with what travail and sorrow we submit to the heavy obligation, when it is forced upon us by our sense of right, of showing him how things ought to be done.

We have been reproached by Ruskin for shutting ourselves up behind park palings and garden walls, regardless of the waste world that moans in misery without, and that has been too much our attitude; but the day of our acquiescence is over. There is that in ourselves which forces us out of our apathy; we have no choice in the matter. When we hear the "Help! help! help!" of the desolate and the oppressed, and still more when we see the awful dumb despair of those who have lost even the hope of help, we must respond. This is often inconvenient to man, especially when he has seized upon a defenceless victim whom he would have destroyed had we not come to the rescue; and so, because it is inconvenient to be exposed and thwarted, he snarls about the end of all true womanliness, cants on the subject of the Sphere, and threatens that if we do not sit still at home with cotton-wool in our ears so that we cannot be stirred into having our sympathies aroused by his victims when they shriek, and with shades over our eyes that we may not see him in his degradation, we shall be afflicted with short hair, coarse skins, unsymmetrical figures, loud voices, tastelessness in dress, and an unattractive appearance and character generally, and then he will not love us any more or marry us. And this is one of the most amusing of his threats, because he has said and proved on so many occasions that he cannot live without us whatever we are. O man! man! you are a very funny fellow now we know you! But take care. The standard of your pleasure and convenience has already ceased to be our conscience. On one point, however, you may reassure yourself. True womanliness is not in danger, and the sacred duties of wife and mother will be all the more honorably performed when women have a reasonable hope of becoming wives and mothers of *men*. But there is the difficulty. The trouble is not because women are mannish, but because men grow ever more effeminate. Manliness is at a premium now because there is so little of it, and we are accused of aping men in order to conceal the side from which the contrast should evidently be drawn. Man in his manners becomes more and more wanting until we seem to be near the time when there will be nothing left of him but the old Adam, who said, "It wasn't me."

Of course it will be retorted that the past has been improved upon in our day; but that is not a fair comparison. We walk by the electric light: our ancestors had only oil-lamps. We can see what we are doing and where we are going, and should be as much better as we know how to be. But where are our men? Where is the chivalry, the truth, and affection, the earnest purpose, the plain living, high thinking, and noble self-sacrifice that make a man? We look in vain among the bulk of our writers even for appreciation of these qualities. With the younger men all that is usually cultivated is that flippant smartness which is synonymous with cheapness. There is such a want of wit amongst them, too, such a lack of variety, such monotony of threadbare subjects worked to death! Their "comic" papers subsist upon repetitions of those three venerable jests, the mother-in-law, somebody drunk, and an edifying deception successfully practised by an unfaithful husband or wife. As they have nothing true so they have nothing new to give us, nothing either to expand the heart or move us to happy mirth. Their ideas of beauty threaten always to be satisfied with the ballet dancer's legs, pretty things enough in their way, but not worth mentioning as an aid to the moral, intellectual, and physical strength that make a man. They are sadly deficient in imagination, too; that old fallacy to which they cling, that because an evil thing has always been, therefore it must always continue, is as much the result of want of imagination as of the man's tricks of evading the responsibility of seeing right done in any matter that does not immediately affect his personal comfort. But there is one thing the younger men are specially good at, and that is giving their opinion; this they do to each other's admiration until they verily believe it to be worth something. Yet they do not even know where we are in the history of the world. One of them only lately, doubtless by way of ingratiating himself with the rest of the Bawling Brotherhood, actually proposed to reintroduce the Acts of the Apostles-of-the-Pavements; he was apparently quite unaware of the fact that the mothers of the English race are too strong to allow themselves to be insulted by the reimposition of another most shocking degradation upon their sex. Let him who is responsible for the economic position which forces women down be punished for the consequence. If any are unaware of cause and effect in that matter, let them read *The Struggle for Life*, which the young master wrote in *Wreckage*. As the workingman says with Christ-like compassion: "They wouldn't be there, poor things, if they were not driven to it."[1]

There are upwards of a hundred thousand women in London doomed to damnation by the written law of man if they dare to die, and to infamy for a livelihood if they must live; yet the man at the head of affairs wonders what it is that we with the power are protesting against in the name of our sex. But *is* there any wonder we women wail for the dearth of manliness when we find men from end to end of their rotten social system forever doing the most cowardly deed in their own code, striking at the defenceless woman, especially when she is down?

The Bawling Brotherhood have been seeing reflections of themselves lately which did not flatter them, but their conceit survives, and they cling confidently to the delusion that they are truly all that is admirable, and it is the mirror that is in fault. Mirrors may be either a distorting or a flattering medium, but women do not care to see life any longer in a glass darkly. Let there be light. We suffer in the first shock of it. We shriek in horror at what we discover when it is turned on that which was hidden away in dark corners, and as we recover ourselves we go to work with a will to sweep them out. It is for us to set the human household in order, to see to it that all is clean and sweet and comfortable for the men who are fit to help us to make home in it. We are bound to raise the dust while we are at work, but only those who are in it will suffer any inconvenience from it, and the self-sufficing and self-supporting are not afraid. For the rest it will be all benefits. The Woman Question is the Marriage Question, as shall be shown hereafter.

Notes

1. Grand is referring to Hubert Crackanthorpe's collection of stories, entitled *Wreckage: Seven Studies* (1893). In the story "The Struggle for Life," a working-class woman sells her body for half-a-crown in order to feed her starving baby. Meanwhile, her husband spends his wages on a prostitute in a brothel.

33. The New Woman and the Old

Introduction

Sarah Grand's "The New Woman and the Old," appearing in 1898 in *Lady's Realm,* and reprinted here from that periodical, provides insight into the struggles of the emerging New Woman and her troubled relationship with the older generation. The legal and political advances of the 1890s seemed to betray the ideals by which traditional women had lived, and with hurt feelings and outraged sensibilities many of them took to the pages of popular journals to decry the effrontery of their "daughters." In the ensuing debate, known as "The Revolt of the Daughters," young feminists attempted to justify themselves and to attain the support and sympathy of their "mothers." Grand's essay is an important commentary on this generational conflict. Keenly aware of women's need for solidarity, Grand attacked those who were unable or unwilling to support emancipation and who continued to espouse ideas about marriage and ideal womanhood whose "time had passed." In her words, women who insisted on defining themselves (and other women) through their relations with men were no less than "traitors to their sex." Attempting to establish the identity of the New Woman, Grand celebrates her capacity for joy, love, and integrity. Rather than an enemy to her mothers, she is the liberator of her future daughters, and while she is capable of making (and admitting to) mistakes, she retains what has always been best in women, but without the same obstacles to her growth. An older New Woman herself, Grand embodied the ideal of cross-generational solidarity and responsible motherhood that she espoused, and she positioned herself as a model for other mature women to follow.

The New Woman and the Old

Where is this New Woman, this epicene creature, this Gorgon set up by the snarly who impute to her the faults of both sexes while denying her the charm of either—where is she to be found, if she exist at all? For my own part, until I make her acquaintance I shall believe her to be the finest work of the imagination which the newspapers have yet produced.

I saw a lady the other day standing beside a bicycle on a country lane. She was a young creature, slender, elegant, admirably built, her figure, set off to the best advantage by the new cycling costume, being evidently undeformed by compression of any kind. Judging by what the papers say of the effect of this costume on the female character, I really should have been afraid to accost her. However, she spoke to me, very courteously asking her way, which she had lost. I directed her, and then she prepared to mount.

"Oh! wait one moment," I exclaimed, emboldened by the charm of her manner. "Do pardon me for asking, but are you the New Woman?"

"I'm sure I don't know," she answered, laughing. "I only know that I enjoy every hour of my life, and that is a new thing for a woman. But pray excuse me. I am hurrying home to put my baby to bed, and get my husband's tea."

She whirled away, leaving me at first under the impression that, of course, she could not be the New Woman. On second thoughts, however, I felt pretty sure that she was—the New Woman and the Old too—new in the perfection of her physique, old in her home-loving proclivities: a stronger, better, more beautiful creature than the blockhead majority can conceive. You may know her for certain by her manners, for she is always gentle and serene. It is the Old Woman who shrieks. Her most prominent characteristic is disloyalty to her own sex. She heaps abuse upon the New Woman whom she does not know; but the New Woman bears her no ill-will for her attacks, which are fine samples of what ought not to be, and help notably to point her own moral. The New Woman is magnanimous by nature, and she can well afford to be so, for all that makes life worth having is hers:—"Give me a large heart: an unloving nature is an unlovely nature," she says. "Make me conspicuous for gentlehood, for courtesy and kindness to young and old, men and women, rich and poor. Give me the country to live in, with the sea in sight, and ample leisure. Give me the society of my fellow creatures to enrich my human nature; and give me hours of sacred solitude to strengthen that in me which is divine. Love me! love me! and let me love you! Laugh at me, and let me laugh back. Laugh with me then. Let us see the fun of it all, and laugh without bitterness; life and love last longer, and are the better of such laughter." So she prays; and all her prayers are answered.

The New Woman confesses that she is full of faults. Doubtless in some phases her vanity is overweening, her knowledge ill-digested, and her grammar shaky; what can you expect of the child? She will improve in time, especially if the Old Woman will kindly continue to bark at her whenever she makes a mistake. So let the Old Woman be reassured; the glory of grammar will not be diminished. Not that there are always faults where the Old Woman finds them. The sentences stand the test of analysis, but doubtless they took the Old Woman's breath away when she read them, and so she paused in the wrong place, which rendered the sense obscure. But, at any rate, the New Woman is progressing, and there are plenty to help and encourage her. She sits down to her work with a smile, for she has won the great heart of the people, and knows that they will like her worst better than the best which the Old Woman has to offer them. Head without heart goes a very small way, and only intoxicates, like stimulant without food; but in the matter of heart the New Woman is well endowed. Altogether she is well endowed. Her health is radiant, her manners charming, her wit taking, her morals unimpeachable, and her will a quantity to be reckoned with. Her faults are the overflow of her exuberant spirits, as, for instance, when the Old Woman is more than usually censorious, and she plays her a trick, she wagers that with a word she will have her out on her quill in a hurry, and waits ready to receive her with a shout of laughter when she appears.

The Old Woman has no notion of progress. She ridicules everything to which she is unaccustomed, as is the way with the ignorant. She is unaccustomed to the practice which the New Woman has adopted, of exposing the sores of Society in order to diagnose its diseases, and find a remedy for them: unaccustomed to the creed that there is still boundless better in men and women to be developed. This is the creed of the New Woman, and the Old Woman ridicules it. Her own belief is that evil will always continue, because it has always been; and she is too conservative to wish it otherwise. The New Woman's strength of expression has shaken the Old Woman, and she accuses her of indelicacy, although, in the same breath, she herself stigmatises some of her own sex with one of the foulest epithets in language. But inconsistency was the keynote of the Old Woman's character, and the weathercock her emblem. The New Woman does not blame her, however, for using the right word on occasion. There are times when elegant phraseology is out of place. A knock-down blow is not to be dealt with dainty fingers. Strong words do good when used with that intent; they disgust us with coarse things. It is the coarse idea elegantly veiled in choice language so as to render it attractive that corrupts the mind, and you will find this done in the Old Woman's works to perfection. When she happens to be by way of improving us, she is apt to be a solemn person, and deadly dull, taking herself far too seriously. The New Woman errs perhaps on the other side. Her sense of humour is always on the alert, and she not only sees when other people are ridiculous, but acknowledges it with a grin when she has made herself so. Good humour is another of her attributes. She cultivates it, and hopes to see the day when nothing will have power to ruffle her equanimity. As it is, she will meet you sympathetically on any ground you like, oppose you with a will, and then make a salve for your wounded feelings, if you get the worst of it, or expect you to do as much for her if she does. She cannot for the life of her comprehend why people should differ with bitterness. The Old Woman has no sense of humour. Search her books through and see if there is a flash of it to relieve the reeking sensuality. She uses sentimentality instead of humour, as an artist sometimes uses a brilliant fugitive colour instead of a duller permanent tint, just to gain the glory of its first effect. Sentimentality is a fugitive effect: it is a disease of the nervous system which finds a different expression of itself in every age. A sentimental person will be kind to a dog and cruel to a child. But humour is ousting sentimentality out of the world, and sentimentality, suffering from the indignity, calls it a coarse proceeding.

The Old Woman cares only for others in so far as they have it in their power to add to her own pleasure in life. She resents the intrusion on her luxury of any mention of the working man. What is he to her but a machine to cultivate her roses? an ugly machine, that should be shut up in a shed directly it is done with. Of course it must have oil enough to keep it from creaking, because the plaintive sound distracts her, but she smiles derisively at the notion that it is worth any other attention, or that it would be possible to polish it if you tried. What is it to her if the man ache in her service, and have no time for any joy in life, and only bread enough to make muscles to work out her whims—he gets his wages. Toil for him, ample leisure for her, only disturbed by anger because some beautiful creature that might have made her happier if alive has been slaughtered. The bird that might have delighted her eyes has been made a feather in another woman's cap, and therefore she is indignant; the weary working-man never costs her a thought so long as he does not disturb her, but if he complains he becomes a bore to be banished. With the New Woman it is different. She sorrows for all who suffer, from the slaves of service to the seals of commerce, from the hunted otter to the humming-bird persecuted for fashion's sake. To be consistent, she and the Old Woman should both be vegetarians, and even then should mourn because the lovely cabbage leaves are cut off in their prime to be boiled; but the New Woman will wager her share of humour against the Old Woman's sentimentality, that if either of them carried their principles to the point of starvation it would not be the Old one.

When man jeers at the Old Woman we resent it for the honour of our sex; but we must confess that she gave him good cause. See how she reasons! Because Bismarck is great, therefore there is no fault to be found with any man![1] Because Lady Jane Grey, the daughter of a duke, was taught Latin and Greek, and otherwise enjoyed the advantage of the best education of her time, therefore it is absurd for modern women to clamour for any privilege they have not got![2] The Old Woman has no sense of comparison, and is a prey to confusion of thought. She would have us believe, in the face of all evidence to the contrary, that the ordinary girl of ability has always had within her reach the necessary means of culture: that the Vicar of Wakefield's wife and daughters were as carefully educated as his sons, or if they were not it was their own fault. She contends that women have nothing to complain of in the way of opportunities, and illustrates the point by insisting that the curate's clever child, living untaught in a country village, without a penny to buy a book, or a friend from whom to borrow one, would succeed if she had it in her, because George Sand, a woman of birth and position, besides being a genius born, succeeded.[3] But even she did not succeed till she gave herself a man's opportunities to develop her powers. Our

Old Woman also maintains that the village doctor's daughter, a girl with a big brain and no occupation, should be satisfied to see her stupid brother sent to school, to enjoy advantages which would have made her life worth having, but are only lost upon him. Mrs. Somerville,[4] having every opportunity, every book, every instrument, and every encouragement, made her mark as also did Elizabeth Barrett Browning under similar circumstances; therefore the Old Woman thinks the village doctor's daughter has nothing to complain of. Was ever B more admirably compared to a bull's foot? Pattis are doubtless born, but where would the perfection of their method be but for the making?[5] Singers have a tale of training to tell that is second to none in severity. No reasonable being could suppose that talent was enough without the means to develop it; but one must not expect too much of the Old Woman; she was never supposed to be a reasonable being. She is of settled prejudices, settled virtues, settled vices, a creature of custom, who has come to a standstill. The New Woman, on the contrary, is altering always. She is progressing by degrees. Attempts are made to check her with theories, but she declines to be bound by these until they have been put to the test of experiment, and their value demonstrated. With her as with other creatures, part of the process of development is unlovely. She is apt to be angular when only half grown, and to exhibit the peculiarities which provoke the abuse which the Old Woman, mistaking her for a full grown specimen with her usual want of discernment, levels at her. Much that the Old Woman says of her then is true, but what I say of her is also true; she is the most complex, most interesting creature on earth. Her progress is in obedience to the law, and the law leads upwards. There is a wee dash of boy in her to relieve the insipidity, but all that is not boy is gentlewoman. Her superiority to the Old Woman shines in her versatility; she can do so many more things in a womanly way. When she takes up a new pursuit the Old Woman derides her. She makes every step in advance painful for her: but when the step is taken, and another advantage gained, the Old Woman comes in cautiously, and seizes more than her share of it. Twenty years ago women were held in such low esteem, in consequence of the tactics of the Old Woman, that they were not safe from insult in the public streets, could not drive in a hansom, mount to the top of an omnibus, live alone in cities, without loss of caste, or make their livelihood in a hundred honest ways now honourably open to them; but the New Woman came, exacted respect, and won it. The Old Woman opposed and bespattered her so long as the struggle lasted, but when the wind changed and the rising tide of public opinion carried the New Woman on triumphantly, then the Old Woman followed her, greedily reaping the benefit of her success, but not giving thanks. The Old Woman is a creature of clothes, and she will adopt any ridiculous or indecent fashion that comes to her by way of the fashion papers; but she cannot be taught to dress herself. She has shown as much of the upper part of her body unclad as she dare for generations, and she has gazed complacently at the bare legs of the ballet too, but she hisses the new bicycling dress like the goose she is. When the battle of the bicycling dress is over, however, the Old Woman will discover that it can be worn as modestly as riding habit or bathing dress, and then she will adopt it, mean Old Woman!

The New Woman is much purer even as she is much greater of nature. She can live on occasion among crowds of human beings without a thought in her mind to sully her delicacy. She believes that men and women can meet together, be herded together for the moment, if you will, under circumstances of the closest intimacy by exigencies of occupation or travel, and not have an objectionable thought among them, and so believing she creates about herself the moral atmosphere she prefers. Grossness is in the mind that entertains it, the nasty mind. The New Woman does things which the Old Woman could not do without thought of evil because the New Woman lives in a more rarified moral atmosphere than the Old one. She knows that thoughts are things, that mind moves mind insensibly, and so she banishes the corrupt mind from her presence, as she banishes the corrupt work from her bookshelves. The Old Woman has not attained to this knowledge, and is satisfied with restrictions imposed upon language. We agree that a nasty-minded young person should neither be allowed to travel nor to associate at college with her superiors. She should be shut up in seclusion with the Old Woman. Nasty-mindedness is contagious, but so also is refinement; and the woman who knows and is not tainted is a finer creature than the one who is not enlightened because she cannot be trusted.

The Old Woman knew her own sex as little as she cared for it—that is to say, not at all. She only recognised other women in their relation to men, and that only in the one sense, the sexual. She sees in our sacred humanity evidence of one function only, and deals with that principally in a state of perversion. Hers were the three-bottle days of sexuality. The New Woman despises any intemperance; besides, she has no time to do more than sip a wholesome draught. She is a well-balanced creature, with innumerable interests in life, and enjoys them all without excess. The Old Woman depended on Man for her pleasures. She liked to be made love too [sic], and so does the New Woman when it is delicately done, and there is not too much of it. But to live only to be loved in that way would be too much sweet to be wholesome. That was the mistake the Old Woman made; she was limited. She had only the one great interest in life, and strove always to prolong it. Her paradise was the passion period; she had no great sympathy with any other phase of nature—which made her a monotonous person, in whom one's interest soon became exhausted. The whole aim and object of her existence was sensual pleasure. The New Woman is a nobler creature. Her face softens at the thought of the little ones. Man may be dear as her lover, but he is dearer still as the father of her children.

The New Woman can be hard on man, but it is because she believes in him and loves him. She recognises his infinite possibilities. She sees the God in him, and means to banish the brute. She has full faith in his ultimate perfection, otherwise she would not tolerate him for a moment. And, alas! for the Old Woman, after the way in which she laid herself out to attract him, man likes the New Woman best. He suffers no pin-pricks of a petty mind in her company. Her admirable temper and fine physique are a lasting charm; and he likes her confidence in him, her frank camaraderie, her sincerity; but more especially is he surprised and delighted to find that she does not pillage him. She is a loyal lady, and wholesome-minded. Her bosom friends need not keep one eye on her and the other on their husbands. Her kisses are for her own, and for the children; and that is more than the Old Woman could say as a rule.

The Old Woman has had her day. Let us hope she enjoyed it. She has taught us what to avoid in life, many thanks to her, although no one is more disgusted than she is at the effect of her works upon us. Gawain was agreeable to the Old Woman doubtless, but only Galahad is good enough for the New. She is arrogant in that; she asks for the best man, and means to have him.

But what the New Woman demands specially is what every man worth the name is glad that she should have—fair play. She objects to the cowardliness which will trade upon a young, ill-educated girl's indolence, love of luxury, and mistaken notions of life; who knows her nature while she herself is kept in ignorance of it, and uses his knowledge to degrade her. That is not fair play. There is no need to interfere between men and women of the world; let them regulate their relations as they please, and take the consequences—they know what they are doing. But the mother in the New Woman aches to protect the young—the young girl from being brutalised by man, and the young boy from falling into the woman's hands after all that was angelic in her has been destroyed by evil association.

Does the Old Woman really think that we, without foreseeing a better day to come, would leave the sacred solitude of our woods, leave the gladness of summer seas, the glory of summer sunset, the songs of birds, the perfume of flowers, the companionship of our friends, and all the ecstatic joys of seclusion, and go forth to fight for any motive but the highest? You, who are not unacquainted with the horrors of lust, stand aside for us. Love is our God, and we go forth at his bidding to deliver his message; but let no one shame himself by saying that we do not suffer in the going.

The Old Woman draws her hood over her head, and sits in darkness that she may not know us for what we are. We are the new generation mentioned by the Master, and already we are knocking at the door. Our knocking is the knell of the Old Woman. No wonder she shudders! But it is useless to resist. She must go. That is inevitable—and it is also pathetic.

Notes

1.   Otto Eduard Leopold, Prince von Bismarck (1815–98). While serving as minister-president and foreign minister of Prussia from 1862, Bismarck orchestrated the unification of Germany. He served as Chancellor of the new German empire from 1871 to 1890.

2.   Lady Jane Grey (1537–54) was granddaughter of Henry VIII's sister. She reigned as Queen of England for nine days.

3.   George Sand. Pseudonym of Amandine-Aurore Lucille Dupin, Baronne Dudevant (1804–76). A famous French novelist who left her husband to lead an independent literary life in Paris.

4.   Mary Fairfax Greig Somerville (1780–1872). Considered the "queen of nineteenth-century science," Somerville published articles as well

as highly regarded scientific books, including *The Mechanism of the Heavens* (1831) and *On Molecular and Microscopic Science* (1868).

5.   Adelina Patti (1843–1919). A coloratura soprano who was one of the most enthusiastically admired operatic stars of the period.

XVI. Vernon Lee
(Violet Paget)

(1856–1935)

Vernon Lee holds a prominent position among both aesthetes and social theorists of late-Victorian intellectual society. Writing beyond the more narrowly defined boundaries of art and literature, Lee was a cultural critic whose domain extended across the Medieval, Renaissance, and contemporary epochs of artistic production in Great Britain and on the continent.

Lee began her life and literary career as Violet Paget, the daughter of relatively affluent English-born parents, Matilda Abadam (whose first husband, Captain Lee-Hamilton, died) and Henry Ferguson Paget, an educator of French ancestry. Born in Boulonge-sur-Mer, France, Lee spent much of her childhood traveling with her parents, especially in Germany, France, and Italy. The family eventually settled at Villa Il Palmerino, San Gervasio, Florence, where Lee resided until her death.

Lee's education was largely conducted at home, where her love of art, literature, and philosophy was fostered by the intellectual pursuits of her mother. During the 1860s, Lee also attended schools in Germany and Switzerland. While studying in Thun, Switzerland, she met Marie Schulpbach, who became one of her most influential teachers. At this time, the Pagets developed a friendship with the Sargent family, who often introduced them to prominent artists and cultural figures of the day. Mrs. Sargent toured Rome with Lee, and proved to be another major influence in the educational formation of this future critic of art and culture. Mrs. Sargent's children, Emily and John Singer Sargent, were among Lee's closest childhood friends. This cosmopolitan atmosphere also influenced Lee's half-brother, Eugene Lee-Hamilton, from whose name she fashioned her pseudonym. A poet and student of literature, Lee-Hamilton consistently encouraged his younger sibling in the intellectual and literary pursuits that would soon exceed his own. Indeed, as early as 1870 *Les Aventures d'une Piece de Monnaie*, written by the thirteen-year-old "Mlle V.P.," was published in the Swiss paper *La Famille*. *Studies of the Eighteenth Century in Italy*, the work that launched her literary career, appeared in 1880. Signed "Vernon Lee," this book met with an immediately favorable reception in England and on the continent. Italy's *Nueva Autologia* said of the author's work, "The severity of his studies and the patience of his research are evident at every step."

In 1881, Lee traveled to England for the first time and instantly assumed a prominent position in English artistic and intellectual society. Among circles that included James Whistler, Ouida (Marie Louise De La Ramée), Oscar Wilde, Henry James and the Humphry Wards, she was known for her wit and conversational skills; she was often revered, although occasionally despised. George Bernard Shaw called her "the noblest Briton of them all," while Max Beerbohm complained that she was always "having a crow to pick, ever so coyly, with Nietzsche . . . or Mr. Carlyle . . . or Mr. H.G. Wells." In 1884, Lee published the novel *Miss Brown*, in which she satirized the "art for art's sake" movement, and thus alienated many of her friends.

Nevertheless, as Lee developed her aesthetic philosophy, she remained ideologically and socially in step with many in the London intellectual scene. Through the Humphry Wards, she met Walter Pater, with whom she developed a close friendship. She even dedicated her next major work, *Euphorion: Studies in the Antique and the Medieval in the Renaissance* (1884), to him. Often differing ideologically from Pater, however, as well as frequently posing explicit challenges to John Ruskin's writing, Lee developed and established her own aesthetic through prolific contributions to journals whose range extended from the popular *Contemporary Review* under the liberal-minded editorship of Percy William Bunting to the more intellectually elite *Fortnightly Review*. Among the most explicit statements of her aesthetic theory is the essay "Art and Life" (1896), reprinted here.

As evidenced in "Art and Life," and more radically in the later "Gospels of Anarchy," Lee began to synthesize aesthetic and social theory during the later 1880s and throughout the 1890s. A concern with contemporary social ills and inequities, as well as a belief in the individual's intellectual refinement as the key to amelioration of these problems, is apparent in the series of "Dialogues" that would later comprise *Baldwin: Being Dialogues on Views and Aspirations* (1886) and *Althea: A Second Book of Dialogues on Aspirations and Duties* (1894).

Later, Lee's sociopolitical liberalism (specifically her lack of nationalist loyalties and the pacifism that her writing openly manifested during the Boer War, the Italo-Turkish War, and at the outbreak of World War One), would lead to her falling out of popular favor, particularly in Great Britain and Italy. This change in reception was exacerbated by the fact that certain British journals would no longer accept her work. Throughout the late 1800s, Lee had contributed the majority of her essays to the *Contemporary Review*, *Fraser's Magazine*, and the *Fortnightly Review*; by 1900, she frequently turned to publishing in American periodicals, such as *The North American Review* and *Atlantic Monthly*.

Late in her career, Lee achieved international success for the fiction, drama, and travel writing that she had been consistently producing along with her critical endeavors. In 1903, she published the five-act romantic drama, *Ariadne in Mantua*, whose popularity carried it through three English editions. Ironically, *Ariadne* and travel essays like those contained in *Genius Loci* (1899), all of which Lee saw as her lesser work, attracted her widest readership.

Lee's life and literary career are reconstructed with some insightful detail in Peter Gunn's biographical study, *Vernon Lee: Violet Paget, 1856–1935* (1964), which concentrates primarily on Lee as a member of Victorian intellectual society, rather than on Lee as a major contributor to contemporary—and future—theoretical dialogues. More recent studies focus on Lee's romantic and intellectual relationships with other women. These studies include Burdett Gardner's *The Lesbian Imagination (Victorian Style): A Psychological and Critical Study of "Vernon Lee"* (1987), and Phyllis Mannocchi's "Vernon Lee and Kit Anstruther-Thomson: A Study of Love and Collaboration Between Romantic Friends" (*Women's Studies* 12 (1986):129–48). For a critical study of Lee's fiction, consult Veneta Colby's *The Singular Anomaly: Women Novelists of the Nineteenth Century* (1970). Lee's obituary in the *Times* (February 14, 1935) provides not only basic biographical information, but also some sense of Lee's reputation among her contemporary readership.

Kathleen Dillon,
Temple University

34. Art and Life
I., III.

Introduction

Vernon Lee's article "Art and Life" appeared in the *Contemporary Review* in May, June, and July, 1896, and is reprinted here from that periodical. By drawing explicit connections between aesthetic beauty and ethical action, and by developing a correlation between artistic form and human existence, "Art and Life" not only attempts a synthesis of the increasingly divergent halves of the late-Victorian self, but also provides an intriguing contrast to the aesthetic standards of judgement established by Walter Pater's "Style" (*Appreciations*, 1889). The first part of "Art and Life" challenges many of the theories held by "persons styled by themselves aesthetes and by others decadents" and advances the notion of the beautiful as fortification of "the spiritual life of the individual." The third part of "Art and Life" develops a discussion of "style" as not only "the organic correspondence between the various parts of the work of art," but also as "the organic interdependence and interchange" of the human form and of behavior. Ultimately, Lee argues for the necessity of a correspondence of interchange between the style of the individual life and that of "the life universal," to which "really aesthetic" thinkers will apply themselves. As is more evident in the dynamic process of questioning and critical reaction outlined later in "Gospels of Anarchy" (1898), this mode of apprehending the universe constitutes an infinite alteration between "being" and "becoming."

Art and Life
I.

One afternoon, in Rome, on the way back from the Aventine, the road-mender climbed on to the tram as it trotted slowly along, and fastened on to its front, alongside of the place of the driver, a big bough of budding bay.

Might one not search long for a better symbol of what we may all do by our life? Bleakness, wind, squalid streets, a car full of heterogeneous people, some very dull, most very common; a laborious jogtrot all the way. But to redeem it all with the pleasantness of beauty and the charm of significance, this laurel branch.

* * *

Our language does not possess any single word wherewith to sum up the various categories of things (made by Nature or made by man, intended solely for the purpose or subserving by mere coincidence) which minister to our organic and many-sided æsthetic instincts, the things which affect us in that absolutely special, unmistakable, and hitherto mysterious manner expressed in the fact of our finding them *beautiful*. It is of the part which such things—whether actually present or merely shadowed in our mind—can play in our life, of the influence of the instinct for beauty on the other instincts making up our nature, that I wish to speak in these pages. And for this reason I have been glad to accept from the hands of chance, and of that road-mender of the tramway, the bay laurel as a symbol of what we have no word to express—the aggregate of all art, all poetry, and particularly of all poetic and artistic vision and emotion.

For the bay laurel—*laurus nobilis* of botanists—happens not merely to be the evergreen, unfading plant into which Apollo metamorphosed, while pursuing, the maiden whom he loved, even as the poet, the artist, turns into immortal shapes his own quite personal and transitory moods; it is a plant of noblest utility, averting, as the ancients thought, lightning from the dwellings it surrounded, even as disinterested love for beauty averts from our minds the dangers which fall on the vain and the covetous; and curing many aches and fevers, even as the contemplation of beauty refreshes and invigorates our spirit. Indeed, we seem to be reading a description no longer of the virtues of the bay laurel, but of the virtues of all beautiful sights and sounds, of all beautiful thoughts and emotions, in reading the following quaint and charming words of an old herbal:

> The bay leaves are of as necessary use as any other in garden or orchard, for they serve both for pleasure and profit, both for ornament and use, both for honest civil uses and for physic; yea, both for the sick and for the sound, both for the living and for the dead. The bay serveth to adorn the house of God as well as of man, to procure warmth, comfort, and strength to the limbs of men and women; . . . . to season vessels wherein are preserved our meats as well as our drinks; to crown or encircle as a garland the heads of the living, and to stick and deck forth the bodies of the dead; so that, from the cradle to the grave we have still use of it, we have still need of it.

The symbol is too perfect to require any commentary. Let me therefore pass on without additional delay to explain, in as few words as possible, why the Beautiful should possess such power for good, and to point out before entering into a detailed account of any of them in especial what the three principal moral functions of æsthetic emotion and contemplation may be said to be. And, first, for the *why*. Beauty, save by a metaphorical application of the word, is not in the least the same thing as goodness, any more than beauty (despite Keats's famous assertion) is the same thing as truth. These three objects of the soul's eternal pursuit have different objects, different laws, and fundamentally different origins. But the energies which express themselves in their pursuit—energies vital, primordial, and necessary even to man's physical survival—have all been evolved under the same stress of adaptation of the human creature to its surroundings; and have therefore, in their beginnings and in their ceaseless growth, been perpetually working in concert, meeting, crossing, and strengthening one another, until they have become indissolubly woven together by a number of great and organic coincidences.

It is these coincidences which all higher philosophy, from Plato downwards, has for ever strained to expound; these coincidences, which all religion and all poetry have taken for granted; and to three of which I desire to call attention, persuaded as I am that the scientific progress of our day will make short work of all the spurious æstheticism and all the shortsighted utilitarianism which have cast doubts upon the intimate and vital connection between beauty and every other noble object of our living. The three coincidences I have chosen are: that between development of the æsthetic faculties and the development of the altruistic instincts; that between development of a sense of æsthetic harmony and a sense of the higher harmonies of universal life; and, before everthing [sic] else, the coincidence between the preference for æsthetic pleasures and the nobler growth of the individual.

The particular emotion produced in us by such things as are beautiful, works of art or of nature, recollections and thoughts as well as sights and sounds, the emotion of æsthetic pleasure has been recognised ever since the beginning of time as of a mysteriously ennobling quality. All philosophers, beginning with Plato, have told us that; and the religious instinct of all mankind has practically proclaimed it, by employing for the worship of the highest powers, nay, by employing for the mere designation of the godhead, beautiful sights and sounds, and words by which beautiful sights and sounds are suggested. Nay, there has always lurked in men's minds, and expressed itself in the metaphors of men's speech—an intuition that the Beautiful is in some manner one of the primordial and, so to speak, cosmic powers of the world. The theories of various schools of mental science, and the practice of various schools of art, the practice particularly of the persons styled by themselves æsthetes and by others decadents, have indeed attempted to reduce man's relations with the great world-power Beauty to mere intellectual dilettantism or sensual superfineness. But the general intuition has not been shaken—the general intuition which felt in Beauty a superhuman, and, in that sense, a truly divine power. And now it must become evident that the methods of modern psychology, of the great new science of body and soul, are beginning to explain the reasonableness of this intuition, or, at all events, to show very plainly in what direction we must look for the explanation thereof. This much can now be asserted, and can be indicated even to those least versed in recent psychological study, to wit, that the power of Beauty, the essential power therefore of art, is due to the relations of certain visible and audible forms with the chief nervous and vital functions of all sensitive creatures; relations established throughout the whole process of human and, perhaps, even of animal evolution; relations seated in the depths of our activities, but radiating upwards even like our vague, organic sense of comfort and discomfort; and permeating, even like our obscure relations with atmospheric conditions, into our highest and clearest consciousness, colouring and altering the whole groundwork of our thoughts and feelings. Such is the primordial and, in a sense, cosmic power of the Beautiful; a power whose very growth, whose constantly more complex nature proclaims its necessary and beneficial action in human evolution. It is the power of making human beings live, for the moment, in a more organically vigorous and harmonious fashion, as mountain air or sea-wind makes them live, but with the difference that it is not merely the bodily, but very essentially the spiritual life, the life of thought and emotion, which is thus raised to unusual harmony and vigour. I may illustrate the matter by a very individual instance, which will bring to the memory of each of my readers the vivifying power[1] of some beautiful sight or sound or beautiful description. I was seated working by my window, depressed by the London outlook of narrow grey sky, endless grey roofs, and rusty elm-tops, when I became conscious of a certain increase of vitality, almost as if I had drunk a glass of wine, because a band somewhere or other had begun to play. Suddenly, after various indifferent pieces, it began a certain piece, by Handel or in Handel's style, of which I have never known the name, but which I have always called for myself the *Te Deum* tune. And then it seemed as if my soul, and according to the sensations, in a certain degree my body even, were caught up on those notes, and were striking out as if swimming in a great breezy sea; or as if it had put forth wings and risen into a great free space of air. And, noticing my feelings, I seemed to be conscious that those notes were being played on me, my fibres becoming the strings, so that as the notes moved and soared and swelled and radiated like stars and suns, I also being identified with sound, having become apparently the sound itself, must needs move and soar with them.

We can all recollect a dozen instances in which architecture, music, painting, or some sudden sight of sea or mountain, has thus affected us; and all poetry, particularly all great lyric poetry—Goethe's, Schiller's, Wordsworth's, and, above all, Browning's—is full of the record of such experience.

I have said that the difference between this æsthetic heightening of our vitality (and this that I have been describing is, I pray you to observe, the æsthetic phenomenon *par excellence*), and such heightening of vitality as we experience from going into fresh air and sunshine or taking fortifying food—the difference between the æsthetic and the mere physiological pleasurable excitement consists herein, that in the case of an impression, not of bodily comfort but of beauty, it is not merely our physical life but our spiritual life which is suddenly rendered more vigorous. We do not merely breathe better and digest better, though that is no small gain, but we seem to *know better*: under the vitalising touch of the Beautiful, our consciousness seems filled with the affirmation of what life is, what is worth being, what among our many thoughts and acts and feelings are real and organic and important, what among the many possible moods is the real, eternal *ourself*.

Such are the great forces of Nature gathered up in what we call the *æsthetic phenomenon*, and it is these forces of Nature which, stolen from heaven by the man of genius or the nation of genius, and welded together in music or architecture, in visual art or written, give to the great work of art its power to quicken the life of our soul.

I hope I have been able to indicate how, by its essential nature, by the primordial power it embodies, all Beauty, and particularly Beauty in art, tends to fortify and refine the spiritual life of the individual.

But this is only half of the question, for, in order to get the full benefit of beautiful things and beautiful thoughts, in order to obtain in the highest potency those potent æsthetic emotions, the individual must undergo a course of self-training, of self-initiation, which in its turn elicits and improves some of the highest qualities of his soul. Nay, in all true æsthetic training there must needs be—as every great writer on art has felt, from Plato to Ruskin, but none has expressed as clearly as Mr. Pater—into all æsthetic training there must needs enter an ethical, almost an ascetic element.

The greatest art bestows pleasure just in proportion as people are capable of buying that pleasure at the price of attention, intelligence, and reverent sympathy. For great art is such as is richly endowed, full of variety, subtlety, and suggestiveness; full of delightfulness enough for a lifetime, the lifetime of generations and generations of men; great art is to its true lovers like Cleopatra to Antony—"age cannot wither it, nor custom stale its infinite variety." Nay, when it is the greatest art of all, the art produced by the marvellous artist, the most gifted race, and the longest centuries, we find ourselves in presence of something which, like Nature itself, contains more beauty, incorporates more thought, and works more miracles than most of us have faculties to fully appreciate. So that, in some of Titian's pictures and Michael Angelo's frescoes, the Olympia Hermes, certain cantos of Dante and plays of Shakespeare, fugues of Bach and scenes of Mozart, we can each of us, looking our closest, feeling our uttermost, see and feel perhaps but a trifling portion of what there is to be seen and felt, leaving other sides, other perfections, to be appreciated by our neighbours; till it comes to pass that we find different persons very differently delighted by the same masterpiece, and accounting most discrepantly for their delight in it.

Now such pleasure as this requires not merely a vast amount of activity on our part, since all pleasure, even the lowest, is the expression of an activity; it requires a vast amount of attention, of intelligence, of what, in races or in individuals, means special training.

There is a sad confusion in men's minds on the very essential subject of pleasure. We tend, most of us, to oppose the idea of pleasure to the idea of work, effort, strenuousness, patience; and, therefore, recognise as pleasures only those which cost none of these things, or as little as possible, pleasures which, instead of being produced through our will and act, impose themselves upon us from outside. In all art— for art stands halfway between the sensual and emotional experiences and the experiences of the mere reasoning intellect—in all art there is necessarily an element which thus imposes itself upon us from without, an element which takes and catches us: colour, strangeness of outline, sentimental or terrible quality, rhythm, modulation or clang which tickles the ear. But the art which thus takes and catches our attention the most easily, asking nothing in return, or next to nothing, is also the poorest art—the oleograph, the pretty woman in the fashion-plate, the caricature, the representation of some domestic or harrowing scene, children being put to bed, babes in the wood, railway accidents, &c.; or again, dance or march music, and aphorisms in verse. It catches your attention, instead of your attention catching it; but it speedily ceases to interest, gives you nothing more, cloys, or comes to a dead stop. It resembles thus far mere sensual pleasures—a savoury dish, a glass of good wine, an excellent cigar, a warm bed, which impose themselves on the nerves without expenditure of attention; with the result, of course, that little or nothing remains, a sensual impression dying, so to speak, childless, a barren, disconnected thing, without place in the memory, unmarried as it is to the memory's clients, thought and human feeling.

If so many people prefer poor art to great, 'tis because they refuse to give, through inability or unwillingness, as much of their soul as great art requires for its enjoyment. And it is noticeable that busy men, coming to art for pleasure when they are too weary for attention or thought, so often prefer the sensation-novel, the music-hall song, and such painting as is but a costlier kind of oleograph; treating all other art as humbug, and art in general as a trifle wherewith to wile away a lazy moment, a trifle about which every man *can know what he likes best*.

Thus it is that great art makes, by coincidence, the same demands as noble thinking and acting. For, even as all noble sports develop muscle, develop eye, skill, quickness and pluck in bodily movement, qualities which are valuable also in the practical business of life; so also the appreciation of noble kinds of art implies the acquisition of habits of accuracy, of patience, of respectfulness and suspension of judgment, of preference of future good over present, of harmony and clearness, of sympathy (when we come to literary art), judgment and kindly fairness, which are all of them useful to our neighbours and ourselves in the many contingencies and obscurities of real life. Now this is not so with the pleasures of the senses; the pleasures of the senses do not increase by sharing, and sometimes cannot be shared at all; they are, moreover, evanescent, leaving us no richer; above all, they cultivate in ourselves qualities useful only for that particular enjoyment. Thus, a highly discriminating palate may have saved the life of animals and savages, but what can its subtleness do nowadays beyond making us into gormandising and winebibbing persons?

Delight in beautiful things and in beautiful thoughts requires, therefore, a considerable exercise of the will and the attention, such as is not demanded by our lower enjoyments. Indeed, it is probably this absence of moral and intellectual effort which recommends such lower kinds of pleasure to a large number of persons. I have said lower *kinds* of pleasure, because there are other enjoyments besides those of the senses which entail no moral improvement in ourselves: the enjoyments connected with vanity. Even if any of us could be sure of being impeccable on these points, we should not be too hard on the persons and the classes of persons who are conscious of no other kind of enjoyment. They are not necessarily base, not necessarily sensual or vain, because they care only for bodily indulgence, for notice and gain. They are very likely not base, but only apathetic, slothful, or very tired. The noble sport, the intellectual problem, the great work of art, the divinely beautiful effect in Nature, require that one should *give oneself;*

the French-cooked dinner as much as the pot of beer; the game of chance, whether with clean cards at a club or with greasy ones in a taproom; the outdoing of one's neighbours, whether by the out-at-elbows heroes of Zola or the polished heroes of Balzac, require no such coming forward of the soul: they *take* us, without any need for our giving ourselves. Hence, as I have just said, the preference for them does not imply original baseness, but only lack of higher energy. We can judge of the condition of those who can taste no other pleasures by remembering what the best of us are when we are tired or ill: vaguely craving for interests, sensations, emotions, variety, but quite unable to procure them through our own effort, and longing for them to come to us from without. Now, in our still very badly organised world, an enormous number of people are condemned by the tyranny of poverty or the tyranny of fashion, to be, when the day's work or the day's business is done, in just such a condition of fatigue and languor, of craving, therefore, for the baser kinds of pleasure. We all recognise that this is the case with what we call *poor people*, and that this is why poor people are apt to prefer the public-house to the picture-gallery or the concert-room. It would be greatly to the purpose were we to acknowledge that it is largely the case with the rich, and that for that reason the rich are apt to take more pleasure in ostentatious display of their properties than in contemplation of such beauty as is accessible to all men. Indeed, it is one of the ironies of the barbarous condition we are pleased to call *civilisation*, that so many rich men—thousands daily—are systematically toiling and moiling till they are unable to enjoy any pleasure which requires vigour of mind and attention, rendering themselves impotent, from sheer fatigue, to enjoy the delights which life gives generously to all those who fervently seek them. And what for? Largely for the sake of those pleasures which can be had only for money, but which can be enjoyed without using one's soul.

* * *

Thus it is that real æsthetic keenness—and æsthetic keenness, as I shall show hereafter, means appreciating beauty, not collecting beautiful properties—means a development of the qualities of patience, attention, reverence, and of that vigour of soul which is not called forth, but rather impaired, by the coarser enjoyments of the senses and of vanity. So far, therefore, we have seen that the capacity for æsthetic pleasure presupposes a certain nobility in the individual. I think I can show that the preference for æsthetic pleasure implies also a happier relation between the individual and his fellows.

But the cultivation of our æsthetic pleasures does not merely necessitate our improvement in certain very essential moral qualities. It tends, as much, in a way, as the cultivation of the intellect and the sympathies, to make us live chiefly in the spirit; in which alone, as philosophers and mystics have rightly understood, there is safety from the worst miseries and room for the most complete happiness. Only, we shall learn from the study of our æsthetic pleasures that while the stoics and mystics have been right in affirming that the spirit only can give the highest good, they have been fatally wrong in the reason for their preference. And we may learn from our æsthetic experiences that the spirit is useful, not in detaching us from the enjoyable things of life, but, on the contrary, in giving us their consummate possession. The spirit—one of whose most precious capacities is that it enables us to print off all outside things on to ourselves, to store moods and emotions, to recombine and reinforce past impressions into present ones—the spirit puts pleasure more into our own keeping, making it more independent of time and place, of circumstances, and, what is equally important, independent of other people's strivings after pleasure, by which our own, while they clash and hamper, are so often fatally impeded.

For our intimate commerce with beautiful things and beautiful thoughts does not exist only, or even chiefly, at the moment of seeing, or hearing, or reading; nay, if the beautiful touched us only at such separate and special moments, the beautiful would play but an insignificant part in our existence.

As a fact, those moments represent very often only the act of *storage*, or not much more. Our real æsthetic life is in ourselves, often isolated from the beautiful words, objects, or sounds; sometimes almost unconscious; permeating the whole of the rest of life in certain highly æsthetic individuals, and, however mixed with other activities, as constant as the life of the intellect and sympathies; nay, as constant as the life of assimilation and motion. We can live off a beautiful object, we can live by its means, even when its visible or audible image is partially, nay, sometimes wholly, obliterated; for the emotional condition can survive the image and be awakened at the mere name, awakened sufficiently to heighten the emotion caused by other images of beauty. We can sometimes feel, so to speak, the spiritual companionship and comfort of a work of art, or of a scene in Nature, nay, almost its particular caress to our whole being, when the work of art or the scene has grown faint in our memory, but the emotion it awakened has kept warm.

Now this possibility of storing for later use, of increasing by combination, the impressions of beautiful things, makes art—and by art I mean all æsthetic activity, whether in the professed artist who creates or the unconscious artist who assimilates—the type of such pleasures as are within our own keeping, and makes the æsthetic life typical also of that life of the spirit in which alone we can realise any kind of human freedom. We shall all of us meet with examples thereof if we seek through our consciousness. That such things existed was made clear to me during a weary period of illness, for which I shall always be grateful, since it taught me, in those months of incapacity for enjoyment, that there is a safe kind of pleasure, a pleasure we can defer. I spent part of that time at Tangier, surrounded by all things which could delight me, but in none of which I took any real delight. I did not enjoy Tangier at the time, but I have enjoyed Tangier ever since, on the principle of the bee eating its honey months after making it. The reality of Tangier, I mean the reality of my presence there, and the state of my nerves, were not in the relation of enjoyment; but the image of Tangier, the remembrance of what I saw and did there, has often since been with my *ego* in the relation of the greatest enjoyment.

After all, is it not often the case with pictures, statues, journeys, and the reading of books? The weariness entailed, the mere continuity of looking or attending, quite apart from tiresome accompanying circumstances, make the apparently real act, what we expect to be the act of enjoyment, quite illusory; like Coleridge, we see, not *feel*, how beautiful things are. Later on, all odious accompanying circumstances are utterly forgotten, eliminated, and the weariness is gone: we enjoy not merely unhampered by accidents, but in the very way our heart desires. For we can choose—our mood unconsciously does it for us—the right moment and right accessories for consuming some of our stored delights; moreover, we can add what condiments and make what mixtures suit us best at that moment. We draw not merely upon one past reality, making its essentials present, but upon dozens. To revert to Tangier (whose experience first brought these possibilities clearly before me), I find I enjoy it in connection with Venice, the mixture having a special roundness of tone or flavour. Similarly, I once heard

Bach's *Magnificat*, with St. Mark's of Venice as a background in my imagination; certain moonlight songs of Schumann have blended wonderfully with remembrances of old Italian villas. King Solomon,[2] in all his ships, could not have carried the things which I can draw, in less than a second, from one tiny convolution of my brain, from one corner of my mind: no Faust[3] that ever lived had spells which could evoke such kingdoms and worlds as any one of us can conjure up with certain words: Greece, the Middle Ages, Orpheus, Robin Hood, Mary Stuart, Ancient Rome, the Far East. And here, as fit illustration of these beneficent powers, which can free us from a life where we are stifled and raise us into a life where we can breathe and grow, let me record my gratitude to a certain young goat, which, on one occasion, turned what might have been a detestable hour into a pleasant one. The goat, or rather kid, a charming gazelle-like creature, with budding horns and broad, hard forehead, was one of my fourteen fellow-passengers in a third-class carriage on a certain bank holiday Saturday. Riding and standing in such crowded misery had cast a general gloom over all the holiday-makers; they seemed to have forgotten the coming outing in sullen hatred of all their neighbours; and I confess that I too began to wonder whether bank holiday was an altogether delightful institution. But the goat had no such doubts. Leaning against the boy who was taking it holiday-making, it tried very gently to climb and butt, and to play with its sulky fellow-travellers. And as it did so it seemed to radiate a sort of poetry on everything: vague impressions of rocks, woods, hedges, the Alps, Italy, and Greece; mythology, of course, and that amusement of "jouer avec des chèvres apprivoisées," which that great charmer M. Renan has attributed to his charming Greek people. And, as I realised the joy of the goat on finding itself among the beech woods and short grass of the Hertfordshire hills, I began also to see my other fellow-travellers no longer as surly people resenting each other's presence, but as happy human beings admitted once more to the pleasant things of life: the goat had quite put me in concert with bank holiday. When it got out of the train at Berkhampstead, the emptier carriage seemed suddenly more crowded, and my fellow-travellers more discontented; but I remained quite pleased, and when I had alighted, found that instead of a horrible journey, I could remember only a rather charming little adventure. That beneficent goat had acted as Pegasus; and on its small back my spirit had ridden off to the places it loves.[4] In this fashion does the true æsthete tend to prefer, even like the austerest moralist, the delights which, being of the spirit, are most independent of circumstances and most in the individual's own power.

The habit of æsthetic enjoyment makes this epicurean into an ascetic. He builds as little as possible on the things of the senses and the moment, knowing how little, in comparison, we have either in our power. For, even if the desired object, person, or circumstance comes, how often does it not come at the wrong hour! In this world, which mankind still fits so badly, the wish and the realisation are rarely in unison, rarely in harmony, but follow each other, most often, like vibrations of different instruments, at intervals which can only jar. The *n'est-ce que cela*, the inability to enjoy, of successful ambition and favoured passionate love is famous; and short of love even and ambition, we all know the flatness of much desired pleasures. King Solomon, who had not been enough of an ascetic, as we all know, and therefore ended off in cynicism, had learned that there is not only satiety as a result of enjoyment, but a sort of satiety also, an absence of keenness, an incapacity for caring, due to the deferring of enjoyment. He doubtless knew, among other items of vanity, that our wishes are often fulfilled without our even knowing it, so indifferent have we become through long waiting, or so changed in our wants.

In a similar way, the modest certainty of all pleasure derived from the Beautiful will accustom the perfect æsthete to seek for the like in other branches of activity. Accustomed to the happiness which is in his own keeping, he will view with suspicion all craving for satisfactions which are beyond his control; he will not ask to be given the moon, and he will not even wish to be given it, lest the wish should grow into a want; he will make the best of candles and glowworms and of distant heavenly luminaries: moreover, being accustomed to enjoy the mere sight of things as much as other folk do their possession, he will probably actually prefer that the moon should be hanging in the heavens, and not on his staircase.

Again, having experience of the æsthetic pleasures which involve, in their sober waking bliss, no wear and tear, no reaction of satiety, he will not care much for the more rapturous pleasures of passion and success, which always cost as much as they are worth. He will be unwilling to run into such debt with his own feelings, having learned from æsthetic pleasure that there are modes of soul which, instead of impoverishing, enrich it.

Thus does the commerce with beautiful things and beautiful thoughts tend to develop in us that healthy amount of asceticism which is necessary for every workable scheme of greater happiness for the individual and the plurality: self-restraint, choice of aims, consistent and thorough-paced subordination of the lesser interest to the greater; above all, what sums up asceticism as an efficacious means towards happiness, preference of the spiritual, the unconditional, the durable, to the temporal, the uncertain, and the fleeting. The intimate and continuous intercourse with the Beautiful teaches us, therefore, the renunciation of the unnecessary for the sake of the possible; it teaches asceticism leading not to indifference and Nirvana, but to higher complexities of vitalisation, to a more complete and harmonious rhythm of individual existence.

*   *   *

In such manner, to resume our symbol of the bay laurel which the road-mender stuck on to the front of that tramcar, can our love for the Beautiful avert, like the plant of Apollo, many of the storms and cure many of the fevers of life.

Art and Life
III.

"To use the beauties of earth as steps long which he mounts upwards, going from one to two, and from two to all fair forms, and from fair forms to fair actions, and from fair actions to fair notions, until from fair notions he arrives at the notion of absolute beauty, and at last knows what the essence of beauty is; this, my dear Socrates," said the prophetess of Mantineia, "is that life, above all others, which man should live, in the contemplation of beauty absolute. Do you not see that in that communion only, beholding beauty with the eye of the mind, he will be enabled to bring forth not images of beauty, but realities; for he has hold not of an image, but of a reality; and bringing forth and educating true virtue to become the friend of God, and be immortal, if mortal man may?"

Such are the æsthetics of Plato, put into the mouth of that mysterious Diotima, who was a wise woman in many branches of knowledge. As we read them nowadays we are apt to smile with incredulity not unmixed with bitterness. Is all this not mere talk, charming and momentarily elating us like so much music; mere beauty which, because we like it, we half voluntarily confuse with *truth*? And, on the other hand, is not the truth of æsthetics, the bare, hard fact, a very different matter? For we have learned that we human creatures shall never know the absolute or the essence, that notions, which Plato took for realities, are mere relative conceptions; that virtue and truth are intellectual abstractions, while beauty is a complex physical, or mainly physical, quality; and every day we are hearing of new discoveries connecting our æsthetic emotions with the structure of eye and ear, the movement of muscles, the functions of nerve centres, nay, even with the action of heart and lungs and viscera. Moreover, all round us schools of criticism and cliques of artists are telling us for ever that so far from bringing forth and educating true virtue, art has the sovereign power, by mere skill and subtlety, of investing good and evil, healthy and unwholesome, with equal merit, and obliterating the distinctions drawn by the immortal gods, instead of helping the immortal gods to their observance.

Thus we are apt to think, and to take the words of Diotima as merely so much lovely rhetoric. But—as my previous chapters have indicated—I think we are so far mistaken. I believe that, although explained in the terms of fantastic, almost mythical metaphysic, the speech of Diotima contains a great truth, deposited in the heart of man by the unnoticed innumerable experiences of centuries and peoples; a truth which the advance of knowledge will confirm and explain. For in that pellucid atmosphere of the Greek mind, untroubled as yet by theoretic mists, there may have been visible the very things which our scientific instruments are enabling us to see and reconstruct piecemeal, great groupings of realty metamorphosed into Fata Morgana cities seemingly built by the gods.

And thus I am going to try to reinstate in others' belief, as it is fully reinstated in my own, the theory of higher æsthetic harmonies, which the prophetess of Mantineia taught Socrates: to wit, that through the contemplation of true beauty we may attain, by the constant purification—or, in more modern language, the constant selecting and enriching—of our nature, to that which transcends material beauty; because the desire for harmony begets the habit of harmony, and the habit thereof begets its imperative desire, and thus on in never-ending alternation.

*   *   *

Perhaps the best way of expounding my reasons will be to follow the process by which I reached them; for so far from having started with the theory of Diotima, I found the theory of Diotima, when I re-read it accidentally after many years' forgetfulness, to bring to convergence the result of my gradual experience.

*   *   *

Thinking about the Hermes of Olympia, and the fact that so far he is pretty well the only Greek statue which historical evidence unhesitatingly gives us as an original masterpiece, it struck me that, could one become really familiar with him, could eye and soul learn all the fulness of his perfection, we should have the true starting-point for knowledge of the antique, for knowledge, in great measure, of all art.

Yes, and of more than art, or rather of art in more than one relation.

Is this superstition a mere myth, perhaps, born of words? I think not. Surely if we could really arrive at knowing such a masterpiece, so as to feel rather than see its most intimate organic principles, and the great main reasons separating it from all inferior works and making it be itself—could we do this, we should know not merely what art is and should be, but, in a measure, what life should be and might become: what are the methods of true greatness, the sensations of true sanity. It would teach us the eternal organic strivings and tendencies of our soul, those leading in the direction of life, leading away from death.

If this seems mere allegory and wild talk, let us look at facts and see what art is. For is not art—inasmuch as it is untroubled by the practical difficulties of existence, inasmuch as it is the free, unconscious attempt of all nations and generations to satisfy outside life, those cravings which life still leaves unsatisfied—is not art an exquisite, sensitive instrument, showing in its delicate oscillations the most intimate movements and habits of soul? Does it not reveal our most recondite necessities and possibilities, by sifting and selecting, reinforcing or attenuating, among the impressions received from without; showing us thereby how we must stand towards nature and life, how we must feel and be?

And this most particularly in those spontaneous arts which, first in the field, without need of adaptations of material or avoidance of the already done, without having to use up the rejected possibilities of previous art, or awaken yet unknown emotions, are the simple, straightforward expression, each the earliest satisfactory one in its own line, of the long unexpressed, long integrated, organic wants and wishes of the great races of men: the arts, for instance, which have given us that Hermes, Titian's pictures, and Michael Angelo's and Raphael's frescoes; given us Bach, Gluck, Mozart, certain serener passages of Beethoven, music of yet reserved pathos, of braced, spring-like strength, learned, select: arts which never go beyond the universal, averaged expression of the soul's desires, because the desires themselves are sifted, limited to the imperishable and unchangeable, like the artistic methods which embody them, reduced to the essential by the long delay of utterance, the long—century long—efforts to utter.

Becoming intimate with such a statue as the Olympia Hermes, and comparing the impressions received from it with the impressions both of inferior works in the same branch of art and with the impressions of equally great works—pictures, buildings, musical compositions—in other branches of art, becoming conversant with the difference between great art and poor art, we gradually become aware of a quality which exists in all good art and is absent in all bad art, and without whose presence those impressions summed up as beauty, dignity, grandeur, are never to be had. This peculiarity, which most people perceive and few people define—explaining it away sometimes as *truth*, or taking it for granted under the name of *quality*—this peculiarity I shall call for convenience' sake *style*; for I think we all admit that the absence or presence of *style* is what distinguishes bad art from good. *Style*, in this sense—and remember that it is this which connoisseurs most usually allude to as *quality*—*style* may be roughly defined as the organic correspondence between the various parts of a work of art, the functional interchange and interdependence thereof. In this sense there is style in every really living thing, for otherwise it could not live. If the muscles and limbs, nay, the viscera and tissues, did not adjust themselves to work together, if they did not in this combination establish a rhythm, a backward-forward, contraction-relaxation, taking-in-giving-out, diastole-systole in all their movements, there would be, instead of a living organism, only an inert mass. In all living things, and just in proportion as they are really alive (for in most real things there is presumably some defect of rhythm tending to stoppage of life), there is bound to be this organic interdependence and interchange. Natural selection, the survival of such individuals and species as best work in with, and are most rhythmical to, their surroundings—natural selection sees to that.

Now in art that which takes the place of natural selection is man's selection; and all forms of art which man keeps and does not send into limbo, all art which man finds suitable to his wants, rhythmical with his habits, must have that same quality of interdependence of parts, of interchange of function. But in the case of art, the organic necessity refers not to outer surroundings, but to man's feeling; in fact, man's emotion constitutes necessity towards art, as surrounding nature constitutes necessity for natural productions. Now man, accustomed to organic harmony, to congruity of action because his own existence, nay, the existence of every cell of him, depends upon it; man, who is accustomed to style because it is only thanks to style that he exists, cannot do without congruity in the impressions he receives from art, cannot do without *style*. Man is one complete microcosm of interchange, of give-and-take, diastole-systole, of rhythm and harmony; and therefore all such things as give him impressions of the reverse thereof, go against him, and in a greater or lesser degree threaten, disturb, paralyse, in a way poison or maim him. Hence he is for ever seeking such congruity, such *style*; and his artistic creativeness is conditioned by the desire for it, nay, is perhaps mainly seeking to obtain it. Whenever he spontaneously and truly creates artistic forms, he obeys the imperious vital instinct for congruity; nay, he seeks to eke out the insufficient harmony between himself and the things which he *cannot* command, the insufficient harmony between the uncontrollable parts of himself, by a harmony created on purpose in the things which he *can* control. To a large extent, man feels himself tortured by discordant impressions coming from the world outside and the world inside him; and he seeks comfort and medicine in harmonious impressions of his own making, in his own strange inward-outward world of art.

This, I think, is the true explanation of that much-disputed-over *ideal*, which, according to definitions, is perpetually being enthroned and dethroned as the ultimate aim of all art: the ideal, the imperatively clamoured-for mysterious something, is neither conformity to an abstract idea, nor conformity to the individual; it is, I take it, simply conformity to man's requirements, to man's inborn and peremptory demand for greater harmony, for more perfect coordination and congruity in his feelings.

Now, when mankind are, in the exercise of the artistic instincts, partially obeying some other call than this one—the desire for money, for fame, or for some intellectual formula—things are quite different, and there is no production of what I have called style. There is no *style* when even great people set about doing pseudo-antique sculpture in Canova-Thorwaldsen[5] fashion because Winckelmann and Goethe have made antique sculpture fashionable; there is no *style* when people set to building pseudo-Gothic in obedience to the Romantic movement and to Ruskin. For neither the desire for making a mark, nor the most conscientious pressure of formula, gives that instinct of artistic congruity which marks even the most rudimentary artistic efforts in the most barbarous ages, when men are impelled merely and solely by the æsthetic instinct. Moreover, where people do not want and need (as they want and need food or drink or warmth or coolness) one sort of effect, that is to say, one arrangement of impressions rather than another, they are sure to be deluded by the mere arbitrary classification, the mere *names* of things. They will think that smooth cheeks, wavy hair, straight noses, limbs of such or such measure, attitude, and expression, set so, constitute the Antique; that clustered pillars, cross vaulting, spandrils, and Tudor roses make Gothic. But the Antique is the particular and all permeating relation between those other ones; and unless you aim at the *specific emotion* of Antique or Gothic, unless you feel the imperious call for the special harmony of either, all the measurements and all the formulas will not avail. While, on the contrary, people without any formula or any attempt at imitation, like the Byzantine architects and those of the fifteenth century, merely because they are obeying their own passionate desire for congruity of impressions, for harmony of structure and function, will succeed in creating brand-new, harmonious, organic art out of the actual details, sometimes the material ruins, of an art which has passed away.

What I have tried to analyse and explain we shall find, by a mere synthetic intuition, of all great art, and most of all, of course, in the very greatest art, in the works of the greatest masters of the greatest artistic periods, in the paintings of Giorgione,[6] Titian, Michael Angelo, Leonardo; in the music of Bach, Gluck, Mozart, and the happier Beethoven; most typically, perhaps, in the statue of Olympia Hermes. If we walk round that statue, allowing by this means the statue, so to speak, to assume its attitude, and—by the indications of muscles which have just fallen into use, and muscles which are just going to leave it—to perform its action, we shall realise that connection, interdependent of parts, that rhythm of interest and importance, which, preventing the spectator from becoming absorbed in any one detail, forcing him to follow the whole life of the figure, makes not only the work itself, but the mind perceiving it, to participate in the fulness of life.

Moreover, if we become intimate with this statue, and intimate in so far with the thoughts and emotions it awakens in ourselves, we shall find that it possesses, besides this congruity within itself which assimilates it to all really living things, a further congruity, not necessarily found in real objects, but which forms the peculiarity of the work of art, a congruity with ourselves; for the great work of art is vitally connected with the habits and wants, the whole causality and rhythm of mankind; it has been adapted thereto as the boat to the sea, as the sea itself to its rocky bed.

*   *   *

In this manner can we learn from art the chief secret of life: the secret of action and reaction, of causal connection, of suitability of part to part, of organism, interchange, and growth.

And when I say *learn*, I mean learn in the least official and the most efficacious way. I do not mean merely that, looking at a statue like the Hermes, a certain fact is borne in upon our intelligence, the fact of all vitality being dependent on harmony. I mean that perhaps, nay probably, without any such formula, without the intellectual perception of any such fact, our whole nature becomes accustomed to a certain repeated experience, our whole nature becomes adapted thereunto, and acts and reacts in consequence, by what we call intuition, instinct. It is not with our intellect alone that we possess such a fact, as we might intellectually possess the fact that twice two is four, or that Elizabeth was the daughter of Henry VIII, knowing casually what we may casually also forget; we possess, in such a way that forgetting becomes impossible, with our whole soul and our whole being, re-living that fact with every breath that we draw, with every movement we make, the first great lesson of art, that vitality means harmony. Let us look at this fact, and at its practical applications, apart from all æsthetic experience.

All life is harmony; and all improvement in ourselves is therefore, however unconsciously, the perceiving, the realising, or the establishing of harmonies, more minute or more universal.

Yes, curious and unpractical as it may seem, harmonies, or, under their humbler separate names—arrangements, schemes, classifications, are the chief means for getting the most out of all things, and particularly the most out of ourselves.

For they mean, first of all, unity of means for the attaining of unity of effect, that is to say, incalculable economy of material, of time, and of effort; and secondly, unity of effect produced, that is to say, economy even greater in our power of perceiving and feeling: nothing to eliminate, nothing against whose interruptions we waste our energy, that is, our power of being impressed in the progress of struggling.

Where there exists harmony one impression leads to, enhances another; we, on the other hand, unconsciously recognise at once what is doing to us, what we in return must do; the mood is indicated, fulfilled, consummated; in plentitude we feel, we are; and in plentitude of feeling and being, we, in our turn, *do*. Neither is such habit of harmony, of scheme, of congruity, a mere device for sucking the full sweetness out of life, although, heaven knows, that were important enough. As much as such a habit husbands, and in a way multiplies, life's sweetness; so likewise does it husband and multiply man's power. For there is no quicker and more thorough mode of selecting among our feelings and thoughts than submitting them to a standard of congruity; nothing more efficacious than the question: "Is such or such a notion or proceeding harmonious with what we have made the rest of our life, with what we wish our life to be?" This is, in other words, the power of the *ideal*, the force of *ideas*, of thought-out, recognised habits, as distinguished from blind helter-skelter impulse. This is what welds life into one, making its forces work not in opposition but in concordance; this is what makes life consecutive, using the earlier act to produce the later, tying together existence in an organic fatality of *must be*: the fatality not of the outside and the unconscious, but of the conscious, inner, upper man. Nay, it is what makes up the *ego*. For the *ego*, as we are beginning to understand, is no mysterious separate entity, still less a succession of disconnected, conflicting, blind impulses; the *ego* is the congruous, perceived, nay, thought-out system of habits, which perceives all incongruity towards itself as accidental and external. Hence, when we ask which are the statements we believe in, we answer instinctively (logic being but a form of congruity) those statements which accord with themselves and with other statements; when we ask, which are the persons we trust? we answer, the persons whose feelings and actions are congruous with themselves and with the feelings and actions of others. And, on the contrary, it is in the worthless, in the degenerate creature, that we note moods which are destructive to one another's object, ideas which are in flagrant contradiction; and it is in the idiot, the maniac, the criminal, that we see thoughts disconnected among themselves, perceptions disconnected with surrounding objects, and instincts and habits incompatible with those of other human beings. Nay, if we look closely, we shall recognise, moreover, that those emotions of pleasure are the healthy, the safe ones, which are harmonious not merely in themselves (as a musical note is composed of even vibrations), but harmonious with all preceding and succeeding pleasures in ourselves, and harmonious, congruous, with the present and future pleasures of others.

*   *   *

The instinct of congruity, of subordination of part to whole, the desire for harmony which is fostered above all things by art, is one of the most precious parts of our nature, if only, obeying its own tendency to expand, we apply it to ever wider circles of being; not merely to the accessories of living, but to life itself.

For this love of harmony and order leads us to seek what is most necessary in our living: a selection of the congruous, an arrangement of the mutually dependent in our thoughts and feelings.

Much of the work of the universe is done, no doubt, by what seems the exercise of mere random energy, by the thinking of apparently disconnected thoughts and the feeling of apparently sporadic impulses; but if the thought and the impulse remained really disconnected and sporadic, half would be lost and half would be distorted. It is one of the economical adaptations of nature that every part of us tends not merely to be congruous with itself, to eliminate the hostile, to beget the similar, but tends also to be connected with other parts; so that, action coming in contact with action, thought in contact with thought, and feeling in contact with feeling, each single one will be strengthened or neutralised by the other. And it is the especial business of what we may call the central consciousness, the dominant thought or emotion, to bring these separate thoughts and impulses, these separate groups thereof, into more complex relations, to continue on a far vaster scale that vital contact, that trying of all things by the great trial of affinity or repulsion, of congruity or incongruity. Thus we try ourselves; and by the self-same process, by the trial of affinity and congruity, the silent forces of the universe try *us*, rejecting or accepting, allowing us, our thoughts, our feelings to live and be fruitful, or condemning us and them to die in barrenness.

Whither are we going? In what shape shall the various members of our soul proceed on their journey; which forming the van, which the rear and centre? Or shall there be neither van, nor rear, nor wedge-like flight?

If this question remains unasked or unanswered, our best qualities, our truest thoughts and purest impulses, may be hopelessly scattered into distant regions, become defiled in bad company, or, at least, barren in isolation; the universal life rejecting or annihilating them.

How often do we not see this! Natures whose various parts have rambled asunder, or have come to live, like strangers in an inn, casually, promiscuously, each refusing to be his brother's keeper: instincts of kindliness at various ends, unconnected, unable to coalesce and conquer; thoughts separated from their kind, incapable of application; and, in consequence, strange superficial comradeships, shoulder-rubbings of true and false, good and evil, become indifferent to one another, incapable of looking each other in the face, careless, unblushing. Nay, worse. For lack of all word of command, of all higher control, hostile tendencies accommodating themselves to reign alternate, sharing the individual in distinct halves, till he becomes like unto that hero of Gautier's[7] witch story, who was a pious priest one half of the twenty-four hours and a wicked libertine the other: all power of selection, of reaction, gone in this passive endurance of conflicting tendencies, all identity gone, save that of a mere feeble outsider looking on at the alternations of intentions and lapses, of good and bad. And the soul of such a person—if, indeed, we can speak of one soul or one person where there exists no unity—becomes like a jangle of notes belonging to different tonalities, alternating and mingling in hideous confusion for lack of a clear thread of melody, a consistent system of harmony, to select, reject, and keep all things in place.

Melody, harmony: the two great halves of the most purely æsthetic of all arts, symbolise, as we might expect, the two great forces of life: consecutiveness and congruity, under their different names of intention, fitness, selection, adaptation. These are what make the human soul like a conquering army, a fleet freighted with riches, a band of priests celebrating a rite. And this is what art, by no paltry formula, but by the indelible teaching of habit, of requirement, and expectation, become part of our very fibre—this is what art can teach to those who will receive its highest lesson.

*   *   *

Those who can receive that lesson, that is to say, those in whom it can expand and ramify to the fulness and complexity which is its very essence—for it happens frequently enough that we learn only a portion of this truth, which by this means is distorted into error. We accept the æsthetic instinct as a great force of Nature; but, instead of acknowledging it as our master, as one of the great lords of life, of whom Emerson spoke, we try to make it our servant. We attempt to get congruity in the details of our everyday existence, and refuse to seek for congruity between ourselves and the life which is greater than ours.

A friend of mine, who had many better ways of spending her money, was unable one day to resist the temptation of buying a beautiful old majolica inkstand, which, not without a slight qualm of conscience, she put into a very delightful old room of her house. The room had an inkstand already, but it was of glass, and modern. "This one is in harmony with the rest of the room," she said, and felt fully justified in her extravagance. It is this form, or rather this degree, of æstheticism, of finer perception, which so often prevents our realising the higher æsthetic harmonies. In obedience to a perception of what is congruous on a small scale we often do oddly incongruous things: spend money we ought to invest, give time and thought to trifles while neglecting to come to conclusions about matters of importance; endure, or even cultivate, persons with whom we have less than no sympathy; nay, sometimes, from a keen sense of incongruity, tune down our thoughts and feelings to the flatness of our surroundings. The phenomenon of what may thus result from a certain æsthetic sensitiveness is discouraging, and I confess that it used sometimes to discourage and humiliate me profoundly. But the philosophy which the prophetess of Mantineia taught Socrates settles the matter, and solves satisfactorily what in my mind I always think of as the question of the majolica inkstand.

Diotima, you will remember, did not allow her disciple to remain engrossed in the contemplation of one kind of beauty, but particularly insisted that he should use various fair forms as steps by which to ascend to the knowledge of ever higher beauties. And this I should translate into more practical language by saying that, in questions like that of the majolica inkstand, we require not a lesser sensitiveness to congruity, but a greater; that we must look not merely at the smaller, but at the larger items of our life, asking ourselves, "Is this harmonious? or is it, seen in some wider connection, even like that clumsy glass inkstand in the oak panelled and brocade hung room?" If we ask ourselves this, and endeavour to answer it faithfully—with that truthfulness which is itself an item of congruity—we may find that, strange as it may seem, the glass inkstand, ugly as it is in itself, and out of harmony with the furniture, is yet more congruous, and that we actually prefer it to the one of majolica.

And it is in connection with this that I think that many persons who are really æsthetic, and many more who imagine themselves to be so, should foster a wholesome suspicion of the theory which makes it a duty to accumulate certain kinds of possessions, to exclusively seek certain kinds of impressions, on the score of putting beauty and dignity into our lives.

Put beauty, dignity, harmony, serenity into our lives. It sounds very fine. But *can* we? I doubt it. We may put beautiful objects, dignified manners, harmonious colours and shapes, but can we put dignity, harmony, or beauty? Can we put them into an individual life; can anything be put into an individual life save furniture and garments, intellectual as well as material? For an individual life, taken separately, is a narrow, weak thing at the very best; and everything we can put into it, everything we lay hold of for the sake of putting in, must needs be small also, merely the chips or dust of great things; or if it have life, must be squeezed, cut down, made so small before it can fit into that little receptacle of our egoism, that it will speedily be a dead, dry thing: thoughts once thought, feelings once felt, now neither thought nor felt, merely lying there inert, as a dead fact, in our sterile self. Do we not see this on all sides, examples of life into which all the dignified things have been crammed and all the beautiful ones, and which yet, despite the statues, pictures, poems, and symphonies within its narrow compass, is yet so far from dignified or beautiful?

But we need not trouble about dignity and beauty coming to our life so long as we veritably and thoroughly *live;* that is to say, so long as we try not to put anything into our life, but to put our life into the life universal. The true, expanding, multiplying life of the spirit will bring us in contact, we need not fear, with beauty and dignity enough, for there is plenty such in creation, in things around us, and in other people's souls; nay, if we but live to our utmost power the life of all things and all men, seeing, feeling, understanding for the mere joy thereof, even our individual life will be invested with dignity and beauty in our own eyes.

But furniture will not do it, nor dress, nor exquisite household appointments; nor any of the things, books, pictures, houses, parks, of which we can call ourselves owners. I say *call* ourselves: for can we be sure we really possess them? And thus, if we think only of our life, and the decking thereof, it is only furniture, garments, and household appointments we can deal with; for beauty and dignity cannot be confined in so narrow a compass.

*   *   *

I have spoken so far of the conscious habit of harmony, and of its conscious effect upon our conduct. I have tried to show that the desire for congruity, which may seem so trivial a part of the mere dilettante's superfineness, may expand and develop into such love of harmony between ourselves and the ways of the universe as shall make us wince at other folks' loss united to our gain, at our deterioration united to our pleasure, even as we wince at a false note or a discordant arrangement of colours.

But there is something more important than conscious choice, and something more tremendous than definite conduct, because conscious choice and conduct are but its separate and plainly visible results. I mean the unconscious way of feeling and organic way of living: that which, in the language of old-fashioned medicine, we might call the complexion or habit of the soul.

This is undoubtedly affected by conscious knowledge and reason, as it undoubtedly manifests itself in both. But it is, I believe, much more what we might call a permanent emotional condition, a particular way of feeling, of reacting towards the impressions given us by the universe. And I believe that the individual is sound, that he is capable of being happy while increasing the happiness of others, or the reverse, according as he reacts harmoniously or inharmoniously towards those universal impressions. And here comes in what seems to me the highest benefit we can receive from art and from all the activities, however little manifested, in visible or audible works, which, as I have said before, are in art merely specialised and made publicly manifest.

The habit of beauty, of style, is but the habit, engrained in our nature by the unnoticed experiences of centuries, of *life* in our surroundings and in ourselves; the habit of beauty is the habit, I believe we shall find, by scientific analysis of Nature's ways and means, of the growing of trees, the flowing of water, the perfect play of perfect muscles, all registered unconsciously in the very structure of our soul. And for this reason every time we experience afresh the particular emotion associated with the quality *beautiful*, we are adding to that rhythm of life within ourselves by recognising the life of all things. There is not room within us for two conflicting waves of emotion, for two conflicting rhythms of life, one sane and one unsound. The two may possibly alternate, but in most cases the weaker will be neutralised by the stronger; and, at all events, they cannot co-exist. We can account only in this manner for the indisputable fact that great emotion of a really and purely æsthetic nature has a morally elevating quality, that as long as it endures—and in finer organisations its effect is never entirely lost—the soul is more clean and vigorous, more fit for high thoughts and high decisions. All understanding, in the wider and more philosophical sense, is but a kind of becoming: our soul experiences the modes of being which it apprehends. Hence the particular religious quality (all faiths and rituals taking advantage thereof) of a high and complex æsthetic emotion; whenever we come in contact with real beauty, we become aware, in an unformulated but overwhelming manner, of some of the immense harmonies of which all beauty is the product; of which all separate beautiful things are, so to speak, the single patterns happening to be in our line of vision, while all around other patterns connect with them, meshes and meshes of harmonies, spread out, outside our narrow field of momentary vision, an endless web, like the constellations which, strung on their threads of mutual dependence, cover and fill up infinitude.

In the moments of such emotional perception, our souls also, ourselves, become in a higher degree organic, alive, receiving and giving out the life of the universe; come to be woven into the patterns of harmonies, made of the stuff of reality, homogeneous with themselves, consubstantial with the universe, like the living plant, the flowing stream, the flying cloud, the great picture or statue.

And in this way is realised, momentarily, but with ever-increasing power of repetition, that which, after the teaching of Diotima, Socrates prayed for—"the harmony between the outer and the inner man."

But this, I know, many will say, is but a delusion. Rapture is pleasant, but it is not necessarily, as the men of the Middle Ages thought, a union with God. And is this the time to revive, or seek to revive it, when science is for ever pressing upon us the conclusion that soul is a function of matter—is this the time to revive discredited optimistic idealisms of an unscientific philosophy?

But if science become omniscient, it will surely recognise and explain the value of such recurring optimistic idealisms; and if the soul be a function of matter, will not science recognise but the more, that the soul is an integral and vitally dependent portion of the material universe?

*   *   *

Be this as it may, one thing seems certain, that the artistic activities are those which bring man into emotional communion with external Nature; and that such emotional communion is necessary for man's thorough spiritual health. Perception of cause and effect, generalisation of law, reduces the universe indeed to what man's intellect can grasp; but in the process of such reduction to the laws of man's thought, the universe is shorn of its very power to move man's emotion and overwhelm his soul. The abstract which we have made does not vivify us sufficiently. And the emotional communion of man with Nature is through those various faculties which we call æsthetic. It is not to no purpose that poetry has for ever talked to us of skies and mountains and waters; we require, for our soul's health, to think about them otherwise than with reference to our material comfort and discomfort; we require to feel that they and ourselves are brethren united by one great law of life. And what poetry suggests in explicit words, bidding us love and be united in love to external Nature; art, in a more irresistible because more instinctive manner, forces upon our feelings, by extracting, according to its various kinds, the various vital qualities of the universe, and making them act directly upon our nerves: rhythms of all sorts, static and dynamic, in the spatial arts of painting and sculpture; in the half spatial, half temporal art of architecture; in music, which is most akin to life, because it is the art of movement and change.

We can all remember moments when we have seemed conscious, even to overwhelming, of this fact. In my own mind it has become indissolubly connected with a certain morning at Venice, listening to the organ in St. Mark's.

Any old and beautiful church gives us all that is most moving and noblest—organism, beauty, absence of all things momentary and worthless, exclusion of grossness, of brute utility and mean compromise, equality of all men before God; moreover, time, eternity, the past, and the great dead. All noble churches give us this; how much more, therefore, this one, which is noblest and most venerable!

It has, like no other building, been handed over by man to Nature; Time moulding and tinting into life this structure already so absolutely organic, so fit to live. For its curves and vaultings, its cupolas mutually supported, the weight of each carried by all; the very colour of the marbles, brown, blond, living colours, and the irregular symmetry, flowerlike, of their natural patterning, are all seemingly organic and ready for vitality. Time has added that, with the polish and dimming alternately of the marbles, the billowing of the pavement, the slanting of the columns, and last, but not least, the tarnishing of the gold and the granulating of the mosaic into an uneven surface: the gold seeming to have become alive and in a way vegetable, and to have faded and shrunk like autumn leaves.

The morning I speak of they were singing some fugued composition, by I know not whom. How well that music suited St. Mark's! The constant interchange of vault and vault, cupola and cupola, column and column, handing on their energies to one another; the springing up of new details gathered at once into the great general balance of lines and forces; all this seemed to find its natural voice in that fugue, to express, in that continuous revolution of theme chasing, enveloping theme, its own grave emotion of life everlasting: Being, becoming; Becoming, being.

It is such an alternation as this, ceaseless, rhythmic, which constitutes the upward life of the soul: that life of which the wise woman of Mantineia told Socrates that it might be learned through faithful and strenuous search for ever widening kinds of beauty, the "life above all," in the words of Diotima, "which a man should live." The life which vibrates for ever between being better and conceiving of something better still; between satisfaction in harmony and craving therefor. The life whose rhythm is that of happiness actual and happiness ideal, alternating for ever, for ever pressing one another into being, as the parts of a fugue, the dominant and the tonic. Being, becoming; becoming, being; idealising, realising; realising, idealising.

Notes

1.   "vivifying power": cf. Samuel Taylor Coleridge's concept of the imagination's power to "volatize" its subject matter in the process of creation (*On the Principles of Genial Criticism*, "Essay Third," 1814).

2.   In the Old Testament, Solomon was a Hebrew King, known for his great wealth and splendor, as well as his many wives.

3.   A legendary magician of the 16th century who sold his soul to the devil in exchange for knowledge and power.

4.   In Greek mythology, Pegasus is a winged horse who is tamed by Bellerophon with the help of a bridle given to him by Athena. Pegasus, the flying horse of the Muses, is also symbolic of poetic inspiration.

5.   Antonio Canova (1757–22). A sculptor from the Romantic Classicism School who, although considered the greatest sculptor of his day, suffered greatly in reputation after his death, due to his at times highly artificialized style.

6.   Giorgione da Castelfranco (1478–1510). A Venetian painter who was the illustrious student of Giovanni Bellini.

7.   Théophile Gautier (1811–72). A French poet, novelist, and journalist known for his extreme romanticism and his vampire stories, most famous of which is *La Morte amoureuse*.

35. Gospels of Anarchy

Introduction

Vernon Lee's "Gospels of Anarchy" first appeared in the *Contemporary Review* in July, 1898, and is reprinted here from that periodical. Written almost two decades after the publication of Lee's earliest work, which centered on aesthetic criticism, this essay instead exhibits her concern with the amelioration of the human condition and advocates a reform that will be enacted through each individual's "anarchic" revolt against "violence" of various sorts. Lee warns against two extremes of erroneous assumption: that humans are inherently good, or that humans are inherently evil. Her argument immediately establishes the individual's capacity for doubt and defiance in the face of dogma as the only attainable "reality" in a universe that is no more than a "sham constructed by human hands."

Upon Lee's death, the *Times* dismissed "Gospels of Anarchy," ranking it among her "less attractive pseudo-political and sociological writings." However, the article does hold attraction in its synthesis of aesthetic and literary criticism with sociological theory. Exemplifying much of the writing in Lee's middle and later career, this essay reveals her attempt to coordinate individual and social reform.

Gospels of Anarchy*

In such of us as not merely live, but think and feel what life is and might be, an inner drama is enacted, full of conflicting emotions, long drawn out over the years, and sometimes never brought to a conclusion.

It begins with the gradual suspicion, as we pass out of childish tutelage, that the world is not at all the definite, arranged, mechanical thing which the doctrine convenient to our elders and our own optimistic egoism have led us to expect; that the causes and results of actions are by no means so simple as we imagined, and that good and evil are not so distinctly opposed as black and white. We guess, we slowly recognise with difficulty and astonishment that this well-regulated structure called the universe or life is a sham constructed by human hands; that the reality is a seething whirlpool of forces seemingly blind, mainly disorderly and cruel, and, at the best, utterly indifferent; a chaos of which we recognise, with humiliation turning into cynicism, that our poor self is but a part and a sample.

Thus we feel. But if we feel long enough, and do not get blunted in the process, we are brought gradually, by additional seeing and feeling, to a totally new view of things. The chaos becomes ordered, the void a firmament, and we recognise with joy and pride that the universe has made us, and that we, perceiving it, have made the universe in our turn; and in so far it is true that "in la sua volontade è nostra pace."

The following notes display, whatever its value, this process of destruction and reconstruction in one particular type of mind; embody, for the benefit of those who constitutionally tend to think alike, and still more of those who are constitutionally bound to think differently, the silent discussions on anarchy and law which have arisen in me as a result of other folks' opinions and of experience of life's complexities and deadlocks.

I.

On the one hand, a revolt against any philosophical system of unity, which many would call a revolt against all philosophy, genuine scepticism. Then the denial that the feeling of obligation can be brought to bear on any fixed point. . . . Morally, we must content ourselves with the various injunctions of wisdom, and with distinct, independent ideals. Something beyond them is, indeed, recognised; but, whereas we were accustomed to place it in the obligatory character of certain prescriptions, we are now told to understand it as a perpetual warning against all dogmatism (H.B. Brewster, "Theories of Anarchy and Law," p. 113).

Such doubts as these must have arisen, most certainly, in all kinds of men at all times, producing worldly wise cynicism in some and religious distress in others. Such doubts as these have lurked, one suspects, at the bottom of all transcendentalism. They are summed up in Emerson's disquieting remark that saints are sad where philosophers are merely interested, because the first see sin where the second see only cause and effect. They are implied in a great deal of religious mysticism, habitually lurking in esoteric depths of speculation, but penetrating occasionally, mysterious subtle gases, to life's surface, and there igniting at contact with the active impulses of men; whence the ambiguous ethics, the questionable ways of many sects originally ascetic. Nay, it is quite conceivable that, if there really existed the thing called the Secret of the Church which Villiers de l'Isle Adam's[1] gambling abbé staked at cards against twenty louis-d'or, it would be found to be, not that *there is no purgatory*, but rather that there is no heaven and hell, no law and no sin.

Be this as it may, all dogmatic religions have forcibly repressed such speculations, transcendental or practical, upon the ways of the universe and of man. And it is only in our own day, with the habit of each individual striking out his practice for himself, and with the scientific recognition that the various religiously sanctioned codes embody a very rough-and-ready practicability; it is only in our own time that people are beginning to question the perfection of established rules of conduct, to discuss the drawbacks of duty and self-sacrifice, and to speculate upon the possible futility of all ethical systems, nay, upon the possible vanity of all ideals and formulas whatever.

But the champions of moral anarchy and intellectual nihilism have made up for lost time, and the books whose titles I have placed at the beginning of these notes contain, systematically or by implication, what one might call the ethics, the psychology, and the metaphysics of negation. These doctrines of the school which denies all schools and all doctrines are, as I hope to show, not of Mephistophelean origin. *The spirit which denies* has arisen, in our days at least, neither from heartlessness nor from levity. On the contrary, and little as the apostles of anarchy may suspect it, it is from a growing sensitiveness to the sufferings of others, and a growing respect for intellectual sincerity, that have resulted such doubts of the methods hitherto devised for diminishing unhappiness and securing truth. And for this reason, if no other, such subversive criticism ought to be of the highest use to the very notions and tendencies which it attacks: we want better laws, better formulas, better ideals; we want a wiser attitude towards laws, formulas, and ideals in general; and this better we shall get only by admitting that we have not already got the best.

Leaving alone the epic feats of the old spirit of duty, the tragedies of Jeanie Deans and Maggie Tulliver, the lesser, though not less admirable, heroism shown us in some of Mary Wilkins's New England stories,[3] we have all of us witnessed the action of that moral training which thwarted personal preferences and repugnances, and victoriously silenced their claims. We have all of us heard of women (particularly in the times of our mothers and grandmothers) refusing the man they loved and marrying the man of whom their parents approved; we still look on, every day, at lives dragged along in hated companionship; at talents—nay, actual vocations—suppressed in deference to family prejudice or convenience; acts of spiritual mutilation so thorough as often to minimise their own suffering; changing the current of life, atrophying organic possibilities in such a way that the victim's subsequent existence was not actively unhappy, and not even obviously barren. Such things still go on all round us. The difference now is that the minor sacrifices are no longer taken for granted by all lookers-on; and the grand, heroic self-immolations no longer universally applauded. There has arisen (it began, not without silly accompaniments enough, and disgusting ones, in the eighteenth century) an active suspiciousness towards all systematic tampering with human nature. We have had to recognise all the mischief we have done by always knowing better than the mechanical and spiritual forces of the universe; we are getting to believe more and more in the organic, the constitutional, and the unconscious; and there is an American book (by the late Mr. Marsh) on the disastrous consequences of cutting down forests, draining lakes, and generally subverting natural arrangements in our greed for immediate advantages, which might be taken, every chapter of it, as an allegorical exhibition of the views to which most people are tending on the subject of religious and social discipline.

We have had to recognise, moreover, that a great deal of all the discipline and self-sacrifice hitherto so universally recommended has been for the benefit of individuals, and even classes, who by no means reciprocated towards their victims; and we cannot deny that there is a grain of truth in Nietzsche's contempt for what he calls the "Ethics of Slaves." And, finally, we see very plainly that the reasonableness and facility of thorough-going self-sacrifice would be amply compensated in another existence: it was rational to give up the present for the future; it is not rational to prefer a future which is problematic to a present which alone is quite certain. In this way have all of us who think at all begun to think differently from our fathers; indeed, we feel upon this point even more than we actually think. We warn people not to give up their possibilities of activity and happiness in deference to the wishes of others. We almost unconsciously collect instances of such self-sacrifice as has entailed the damage of others, instances of the tissues of the social fabric being insidiously rotted through the destruction of one of its human cells; and these instances, alas! are usually correct and to the point. We even invent, or applaud the invention of, other instances which are decidedly far-fetched: for instance, Mrs. Alving producing her son's hereditary malady by not acquiescing more openly in his father's exuberant *joy of life*; and Pastor Rosmer destroying, by his scruples, the resources for happiness of the less scrupulous Rebecca.[4]

I have chosen these examples on purpose, for they have enabled me to give a name to those portions of the anarchical tendencies of our day; we are, all of us who look a little around us and feel a little for others, more or less infected with *Ibsenism*, conscious or unconscious followers of the Ibsenite gospel which Mr. Bernard Shaw preaches with jaunty fanaticism. This seems, on the whole, a very good thing. Except, perhaps, in the question of manners, of courtesy, particularly between the sexes (æsthetic superfluities, but which help to make life liveable), I feel persuaded that even the most rabid Ibsenism will be advantageous. The more we let nature work for us, the more we employ our instincts and tendencies, instead of thwarting them, the less will be the waste, the greater the achievement. But in all cases like this there is apt to be a drawback: alongside of a great gain, a certain loss, and this we should do our utmost to minimise. The old conception of duty was warped by the fearful error of thinking that human nature is bad; or, as we moderns would express it, that the instincts of the individual are hostile to the community. This was, calmly looked at, monstrous. But are we not, perhaps, on the brink of a corresponding error, less enormous of course, but large enough to grow a fine crop of misery? The error, I mean, of taking for granted that human nature is already entirely good; that the instincts, desires, nay, interests of the individual are necessarily in accordance with the good of the community. The Ibsenian theory is right in saying that there are lots of people, a majority, even, who had much better have had their own way. But is the Ibsenian theory right in supposing that certain other persons (and there may be strands of such in the best of us), persons like Captain Alving, or Rebecca West, or Hedda Gabler, or the Master Builder,[5] would have become harmless and desirable if no one had interfered with their self-indulgence, their unscrupulousness, their inborn love of excitement, or their inborn *ego*-mania? Surely not. There is not the smallest reason why the removal of moral stigma and of self-criticising ideals should reduce these people's peculiar instincts (and these people, I repeat, are mere types of what is mixed up in most of us) to moderation.

Nor is moderation the remedy for all evils. There are in us tendencies to feel and act which survive from times when the mere preservation of individual and of race was desirable quite unconditionally; but which, in our altered conditions, require not moderating, but actually replacing by something more discriminating, less wasteful and mischievous. Vanity, for instance, covetousness, ferocity, are surely destined to be evolved away, the useful work they once accomplished being gradually performed by instincts of more recent growth which spoil less in the process. Improvement, in the moral life as in any other, is a matter of transformation. Now, if we are to use our instincts, our likings and dislikings, to carry us from narrower circles of life to wider ones, we must work unceasingly at reconstituting those likings and dislikings themselves. The evolution by which our *ego* has become less incompatible with its neighbours has taken place largely by the mechanism of ideals and duties, of attaching to certain acts an odium sufficient to counterbalance their attraction, till it has become more and more difficult to thoroughly enjoy oneself at other folks' cost.

Ibsenians are apt to ask whether it was not horrible that Claudio should be put to death because Isabella stickled about chastity, that an innocent Effie Deans should be hanged because Jeanie had cut-and-dried ideas of veracity;[6] that Brutus's son should die because his father was so rigidly law-abiding. But it would have been far more horrible for the world at large if people had always been ready to sacrifice chastity, veracity, or legality to family feelings; indeed, could such have been the case, the world, or at least humankind, would probably have gone to pieces before Claudio, or Effie, or the son of Brutus had been born. Cut-and-dried notions of conduct are probably exactly commensurate with moral slackness. We do not require to deter people from what they do not want to do, nor to reward them for what they would do unrewarded. The very difficulty of acting spontaneously in any given way demands the formation of more or less unreasoning habits; the difficulty of forming desirable habits demands the coercive force of public opinion; and the insufficient power of mere opinion necessitates that appeal to brute force which is involved in all application of the law. The oversight of Ibsenian anarchists (whatever Ibsen's individual views on the subject) is that of imagining that duties, ideals, laws, can be judged by examining their action in the individual case; for their use, their evolutional *raison d'être*, is only for the general run.

The champions of the *Will of the Ego*, whether represented by bluff Bernard Shaw or by ambiguous Maurice Barrès,[7] start from the supposition that because the individual is a concrete existence, while the species is obviously an abstraction, the will of the individual can alone be a reality, and the will of the species must be a figment. They completely forget that there is not one concrete individual, but an infinite number of concrete individuals, and that what governs the world is, therefore, the roughly arranged will of all these concrete individuals. The single individual may *will to live* as hard as he can, will to expand, assimilate, reproduce, cultivate his *moi*, or anything else besides, but the accomplishment of that will of his—nay, the bare existence of himself and his will—depends entirely upon the will of the species. Without the permission of that abstract entity which he considers a figment, the concrete and only really real individual would never have realised his individual existence at all. This is not saying that his own will is not to react against the will of the species; for the will of the species is merely the averaged will of its component individuals, and as the individual will alters, so must the averaged will differ. The opinions and ideals and institutions of the present and the future are unconsciously, and in some cases consciously, modified, however infinitesimally, by the reactions of every living man and woman; and the more universal this atomic individual modification, the higher the civilisation, the greater the bulk of happiness attained and attainable. Meanwhile ideals, commandments, institutions are, each for its own time, so many roads, high roads, if not royal roads, to the maximum of good behaviour possible in any given condition. Without them, people would have to carry their virtuous potentialities through bogs and briars, where most of them would remain sticking. Succeeding generations, knowing more of the soil and employing more accurate measurements; making, moreover, free use of blasting powder, may build shorter and easier roads, along which fewer persons will die; roads also in a great variety of directions, that every one may get near his real destination. And the more each individual keeps his eyes open to the inconveniences and dangers of the existing roads to righteousness, and airs his criticisms thereof, the better: for the majority, which is as slow as the individual is quick, is not likely to destroy the old thoroughfares before having made itself new ones. The Ibsenian anarchists are right in reminding us that there is really nothing holy in such a road; for holiness is a quality, not of institutions, but of character, and a man can be equally holy along a new road as along an old one; alas! as holy along a wrong road as along a right one. But we, on the other hand, must remind the Ibsenians that new or old, right or wrong, such high roads are high roads, not to the advantage of the single individual at any given moment, but of the majority at most times, or, at least, of the majority composed of the most typical individuals.

II.

After our doubts regarding the validity of the ideals and institutions to which society expects each individual voluntarily to conform come doubts, even more necessary and natural, concerning the majesty of the methods by which society enforces its preference on such individuals as fail to conform spontaneously thereunto.

Such doubts as these are by no means due to the growth of sympathy only, to what is called, and sometimes really is, mere sentimental weakness. Together with disbelief in a theologically appointed universe, we have witnessed the growth of respect both for fact and for logic; and, as a consequence, we no longer regard the infringement of a human law as the rebellion to the will of God. We have replaced the notion of *sin* by the notion of *crime*, and the particular act which we happen to call a crime is no longer, in our eyes, a detached and spontaneously generated fact in a single individual life, but the result of a dozen converging causes, of which this individual character may be only one, while the constitution of surrounding society is sure to be another of the determinants. We recognise also that while, on the one hand, the capacity for committing certain acts intolerable to the majority does not imply an utter worthlessness of character in many other directions; on the other hand, the thorough-going perversity which renders an individual criminal an unmitigated evil to his fellow-creatures involves constitutional and irresistible tendencies which are incompatible with any notion of responsibility. All this comes to saying that the coercion and punishment of offenders has become a question not of morality, but of police; that it has ceased to be a sort of holy sacrifice to God, and grown to be a rough-and-ready way of getting rid of a nuisance. And this has altered our feelings from the self-complacency of a priest to the humiliation of an unwilling scavenger. We are getting a little ashamed of the power to imprison, bully, outlaw, destroy either life or life's possibilities, which constitutes the *secular arm* of all theoretic morality.

Is such a feeling mistaken? Surely only inasmuch as it would turn a desirable possibility for the future into an unmanageable actuality in the present. Since, however much we may admit that bodily violence, and the kind of discipline dependent thereupon, are necessary in the present, and will be necessary for longer than we dare foresee in the future, we must open our eyes to the fact that all progress represents a constant diminution thereof; and we must be careful that all our methods (even the methods including authoritativeness and violence) shall tend to the eventual disappearance of violence towards human beings and authoritativeness towards adults, violence remaining our necessary method with brutes and authoritativeness with children, but even in these relations diminishing to the utmost. For violence, and the discipline founded on violence (as distinguished from self-discipline sprung from intelligence and adaptability) means not merely suffering, but wastefulness worse than suffering, because it entails it: waste of the possibilities of adaptation in him who exerts it, as well as of constitutional improvement in him who suffers from it. Waste above all of the *Reality*, the reality which must be slightly different in every individual case, reality containing the possibilities of new arrangements and new faculties; reality which we cruelly disregard whenever we treat individual cases as merely typical, whenever we act on the one half of a case containing similarity, and neglect the other half of the case containing difference. Such wastefulness of method is necessary just in proportion as we are deficient in the power of selecting, preferring, and postponing, the powers of self-sacrifice. Violence over body and over mind; violence against the will of others; violence against fact; these represent the friction in the imperfect mechanism of life; and progress is but the substitution of human mechanism more and more delicate and solid, through which the movement is ever greater, the friction ever less.

Meanwhile, do we possess a human mechanism as good as it might be? Tolstoi, Ibsen, the author of the very suggestive dialogues on Anarchy and Law, even egoistic decadents like Maurice Barrès, the whole heterogeneous crusade of doubt and rebellion, are doing good work in showing that we have not; in forcing us to consider what proportions of subtlety and clumsiness, of movement and of friction, of utility and waste, are represented by the system of coercion and punishment accepted in our days. And such an examination will surely prove that in this matter we have developed our ingenuity less (sometimes atrophied it), and proceeded with far greater hurry and slovenliness than with any of the other products of civilisation. Try and imagine where building, agriculture, manufacture, any of the most common crafts would be had it been carried on throughout the centuries as we still carry on the moralisation of mankind; if stone, brick, soil, manure, raw material, let alone the physical and chemical laws, had been treated in the rough-and-ready manner in which we treat human thought and impulse. But the fact is that we have required food, clothing, and shelter so bitterly hitherto, that all our best intelligence and energy have gone to diminish wastefulness in their production; and no time has remained, no power of discrimination, for making the best of intellectual and moral qualities. Indeed, we have dealt, and we deal only, with the *bad* moral qualities of mankind; those that can be seen in spare five minutes and with a rushlight; nay, those which are stumbled over in the dark and kicked into corners. We may hope for improvement almost in proportion as we recognise that destruction is the expression not of responsibility towards heaven on the part of the malefactor, but of incapacity and hurry on the part of those whom the malefactor damages. For here even as in the question of duties and ideals, what we are suffering from is lack of discrimination, paucity of methods, insufficiency of formulas; and what we want is not less law, but more law; law which will suit the particular case which is a reality and has results, not merely the general run, which is an abstraction and takes care of itself.

Out of these various doubts about standards of conduct and social arrangements there arises gradually a central core of doubt, to which the others can be logically reduced; the doubt, namely, whether the individuality is not cramped, enfeebled, rendered unfit for life, by obedience to any kind of abstraction, to anything save its own individual tendencies. Oddly enough, the psychological theory had in this matter preceded the thoroughgoing practical application; and the essential principles of subsequent anarchical views were expressed by the earliest and the least read of anarchist writers, Max Stirner (Kaspar Schmidt), who died so long ago as 1856.

Max Stirner builds up his system—for his hatred of system is expressed in elaborately systematic form—upon the notion that the *Geist*, the intellect which forms conceptions, is a colossal cheat for ever robbing the individual of its due, and marring life by imaginary obstacles; a wicked sort of archimago, whose phantasmagoria, duty, ideal, vocation, aim, law, formula, can be described only by the untranslatable German work *Spuk*, a decidedly undignified haunting by bogies. Against this kingdom of delusion the human individual—*der Einzige*—has been, since the beginning of time, slowly and painfully fighting his way; never attaining to any kind of freedom, but merely exchanging one form of slavery for another, slavery to the religious delusion for slavery to the metaphysic delusion, slavery to divine right for slavery to civic liberty; slavery to dogma, commandment, heaven and hell, for slavery to sentiment, humanity, progress—all equally mere words, conceits, figments, by which the wretched individual has allowed himself to be coerced and martyrised; the wretched individual who alone is a reality. This is the darkest, if not the deepest, pit of anarchical thought; and through its mazes Stirner drags us round and round for as long a time as Kant requires for his Categories, or the author of the *Imitation* for the love of God—both of which, by the way, are good examples of *Spuk*. But even as Dante clambered out of hell by continuing the way he had come down, so we also can emerge from Stirner's negations by pursuing the arguments which had led into them. And, having got to the individual as the only and original reality, we can work our way back to those subsidiary and contingent realities, the individual's duties, ideals, and institutions.

There is nothing real, says Stirner, but the various conditions of the individual; the rest is delusion, *Spuk*. But if only the *ego* is real, how can anything else interfere with it? If such abstractions and figments as God, state, family, morality, or whatever the name of the particular bogey, can cramp, cabin, maim our individuality; then, since our individuality alone has reality, these various delusions must be a part of our own individuality. Free yourselves, says Stirner, from your own ideas. But our ideas, whether spontaneously generated in ourselves or assimilated from others, must, in order to have real powers such as we attribute to them, be a part of ourself: and if we sacrifice any other part of ourself to those ideas, it is a proof that they, and not the sacrificed part, must be, at that particular conjunction of circumstances, the dominant part of our *ego*. Stirner's psychology admits love for individuals as a determinant of action; and similarly regard for the reciprocity of self-interest. But is not love for mankind, however vague the mankind, and regard for principle, however abstract the principle, quite as much a real active power of our nature? If Stirner is made uncomfortable, as he says, by the frown on the face of his beloved, and "kisses the frown away"—to rid himself of his discomfort; why, so are other *egos*—less numerous, but not less real—made uncomfortable by the look of pain in men and women whom they do not care for, nay, by the mere knowledge that men and women, nay, animals, whom they have never seen, are suffering, or are likely to suffer: and, in certain *egos*—rarest, but most efficaciously real—there will arise an impulse— yes, something so irresistibly real as a constitutional impulse—to sacrifice everything for the sake of diminishing that unseen, that possible suffering: present suffering in hospitals, in factories, in slums, in prisons, or future suffering in hell.

And similarly there are *egos* which are made as wretched by the neglect of some civic or religious duty as Stirner could possibly be by skipping a meal or losing a night's sleep. It is quite a different question whether such ideas as these, ideas whose coercive power reveals them an integral part of the *ego*, happen or not to coincide with the courses most desirable for the total welfare either of one single *ego* or of a great number of *egos*: the point at issue is whether or not such active factors in life can be treated as separate from life itself; it is a different question similarly whether any more egoistic preference, say for alcohol or gambling, happens in the long run to tally with the *ego's* advantage. Stirner, indeed, entrenches himself behind the notion that wherever there exists any kind of overmastering desire, need, or idea, the *ego* ceases to exist. But, as a psychological fact, at any given moment of reality, some desire, need, or idea, or group of desires, needs or ideas, must inevitably be having the mastery, otherwise impulse would disappear and action of all kinds cease. For the *ego* which refuses to be dominated by any particular idea or any particular desire, be it externalized as humanity, duty, or merely tobacco or bottle, is an *ego* dominated by some other idea or desire, by the idea or desire that it ought to be free from such domination in particular, or from all conscious domination in general. But as to an *ego* which, at any given moment, is otherwise than dominated by some feeling, impulse, or thought, that kind of *ego* is, oddly enough, exactly the thing which Stirner is waging war against—an abstraction, a nonentity, a figment of logic, of which we have no practical experience. Yes, indeed, nothing but the *ego* is efficient, since, to be efficient, everything else must have been absorbed into or must impinge upon it.

This anarchical psychology of Stirner's (and something similar, however unformulated, exists in the mind also of Maurice Barrès and of Bernard Shaw) brings home to me how much we stand in need of a new science of will, thought, and emotion; or, rather, of the practical application of such a science of the soul as recent years have already given us. It would put us equally above the new-fangled theories of freeing the *ego* by abolishing ideals and habits, and the old-fashioned notions of thwarting the *ego* in the name of morality. For it would show that the *ego* is not the separate momentary impulse, but the organic hierarchy of united graduated impulses; a unity which being evolved by contact with similar unities, can be made as harmonious with them as the mere separate impulses, referring to mere partial and momentary relations, are likely to be the reverse. This being understood, we shall seek less for the outer discipline, the constraining of the individual by society, than for the inner discipline, the subordination of the individual's lesser and also less durable motives to the greater and more durable. We shall, once we have really conceived this organic unity of the individual, desist from our wasteful and cruel attempts to reduce all men to one pattern, to extract from all the same kind of service. But in such healthy development of the *ego*, in such organic, inner discipline, the conscious reference to standards, the conscious desire for harmony, will be an indispensable means. Duties and ideals will again be valued above all things; not, indeed, as intellectual formulas, but as factors of habitual emotional conditions. For the chief value of duty or ideal is the capacity fostered thereby of being dutiful, of acting in accordance with an ideal. Among the great gifts for which we must thank the theological systems of the past, the puritan element in every creed, the most valuable are not the the tables of permissions and prohibitions, always variable, and still very rough and ready. The splendid work of Puritanism is the training, nay, the conception, of a real individuality, the habit of self-dominion, of postponing, foregoing the immediate, momentary and temporal for the sake of a distant, permanent, and, inasmuch as intellectually recognised, spiritual something. The moral value of Jeanie Deans is not in her conviction that under no circumstances must a lie be told (although her conviction was correct in 999 cases out of 1000), but in her incapacity of telling a lie so long as she was convinced against it. Puritanism is psychologically right in its implicit recognition of the superiority of the habitual condition of feeling over the transient impulse. For *what I habitually wish to be* represents, or ought to represent, the bulk of my nature and organisation more really than *what at a given moment I actually am*. If individualism is to triumph, if any good is to come (and it doubtless will) out of contemporary anarchic theories of the ego, it will be by an increase rather than a diminution of the healthy Puritan element. It is, after all, the Puritans in temper who have done all successful rebellion against items of Puritan codes; whereas the egoist of the modern type is, nine times out of ten, the sort of person who tolerates evil for want of the self-discipline and consistency necessary to stop it.

   After the psychology of anarchy comes its metaphysics, or, I would almost say, its theology. Theology, because, not satisfied with appealing to our reason, it meddles with the instincts which seek for the quality we call *divine*, and for the emotions that quality awakens; and theology also, because it occasionally even suggests the making of new gods, the creation of a strange metaphorical Olympus. Like all other theology, it is esoteric and exoteric; it has its treatises of highest metaphysical subtlety; and its little popular catechisms, as full of explicit absurdities. Such a catechism as this was made up by the late J.A. Symonds out of the opinions, or what he took to be the opinions, of Walt Whitman. It is the declaration of the equal rights and equal dignity of all the parts of man's nature; and implicitly therefore of the foolishness of all the hierarchies which various creeds and various systems of ethics have set up in the soul and life of mankind. It is characteristically different in tone from the anarchical utterances of the egotistic decadent Barrès and the metaphysical Nihilist Stirner; it is eminently Anglo-Saxon in a sort of unconscious optimistic cant. Its subversiveness consists in an attempt to set things right; but it does so, not by pleading that nothing is evil, but rather by insisting that everything is good. The democratic view, as it is called, of Whitman, as expounded by Symonds, consists in asserting that all things are equally divine.

Now if you start with identifying *divine* with *divinely ordained*, and identify the divinity with the bare fact of existence, then all things are certainly portions of the divinity, and, in so far, *divine*. But if all things are in this sense *divine*, then divine ceases to be a quality which evokes any sense of preference; then *divine* is no longer an expression commensurate with esteem, still less legitimately productive of emotional satisfaction; if all things are divine, why then some may be divine and honourable, and others divine, and dishonourable. There is something akin in this anarchic theology to the juggling with the word *value* of Karl Marx and his followers. It is the acceptance of the emotional quality of a word after emptying out the meaning which had produced it. Good, noble, divine; a hierarchy of words denoting such qualities as we think especially desirable, denoting the fuller possession of that which we esteem most highly in ourselves, be it strength or beauty, moral or intellectual helpfulness; words which awaken in our mind the sense of approval, of respect, and finally of reverence and wonder. Perform a little sleight-of-hand, and shuffle *divinity* with *God*, *God* with *Nature*, *Nature* with *Being*, and you contrive to awaken that emotion of rareness, superiority, wonderfulness, in connection with . . . with what? O irony of self-delusion! with *everything equally*.

This subversion of all appreciation is the furthest possible from being, as Whitman seems to have imagined, and as Symonds reiterates, a highly scientific thought. For science teaches us that all life, and especially the life we human beings call *progress*, is not a mere affirmation, so to speak, of mere passive being, of "what is—is"—but a selection and rejection, the perpetual assertion of fitness against unfitness, a constant making of inequality. To our feelings, and to our mind (unless it become a word without intellectual and emotional meaning) the *divine* is the supremely desirable. According to our condition that desirable has inevitably shifted quarters, but it has always been, and must always be, the exceptional, the exceptional which becomes, perhaps, by dint of our seeking it, the rule; our desires being set free to seek something new, some other rare thing which we would fain to make common. And in this way our spiritual progress has consisted, most probably, in the gradual relegation to the obscure, half-conscious, automatic side of our nature of instincts and functions which have once been uppermost; in the gradual raising the level of the desirable, the contemplated above the necessities of the moment and the body, above the interest of the ego. There is no place for democracy *à la* Whitman in the soul; its law is co-ordination, subordination, hierarchy.

The "Theories of Anarchy and Law," of Mr. H.B. Brewster, is unknown to the public just in proportion, I should say, to its merits. It takes no ordinary reader to appreciate its subtlety of analysis and boldness of hypothesis; and the marvellous impartiality which sees every side of every argument equally, and refrains from all judgement, is positively distressing even to the most admiring reader, who seeks in vain for something to attack or to espouse, who gropes, blinded by excess of light, for the unclutchable personality of the author. Behind which of the speakers of these dialogues shall we look for the author? At which moment does he shift from the one side to the other? Is Mr. Brewster on the whole for or against intellectual and ethical Nihilism? Be this as it may, the book is on the whole a perfect gospel of anarchy, because, in the first place, the anarchical opinions, although they represent only one quarter of the doctrines represented, are those we are least accustomed to and consequently most impressed by; and because, in the second place, the very impartiality, the refusal to decide, to commend and condemn, leaves an impression of the utter vanity of all formula and all system.

It is, therefore, only as an expression of anarchic tendencies that I wish, in this connection, to mention the book. And principally because it affords, in the most remarkable form, the chief thought of what I should call the transcendental theology of anarchy. I use the word theology once more advisedly. For Mr. Brewster has separated from the various practical and speculative items which held it in solution, and distilled into the subtlest essence, a transcendental principle which lurks, however unperceived, in all anarchic writings, a transcendental equivalent of the old Persian and Manichean dualism. At the end of all the doubts, doubts about ideals, duties, institutions, formulas, whether they are good or evil, arises the final doubt: have we a right to prefer good to evil? Does the universe live only in the being of God; does the universe not live equally in the being of Satan? The pessimistic philosophers of our century have accustomed us to conceive of forces in creation which are irreconcileable with benevolence. The later Darwinism is training us to perceive that in the process of evolution there is, alongside of the selection of the fittest, the rendering even unfitter of the initially unfit, degenerative tendencies as well as tendencies to adaptation. We have had to admit that destruction is a factor in all construction. The doubt arises, may not destruction be just as great a power as construction? Not as its servant, but as its rival, its equal. Are we not Pharisees in condemning all persons and instincts unsuitable, forsooth, to the purposes of our race and civilisation, when those persons and instincts are as much realities as any others? Are we not Philistines in condemning all views of life which do not square with our particular intellectual organisation? Is not what we call evil a reality, and does chaos perhaps not exist as truly as order? Shall we not recognise the great dualism?

By no means. We are so constituted that evil cannot please nor chaos satisfy us; and our constitution must be, for us, the law of the universe. For we conceive the universe only in terms of our own existence, and the qualities we attribute to it are only modes of our own feeling. All we can be sure of about good and evil, chaos and order, is that they are conceptions of ours; are they conceptions, and if so, to what extent corresponding, of anything else? We cannot tell. What we call forces of destruction and disorder are such to us; nay, they are forces perhaps only to us; it is only through our own aversion that we know of destruction and disorder at all. The origin of all such doubts, and their solution also, lies in the nature of the doubter. In the little world which our faculties, our spiritual and practical needs, as well as our bodily senses, have created for us out of the infinite unknown universe, it is our human instincts which decide, as they have determined, everything. And among the ideas they have set on foot they decide for good against evil, for order against chaos.

These discussions on anarchy and law, these struggles between what we have and what we want, should give a result more practically important than even the most important application in practice; for, in our life, a habit of feeling and thinking, an attitude, is of wider influence than a rule of conduct. The attempt to verify our moral compass, the deliberate readiness to do so, might result in the safest kind of spiritual peace. For, to be able to see in all that we call *bad*, *wrong*, *false*, the cause and effect, the immense naturalness and inevitableness, its place in the universe as distinguished from its place in our own liking or convenience; to be able to face *fact* as *fact*, as something transcending all momentary convenience or pleasantness; yet at the same time to preserve our human preferences, to exercise our human selection all the more rigidly because we know that it is *our* selection, reality offering more, but we accepting only what we choose; such a double attitude would surely be the best. It would be the only attitude thoroughly true, just, kind, and really practical, giving us peace and dignity and energy for struggle without hoodwinking or arrogance. It would be more respectful both to our own nature and to the nature which transcends ours to recognise that what mankind wants it wants because it is mankind; and to leave off claiming from the university conformity to human ideals and methods.

The sense of this (however vague) has been furthered by occasional fortunate conditions of civilisation, and it is, most probably, constitutional in certain happily balanced natures. It is what gives the high serenity to men of the stamp of Plato and Goethe and Browning; they can touch everything, yet remain with preferences unaltered. Perhaps we may all some day attain, by employing equally our tendencies to doubt and our tendencies to believe, to such a fearless, yet modest, recognition of what is, and also of what we wish it to be.

Notes

*   1. George Bernard Shaw: "The Quintessence of Ibsenism."
    2. Maurice Barrès: "L'Ennemi des Lois."
        "   "   "Le Jardin de Bérénice."
        "   "   "Un Homme Libre."
    3. Max Stirner: "Der Einzige und sein Eigenthum."
    4. J.A. Symonds: "Walt Whitman."
    5. H.B. Brewster: "Theories of Anarchy and Law." [Lee's note]

1. A reference to Jean-Marie-Mathias-Philippe-Auguste, comte de Villiers de l'Isle-Adam (1838–89), a French poet, dramatist, and short-story writer whose work often dealt with the occult.

2. Jeanie Deans is David and Christian Deans's daughter in Sir Walter Scott's *Heart of Midlothian* (1818); Maggie Tulliver is the protagonist of George Eliot's *The Mill on the Floss* (1860); Mary Eleanor Wilkins Freeman (1852–1930) was best known for her short stories about frustrated characters who lived in rural New England villages.

3. References to characters in Henrik Ibsen's dramas. In *Ghosts* (1881), Oswald Alving is the son of a vicious father whose memory has been cloaked by his wife after his death. Oswald becomes a mere physical wreck and in the end begs his mother to give him morphia so that he can commit suicide. In *Rosmersholm* (1886), Pastor Rosmer's wife commits suicide, and Rosmer falls under the influence of his wife's former companion, Rebecca West. After scandals arise, Rosmer asks Rebecca to marry him, but she refuses, due to her conscience. Eventually they both throw themselves into a mill-dam.

4. References to the protagonists in Henrik Ibsen's dramas, *Hedda Gabler* (1890), and *The Master Builder* (1892).

5. Isabella is Claudio's sister in Shakespeare's *Measure for Measure*; Effie Deans is Jeanie Deans's sister in Scott's *Heart of Midlothian* (1818).

6. (Auguste-)Maurice Barrès (1862–1923). French writer and politician who was also an influential nationalist.